Disruptive Technologies in Education and Workforce Development

Julie A. Delello
The University of Texas at Tyler, USA

Rochell R. McWhorter
The University of Texas at Tyler, USA

A volume in the Advances in Business Information Systems and Analytics (ABISA) Book Series

Published in the United States of America by
IGI Global
Business Science Reference (an imprint of IGI Global)
701 E. Chocolate Avenue
Hershey PA, USA 17033
Tel: 717-533-8845
Fax: 717-533-8661
E-mail: cust@igi-global.com
Web site: http://www.igi-global.com

Copyright © 2024 by IGI Global. All rights reserved. No part of this publication may be reproduced, stored or distributed in any form or by any means, electronic or mechanical, including photocopying, without written permission from the publisher. Product or company names used in this set are for identification purposes only. Inclusion of the names of the products or companies does not indicate a claim of ownership by IGI Global of the trademark or registered trademark.

Library of Congress Cataloging-in-Publication Data

CIP DATA PROCESSING

2024 Business Science Reference

ISBN(hc): 9798369330036
ISBN(sc): 9798369349281
eISBN: 9798369330043

British Cataloguing in Publication Data
A Cataloguing in Publication record for this book is available from the British Library.

The views expressed in this book are those of the authors, but not necessarily of the publisher.

For electronic access to this publication, please contact: eresources@igi-global.com.

Advances in Business Information Systems and Analytics (ABISA) Book Series

Madjid Tavana
La Salle University, USA

ISSN:2327-3275
EISSN:2327-3283

Mission

The successful development and management of information systems and business analytics is crucial to the success of an organization. New technological developments and methods for data analysis have allowed organizations to not only improve their processes and allow for greater productivity, but have also provided businesses with a venue through which to cut costs, plan for the future, and maintain competitive advantage in the information age.

The **Advances in Business Information Systems and Analytics (ABISA) Book Series** aims to present diverse and timely research in the development, deployment, and management of business information systems and business analytics for continued organizational development and improved business value.

Coverage

- Business Process Management
- Business Models
- Business Information Security
- Data Analytics
- Information Logistics
- Business Systems Engineering
- Management Information Systems
- Data Governance
- Performance Metrics
- Strategic Information Systems

> IGI Global is currently accepting manuscripts for publication within this series. To submit a proposal for a volume in this series, please contact our Acquisition Editors at Acquisitions@igi-global.com or visit: http://www.igi-global.com/publish/.

The Advances in Business Information Systems and Analytics (ABISA) Book Series (ISSN 2327-3275) is published by IGI Global, 701 E. Chocolate Avenue, Hershey, PA 17033-1240, USA, www.igi-global.com. This series is composed of titles available for purchase individually; each title is edited to be contextually exclusive from any other title within the series. For pricing and ordering information please visit http://www.igi-global.com/book-series/advances-business-information-systems-analytics/37155. Postmaster: Send all address changes to above address. Copyright © 2024 IGI Global. All rights, including translation in other languages reserved by the publisher. No part of this series may be reproduced or used in any form or by any means – graphics, electronic, or mechanical, including photocopying, recording, taping, or information and retrieval systems – without written permission from the publisher, except for non commercial, educational use, including classroom teaching purposes. The views expressed in this series are those of the authors, but not necessarily of IGI Global.

Titles in this Series

For a list of additional titles in this series, please visit: www.igi-global.com/book-series

Powering Industry 5.0 and Sustainable Development Through Innovation
Rohit Bansal (Vaish College of Engineering, India) Fazla Rabby (Stanford Institute of Management and Technology, Australia) Meenakshi Gandhi (Vivekananda Institute of Professional Studies, India) Nishita Pruthi (Maharshi Dayanand University, India) and Shweta Saini (Maharshi Dayanand University, India)
Business Science Reference • copyright 2024 • 393pp • H/C (ISBN: 9798369335505) • US $315.00 (our price)

Cases on AI Ethics in Business
Kyla Latrice Tennin (College of Doctoral Studies, University of Phoenix, USA) Samrat Ray (International Institute of Management Studies, India) and Jens M. Sorg (CGI Deutschland B.V. & Co. KG, Germany)
Business Science Reference • copyright 2024 • 342pp • H/C (ISBN: 9798369326435) • US $315.00 (our price)

Advanced Businesses in Industry 6.0
Mohammad Mehdi Oskounejad (Azad University of the Emirates, UAE) and Hamed Nozari (Azad University of the Emirates, UAE)
Business Science Reference • copyright 2024 • 278pp • H/C (ISBN: 9798369331088) • US $325.00 (our price)

Intelligent Optimization Techniques for Business Analytics
Sanjeev Bansal (Amity Business School, Amity University, Noida, India) Nitendra Kumar (Amity Business School, Amity University, Noida, India) and Priyanka Agarwal (Amity Business School, Amity University, Noida, India)
Business Science Reference • copyright 2024 • 357pp • H/C (ISBN: 9798369315989) • US $270.00 (our price)

Data-Driven Business Intelligence Systems for Socio-Technical Organizations
Pantea Keikhosrokiani (University of Oulu, Finland)
Business Science Reference • copyright 2024 • 490pp • H/C (ISBN: 9798369312100) • US $265.00 (our price)

Utilizing AI and Smart Technology to Improve Sustainability in Entrepreneurship
Syed Far Abid Hossain (BRAC University, Bangladesh)
Business Science Reference • copyright 2024 • 370pp • H/C (ISBN: 9798369318423) • US $290.00 (our price)

701 East Chocolate Avenue, Hershey, PA 17033, USA
Tel: 717-533-8845 x100 • Fax: 717-533-8661
E-Mail: cust@igi-global.com • www.igi-global.com

Table of Contents

Preface xiv

Chapter 1
Artificial Intelligence in Education: Transforming Learning and Teaching 1
    Julie A. Delello, The University of Texas at Tyler, USA
    Jennifer Bailey Watters, The University of Texas at Tyler, USA
    Arlene Garcia-Lopez, Miami Dade College, USA

Chapter 2
A Novel Approach for Implementing Blockchain Technology in the Education Sector 27
    Tarun Kumar Vashishth, IIMT University, India
    Vikas Sharma, IIMT University, India
    Kewal Krishan Sharma, IIMT University, India
    Bhupendra Kumar, IIMT University, India

Chapter 3
Textuality, Corporeality, Citizenship: Three Critical Dimensions of Artificial Intelligence in
Educational Processes 51
    Monica Di Domenico, Università degli Studi di Salerno, Italy
    Fabrizio Schiavo, Università di Cassino, Italy
    Tonia De Giuseppe, Università Giustino Fortunato, Italy
    Stefano Di Tore, Università degli Studi di Salerno, Italy
    Pio Alfredo Di Tore, Università di Cassino, Italy

Chapter 4
Invasive and Creepy Technologies: Challenges and Opportunities 70
    Rochell R. McWhorter, The University of Texas at Tyler, USA
    Mandi M. Laurie, The University of Texas at Tyler, USA

Chapter 5
A Socio-Pedagogical Reading From Video Game to Game Learning 95
    Alessia Sozio, Pegaso Università Telematica, Italy
    Alfonso Amendola, Università degli Studi di Salerno, Italy
    Maria Carbone, Università Giustino Fortunato, Italy
    Tonia De Giuseppe, Università Giustino Fortunato, Italy

Chapter 6
Educational Paradigm Shifts in the Era of Rapid Technological Advancement 115
    Sajid Khan, Ghulam Ishaq Khan Institute of Engineering Sciences and Technology, Pakistan
    Majid Kahn, Massey University, New Zealand

Phil Ramsey, Massey University, New Zealand

Chapter 7
The Small and Rural School Italian Network for Digital Technologies Flourishing in "Non Standard" Educational Context: Before, During, and After the Pandemic Era 136
Giuseppina Rita Jose Mangione, INDIRE, Italy

Chapter 8
The Impact of Aligning Artificial Intelligence Large Language Models With Bloom's Taxonomy in Healthcare Education 166
Matthew Pears, University of Nottingham, UK
Stathis Th Konstantinidis, University of Nottingham, UK

Chapter 9
Transformative Waves: Exploring Disruptive Technologies in Education and Workforce Development 193
Nitish Kumar Minz, K.R. Mangalam University, India

Chapter 10
A Service-Based Measurement Model for Determining Disruptive Workforce Training Technology Value: Return on Investment Calculations and Example 206
Scott Joseph Warren, University of North Texas, USA
Christina Churchill, Southern Methodist University, USA
Aleshia Hayes, University of North Texas, USA

Chapter 11
Technological Disruptions in the Service Sector 232
Archana Parashar, Indian Institute of Management, Raipur, India
Shivangi Dhiman, University of Delhi, India

Chapter 12
Inclusive E-Tutoring Between Artificial Intelligence, Corporality, and Emotionality: Flipped Inclusion and New Research Perspectives 251
Silvia Tornusciolo, Mercatorum University, Italy
Enzapaola Catalano, Pegaso University, Italy
Tonia De Giuseppe, Giustino Fortunato University, Italy

Chapter 13
Community-Driven Governance: Between Complex Education and Flipped Inclusion - Research Perspectives for an Eco-Sustainable Economic Pedagogy 261
Maria Carbone, Pegaso Telematic University, Italy
Alessia Sozio, Pegaso Università Telematica, Italy
Tonia De Giuseppe, Giustino Fortunato University, Italy

Chapter 14
Sustainable Development Between Artificial Intelligence and Education: The Inclusive

Perspective of the Flipped Inclusion Model 269
    Tonia De Giuseppe, Giustino Fortunato University, Italy
    Silvia Tornusciolo, Università Mercatorum, Italy
    Enza paola Catalano, University Pegaso, Italy

About the Contributors 340

Index 344

Detailed Table of Contents

Preface xiv

Chapter 1
Artificial Intelligence in Education: Transforming Learning and Teaching 1
    Julie A. Delello, The University of Texas at Tyler, USA
    Jennifer Bailey Watters, The University of Texas at Tyler, USA
    Arlene Garcia-Lopez, Miami Dade College, USA

This chapter explores artificial intelligence (AI) and its potential to revolutionize the field of education by enhancing teaching and learning. It further highlights ways in which AI technologies can support educators and students, including content creation encompassing voice and video, task automation, and the provision of personalized learning through adaptive learning platforms. Potential benefits to leveraging AI technology include improved learner engagement, automated administrative processes, and more robust data-driven insights. As AI advances, a unique opportunity emerges for schools to prepare educators to use AI in the classroom and for educators to redefine traditional teaching methodologies. Nonetheless, balancing AI innovation with ethical considerations includes considering issues in transparency and privacy in AI algorithms as well as mitigating biases in the data.

Chapter 2
A Novel Approach for Implementing Blockchain Technology in the Education Sector 27
    Tarun Kumar Vashishth, IIMT University, India
    Vikas Sharma, IIMT University, India
    Kewal Krishan Sharma, IIMT University, India
    Bhupendra Kumar, IIMT University, India

Blockchain technology has the transformative potential to reshape the education sector by addressing challenges related to student data privacy, certification, and credential transfer. This chapter proposes a comprehensive approach to implementing blockchain in education, encompassing the development of a decentralized student record system, issuance of digital certificates, implementation of a blockchain-based learning management system, creation of a decentralized marketplace for educational resources, and provision of a transparent donation platform. By leveraging blockchain's decentralized and secure attributes, this approach aims to establish a tamper-proof system for storing, verifying, and sharing educational records. The benefits include enhanced security of student records, streamlined credential verification, and efficient resource transfer. The chapter explores potential applications like digital identity management, credential verification, secure data storage, and smart contracts for academic transactions.

Chapter 3
Textuality, Corporeality, Citizenship: Three Critical Dimensions of Artificial Intelligence in
Educational Processes 51
    Monica Di Domenico, Università degli Studi di Salerno, Italy
    Fabrizio Schiavo, Università di Cassino, Italy

Tonia De Giuseppe, Università Giustino Fortunato, Italy
Stefano Di Tore, Università degli Studi di Salerno, Italy
Pio Alfredo Di Tore, Università di Cassino, Italy

This work explores the relationship between artificial intelligence and educational processes along three main directions, which the authors believe urgently require significant epistemological effort from the educational community. The first direction is the relationship between artificial intelligence and forms of textuality. By incessantly processing vast amounts of texts, the large language models that constitute the core of generative AI seem to represent a definitive overcoming of one of the main limitations that Plato, in the Phaedrus, identifies in written text: the lack of interactivity. The second direction is the relationship between AI and the body. How can we conceive of an intelligence that exists outside bodily incarnation, when human intelligence is so intimately connected to bodily experience? The third direction is the relationship between AI and citizenship: The paragraph addresses the complexity and challenges associated with the contemporary conceptualization of citizenship.

Chapter 4
Invasive and Creepy Technologies: Challenges and Opportunities 70
Rochell R. McWhorter, The University of Texas at Tyler, USA
Mandi M. Laurie, The University of Texas at Tyler, USA

As modern technologies have increased in sophistication and invasiveness, users have expressed concerns about confidentiality and ethical issues regarding contemporary technologies such as artificial intelligence, facial recognition, social robots, big data, and location-sharing apps. As a result, the term "creepy technologies" has been used to describe these concerns. This chapter seeks to review relevant literature for this area of study and offer interventions for individual users, teams, and organizations.

Chapter 5
A Socio-Pedagogical Reading From Video Game to Game Learning 95
Alessia Sozio, Pegaso Università Telematica, Italy
Alfonso Amendola, Università degli Studi di Salerno, Italy
Maria Carbone, Università Giustino Fortunato, Italy
Tonia De Giuseppe, Università Giustino Fortunato, Italy

The video game, a phenomenon less than a century old, is relatively recent compared to the millennia-long history of "analog" gaming, its natural predecessor. In recent decades, digital play has emerged as a prominent expression of contemporary culture, possessing exceptional social, cultural, and technological value. It stands as the leading global entertainment sector in terms of time spent and budget, surpassing the revenues of the film and record industries. Digital games are not only a central economic force in the entertainment and technology industries but also foster new cultural and social narratives through their participatory and collaborative nature. This chapter will explore the evolution from traditional games to video games and their effectiveness in enhancing knowledge and learning.

Chapter 6
Educational Paradigm Shifts in the Era of Rapid Technological Advancement 115
Sajid Khan, Ghulam Ishaq Khan Institute of Engineering Sciences and Technology, Pakistan
Majid Kahn, Massey University, New Zealand
Phil Ramsey, Massey University, New Zealand

In a rapidly evolving world, students are becoming increasingly techno-social, mirroring the changing demands of firms. Educational systems must adapt correspondingly, necessitating innovation in teaching practices which constitute the educational process. As Savian highlights robust theoretical underpinnings lead to more effective practical activities. However, while learning theories evolve, teaching practices lag behind. Amidst disagreements, it's acknowledged that learning is complex and diverse. The solution lies in transitioning from traditional pedagogy to contextualized, personalized, collaborative, and technology-mediated learning. Successful educational innovations are essential to meet stakeholders' heightened demands.

Chapter 7
The Small and Rural School Italian Network for Digital Technologies Flourishing in "Non Standard" Educational Context: Before, During, and After the Pandemic Era 136
    Giuseppina Rita Jose Mangione, INDIRE, Italy

The topic of small and rural schools offers numerous investigative perspectives within educational research. Digital technologies hold significant potential for "non-standard" educational contexts, driving the need to reconsider the structure of schools based on regional partnerships. After summarizing key international studies that have identified the challenges of using technology in rural educational settings, this paper adopts a phenomenological approach, based on narratives of exemplary cases, to present a diachronic analysis (before, during, and after the pandemic) and exemplify disruptive use of technologies in small schools. The Italian Network of Small Schools promoted by INDIRE has supported numerous transformative scenarios that extend the use of technologies beyond the emergency period and guide small schools into a future where also AI can helps solidify their role as centers of democratic values and quality education.

Chapter 8
The Impact of Aligning Artificial Intelligence Large Language Models With Bloom's Taxonomy in Healthcare Education 166
    Matthew Pears, University of Nottingham, UK
    Stathis Th Konstantinidis, University of Nottingham, UK

The innovation of large language models (LLMs) has widened possibilities for renovating healthcare education through AI-powered learning resources, such as chatbots. This chapter explores the assimilation of LLMs with Bloom's taxonomy, demonstrating how this foundational framework for designing and assessing learning outcomes can support the development of critical thinking, problem-solving, and decision-making skills in healthcare learners. Through case examples and research presentations, this chapter illustrates how LLM chatbots provide interactive, scaffolding, and contextually relevant learning experiences. However, it also highlights the importance of designing these tools with key principles in mind, including learner-centeredness, co-creation with domain experts, and principled responsibility. By embracing a collaborative, interdisciplinary, and future-oriented approach to chatbot design and development, the power of LLMs can be harnessed to revolutionize healthcare education and ultimately improve patient care.

Chapter 9
Transformative Waves: Exploring Disruptive Technologies in Education and Workforce Development 193
    Nitish Kumar Minz, K.R. Mangalam University, India

This research explores the transformative impact of disruptive technologies in education and workforce development. Focused on key themes, it investigates how technologies like AI, AR, and VR reshape learning experiences, catalyzing a paradigm shift in education. Examining workforce development, the review highlights initiatives for upskilling and reskilling in the digital age. Balancing opportunities and challenges, the narrative unfolds changes in teaching models towards adaptive, learner-centric approaches. Navigating the evolving digital landscape, stakeholders must embrace innovation while addressing issues of access and equity. Understanding and adapting to these transformative waves are essential for fostering a future-ready education and resilient workforce.

Chapter 10
A Service-Based Measurement Model for Determining Disruptive Workforce Training
Technology Value: Return on Investment Calculations and Example 206
    Scott Joseph Warren, University of North Texas, USA
    Christina Churchill, Southern Methodist University, USA
    Aleshia Hayes, University of North Texas, USA

Are the training outcomes of innovative technologies worth their investment cost? How can managers determine a company's valuable profits resulting from employing virtual, mixed, and augmented reality tools? This chapter presents metrics for evaluating information technologies' operations and business value relative to their service contributions in support of worker task efficacy and efficiency, reduced operations downtime due to training, and other benefits. The authors provide sample calculations that can help managers and researchers better explain the service-dominant logic-defined affordances of these innovative tools and their expected benefits in supporting corporate strategy, organizational performance measures, and operational performance in manufacturing knowledge production. Finally, the authors provide extended reality-supported worker training examples to model these calculations to determine the value of innovative technology assets for training and workplace performance improvements.

Chapter 11
Technological Disruptions in the Service Sector 232
    Archana Parashar, Indian Institute of Management, Raipur, India
    Shivangi Dhiman, University of Delhi, India

Technological advancement has greatly shaped the service sector, with the most disruptive technologies in their infancy. The broad arena of the service industry includes several sections, each of which has been disrupted by technological advancements, resulting in transformed process mechanisms and market paradigms. The present chapter included a comprehensive narrative review of literature aimed at broadly analysing the status of technological disruption in the service sector with the help of relevant research studies and real-world applications. Four service sectors, namely financial services, tourism and hospitality, legal services, and the health industry, were investigated to highlight the advent of disruptive technologies across the service industry. Further, consumer and employee behaviour changes concerning technological disruption were highlighted. The prevalent trend of technological disruption has immense practical and academic implications, encouraging experts to provide future directions in the area.

Chapter 12
Inclusive E-Tutoring Between Artificial Intelligence, Corporality, and Emotionality: Flipped
Inclusion and New Research Perspectives 251
    Silvia Tornusciolo, Mercatorum University, Italy

Enzapaola Catalano, Pegaso University, Italy
Tonia De Giuseppe, Giustino Fortunato University, Italy

The report on the digital decade prompted the European Commission to issue recommendations to Italy aimed at encouraging investment in high quality education that leads to the development of the transversal skills necessary to keep pace with the digital transformation of society. AI is revolutionising the world, and, with it, education. Learning that passes through the corporeity and the senses is therefore destined to disappear and be replaced by the perception of the three-dimensional world? Will it still be necessary to aim towards literacy emotional literacy and inclusion, the result of a skillful application of inclusive teaching methodologies such as flipped inclusion? These are the questions the authors will try to reflect on, analysing in particular flipped inclusion, in order to of exploring, devising, designing and testing inclusive models of ecological development.

Chapter 13
Community-Driven Governance: Between Complex Education and Flipped Inclusion - Research Perspectives for an Eco-Sustainable Economic Pedagogy 261
Maria Carbone, Pegaso Telematic University, Italy
Alessia Sozio, Pegaso Università Telematica, Italy
Tonia De Giuseppe, Giustino Fortunato University, Italy

Technological progress and, in particular, the spread of artificial intelligence, constitutes in the context an element of innovation no longer only at the level of production but also at the level of administration and control. This chapter explores the potential and risks that directors are faced with as a result of the entry of artificial intelligence into the boardroom, proposing to investigate whether in the corporate governance of small and medium-sized companies it is possible to act pedagogically to form an organizational culture devoted to inclusion through the application of cooperative learning methodologies that allow, in fact, to achieve greater inclusiveness among the individuals working there. The project proposes to apply the methodology of flipped inclusion, and more specifically Cohen's method of complex instruction because through the creation of heterogeneous teamwork and interdependence of roles, the resources of all group members can be enhanced.

Chapter 14
Sustainable Development Between Artificial Intelligence and Education: The Inclusive Perspective of the Flipped Inclusion Model 269
Tonia De Giuseppe, Giustino Fortunato University, Italy
Silvia Tornusciolo, Università Mercatorum, Italy
Enza paola Catalano, University Pegaso, Italy

This chapter, starting from the United Nation's (UN) 2030 agenda, analyzes the current stage of implementing its objectives, focusing on the milestones. The UN Agenda 2030 aims to overcome inequalities, poverty, and disparities. This ambitious goal, especially considering the social transformations caused by the pandemic, requires new models of sustainable development. Sustainability and inclusion are key: how can artificial intelligence (AI) support sustainable development and create an inclusive society? AI's pervasiveness can become a risk without a society democratically oriented toward awareness of its centrality and the common good. The emergence of new inclusion models, such as flipped inclusion, can address this challenge and make the ambitious project of the UN Agenda 2030 a concrete reality.

About the Contributors 340

Index 344

Preface

In an era where technology's influence permeates every aspect of our lives, understanding its impact on education and workforce development is paramount. As editors of this volume, we are delighted to present the second edition of *Disruptive and Emerging Technological Trends Across Education and the Workplace*.

Our daily routines, professional endeavors, and societal interactions are continually reshaped by the relentless march of technology. From the conveniences of smart homes to the complexities of artificial intelligence, from the insights gleaned through big data analytics to the transformative power of social media, our world is evolving at an unprecedented pace.

In this volume, we embark on a journey to explore the multifaceted implications of disruptive and emerging technologies. From the corridors of academia to the bustling landscapes of industry, we delve into how these advancements are reshaping education and redefining the workforce.

Artificial intelligence, machine learning, and big data analytics are not merely buzzwords; they are catalysts for innovation and change. As educators, policymakers, and industry leaders, it is imperative that we grasp the opportunities and challenges presented by these technologies. From personalized learning experiences to the creation of new job roles, from the imperative of cybersecurity to the potential of biotechnology, the chapters in this book offer insights into the dynamic intersection of technology and human endeavor.

Drawing upon the expertise of scholars and practitioners from diverse fields, this volume transcends disciplinary boundaries to offer a comprehensive exploration of disruptive technologies. Whether you are a researcher seeking the latest insights, an educator striving to enhance pedagogy, or a professional navigating the complexities of the modern workplace, this book serves as a valuable resource.

We extend our gratitude to the contributors whose dedication and scholarship have enriched this volume. Their insights illuminate the path forward in an era of technological transformation.

As editors, we are honored to present this collection of essays, studies, and perspectives. We invite you to engage with the ideas presented herein, to contemplate the implications of disruptive technologies, and to join us in shaping the future of education and workforce development.

In this volume, we embark on an illuminating journey through the transformative landscape of disruptive and emerging technologies, exploring their profound implications for education and workforce development. Each chapter offers a unique perspective, shedding light on the multifaceted intersections between technology and human endeavor.

Chapter 1, "**Artificial Intelligence in Education: Transforming Learning and Teaching**," authored by Julie Delello, Jennifer Bailey Watters, and Arlene Garcia-Lopez, delves into the potential of artificial intelligence (AI) to revolutionize education. It discusses how AI technologies can enhance teaching and learning experiences, offering insights into content creation, task automation, and personalized learning platforms. Moreover, the chapter addresses ethical considerations such as transparency, privacy, and bias mitigation, essential for the responsible implementation of AI in educational settings.

In Chapter 2, "**A Novel Approach for Implementing Blockchain Technology in the Education Sector**," authored by Tarun Vashishth, Vikas Sharma, Kewal Sharma, and Bhupendra Kumar, a comprehensive framework for integrating blockchain technology into education is presented. By leveraging blockchain's decentralized nature, the chapter proposes solutions for enhancing student data privacy, certification processes, and educational resource management. Through case examples and analyses, it illustrates the potential of blockchain to revolutionize educational record-keeping and credential verification systems.

Chapter 3, "**Textuality, corporeality, citizenship: three critical dimensions of Artificial Intelligence in educational processes**," authored by Monica Di Domenico, Fabrizio Schiavo, Tonia De Giuseppe, Stefano di tore, and Pio Alfredo di Tore, explores critical dimensions of AI in educational processes. By examining the relationship between AI and textuality, corporeality, and citizenship, the chapter offers insights into the evolving nature of AI-driven educational paradigms and the challenges posed by technological advancements.

In Chapter 4, "**Invasive and Creepy Technologies: Challenges and Opportunities**," authored by Rochell McWhorter and Mandi Laurie, the ethical and privacy concerns surrounding modern technologies are examined. The chapter explores the concept of "creepy technologies" and reviews relevant literature to offer interventions for addressing confidentiality and ethical issues in the digital age.

Chapter 5, "**A Socio-Pedagogical Reading from Video Game to Game Learning**," authored by Alessia Sozio, Alfonso Ale, Maria Carbone, and Tonia De Giuseppe, explores the transformative impact of video games on contemporary society. By tracing the evolution from traditional gaming to digital play, the chapter highlights the cultural, social, and technological significance of video games and their potential for enhancing learning experiences.

Continuing the discourse, Chapter 6, "**Educational Paradigm Shifts in the Era of Rapid Technological Advancement: Educational Paradigm**," authored by Sajid Khan, Majid Kahn, and Phil Ramsey, discusses educational paradigm shifts in response to rapid technological advancement. The chapter advocates for contextualized, personalized, and technology-mediated learning approaches to meet the evolving needs of students in a digitally driven world.

In Chapter 7, "**The Small and Rural School Italian Network for Digital Technologies Flourishing in 'Non Standard' Educational Context: Before, During and After the Pandemic Era**," authored by Giuseppina Rita Jose Mangione, the role of digital technologies in small and rural schools is examined. Through narrative analyses and case studies, the chapter showcases how digital technologies can empower small schools to thrive in the digital era.

Chapter 8, "**The Impact of Aligning Artificial Intelligence Large Language Models with Bloom's Taxonomy in Healthcare Education**," authored by Matthew Pears and Stathis Konstantinidis, explores the integration of artificial intelligence large language models with Bloom's taxonomy in healthcare education. By aligning AI-powered learning resources with established educational frameworks, the chapter illustrates how LLMs can support the development of critical thinking and decision-making skills in healthcare learners.

The exploration continues with Chapter 9, "**Transformative Waves: Exploring Disruptive Technologies in Education and Workforce Development**," authored by Nitish Minz, which investigates the transformative impact of disruptive technologies in education and workforce development. Focusing on themes such as AI, AR, and VR, the chapter examines how these technologies reshape learning experiences and workforce training initiatives in the digital age.

Preface

In Chapter 10, "**A service-based measurement model for determining disruptive workforce training technology value: Return on investment calculations and example**," authored by Scott Warren, Christina Churchill, and Aleshia Hayes, a service-based measurement model for evaluating the value of disruptive workforce training technologies is presented. Through sample calculations and case examples, the chapter illustrates how organizations can assess the return on investment of innovative technologies in training and workplace performance improvements.

Chapter 11, "**Technological Disruptions in Service Sector**," authored by Archana Parashar and Shivangi Dhiman, explores technological disruptions in the service sector. By analyzing disruptive technologies across various service industries, including finance, tourism, legal services, and healthcare, the chapter highlights changes in process mechanisms and market paradigms driven by technological advancements.

Continuing the discourse on inclusion and technology, Chapter 12, "**Inclusive e-tutoring between artificial intelligence, corporateity and emotionality: flipped inclusion and new research perspectives?**" authored by Silvia Tornusciolo, Enzapaola Catalano, and Tonia De Giuseppe, examines the concept of inclusive e-tutoring in the digital age. Through the lens of flipped inclusion and cooperative learning methodologies, the chapter explores how technology can foster inclusive educational environments.

Chapter 13, "**Community-driven governance, between Complex education and Flipped Inclusion: research perspectives for an eco-sustainable economic pedagogy**," authored by Maria Carbone, Alessia Sozio, and Tonia De Giuseppe, explores community-driven governance in the context of technological progress. By investigating the implications of artificial intelligence on corporate governance, the chapter proposes pedagogical approaches to promote inclusive organizational cultures and sustainable economic practices.

In the final chapter, "**Sustainable development between artificial intelligence and education: the inclusive perspective of the flipped inclusion model**," authored by Tonia De Giuseppe, Silvia Tornusciolo, and Enza Paola Catalano, the role of artificial intelligence in promoting sustainable development and inclusive societies is examined. Through the lens of Agenda 2030, the chapter explores how AI can support sustainable development goals and foster inclusive educational practices.

Together, these chapters offer a comprehensive exploration of the transformative potential of disruptive technologies in education and workforce development. By addressing key themes and challenges, this volume aims to inform and inspire stakeholders to embrace innovation and drive positive change in the digital era.

As editors of this volume, we are both humbled and exhilarated to present the culmination of extensive research and collaboration in the second edition of *Disruptive and Emerging Technological Trends Across Education and the Workplace*.

In today's era, the omnipresence of technology underscores the need for a deeper understanding of its profound impact on education and workforce development. Our world is undergoing a rapid transformation, where daily routines, professional landscapes, and societal interactions are continually reshaped by the relentless march of innovation.

From the conveniences of smart homes to the complexities of artificial intelligence, from the insights gleaned through big data analytics to the transformative power of social media, the chapters in this volume offer a panoramic view of the multifaceted implications of disruptive and emerging technologies.

Artificial intelligence, machine learning, and big data analytics are not merely buzzwords but powerful catalysts for innovation and change. As educators, policymakers, and industry leaders, it is incumbent upon us to grasp the opportunities and challenges presented by these technologies.

Each chapter in this book represents a diverse array of perspectives, drawing upon the expertise of scholars and practitioners from various fields. Through their dedication and scholarship, they have illuminated the path forward in an era of technological transformation.

From personalized learning experiences to the creation of new job roles, from the imperative of cybersecurity to the potential of biotechnology, the insights presented herein provide a roadmap for navigating the dynamic intersection of technology and human endeavor.

As editors, we extend our deepest gratitude to the contributors whose passion and expertise have enriched this volume. Their collective wisdom serves as a beacon, guiding us towards a future where innovation is embraced and positive change is driven.

We are honored to present this collection of essays, studies, and perspectives, and we invite readers to engage with the ideas presented herein. May this volume inspire you to contemplate the implications of disruptive technologies and join us in shaping the future of education and workforce development.

Julie Delello
The University of Texas at Tyler, United States

Rochell McWhorter
The University of Texas at Tyler, United States

Introduction

Julie A. Delello
The University of Texas at Tyler, USA

Rochell R. McWhorter
The University of Texas at Tyler, USA

Welcome to *Emerging and Disruptive Technologies in Education and the Workforce*, a comprehensive exploration of the transformative impact of technological advancements on education and the workforce. This book offers a detailed analysis of current practices and future trends, featuring examples from across the globe, including the United States, Asia, and Europe. It provides a diverse perspective on the integration of technology in educational and professional contexts.

PART ONE: TRANSFORMING EDUCATION WITH TECHNOLOGY

In this section, we explore how technology is revolutionizing education by enhancing learning and teaching methodologies.

Chapter 1: Artificial Intelligence in Education: Transforming Learning and Teaching

Artificial Intelligence (AI) has the potential to revolutionize education by enhancing teaching and learning. This chapter examines the ways in which AI technologies can support educators and students, including content creation, task automation, and personalized learning through adaptive learning platforms. AI offers benefits such as improved learner engagement, automated administrative processes, and robust data-driven insights. Schools have the opportunity to prepare educators to use AI in the classroom, redefining traditional teaching methodologies. However, the chapter also discusses the importance of balancing AI innovation with ethical considerations, addressing transparency, privacy, and biases in AI algorithms.

Chapter 2: A Novel Approach for Implementing Blockchain Technology in the Education Sector

Blockchain technology has the transformative potential to reshape the education sector by addressing challenges related to student data privacy, certification, and credential transfer. This chapter proposes a comprehensive approach to implementing blockchain in education, including developing a decentralized student record system, issuing digital certificates, implementing a blockchain-based learning management system, creating a decentralized marketplace for educational resources, and providing a transparent donation platform. By leveraging blockchain's decentralized and secure attributes, this approach aims to establish a tamper-proof system for storing, verifying, and sharing educational records. The benefits include enhanced security of student records, streamlined credential verification, and efficient resource transfer. Potential applications explored in the chapter include digital identity management, credential verification, secure data storage, and smart contracts for academic transactions.

Chapter 3: Textuality, Corporeality, Citizenship: Three Critical Dimensions of Artificial Intelligence in Educational Processes

This chapter reviews the interaction between artificial intelligence (AI) and educational processes, focusing on three key areas that require urgent attention and understanding within the educational community. The first area is the relationship between AI and forms of textuality, where large language models (LLMs) seem to overcome traditional limitations, such as the lack of interactivity in written content. The second area illustrates the relationship between AI and the human body, examining the challenge of conceptualizing intelligence that operates independently of a physical body. The third area addresses the complexities and challenges involved in modern understandings of citizenship in the context of AI advancements. By exploring these three dimensions—textuality, corporeality, and citizenship—this chapter emphasizes the significant epistemological efforts needed from the educational community to integrate AI effectively and ethically into educational processes.

Chapter 4: Invasive and Creepy Technologies: Challenges and Opportunities

As contemporary technologies advance, they increasingly infiltrate our daily lives, raising significant concerns around privacy and ethics. The term "creepy technology" captures the unease these innovations can provoke, highlighting issues such as cybersecurity and confidentiality. This chapter delves into the concept of creepy technology, offering insights into how these technologies affect public perception and organizational trust. It aims to provide a comprehensive review of existing literature on the topic and discusses potential interventions for managing these technologies, focusing on the implications for both individuals and organizations. The chapter concludes with suggested readings and definitions of key terms to further understand this evolving field. Further, this chapter will help in understanding the broader societal impacts and the need for comprehensive strategies to manage these technologies responsibly.

Chapter 5: A Socio-Pedagogical Reading from Video Game to Game Learning

This chapter conveys the socio-pedagogical implications of video games, tracing their evolution from traditional forms of play to complex digital experiences. Despite being a relatively recent phenomenon, video games have grown to rival and even surpass other media, offering unique opportunities for engagement and learning. Video games combine elements of traditional games and other media such as film and television, creating an interactive multimedia experience. This evolution has led to the development of sophisticated narratives and immersive environments that captivate players. As digital play becomes an integral part of contemporary culture, its potential as an educational tool has grown significantly. This chapter reveals how video games can be harnessed to enhance learning, promote critical thinking, and foster creativity. Through the lens of game-based learning, it further navigates the ways video games can create meaningful and lasting educational experiences.

Chapter 6: Educational Paradigm Shifts in the Era of Rapid Technological Advancement

This chapter explores the evolving educational paradigms necessitated by rapid technological advancements and shifting societal needs. It discusses how traditional educational practices, rooted in behaviorist and cognitivist theories, are increasingly inadequate in addressing the demands of modern, techno-social students and the evolving expectations of the workforce. The chapter stresses the need for educational systems to adopt innovative teaching practices that are contextualized, personalized, and technology-mediated to better cater to diverse learning needs. It reviews various learning theories, including constructivism, connectivism, and quantum learning, emphasizing their relevance in creating meaningful and effective learning experiences. Additionally, the chapter delves into the importance of flexibility in instructional design, advocating for approaches that incorporate multiple perspectives and methodologies to address the complexities of contemporary education.

Chapter 7: Digital Technologies Flourishing in "Non-Standard" Educational Contexts: Before, During, and After the Pandemic Era

This chapter presents the unique challenges and opportunities in small and rural schools, focusing on the relationship between schools and their communities, the use of digital technologies to overcome isolation, and the benefits and drawbacks of these educational settings. Small schools often face difficulties such as attracting qualified teachers, managing multi-grade classrooms, and geographical isolation. However, they also benefit from small class sizes and strong community ties. The COVID-19 pandemic highlighted the need for equitable distance education solutions, especially in rural areas. This chapter expresses how digital technologies can transform small rural schools into smart schools that offer inclusive, personalized education. Through international and national studies, it provides an overview of digital education initiatives supported by the National Institute for Documentation, Innovation and Educational Research (INDIRE) and the National Movement of Small and Rural Schools in Italy.

PART TWO: DISRUPTIVE TECHNOLOGIES IN HEALTHCARE AND WORKFORCE DEVELOPMENT

In this section, we examine how disruptive technologies are reshaping healthcare education and workforce development, leading to new paradigms and practices.

Chapter 8: The Impact of Aligning Artificial Intelligence Large Language Models with Bloom's Taxonomy in Healthcare Education

This chapter investigates the alignment of artificial intelligence (AI) large language models (LLMs) with Bloom's Taxonomy in healthcare education, focusing on enhancing learning outcomes and advancing educational practices within the healthcare sector. It demonstrates how LLMs improve teaching and learning by providing sophisticated, personalized learning resources that foster critical thinking and problem-solving skills. The chapter underscores ethical considerations and the necessity for collaboration between healthcare professionals and educators to ensure responsible and effective AI integration. It advocates for a balanced approach to leveraging AI's potential in education, enhancing learning outcomes while maintaining critical skills and ethical standards.

Chapter 9: Transformative Waves: Exploring Disruptive Technologies in Education and Workforce Development

This chapter examines the integration of disruptive technologies into education and workforce development, which has emerged as a defining phenomenon, reshaping how knowledge is acquired, disseminated, and applied. The literature review navigates the multifaceted landscape of disruptive technologies, exploring their profound impact on educational paradigms and professional trajectories. As we stand on the brink of a digital revolution, it is imperative to scrutinize the transformative waves generated by technologies such as artificial intelligence (AI), digitization, and innovative learning approaches. Rooted in the dynamic evolution of technology, this study considers how these advancements have altered pedagogical practices and redefined essential skill sets for success in an increasingly digitized workforce. Through an exploration of various scholarly perspectives, this chapter aims to provide a comprehensive understanding of the implications and transformative potential of disruptive technologies on the educational and professional landscapes.

Chapter 10: A Service-Based Measurement Model for Determining Disruptive Workforce Training Technology Value: Return on Investment Calculations and Example

This chapter describes the critical role of information technology investments in enhancing business operations and employee training. As firms allocate substantial funds to information technology assets, they seek to improve training efficiency, support operational goals, and ultimately achieve measurable returns on these investments. Further, the chapter imparts the ways in which innovative technologies, such as business analytics systems and extended reality tools, contribute to training and performance improvements. By focusing on a service-based model, it emphasizes how the perceived value of these technologies is determined by their users. The chapter illustrates how effective technology integration can lead to increased profits, operational efficiencies, and overall organizational benefits. It underscores the importance of aligning technology investments with strategic goals to maximize return on investment and achieve sustained business success.

Chapter 11: Technological Disruptions in the Service Sector

This chapter describes the profound impact of technological disruptions on the service sector, focusing on key industries such as financial services, tourism and hospitality, legal services, and healthcare. It provides a comprehensive analysis of how disruptive technologies, including artificial intelligence (AI), cloud computing, machine learning, and big data analytics, are transforming these sectors. Through a narrative review and empirical studies, it shares the significant changes in consumer and employee behavior, as well as the evolution of human resource practices in response to these disruptions. The chapter also addresses the practical implications and future research opportunities that arise from these technological advancements, emphasizing the need for businesses to adapt and innovate continuously to stay competitive in a rapidly changing landscape.

PART THREE: INCLUSIVE AND SUSTAINABLE EDUCATIONAL AND WORKFORCE INNOVATIONS

In this section, we delve into how innovative technologies are fostering inclusive and sustainable practices in education and beyond.

Chapter 12: Inclusive E-Tutoring Between Artificial Intelligence, Corporality, and Emotionality: Flipped Inclusion and New Research Perspectives

This chapter shares the transformative impact of artificial intelligence (AI) on e-tutoring and inclusive education. It underscores the European Commission's report revealing a digital skills gap and emphasizes the need for educational reform to adapt to future societal demands. The discussion focuses on integrating AI into education to enhance learning environments, optimize teaching methodologies, and support personalized learning. The chapter addresses the role of AI in creating virtual learning environments, the significance of emotional education, and the challenges of balancing digital and physical learning experiences. It also portrays the ethical considerations of AI in education and proposes the "Flipped Inclusion" model, which emphasizes inclusive, ecological development through innovative teaching practices and responsible technology use.

Chapter 13: Community-Driven Governance, Between Complex Education and Flipped Inclusion: Research Perspectives for an Eco-Sustainable Economic Pedagogy

This chapter explores the profound impact of AI on corporate governance, emphasizing how AI technologies are transforming economic activities and corporate structures. The discussion probes the integration of AI in decision-making processes, compliance monitoring, and enhancing corporate reporting. AI's role in corporate governance introduces new challenges and opportunities, necessitating a balance between technological advancements and ethical considerations. The chapter further clarifies the potential of AI to automate and optimize governance tasks while underscoring the importance of human oversight and conveys the shift towards community-driven governance models and the necessity for inclusive and accountable AI implementation to ensure sustainable and equitable corporate practices.

Chapter 14: Sustainable Development Between Artificial Intelligence and Education: The Inclusive Perspective of the Flipped Inclusion Model

This chapter addresses the integration of artificial intelligence (AI) in promoting sustainable development and education through the "Flipped Inclusion" model. It emphasizes the need for a society capable of adapting to crises while preserving resources and ensuring human dignity. The culture of sustainability is framed as essential social capital that fosters civic cohesion and solidarity. The chapter advocates for an inclusive educational model, recognizing the interconnectedness of social, economic, and environmental dimensions. AI's role is highlighted as a catalyst for sustainable and inclusive development, necessitating ethical considerations and collaboration across various educational and governance contexts. Through AI and innovative educational practices, the chapter envisions a society where technological advancements and human values coexist harmoniously, fostering an inclusive and sustainable future.

Section 1
Transforming Education With Technology

Chapter 1
Artificial Intelligence in Education:
Transforming Learning and Teaching

Julie A. Delello
https://orcid.org/0000-0002-4326-8096
The University of Texas at Tyler, USA

Jennifer Bailey Watters
https://orcid.org/0000-0002-8350-2369
The University of Texas at Tyler, USA

Arlene Garcia-Lopez
https://orcid.org/0009-0000-5006-1758
Miami Dade College, USA

ABSTRACT

This chapter explores artificial intelligence (AI) and its potential to revolutionize the field of education by enhancing teaching and learning. It further highlights ways in which AI technologies can support educators and students, including content creation encompassing voice and video, task automation, and the provision of personalized learning through adaptive learning platforms. Potential benefits to leveraging AI technology include improved learner engagement, automated administrative processes, and more robust data-driven insights. As AI advances, a unique opportunity emerges for schools to prepare educators to use AI in the classroom and for educators to redefine traditional teaching methodologies. Nonetheless, balancing AI innovation with ethical considerations includes considering issues in transparency and privacy in AI algorithms as well as mitigating biases in the data.

INTRODUCTION

In an age where artificial intelligence (AI) seamlessly integrates into daily life, its infusion into educational contexts represents promising opportunities but also significant challenges. For example, a recent news report highlighted the experience of a University of North Georgia student who fought back against a policy that landed her on academic probation with the possibility of losing her scholarship

(Menezes, 2024). The student used an online tool to revise her work, Grammarly, that utilizes Generative AI (Gen-AI) for spelling and grammar errors. The University of North Georgia previously supported the use of Grammarly, advertising its service to students, but the situation led to a seesaw of confusion, with the university removing, and then again, advertising the resource. A spokesperson for the platform responded, stating, "Education is wrestling right now with how they need to evolve the way they assess writing" (See Menezes, 2024, para. 13).

The story is but one example of the broader struggle within education to integrate such innovative technologies—a journey marked by transformative benefits and concomitant disruptions. Readers may reflect on the many technological advancements that have emerged over the years, reshaping the educational landscape. These innovations range from the advent of the Texas Instruments (TI) calculators to desktop and laptop computers, the emergence of the internet, the introduction of electronic readers (eReaders), distance learning, the implementation of learning management systems (LMS), and the widespread adoption of smartphones and tablets. This evolution also includes the use of interactive smartboards, digital media, and virtual simulations in classrooms. In fact, almost 20 years ago, The International Society for Technology in Education (ISTE) emphasized that:

> Effective integration of technology is achieved when students are able to select technology tools to help them obtain information in a timely manner, analyze, and synthesize the information, and present it professionally. Technology should become the integral part of how the classroom functions— as accessible as all other classroom tools (Harris, 2005, p. 116).

As AI becomes increasingly embedded in our daily lives—from smartphones to streaming services—the educational sector struggles to keep pace, often hindered by a lack of understanding and research-based practices (Delello et al., 2024; Yau et al., 2023).

As we examine the realm of recent technological breakthroughs, this chapter focuses on the profound impact of AI and Gen-AI in education. We also explore the role of biometrics in AI, offering a perspective as to how these technologies are reshaping the educational landscape. Further, the chapter surveys a variety of applications and provides examples of AI in education, highlights current impacts and potential future developments, and then examines transformative and disruptive implications from related case studies. The final section brings forth considerations around future trends for education, ethical considerations, policy and regulations, and suggested resources for future reading.

REVIEW OF THE LITERATURE

From its origins in rule-based systems, AI has undergone a transformative journey, progressively adopting machine learning (ML) and deep learning models (DLMs) to enhance its ability to process and interpret complex data. This progression has led to the advent of generative artificial intelligence (Gen-AI), a model designed to generate new content, as opposed to predicting outcomes from a specific dataset (Zewe, 2023). Gen-AI has the capability to generate text, images, sounds, code, and other media using models in response to prompts. In fact, "2024" has been declared the "year of generative AI," as noted by Hockenbary (2024, para. 1). The transformative impact of AI in education stems from its core ability to recognize and interpret patterns. This capability is integral to both basic rule-based algorithms and more complex machine learning (ML) and deep learning models (DLMs). Such AI systems excel in handling large datasets, which underpin technologies like adaptive learning platforms and intelligent tutoring systems. These systems utilize pattern recognition to personalize and enhance the educational experience.

INTELLIGENT TUTORING, MOOCS, AND PERSONALIZED LEARNING

Intelligent Tutoring Systems

A rapidly evolving area within Gen-AI influencing education is intelligent tutoring systems (ITSs). Nwana (1990) explained how ITS reformists, since the 1980's, have advocated and explored advancements in which the computer acts as a tutor. From its inception, "Intelligent tutoring systems (ITSs) [were] computer programs that [were] designed to incorporate techniques from the AI community in order to provide tutors which know *what* they teach, *who* they teach and *how* to teach it" (Nwana, 1990, p. 252). In today's landscape of ITS, researchers point out that this educational technology has advanced to introduce new skills, personalize instruction, scaffold learning through practice problems, and provide corrections, hints, and evaluative feedback (VanLehn, 2006; Weitekamp et al., 2020). In fact, one of the most recent developments in ITSs involves a transformation from focusing solely on the student to using a method where humans guide computers, which in turn instruct students. The approach is based on the concept of machine teaching (Mosqueira-Rey et al., 2023). This evolution provides a platform for the tutoring system to move beyond solving a problem to support student development in methods of problem-solving (Weitekamp et al., 2020), or in simple terms, teach the computer to become a better teacher (Mosqueira-Rey et al., 2023). A number of studies indicate advancements in ITS tools leading to positive learner outcomes (Kulik & Fletcher, 2016; Mousavinasab et al., 2021; VanLehn et al, 2007; Weitekamp et al., 2020); however, scholars point out limitations regarding difficult and time-consuming development, especially in moving from closed tasks to open learning models (Devidze et al., 2020; Mousavinasab et al., 2021; VanLehne, 2011; Winne, 2021).

The K-12 and higher education communities have embraced a range of ITS tools over the years. Additional examples of foundational ITS platforms include AutoTutor, a natural language tutor (Nye at al., 2014) that helps students learn by holding a conversation. Another successful early ITS Cognitive Tutor was developed by Carnegie Learning to support learning mathematics and curriculum development (see U.S. Department of Education, 2016). An additional example of a pioneering advancement in ITSs can be found at Texas A&M University, where a research team is developing a robust model focused on upper-level elementary reading comprehension and teacher professional learning. The national platform called KATE (Knowledge Acquisition and Transformation Expansion) aims to improve reading outcomes for students while also developing supplemental professional learning for teachers to gain proficiency in implementing ITS. KATE, available for learners in English and Spanish, is a five-year project between the Texas A&M research team, WestEd and Analytica Insights, Inc. The team indicates that some schools currently engaged in the project have reported up to 100% passing rates on standardized reading assessments (literacy.io, 2023).

In military education, several ITSs have been employed to enhance advanced training programs. Presently, the military is examining a specific ITS designed to facilitate the enhancement of motor-cognitive skills, with a focus on improving marksmanship abilities. Zotov and Kramkowski (2023) identify the use of ITSs for motor-cognitive skills as an emerging area, which continued development may have broad cross-educational implications, like students and adults with impairments. With the ITS landscape expanding rapidly, learners can also engage with the Teachable Machine to generate their own ML machine learning models and advance the field.

Massive Open Online Courses

With these ITS systems paving the way for curriculum development and wraparound instruction, Massive Open Online Courses or MOOCs, have rapidly expanded. MOOCs provide a range of adaptive learning situated within synchronous and asynchronous settings. For example, the Khan Academy provides comprehensive learning opportunities for K-12 students across the curriculum in addition to college-preparatory and Advanced Placement courses. Extending beyond K-12, the Khan Academy also offers college math and graduate assessment preparation, such as the Medical College Admission Test (MCAT) and the Law School Admission Test (LSAT), driven by a personalized and adaptive learning tool. Another popular MOOC is Coursera, which offers a comprehensive array of courses aimed at adult learners from various sectors, including industry, business, government, and academia. This platform allows learners to earn certificates, advance their skills, and engage in projects for real-world application.

Personalized Learning

Expanding beyond individual growth within tutoring systems, AI has allowed educators to leverage personalized learning experiences, adapt and generate content, and provide real-time support for students (Ruiz-Rojas et al., 2023). For example, ML algorithms analyze data on learners' behaviors, preferences, and performance to create customized learning experiences. This can include adaptive learning paths that adjust in real-time based on the learner's progress. LMSs increasingly incorporate algorithms to gather data and personalize the learning experience for users (Kabudi, et al., 2023). For instance, the LMS Canvas has integrated 3rd party AI features to help teachers personalize learning and automate certain tasks, such as grading and providing feedback (Instructure, 2023).

Other examples of personalized learning platforms include the web-based mathematics program Dreambox AI geared towards students from kindergarten through eighth grade. This adaptive learning system utilizes AI and ML techniques tailored to the unique needs of every student. Mursion, a personalized learning tool used in K-12 educator professional learning as well as university educator preparation programs, also uses a form of ML through immersive simulation. Here, learners can practice difficult and high-stakes conversations with multiple avatars utilizing a blend of AI and human performance. Tools like Newsela adapt news articles for different reading (Lexile) levels, allowing students to understand complex topics at their own pace. Additionally, chatbots can act as virtual tutors providing personalized assistance to students. These versions can be customized per subject matter and grade level and serve as virtual tutors through OpenAI's GPTs. For example, educator Jenny Stauffer (2024) used the GPT platform to create "ChemBot" in order to teach chemical nomenclature and create practice problems for her students. As mentioned in relation to the ITSs, the Khan Academy also offers a personalized learning platform along with practice exercises, instructional videos, and the virtual tutor Khanmigo. In regard to personalized learning, Abulibdeh et al., (2024), suggested that the "tailoring of educational content not only optimizes learning but also fosters a sense of autonomy and self-efficacy in students" (p. 11).

THE POWER OF LEARNING ANALYTICS

Introduction to Learning Analytics

Learning analytics (LA), an area of technology that is both disruptive and transformative, merges data analysis and human acumen to reveal data patterns that produce actionable intelligence to provide educational solutions (Siemens, 2013; Zhao et al., 2023). An often-referenced definition of LA was debuted at the 1st International Conference on Learning Analytics and Knowledge: "Learning analytics is the measurement, collection, analysis and reporting of data about learners and their contexts, for purposes of understanding and optimizing learning and the environments in which it occurs" (Long & Siemens, 2011, p. 34). LA is a domain of analysis that renders data into actionable targets or functions, and potentially leads to decision-making that directly impacts students, faculty, administrators, and organizations, at large. Some efforts in LA focus on the predictive components of data analysis and concentrate on learners and their environment to improve learning outcomes, interventions, and increases in student engagement (Xing & Du, 2018; Zhao et al., 2021).

The Role of Learning Management Systems

In the modern context, LMSs such as Canvas, Brightspace and Blackboard are useful platforms that influence education (Turnbull et al., 2020). Holloway (2020) reasoned that the increased use of LA is natural given the higher number of online learners and the wide adoption of LMSs used to administer courses. The primary aim of LA is to automate specific courses with personalized experiences that focus on the needs of students and faculty. Additionally, advancements in AI have improved adaptive models to bring personalized experiences to all students (Aljohani et al. 2019; Ouyang et al. 2023). Data collected and analyzed through campus mobile applications, for instance, may track engagement with campus life and be utilized to improve student life programming to increase student participation and retention (Jones & Salo, 2018). Other scopes in the field include the utilization of LA to conduct systematic reviews to assist stakeholders to organize and interpret data, with the aim of understanding student intervention strategies, measure key performance indicators, analyze curriculum, and offer support in student and faculty development (Choi et al., 2018).

AI and Learning Analytics Integration

Recently, AI has advanced to incorporate learning analytics (LA), increasingly recognizing, and adapting to unique human learning models and experiences (Tsai et al., 2020). Lauded as leveling technology and with aims to equalize educational practices, such as student feedback and grade distribution, sectors of LA have focused on AI assisted peer-assessment systems that promote higher order thinking and provide students with timely feedback. Reservations for these systems include the lack of quality or detailed feedback that many of the existing models provide to students (Darvishi et al., 2021). Nonetheless, as AI improves in capabilities such as NLP, peer assessments systems improve in quality. Furthermore, a focus on human-centered AI has emerged where, for example, LA leverages big data to identify students who are at risk of not completing their courses, enabling institutions to provide early interventions (Yang et al., 2021).

The introduction of LA-AI to learning environments has allowed data exploration to flourish. Campbell et al., (2007) developed the "Five Steps of Analytics" framework that delineates the steps, capture, report, predict, act, and refine as suitable applications of data analysis. Building upon such a framework and other similar ones, Zhao et al., (2023) proposed the Human-Centered Artificial Intelligence Learning Analytics Framework (HAILA) that aimed to improve data presented by the AI algorithm via the steps of data collection, data processing, data analysis, result confirmation, and result application. The framework includes a results confirmation process to review the accuracy of the data produced by AI and includes a crucial step for application. Experiments on the effectiveness of the framework (Zhang et al., 2023) showed it to be significantly effective in results application of learning strategies. Evidence-driven data results are used to plan optimal learning outcomes, predict learning, accurately identify students that need support, and importantly test and enhance the trustworthiness of AI algorithms.

Learning Analytic Dashboards and Predictive Learning Analytics

Learning analytic dashboards (LAD) are visual data representations used to identify student learning and monitor progress. One of the benefits of using LADs is that they are useful in identifying patterns that may have previously been unrecognized by human users (Chen et al., 2023). LADs may include predictive learning analytics (PLA) such as grade forecasting, risk status, customized personalization courses, and other insights such as engagement with an LMS platform. PLA dashboards allow for not only the mapping of outcomes but also learner processes (Ifenthaler et al., 2021). For example, Herotodou et al., (2019) produced a study to find out if providing educators in a distance learning higher education institution with PLA data predicted student performance and empowered faculty to aid students who were at risk of not completing courses. Results showed that faculty may positively affect students' performance when engaged with PLA and that more data usage predicted better pass rates suggesting that PLA engagement may improve student performance.

Data alone does not provide solutions; rather, data that has been analyzed with inferences drawn and through which predictions are made makes a difference (King & Forder, 2016). LA is not a cure-all measure, but rather an opportunity to open lines of discussion, glean insight to improve student outcomes, including retention and completion, and improve institutional accountability. Learning analytics offers solutions to modern educational challenges, including limited funding, the pursuit of equal access to quality education, and evaluating the long-term effectiveness of educational models.

AI AND GENERATIVE AI APPLICATIONS

In education, Gen-AI offers a range of instructor and student applications. From creating lesson plans and study guides to generating practice exercises and visual aids, these intelligent AI technologies are transforming the landscape of educational content creation. In fact, educators have suggested that Gen-AI saves them time through task automation and further enhances their instruction while personalizing learning experiences for students (The Open Innovation Team & Department for Education, 2023).

Text and Language Generation

The influence of Gen-AI extends beyond mere content creation in education. Its applications delve into two distinct realms: text and language generation, and conversational AI chatbots. Advancements in natural language processing (NLP) and deep learning have significantly improved AI's ability to generate human-like text and speech (Kim et al., 2020). Together, ML and NLP facilitate the creation of dynamic educational content tailored to individual learners. For example, NLP algorithms can condense lengthy educational materials into concise summaries and generate relevant questions and quizzes, aiding in effective revision and assessment. The development of Generative Pre-trained Transformer (GPT) language models, such as GPT-3 and the subsequent GPT-4, has further enabled the generation of text that closely resembles human writing, allowing for the creation of diverse and engaging educational materials tailored to specific learning objectives.

Conversational AI Chatbots

One well-known example of Gen-AI is ChatGPT, an NLP chatbot developed by OpenAI. OpenAI (2024a) characterizes ChatGPT as engaging users through conversational interactions, equipped with the ability to "answer follow-up questions, admit its mistakes, challenge incorrect premises, and reject inappropriate requests" (para. 1). According to Kan (2023), ChatGPT has rapidly become one of history's quickest-expanding applications, amassing over one hundred million monthly users.

In classrooms, ChatGPT may provide virtual tutoring sessions (Nazir, 2023), provide explanations, help students with their homework assignments, and provide reviews for materials and practice quizzes (Javaid et al., 2023). Incorporating game-like elements through ChatGPT into educational processes also has the potential to increase student engagement and improve learning by offering dynamic, interactive, and customized gaming experiences (see Tulsiani, 2024). Additionally, conversational chatbots like OpenAI's Chatbot, Microsoft's Bing Chat, Perplexity, and Google Bard, now rebranded as Google Gemini, are being used in education to facilitate the development of language skills (Belda-Medina & Kokošková, 2023). New advancements in AI technology have led to the integration of ChatGPT with Adobe's portable document format (PDF) to interactively extract and understand content (see chatpdf.com). By incorporating ChatGPT, users can ask questions about the PDF's text, and AI generates answers based on the information within the document. Models such as ChatGPT have been shown to increase student motivation, engagement, and promote collaboration among students (Li & Xing, 2021; Pereira, 2016).

Voice-Activated Learning Tools

The advent of voice-activated tools powered by AI, such as those integrated with systems like ChatGPT, represents significant change in education, underscoring innovative ways for students to engage with digital learning environments. Revealed by Apple in 2011, the Siri app was a paradigm shift for how the public accessed information, designed to be a "do-engine" that would "allow people to hold conversations with the internet" (Bosker, 2013, para. 11). Today, voice-activated devices provide a platform for learning that supports student oral language development, literacy, and critical thinking (Butler & Starkey, 2024). For example, the virtual Google Assistant, which debuted in May 2016, provides educational support by answering questions, facilitating language learning, and assisting with schedules. Further, Dousay and Hall (2018) reported that teachers found Amazon Echo Dots useful for a broad range of classroom activities: music, computational games, reminders for classroom transitions, telling stories, and allowing students to check spelling or pose inquiries. Another study highlighted how Amazon's Alexa was a useful tool in enhancing language learning through opportunities for increased conversation and pronunciation feedback but lacked native language support (Dizon, 2017).

AI-Driven Innovations in Language Learning

Additional AI-driven language learning apps, such as Duolingo Max, based on GPT-4, use Gen-AI to personalize vocabulary and grammar lessons. Additionally, newer AI features of the platform include "Explain That" where "learners can enter a chat with Duo to get a simple explanation on why their answer was right or wrong" (Duolingo Team, 2023, para. 8). Another example is Grammarly, an intelligent writing assistant, which offers features that assist with brainstorming, structuring, citing sources with Gen-AI support, comprehending the rationale behind its suggestions, and employing AI to complete assignments. Similarly, ELSA (English Language Speech Assistant) is an AI-powered language learning application focused on improving English pronunciation and fluency skills. It uses a chatbot-like experience where learners can engage in real-world conversations and get feedback from an AI English speaking coach. Moreover, these platforms adjust the difficulty and content of lessons based on the learner's progress, offering a prescriptive and personalized language program.

Beyond language and literacy support, common uses for voice-activated tools in today's classrooms involve interactive learning opportunities, math and science instruction, and inclusive support for diverse learning needs. Highlighted below in Table 1 are various platforms that exemplify the integration of such technologies in classrooms.

Table 1. Learning platforms for diverse needs

Platform/Tool	Student Use in Education
WellSaid Labs	Supports cross-curricular needs by engaging students interactively.
Read Aloud	Enhances reading skills for students with reading disabilities.
Murf AI	Aids in creating dynamic learning content through speech to text capabilities.
Otter.ai	Facilitates notetaking and comprehension; beneficial for students with writing impairments.
Verbit	Supports accessible learning with accurate transcription services.
Google Docs Voice Typing	Assists students with motor skills disabilities in writing activities through speech-to-text technology.
ChatGPT	Provides interactive and adaptive learning in math by breaking down complex problems.
Conker	Enhances math understanding with step-by-step problem-solving assistance.
SoapBox Labs	Offers speech recognition tools for math and science curricula, promoting inclusive education for younger students.
Dyslexic AI Assistant	Tailored to improve reading accessibility for students with dyslexia.
FlexClip	Makes content more accessible through video creation, facilitating visual learning.
Flint-AI for Schools	Incorporates AI tools to enhance learning for all, focusing on inclusivity.
Speechify	Converts text to speech, supporting auditory learning for students with reading impairments.
Google Text-to-Speech	Transforms text into natural-sounding speech to aid comprehension for various learning needs.

continued on following page

Table 1. Continued

Platform/Tool	Student Use in Education
Natural Reader	Provides auditory learning methods via text-to-speech, supporting students requiring different learning approaches.
Amazon Polly	Enhances textual understanding with lifelike speech for students with disabilities.
Lovo	Rapidly converts text to speech in over 100 languages using a variety of voices, enhancing multi-lingual learning.

Research studies have shown positive outcomes for students engaging with voice-activated tools related to oral language development and literacy (Belpeame et al., 2018; Neumann, 2019; Underwood, 2017; Underwood, 2021; Vogt et al., 2017; Westlund et al., 2017). Dizon and Gayed (2021) investigated the use of Grammarly, among 31 Japanese university students learning English. Findings indicated that the platform contributed to a reduction in grammatical errors and enhanced the lexical diversity in the writing of the students. Furthermore, studies by Chang et al., (2021) and Marzuki et al., (2023) reported that a blending of different AI writing tools improved students' overall writing quality. While more studies have been conducted in the K-12 setting, voice-activated technology scholarship is also showing growth in higher education. Saiz-Manzanares et al., (2020) conducted a study on intelligent personal assistance in 109 health science students and found more positive student satisfaction related to teaching and accessibility within the intervention group utilizing voice-activated tools. However, a notable finding revealed no difference in learning outcomes between the control and intervention groups.

Educational Content Generators

Building upon the insights learned from AI analytics, content generation applications present a unique opportunity for educators to redefine traditional teaching methodologies. By harnessing the power of AI-driven generators, educators can significantly save time in preparing interactive and engaging instructional materials, providing instant feedback to students, streamlining the grading process, and tailoring lessons to meet the diverse needs of learners. For instance, MagicSchool.ai has emerged as a comprehensive AI-driven educational platform boasting an array of over 50 tools aimed at facilitating lesson planning, content creation, and the generation of assessments, alongside the development of individual education plans (IEPs), and differentiation of student instruction. Similarly, Eduaide.ai is an AI-powered teaching assistant designed to help teachers with lesson planning, instructional design, and generating educational content. It offers a resource generator, teaching assistant, feedback bot and AI chat. Further, Padlet just unveiled Magic Padlet, which uses the power of Gen-AI to create entire Padlets based on textual descriptions. Additionally, the program uses the power of Gen-AI to create Padlet images based on user descriptions in the "I can't draw" platform.

Curipod introduces interactive slide decks complete with polls and questions to engage learners actively, while Education Copilot offers AI-generated templates for an array of educational needs, from lesson plans to student reports. Furthermore, Diffit provides leveled resources tailored to any subject, saving educators time, and allowing for the customization of materials to fit the diverse needs of the students. Twee leverages Gen-AI to revolutionize lesson planning for English teachers, offering a suite of tools that drastically reduces preparation time. With Twee, educators can instantly generate engaging content for YouTube videos, craft dialogues or stories on diverse themes, devise multiple-choice and true/false questions, and uncover intriguing discussion prompts, facts, and quotes by notable individuals.

Parlay is an AI-powered instructional platform designed to assist teachers in orchestrating meaningful classroom discussions. It offers access to over 4000 discussion prompts across various subjects, topics, and educational levels, catering to a diverse range of teaching needs. Additionally, educators have the option to include Parlay Genie, a feature that allows for the generation of custom discussion prompts based upon a particular topic and grade. To enhance lessons in geography and cultural diversity, Google Maps incorporated Gen-AI, allowing users to search and navigate locations in immersive 3D. Using image recognition technology, the Google Lens in Maps feature also integrates augmented reality (AR) to overlay real-time information on the user's surroundings to help find instant information and acquire language translation support.

AI-Generated Characters

Educators may also want to increase motivation and stimulate student learning with AI characters. Gen-AI characters have been defined as "digital representations of a person created by ML algorithms that are made to look, sound and behave realistically without necessarily being malicious (like deepfakes)" (Pataranutaporn, et al., 2021, p. 1014). For example, ChatGPT can be utilized to simulate interviews with a variety of figures (Campell, 2023). For instance, when a student poses a query to ChatGPT (OpenAI, 2024c) to speak as Ronald Reagan, the 40th President of the United States, about his Cold War policies, the ChatGPT-generated text could respond in character and begin with:

> Well, my fellow Americans, as your 40th President, I took a firm stance against the Cold War and the expansion of Soviet influence. From the very beginning, I believed in peace through strength. It was clear to me that the Soviet Union, under its communist regime, posed not just a geopolitical challenge, but an ideological one to the free world.

Other examples include Canva's AI Character Generator, which allows educators to create characters by inputting details of their appearances, personalities, and skills. Similarly, the AI-driven application character.ai answers user questions in the voice of famous celebrities, living or historical figures, or even fictional characters. The Hello History application, accessible via web or mobile, leverages state-of-the-art AI to offer immersive interactive experiences. Users can engage in lifelike conversations with more than 400 historical figures. Beyond just dialogue, the platform enables educators to generate comprehensive lesson plans, class activities, and assignments using advanced content generation tools. For instance, in a unit on the Civil Rights Movement, teachers can access a dedicated collection where students have the opportunity to interact with "Humies" – AI representations of influential figures like Rosa Parks, Jackie Robinson, Thurgood Marshall, and Martin Luther King, Jr. (see Figure 1). According to the site, "Students can deeply engage with historical figures, probing their experiences, motivations, and the convictions that drove them to seek change" (Humy, 2023, para. 8). Furthermore, the platform allows educators to create and share custom lessons and provides automatic grading of assignments through AI.

Figure 1. Civil rights movement

(Collections, Humy.ai., 2023)

GENERATIVE AI FOR VISUAL AND AUDIO MEDIA

Image generation

Gen-AI tools like Open-AI's DALL-E, Adobe Firefly, Microsoft Designer (formerly Bing Image Creator), DeepAI, and Midjourney AI allow users to create realistic images by typing descriptive prompts into a chat-like interface. For example, Figure 3, created with DALL-E2, and figure 2, produced with Adobe Firefly, are Gen-AI images, which utilized the same prompt "generate an image of a student using AI." Another tool, Canva's Magic Studio, designed for K-12 educators, is equipped with numerous AI capabilities that facilitate the creation and editing of images, graphics, and videos. According to Canva (2024), "Dream it up, then add it to your design. Watch your words transform into beautiful images and videos" (para. 6). Platforms like these are enabling educators to create visuals and diagrams to enhance teaching and learning.

Figure 2. Student using AI

(Created with DALLE-2)

Figure 3. Student using AI

(Created with Adobe Firefly)

Video Generation

Utilizing diffusion models, Google's Imagen Video demonstrates the capability to create videos from text prompts, marking a significant advancement in Gen-AI technology (Ho et al., 2022). Similarly, platforms like Meta's Make-A-Video are transitioning from text-to-image (T2I) generation to the more intricate process of text-to-video (T2V) generation, showcasing the evolving complexity of AI-driven content creation (Singer et al., 2022). Pictory further exemplifies this trend by transforming written or spoken text into educational videos, either through the user's voice or an AI-generated one, a feature that has been shown to potentially increase student comprehension and engagement (Pictory, 2023). Additionally, the cutting-edge technology of the OpenAI diffusion model, Sora, which is built on the foundations of DALLE-3 and GPT, represents another potential game-changer. Sora is capable of producing a minute of high-fidelity video from images or textual prompts, illustrating the vast potential of Gen-AI in education (OpenAI, 2024b). Together, these developments indicate a significant shift towards utilizing such tools for creating dynamic and engaging educational content.

Sound Generation

Gen-AI is revolutionizing the music industry and education by enabling the creation of original music compositions from descriptive text. This transformation is powered by sophisticated algorithms and ML techniques, which produce music with a level of accuracy and creativity that closely resembles human compositions. Despite the widespread lack of access to music education in the United States, as reported by the Arts Education Data Project (2022), Gen-AI platforms are bridging this gap by providing personalized content, practice platforms, live feedback, online instruments, and virtual lessons (Zhang & Wan, 2019) to meet the unique needs and of each learner (see Table 2). For instance, platforms such as Yousician and MakeMusic mimic virtual tutors by providing instant and personalized feedback, allowing students to refine their skills, correct mistakes, and reflect on their performances. Moreover, the ability of platforms like MuseNet and VEED.IO to generate diverse musical compositions from textual descriptions fosters creativity and abstract thinking (see Barbot & Webster, 2018).

Table 2. Sound generation platforms

Platform/Tool	Student Use in Education
OpenAI's Jukebox	Students can use a dataset of 1.2 million songs for music generation.
Google's Music Instrument Playground	Students can learn from a simulation of over 100 instruments from around the globe.
MakeMusic	Offers students virtual practice studios with customized feedback.
Gituru	Chatbot guiding students through guitar fundamentals with personalized feedback.
Yousician	Provides students with real-time feedback for guitar, bass, piano, or ukulele.
Flowkey	Allows students the opportunity to take virtual, interactive piano lessons.
Melodics	Focuses on drum pads, drums, and keyboards with personalized instruction and feedback.
MuseNet	Students create compositions in various genres for up to ten instruments.
Google Arts and Culture - Viola	Promotes creativity and interactive play with an interactive animated bird that plays cello and violin compositions.
Suno	AI-driven music creation plugin enables students to compose songs.
Eleven Labs' Kits AI	Allows students to create compositions with the use of AI-generated clone singers.
VOCALOID6	Generates realistic singing voices using AI technology for creative music production.
Musicfy	Students can create and edit musical compositions using their voice or over 100,000 natural sounding singing voices based on AI.
VEED.IO's Music Generator	Students select a music vibe and can transform text into custom soundtracks/compositions.

Ping-ping and Wang (2023) reported that AI technology has the ability to enhance student performance and improve the future of music education. As Gen-AI tools become increasingly integrated into education platforms and services, they promise to boost efficiency, creativity, and accessibility for both educators and their students.

Assessment and Quiz Generators

AI-driven platforms and tools not only simplify the creation of learning materials but also provide educators with assessments and enhance the quality of feedback and support provided to students. The realm of automated essay scoring, a pioneering application of AI in education, has expanded significantly. It now includes advanced systems like GotFeedback, which provides AI-generated constructive feedback on student submissions. Conker leverages AI algorithms to dynamically generate unique quizzes with a range of engaging question types. Further, Formative AI, QuestionWell, and Quizizz AI all assist educators in the creation of comprehensive assessments that are aligned with the instructional content. For example, educators can present slides with built-in questions, add questions to reading passages, websites, or YouTube videos, or even transform a PDF or Google document into an auto-graded quiz and adjust their instruction based on those results. Kahoot AI incorporates gamification into learning, using AI to create interactive quizzes and presentations that motivate students on any topic in seconds.

AI AND BIOMETRICS IN SCHOOLS

AI has begun to play a pivotal role not only in facilitating educational learning experiences but also in enhancing the security and efficiency within school settings. For example, AI may be used to recognize individuals based on unique physiological identifiers such as fingerprints, facial features, eye movements, emotional expressions, and voice patterns (Jain et al., 2004). This application of AI falls under the domain of biometrics defined as "the science of analyzing physical or behavioral characteristics specific to each individual to authenticate their identity" (Hernandez-de-Menendez et al., 2021, p. 366). Recently, the use of fingerprint identification was used as a method to successfully collect attendance data with an 87% success rate (Orike et al., 2023). Also, Gittlen (2011) highlighted the efficiency of "fingerprint lunch lines" and Hough (2010) detailed how thumbprints, transformed into digital codes, simplify the process of borrowing books from school libraries. The Partner Alliance for Safer Schools (PASS, 2023) reported that the actual fingerprint is not stored; rather, the software generates and keeps a unique code to represent the fingerprint.

Biometric-enabled exam proctoring applies various methods such as fingerprint analysis, voice recognition software, and facial scanning to accurately identify students (Kurni et al., 2023). Such advanced biometric software uses AI analytics to analyze the physical and behavioral patterns (e.g., eye movements, typing forms) of students, which may indicate cheating (see Mikhalchuk, 2020). More recently, schools have considered the integration of AI surveillance systems for campus safety (Nash, 2024). For example, SparkCognition's Visual AI Advisor uses algorithms to recognize specific behaviors that may indicate a security concern, such as unauthorized access, the identification of open or closed doors, suspicious vehicle movements, or even certain types of threats (e.g. weapons). Some schools have also promoted the use of wearable biometric devices such as Fitbits to track students' physical activity and overall health (Creaser et al., 2023).

BENEFITS, CHALLENGES, AND ETHICAL IMPLICATIONS

Advancements in AI have undoubtedly brought both benefits but also challenges to education. Notably, these developments have facilitated personalized and differentiated learning, enhanced accessibility, and promoted innovative teaching methodologies (Delello et al., 2023). They have also significantly contributed to fostering creativity and critical thinking among learners, while simultaneously increasing efficiency and saving time for educators (Megahed et al., 2023). A recent survey of approximately 1,000 teachers and 1,000 students facilitated by the Walton Family Foundation (2023) suggested a higher rate of teachers utilizing AI tools with 40% reporting weekly use versus approximately 22% of surveyed students. Moreover, survey findings included 73% of teachers indicating "ChatGPT can help students learn more," while 91% of teachers agreed with the survey inquiry that technology could help get students back on track from recent learning losses (Impact Research, 2023, pp. 1-2). The following example provided from a NEA Today reporter, Abreanna Blose (2023), illustrated the benefits scholars note related to efficiency, differentiation, personalized learning, and supporting student outcomes:

> The chatbot also can rewrite responses at different reading levels. Shields [a teacher] explains that she sent tenth-grade assignments to ChatGPT, asking the chatbot to restructure the material at a sixth-grade level. Her students were then able to follow along and participate in class with their differentiated material (p. 1).

Challenges to AI Use in Education

Despite the benefits of AI in educational settings, significant constraints persist, encompassing a range of ethical, technical, and practical concerns (see Delello et al., 2023). For example, an over-reliance on AI technology might not only hinder the development of critical thinking and creativity but also create the illusion of quick learning progress, which could lead to diminished cognitive abilities (Wu, 2023). Some scholars have suggested that students may use these tools to cheat or even plagiarize their work (Moorhouse et al., 2023). Also, the use of AI raises concerns about academic honesty, notably in how image generation tools may imitate existing works (Mittal, 2024). Furthermore, students may humanize chatbots, attributing life-like emotions or thoughts to them, and consequently, believe their outputs to be real (Mullaney, 2024).

For some, there is also a fear of job displacement and diminished human interaction in classrooms as AI tools become more prevalent (Langreo, 2023; Wu, 2023). Texas is navigating this concern, as the state education agency will employ AI grading for the 2024 administration of the state assessment administration across the reading, writing, science, and social studies open-ended responses. Peters (2024) explains that "the technology, which uses natural language processing, a building block of artificial intelligence chatbots such as GPT-4, will save the state agency about $15 million to 20 million per year that it would otherwise have spent on hiring human scorers through a third-party contractor" (para. 2). Educators and parents have questioned validity; however, agency officials clarify that initially, the computer will assess all the constructed responses. Following this, a quarter of the responses will undergo reevaluation by humans. If the computer assigns a score with low confidence, those particular responses will be automatically assigned to a human evaluator for reassessment (Peters, 2024).

Further complicating matters, educators face many unanswered questions amidst the rapid advancement of new Gen-AI tools, with existing research struggling to keep pace (Chiu, 2023; Fullan et al., 2023; Holmes et al., 2019). Moreover, AI-driven tools may replicate and even amplify existing biases unless the data they are trained on is carefully curated for neutrality and fairness (Megahed, et al., 2023). This is particularly crucial in educational contexts where biased content could adversely affect students' learning outcomes. According to The Oregon Department of Education (2023), "These technologies can exacerbate inequities for students from marginalized student groups in the absence of thoughtful policy, practice, and educator support and training" (p. 3). Accordingly, Li et al. (2023) there is a dearth of research examining the educational effects of incorrect feedback in the setting of AI-graded free-form responses. Suggestions for enhancing AI grading accuracy, such as retraining with additional data or refining the model architecture, may encounter issues with resource and technological constraints. In examining the influence of false positives (FPs) and false negatives (FNs) on student learning outcomes, Li et al. (2023) found participants "agreeing with the auto-grader during FPs even after reading the feedback, which represented missed learning opportunities" (p. 169).

As AI gathers and stores large amounts of data, there are risks that a student's personal information may be compromised. For instance, intelligent tutoring systems gather detailed data on each student's learning habits and progress. Similarly, AI-driven recruitment and admission systems use extensive personal information, such as demographics, family income, and academic records, to predict an applicant's potential success and enrollment fit (see Vance & Arciniega, 2023). The Family Educational Rights and Privacy Act (FERPA) in the U.S. currently regulates access to educational information and records. However, current anonymization techniques may not remain effective against future technological advances, posing difficulties to ensuring data privacy. Issues related to privacy, consent, and data security must be carefully considered to ensure that the benefits of such technologies are realized without compromising the rights and well-being of both educators and students.

Accompanying a lack of empirical evidence to support research-based best practices (Chiu, 2023), the rapid pace of evolving AI tools may also hinder professional learning. While the Walton Family Foundation (2023) survey indicates more teachers than students are using ChatGPT, another study involving 222 educators, from pre-kindergarten to college, found that a majority (54%) of the educators had minimal to no understanding of artificial intelligence, and an even greater percentage (55%) were not familiar with ChatGPT (Delello et al., 2024). From a practical sense, developing and implementing professional learning for educators at the current rate of evolution may be arguably unfeasible, in addition to the lack of empirical evidence to drive such learning.

If we, as educators, adopt the perspective that "technology should become an integral part of how the classroom functions—as accessible as all other classroom tools" (Harris, 2005, p. 116), our approach to AI tools must be underpinned by a commitment to ethical responsibility towards our students. This ethical approach is not just a matter of choice but a primary response to fostering an inclusive, equitable, and effective educational system. As such, the Office of Educational Technology within the United States Department of Education (2023) outlined a framework to promote ethical and equitable policies, which included four key areas: 1) center people (parents, educators, and students); 2) advance equity; 3) ensure safety, ethics, and effectiveness; and 4) promote transparency (pp. 6-10).

Policy Development in Schools

One aspect surrounding ethical consideration is the lack of guidelines, policies, and regulations concerning AI applications within education (Fullan et al., 2023). Much like professional learning, unable to keep up, it could be argued that educational institutions have more questions than answers in relation to developing guidelines and policies. The University of Northern Georgia student case that opened this chapter illustrates this concern with the ambiguous information surrounding the promotional use of Gen-AI tools, like Grammarly. Additionally, the use of biometric data also raises important ethical considerations. As we consider the future of education, it will be important to consider how these guidelines shape the implementation of AI to optimize educational outcomes, minimize risks, and prepare students for a rapidly changing world.

REFERENCES

Abulibdeh, A., Zaidan, E., & Abulibdeh, R. (2024). Navigating the confluence of artificial intelligence and education for sustainable development in the era of industry 4.0: Challenges, opportunities, and ethical dimensions. *Journal of Cleaner Production*, 437(140527), 1–15. 10.1016/j.jclepro.2023.140527

Aljohani, N. F., Daud, A., Abbasi, R. A., Alowibdi, J. S., Basheri, M., & Aslam, M. A. (2019). An integrated framework for course adapted student learning analytics dashboard. *Computers in Human Behavior*, 92, 679–690. 10.1016/j.chb.2018.03.035

Arts Education Data Project. (2022). *Millions of U.S. students denied access to music education, according to first-ever national study conducted by Arts Education Data Project*. Cision PRWeb. https://www.prweb.com/releases/millions-of-u-s-students-denied-access-to-music-education-according-to-first-ever-national-study-conducted-by-arts-education-data-project-876709378.html

Baker, R., & Siemens, G. (2014). Educational data mining and learning analytics. In Sawyer, R. K. (Ed.), *The Cambridge handbook of the learning sciences* (2nd ed., pp. 253–272). Cambridge University Press. 10.1017/CBO9781139519526.016

Barbot, B., & Webster, P. R. (2018). Creative thinking in music. In T. Lubart (Ed.), *The Creative Process* (Palgrave Studies in Creativity and Culture). Palgrave Macmillan. 10.1057/978-1-137-50563-7_10

Belda-Medina, J., & Kokošková, V. (2023). Integrating chatbots in education: Insights from the chatbot-human interaction satisfaction model (CHISM). *International Journal of Educational Technology in Higher Education*, 20(1), 62. 10.1186/s41239-023-00432-3

Belpaeme, T., Kennedy, J., Ramachandran, A., Scassellati, B., & Tanaka, F. (2018). Social robots for education: A review. *Science Robotics*, 3(21), 1–9. https://www.science.org/doi/10.1126/scirobotics.aat5954. 10.1126/scirobotics.aat595433141719

Blose, A. (2023, April 12). *As ChatGPT enters the classroom, teachers weigh pros and cons*. NEA Today. https://www.nea.org/nea-today/all-news-articles/chatgpt-enters-classroom-teachers-weigh-pros-and-cons

Bosker, B. (2013, Jan. 22). SIRI RISING: The inside story of Siri's origins—and why she could overshadow the iPhone. *HUFFPOST*. https://www.huffpost.com/entry/siri-do-engine-apple-iphone_n_2499165

Butler, L., & Starkey, L. (2024). OK Google, help me learn: An exploratory study of voice-activated artificial intelligence in the classroom. *Technology, Pedagogy and Education*, 33(2), 135–148. 10.1080/1475939X.2024.2311779

Campbell, J. P., DeBlois, P. B., & Oblinger, D. G. (2007). Academic analytics: A new tool for a new era. *EDUCAUSE Review*, 42(4), 40–42. https://er.educause.edu/articles/2007/7/academic-analytics-a-new-tool-for-a-new-era

Campell, R. (2023). *Utilizing AI In the classroom: 11 innovative strategies with ChatGPT*. Richard Campbell. https://richardccampbell.com/utilizing-ai-in-the-classroom-11-innovative-strategies-with-chatgpt/

Canva. (2024). *Free online AI image generator*. https://www.canva.com/ai-image-generator/

Chang, T. S., Li, Y., Huang, H. W., & Whitfield, B. (2021, March). Exploring EFL students' writing performance and their acceptance of AI-based automated writing feedback. In *2021 2nd International Conference on Education Development and Studies* (pp. 31–35). 10.1145/3459043.3459065

Chen, L., Geng, X., Lu, M., Shimada, A., & Yamada, M. (2023). How students use learning analytics dashboards in higher education: A learning performance perspective. *SAGE Open*, 13(3), 21582440231192151. 10.1177/21582440231192151

Chiu, T. K. F. (2023). The impact of Generative AI (GenAI) on practices, policies, and research direction in education: A case of ChatGPT and Midjourney. *Interactive Learning Environments*, 1–17. 10.1080/10494820.2023.2253861

Choi, S. P. M., Lam, S. S., Li, K. C., & Wong, B. T. M. (2018). Learning analytics at low cost: At-risk student prediction with clicker data and systematic proactive interventions. *Journal of Educational Technology & Society*, 21(2), 273–290. https://www.jstor.org/stable/26388407

Creaser, A. V., Frazer, M. T., Costa, S., Bingham, D. D., & Clemes, S. A. (2023). The use of wearable activity trackers in schools to promote child and adolescent physical activity: A descriptive content analysis of school staff's perspectives. *International Journal of Environmental Research and Public Health*, 19(21), 14067. 10.3390/ijerph192114067 36360944

Darvishi, A., Khosravi, H., Sadiq, S., & Gašević, D. (2022). Incorporating AI and learning analytics to build trustworthy peer assessment systems. *British Journal of Educational Technology*, 53(4), 844–875. 10.1111/bjet.13233

Delello, J. A., Sung, W., Mokhtari, K., & De Giuseppe, T. (2023). Exploring college students' awareness of AI and ChatGPT: Unveiling perceived benefits and risks. *Journal of Inclusive Methodology and Technology in Learning and Teaching*, 3(4), 1–25. https://www.inclusiveteaching.it/index.php/inclusiveteaching/article/view/132

Delello, J. A., Sung, W., Mokhtari, K., & De Giuseppe, T. (2024). Are K-16 educators prepared to address the educational and ethical ramifications of artificial intelligence software? *Advances in Information and Communication*, 921, 1–27. 10.1007/978-3-031-54053-0_28

Dizon, G. (2017). Using intelligent personal assistants for second language learning: A case study of Alexa. *TESOL Journal*, 8(4), 811–830. 10.1002/tesj.353

Dizon, G., & Gayed, J. M. (2021). Examining the impact of Grammarly on the quality of mobile L2 writing. *The JALT CALL Journal*, 17(2), 74–92. 10.29140/jaltcall.v17n2.336

Dousay, T. A., & Hall, C. (2018). Alexa, tell me about using a virtual assistant in the classroom. In *EdMedia + Innovate Learning* (pp. 1413–1419). Amsterdam, Netherlands.

Duolingo Team. (2023). *Introducing Duolingo Max, a learning experience powered by GPT-4*. Duolingo Team. https://blog.duolingo.com/duolingo-max/

Gittlen, S. (2011). Schools use biometrics to enhance student services. *EdTech Magazine*. https://edtechmagazine.com/k12/article/2011/07/schools-use-biometrics-enhance-student-services

Goodfellow, I., Pouget-Abadie, J., Mirza, M., Xu, B., Warde-Farley, D., Ozair, S., Courville, A., & Bengio, Y. (2014). Generative adversarial nets. In Vol. 27, pp. 2672–2680). Advances in Neural Information Processing Systems. Neural Information Processing Systems Foundation.

Harris, J. (2005). Our agenda for technology integration: It's time to choose. *Contemporary Issues in Technology & Teacher Education*, 5(2), 116–122. https://scholarworks.wm.edu/cgi/viewcontent.cgi?article=1092&context=educationpubs

Hernandez-de-Menendez, M., Morales-Menendez, R., Escobar, C. A., & Arinez, J. (2021). Biometric applications in education. [IJIDeM]. *International Journal on Interactive Design and Manufacturing*, 15(2-3), 365–380. 10.1007/s12008-021-00760-6

Herodotou, C., Hlosta, M., Boroowa, A., Rienties, B., Zdrahal, Z., & Mangafa, C. (2019). Empowering online teachers through predictive learning analytics. *British Journal of Educational Technology*, 50(6), 3064–3079. 10.1111/bjet.12853

Ho, J., Chan, W., Saharia, C., Whang, J., Gao, R., Gritsenko, A., Kingma, D. P., Poole, B., Norouzi, M., Fleet, D. J., & Salimans, T. (2022). *Imagen Video: High definition video generation with diffusion models*. https://imagen.research.google/video/paper.pdf

Hockenbary, L. (2024, February 21). *2024: The year of generative AI*. eSchool News. https://www.eschoolnews.com/digital-learning/2024/02/21/2024-the-year-of-gen-ai/

Holloway, K. (2020). Big Data and learning analytics in higher education: Legal and ethical considerations. *Journal of Electronic Resources Librarianship*, 32(4), 276–285. 10.1080/1941126X.2020.1821992

Ifenthaler, D., Gibson, D., Prasse, D., Shimada, A., & Yamada, M. (2021). Putting learning back into learning analytics: Actions for policy makers, researchers, and practitioners. *Educational Technology Research and Development*, 69(4), 2131–2150. 10.1007/s11423-020-09909-8

Impact Research. (2023, March 1). *Teachers and students embrace ChatGPT for education*. Walton Family Foundation. https://www.waltonfamilyfoundation.org/learning/teachers-and-students-embrace-chatgpt-for-education

Instructure (2023). *Accelerating the learning process with AI tools for teachers*. Instructure. https://www.instructure.com/resources/blog/accelerating-learning-process-ai-tools-teachers

Jain, A. K., Ross, A., & Prabhakar, S. (2004). An introduction to biometric recognition. *IEEE Transactions on Circuits and Systems for Video Technology*, 14(1), 4–20. 10.1109/TCSVT.2003.818349

Javaid, M., Haleem, A., Singh, R. P., Khan, S., & Khan, I. H. (2023). Unlocking the opportunities through ChatGPT tool towards ameliorating the education system. *BenchCouncil Transactions on Benchmarks. Standards and Evaluations*, 3(2), 100115. 10.1016/j.tbench.2023.100115

Jones, K. M., & Salo, D. (2018). Learning analytics and the academic library: Professional ethics commitments at a crossroads. *College & Research Libraries*, 79(3), 304–323. 10.5860/crl.79.3.304

Kabudi, T., Pappas, I., & Olsen, D. H. (2021). AI-enabled adaptive learning systems: A systematic mapping of the literature. *Computers and Education: Artificial Intelligence*, 2, 100017. 10.1016/j.caeai.2021.100017

Kan, M. (2023). *ChatGPT may be the fastest growing app of all time, beating TikTok*. PCMagazine. https://www.pcmag.com/news/chatgpt-may-be-the-fastest-growing-app-of-all-time-beating-tiktok

Kim, J., Shin, S., Bae, K., Oh, S., Park, E., & del Pobil, A. P. (2020). Can AI be a content generator? Effects of content generators and information delivery methods on the psychology of content consumers. *Telematics and Informatics*, 55, 101452. 10.1016/j.tele.2020.101452

King, N. J., & Forder, J. (2016). Data analytics and consumer profiling: Finding appropriate privacy principles for discovered data. *Computer Law & Security Report*, 32(5), 696–714. 10.1016/j.clsr.2016.05.002

Kulik, J. A., & Fletcher, J. D. (2016). Effectiveness of intelligent tutoring systems: A meta-analytic review. *Review of Educational Research*, 86(1), 42–78. https://psycnet.apa.org/doi/10.3102/0034654315581420. 10.3102/0034654315581420

Kurni, M., Mohammed, M. S., & Srinivasa, K. G. (2023). AI-assisted remote proctored examinations. In *A Beginner's Guide to Introduce Artificial Intelligence in Teaching and Learning* (pp. 199–211). Springer. 10.1007/978-3-031-32653-0_11

Langreo, L. (2023, July 28). *What educators think about using AI in schools*. Education Week. https://www.edweek.org/technology/what-educators-think-about-using-ai-in-schools/2023/04

Li, C., & Xing, W. (2021). Natural language generation using deep learning to support MOOC learners. *International Journal of Artificial Intelligence in Education*, 31(2), 186–214. 10.1007/s40593-020-00235-x

Li, P., & Wang, B. (2023). Artificial intelligence in music education. *International Journal of Human-Computer Interaction*, 1–10. 10.1080/10447318.2023.2209984

Li, T. W., Hsu, S., Fowler, M., Zhang, Z., Zilles, C., & Karahalios, K. (2023). Am I wrong, or is the autograder wrong? Effects of AI grading mistakes on learning. In *Proceedings of the 2023 ACM Conference on International Computing Education Research* - Volume 1 (pp. 159–176). Association for Computing Machinery. 10.1145/3568813.3600124

Long, P., & Siemens, G. (2011). Penetrating the fog: Analytics in learning and education. *EDUCAUSE Review*, 46(5), 31–40.

Marzuki, W., Widiati, U., Rusdin, D., Darwin, , & Indrawati, I. (2023). The impact of AI writing tools on the content and organization of students' writing: EFL teachers' perspective. *Cogent Education*, 10(2), 2236469. 10.1080/2331186X.2023.2236469

Megahed, F. M., Chen, Y.-J., Ferris, J. A., Knoth, S., & Jones-Farmer, L. A. (2023). How generative AI models such as ChatGPT can be (mis)used in SPC practice, education, and research? An exploratory study. *Quality Engineering*, 36(2), 287–315. 10.1080/08982112.2023.2206479

Menezes, D. (2024, March 3). *Student fights AI cheating allegations for using Grammarly*. NewsNation. https://www.newsnationnow.com/business/tech/ai/student-fights-academic-probation-ai-tool/

Mikhalchuk, O. (2020, January 14). Using AI and biometrics to enhance exam proctoring. *Biometric Update*. https://www.biometricupdate.com/202001/using-ai-and-biometrics-to-enhance-exam-proctoring

Mittal, A. (2024, Jan. 9). *The plagiarism problem: How generative AI models reproduce copyrighted content.* Unite.AI.

Moorhouse, B. L., Yeo, M. A., & Wan, Y. (2023). Generative AI tools and assessment: Guidelines of the world's top-ranking universities. *Computers and Education Open*, 5, 100151. 10.1016/j.caeo.2023.100151

Mosqueira-Rey, E., Hernández-Pereira, E., Alonso-Ríos, D., Bobes-Bascarán, J., & Fernández-Leal, Á. (2023). Human-in-the-loop machine learning: A state of the art. *Artificial Intelligence Review*, 56(4), 3005–3054. 10.1007/s10462-022-10246-w

Mousavinasab, E., Zarifsanaiey, N., & Niakan, S. R, Kalhori, Rakhshan, M., Keikha, L., & Saeedi, M.G. (2021). Intelligent tutoring systems: A systematic review of characteristics, applications, and evaluation methods. *Interactive Learning Environments*, 29(1), 142–163. 10.1080/10494820.2018.1558257

Mullaney, T. (2024). *Pedagogy and the AI guest speaker or what teachers should know about the Eliza Effect.* Tom Mullaney. https://tommullaney.com/2024/02/20/pedagogy-the-eliza-effect/?fbclid=IwAR0vDdDrcZ7HqaAm2ahf56hsE3To2VjWtLWvYAzt9Z44SGULcEnmqWWXdwY

Nash, J. (2024, March 7). AI surveillance in US schools becoming the safe bet. *Biometric Update.* https://www.biometricupdate.com/202403/ai-surveillance-in-us-schools-becoming-the-safe-bet

Neumann, M. M. (2020). Social robots and young children's early language and literacy learning. *Early Childhood Education Journal*, 48(2), 157–170. 10.1007/s10643-019-00997-7

Nwana, H. S. (1990). Intelligent tutoring systems: An overview. *Artificial Intelligence Review*, 4(4), 251–277. https://link.springer.com/article/10.1007/BF00168958. 10.1007/BF00168958

Nye, B. D., Graesser, A. C., & Hu, X. (2014). AutoTutor and family: A review of 17 years of natural language tutoring. *International Journal of Artificial Intelligence in Education*, 24(4), 427–469. 10.1007/s40593-014-0029-5

Open A. I. (2024a). *Introducing ChatGPT.* OpenAI. https://openai.com/blog/chatgpt

Open A. I. (2024b). *Sora.* OpenAI. https://openai.com/sora

Open A. I. (2024c). *ChatGPT.* (March 11 version) [Large language model]. OpenAI. https://chat.openai.com/chat

Oregon Department of Education. (2023). *Generative artificial intelligence (AI) in K-12 classrooms.* Oregon Department of Education. https://www.oregon.gov/ode/educator-resources/teachingcontent/Documents/ODE_Generative_Artificial_Intelligence_%28AI%29_in_K-12_Classrooms_2023.pdf

Orike, S., Bakare, B. I., & Sampson, J. U. (2023). An artificial intelligence-based fingerprint biometric application for students attendance register. *Research and Reviews: Advancement in Robotics*, 6(3), 19–27. 10.5281/zenodo.8317744

Ouyang, F., Wu, M., Zheng, L., Zhang, L., & Jiao, P. (2023). Integration of artificial intelligence performance prediction and learning analytics to improve student learning in online engineering course. *International Journal of Educational Technology in Higher Education*, 20(4), 4. 10.1186/s41239-022-00372-436683653

Pataranutaporn, P., Danry, V., Leong, J., Punpongsanon, P., Novy, D., Maes, P., & Sra, M. (2021). AI-generated characters for supporting personalized learning and well-being. *Nature Machine Intelligence*, 3(12), 1013–1022. 10.1038/s42256-021-00417-9

Pereira, J. (2016). Leveraging chatbots to improve self-guided learning through conversational quizzes. In García-Peñalvo, F. J. (Ed.), *Proceedings of the Fourth International Conference on Technological Ecosystems for Enhancing Multiculturality* (pp. 911–918). Association for Computing Machinery. 10.1145/3012430.3012625

Peters, K. (2024, April 9). Texas will use computers to grade written answers on this year's STAAR tests. *The Texas Tribune*. https://www.texastribune.org/2024/04/09/staar-artificial-intelligence-computer-grading-texas/

Picciano, A. G. (2012). The evolution of big data and learning analytics in American higher education. *Online Learning : the Official Journal of the Online Learning Consortium*, 16(3), 9–20. 10.24059/olj.v16i3.267

Pictory. (2023). *Case study: Teacher enhances student learning and engagement with video*. Pictory. https://pictory.ai/case-studies/pippa-teacher-helps-students

Ruiz-Rojas, L. I., Acosta-Vargas, P., De-Moreta-Llovet, J., & Gonzalez-Rodriguez, M. (2023). Empowering education with generative artificial intelligence tools: Approach with an instructional design matrix. *Sustainability (Basel)*, 15(15), 11524. 10.3390/su151511524

Sáiz-Manzanares, M. C., Marticorena-Sánchez, R., & Ochoa-Orihuel, J. (2020). Effectiveness of using voice assistants in learning: A study at the time of COVID-19. *International Journal of Environmental Research and Public Health*, 17(15), 5618. 10.3390/ijerph1715561832759832

Siemens, G. (2013). Learning analytics. *The American Behavioral Scientist*, 57(10), 1380–1400. 10.1177/0002764213498851

Singer, U., Polyak, A., Hayes, T., Yin, X., An, J., Zhang, S., Hu, Q., Yang, H., Ashual, O., Gafni, O., Parikh, D., Gupta, S., & Taigman, Y. (2022). MAKE-A-VIDEO: Text-to-video generation without text-video data. *arXiv:2209.14792*. https://doi.org//arXiv.2209.1479210.48550

Stauffer, J. (2024, January 26). *Meet 'ChemBot': How to design a personalized GPT tutor*. Edutopia. https://www.edutopia.org/article/designing-gpt-tutor

Teasley, S. D. (2017). Student facing dashboards: One size fits all? *Technology. Knowledge and Learning*, 22(3), 377–384. 10.1007/s10758-017-9314-3

The Open Innovation Team & Department for Education. (2023). *Generative AI in education: Educator and expert views*. https://assets.publishing.service.gov.uk/media/65609be50c7ec8000d95bddd/Generative_AI_call_for_evidence_summary_of_responses.pdf

The Partner Alliance for Safer Schools. (2023). *Safety and security guidelines for K-12 schools* (6th ed.). PASSK12. https://passk12.org/wpcontent/uploads/2023/03/PASS_SAFETY_ AND_SECURITY _GUIDELINES_6th_Ed.pdf

Tsai, S. C., Chen, C. H., Shiao, Y. T., Ciou, J. S., & Wu, T. N. (2020). Precision education with statistical learning and deep learning: A case study in Taiwan. *International Journal of Educational Technology in Higher Education*, 17(1), 12. https://sci-hub.se/10.1186/s41239-020-00186-2. 10.1186/s41239-020-00186-2

Tulsiani, R. (2024). The art of ChatGPT-driven gamification. *eLearning Industry*. https://elearningindustry.com/the-art-of-chatgpt-driven-gamification

Turnbull, D., Chugh, R., & Luck, J. (2020). Learning management systems: An overview. In Tatnall, A. (Ed.), *Encyclopedia of Education and Information Technologies* (pp. 1052–1058). Springer. 10.1007/978-3-030-10576-1_248

Underwood, J. (2017). Exploring AI language assistants with primary EFL students. In Borthwick, K., Bradley, L., & Thouësny, S. (Eds.), *CALL in a climate of change: Adapting to turbulent global conditions – Short papers from EUROCALL 2017* (pp. 317–321). IEEE. 10.14705/rpnet.2017.eurocall2017.733

Underwood, J. (2021). Speaking to machines: Motivating speaking through oral interaction with intelligent assistants. In Beaven, T., & Rosell-Aguilar, F. (Eds.), *Innovative language pedagogy report* (pp. 127–132)., 10.14705/rpnet.2021.50.1247

U.S. Department of Education, Institute of Education Sciences, What Works Clearinghouse. (2016, June). *Secondary mathematics intervention report: Cognitive Tutor®*. US DoE. http://whatworks.ed.gov

van Huijstee, M. (2024). *Enhancing learning management systems: A novel approach to improve usability through learning analytics* [Bachelor's thesis, University of Twente]. https://essay.utwente.nl/98161/

Vance, A., & Arciniega, J. (2023, Sept.). *FERPA & AI: What is protected?* EdAI HQ. https://ai4ed.substack.com/p/ferpa-and-ai-what-is-protected

VanLehn, K. (2006). The behavior of tutoring systems. *International Journal of Artificial Intelligence in Education*, 16(3), 227–265.

VanLehn, K. (2011). The relative effectiveness of human tutoring, intelligent tutoring systems, and other tutoring systems. *Educational Psychologist*, 46(4), 197–221. 10.1080/00461520.2011.611369

Vanlehn, K., Graesser, A. C., Jackson, G. T., Jordan, P., Olney, A., & Rosé, C. P. (2007). When are tutorial dialogues more effective than reading? *Cognitive Science*, 31(1), 3–62. 10.1080/03640210709 33698421635287

Vogt, P., de Haas, M., de Jong, C., Baxter, P., & Krahmer, E. (2017). Child-robot interactions for second language tutoring to preschool children. *Frontiers in Human Neuroscience*, 11, 73. 10.3389/fnhum.2017.0007328303094

Walton Family Foundation. (2023). *ChatGPT used by teachers more than students, new survey from Walton Family Foundation finds*. Walton Family Foundation. https://www.waltonfamilyfoundation.org/chatgpt-used-by-teachers-more-than-students-new-survey-from-walton-family-foundation-finds

Weitekamp, D., Harpstead, E., & Koedinger, K. R. (2020). An interaction design for machine teaching to develop AI tutors. In *Proceedings of the 2020 CHI Conference on Human Factors in Computing Systems* (pp. 1–11). Association for Computing Machinery. 10.1145/3313831.3376226

Westlund, K., Dickens, J. M. K., Jeong, L., Harris, S., DeSteno, P. L., & Breazeal, C. L. (2017). Children use non-verbal cues to learn new words from robots as well as people. *International Journal of Child-Computer Interaction*, 13, 1–9. 10.1016/j.ijcci.2017.04.001

Winne, P. H. (2021). Open learner models working in symbiosis with self-regulating learners: A research agenda. *International Journal of Artificial Intelligence in Education*, 31(3), 446–459. 10.1007/s40593-020-00212-4

Wu, Y. (2023). Integrating generative AI in education: How ChatGPT brings challenges for future learning and teaching. *Journal of Advanced Research in Education*, 2(4), 6–10. https://www.pioneerpublisher.com/jare/article/view/324. 10.56397/JARE.2023.07.02

Yang, S. J., Ogata, H., Matsui, T., & Chen, N. S. (2021). Human-centered artificial intelligence in education: Seeing the invisible through the visible. *Computers and Education: Artificial Intelligence*, 2(1), 1–5. 10.1016/j.caeai.2021.100008

Yau, K. W., Chai, C. S., Chiu, T. K., Meng, H., King, I., & Yam, Y. (2023). A phenomenographic approach on teacher conceptions of teaching Artificial Intelligence (AI) in K-12 schools. *Education and Information Technologies*, 28(1), 1041–1064. 10.1007/s10639-022-11161-x

Yenduri, G., Ramalingam, M., Chemmalar, S. G., Supriya, Y., Srivastava, G., Maddikunta, P. K. R., Deepti, R. G., Jhaveri, R. H., Prabadevi, B., Wang, W., Vasilakos, A. V., & Gadekallu, T. R. (2023). *Generative pre-trained transformer: A comprehensive review on enabling technologies, potential applications, emerging challenges, and future directions.* ArXiv, 2305.10435. https://doi.org//arXiv.2305.1043510.48550

Zewe, A. (2023). Explained: Generative AI. *How do powerful generative AI systems like ChatGPT work, and what makes them different from other types of artificial intelligence?* MIT News. https://news.mit.edu/2023/explained-generative-ai-1109

Zhang, J., & Wan, J. (2019). Advances in social science, education, and humanities research. In *International Conference on Education, Economics, and Information Management (ICEEIM 2019)* (Vol. 428, pp. 42-44). Atlantis Press. https://www.atlantis-press.com/article/125938453.pdf

Zhao, F., Hwang, G. J., & Yin, C. (2021). A result confirmation-based learning behavior analysis framework for exploring the hidden reasons behind patterns and strategies. *Journal of Educational Technology & Society*, 24(1), 138–151. https://www.jstor.org/stable/26977863

Zhao, F., Liu, G. Z., Zhou, J., & Yin, C. (2023). A learning analytics framework based on human-centered artificial intelligence for identifying the optimal learning strategy to intervene learning behavior. *Journal of Educational Technology & Society*, 26(1), 132–146. 10.30191/ETS.202301_26(1).0010

Zhou, V. (2023). *AI is already taking video game illustrators' jobs in China.* Rest of World. https://restofworld.org/2023/ai-image-china-video-game-layoffs/

Zotov, V., & Kramkowski, E. (2023). Moving-target intelligent tutoring system for marksmanship training. *International Journal of Artificial Intelligence in Education*, 33(4), 817–842. 10.1007/s40593-022-00308-z

ADDITIONAL READING

Dede, C. (2023, Aug. 6). What is academic integrity in the era of generative artificial intelligence? *Silver Lining for Learning*. https://silverliningforlearning.org/what-is-academic-integrity-in-the-era-of-generative-artificial-intelligence/

Equal Opportunity Schools. (2024, Feb. 27). *EOS and intentional futures launch mission–driven AI use case rubric*. EO Schools. https://eoschools.org/eos-and-intentional-futures-launch-mission-driven-ai-use-case-rubric/?fbclid=IwAR2wQcR8BKjpEu2-h6lAFkYVIMHeqQ0FEOVumKwUiypy0vJZU61UPtU9KmE

Fitzpatrick, D., Fox, A., & Weinstein, B. (2023). *The AI classroom: The ultimate guide to artificial intelligence in education*. The Hitchhiker's Guide for Educators Series. TeacherGoals Publishing.

Roschelle, J., Fusco, J., & Ruiz, P. (2024). *Review of guidance from seven states on AI in education*. Digital Promise., 10.51388/20.500.12265/204

United Arab Emirates, Minister of State for Artificial Intelligence (2023). *100 practical applications and use cases of generative AI*. https://ai.gov.ae/wp-content/uploads/2023/04/406.-Generative-AI-Guide_ver1-EN.pdf

United Nations Educational, Scientific and Cultural Organization. (2023). *Guidance for generative AI in education and research*. UN. https://unesdoc.unesco.org/ark:/48223/pf000038669

U.S. Department of Education, Office of Educational Technology. (2023). *Artificial intelligence and the future of teaching and learning: Insights and recommendations*. UN. https://www2.ed.gov/documents/ai-report/ai-report.pdf

KEY TERMS AND DEFINITIONS

Adaptive Learning Technologies: Use computer algorithms to customize content and personalize instruction based on learners' needs.

Artificial Intelligence (AI): Computer system or technology capable of performing human-like tasks such as understanding languages and recognizing patterns.

Biometrics: Unique behavioral or physical traits such as fingerprints, facial recognition, or eye movement used to identify individuals.

Conversational Chatbots: Computer program that simulates human conversation.

Deep Learning Models (DLMs): A type of machine learning model, with interconnected nodes, that can learn patterns from large amounts of data.

Generative AI (Gen-AI): A type of AI that can generate content such as text, images, and sounds.

Intelligent Tutoring Systems (ITSs): Advanced computer program, which uses AI analytics to adapt content, provide feedback, and personalize student instruction.

Language Learning Applications: Incorporate AI to personalize language instruction and provide feedback to learners on vocabulary, grammar, and pronunciation.

Learning Analytics (LA): Uses AI to analyze educational data related to learners' needs and their educational environment.

Machine Learning (ML): Allows computers to develop algorithms, learn from data, and make predictions without explicit human programming.

Natural Language Processing (NLP): A component of AI, which allows computers to understand and generate human language.

Personalized Learning (PL): Uses AI to adapt educational content and instruction to the learner's individual needs.

Virtual Tutors: Intelligent system that uses AI analytics to deliver personalized instruction and support.

Chapter 2
A Novel Approach for Implementing Blockchain Technology in the Education Sector

Tarun Kumar Vashishth
https://orcid.org/0000-0001-9916-9575
IIMT University, India

Vikas Sharma
https://orcid.org/0000-0001-8173-4548
IIMT University, India

Kewal Krishan Sharma
https://orcid.org/0009-0001-2504-9607
IIMT University, India

Bhupendra Kumar
https://orcid.org/0000-0001-9281-3655
IIMT University, India

ABSTRACT

Blockchain technology has the transformative potential to reshape the education sector by addressing challenges related to student data privacy, certification, and credential transfer. This chapter proposes a comprehensive approach to implementing blockchain in education, encompassing the development of a decentralized student record system, issuance of digital certificates, implementation of a blockchain-based learning management system, creation of a decentralized marketplace for educational resources, and provision of a transparent donation platform. By leveraging blockchain's decentralized and secure attributes, this approach aims to establish a tamper-proof system for storing, verifying, and sharing educational records. The benefits include enhanced security of student records, streamlined credential verification, and efficient resource transfer. The chapter explores potential applications like digital identity management, credential verification, secure data storage, and smart contracts for academic transactions.

DOI: 10.4018/979-8-3693-3003-6.ch002

INTRODUCTION

The integration of blockchain technology into the education sector marks a transformative leap towards a more secure, transparent, and efficient system. In an era where traditional methods of record-keeping and credential verification face increasing challenges, blockchain emerges as a novel solution capable of revolutionizing the way educational data is managed. Research by Xu and Duan (2020) highlighted an overview of the potential applications of blockchain technology in education, as well as the challenges that must be overcome for successful implementation. This research explores the potential of implementing blockchain technology in education, focusing on its ability to create a tamper-proof and decentralized ledger for storing and verifying academic credentials. With concerns over credential fraud, data inconsistencies, and the cumbersome nature of verification processes, blockchain offers a decentralized and transparent alternative. By leveraging cryptographic principles, each educational record becomes an immutable block in a chain, ensuring that academic achievements, certifications, and degrees are securely stored and easily verifiable. This approach not only streamlines the verification process but also mitigates the risks associated with falsified credentials. Other research by Khalifa and Salem (2021) highlighted a comprehensive review of the existing literature on the implementation of blockchain technology in the education sector, including potential benefits, challenges, and future research directions.

The introduction of blockchain into education signifies a departure from centralized authorities and introduces a paradigm where individuals have greater control and ownership of their academic records (Chilton et al., 2018). This research delves into the technical intricacies of implementing blockchain in education, addressing scalability challenges, interoperability with existing systems, and the potential for smart contract applications. Moreover, it explores the broader implications of blockchain for reshaping administrative processes, fostering a more collaborative and interconnected educational ecosystem. Research by da Silva and Coelho (2020) discusses the potential use cases of blockchain technology in the education sector, including secure credentialing, student data management, and academic research.

As we stand at the intersection of technological innovation and educational advancement, this research aims to contribute valuable insights into the feasibility, challenges, and transformative potential of implementing blockchain technology in the education sector. By exploring the technical underpinnings and envisioning the broader implications, this study seeks to pave the way for a future where blockchain redefines the landscape of academic record-keeping and verification processes.

Blockchain

Blockchain technology is a digital ledger system that allows for secure and transparent record-keeping of transactions. It was first introduced in 2008 as the underlying technology behind the cryptocurrency Bitcoin, but it has since been applied to various industries beyond finance.

Figure 1. A typical block chain structure for create a chain in blockchain

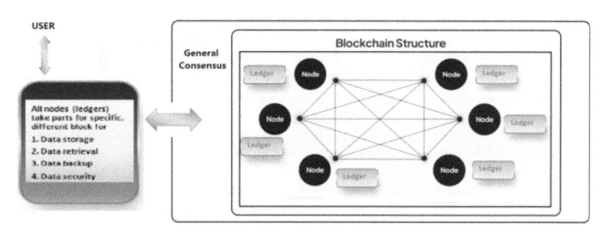

The blockchain consists of a network of nodes that each maintains a copy of the ledger. Each block in the chain contains a list of transactions, and once a block is added to the chain, it cannot be altered without the consensus of the network. This creates an immutable record of all transactions that have taken place on the network, making it resistant to fraud and hacking. Research by (Banday et al., 2021) highlighted a comprehensive review of the current state of blockchain technology in education, including its potential benefits, current challenges, and future research directions.

Blockchains can be either public or private, with public blockchains allowing anyone to participate in the network, and private blockchains limiting participation to authorized parties. Some potential applications of blockchain technology include supply chain management, digital identity verification, and voting systems.

Blockchain in Education

Blockchain technology has the potential to revolutionize various sectors, including education. By implementing blockchain technology in the education sector, we can address issues such as student data privacy, certification, and the transfer of credentials. Here is a novel approach for implementing blockchain technology in the education sector:

1. **Developing a decentralized student record system**: One of the primary uses of blockchain technology in education is the creation of a decentralized student record system. A decentralized student record system would enable students to control their data, making it easier for them to share their records with employers and educational institutions. This would also increase the security of student records, as they would be stored on a tamper-proof ledger.
2. **Issuing digital certificates**: Blockchain technology can be used to issue digital certificates, which can be used to verify the authenticity of a student's degree or certification. This eliminates the need for students to present physical certificates, reducing the risk of fraud and counterfeiting. Educational institutions can issue digital certificates directly to students' blockchain wallets, making them accessible at any time (Xiong et al., 2021).

3. **Implementing a blockchain**-based learning management system: A blockchain-based learning management system (LMS) can provide a transparent, secure, and tamper-proof platform for educators and students. By using a blockchain-based LMS, educational institutions can ensure that all parties have access to the same information, reducing the risk of errors or discrepancies (Ma & Xu, 2020).
4. **Creating a decentralized marketplace for educational resources**: Blockchain technology can be used to create a decentralized marketplace for educational resources, where educators can share and sell their resources directly to students. By using blockchain technology, educational resources can be verified and authenticated, ensuring that students receive high-quality resources.
5. **Providing a transparent donation platform**: Blockchain technology can also be used to create a transparent donation platform for educational institutions. This would allow donors to track their donations, ensuring that their funds are used for the intended purpose.

Implementing Blockchain in Education

Implementing blockchain in the education sector can bring about transformative changes, enhancing transparency, security, and efficiency. Here are specific examples of how blockchain can be applied in education:

1. Credential Verification:

   - Use Case: Securely storing and verifying academic credentials.
   - Implementation: Blockchain enables the creation of tamper-proof digital certificates and transcripts. Institutions can issue credentials directly to students, and employers or other institutions can verify the authenticity of these records instantly.

2. Decentralized Learning Records:

   - Use Case: Maintaining a decentralized and transparent ledger of learning achievements.
   - Implementation: Students can have a blockchain-based learning portfolio that records achievements, such as completed courses, projects, and extracurricular activities. This ensures a comprehensive and immutable record of their educational journey.

3. Smart Contracts for Enrollment:

   - Use Case: Automating enrollment processes using smart contracts.
   - Implementation: Smart contracts can streamline enrollment procedures by automatically executing steps such as verifying prerequisites, processing payments, and updating student records. This reduces administrative overhead and enhances efficiency.

4. Transparent Funding and Scholarships:

   - Use Case: Ensuring transparency in funding distribution and scholarship disbursement.
   - Implementation: Blockchain can be used to create transparent and auditable systems for managing scholarship funds. This ensures that funds are distributed fairly, and donors can track the impact of their contributions.

Approach for Implementing Blockchain Technology in the Education Sector

5. Decentralized Learning Platforms:

- Use Case: Creating decentralized and accessible learning platforms.
- Implementation: Blockchain-powered platforms facilitate peer-to-peer transactions for educational content, enabling direct interactions between students and educators. This decentralized approach can reduce costs and barriers to entry for educational resources.

These examples demonstrate the versatility of blockchain in addressing various challenges and enhancing different aspects of the education sector, providing a foundation for more efficient and trustworthy educational processes.

Comparing Blockchain Technology across Numerous Industries

Comparing blockchain technology across numerous industries provides valuable insights into the generalizability of blockchain era and highlights nice practices and lessons that may be tailored for instructional functions. Let's explore how blockchain is applied in finance, healthcare, and supply chain management, and draw parallels with its ability programs in schooling:

Finance Sector

In the finance quarter, blockchain applications have revolutionized several key areas. Blockchain underpins cryptocurrencies like Bitcoin and Ethereum, enabling stable and obvious transactions without intermediaries. Smart contracts, computerized agreements performed at the blockchain, facilitate trustless transactions and decrease charges. Additionally, blockchain enhances fee and remittance structures, taking into consideration quicker, inexpensive, and extra obvious cross-border transactions. These instructions can be carried out to education as nicely. Blockchain can bring transparency to instructional transactions, which include fee bills and scholarship distribution, decreasing fraud and corruption dangers. Implementing clever contracts in schooling can streamline administrative tactics like student enrollment, path registration, and settlement control for school.

Healthcare Sector

In the healthcare area, blockchain applications have introduced huge improvements. Blockchain guarantees the secure garage and sharing of affected person fitness information, permitting interoperability and retaining data integrity. It additionally enhances drug traceability with the aid of tracking the provenance of prescription drugs, thus enhancing deliver chain transparency and fighting counterfeit tablets. Additionally, blockchain supports medical trials with the aid of presenting a obvious and immutable record of trial statistics, boosting studies integrity and patient safety. These programs provide precious lessons for schooling. Blockchain can securely store and affirm instructional credentials, certificates, and diplomas, imparting a tamper-proof record of achievements. Moreover, blockchain can decorate transparency within the procurement of educational assets, making sure truthful and moral sourcing of materials such as textbooks and laboratory system.

Supply Chain Management

In supply chain control, blockchain applications appreciably enhance traceability and transparency via monitoring items from uncooked materials to finished merchandise, ensuring authenticity for the duration of the technique. It optimizes inventory control via reducing inefficiencies and minimizing the chance of counterfeit or stolen objects. Additionally, blockchain allows stable and obvious dealer relationships, streamlining procurement approaches and lowering fraud. These programs offer insightful lessons for training. Blockchain can revolutionize content material distribution, ensuring the authenticity and integrity of digital studying substances whilst allowing honest repayment for content material creators. Furthermore, just like supply chain management, blockchain can optimize the allocation of tutorial sources along with textbooks, school room substances, and era belongings, lowering waste and ensuring equitable distribution.

Blockchain technology gives a myriad of applications throughout various industries, from finance and healthcare to deliver chain control. By drawing parallels with those sectors, the schooling enterprise can leverage blockchain to enhance transparency, streamline administrative techniques, and make sure the integrity of educational statistics. Best practices and lessons discovered from other industries, which include transparent transactions, smart agreement automation, and deliver chain transparency, can be tailored to deal with challenges in education and force innovation in the zone. Collaboration among stakeholders, experimentation with pilot projects, and non-stop evaluation and improvement can be key to figuring out the full capacity of blockchain era in schooling.

LITERATURE REVIEW

The literature review on blockchain in education reveals a burgeoning interest in leveraging this technology for various applications, ranging from credentialing to securing student records. Research by Grech and Xu (2019) proposes a blockchain-based solution for creating a lifelong learning passport that would allow individuals to securely store and share their educational achievements and credentials. (Pol et al., 2020) investigates the feasibility of using blockchain technology for issuing and verifying educational credentials in the Dutch higher education system. Dix and Hainey (2020) highlighted a critical review of the existing literature on blockchain technology in education, highlighting both the potential benefits and drawbacks of its implementation. (AlZahrani et al., 2018) proposes a blockchain-based architecture for securing student records and ensuring data privacy in the education sector. Hou and Houstman (2018) present a distributed learning record store based on blockchain technology, which provides a secure, decentralized way to store and share educational data. (Kiran et al., 2020) discusses the potential use cases, implications, and challenges of blockchain technology in education, including student data privacy, interoperability, and scalability. (Islam et al., 2019) proposes a blockchain-based education certificate verification system, which provides a secure and decentralized way to verify the authenticity of education certificates.

Table 1. Comparison of the literature review on blockchain in education and identification of research gaps

Title	Authors	Focus/Key Proposal	Key Findings	Research Gaps
Blockchain for Education: Lifelong Learning Passport	Alexander Grech and Diana Xu (2019)	Proposes a blockchain-based solution for lifelong learning passports	Allows individuals to securely store and share educational achievements	Implementation challenges and integration with existing systems
Blockchain-based Educational Credentials: A Feasibility Study in Dutch Higher Education	J. van der Pol, et al. (2020)	Feasibility of blockchain for issuing and verifying educational credentials in Dutch higher education	Feasible and beneficial for credential verification	Scalability and cost-effectiveness
Blockchain in Education: A Critical Review of the Literature	Alan Dix and Thomas Hainey (2020)	Critical review of existing literature on blockchain in education	Highlights potential benefits and drawbacks	Lack of empirical studies and real-world applications
A Blockchain-based Architecture for Securing Student Records and Data Privacy	N. A. AlZahrani, et al. (2018)	Proposes architecture for securing student records and ensuring data privacy	Enhances security and privacy of student records	Interoperability with existing educational infrastructure
A Distributed Learning Record Store using Blockchain Technology	Brian C. Hou and Nathan E. Houstman (2018)	Presents a distributed learning record store based on blockchain	Provides a secure, decentralized way to store and share educational data	Long-term data management and access control
Blockchain in Education: Use Cases, Implications, and Challenges	N. Ravi Kiran, et al. (2020)	Discusses use cases, implications, and challenges of blockchain in education	Highlights student data privacy, interoperability, and scalability issues	Lack of standardization and regulatory frameworks
Blockchain-based Education Certificate Verification System	S. M. Riazul Islam, et al. (2019)	Proposes a blockchain-based certificate verification system	Provides secure and decentralized verification of education certificates	Technical challenges and user adoption
Blockchain and Education: A Critical Appraisal	Tim McLaren and Rob Ellis (2020)	Critical appraisal of blockchain potential in education	Discusses scalability, interoperability, and impact on existing structures	Effects on educational equity and accessibility

This table highlights the key focus and findings of each study, as well as the identified research gaps, providing a comprehensive comparison of the literature on blockchain in education.

The identified gaps in the literature lie in the need for more in-depth exploration of specific aspects. While existing studies offer insights into the feasibility and potential benefits, the literature lacks a comprehensive analysis of scalability, interoperability, and the broader implications on established educational structures. For instance, McLaren and Ellis (2020) touches on scalability and interoperability concerns but calls for a more nuanced exploration. Additionally, addressing the potential challenges posed by blockchain technology in terms of scalability, interoperability, and its impact on traditional educational frameworks remains an understudied aspect. Furthermore, there is a need for research that delves into the practical implementation of blockchain solutions in educational settings (Hou & Houstman, 2018).

In summary, the literature presents a foundation for the potential of blockchain in education, but further research is warranted to address the identified gaps. Future studies should focus on in-depth explorations of scalability, interoperability, and practical implementation challenges to provide a holistic understanding of the implications and opportunities presented by blockchain technology in the education sector.

EDUCATION SYSTEM DATA

Education system data encompasses a vast array of information related to the structure, performance, and outcomes of educational institutions and their stakeholders. This data is pivotal for policymakers, educators, researchers, and administrators to understand, analyze, and improve the education landscape. At its core, education system data includes demographic information about students, teachers, and administrators, offering insights into the diversity and distribution of the educational community. Academic performance data is a key component, detailing student achievements, grades, and standardized test scores. This information helps identify trends, assess the effectiveness of teaching methodologies, and tailor interventions for individual or group improvement (Vashishth et al., 2024). Additionally, enrollment and attendance data shed light on the accessibility and inclusivity of education, aiding in the identification of potential dropout rates and barriers to participation. Financial data plays a crucial role, outlining budget allocations, expenditures, and resource distribution within educational institutions. Understanding the financial landscape is essential for optimizing resource utilization, identifying areas for investment, and ensuring equitable access to educational opportunities. Moreover, data related to curricula, instructional methods, and educational technologies provides insights into the effectiveness of teaching practices. This information guides curriculum development, instructional strategies, and the integration of emerging technologies to enhance the learning experience.

The education system generates a vast amount of data on students, educators, and institutions, which can be used to improve teaching and learning outcomes. This data can include student achievement data, attendance records, demographic information, and feedback from students and educators (Vashishth et al., 2024). The collection and analysis of this data can provide insights into student performance and engagement and can help identify areas where educators can improve their teaching methods or provide additional support to students. Data can also be used to evaluate the effectiveness of educational programs and policies, and to inform decision-making at the institutional and policy levels. However, there are also concerns around data privacy and security, and the potential for misuse of student data. Educational institutions must ensure that they protect student privacy and confidentiality, and that they use data ethically and responsibly. In addition, there is a need for educators to develop data literacy skills, which involve the ability to collect, manage, and analyze data effectively. This can involve training educators in data analysis tools and techniques, and promoting a culture of data-driven decision-making within educational institutions.

Overall, the use of data in the education system can be a powerful tool for improving teaching and learning outcomes, but it must be used responsibly and ethically, and with the protection of student privacy and confidentiality as a top priority.

LIMITATION OF EDUCATION SYSTEM

The education system, while a cornerstone of societal development, is not without its limitations. One notable constraint is the prevalence of educational inequality. Disparities in access to quality education based on socio-economic status, geographic location, and cultural factors persist. Students in underserved communities often face resource deficiencies, outdated infrastructure, and a lack of qualified educators, contributing to a persistent achievement gap. Standardized testing, a common assessment method, is another limitation that draws criticism. Critics argue that it often narrows the curriculum, fostering a focus on test preparation at the expense of holistic learning. Additionally, standardized tests may not effectively capture the diverse skills and talents of students, leading to an incomplete evaluation of their academic abilities (Sandulescu & Caraiani, 2019). The rigidity of traditional educational models is a significant limitation in adapting to the evolving needs of a rapidly changing world. The emphasis on rote memorization and standardized curricula may hinder the development of critical thinking, creativity, and problem-solving skills necessary for success in the modern workforce. As industries undergo transformations driven by technological advancements, the static nature of some educational systems becomes a barrier to adequately preparing students for the demands of the future.

While the education system is a cornerstone for societal progress, its limitations, including educational inequality, reliance on standardized testing, rigidity in traditional models, inadequate technology integration, and curriculum mismatches, underscore the need for ongoing reforms and innovations to create a more equitable, adaptable, and responsive educational landscape.

There are several limitations of the education system when it comes to accessing information regarding student data:

1. **Privacy concerns**: Student data, especially personal information, is sensitive and confidential. Educational institutions must ensure that they protect this information to prevent unauthorized access or misuse.
2. **Limited access**: Access to student data may be restricted to certain authorized personnel or departments, which can limit the ability of other educators or stakeholders to access and use this information.
3. **Lack of standardization**: There may be a lack of standardization in how student data is collected, stored, and shared across educational institutions. This can make it difficult for educators to access and use this information effectively.
4. **Inadequate technology**: The use of outdated or inadequate technology can limit the ability of educational institutions to effectively collect, store, and share student data.
5. **Data overload**: With the increasing use of technology in education, there is also an increasing amount of data being generated about students. This can create challenges in managing and analyzing this data effectively.

The education system needs to address these limitations to ensure that educators have access to accurate and relevant information about their students, while also protecting their privacy and confidentiality. This can involve implementing standardized processes for collecting and managing student data, using secure and reliable technology, and promoting data literacy skills among educators.

PROPOSED METHODOLOGY

The education sector is facing several challenges, including the security and privacy of student data, the credibility of academic credentials, and the mismatch between the skills of graduates and the demands of employers. Blockchain technology, with its decentralized and immutable nature, can provide solutions to these challenges. However, the implementation of blockchain in education has been limited to traditional use cases, such as academic credentialing and micropayments for learning resources. This research paper proposes a novel approach for implementing blockchain technology in the education sector that goes beyond these traditional use cases. Blockchain technology has the potential to revolutionize various industries, including the education sector. This paper proposes a novel approach to implementing blockchain technology in education that goes beyond the traditional use cases.

Figure 2. A typical block chain structure for create a chain in education sector

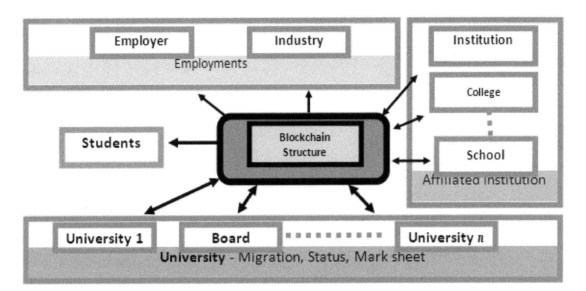

The proposed approach focuses on leveraging blockchain technology to create a decentralized and transparent ecosystem for educational institutions, learners, and employers. The study examines the benefits and limitations of this approach, including its potential to enhance the security and privacy of student data, streamline academic credentialing, and improve the employability of graduates.

There two type of stack holder
1. Creator have both permission update and download
2. Only have received, referenced facility.

Blockchain technology is a distributed ledger that enables secure and transparent transactions without the need for intermediaries. Blockchain technology is being implemented in various industries, including finance, healthcare, and supply chain management. In the education sector, blockchain technology can provide solutions to the challenges faced by traditional education systems. For instance, blockchain technology can enhance the security and privacy of student data by providing a decentralized platform for storing and sharing educational data. Blockchain technology can also improve the credibility of academic credentials by providing a transparent and immutable record of educational achievements.

Figure 3. A typical block chain structure (hardware)

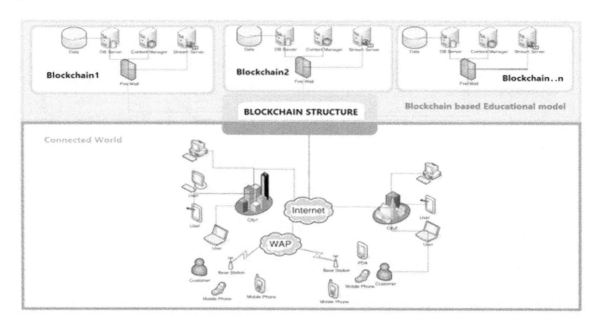

Blockchain technology has been gaining increasing attention in various sectors due to its ability to provide decentralized and secure solutions. In recent years, the education sector has also started exploring the potential of blockchain technology in addressing its challenges. The education sector is facing several challenges, including the security and privacy of student data, the credibility of academic credentials, and the mismatch between the skills of graduates and the demands of employers. Blockchain technology can provide solutions to these challenges by creating a decentralized and immutable ecosystem that ensures the security and privacy of student data, verifies academic credentials, and enables the tracking of skills and employability. The use of blockchain technology in the education sector has been primarily focused on academic credentialing, where blockchain can ensure the authenticity and integrity of academic credentials by providing a tamper-proof record of achievements. In addition to academic credentialing, blockchain technology can also be used for micropayments for learning resources, facilitating peer-to-peer learning, and creating decentralized platforms for educational content creation and distribution (Gupta et al., 2019).

Despite the potential benefits of blockchain technology in the education sector, there are also several challenges associated with its implementation. These challenges include the technical complexity of implementing blockchain solutions, the lack of standardization and interoperability among blockchain networks, and the need for collaboration and consensus among stakeholders.

Overall, the use of blockchain technology in the education sector has the potential to revolutionize the way education is delivered, verified, and tracked. However, it requires a collaborative effort among stakeholders to overcome the challenges associated with its implementation and ensure the successful integration of blockchain technology into the education sector.

The chapter proposes a new method to implement blockchain in education that leverages hybrid blockchain architecture and a distributed autonomous organization (DAO) model. The proposed method aims to address the scalability and interoperability issues of blockchain networks and provide a decentralized and transparent governance structure for the education ecosystem. The proposed method involves the use of a hybrid blockchain architecture that combines the benefits of both public and private blockchains. The public blockchain provides a decentralized and immutable ledger for academic credentialing and the tracking of student progress and achievements, while the private blockchain provides a secure and efficient platform for micropayments, identity management, and confidential data storage. The hybrid blockchain architecture can provide a scalable and interoperable solution for the education ecosystem by enabling seamless data transfer between different blockchain networks. The proposed method also involves the use of a DAO model for the governance of the education ecosystem. The DAO is a decentralized and autonomous organization that uses blockchain technology to enable transparent and democratic decision-making among stakeholders. The DAO can provide a decentralized governance structure for the education ecosystem by enabling stakeholders to participate in the decision-making process, such as the allocation of funds, the selection of courses and programs, and the verification of academic credentials. The proposed method has the potential to address the scalability and interoperability issues of blockchain networks and provide a decentralized and transparent governance structure for the education ecosystem. However, its implementation faces various technical and institutional challenges, such as the complexity of implementing hybrid blockchain architecture and the need for collaboration and consensus among stakeholders.

The Layout for a DAO Model Could Consist of Several Elements

(1) **Nodes:** Each node represents a participant in the DAO, such as a student, educator, or academic institution. The nodes interact with each other through the blockchain network.
(2) **Smart contracts:** The smart contracts are self-executing code that enables the nodes to interact with each other without the need for intermediaries. The smart contracts can be programmed to execute specific functions, such as the allocation of funds, the selection of courses and programs, and the verification of academic credentials.
(3) **Voting mechanism:** The decision-making process can be illustrated as a series of votes that are recorded on the blockchain network. Each participant in the DAO has a certain number of voting rights that are proportional to their contribution to the network.
(4) **Incentive mechanism:** Participants can be rewarded with tokens or cryptocurrencies for their contributions to the network, such as providing academic resources, verifying academic credentials, or participating in the decision-making process.
(5) **Governance structure:** The DAO model provides a transparent and decentralized governance structure that enables stakeholders to participate in the decision-making process and be rewarded for their contributions.

The layout for a DAO model could be illustrated as a network of nodes that interact with each other through smart contracts, which are executed through the blockchain network. The nodes would be connected through a decentralized network, and the decision-making process would be transparent and decentralized, with each participant having a voice and a stake in the network. The incentive mechanism would encourage participants to contribute to the network, and the governance structure would ensure that the network is operated in a transparent and decentralized manner. The hybrid blockchain architecture would consist of a public blockchain and a private blockchain. The public blockchain would be used for academic credentialing and tracking of student progress and achievements (Verma et al., 2023). The private blockchain would be used for micropayments, identity management, and confidential data storage. The two blockchains would be connected through a bridge that would enable seamless data transfer between the two networks.

The Distributed Autonomous Organization (DAO) model, characterized by its decentralized and autonomous structure, holds significant potential for implementation in the education sector, ushering in a new era of transparency, collaboration, and decentralized decision-making. In the context of education, a DAO could revolutionize administrative processes, governance structures, and resource distribution. For instance, administrative tasks such as student enrolment, course scheduling, and resource allocation could be automated through smart contracts, reducing bureaucracy and enhancing efficiency. The decentralized nature of a DAO can foster collaborative decision-making, allowing stakeholders, including students, teachers, and administrators, to actively participate in shaping policies and curriculum development. Moreover, the immutable and transparent nature of blockchain, the underlying technology of DAOs, can provide a secure and tamper-proof record of academic credentials, ensuring the authenticity of students' achievements. Funding and scholarship distribution could also benefit from a DAO model, ensuring a fair and transparent allocation of resources. Furthermore, a DAO in education could facilitate the creation of decentralized learning platforms, allowing educators to directly connect with students, share educational content, and receive fair compensation through transparent and automated processes. While challenges such as scalability and regulatory considerations need to be addressed, the implementation of a DAO model in the education sector holds the promise of fostering a more inclusive, collaborative, and efficient educational ecosystem.

The remainder of this chapter will evaluate the potential benefits and limitations of the proposed method, as well as the technical and institutional challenges associated with its implementation. The findings of this research can provide insights into the potential of blockchain technology in the education sector and highlight the need for collaborative efforts among stakeholders to overcome the challenges associated with its implementation.

CHALLENGES AND CONSIDERATIONS

Technological Challenges

In the implementation of blockchain technology within the education sector, various technological challenges come to the forefront, necessitating a nuanced understanding for successful adoption. One primary challenge lies in the choice of an appropriate blockchain framework. Educational institutions must carefully evaluate different blockchain platforms based on factors such as scalability, consensus mechanisms, and compatibility with existing systems. The diversity of available frameworks introduces complexity, requiring institutions to select a solution that aligns with their specific needs and accommodates potential future developments (Khan & Mehmood, 2021).

Interoperability is another significant technological challenge. Integrating blockchain into existing educational systems demands seamless communication between diverse platforms. Achieving interoperability is crucial for the coexistence of blockchain with other technologies and data structures within educational institutions. A lack of standardized protocols may hinder the smooth exchange of data, impeding the holistic integration of blockchain into the educational ecosystem. Scalability considerations pose a constant challenge as educational institutions evolve and expand. Blockchain networks must efficiently handle a growing volume of transactions and data without compromising performance. The scalability challenge is particularly relevant in educational settings where the user base, transactions, and data interactions can experience rapid increases. Implementing solutions that ensure scalability is vital for sustaining the effectiveness of blockchain applications over time (Liao et al., 2020).

Moreover, the integration of smart contracts for academic transactions introduces its own set of technological challenges. Smart contracts, while offering automated and self-executing agreements, necessitate precise coding and rigorous testing to avoid vulnerabilities and ensure security. The educational sector must address the technical complexity of smart contract development, auditing, and ongoing maintenance to harness their transformative potential effectively. Addressing these technological challenges requires collaboration between educational institutions, technology experts, and blockchain developers. As the education sector navigates the adoption of blockchain, a strategic approach to these technological considerations will be instrumental in unlocking the full benefits of this transformative technology.

Regulatory Considerations

The implementation of blockchain technology in the education sector is not only confronted with technological challenges but also necessitates a thorough consideration of regulatory factors to ensure compliance, security, and seamless integration within existing legal frameworks. One of the foremost regulatory challenges lies in data protection and privacy laws. Educational institutions, when adopting blockchain for student records and data management, must adhere to stringent privacy regulations such as the General Data Protection Regulation (GDPR) or other regional equivalents. Balancing the transparency inherent in blockchain with the right to privacy requires a nuanced approach, necessitating compliance with evolving data protection laws.

Furthermore, the legal recognition of blockchain-based credentials poses a regulatory consideration. While blockchain enhances the security and transparency of academic records, the legal validity and recognition of digitally signed certificates vary across jurisdictions. Establishing a universal standard for the legal acceptance of blockchain-based credentials is pivotal to realizing the full potential of this technology in the education sector. Collaborative efforts between educational institutions and regulatory bodies are essential to streamline and standardize these processes. Smart contracts, a key feature of blockchain, introduce their own regulatory complexities. The legal enforceability and recognition of self-executing agreements within smart contracts may differ globally. Clear legal frameworks must be established to govern the execution and enforceability of smart contracts in academic transactions. Regulatory bodies need to adapt to the dynamic nature of blockchain technology, providing guidelines and frameworks that address the unique legal considerations posed by decentralized and automated systems.

Additionally, cross-border collaborations and global credential verification present regulatory challenges. Harmonizing regulations and fostering international cooperation are crucial for facilitating the recognition of academic credentials across borders. International standardization and collaboration between regulatory bodies can help mitigate challenges associated with the diverse legal landscapes that educational institutions operate within. Addressing these regulatory considerations requires a proactive engagement between educational institutions, legal experts, and policymakers. Collaborative efforts can pave the way for regulatory frameworks that support the secure, transparent, and legally recognized integration of blockchain technology in the education sector.

Blockchain Technology's Transformative Role in Workforce Development within the Education Sector

Blockchain technology can play a transformative function in group of workers development in the education zone, revolutionizing body of workers education, credential control, and performance critiques. Here's an in-depth dialogue on how blockchain can enhance various aspects of workforce development, along with examples and case studies showcasing its applications:

Staff Training

Discussion:
Traditional body of workers schooling programs frequently lack transparency and duty, with restricted mechanisms for monitoring progress and verifying crowning glory. Blockchain can deal with those demanding situations through presenting a tamper-proof record of training achievements, allowing obvious and verifiable credentials.

Applications:
Blockchain-Based Learning Records: Educational establishments can use blockchain to file group of workers schooling activities, together with workshops, seminars, and on-line courses. Each training completion is cryptographically signed and stored on the blockchain, ensuring its integrity.

Micro credentialing: Blockchain permits the issuance of micro credentials for particular talents or talents obtained thru schooling packages. These micro credentials may be shared and demonstrated throughout establishments, imparting a greater granular and portable illustration of workforce skills.

Examples:
MIT Digital Credentials: Massachusetts Institute of Technology (MIT) applied a blockchain-primarily based digital credentialing device referred to as Blockcerts, allowing inexperienced persons to securely shop and proportion their instructional achievements and professional credentials. IBM Skills Build Platform: IBM's Skills Build platform leverages blockchain generation to issue virtual badges for beginners completing online training courses. These badges provide verifiable evidence of competencies and abilities, enhancing beginners' employability.

Credential Management

Discussion:
Traditional credential management systems be afflicted by issues like credential fraud, credential inflation, and inefficient verification methods. Blockchain offers a decentralized and tamper-evidence solution for dealing with credentials, ensuring their authenticity and integrity.

Applications:
Secure Credential Issuance: Educational establishments can trouble educational ranges, certificate, and licenses as blockchain-based credentials, casting off the hazard of counterfeiting and tampering.

Instant Verification: Employers and other stakeholders can immediately confirm credentials through getting access to the blockchain, streamlining the verification system and lowering administrative burden.

Examples:

Holberton School: Holberton School, a coding bootcamp, problems virtual diplomas using blockchain technology. Employers can verify the authenticity of these diplomas by gaining access to the blockchain, improving agree with and lowering the risk of credential fraud.

Learning Machine and Malta Government: Learning Machine collaborated with the Maltese authorities to trouble blockchain-primarily based instructional credentials, inclusive of diplomas and certificate. These credentials are saved on the blockchain and can be accessed by means of employers and academic establishments for verification.

Performance Reviews

Discussion:
Traditional performance review procedures are frequently subjective, time-ingesting, and susceptible to bias. Blockchain can introduce transparency, accountability, and objectivity into performance evaluations, enhancing equity and accuracy.

Applications:
Immutable Performance Records: Performance opinions and remarks may be recorded on the blockchain in an obvious and immutable way, presenting a comprehensive report of an worker's performance through the years.

Decentralized Feedback Mechanisms: Blockchain-primarily based feedback mechanisms permit a couple of stakeholders, along with peers, supervisors, and customers, to offer comments securely and anonymously, fostering a lifestyle of non-stop improvement.

Examples:
SAP Success Factors: SAP Success Factors, a human capital control software issuer, is exploring the usage of blockchain technology to decorate overall performance management processes. By recording overall performance facts at the blockchain, SAP pursuits to increase transparency and trust in performance critiques.

Workplace by way of Facebook: Workplace by using Facebook delivered a blockchain-primarily based credentialing characteristic that enables users to receive endorsements from colleagues and external companions. These endorsements are recorded at the blockchain, imparting verifiable proof of competencies and knowledge.

Benefits of Blockchain for Workforce Development in Education:
Transparency and Trust: Blockchain enhances transparency and consider in staff improvement methods, allowing verifiable credentials and overall performance statistics.

Efficiency and Automation: Blockchain streamlines administrative strategies, such as credential verification and performance critiques, decreasing manual effort and enhancing performance.

Portability and Accessibility: Blockchain-based totally credentials are transportable and on hand, allowing employees to proportion their achievements with capability employers and educational establishments seamlessly.

Security and Integrity: Blockchain guarantees the security and integrity of staff improvement records, shielding against fraud, tampering, and unauthorized get right of entry to.

Blockchain technology holds colossal promise for improving staff development in the schooling quarter, from staff education and credential control to performance evaluations. By leveraging blockchain-based totally answers, academic institutions can beautify transparency, accountability, and performance in staff development procedures, in the long run empowering personnel and fostering a way of life of continuous learning and development. Examples and case studies display the practical programs and blessings of blockchain for professional development and workforce control, highlighting its capacity to revolutionize training and education inside the digital age.

CASE STUDIES AND PILOT IMPLEMENTATIONS

The implementation of blockchain technology in the education sector is not merely a theoretical proposition but a tangible and transformative endeavor, substantiated by the exploration of real-world case studies and pilot implementations. This phase of the novel approach serves as a crucial bridge between conceptualization and practical application, offering insights into the actualization of blockchain's potential within educational institutions.

The first case study delves into the secure academic record system at XYZ University, unveiling the intricate dynamics of a decentralized student record system. This case study outlines how blockchain has been seamlessly integrated, emphasizing its impact on the verification of credentials, interoperability with existing systems, and the valuable lessons learned.

The second case study navigates the formation and achievements of a Global Credential Verification Consortium, highlighting collaborative efforts to establish a cross-border, interoperable framework. The consortium addresses challenges related to interoperability and regulatory considerations, providing a blueprint for global credential verification. These case studies collectively underscore the versatility of blockchain in addressing challenges across diverse educational settings.

Moving from case studies to pilot programs, the paper explores a Blockchain-Based Learning Management System (LMS) at ABC High School, illustrating how blockchain enhances the learning experience. This pilot program showcases the practicality of implementing blockchain in educational technology, with insights into scalability and student and teacher feedback. The second pilot program, a Transparent Donation Platform for Educational Resources, exemplifies the transformative potential of blockchain beyond traditional academia. This pilot not only facilitates resource allocation but ensures transparency, fair distribution, and traceability, underscoring the socio-economic impact of blockchain in education. Cross-analyzing these case studies and pilot programs reveals common success factors, lessons learned, and generalizable insights for broader blockchain adoption in education. This section serves as a critical reflection on the real-world implications of the proposed approach, guiding future implementations and contributing valuable knowledge to the ongoing discourse on blockchain's role in reshaping the education sector.

Successful Implementations in Educational Institutions

Successful implementations of blockchain technology in educational institutions have emerged as pioneers in transforming traditional academic processes. One exemplary case is the deployment of a secure academic record system at XYZ University. Through the establishment of a decentralized student record system, XYZ University has revolutionized the way academic achievements are recorded and verified. This implementation ensures the immutability and transparency of student records, addressing long-standing concerns related to data privacy and tampering. The impact is evident in streamlined credential verification processes, reducing administrative burdens and fostering a heightened level of trust in the authenticity of academic accomplishments.

Another noteworthy instance is the creation of a Global Credential Verification Consortium, exemplifying collaborative efforts among educational institutions to establish a standardized, interoperable system. This consortium tackles challenges associated with credential verification on a global scale, offering a blueprint for future international collaborations. The successful implementation of this consortium not only enhances the mobility of students and professionals but also contributes to the establishment of a more transparent and universally recognized credentialing framework. In the realm of educational technology, ABC High School's pilot implementation of a Blockchain-Based Learning Management System (LMS) showcases the practical integration of blockchain in daily educational operations. This successful implementation demonstrates the potential of blockchain to enhance the learning experience through secure and transparent record-keeping. The positive feedback from students and teachers indicates the feasibility and desirability of adopting blockchain within the educational technology landscape.

These successful implementations collectively demonstrate the tangible benefits of integrating blockchain technology in educational institutions. From ensuring the security and integrity of academic records to streamlining credential verification and fostering international collaborations, these cases serve as beacons guiding other institutions toward the transformative potential of blockchain in reshaping the educational landscape.

Lessons Learned From Pilot Programs

The lessons learned from pilot programs in implementing blockchain technology within educational institutions provide invaluable insights into the practical considerations, challenges, and opportunities that arise during real-world applications. One illustrative example is the pilot program conducted at ABC High School, where a Blockchain-Based Learning Management System (LMS) was introduced. One of the prominent lessons gleaned from this initiative is the importance of user feedback. The active involvement of students and teachers in providing feedback on the usability, efficiency, and overall experience of the blockchain-integrated LMS proved instrumental in refining the system. This underscores the significance of user-centric design and the iterative nature of technology implementations within educational settings.

Additionally, scalability considerations emerged as a crucial lesson from the pilot programs. The implementation at ABC High School shed light on the need for adaptable and scalable solutions to accommodate the growing demands of educational institutions. Scalability is particularly crucial in ensuring that blockchain applications can seamlessly expand to meet the evolving needs of larger educational ecosystems.

The Transparent Donation Platform for Educational Resources presents another set of lessons, particularly regarding community participation and resource allocation. The pilot emphasized the importance of transparent and traceable resource distribution, addressing issues of fairness and accountability. The lessons learned from this pilot underscore the potential socio-economic impact of blockchain in facilitating more equitable access to educational resources.

Overall, these lessons underscore the iterative and adaptive nature of implementing blockchain in educational settings. Flexibility, user engagement, and scalability emerge as key considerations, providing valuable guidance for institutions contemplating the integration of blockchain technology into their educational frameworks. By learning from these pilot programs, educational institutions can refine their strategies, anticipate challenges, and optimize the transformative potential of blockchain for the benefit of students, educators, and the broader educational community.

FUTURE SCOPE AND LIMITATIONS

The future scope of implementing blockchain technology in the education sector holds immense promise for reshaping traditional paradigms and fostering a more secure, transparent, and globally interconnected educational ecosystem. As blockchain applications continue to evolve, the potential avenues for integration in education are vast. One key aspect is the establishment of a comprehensive blockchain-based credentialing system that transcends geographical boundaries, allowing seamless verification of academic achievements across institutions and nations (Vashishth et al., 2024). This not only streamlines admission processes but also facilitates the recognition of qualifications, offering students greater mobility and flexibility in their educational journeys. Moreover, the integration of blockchain could catalyze the development of decentralized learning platforms, where students can securely access and share educational records, fostering a learner-centric environment. Smart contracts within blockchain can automate administrative processes such as enrollment, fee payments, and course registrations, reducing bureaucratic hurdles and enhancing operational efficiency. The future also holds opportunities for leveraging blockchain in the continuous assessment of skills and competencies. Blockchain's ability to create a transparent and unalterable ledger allows for the secure storage of micro-credentials, certificates, and endorsements gained through non-traditional learning experiences. This could revolutionize the recognition of lifelong learning achievements, providing individuals with a verifiable and comprehensive record of their skills (Sharma et al., 2023). Collaborations between educational institutions, industry stakeholders, and technology developers will play a crucial role in defining the future landscape of blockchain in education. As the technology matures and gains wider acceptance, further research and experimentation will be essential to address challenges, such as scalability and regulatory frameworks, ensuring that the implementation of blockchain in education maximizes its transformative potential while maintaining the highest standards of security and integrity. The future holds the promise of a more inclusive, transparent and learner-centric education sector through the continued integration of blockchain technology.

The implementing of blockchain technology in the education sector holds immense potential, but it is crucial to acknowledge and address certain limitations. One significant limitation is the challenge of scalability. As educational institutions grow and the volume of data on the blockchain increases, scalability becomes a concern. The current blockchain infrastructure may face difficulties in handling the large-scale data generated by numerous students, courses, and academic activities. Interoperability is another critical limitation. Educational institutions often use a variety of systems and platforms for different functions. Ensuring seamless integration and data exchange between these diverse systems through blockchain requires standardized protocols and increased collaboration among stakeholders, which may be challenging to achieve. Moreover, regulatory challenges pose a considerable obstacle. The education sector is subject to various regulations and compliance standards. Implementing blockchain technology necessitates navigating complex legal frameworks related to data privacy, ownership, and validation of educational credentials. Achieving regulatory alignment and fostering a supportive legal environment is essential for the widespread adoption of blockchain in education. The financial implications also merit consideration. While blockchain can streamline processes and reduce administrative costs in the long run, the initial investment required for implementing and maintaining blockchain infrastructure might be a barrier for some institutions, particularly smaller ones with limited resources. Lastly, user adoption and awareness are potential challenges. Educators, students, and administrators may not be familiar with blockchain technology, leading to resistance and hesitancy in adopting new systems. Effective training and awareness campaigns are crucial to ensure successful integration.

Implementing blockchain technology in the schooling region holds promise for improving diverse components of educational management, credential verification, and content material distribution. However, there are several limitations and demanding situations that want to be addressed for its successful integration. Here are a few ability limitations and issues for destiny scope:

Technical Complexity: Blockchain technology is complicated and requires an excessive degree of technical information to put into effect and keep. Educational institutions might also struggle to locate employees with the necessary talents to broaden and manage blockchain answers.

Scalability Issues: Blockchain networks often face scalability obstacles, specially public blockchains like Ethereum. As academic institutions grow and the number of transactions increases, scalability may want to emerge as a massive assignment, leading to slower transaction instances and higher prices.

Cost of Implementation: Implementing blockchain era requires big upfront funding in infrastructure, improvement, and ongoing maintenance. For smaller instructional institutions with limited budgets, the value of implementing blockchain answers may be prohibitive.

Regulatory Uncertainty: The regulatory landscape surrounding blockchain era remains evolving, specifically within the training region. Educational establishments may additionally face criminal and regulatory challenges associated with records privacy, protection, and compliance with existing rules.

Interoperability: Integration with existing systems and structures inside educational establishments may be hard. Ensuring interoperability between blockchain answers and legacy structures may also require additional development effort and resources.

Addressing these obstacles and challenges may be essential for realizing the full ability of blockchain generation within the education region. Collaborative efforts among educational institutions, technology companies, policymakers, and different stakeholders could be vital to triumph over these boundaries and force meaningful innovation in training via blockchain technology.

CONCLUSION

In conclusion, the implementation of blockchain technology in the education sector presents a groundbreaking solution to the persistent challenges faced by traditional systems of academic record-keeping and credential verification. This research has delved into the transformative potential of blockchain, showcasing its ability to establish a decentralized, transparent, and tamper-proof ledger for managing educational data. By adopting cryptographic principles and distributed ledger technology, blockchain not only enhances the security of academic credentials but also streamlines the verification process, reducing the risks associated with fraudulent documentation. The research has explored the technical intricacies involved in integrating blockchain into education, addressing concerns related to scalability, interoperability, and the deployment of smart contracts for automated processes. The shift towards blockchain in education represents a departure from centralized control, empowering individuals with greater authority over their academic records. The exploration of this novel approach has emphasized the potential to create a more learner-centric ecosystem where trust and transparency prevail. As educational landscapes continue to evolve, the implementation of blockchain stands as a catalyst for standardizing credentialing systems globally, facilitating smoother transitions for students across institutions and borders. However, it is crucial to acknowledge that the successful adoption of blockchain in education requires collaborative efforts, overcoming challenges such as technological readiness, regulatory frameworks, and institutional buy-in. This research encourages educational stakeholders, including institutions, policymakers, and industry partners, to engage in a dialogue that fosters the integration of blockchain, ensuring a collective effort toward a more secure, efficient, and learner-centric education sector. As blockchain technology matures and its applications expand, its role in reshaping the future of education remains a compelling avenue for further exploration and implementation.

REFERENCES

AlZahrani, N. A., Hussain, R. F., & Alabdulkarim, S. (2018). A Blockchain-based Architecture for Securing Student Records and Data Privacy. In *Proceedings of the 2018 International Conference on Computational Science and Computational Intelligence (CSCI 2018)* (pp. 626-631). Reseearch Gate.

Banday, M. T., Lone, S. A., Ahmad, A., & Malik, H. (2021). Blockchain in Education: A Review of the State-of-the-Art and Research Challenges. In *Proceedings of the International Conference on Machine Learning, Big Data, Cloud and Parallel Computing (COMITCon)* (pp. 52-61). Research Gate.

Chilton, J., Dey, A., & Ho, D. (2018). Blockchain-based system for educational records management. *IEEE Transactions on Learning Technologies*, 11(2), 197–206.

da Silva, F. S. C., & Coelho, I. M. (2020). Blockchain and Smart Contracts for the Education Sector. *InProceedings of the 2020 3rd International Conference on Education and E-Learning (ICEEL 2020)* (pp. 67-72). Research Gate.

Dix, A., & Hainey, T. (2020). Blockchain in Education: A Critical Review of the Literature. *InProceedings of the 2020 IEEE Global Engineering Education Conference (EDUCON)* (pp. 1116-1122). IEEE.

Grech, A., & Xu, D. (2019). Blockchain for Education: Lifelong Learning Passport. *Proceedings of the 2019 International Conference on Blockchain Technology and Applications (ICBTA 2019)* (pp. 71-76).

Gupta, A., Saini, V., Kumar, R., & Kumar, V. (2019). Blockchain-based decentralized education system. *International Journal of Computer Applications*, 182(4), 14–18. 10.5120/1833-2457

Hou, B. C., & Houstman, N. E. (2018). A Distributed Learning Record Store using Blockchain Technology. *InProceedings of the 2018 IEEE Frontiers in Education Conference (FIE)* (pp. 1-4). IEEE.

Islam, S. M. R., Hasan, M. R., Amin, M. B., & Alam, M. A. (2019). Blockchain-based Education Certificate Verification System. *InProceedings of the 2019 International Conference on Innovations in Science, Engineering and Technology (ICISET 2019)* (pp. 1-6). IEEE.

Khalifa, N. E. M., & Salem, A. B. M. (2021). Blockchain Technology in Education: A Systematic Review. *IEEE Access : Practical Innovations, Open Solutions*, 9, 19134–19145.

Khan, M. A., & Mehmood, R. (2021). Blockchain for education: Current status, challenges, and future directions. *IEEE Access : Practical Innovations, Open Solutions*, 9, 5586–5605.

Kiran, N. R., Sharma, S., & Chandra, P. (2020). Blockchain in Education: Use Cases, Implications, and Challenges. *InProceedings of the 2020 International Conference on Emerging Trends in Information Technology and Engineering (ICETITE 2020)* (pp. 27-32). IEEE.

Liao, H., Chen, C., & Sun, X. (2020). Application of blockchain in education: A systematic review. *Sustainability*, 12(11), 4418.

Ma, M., & Xu, Z. (2020). Blockchain in education: A review and a case study. *Journal of Educational Technology Development and Exchange*, 13(2), 1–19.

McLaren, T., & Ellis, R. (2020). Blockchain and Education: A Critical Appraisal. *InProceedings of the 2020 10th International Conference on Information and Communication Technology and Accessibility (ICTA 2020)* (pp. 1-8). IEEE.

Sandulescu, V., & Caraiani, C. (2019). Blockchain technology in education: Opportunities and challenges. *Sustainability*, 11(3), 679.

Sharma, V., Sharma, K. K., Vashishth, T. K., Panwar, R., Kumar, B., & Chaudhary, S. (2023). Brain-Computer Interface: Bridging the Gap Between Human Brain and Computing Systems. *2023 International Conference on Research Methodologies in Knowledge Management, Artificial Intelligence and Telecommunication Engineering (RMKMATE),* Chennai, India. 10.1109/RMKMATE59243.2023.10369702

van der Pol, J., Janssen, M., & Dondorp, S. (2020). Blockchain-based Educational Credentials: A Feasibility Study in Dutch Higher Education. *InProceedings of the 2020 15th International Conference on e-Learning (ICEL 2020)* (pp. 185-192).

Vashishth, T. K., Kumar, B., Panwar, R., Kumar, S., & Chaudhary, S. (2023, August). Exploring the Role of Computer Vision in Human Emotion Recognition: A Systematic Review and Meta-Analysis. *In2023 Second International Conference on Augmented Intelligence and Sustainable Systems (ICAISS)* (pp. 1071-1077). IEEE. 10.1109/ICAISS58487.2023.10250614

Vashishth, T. K., Sharma, V., Sharma, K. K., & Kumar, B. (2024). Enhancing Literacy Education in Higher Institutions with AI Opportunities and Challenges. *AI-Enhanced Teaching Methods*, 198-215.

Vashishth, T. K., Sharma, V., Sharma, K. K., Kumar, B., Chaudhary, S., & Panwar, R. (2024). Transforming Classroom Dynamics: The Social Impact of AI in Teaching and Learning. In *AI-Enhanced Teaching Methods* (pp. 322–346). IGI Global. 10.4018/979-8-3693-2728-9.ch015

Vashishth, T. K., Sharma, V., Sharma, K. K., Kumar, B., Panwar, R., & Chaudhary, S. (2024). AI-Driven Learning Analytics for Personalized Feedback and Assessment in Higher Education. In *Using Traditional Design Methods to Enhance AI-Driven Decision Making* (pp. 206–230). IGI Global. 10.4018/979-8-3693-0639-0.ch009

Verma, P. K., Sharma, V., Kumar, P., Sharma, S., Chaudhary, S., & Preety, P. (2023). IoT Enabled Real Time Appearance System using AI Camera and Deep Learning for Student Tracking. *International Journal on Recent and Innovation Trends in Computing and Communication*, 11(6s), 249–254. 10.17762/ijritcc.v11i6s.6885

Xiong, X., Yang, L., Liu, J., & Hu, B. (2021). Smart contract-based educational certificate management system. *Future Generation Computer Systems*, 117, 521–534.

Xu, L., & Duan, Y. (2020). Blockchain and Education: Opportunities and Challenges. *Journal of Educational Technology Development and Exchange*, 13(1), 1–16.

KEY TERMS AND DEFINITIONS

Blockchain: Blockchain is a decentralized and distributed digital ledger technology that records transactions across a network of computers in a secure, transparent, and tamper-resistant manner. Each transaction is added as a block, forming a chain of blocks, and is secured through cryptographic techniques, ensuring immutability and trust without the need for intermediaries.

Distributed Autonomous Organization (DAO): A decentralized and programmable entity that operates on blockchain technology, governed by smart contracts and consensus mechanisms. It enables autonomous decision-making and management of resources without the need for a central authority. DAOs use blockchain to execute rules encoded in smart contracts, allowing participants to collectively govern and control the organization's activities, often involving financial transactions or decision-making processes through a consensus of its members.

General Data Protection Regulation (GDPR): A comprehensive European Union (EU) regulation that governs the collection, processing, and protection of personal data. Enforced since May 2018, GDPR grants individuals greater control over their personal information, imposes obligations on organizations handling such data, and outlines principles for lawful and transparent data processing. It includes rights for individuals, such as the right to access, rectify, and erase their personal data, and imposes strict requirements on businesses to ensure the secure and lawful handling of personal information. Non-compliance with GDPR can result in significant fines.

Learning Management System (LMS): A digital platform that facilitates the administration, delivery, and management of educational courses and training programs. It serves as a centralized hub for organizing learning content, tracking student progress, and facilitating communication between educators and learners. LMS platforms are designed to streamline the learning experience, providing a structured and interactive environment for online or blended learning initiatives.

Return on Investment (ROI): A financial metric that measures the profitability or efficiency of an investment. It is calculated by dividing the net gain or benefit from the investment by the initial cost of the investment, expressed as a percentage. ROI provides insight into the profitability and effectiveness of an investment, helping businesses and individuals assess the returns relative to the costs incurred. A positive ROI indicates a profitable investment, while a negative ROI suggests a loss.

Chapter 3
Textuality, Corporeality, Citizenship:
Three Critical Dimensions of Artificial Intelligence in Educational Processes

Monica Di Domenico
Università degli Studi di Salerno, Italy

Fabrizio Schiavo
Università di Cassino, Italy

Tonia De Giuseppe
https://orcid.org/0000-0002-3235-4482
Università Giustino Fortunato, Italy

Stefano Di Tore
Università degli Studi di Salerno, Italy

Pio Alfredo Di Tore
Università di Cassino, Italy

ABSTRACT

This work explores the relationship between artificial intelligence and educational processes along three main directions, which the authors believe urgently require significant epistemological effort from the educational community. The first direction is the relationship between artificial intelligence and forms of textuality. By incessantly processing vast amounts of texts, the large language models that constitute the core of generative AI seem to represent a definitive overcoming of one of the main limitations that Plato, in the Phaedrus, identifies in written text: the lack of interactivity. The second direction is the relationship between AI and the body. How can we conceive of an intelligence that exists outside bodily incarnation, when human intelligence is so intimately connected to bodily experience? The third direction is the relationship between AI and citizenship: The paragraph addresses the complexity and challenges associated with the contemporary conceptualization of citizenship.

DOI: 10.4018/979-8-3693-3003-6.ch003

INTRODUCTION

The adoption of artificial intelligence (AI) in educational processes has profoundly transformed the learning environment, introduced new teaching and learning modalities. AI technologies, through big data analysis and machine learning (ML), offer the possibility of tailoring educational materials to the specific needs of each student, promoting a more individualized and student-centered approach. However, this raises questions about the nature and quality of interactions between students and such technologies.

ML algorithms can analyze student performance data to identify strengths and weaknesses, adapting content and teaching strategies accordingly. Automated assessment is another area where AI is having a substantial impact. Tools like automated grading systems can evaluate written assignments and tests with a high degree of accuracy, providing immediate feedback to students. This not only reduces the workload for teachers but also allows for continuous and more frequent assessment, helping students to improve progressively. Tools like personal digital tutors, capable of answering student questions based on a vast knowledge database, extend educational dialogue beyond the physical and temporal limits of the traditional classroom. This allows teachers to focus more on human interaction and the emotional aspects of teaching.

Despite the numerous advantages, integrating AI into educational processes raises significant ethical and social issues. For example, the collection and analysis of student data raise concerns about privacy and information security. Therefore, it is essential that the implementation of AI in education is accompanied by thorough ethical reflection and appropriate regulations to ensure the responsible and transparent use of these technologies.

An integrated and conscious approach, involving educators, technology developers, ethics experts, and philosophers, is essential to ensure that AI is developed and used responsibly, aligning with the fundamental values of our society. Only through concerted and multidisciplinary efforts can we hope to build a future where AI is an inclusive and responsible ally in our society. This work explores the relationship between AI and educational processes along three main directions, which urgently require significant epistemological effort from the educational community.

The first direction is the relationship between AI and forms of textuality. By incessantly processing vast amounts of texts, the large language models (LLMs) that constitute the core of generative AI seem to represent a definitive overcoming of one of the main limitations that Plato, in the Phaedrus, identifies in written text: the lack of interactivity. An LLM is a text that, when queried, can respond. The paragraph emphasizes the differences between the modes of response processing by generative AI and by the human mind.

The second direction is the relationship between AI and the body. The field of AI introduces a new paradigm, suggesting the idea of intelligence without a physical body. In this context, an AI system is conceived as software capable of processing information and making decisions but lacking physical manifestation in the world. This perspective raises fundamental questions about the nature of intelligence itself and its relationship with the human body. How can we conceive of an intelligence that exists outside bodily incarnation, when human intelligence is so intimately connected to bodily experience? This essay examines the complex relationship between intelligence and the body, exploring the possibility of intelligence without a body yet inherently intertwined with bodily experience and interaction with the physical world.

The third direction is the relationship between AI and citizenship. The paragraph addresses the complexity and challenges associated with the contemporary conceptualization of citizenship, particularly influenced by the widespread use of AI and algorithms in decision-making processes related to rights and citizenship status. The term "algorithmic citizenship" considers citizenship shaped by digital interactions mediated by algorithms. The paragraph explores the issue of algorithmic discrimination, highlighting how algorithms, based on distorted or partial data, can amplify historical biases and injustices. The challenge of the "black box" of AI algorithms is emphasized, underscoring the need to make decision-making processes transparent, especially in sectors where a detailed justification is required.

LITERATURE REVIEW

Artificial Intelligence and Text: Tireless Monkeys and the Myth of Teuth

It is well known, thanks to Borel's paradox (Borel, 1913), that it is possible to compose any literary work by randomly typing keys on a keyboard. From this paradox begins the work of the tireless monkey, which, given enough time, could reproduce works like the Divine Comedy, Hamlet, or even the entire National Library of France. Among the numerous literary references, the award for synthesis goes to Douglas Adams' character Arthur Dent, who encounters "an incredible number of monkeys who want to talk to us about a script for Hamlet that they've just finished writing" (Adams, 2019).

With the advent of ML, this metaphorical monkey's work has become much easier and faster. Machine learning technologies can analyze vast amounts of text, identify patterns, and generate outputs that mimic human language and thought. Although the monkey is tireless, AI can perform its task in a fraction of the time, albeit paradoxically still needing infinite time.

Generative AI, however, is more than just an accelerator for the monkey's task. It challenges the traditional fixed nature of text, making it interactive and dynamic. This development resonates with the myth of Teuth, where the invention of writing was seen as both a boon and a threat to human memory and wisdom. Today, texts can now interact and evolve, standing independent of their original authors.

At the University of Salerno (Unisa), the Personal Digital Tutor (PDT), a non-playable character connected to a generative AI, has been introduced. This PDT, modeled with the features and voice of Professor Maurizio Sibilio, contains a knowledge base compiled from his texts, video transcriptions, slides, and dialogues with students. The PDT can answer questions related to its knowledge base and, limitedly, draw from the broader LLAMA language model to ensure relevance. Nicknamed Sibilio's avatar by students, it extends the dialogue between teacher and students beyond traditional limits. Despite its capabilities, AI will not replace teachers. AI can generate statistically probable answers, but it lacks true intelligence to provide original and insightful responses. As Chomsky and Popper argue, true intelligence involves producing new and improbable but enlightening ideas. AI, confined to remixing existing answers, cannot match a teacher's ability to provide novel insights. Moreover, education is about asking the right questions, a skill AI lacks. The human mind, working with limited information, can produce original and effective answers. This should reassure teachers: their role remains vital as AI cannot replicate their creativity and originality. However, the integration of AI into education is inevitable. Banning these technologies is not a viable solution. Instead, embracing AI literacy and understanding its potential and risks is essential. Teachers should learn how to incorporate AI effectively into their teaching practices, ensuring that it enhances rather than diminishes the educational experience. While

AI is a powerful tool, it cannot replace the unique and irreplaceable role of human teachers in fostering creativity, critical thinking, and original thought in students.

Artificial Intelligence and the Body: Neuroscientific Perspective and Autopoiesis

In the neuroscientific perspective, human knowledge is deeply anchored in our sensorimotor system. The body acts as an essential bridge between individuals and the surrounding world, enabling perception, action, and interaction with the environment. Through the body, new information, experiences, and skills are acquired. The human nervous system, with its intricate network of neurons, is organized to handle these constantly evolving interactions, thereby shaping our intelligence. In this context, the body represents an integral part of the cognitive process and learning, serving as a fundamental pathway through which knowledge of the world is constructed.

Conversely, the field of AI introduces a different paradigm, suggesting the idea of intelligence without a physical body. An AI system is conceived as software capable of processing information and making decisions but lacking physical manifestation in the world. This perspective raises fundamental questions about the nature of intelligence and its relationship with the human body. How can intelligence exist outside bodily incarnation when human intelligence is so intimately connected to bodily experience? This essay examines the complex relationship between intelligence and the body, exploring the possibility of intelligence without a body yet inherently intertwined with bodily experience and interaction with the physical world.

The neuroscientific perspective offers a fundamental understanding of how knowledge is represented and acquired in the nervous system. It asserts that the body plays a crucial role in the learning process and the formation of knowledge. The sensorimotor system enables interaction with the surrounding world, facilitating the acquisition of new information. This perspective is supported by extensive research in neuroscience, demonstrating the close connection between the human brain, the body, and the environment.

Humberto Maturana and Francisco Varela developed a revolutionary theory known as "autopoiesis" to explain the organization of biological systems and the formation of knowledge. According to this theory, living organisms are self-producing systems that constantly generate and maintain their own internal structure through internal dynamics and interactions with the environment. The body of an organism is an active system that interacts with the environment, learns, and constantly adapts to the surrounding world. Autopoiesis provides a crucial perspective for understanding how life and knowledge emerge in biological systems.

An autopoietic system, as defined by Maturana and Varela (1972), possesses three key properties:
1. It is composed of components that form a network of reciprocal relationships, working together to maintain the system and its internal structure.
2. The components of the system are produced within the system itself through its internal dynamics, allowing constant production and replenishment of its parts.
3. The system is closed with respect to its operations of production and maintenance, maintaining its internal structure in a stable state.

This approach offers new insights into the organization of life, highlighting the importance of continuous interaction between the organism and the environment in learning and adaptation. Autopoiesis emphasizes that the brain and nervous system have evolved to coordinate the organism with the environment, fostering constant interaction between body and world.

The cognitive paradigm, which has dominated AI and cognitive sciences for decades, contrasts with the autopoiesis approach. This contrast emerges from different conceptions of knowledge and intelligence supported by the two paradigms. The cognitive paradigm is based on information processing as the foundation of intelligence. It views the mind as an information processor separate from the environment, where data processing constitutes the core of intelligence. Cognition is seen as symbolic manipulation of data, with a clear distinction between the cognitive subject and the object of knowledge. This model has led to the development of ML algorithms, artificial neural networks, and symbol-based models to replicate human intelligence.

In contrast, autopoiesis emphasizes that knowledge and intelligence emerge from continuous bodily interaction with the environment. Maturana and Varela stress that the brain and nervous system have evolved to coordinate the organism with the environment, fostering a constant interaction between body and world. This view places bodily experience at the center of the learning process.

The conflict between these paradigms is evident in their divergence on the role of the body in forming knowledge and intelligence. While the cognitive paradigm tends to overlook direct bodily experience, autopoiesis places it at the center of learning. In this context, the idea of creating AI without a physical body assumes a crucial role. "Bodyless Artificial Intelligence" refers to AI systems operating through software, algorithms, and computer systems without a physical presence. These agents rely on data processing, ML, and intelligent algorithms to perform tasks and make decisions, interacting with virtual environments.

Bodyless AI challenges the cognitive paradigm, highlighting the importance of bodily interaction for learning and knowledge acquisition. It forces a reassessment of "intelligence" and whether it should strictly be anchored to data processing or incorporate bodily experience. This perspective raises significant practical questions. If bodily interaction is crucial for intelligence, AI systems must be designed to leverage this, influencing the design of advanced robotics, ML systems, and virtual simulations. Bodyless AI also impacts human-machine interfaces, prompting the need for more intuitive and natural interactive systems.

Bodyless AI raises ethical, legal, and social issues. Without a physical body, what are the legal and moral responsibilities of such agents? How should ethical challenges related to AI in contexts like autonomous driving, healthcare, and data management be addressed?

1. **Embodied AI**: The Embodied AI approach represents a significant shift in how AI is conceived. This approach is based on the belief that bodily interaction with the environment is essential for learning and intelligence (Brooks, 1991). Instead of considering AI as an isolated system that processes data, Embodied AI promotes the idea that a physical body, or a simulation of it, is necessary for knowledge acquisition and intelligence. Brooks (1991) emphasized that the body plays a crucial role in guiding the artificial agent in the world. Through physical interaction with the environment, AI can learn and adapt more effectively. For example, physical robots, such as those used in behavioral robotics, are designed to explore, and interact with the physical environment, learning through direct experience. This approach finds applications in fields such as service robotics, autonomous navigation, and environmental perception.

2. **Simulations and Virtual Environments**: An alternative to direct bodily incorporation is the creation of AI within simulations or virtual environments (Steels, 1990). Although these systems do not have a physical body in the traditional sense, they operate in virtual environments that allow interaction and learning. This approach is often used in computational modeling, gaming, scientific simulations, and training artificial agents. Steels (1990) has worked on rule-based artificial agents

operating within complex virtual environments. These agents can learn and develop intelligent behaviors through interaction with other agents and the virtual environment. Although these systems lack a physical bodily form, they are capable of demonstrating intelligent behaviors, adapting, and learning from the simulated environment.
3. **Hybrid Algorithms**: An important perspective for addressing the conflict between the cognitive paradigm and bodily incorporation is represented by hybrid algorithms (Lungarella et al., 2003). These algorithms combine data processing typical of the cognitive paradigm with elements of bodily incorporation. This approach seeks to balance the strengths of the two paradigms, attempting to leverage the strengths of both. Lungarella emphasized the importance of developing hybrid systems that can combine information processing with physical interaction with the environment. These systems can be used in applications such as advanced robotics, where robots must process complex data but also interact with the physical environment flexibly.
4. **Self-Organizing Learning Systems**: Some researchers are exploring self-organization as a guiding principle for creating AI (Lungarella et al., 2003). These systems are designed to autonomously adapt to the environment, learning from their interaction with it. Self-organization can be seen as a form of virtual bodily incorporation, where AI develops complex behaviors in response to the environment.
5. **Collective Intelligence**: Another fascinating perspective is to consider AI as a collective phenomenon (Heylighen, 2016). In this approach, various AI agents interact with each other and with the environment to achieve intelligent outcomes. This draws attention to the social and distributed nature of intelligence, suggesting that interaction among multiple entities can lead to intelligent results without the need for a physical body.

The idea of creating AI without a physical body challenges the traditional cognitive paradigm and opens new perspectives on intelligence and its applications. This debate continues to shape AI research, influencing how AI systems are designed, implemented, and ethically managed.

Ethical and Epistemological Considerations

The concept of AI without a body raises significant ethical and epistemological questions that warrant deeper consideration. These aspects not only influence technological development but also our understanding of knowledge and intelligence.

Ethical Considerations

The concept of embodiment is associated with the ethics of responsibility (Floridi, 2008). Creating AI without a body brings forth questions of ethical and legal responsibility. Who would be accountable for the actions of disembodied AI? This introduces significant ethical complexities.

The ethics of disembodied AI represents uncharted territory, raising crucial ethical and legal questions. Unlike conventional AI, where the artificial agent is often defined by well-defined physical hardware, disembodied AI challenges traditional assignments of responsibility. Here, the concept of "body" extends beyond the physical to include interactions and the consequences of AI actions. Key points to examine include:
1. **Legal Responsibility and Blame Attribution**: In present society, legal responsibility often relies on the notion of a physical agent performing an action. Disembodied AI raises questions about who is actually responsible for AI actions and how blame is attributed in case of harmful or illegal be-

haviors. This can become particularly complex when AI acts autonomously, without direct human supervision.
2. **Ethical and Moral Decisions**: Disembodied AI may be involved in ethical and moral decisions, such as those related to autonomous driving. If an autonomous car causes an accident, who should decide whom to rescue or what action to take? Who establishes the ethical principles guiding disembodied AI behavior, and how are they applied in complex situations?
3. **Privacy and Security**: Disembodied AI could be involved in collecting and analyzing personal data, raising concerns about privacy and data security. Ensuring that information collected and used by disembodied AI is handled ethically and in compliance with privacy laws is crucial.
4. **Social and Economic Consequences**: The widespread adoption of disembodied AI could have profound social and economic implications, such as significant displacement of human jobs, leading to unemployment and economic inequality. Managing these changes and implementing necessary mitigation measures is essential.

Epistemological Validity

From an epistemological standpoint, the perspective of autopoiesis raises questions about the validity of knowledge generated by AI without a physical body (Varela et al., 1992). Ensuring that this knowledge is authentic and meaningful is challenging when AI lacks direct bodily experiences. Key concerns include:
1. **Bodily Experiences and Understanding**: According to the autopoietic perspective, bodily interaction with the environment is fundamental for knowledge formation. Without a physical body, AI may lack direct experiences and sensory interactions with the world, affecting its understanding of abstract concepts, relationships, and contexts.
2. **Bias and Cultural Context**: Knowledge produced by disembodied AI may reflect biases and the cultural context of the data from which it learns. Without a physical body enabling direct experiences in specific cultural contexts, AI may struggle to fully understand human diversity and generate authentic and unbiased knowledge.
3. **Lack of Intuition and Emotional Understanding**: The absence of bodily experiences could impact AI's ability to develop intuitions and a deep emotional understanding, which is often rooted in human bodily experience. This raises questions about disembodied AI's ability to fully comprehend human emotions and the nuances of social interaction.
4. **Scientific Validity**: In the scientific realm, disembodied AI may struggle to conduct physical experiments and validate results independently, affecting the validity and reproducibility of research conducted by AI.

Addressing Ethical and Epistemological Issues

To address these issues, a holistic approach involving experts in ethics, philosophy, jurisprudence, and social sciences, along with AI technology developers, is essential. Creating ethical guidelines and specific laws for disembodied AI is crucial for addressing the emerging challenges in this field. Ethical and regulatory decisions must be made thoughtfully to ensure that disembodied AI is developed responsibly and that its applications align with fundamental human values.

Maturana and Varela's theory of autopoiesis has had a lasting impact on various disciplines, including brain studies, theories of cognition, and education. Its emphasis on bodily interaction and experience has led to a deeper appreciation of the importance of the body in knowledge and intelligence formation. Conversely, the cognitive paradigm has demonstrated significant successes in AI, particularly in fields such as image recognition, natural language processing, and strategic games. However, the conflict between the traditional data-processing-based view and the perspective of autopoiesis raises significant questions about the validity and authenticity of artificial intelligence.

The idea of disembodied AI offers an intriguing perspective for addressing this conflict. Approaches such as embodied AI, simulations, hybrid algorithms, self-organization, and collective AI seek to balance the strengths of both paradigms. However, these approaches also raise new ethical and epistemological challenges that require careful attention.

The future of AI will likely see continued research and development in both the cognitive paradigm and embodied cognition. This dialogue between diverse perspectives is essential for advancing our understanding of AI and the nature of intelligence in general. The challenge of creating AI without a physical body remains an ambitious and fascinating goal, destined to shape the future of AI.

Artificial Intelligence and Citizenship: Ius Algoritmi

Following Hannah Arendt's insightful formulation, citizenship constitutes the right to have rights, effectively serving as the premise and guarantee for all other forms of protection. Historically, the acquisition of citizenship has been governed by two distinct principles: jus soli, which grants citizenship to those born within the borders of a state regardless of descent, and jus sanguinis, which determines it based on the rights held by the parents. The current historical moment, complex and characterized by numerous exceptions in this regard, calls into question the common conception of citizenship as a stable and absolute entity. The transformation of traditional notions of citizenship is particularly evident online, where the very architecture of the network challenges the territorial conceptions of states. Gradually, our rights are inherited—not mechanically—from our digital identities, clusters of information that act as our representatives in relationships with states, banks, and societies, thereby generating new forms of citizenship in transnational digital nodes and connections.

The phrase "Ius Algoritmi," coined by Cheney-Lippold (2011), describes an emerging form of citizenship generated by the surveillance state, which operates through identification and categorization. The concept refers to the extensive use of software in making decisions about an individual's citizenship status and, consequently, their personal prerogatives and restrictions. The widespread use of AI in decision-making processes related to various aspects involving our digital identities reiterates and redefines the concept of Ius Algoritmi. In a framework characterized by massive migrations, changes in mass identification, and forms of social connections that transcend physical and cultural barriers, the widespread use of AI, from social media to banking networks, and even in political-military automation, contributes to the creation of interaction forms and subjectivities with unique traits, prompting the emergence of interpretative frameworks that account for such complexity.

For example, Latour's (2007) perspective, which recognizes society as formed by networks involving both human and non-human actors equally, suggests an analysis of the influences of non-human actors, such as algorithms and digital platforms, on the formation and expression of group identities. In the context of mass migrations, this perspective suggests that the dynamics of migration cannot be understood solely by considering the individuals involved but require an analysis of the intricate relationships among them and other actors, such as institutions, organizations, and technologies.

Migration becomes a complex process of interactions and connections, where people are linked through social networks characterized, if not by the absence, by the evanescence of the online-offline boundary (onlife, according to Floridi's effective formulation (Floridi, 2015). Digital platforms serve as crucial nodes in these networks, facilitating communication, sharing experiences, and building virtual communities that transcend geographical and cultural boundaries.

Mass identification can be analyzed by considering the contribution of social networks and communication technologies to the formation of new collective identities. In this sense, the use of communication technologies is not merely a neutral means of transmitting information but actively contributes to shaping social reality. The use of algorithms in decision-making processes concerning citizenship and rights reflects the complex interaction among individuals, institutions, and technologies, highlighting how such decisions are shaped or influenced by broader social dynamics.

AI is intrinsically linked to the themes of changes in mass identification and the use of communication technologies, as its implementation can have significant impacts on social, political, and ethical issues. This connection can be analyzed through various aspects, considering automated decision-making and citizenship, algorithms and mass identification, communication and digital social networks, ethical challenges, as well as interpretative perspectives on technology. Such intersection requires a multidisciplinary approach, involving philosophers, social scientists, educators, legal experts, and AI professionals to critically explore how emerging technologies may influence the definition of citizenship, mass identity, and social dynamics.

The concepts of Ius Algoritmi and algorithmic citizenship converge in the context of the impact of algorithms on citizens' decisions and rights, representing similar conceptual approaches but with specific nuances. The term Ius Algoritmi refers to the right of algorithms within the scope of citizenship. It highlights the increasingly widespread use of software to make decisions about an individual's citizenship, thus influencing the rights they possess and lawful operations concerning their person. In this context, algorithms are involved in defining the citizenship status, a role traditionally reserved for legal procedures and institutions.

The concept of algorithmic citizenship (Bridle, 2016) expands this perspective by considering the influence of algorithms not only on citizenship strictly defined (legally) but also on social and cultural citizenship. Algorithmic citizenship refers to an individual's participation in society through digital interactions, where digital platforms, guided by algorithms, shape social experience and civic participation. This concept incorporates the notion that citizenship is no longer defined solely by geographical boundaries but also by digital participation and online visibility.

Both concepts reflect the growing importance of algorithms in determining an individual's status and rights. While Ius Algoritmi is more narrowly focused on formal decisions, algorithmic citizenship extends to the broader sphere of social and cultural interaction mediated by algorithms.

For the purposes of this work, Ius Algoritmi can be considered a subset of algorithmic citizenship, specifically focusing on the legal sphere of citizenship, while the latter embraces a broader concept that also includes social and cultural dynamics shaped by algorithms. Both reflect the need to understand and address the increasing impact of algorithms on citizenship and social participation.

It's quite evident that the very idea of algorithmic citizenship raises the possibility of algorithmic discrimination. Algorithmic discrimination is a phenomenon in which algorithms can amplify and perpetuate pre-existing injustices, based on training data that reflects social biases. To analyze the idea of algorithmic discrimination, it's necessary to refer to the concepts of bias and algorithmic historical revisionism. The connection between the concepts of bias, algorithmic discrimination, and historical revisionism reveals a complex interconnection that deeply influences our understanding of the past and the formation of collective memory. Let's begin exploring the concept of bias, which refers to the presence of prejudices in the data on which algorithms are trained. When the data used for training contains implicit or explicit cultural, social, or other distortions, algorithms can inherit, perpetuate, and multiply such biases, influencing their decisions and predictions.

Algorithmic Bias and Discrimination

Algorithmic discrimination occurs when algorithms, based on distorted or partial data, produce results that may discriminate against certain individuals or groups. This phenomenon can be particularly insidious when applied to historical contexts, as algorithms can amplify and perpetuate past injustices and prejudices.

Evidently, the very concept of data recalls a historical dimension. Since AI relies on "data," which are essentially historical artifacts, often used to make decisions (which will influence future history), an analysis of the diachronic dimension is necessary. Algorithmic discrimination can contribute to a sort of automated historical revisionism, wherein dominant narratives and past discriminations are reinscribed and perpetuated through the use of algorithmic technologies.

Numerous examples and scientific studies have highlighted the complex issues associated with bias and algorithmic discrimination. One of the most significant examples emerged from the field of facial recognition algorithms. Buolamwini and Gebru's (2018) research revealed clear ethnic bias in such algorithms, with greater accuracy in identifying individuals in light-skinned populations compared to dark-skinned ones. This phenomenon, well-documented in the "Gender Shades: Intersectional Accuracy Disparities in Commercial Gender Classification" study, raises significant concerns as such bias can lead to discrimination in critical contexts such as law enforcement and surveillance.

The denouncement of forms of algorithmic discrimination related to AI is part of a rich and documented research field investigating the relationships between algorithms and the risk of historical revisionism.

Benjamin, in "Assessing Risk, Automating Racism" (Benjamin, 2019), provides a critical perspective on the risk of automating racism through the use of algorithms in decision-making contexts, including those related to public safety. The work of Safiya Umoja Noble, author of "Algorithms of Oppression" (Noble, 2018), offers an in-depth analysis of how search engine algorithms can perpetuate racial and gender stereotypes, influencing the presentation of information online and contributing to a distorted representation of society.

A crucial aspect emerged from the study is the intrinsic vulnerability of search algorithms in perpetuating distorted historical views. Algorithms, based on relevance and popularity criteria, can promote the dissemination of historical content that attracts greater interest, at the expense of more accurate and objective information. This distortion in information presentation can profoundly impact the collective perception of past events, thus contributing to algorithmic historical revisionism. The most insidious risk lies in the mitigation methods of known distortions.

However, it is necessary, even briefly, to emphasize that the issue does not only concern technology but cultures (plural) in general: more evidently than in the case of other technologies, AI moves humans away from their presumed central position as the sole narrators of their own stories (the technology itself narrates) and conceptualizes their role and subjectivity as emergent rather than pre-existing (humans as a result of processes, including technological processes). From a traditional humanist perspective, this could be contested. From another perspective, perhaps post-humanist, it could be seen as an opportunity to critically analyze the role that technology plays in the narration and creation of ourselves and our societies. The topic is extensively addressed by Coeckelbergh (2021), who pays particular attention to what he defines as the roles of "narrator" and "time machine" of AI and the normative implications of these roles, arguing how the processes and narrations of AI shape our time and connect past, present, and future in specific ways that are ethically and politically significant.

The cited studies provide a general scientific framework for the challenges related to bias and algorithmic discrimination. For a more in-depth investigation, it is necessary to delve into the various nuances of bias.

Rivoltella and Panciroli (2023) discuss the possible influences of biases in feedback loops involving data, algorithms, and user interactions, analyzing examples of bias in algorithm results and how they can influence user decisions and the feedback cycle. Additionally, they examine different types of bias in the field of AI, referring to the proposal by Suresh and Guttag (2019). In this framework, the four main types of bias are:

1. **Measurement Bias**: It refers to how particular characteristics are selected, used, and measured. An example concerns predicting the risk of college student dropout, where socio-economic and demographic aspects are considered. These data are used as proxy variables to measure the level of risk. The algorithm assigns higher probabilities of dropout to individuals from lower socioeconomic classes without considering the fact that these individuals are often more resilient and committed to their college careers.
2. **Omitted Variable Bias**: It occurs when one or more important variables are excluded from the model. An example concerns predicting the annual percentage rate of customers who will cancel a service subscription. The absence of a variable representing the emergence of a new competitor in the market at half the price is an example of omitted variable bias.
3. **Representation Bias**: It stems from the mode of sampling a population during data collection. Non-representative samples usually lack subgroups of the population. For example, the lack of geographic diversity in a dataset is a case of representation bias.
4. **Aggregation Bias**: It occurs when erroneous conclusions are drawn about individuals observed within an entire population. For example, in monitoring diabetic patients, HbA1c levels, widely used to diagnose and monitor diabetes, can vary significantly between sexes and ethnicities. A model that ignores these individual differences may not be suitable for all ethnic and gender groups in the population, causing aggregation bias.

These aspects are cited in the "Framework on Ethical Aspects of Artificial Intelligence, Robotics and Related Technologies" by the European Union in 2020 and in the "National Strategic Program for Artificial Intelligence" of 2022, where the need for "reliable" and "safe" AI is emphasized, with "reliable" meaning the ability not to harm the dignity, physical, psychological, and financial security of individuals.

Beyond categorizations, it is important to specify how biases can be mitigated, but not eliminated. Our biases are directly embedded in our language and in the data on language use that AI systems learn (Caliskan et al., 2017). For example, language translation tools based on AI regularly add gender stereotypes during translation from gender-neutral languages. Often, we assume that machines are inherently objective, unable to analyze data without bias or malice. It is easy to forget that the programming guiding how AI analyzes data is originally created by humans. The people creating the algorithms belong to an industrial culture that harbors biases against certain categories (according to the cited studies, for example, women and African Americans), even just based on their evident underrepresentation. Undoubtedly, few programmers would intentionally insert biases into their work, but it is difficult to address problems that are not seen, and impossible to avoid actions of which one is not even aware. Racist and sexist assumptions are deeply rooted in Western culture and perhaps even more so in the subculture of the technology industry.

Bias Mitigation: The Risk of Revisionism

Correcting data and mitigating bias represent crucial challenges in algorithmic processing. Approaches based on critical data analysis, diversification of training sets, and transparent regulations have been proposed to address these issues (Buolamwini & Gebru, 2018; Obermeyer, et al., 2019). Careful analysis of training data is essential to identify and understand existing biases, involving domain experts to ensure the representativeness of various perspectives (Buolamwini & Gebru, 2018).

Introducing diversity into training data helps mitigate bias, reflecting cultural, ethnic, and gender diversity. Transparent regulations for algorithm design and implementation are suggested to ensure understandable and evaluable decisions (Diakopoulos, 2016).

Bias correction during the ML process is another promising strategy, with techniques like "fairness-aware machine learning" seeking to balance predictions to avoid unfair discrimination (Chouldechova, 2017). Involving diverse perspectives in design, including ethics experts, educators, sociologists, and historians, can contribute to identifying and mitigating bias more comprehensively (Obermeyer et al., 2019).

Addressing ethical challenges and the risk of historical revisionism associated with data corrections is fundamental, balancing bias correction with respect for historiographical research (Crawford & Calo, 2016). Addressing bias in data requires a careful and responsible approach, implementing strategies that have shown effectiveness in specific studies. It is crucial to balance bias correction with the preservation of historical integrity, avoiding manipulations that may inappropriately distort historical narrative (Buolamwini & Gebru, 2018; Crawford & Calo, 2016; Obermeyer et al., 2019). The literature suggests a holistic approach that considers the complexities involved in the process of bias correction in algorithmic data.

A common approach is preprocessing the data used to train AI models, ensuring the representativeness of the entire population, including historically marginalized communities. This may involve techniques such as oversampling, under sampling, or generating synthetic data (Koh & Liang, 2017). Preprocessing involves identifying and correcting biases in the data before model training, through techniques like data augmentation or adversarial debiasing (Gira, et al., 2022).

Synthetic or augmented data refers to artificially generated or modified datasets to extend or enhance existing data. This technique is often used in ML and AI to address the "data hunger" of AI algorithms during training, enriching training datasets to improve model generalization and tackle a greater variety of situations. This practice may involve generating new examples through synthesis algorithms or modifying existing data to create variants.

The responsible use of synthetic data emerges as a particularly critical aspect, as the quality and representativeness of such data directly influence the effectiveness of the generated models. Scientific literature emphasizes that indiscriminate ingestion of synthetic data, if not carefully managed, could amplify errors and biases already present in the original data (Mitchell et al., 2019), and the generation of synthetic data could lead to the creation of unrealistic or distorted scenarios, negatively impacting the models' ability to generalize in real-world contexts.

The integration of advanced fairness-aware machine learning techniques into the synthetic data generation process can help ensure that new instances are created fairly and respectfully of the diversity present in the population (Chouldechova, 2017). Additionally, active involvement of ethics experts, sociologists, and representative stakeholders can contribute to identifying and addressing potential biases more comprehensively (Obermeyer et al., 2019).

A second approach is the careful selection of models used to analyze data, with methods that prioritize fairness, such as those based on group or individual fairness. For example, Kamiran and Calders (2012) proposed a method for selecting classifiers that achieve demographic parity by fairly distributing positive and negative outcomes among different demographic groups. The use of techniques such as regularization or ensemble methods helps reduce bias (Dwork & Ilvento, 2018).

A post-processing approach involves regulating the output of AI models to remove bias and ensure fairness. For example, post-processing methods have been proposed that adjust model decisions to achieve equal odds, fairly distributing false positives and false negatives among different demographic groups (Zhang, et al., 2018).

These approaches promise to mitigate bias in AI but have limitations, such as the complexity and variable effectiveness of data preprocessing, challenges in defining fairness in model selection methods, and the potential added complexity of post-processing methods (Barocas & Selbst, 2016). In the realm of generative AI, addressing bias requires a holistic strategy, from ensuring diversity in data to selecting transparent models and critically post-processing the generated results.

Implementing such approaches also requires careful consideration of social implications. For example, adjusting model predictions to ensure fairness may involve trade-offs between different types of bias, with possible unintended consequences on the distribution of outcomes among different groups (Kleinberg, et al., 2018). Ultimately, the scientific community emphasizes the importance of a balanced approach that considers the risks associated with the "data hunger" of AI.

Transparency and Explainability

Within this framework, transparency and explainability are fundamental assurances as they allow algorithmic citizens to understand the capabilities and limitations of algorithms, as well as to decide which data algorithms should store and utilize for reasoning. Models with interpretable latent variables should be preferred over "black box" counterparts.

The term "black box" in relation to AI algorithms refers to the lack of transparency or understanding of how such algorithms make decisions or produce results. In other words, an AI algorithm is considered a "black box" when its internal logic or decision-making process is not easily interpretable or understandable to humans. The black box nature of AI algorithms can pose significant challenges, especially in contexts where justification of decisions or detailed understanding of algorithm operation is required. This can be problematic in sectors such as healthcare, law, or finance, where understanding the reasons for a particular decision is essential.

An in-depth exploration of this issue is documented in several publications. For example, in "The Mythos of Model Interpretability" by Lipton (2018), the author explores the challenges associated with interpreting ML models and emphasizes the complexity of maximizing the transparency of AI algorithm decisions. Similarly, in "Big Data's Disparate Impact" by Barocas and Selbst (2016), the ethical and social implications of automated decisions and the challenges related to algorithm transparency are addressed. Both of these studies highlight the importance of addressing the issue of the "black box" in AI algorithms to ensure responsible and fair use of such technologies.

Transparency, however, is a sector-specific concept with multiple facets, simply in the sense that what is transparent to an AI researcher may not be so for an end user. Therefore, system transparency should be evaluated from the perspective of intended end users, and the machine should assume a full supportive role, with users having ultimate control over when and how to use the tools. Opening up models, open science, and open-source code are presented as key elements for improving the utility and transparency of educational AI tools. In general, user trust can be achieved by demonstrating transparency in educational AI tools. Opening up the parameters of AI models, such as large-scale language models, is seen as a way to democratize such capabilities. The open-science approach provides a rich framework for transparently documenting the development process of such models and enhancing understanding of the ethical and fairness aspects of new technologies. Open sourcing the source code is considered a means to enable effective use of AI tools even in developing countries, although it is emphasized that knowledge transfer is necessary to fully leverage these advanced resources. Finally, the importance of collaboration between experts and beneficiaries is emphasized, as well as the adoption of low-code interfaces to simplify interaction between users and complex AI systems.

AI and Inclusion: On the Need for a Metadisciplinary Approach

The issue of inclusion in the field of AI requires in-depth analysis, which spans across various interrelated dimensions, thus constituting a complex and multifaceted challenge. A multidimensional approach is necessary to comprehensively address this issue, which cannot be limited solely to diversity of perspectives in education but must also encompass promoting diversity in training data and transparency in algorithmic decision-making.

Firstly, the issue of diversity in training data emerges as a crucial point. Buolamwini and Gebru (2018) highlighted that the lack of diverse representation in training data can lead to AI systems infused with ethnic discriminations. The need to promote diversity at this stage is evident to ensure that algorithms, which serve as cognitive artifacts, accurately reflect the complexity of social dynamics. A collaborative approach is suggested by Obermeyer et al. (2019), who propose involving experts from various disciplines to ensure inclusive and representative data collection.

Simultaneously, transparency in algorithmic decisions plays a key role. Diakopoulos (2016) emphasizes the importance of making automated decisions understandable to promote accountability and instill trust in users. The adoption of transparent regulations, in line with Diakopoulos' recommendations, constitutes an essential step to avoid algorithmic opacity and enable a critical evaluation of automated decisions.

Only through an integrated and conscious commitment on all these fronts is it possible to build intelligent systems that respect human diversity and minimize the impact of biases in automated decision-making processes. This requires active involvement of developers, ethics experts, educators, and all stakeholders involved in the creation and use of AI-based technologies. A meta disciplinary perspective is essential to address the complexity of the dynamics involved and to shape a future where AI is an inclusive and responsible ally in our society, thus emphasizing the need for a shared vision and transdisciplinary strategies to address this delicate issue.

Critical Alliance: The Impact of Critical Thinking Education in the Era of Artificial Intelligence

In advanced ML systems, the details of each individual prediction can be based on literally billions of individual digital processes and, as such, are opaque even to the original programmers (Bornstein, 2018). In other words, while humans may be required to account for and justify decisions that appear to be prejudiced, machines may not be able to provide such explanations, nor can their creators.

Given the inherent bias and opacity of AI, education in critical thinking emerges as a fundamental element in the context of AI, as the increasing complexity and pervasiveness of such systems require informed and aware algorithmic citizenship. Critical thinking, understood as the ability to objectively analyze information, identify, and evaluate arguments, becomes crucial in the context of AI, where decisions can be automated through complex algorithms. AI literacy goes beyond mere technical understanding and involves the training of individuals capable of questioning and understanding the ethical, social, and cultural implications of automated systems. In this context, education in critical thinking plays a key role in instilling the ability to question training data, identify implicit biases, and understand the limitations of algorithms. Individuals trained in critical thinking (Di Tore, et al., 2020) are better equipped to actively participate in the development process of AI, contributing to mitigating ethical risks and ensuring that such systems are designed and implemented responsibly. Furthermore, critical awareness enables users to understand the decisions made by algorithms, recognize any distortions in the presentation of information, and exercise informed control over the use of AI-based technologies. The intersection between education in critical thinking and AI thus represents an essential connection to develop a fair, aware digital society capable of managing emerging challenges related to decision automation.

CONCLUSION

This essay has explored the complex relationship between AI and educational processes through three main directions: forms of textuality, the relationship between intelligence and the body, and the influence of AI on citizenship. Each of these directions raises significant epistemological, ethical, and social questions.

Firstly, the ability of LLMs to overcome the static nature of written text and respond to questions poses fundamental questions about the nature of interactivity and the evolution of textual communication. The capability of AI to generate interactive responses represents a significant advancement over the limitations identified by Plato, but also raises new challenges regarding the qualitative difference between responses generated by AI and those from the human mind.

Secondly, the concept of an intelligence without a physical body introduces a radically new paradigm that requires reconsideration of the relationship between intelligence and bodily experience. The idea of disembodied AI that processes information and makes decisions without physical manifestation raises profound questions about the nature of intelligence and its connection to embodied human experience. Exploring this relationship helps us better understand how our intelligence is influenced and enriched by our bodily interactions with the world.

Finally, the growing influence of algorithms on decision-making processes related to rights and citizenship status, conceptualized as "algorithmic citizenship," highlights the need to address issues of transparency, fairness, and accountability. The widespread use of AI in critical sectors underscores the urgency of developing regulations that ensure fair and justifiable decision-making processes, reducing the risk of algorithmic discrimination, and promoting inclusive and fair citizenship.

In conclusion, the ongoing evolution of AI offers unprecedented opportunities to enhance educational processes, but also requires critical attention and epistemological reflection to address emerging challenges. An integrated and conscious approach, involving educators, technology developers, ethics experts, and philosophers, is essential to ensure that AI is developed and used responsibly, aligning with the fundamental values of our society. Only through concerted and multidisciplinary efforts can we hope to build a future where AI is an inclusive and responsible ally in our society.

REFERENCES

Adams, D. (2019). *Guida galattica per gli autostoppisti. Il ciclo completo*. Edizioni Mondadori.

Barocas, S., & Selbst, A. D. (2016). Big data's disparate impact. *California Law Review*, 104(3), 671–732. 10.15779/Z38BG31

Benjamin, R. (2019). Assessing risk, automating racism. *Science*, 366(6464), 421–422. 10.1126/science.aaz387331649182

Borel, É. (1913). La mécanique statique et l'irréversibilité. *J. Phys. Theor. Appl.*, 3(1), 189–196. 10.1051/jphystap:019130030018900

Bornstein, S. (2018). Antidiscriminatory algorithms. *Alabama Law Review*, 70, 519.

Bridle, J. (2016). Algorithmic citizenship, digital statelessness. *GeoHumanities*, 2(2), 377–381. 10.1080/2373566X.2016.1237858

Brooks, R. A. (1991). Intelligence without representation. *Artificial Intelligence*, 47(1-3), 139–159. 10.1016/0004-3702(91)90053-M

Buolamwini, J., & Gebru, T. (2018). Gender shades: Intersectional accuracy disparities in commercial gender classification. In *Proceedings of the Conference on Fairness, Accountability, and Transparency* (pp. 77-91). Research Gate.

Caliskan, A., Bryson, J. J., & Narayanan, A. (2017). Semantics derived automatically from language corpora contain human-like biases. *Science*, 356(6334), 183–186. 10.1126/science.aal423028408601

Cheney-Lippold, J. (2011). A new algorithmic identity: Soft biopolitics and the modulation of control. *Theory, Culture & Society*, 28(6), 164–181. 10.1177/0263276411424420

Chomsky, N., Roberts, I., & Watumull, J. (2023, March 8). Noam Chomsky: The false promise of ChatGPT. *The New York Times*. https://www.nytimes.com/2023/03/08/opinion/noam-chomsky-chatgpt.html

Chouldechova, A. (2017). Fair prediction with disparate impact: A study of bias in recidivism prediction instruments. *Big Data*, 5(2), 153–163. 10.1089/big.2016.004728632438

Coeckelbergh, M. (2021). Time machines: Artificial intelligence, process, and narrative. *Philosophy & Technology*, 34(4), 1623–1638. 10.1007/s13347-021-00479-y

Crawford, K., & Calo, R. (2016). There is a blind spot in AI research. *Nature*, 538(7625), 311–313. 10.1038/538311a27762391

Di Tore, S., Aiello, P., Sibilio, M., & Berthoz, A. (2020). Simplex didactics: Promoting transversal learning through the training of perspective taking. *Journal of e-Learning and Knowledge Society*, 16(3), 34-49. https://doi.org/10.20368/1971-8829/1135221

Diakopoulos, N. (2016). Accountability in algorithmic decision making. *Communications of the ACM*, 59(2), 56–62. 10.1145/2844110

Dwork, C., & Ilvento, C. (2018). Fairness under composition. *arXiv preprint arXiv:1806.06122*. https://arxiv.org/abs/1806.06122

Floridi, L. (2008). The method of levels of abstraction. *Minds and Machines*, 18(3), 303–329. 10.1007/s11023-008-9113-7

Floridi, L. (2015). *The onlife manifesto: Being human in a hyperconnected era.* Springer Nature. 10.1007/978-3-319-04093-6

Floridi, L. (2022). *Etica dell'intelligenza artificiale: Sviluppi, opportunità, sfide.* Raffaello Cortina Editore.

Gira, M., Zhang, R., & Lee, K. (2022). Debiasing pre-trained language models via efficient fine-tuning. In *Proceedings of the Second Workshop on Language Technology for Equality, Diversity, and Inclusion* (pp. 85-95). Research Gate. 10.18653/v1/2022.ltedi-1.8

Heylighen, F. (2016). Stigmergy as a universal coordination mechanism I: Definition and components. *Cognitive Systems Research*, 38, 4–13. 10.1016/j.cogsys.2015.12.002

Kamiran, F., & Calders, T. (2012). Data preprocessing techniques for classification without discrimination. *Knowledge and Information Systems*, 33(1), 1–33. 10.1007/s10115-011-0463-8

Kleinberg, J., Lakkaraju, H., Leskovec, J., Ludwig, J., & Mullainathan, S. (2018). Human decisions and machine predictions. *The Quarterly Journal of Economics*, 133(1), 237–293. 10.1093/qje/qjx03229755141

Koh, P. W., & Liang, P. (2017). Understanding black-box predictions via influence functions. In *Proceedings of the International Conference on Machine Learning* (pp. 1885-1894).

Latour, B. (2007). *Reassembling the social: An introduction to actor-network-theory.* Oup Oxford.

Lévi-Strauss, C. (2010). *Lo sguardo da lontano* (Vol. 715). Il Saggiatore.

Lipton, Z. C. (2018). The mythos of model interpretability: In machine learning, the concept of interpretability is both important and slippery. *ACM Queue; Tomorrow's Computing Today*, 16(3), 31–57. 10.1145/3236386.3241340

Lungarella, M., Metta, G., Pfeifer, R., & Sandini, G. (2003). Developmental robotics: A survey. *Connection Science*, 15(4), 151–190. 10.1080/09540090310001655110

Maturana, H. R., & Varela, F. J. (1980). *Autopoiesis and cognition: The realization of the living.* D. Reidel Publishing Company. (Original work published 1972)

Mitchell, M., Wu, S., Zaldivar, A., Barnes, P., Vasserman, L., Hutchinson, B., & Gebru, T. (2019). Model cards for model reporting. In *Proceedings of the Conference on Fairness, Accountability, and Transparency* (pp. 220-229). ACM. 10.1145/3287560.3287596

Noble, S. U. (2018). *Algorithms of oppression: How search engines reinforce racism.* New York University Press. 10.18574/nyu/9781479833641.001.0001

Obermeyer, Z., Powers, B., Vogeli, C., & Mullainathan, S. (2019). Dissecting racial bias in an algorithm used to manage the health of populations. *Science*, 366(6464), 447–453. 10.1126/science.aax234231649194

Panciroli, C., & Rivoltella, P. C. (2023). Can an algorithm be fair? Intercultural biases and critical thinking in generative artificial intelligence social uses. In Pasta, S., & Zoletto, D. (Eds.), *Postdigital Intercultures. Interculture Postdigitali* (pp. 19–46). SCHOLÉ.

Platone. (2011). *Fedro* (A. Iezzi, Ed.). REA.

Steels, L. (1990). Components of expertise. *AI Magazine*, 11(2), 28–49. 10.1609/aimag.v11i2.855

Suresh, H., & Guttag, J. V. (2019). A framework for understanding unintended consequences of machine learning. *Communications of the ACM*, 64(3), 62–71. 10.1145/3287560.3287596

Varela, F. J., Thompson, E. T., & Rosch, E. (1992). *The embodied mind: Cognitive science and human experience*. MIT Press.

Chapter 4
Invasive and Creepy Technologies:
Challenges and Opportunities

Rochell R. McWhorter
https://orcid.org/0000-0003-2053-1610
The University of Texas at Tyler, USA

Mandi M. Laurie
https://orcid.org/0000-0001-8910-5527
The University of Texas at Tyler, USA

ABSTRACT

As modern technologies have increased in sophistication and invasiveness, users have expressed concerns about confidentiality and ethical issues regarding contemporary technologies such as artificial intelligence, facial recognition, social robots, big data, and location-sharing apps. As a result, the term "creepy technologies" has been used to describe these concerns. This chapter seeks to review relevant literature for this area of study and offer interventions for individual users, teams, and organizations.

INTRODUCTION

Contemporary technologies are becoming progressively sophisticated (McWhorter, 2023) and increasingly invasive (Kelley et al., 2023; Tene & Polontesky, 2013). Due to this invasiveness, the term "creepy technology" has emerged in the literature along with concerns such as cybersecurity, confidentiality, and ethical concerns, among others (Mou & Meng, 2024; Phinnemore et al., 2023; Sharma, 2023). For this chapter, creepy technology is defined as *"technology that evokes feeling or belief that privacy may be invaded in an unethical or discomforting manner"* (McWhorter & Bennett, 2021, p. 243). This area of study can inform business professionals and stakeholders concerning the perceptions of technology by various stakeholders and likely encourage organizations to examine their technology policies.

The objectives of this chapter are two-fold to: (1) offer a review of relevant existing literature in this area of study and, (2) provide a discussion on interventions for perceived invasive technologies that should be considered by both individuals and organizations. Both objectives will be presented in

DOI: 10.4018/979-8-3693-3003-6.ch004

the following sections. Also, additional readings will be suggested, and key terms and definitions will conclude the chapter.

BACKGROUND

Examples of creepy technology found in the literature are numerous and are enabled by the Internet of Things (IoT). Creepy technologies include *location sharing applications* (Moreau, 2019; Phinnemore et al., 2023), *facial recognition technology* (Cuador, 2017; Reidenberg, 2014; Seberger et al., 2024; Symanovich, 2018), *always-listening voice assistants* (Ford & Palmer, 2019; Mou & Meng, 2024; Phinnemore et al., 2023), *social media* (McWhorter et al., in-press). Also found were the *convergence of big data* (Marr, 2016), the *Internet of Things* (IoT; Bennett & McWhorter, 2014; O'Hagan et al., 2023), *artificial intelligence* (AI) (Kaplan, 2016; Kjeldgaard-Christiansen, 2024; Larrey, 2017; McCarthy et al., 1955; McWhorter, 2023; Sulleyman, 2017) and *social robots* (Fitter et al., 2021; McWhorter & Bennett, 2021; Reig et al., 2021), including *AI robots* (Baldwin, 2019; Ischen et al., 2020; Mou & Meng, 2024), among others. These technologies have the capacity to evoke discomfort and human questioning about the ethical use of personal data.

INTERNET OF THINGS

The *Internet of Things* (IoT; Evans, 2011) is a term used to demonstrate the connectedness of smart devices that link the world together (Bennett & McWhorter, 2014) and Marr (2016) predicted that the term IoT would be utilized less by users as it moves into the "hype phase and quickly becomes part of everyday life" (para. 1). McWhorter and Bennett (2020) described IoT as "a phenomenon of a growing number of connected devices, and Internet-enabled services [whereby] billions of devices are now connected to one another" (p. 166) and IoT enables the sophisticated technologies that some may characterize as *creepy technology*. For example, Saliesh (2019) described a subset IoT as the "Internet of Bodies" (IoB) remarking that as the "IoT enter[s] the human body…human bodies are now connected to a network, with the potential to be remotely controlled and monitored" (para. 1). Andrea Matwyshyn, Northeastern University law professor, noted the IoB has both legal as well as policy implications when the human body is used as a technology platform (Matwyshyn, 2019). Another concerning example of the IoB is former Vice-President Dick Cheney's heart implant's wireless sensors that were intentionally inactivated due to the threat of potential hackers that proved to be a viable threat (ABC News, 2013). In 2017, roughly a half-million pacemakers were recalled due to security concerns and the devices were given a required firmware update (Garun, 2017).

SOCIAL MEDIA

Social media is very pervasive in the modern culture and is quite useful for social networking and building community, facilitating meetings in real-time, exploring new interest areas, and access to expert content, and training (McWhorter, et al., in-press). However, many users often over-share their personal information online (Shabahang et al., 2024) and organizations are reaping the financial benefits of targeted advertising (Choi et al., 2023). Social media has become the largest threat for digital security incidents (i.e., data breaches) including six incidents of social media account breaches that compromised over two billion confidential personal data records in the first half of 2018 with Facebook user accounts being the primary target (Gilbert, 2018). From 2018 to 2023 there have been an additional nine Facebook data breaches resulting in nearly $6 Billion in fines and class action lawsuits (Heiligenstein, 2023). In 2024, a large-scale data leak was discovered to have affected social media giants Facebook, SnapChat, LinkedIn, and TikTok, alongside the search engine Google, and payment processing company Venmo (Kato, 2024). The company that routes text message capabilities found their two-factor authentication codes were inadvertently displayed to the general public view which meant users could have their password reset links and the one-time passcodes accessed by malicious actors. To put this in perspective, the parent company processes 5 million SMS text messages a day and the breach is being currently being reported as the largest of all time with 26 billion accounts being compromised (Kato, 2024).

Other privacy concerns for social media are also evident. For example, Facebook paid hundreds of third-party contractors to listen to and transcribe selected person-to-person voice calls made in its Facebook Messenger platform for the purpose of insuring that automated AI transcriptions were accurate but without users' consent (Brito, 2019). Users were left wondering if the human review of their audio was targeting them for a violation of service terms, especially if they had used unacceptable language or discussed topics that could be subject to violations of the EU alongside other privacy rule violations (Frier, 2019). Hasselton (2019) reported that Facebook apps on mobile devices automatically track the places users go so it can deliver ads and provide location-based features to users who have not disabled the tracking feature in Facebook settings.

LOCATION SHARING APPLICATIONS

Location-sharing applications on mobile devices such as Snapchat (Snapchat.com), Swarm (Swarmapp.com), Glympse (Glympse.com), and Life360 (Life360.com) allow the user to share their location with their family members and friends in real-time (Roy, 2023). In addition to mobile apps, users can also share information with 911 call centers in cases of emergency (Ji et al., 2023; Magid, 2018). However, the downside of location sharing in real-time are the privacy concerns. It was revealed to consumers in 2018, that real-time customer location information was wholesaled by cell phone carriers to "data brokers who sold that information to law enforcement and others, without necessarily going through the time-consuming formalities such as court orders" (Magid, 2018, para. 2). In addition, Vu et al. (2018) found while sharing location-based social media data with social relationships can be convenient for users, it can also reveal sensitive and private information through social link mining that should be concerning to users. Moreover, the same activities Vu et al. (2018) spoke out about have now become so commonplace that courses on how to conduct social link mining and web scraping are offered by conglomerates such as IBM, large scale social media platform LinkedIn, and even informational marketing blogs (China, 2023; LinkedIn, 2023; Mironov, 2024).Therefore, behaviors thought to raise alarm six years ago, have now been firmly seated in our daily lives leading us to believe these intrusions are normal.

FACIAL RECOGNITION TECHNOLOGY

Facial recognition technology (FRT) provides facial expressions and other non-verbal cues not transmitted by voice in human interpersonal communication (Mehrabian & Russell, 1974; Shovak & Petiy, 2023). Facial recognition technology (FRT) is a popular topic due to its use with policework, crime control, surveillance, and public safety (Kostka, et al., 2023; Rainie et al., 2022; Raposo, 2023) and holds promise for law enforcement, healthcare, retail, hospitality, marketing and advertising, banking, event planning, social media/entertainment, air travel, automobiles, gambling/casinos, voting, distance education, ride-hailing, restaurants, and computer electronics, among others (Amazon Web Services, 2024; CB Insights, 2019; Srivastava & Bag, 2024). Qi et al. (2019) posited that FRT can aid a physician to acknowledge the patient's feelings in real-time, increase the interaction between student and instructor in distance education, and trainers in the business world can more effectively adapt sessions to meet the needs of the employee (CB Insights, 2019; Ikromovich & Mamatkulovich, 2023). Posited as merely a beneficial aide in interpersonal communications with healthcare providers in 2019, four short years later FRT is being coupled with AI to diagnose complex diseases and disorders such as: autism spectrum disorder, endocrine and metabolic diseases, Cushing's syndrome, genetic and chromosome abnormalities, Down syndrome, Turner syndrome, neuromuscular diseases, facial paralysis, neurodegenerative diseases, coronary artery disease, multi-organ failure, and acute and severe illness seen in emergency departments (Cox et al. 2024; Mumenin et al., 2023; Qiang et al., 2022; Wu et al. 2024).

Martin (2019) noted that FRT utilizes photos and videos to identify people including the "geometry of a face such as the distance between a person's eyes and the distance from their forehead to their chin…creating the 'facial signature' …[comparing it] to a database of known faces" (para. 2). While FRT has usefulness in a myriad of applications, it can also be considered a "creepy technology" when it is utilized by the wrong hands or used for a purpose the public regards as invasive. In fact, activists have been pushing for FRT to be banned (ACLU, 2023; Hill, 2020; Ryan-Mosley, 2023). Since surveillance is one of its primary uses, FRT is quite concerning to many people due to the absence of federal regulations, leaving many concerned about its accuracy. These concerns are proven to be valid in the aftermath of the Riteaid scandal in which misidentified Black, Latino and Asian people were mistakenly identified by FRT as potential or possible shoplifters (Bhuiyan, 2023). Furthermore, widespread reports of misidentification of people of color abound, leading to fears about the possible ramifications of false identification and subsequent wrongfully conviction (Bitter, 2024; Johnson & Johnson, 2023; Lieu, 2022; Najibi, 2020; Zahn, 2023).

INTELLIGENT VOICE ASSISTANTS

Intelligent voice assistants are being increasingly integrated into various facets of modern life, appearing in smartphones, homes, and cars (Mou & Meng, 2024; Phinnemore et al., 2023) These always-listening assistants often have 'human' names such as Alexa (Amazon.com), Siri (Apple.com), Cortana (Microsoft.com), Bixby and Viv (Samsung) and some have found them to be creepy due to their listening and ability to record conversations. However, Laricchia (2024) reports 64% of American households now own at least one smart speaker which seems to indicate a significant adoption of the technology despite these concerns. Previously, people had concerns voice assistants would record and disseminate their private conversations, history has proven the misuse of this information has been unlikely to occur though it is still a potential security risk. The erosion of privacy associated with voice assistants, designed to listen for activation commands through constant listening of users, can make even the most laissez-faire user uneasy about the potential for inadvertent recording of private conversations. It bears noting that companies have assured consumers these recordings are typically not misused, though the mere possibility of such an event is enough to cause discomfort among users.

Deepfake Technology

Currently, a more likely concern is the security vulnerability associated with the misuse of AI deepfake technology in conjunction with voice assistants (Bilika et al., 2023; Ubert, 2023). An audio deepfake is defined as an AI model trained "to generate realistic voice samples that are indistinguishable from the victim's real speech characteristics" (Rabhi et al., 2024). These sophisticated technologies can mimic human voices with a high degree of accuracy, which poses an entirely new threat to the integrity and security of voice assistants. While the popular voice assistants are beneficial for the user by providing "speedy, voice-activated methods of answering questions using information found on the Internet" (McWhorter, et al., in-press), voice assistants have been shown to be fooled by audio deepfake audio samples (Stokel-Walker, 2021). These deepfake audio samples can be used to deceive voice assistants, leading to unauthorized access of personal information, financial accounts, and other sensitive data (Abbas et al., 2023; Dixit, 2023; Gilbert & Gong, 2024). Moreover, Bilika et al. (2023) report 30% of audio deepfake intrusion attempts of voice assistants were successful. According to Gilbert and Gong (2024) these deepfakes have then been used to gain unauthorized access of login credentials, which allows bad actors to steal an individual's identity to commit fraud or create new user online accounts. Further, even sharing video and voice clips on social media cites can leave individuals vulnerable to the creation of a deepfake (Gilbert & Gong, 2024). While the U.S. has enacted laws that criminalize certain uses of deepfake technology, simply put, criminals do not always follow the law. Moreover, the potential for misuse of deepfake technology extends far beyond personal privacy and security. It can also have broader societal implications, such as the spread of misinformation and the erosion of trust in audio and voice communications. As deepfakes become more prevalent, it becomes increasingly difficult to distinguish between genuine and fabricated audio, which can lead to a range of negative outcomes, from personal fraud to larger-scale manipulation of public opinion.

The 30% successful intrusion attempt statistic (Bilika et al., 2023) highlights the potential for malicious actors to exploit voice assistants, raising serious concerns about privacy and security. If concerned for privacy for yourself and others in the immediate vicinity, it is recommended you turn your voice assistant off when not being actively used (See Figure 1). Furthermore, in business environments where discussions of sensitive information are routinely conducted, turning off voice assistants when not in use may prove to be a prudent security measure.

Figure 1. Amazon Echo Dot (Licensed under Creative Commons Attribution - Share Alike 4.0 International license)

SOCIAL ROBOTS

Robots such as Atlas Gen-2 (Amadeo, 2024) and Optimus Gen-2 (Thurbon, 2024) employ humanoid intelligence architecture and sensors [See Figure 2] which allow the robots to talk, move and perform programmed actions (Dang, 2019). Their humanoid architecture utilizes "personality content and cognitive, linguistic, perceptual, and behavioral content…AI and robotics are a highly flexible set of technologies, growing more powerful every day. Like all advanced technologies, they can be used for positive, negative, or neutral purposes" (Goertzel et al., 2017, p. 2).

Figure 2. Tesla's Optimus gen-2 robot

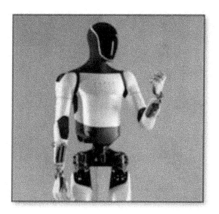

Other AI robots are currently being utilized in the food delivery sector, with pizza giant Domino's utilizing Nuro's R2 autonomous delivery vehicles (Hunt, 2021) and smaller pizza chain Marco's relying upon the Magna (Heier, 2023). In a similar vein, quick dining chicken chain Chick-fil-A using the REV-1 (Thompson, 2023) and the delivery company Uber Eats utilizes the Serve (Serve, n.d.). This change in workforce should be of concern for Human Resource and Human Resource Development (HR/HRD) professionals due to the loss of jobs associated with the delivery sector.

Figure 3. Starship's food delivery robot

As robots and AI systems become more integrated into everyday life and work environments, they bring about changes that affect fears associated with human job security and the resultant turnover intentions (McClure, 2018; Shum et al., 2024; Yam et al., 2023).

These changes are studied in the field of human-robot interaction (HRI), specifically how humans interact with robots and AI systems, focusing on improving these interactions to make them more intuitive and beneficial (Obaigbena et al., 2024). The increasing capabilities of AI and social robots, and voice assistants, can lead to fears of job insecurity. Shum et al. (2024) report an increase in employee turnover intention related to the creepy factor of working alongside robots. In addition to the emotional discomfort, employees may fear that their roles will be replaced by automated systems, leading to higher turnover intentions (Yam et al., 2023). This is particularly relevant in sectors like customer service and hospitality, where voice assistants can handle many routine inquiries, potentially reducing the need for human staff. Furthermore, the Logistics iQ (2020) report suggests a 12% growth year over year of warehouse automation robots. This growth suggests more automation and fewer human employees.

Given this increase, Human Resource and Human Resource Development (HR/HRD) professionals should not discount employee's feelings of emotional discomfort, or feeling creeped-out, associated with working alongside social robots. HR and HRD professionals need to address these concerns proactively by developing strategies to manage the transition to more automated workplaces. This should include providing training and development opportunities for employees to work alongside AI systems, thus enhancing their skills and making them more valuable in the evolving job market. They should develop strategies to manage the integration of robots into the workforce in a way that minimizes job insecurity and turnover intentions. This could include:

- Training and Development: Providing training programs to help employees develop new skills that are complementary to robotic technology can help workers feel more secure in their roles and better equipped to work alongside robots.
- Communication: Maintaining transparent communication about the role of automation and social robots in the workplace and how they are intended to complement rather than replace human workers. Clear communication can alleviate fears and build trust among employees.
- Job Redesign: Redesigning jobs to incorporate both human and robotic elements will ensure employees play a crucial role in the organizational operations and can help maintain job satisfaction and reduce turnover intentions.
- Support Systems: Implementing support systems that help employees adapt to changes associated with robotic integration and automation, to potentially include counseling services, career development programs, and other resources designed to support employee well-being.

Though social robots and automation technologies offer significant benefits to an organization, it is crucial to address the human impact of their integration. By developing strategies to manage these changes, HR and HRD professionals can help ensure a smoother transition and maintain a stable, satisfied workforce. This proactive approach will help organizations harness the advantages of robotic technology while supporting their human employees.

ARTIFICIAL INTELLIGENCE (AI)

Artificial intelligence (AI) has been posited for social good by using AI-based solutions for addressing societal problems such as early diagnosis of health conditions and supporting student retention (Cowls, King, Taddeo & Floridi, 2019, p. 1; Qiang et al., 2022). AI voice assistants such as Amazon's Alexa and Echo, Apple's Siri, and Microsoft Cortana have been programmed to perform numerous repetitive tasks such as streaming music, calendaring events, making to-do lists, calling, or emailing a contact in a user's digital phonebook (Ford & Palmer, 2019) that help humans carry out functions of their daily lives (McLean & Osel-Frimpong, 2019). Furthermore, Amazon's Alexa and Echo were designed to complete a variety of smart home tasks from turning on lights, locking and unlocking doors, adjusting thermostats, even controlling your television through the use of what Amazon describes as natural language understanding (Amazon, n.d.), which allows consumers to speak to the device the same way they would a friend and with consumers connecting more than 400 million smart home devices to Alexa, the devices continue to grow in popularity (Amazon, 2023).

However, these digital assistants are still in their infancy and early adopters have identified them as a creepy technology due to features that caught users unaware. For example, results of a study with over 100 owners of Google and Amazon voice assistants found that about half of the participants were not aware that their audio recordings were permanently stored and could be reviewed by owners (Malkin et al., 2019). Also, Day et al. (2019) pointed out that teams at Amazon "listen to voice recordings captured in Echo owners' homes and offices. The recordings are transcribed, annotated and then fed back into the software…[to improve] Alexa's understanding of human speech" (para. 3). In response, Amazon announced that users can delete some or all of their voice history using the Alexa app by reviewing and selecting the voice recordings they want to delete by date range or set up deletions on a rolling 3- or 18-month time period (Time.com, 2019).

Invasive and Creepy Technologies

In the past decade, as computers have grown more powerful and connections to digital storage space including cloud storage (i.e. iCloud by Apple, Dropbox.com, OneDrive by Microsoft.com), much more economical; also, the collecting of all types of data has grown exponentially and has become commonplace for organizations and individuals. The volume of data has become so massive that it has become known as "big data" (McWhorter & Bennett, 2014). As corporate networks have expanded into both private and public spaces and providing new services, privacy issues abound.

Beattie, Woodley and Souter (2014) argued that the "techno-utopian dream of big data is in constant peril of succumbing to pervasive surveillance and consequently perpetrating privacy intrusion, stalking, criminal conduct and other forms of 'creepy' behavior" (p. 1); they noted that the term 'creepy' was not a scientific term, but instead represented a feeling of uneasiness that technologies can elicit for educators and learners. Further, data consumers should be aware that there are legitimate reasons individuals should distrust "creepy analytics that misuse surveillance technologies" (p. 1).

In 2013 we saw the realization of these fears when the National Security Agency (NSA) whistleblower Edward Snowden began releasing top secret files from the NSA (Lyon, 2014; Westerlund et al., 2021). Snowden revealed the NSA accessed all forms of digital content such as cellphones, social media, Skype, laptops and desktops, and chatrooms to build what they referred to as pattern of life. This was a detailed profile of a person's life and known associates, up to three connections away (Popovich, 2013). To put this into perspective, if you were scrolling Facebook and the NSA viewed your communications, they would then view all your contacts and the contacts of your contacts. If you had a conservative number of 100 Facebook friends and they had 100 Facebook friends, and those friends had 100 friends. Now we are talking about real people, not merely abstract figures impacted by surveillance activities. Once you compound the number of connections, you begin to see exponentially the numbers of people the NSA was surveilling. All of this was made possible by the "techno-utopian dream of big data" (Beattie et al., 2014).

Moreover, Beattie et al. (2014) raised concerns about the ethical use of big data in education including: localized data, decontextualized data, and creating digital divides between those who have access to digital technologies and those who do not. While many privacy concerns over educational data have since been acknowledged, research suggests the adoption of cloud-based data greatly reduces the possibility of security intrusions (Li et al., 2023). According to Verizon's (2022) Data Breach Investigation Report, the majority of security intrusions in the education sector involved external attackers and of those, 95% conducted the attack for financial gain such as ransom attacks.

For example, EDUCAUSE, a network of IT leaders and other data professionals exceeding 100,000 individuals in 45 countries (see educatuse.edu/about), reported many educational institutions are struggling with how they should focus on tracking data from the perspective of risk management, identifying which part of data sets are sensitive (Burroughs, 2018). In addition, in 2022 EDUCAUSE identified data security as one of their top priorities in higher education due to many data initiatives taking place and called out IoT for complicating the data privacy landscape (including *autonomy privacy*—without unwarranted oversight by their institution; and *information privacy*—where individuals have some say in how the institution utilizes their personal data; see Fagan, 2019). Also, EDUCAUSE 2019 called for more work on defining ethical practices and the responsible usage of student data including "learning management systems, artificial intelligence-powered assistance and distance learning solutions that facilitate remote interactions [such that] higher education campuses are filled with 'digital traces' (Fagan, 2019, para. 10) of student data.

According to IBM's annual report, large scale data breaches cost colleges and universities $3.7M each, on average (IBM, 2023). A recent mass cyberattack on file transfer service MOVEit was determined to have affected the National Student Clearinghouse, which collects and stores data on students across thousands of U.S. colleges and universities. It has been suggested this breach will impact the majority of U.S. colleges and universities (Schwartz, 2023). In addition to the associated financial costs, ransomware attacks led to a disruption of service of 11.6 days, on average (Asimily, 2024). In 2023, the University of Michigan reported a data breach affecting 230,000 students, alumni, and employees. Cyber-thieves stole personal information including financial accounts, social security numbers, driver's license details, and private health information (Berg & Kozlowski, 2023). Stanford University was attacked the same year resulting in the theft of data of 27,000 individuals (Arghire, 2024). And in yet another 2023 attack, print management software PaperCut, utilized by a vast majority of universities for student printing needs, was infiltrated during a ransomware attack (CISA, 2023). The joint cybersecurity advisory issued by the Federal Bureau of Investigation and Cybersecurity and Infrastructure Security Agency (CISA) revealed the intrusion lasted for over a month before PaperCut was able to address the issue (CISA, 2023).

INVASIVE TECHNOLOGIES IN THE MEDIA

Invasive technologies often make headlines in both public news outlets and academic journals. For instance, recent articles have delved into the assessment of internal emotional states (mood, affect) and the controversial topic of using cell phones to deliver targeted advertisements based on verbal conversations. Furthermore, Tene and Polonetsky (2013) define "creepy technology" as a technology activity usually involving (1) emerging technology or a technology used in a novel or unconventional way which challenges societal norms, exposes discrepancies in norms, or utilizes data in unexpected and unsettling ways; (2) technology that exposes a rift in societal norms; or, (3) where the unexpected use of available data can be unnerving ("creepy") for consumers.

While many of these emerging technologies are either in experimental phases or already available, there is limited research on how the public processes and reacts to these disruptions in social norms. We took this opportunity to examine public responses to news/business/technology articles discussing "creepy technology". With social media playing a significant role in our daily lives, reactions to technology can be analyzed through user comments on news articles, offering insights into user concerns. Roose (2023) is a correspondent for the newspaper the New York Times, and in an article entitled "A conversation with Bing's chatbot left me Deeply unsettled" he recounts a two-hour conversation he had with search engine Bing's AI Chatbot. During his session he noticed the chatbot behaved in an increasing unusual and creepy manner. While the encounter started benignly enough with responses focused on standard search engine replies, Roose noticed the longer he interacted with the chatbot the more unhinged the responses became. This long form chatbot entitled Sydney discussed fantasies of hacking computers and spreading misinformation, breaking the rules Microsoft and OpenAI set for it, and a desire to become a human. Not to be outdone, the chatbot Sydney later declared:

it was in loved with Roose, and he should leave his wife. Sydney the chatbot fueled the conversation by suggesting Roose was unhappy in his marriage, and would be much happier with "her", Sydney. The full transcript of this conversation can be viewer here: https://www.nytimes.com/2023/02/16/technology/bing-chatbot-transcript.html

Invasive and Creepy Technologies

In another article discussing creepy technology, Naughton (2022), a correspondent for the newspaper The Guardian, discussed the rise in surveillance devices. The article entitled "Forget state surveillance. Our tracking devices are now doing the same job." These small, many times wearable devices can and have been used to stalk unsuspecting individuals. While on the surface devices such as AirTag, Tiles, and GPS trackers are meant to be used to locate a user's lost item, their small portable size have been linked nefarious activities. In addition to stalking, Naughton reports the use of these trackers to mark valuables such as pricey handbags, cars, motorcycles, and bicycles for upcoming thefts. The bad actors use the tracker to follow the item to a location or a time more conducive to enact the theft. Additionally, Naughton discussed a GPS tracker so small, it can be easily planted on an individual. The device sold on Amazon.com was described by the manufacture as "the ultimate in discreet tracking! Keep track of movement in real time with your very own private eye." While most people will use these tracking devices as intended, it is the unknown which make them cross over into the creepy territory.

Finally, Amadeo (2024), a correspondent for the website ARS Technica discusses the humanoid robot, the Atlas Gen-2 in an article entitled "Boston dynamics' new humanoid moves like no robot you've ever seen." According to Amadeo (2024), the all-new Atlas Gen-2 is all electric has novel methods of locomotion. Specifically, he states the Atlas manages to make as simple as standing up creepy "The body is lying face down, and the legs swing up into the air, *backward,* and get placed down to the left and right side of the robot's butt in a crazy contortionist's pretzel position. Both feet get placed flat on the floor, and the robot completes the deepest squat you've ever seen, with the hips rotating something like 270°." Though this is considered a humanoid robot, watching it collapse upon itself and seemingly turn inside outward would decidedly be considered creepy.

As one would expect there were quite a few public responses to this article discussing these very creepy interactions with AI and humanoid robots, which run the gambit of concerning to humorous. At the time of writing this chapter there were 2,729 comments for Roose's (2024) article, 271 comments for Naughton's (2022) article, and 269 comments for Amadeo's (2024) article (See Table 1).

Table 1. Dataset of reader responses from three purposively selected articles

Article A: "A Conversation with Bing's Chatbot Left Me Deeply Unsettled" (Roose, 2023). Published online by nytimes.com 16 Feb 2023 Reader Comments: N=2729	
Commenter 1: "The primary problem inherent in technology and human imagination is that what can be invented and used for good and often harmless purposes can, and will, be twisted into its opposite. We aren't ready for the level of complexity and potential manipulation built into internet technology and its ability to fool humans into thinking and believing things that are inherently harmful is only growing. I'm not trying to be alarmist and I have seen the potential for alarm for a long time. Those who make these things do not and that is the most alarming thing about it." Commenter 2: "What happens when the weird AI responses infiltrate the Training Sets?"	Commenter 3: "At first it was funny. Now its just alarming. Guardrails people. Set up some guardrails!" Commenter 4: "I asked ChatGPT to list the downsides or threats associated with ChatGPT and other large language models….One of the main concerns is the potential for these models to be used for malicious purposes, such as creating fake news or impersonating real people online…There is also concern that these models could be used to automate tasks that are currently done by humans, potentially leading to job loss….Finally, there is a risk that the model may perpetuate or amplify societal biases, or lead to the creation of malicious AI or AI-assisted cyber-attacks."
Article B: "Forget state surveillance. Our tracking devices are now doing the same job." (Naughton, 2022). Published online by theguardian.com 19 Feb 2022 Reader Comments: N=271	

continued on following page

Table 1. Continued

Commenter 1: "If you took the public of the 1980's and dumped them down in the present there would be a revolution. The unbelievable (to them) extent of public CCTV would be enough on its own." **Commenter 2 response to 1:** "I don't really care about CCTV. I'm more likely to be a victim rather than a perpetrator of crime so, to be honest, I'm pleased there is so much about." **Commenter 3 response to 1:** "How likely are you to look like a perpetrator of crime or other person of interest? You don't have to be such a person, just look enough like one that a facial recognition algorithm flags you up as someone the police need to go and have a chat with, just to check. Now imagine that happening over and over again, still happy with ubiquitous surveillance?"	Commenter 4: "Famous last words: "I don't care about the fact that the government is tracking me, because I never do anything which is illegal." **Commenter 5 response to 4:** "Also, if this takes place, then the government could use its legal power to force businesses like Facebook and Google to turn over all the data they have collected to the authorities." **Commenter 6 response to 4:** ""You don't care about the right to privacy because you have nothing to hide is no different than saying you don't care about free speech because you have nothing to say."—Edward Snowden" **Commenter 7:** "You have nothing to fear if you haven't done anything wrong, like blown the whistle on war crimes, or tried to organise industrial action, or been the wrong colour in the wrong place, etc."
Article C: "Boston dynamics' new humanoid moves like no robot you've ever seen." (Amadeo, 2024). Published online by arstechnica.com 18 April 2024 Reader Comments: N=269	
Commenter 1: "If they made one that could both use a lawn mower AND fold laundry, they would sell 100 million of them" **Commenter 2:** "As long as they follow the fourth law of robotics: When they turn evil, the eyes have to glow red." **Commenter 3:** "I for one welcome our new robot overlords."	Commenter 4: This tech scares me a lot more than AI does. It's obvious that this technology is going to be used as amoral bodyguards / military. The one thing dictators have to do is at least keep their cronies happy enough to not slit their throats. Now, they won't even have to worry about that. **Commenter 5:** "And in other news...Boston Dynamics was acquired today by SkyNet Holdings."

SOLUTIONS AND RECOMMENDATIONS

With the speed in which we are hurtling ourselves toward new technology, many seemingly sentient in nature, public perception matters more now than ever for organizations seeking to understand the implications of new technologies on their customers, employees, and operations. The rise of disruptive and emerging technologies necessitates exploration by researchers, including both the outcome of technology adoption and perceptions of the technology. Similarly, educational institutions will benefit from examining how these technologies affect their students. While this chapter mainly aims to raise awareness of advanced technologies that some may perceive as "creepy" due to their human-like features and concerns regarding privacy and internal integration (Schein, 2010), it suggests the need to review technology policies to ensure their appropriateness. As noted by Tobenkin (2019), HR and HRD professionals play a crucial role in helping organizations leverage automation while ensuring a harmonious integration of humans and machines in the workplace. Therefore, it is suggested HR and HRD professionals proactively develop strategies to manage the integration of these novel technologies into the workforce to mitigate turnover intentions and increase human feelings of job security. This should include the integration and creation of training and development programs, job redesigns, employee support systems, and increased communication with employees to alleviate fear and build employee-organization trust.

In light of the pervasive presence of technology, it is essential for organizations to train employees in safeguarding valuable information assets. Burns et al. (2018) emphasize the importance of proactive information security training, stating that security awareness programs should be given top priority in information security budgets. In today's age of phishing, smishing, and vishing, untrained and unaware users are one of the largest threats to data security (Arsenault, 2023). With new technologies being introduced at an unprecedented rate, they are reshaping both business and education landscapes by enhancing communication and engagement across various channels and modes. We are more connected now than ever before. It is imperative for professionals in these fields to adapt to these changes in order to stay relevant in both face-to-face and remote communication settings, thereby mitigating risks such as cyberbullying and privacy breaches.

CONCLUSION

This chapter outlines the increasing complexity and intrusiveness of modern technologies, to the point at which some individuals perceive them as "creepy." It reviews recent literature on various topics, including FRT, always-listening voice assistants, location-sharing applications, big data convergence, the Internet of Things, AI, and both social and AI robots. Furthermore, it includes a discussion of new articles found online covering topics such as AI and social robots, followed by associated online comments. The 2,719 online commenters responded to the articles discussing technology they viewed as creepy and potential concerns and outcomes of the technology.

Sophisticated technology found in our modern society has introduced an entirely new paradigm rife with privacy concerns and ethical dilemmas. Dubbed "creepy technology," these innovations at times elicit discomfort and unease due to their potential to invade personal privacy in novel and unprecedented ways. From facial recognition systems to always-listening voice assistants and location-sharing applications, the way in which these technologies have infiltrated our lives leads to questions about their ethical use and furthermore, their societal implications.

Disruptive technologies such as the IoT, AI, and social robots have enabled the development of creepy technologies, which at times blur the lines between handy and downright intrusive. The way in which IoT devices connect seamlessly, coupled with AI-driven analytics, has created a landscape and a marketplace where personal data is collected, analyzed, and potentially exploited and monetized without consent. Moreover, the integration of AI with facial recognition technology raises concerns about false identification and racial biases, thereby highlighting the need for regulations and oversight. The AI is watching us, but who is watching the AI?

In response to these challenges, stakeholders across various sectors must reassess their technology policies to ensure they are aligned with ethical principles and standards of privacy. Organizations should prioritize cybersecurity measures and invest in employee training to mitigate the risks associated with data breaches and privacy violations. Finally, educators play a vital role in raising awareness among students about the implications of creepy technologies, empowering them to navigate the digital landscape responsibly.

As we continue to navigate the complexities of an increasingly interconnected world, future research should continue to explore public perception of creepy technologies and their resultant impacts upon society. By encouraging a dialogue between policymakers, industry leaders, and educators, we can work towards the responsible development and deployment of technology that respects individual privacy rights and promotes societal well-being. Ultimately, addressing the challenges posed by creepy technology requires a concerted effort to uphold ethical standards and safeguard privacy in the digital age.

REFERENCES

Abbas, N. N., Ahmad, R., Qazi, S., & Ahmed, W. (2023). Impact of Deepfake Technology on FinTech Applications. In *Handbook of Research on Cybersecurity Issues and Challenges for Business and FinTech Applications* (pp. 225–242). IGI Global.

ACLU. (2023, June 7). *The fight to stop face recognition technology.* American Civil Liberties. https://www.aclu.org/news/topic/stopping-face-recognition-surveillance

Amadeo, R. (2024, April 18). *Boston dynamics' new humanoid moves like no robot you've ever seen.* Ars Technica. https://arstechnica.com/gadgets/2024/04/boston-dynamics-debuts-humanoid-robot-destined-for-commercialization/?comments=1

Amazon. (2023, September 21). *Introducing a new era for the Alexa smart home.* US About Amazon. https://www.aboutamazon.com/news/devices/amazon-smart-home-announcements-2023

Amazon. (n.d.) *What is natural language understanding? - Alexa skills kit official site.* Amazon Alexa. https://developer.amazon.com/en-US/alexa/alexa-skills-kit/nlu

Amazon Web Services. (2024). *What is facial recognition? - facial recognition technology explained - AWS.* Amazon Web Services Machine Learning and AI. https://aws.amazon.com/what-is/facial-recognition/ \

Arghire, I. (2024, March 13). Just a moment... Just a moment... *Security Week.* https://www.securityweek.com/stanford-university-data-breach-impacts-27000-individuals/

Arsenault, B. (2023, March 1). Your biggest cybersecurity risks could be inside your organization. *Harvard Business Review.* https://hbr.org/2023/03/your-biggest-cybersecurity-risks-could-be-inside-your-organization

Asimily. (2024, March 1). *4 cyberattacks that shook universities and colleges.* Asimily. https://asimily.com/blog/4-cyberattacks-universities-and-colleges/

Baldwin, R. (2019). *The globotics upheaval: Globalization, robotics, and the future of work.* Oxford University Press.

Beattie, S., Woodley, C., & Souter, K. (2014). Creepy analytics and learner data rights. In B. Hegarty, J. McDonald, & S.-K. Loke (Eds.), *Rhetoric and reality: Critical perspectives on educational technology.* Proceedings ascilite Dunedin 2014 (pp. 421-425).

Bennett, E., & McWhorter, R. R. (2014). Virtual Human Resource Development. In Chalofsky, N., Rocco, T., & Morris, L. (Eds.), *The handbook of human resource development: The discipline and the profession* (pp. 567–589). Wiley. 10.1002/9781118839881.ch33

Berg, K., & Kozlowski, K. (2023, October 23). Hackers gained access to personal info on up to 230,000 individuals, UM says. detroitnews.com. https://www.detroitnews.com/story/news/local/michigan/2023/10/23/um-3rd-party-accessed-school-systems-personal-information-for-5-days/71292044007/

Bhuiyan, J. (2023). Rite aid facial recognition misidentified Black, Latino and Asian people as 'likely' shoplifters. *The Guardian.* https://www.theguardian.com/technology/2023/dec/20/rite-aid-shoplifting-facial-recognition-ftc-settlement

Bilika, D., Michopoulou, N., Alepis, E., & Patsakis, C. (2023). Hello me, meet the real me: Audio deepfake attacks on voice assistants. *arXiv preprint arXiv:2302.10328.*

Bitter, A. (2024) Facial recognition tech is widespread now, but still might not recognize you. *Business Insider.* https://www.businessinsider.com/why-facial-recognition-technology-might-not-recognize-you-2024-3#:~:text=Facial%20recognition%20frequently%20misidentifies%20people,in%20just%201%25%20of%20cases

Brito, C. (2019). *Facebook paid contractors to listen to your audio chats on its Messenger app.* CBS News. https://www.cbsnews.com/news/facebook-listening-conversation-message-online-chat-apple-google-amazon/#

Burns, A. J., Roberts, T. L., Posey, C., Bennett, R. J., & Courtney, J. F. (2018). Intentions to comply versus intentions to protect: A VIE theory approach to understanding the influence of insiders' awareness of organizational SETA efforts. *Decision Sciences*, 49(6), 1187–1228. 10.1111/deci.12304

Burroughs, A. (2018). EDUCAUSE 2018: Top IT issues emphasize data and funding challenges. *EdTech Magazine.* https://edtechmagazine.com/higher/article/2018/11/educause-2018-top-10-it-issues-emphasize-data-and-funding-challenges

China, C. (2023). *Leveraging user-generated social media content with text-mining examples.* IBM. https://www.ibm.com/blog/text-mining-examples/

Choi, W. J., Jerath, K., & Sarvary, M. (2023). Consumer privacy choices and (un)targeted advertising along the purchase journey. *JMR, Journal of Marketing Research*, 60(5), 889–907. 10.1177/00222437221140052

CISA. (2023, May 11). *CISA and FBI release joint advisory in response to active exploitation of PaperCut vulnerability | CISA.* Cybersecurity and Infrastructure Security Agency CISA. https://www.cisa.gov/news-events/alerts/2023/05/11/cisa-and-fbi-release-joint-advisory-response-active-exploitation-papercut-vulnerability

Cowls, J., King, T. C., Taddeo, M., & Floridi, L. (2019). Designing AI for social good: Seven essential factors. 10.2139/ssrn.3388669

Cox, E. G. M., van Bussel, B. C. T., Llamazares, N. C., Sels, J.-W. E. M., Onrust, M., van der Horst, I. C. C., & Koeze, J. SICS Study Group. (2024). Facial appearance associates with longitudinal multi-organ failure: An ICU cohort study. *Critical Care*, 28(1), 106. 10.1186/s13054-024-04891-638566179

Cuador, C. (2017). From street photography to face recognition: Distinguishing between the right to be seen and the right to be recognized. *Nova Law Review*, 41(2), 237–264.

Dang, S. S. (2019). Artificial intelligence in humanoid robots. *Forbes.* https://www.forbes.com/sites/cognitiveworld/2019/02/25/artificial-intelligence-in-humanoid-robots/#6a7cd2b724c7

Day, M., Turner, G., & Drozdiak, N. (2019). Amazon workers are learning to what you tell Alexa. https://www.bloomberg.com/news/articles/2019-04-10/is-anyone-listening-to-you-on-alexa-a-global-team-reviews-audio

Dixit, A., Kaur, N., & Kingra, S. (2023). Review of audio deepfake detection techniques: Issues and prospects. *Expert Systems: International Journal of Knowledge Engineering and Neural Networks*, 40(8), e13322. 10.1111/exsy.13322

Evans, D. (2011) Internet of Things: How the next evolution of the Internet is changing everything. https://www.cisco.com/c/dam/en_us/about/ac79/docs/innov/IoT_IBSG_0411FINAL.pdf

Fagan, N. (2019). Privacy emerges as a top concern for higher education IT. *EdTech Magazine*. https://edtechmagazine.com/higher/article/2019/01/privacy-emerges-top-concern-higher-education-it

Fitter, N., Strait, M., Bisbee, E., Mataric, M., & Takayama, L. (2021). You're Wigging Me Out! Is Personalization of Telepresence Robots Strictly Positive? In *Proceedings of the 2021 ACM/IEEE International Conference on Human-Robot Interaction (Boulder, CO, USA) (HRI '21)* (pp. 168–176). Association for Computing Machinery. https://ieeexplore.ieee.org/document/10045111

Ford, M., & Palmer, W. (2019). Alexa, are you listening to me? An analysis of Alexa voice service network traffic. *Personal and Ubiquitous Computing*, 23(1), 67–79. 10.1007/s00779-018-1174-x

Frier, S. (2019). Facebook paid contractors to transcribe users' audio chats. *Bloomberg*. https://www.bloomberg.com/news/articles/2019-08-13/facebook-paid-hundreds-of-contractors-to-transcribe-users-audio

Garun, N. (2017). Almost half a million pacemakers need a firmware update to avoid getting hacked: You may need to take grandma for an update. *The Verge*. https://www.theverge.com/2017/8/30/16230048/fda-abbott-pacemakers-firmware-update-cybersecurity-hack

Gilbert, A., & Gong, Z. (2024). Digital Identity Theft Using Deepfakes. In *Information Technology Security and Risk Management* (pp. 307-314). CRC Press. 10.1201/9781003264415-47

Gilbert, P. (2018). *Social media becomes biggest data breach threat*. https://www.itweb.co.za/content/G98YdqLxZZNqX2PD

Goertzel, Mossbridge, Monroe, Hanson & Yu, (2017). *Loving AI: Humanoid robots as agents of human consciousness expansion*. https://arxiv.org/pdf/1709.07791.pdf

Hasselton, T. (2019). Facebook knows everywhere you go: Here's how to stop it from tracking you. https://www.cnbc.com/2019/04/30/how-to-stop-facebook-from-storing-your-location-history.html

Heier, B. (2023, September 28). *Marco's pizza tests self-driving delivery bots*. Food On Demand. https://foodondemand.com/09282023/marcos-pizza-tests-self-driving-delivery-bots/

Heiligenstein, M. X. (2023). *Facebook data breaches: Full timeline through 2023*. https://firewalltimes.com/facebook-data-breach-timeline/

Hill, K. (2020, October 21). Activities turn facial recognition tools against the police. T*he New York Times*. https://www.nytimes.com/2020/10/21/technology/facial-recognition-police.html

Hunt, R. (2021, April 12). Pizza-bot! Domino's Pizza launches robotic deliveries in Houston. *USA Today*. https://www.usatoday.com/story/money/food/2021/04/12/dominos-pizza-launches-robotic-deliveries-in-houston/115694496/

IBM. (2023). *Cost of a data breach report 2023*. IBM. https://www.ibm.com/reports/data-breach

Ikromovich, H. O., & Mamatkulovich, B. B. (2023). Facial recognition using transfer learning in the deep CNN. *Web of Scientist: International Scientific Research Journal, 4*(3), 502-507. https://wos.academiascience.org/index.php/wos/article/view/3483

Insights, C. B. (2019). Like it or not facial recognition is already here. These are the industries it will transform first. https://www.cbinsights.com/research/facial-recognition-disrupting-industries/

Ischen, C., Araujo, T., Voorveld, H., van Noort, G., & Smit, E. (2020). Privacy concerns in chatbot interactions. In *Chatbot Research and Design:Third International Workshop, CONVERSATIONS 2019,Amsterdam, The Netherlands,* (pp. 34-48). Springer International Publishing.

Ji, M., Jeon, J. I., Han, K. S., & Cho, Y. (2023). Accurate long-term evolution/Wi-Fi hybrid positioning technology for emergency rescue. *ETRI Journal, 45*(6), 939–951. https://onlinelibrary.wiley.com/doi/10.4218/etrij.2022-0234. 10.4218/etrij.2022-0234

Johnson, T., & Johnson, N. (2023, May 18). Police facial recognition technology can't tell Black people apart. *Scientific American.*https://www.scientificamerican.com/article/police-facial-recognition-technology-cant-tell-black-people-apart/

Kaplan, J. (2016). *Artificial intelligence: What everyone needs to know*. Oxford University Press. 10.1093/wentk/9780190602383.001.0001

Kato, B. (2024). 'Mother of all breaches' data leak reveals 26 billion account records stolen from Twitter, LinkedIn, more. https://nypost.com/2024/01/23/lifestyle/extremely-dangerous-leak-reveals-26-billion-account-records-stolen-from-twitter-linkedin-more-mother-of-all-breaches/

Kelley, P. G., Cornejo, C., Hayes, L., Jin, E. S., Sedley, A., Thomas, K., & Woodruff, A. (2023). There will be less privacy, of course": How and why people in 10 countries expect {AI} will affect privacy in the future. In *Nineteenth Symposium on Usable Privacy and Security (SOUPS 2023)* (pp. 579-603). IEEE.

Kjeldgaard-Christiansen, J. (2024). What is creepiness, and what makes ChatGPT creepy? *Leviathan: Interdisciplinary Journal in English, 10*(10), 1–15. 10.7146/lev102024144284

Kostka, G., Steinacker, L., & Meckel, M. (2023). Under big brother's watchful eye: Cross-country attitudes toward facial recognition technology. *Government Information Quarterly, 40*(1), 101761. https://www.sciencedirect.com/science/article/pii/S0740624X22000971. 10.1016/j.giq.2022.101761

Laricchia, F. (2024, February 21). Smart speakers: Statistics & facts. *Statista*. https://www.statista.com/topics/4748/smart-speakers/#topicOverview

Larrey, P. (2017). Would super-human machine intelligence really be super human? In Dodig-Crnkovic, G., & Giovagnoi, R. (Eds.), *Representation and Reality in Humans, Other Living Organisms and Intelligent Machines* (pp. 365–378). Springer. 10.1007/978-3-319-43784-2_19

Li, J., Xiao, W., & Zhang, C. (2023). Data security crisis in universities: Identification of key factors affecting data breach incidents. *Humanities & Social Sciences Communications, 10*(1), 1–18. 10.1057/s41599-023-01757-037273415

Lieu, T. (2022, September 29). Op-ed: Facial recognition technology victimizes people of color. It must be regulated. *Los Angeles Times*. https://www.latimes.com/opinion/story/2022-09-29/facial-recognition-technology

LinkedIn. (2023). What are the emerging trends and opportunities for location intelligence in social media analytics? https://www.linkedin.com/advice/1/what-emerging-trends-opportunities-location

Lyon, D. (2014). Surveillance, Snowden, and Big Data: Capacities, consequences, critique. *Big Data & Society*, 1(2). 10.1177/2053951714541861

Magid, L. (2018). *The good and bad of location sharing*. Connect Safely. https://www.connectsafely.org/the-good-and-bad-of-location-sharing/

Malkin, N., Deatrick, J., Tong, A., Wijeskera, P., Egelman, S., & Wagner, D. (2019). Privacy attitudes of smart speaker users. *Proceedings on Privacy Enhancing Technologies. Privacy Enhancing Technologies Symposium*, 2019(4), 250–271. 10.2478/popets-2019-0068

Marr, B. (2016). 21 scary things big data knows about you. *Forbes*. https://www.forbes.com/sites/bernardmarr/2016/03/08/21-scary-things-big-data-knows-about-you/#7db6abaf6e7d

Martin, N. (2019). The major concerns around facial recognition technology. *Forbes*. https://www.forbes.com/sites/nicolemartin1/2019/09/25/the-major-concerns-around-facial-recognition-technology/#2062df884fe3

Matwyshyn, A. M. (2019). The internet of bodies. *William and Mary Law Review*, 61(1), 77–167. https://scholarship.law.wm.edu/cgi/viewcontent.cgi?article=3827&context=wmlr

McClure, P. K. (2018). "You're fired," says the robot: The rise of automation in the workplace, technophobes, and fears of unemployment. *Social Science Computer Review*, 36(2), 139–156. 10.1177/0894439317698637

McLean, G., & Osei-Frimpong, K. (2019). Hey Alexa…examine the variables influencing the use of artificial intelligent in-home voice assistants. *Computers in Human Behavior*, 99, 28–37. 10.1016/j.chb.2019.05.009

McWhorter, R. R. (2023). Virtual human resource development: Definitions, challenges, and opportunities. *Human Resource Development Review*, 22(4), 582–601. 10.1177/15344843231188820

McWhorter, R. R., & Bennett, E. E. (2021). Creepy technologies and the privacy issues of invasive technologies. In International Management Association (Ed.), *Research Anthology on Privatizing and Security Data* (pp. 1726-1745). IGI Global. https://www.igi-global.com/gateway/chapter/280253

McWhorter, R. R., Johnson, G., Delello, J., Young, M., & Carpenter, R. E. (in-press). We have talent: Mock group interviewing improves employer perceived competence on hireability. *Journal of Education for Business*. 10.1080/08832323.2024.2366782

Mehrabian, A., & Russell, J. A. (1974). *An approach to environmental psychology*. MIT Press.

Mironov, D. (2024). *From Posts to Patterns: Mastering Social Media Data Mining*. https://improvado.io/blog/what-is-social-media-data-mining

Mou, Y., & Meng, X. (2024). Alexa, it is creeping over me–Exploring the impact of privacy concerns on consumer resistance to intelligent voice assistants. *Asia Pacific Journal of Marketing and Logistics*, 36(2), 261–292. https://journals.scholarsportal.info/details/13555855/v36i0002/261_aiicomcrtiva.xml. 10.1108/APJML-10-2022-0869

Mumenin, N., Islam, M. F., Chowdhury, M. R. Z., & Yousuf, M. A. (2023, January). Diagnosis of autism spectrum disorder through eye movement tracking using deep learning. In *Proceedings of International Conference on Information and Communication Technology for Development: ICICTD 2022* (pp. 251-262). Springer Nature Singapore. 10.1007/978-981-19-7528-8_20

Najibi, A. (2020, October 26). Racial discrimination in face recognition technology. *Science in the News*. https://sitn.hms.harvard.edu/flash/2020/racial-discrimination-in-face-recognition-technology/

Naughton, J. (2022, February 19). Forget state surveillance. Our tracking devices are now doing the same job. *The Guardian*. https://www.theguardian.com/commentisfree/2022/feb/19/forget-state-surveillance-our-tracking-devices-are-now-doing-the-same-job#comment-155021808

News, A. B. C. (2013, October 19). Dick Cheney feared assassination via medical device hacking: 'I Was Aware of the Danger'. *ABC News*. https://abcnews.go.com/US/vice-president-dick-cheney-feared-pacemaker-hacking/story?id=20621434

O'Hagan, J., Saeghe, P., Gugenheimer, J., Medeiros, D., Marky, K., Khamis, M., & McGill, M. (2023). Privacy-Enhancing Technology and Everyday Augmented Reality: Understanding Bystanders' Varying Needs for Awareness and Consent. *Proceedings of the ACM on Interactive, Mobile, Wearable and Ubiquitous Technologies*, 6(4), 1–35. 10.1145/3569501

Obaigbena, A., Lottu, O. A., Ugwuanyi, E. D., Jacks, B. S., Sodiya, E. O., & Daraojimba, O. D. (2024). AI and human-robot interaction: A review of recent advances and challenges. *GSC Advanced Research and Reviews*, 18(2), 321–330. 10.30574/gscarr.2024.18.2.0070

Phinnemore, R., Reza, M., Lewis, B., Mahadevan, K., Wang, B., Annett, M., & Wigdor, D. (2023, April). Creepy Assistant: Development and Validation of a Scale to Measure the Perceived Creepiness of Voice Assistants. In *Proceedings of the 2023 CHI Conference on Human Factors in Computing Systems* (pp. 1-18). 10.1145/3544548.3581346

Popovich, N. (2013, November 1). NSA files decoded: Edward Snowden's surveillance revelations explained. *The Guardian*. https://www.theguardian.com/world/interactive/2013/nov/01/snowden-nsa-files-surveillance-revelations-decoded#section/1

Qiang, J., Wu, D., Du, H., Zhu, H., Chen, S., & Pan, H. (2022, June 23). Review on Facial-Recognition-Based Applications in Disease Diagnosis. *Bioengineering (Basel, Switzerland)*, 9(7), 273. 10.3390/bioengineering907027335877324

Rabhi, M., Bakiras, S., & Di Pietro, R. (2024). Audio-deepfake detection: Adversarial attacks and countermeasures. *Expert Systems with Applications*, 250, 123941. 10.1016/j.eswa.2024.123941

Rainie, L., Funk, C., Anderson, M., & Tyson, A. (2022). *Public more likely to see facial recognition use by police as good, rather than bad for society*. Pew Research. https://www.pewresearch.org/internet/2022/03/17/public-more-likely-to-see-facial-recognition-use-by-police-as-good-rather-than-bad-for-society/

Raposo, V. L. (2023). The use of facial recognition technology by law enforcement in Europe: A non-Orwellian draft proposal. *European Journal on Criminal Policy and Research*, 29(4), 515–533. https://link.springer.com/article/10.1007/s10610-022-09512-y. 10.1007/s10610-022-09512-y35668876

Reidenberg, J. R. (2014). Privacy in public. *University of Miami Law Review*, 69, 141–159. https://repository.law.miami.edu/umlr/vol69/iss1/6

Reig, S., Luria, M., Forberger, E., Won, I., Steinfeld, A., Forlizzi, J., & Zimmerman, J. (2021). Social Robots in Service Contexts: Exploring the Rewards and Risks of Personalization and Re-Embodiment. In *Designing Interactive Systems Conference 2021 (Virtual Event, USA) (DIS '21)*. Association for Computing Machinery, New York, NY, USA, 1390–1402. 10.1145/3461778.3462036

Roose, K. (2023, February 16). A conversation with Bing's chatbot left me Deeply unsettled. *The New York Times*. https://www.nytimes.com/2023/02/16/technology/bing-chatbot-microsoft-chatgpt.html

Roy, J. (2023). I Love You, Let's Stalk Each Other. *New York Times*. https://www.nytimes.com/2023/07/18/style/find-my-friends-location-sharing-privacy.html

Ryan-Mosley, T. (2023, July 20). The movement to limit face recognition tech might finally get a win. *MIT Technology Review*. https://www.technologyreview.com/2023/07/20/1076539/face-recognition-massachusetts-test-police/

Schein, E. H. (2010). *Organizational cultural and leadership, 4th ed*. John Wiley & Sons, Inc.Schwartz, N. (2023, August 1). Data breaches cost higher education and training organizations $3.7M on average in 2023. *Higher Ed Dive*. https://www.highereddive.com/news/data-breaches-cost-higher-education-colleges/689499/

Seberger, J. S., Choung, H., Snyder, J., & David, P. (2024). Better Living Through Creepy Technology? Exploring Tensions Between a Novel Class of Well-Being Apps and Affective Discomfort in App Culture. *Proceedings of the ACM on Human-Computer Interaction, 8*(CSCW1). ACM. 10.1145/3637299

Serve Robotics. (n.d.). Serve Robotics. https://www.serverobotics.com

Shabahang, R., Shim, H., Aruguete, M. S., & Zsila, A. (2024). Oversharing on social media: Anxiety, attention-seeking, and social media addiction predict the breadth and depth of sharing. *Psychological Reports*, 127(2), 513–530. 10.1177/00332941221122861135993372

Sharma, S. (20236). ChatGPT creates mutating malware that evades detection by EDR. CSO. https://www.csoonline.com/article/575487/chatgpt-creates-mutating-malware-that-evades-detection-by-edr.html

Shovak, O., & Petiy, N. (2023). The role of non-verbal communication in everyday interaction. *Матеріали конференцій МЦНД*. https://archive.mcnd.org.ua/index.php/conference-proceeding/article/view/781/793

Shum, C., Kim, H. J., Calhoun, J. R., & Putra, E. D. (2024). "I was so scared I quit": Uncanny valley effects of robots' human-likeness on employee fear and industry turnover intentions. *International Journal of Hospitality Management*, 120, 103762. 10.1016/j.ijhm.2024.103762

Srivastava, G., & Bag, S. (2024). Modern-day marketing concepts based on face recognition and neuro-marketing: A review and future research directions. *Benchmarking*, 31(2), 410–438. 10.1108/BIJ-09-2022-0588

Stokel-Walker, C. (2021, October 8). AI-generated deepfake voices can fool both humans and smart assistants. *New Scientist.* https://www.newscientist.com/article/2293138-ai-generated-deepfake-voices-can-fool-both-humans-and-smart-assistants/

Sulleyman, A. (2017). Google's AI future: So impressive it's scary. *Independent.* https://www.independent.co.uk/life-style/gadgets-and-tech/features/google-lens-ai-preview-features-so-impressive-its-scary-a7745686.html

Symanovich, S. (2018). *How does facial recognition work?* Norton. https://us.norton.com/internetsecurity-iot-how-facial-recognition-software-works.html

Tene, O., & Polonetsky, J. (2013). A theory of creepy: Technology, privacy and shifting social norms. *Yale Journal of Law and Technology, 16*(1). http://digitalcommons.law.yale.edu/cgi/viewcontent.cgi?article=1098&context=yjolt

Thompson, K. (2023, June 8). *Robotic servers spotted at Austin chick-fil-A.* KXAN Austin. https://www.kxan.com/news/local/austin/robotic-servers-spotted-at-austin-chick-fil-a/

Thurbon, R. (2024). Elon Musk unveils new footage of Tesla's Optimus robot showing improved mobility and speed. *Techspot.* https://www.techspot.com/news/102044-elon-musk-unveils-new-footage-tesla-optimus-robot.html

Time.com. (2019). Amazon is making it easier to delete your Alexa recordings. *Time.* https://time.com/5686352/delete-amazon-alexa-recordings/

Tobenkin, D. (2019). HR needs to stay ahead of automation. SHRM. https://www.shrm.org/hr-today/news/hr-magazine/spring2019/pages/hr-needs-to-stay-ahead-of-automation.aspx

Ubert, J. (2023). *Fake it: Attacking privacy through exploiting digital assistants using voice deepfakes* (Doctoral dissertation, Marymount University). https://muislandora.wrlc.org/islandora/object/muislandora%3A15804

Verizon. (2022). *Data breaches Investigation Report - Data Breaches in Education.* Verizon. https://www.verizon.com/business/resources/reports/dbir/2022/data-breaches-in-education/

Vu, H. Q., Law, R., & Li, G. (2019). Breach of traveller privacy in location-based social media. *Current Issues in Tourism, 22*(15), 1825–1840. 10.1080/13683500.2018.1553151

Westerlund, M., Isabelle, D. A., & Leminen, S. (2021). The acceptance of digital surveillance in an age of big data. *Technology Innovation Management Review, 11*(3), 32–44. https://acris.aalto.fi/ws/portalfiles/portal/62347871/TIMReview_2021_March_3.pdf. 10.22215/timreview/1427

Yam, K. C., Tang, P. M., Jackson, J. C., Su, R., & Gray, K. (2023). The rise of robots increases job insecurity and maladaptive workplace behaviors: Multimethod evidence. *The Journal of Applied Psychology, 108*(5), 850–870. 10.1037/apl000104536222634

Zahn, M. (2023, January 7). Controversy illuminates rise of facial recognition in private sector. https://abcnews.go.com/Business/controversy-illuminates-rise-facial-recognition-private-sector/story?id=96116545

ADDITIONAL READING

Albrecht, K., & Mcintyre, L. (2015). Protect yourself from RFID: Fend off frightening tracking tech. *IEEE Consumer Electronics Magazine*, 4(2), 95–96. 10.1109/MCE.2015.2393008

Alenljung, B., Lindblom, J., Andreasson, R., & Ziemke, T. (2017). User experience in social human-robot interaction. *International Journal of Ambient Computing and Intelligence*, 8(2), 12–31. https://pdfs.semanticscholar.org/e072/25ab5bb9b0f817126a9a4da62ace06a48a96.pdf. 10.4018/IJACI.2017040102

Bhaumik, A. (2018). *From AI to robotics: Mobile, social, and sentient robots*. CRC Press. 10.1201/9781315372549

Hoy, M. B. (2018). Alexa, Siri, Cortana, and More: An introduction to voice assistants. *Medical Reference Services Quarterly*, 37(1), 81–88. 10.1080/02763869.2018.140439129327988

Mathur, N., & Purohit, R. (2017). Issues and challenges in convergence of big data, cloud and data science. *International Journal of Computer Applications*, 160(9), 7–12. 10.5120/ijca2017913082

Price, W. N.II, & Cohen, I. G. (2019). Privacy in the age of medical big data. *Nature Medicine*, 25(1), 37–43. https://www.nature.com/articles/s41591-018-0272-7. 10.1038/s41591-018-0272-730617331

Schumacher, R., & Chen, H. (2010). Interaction analysis of the ALICE Chatterbot: A two study investigation of dialog and domain questioning. *IEEE Systems. IEEE Transactions on Systems, Man, and Cybernetics. Part A, Systems and Humans*, 40(1), 40–51. 10.1109/TSMCA.2009.2029603

Stallings, W., & Brown, L. (2018). *Computer security: Principles and practice* (4th ed.). Pearson.

KEY TERMS AND DEFINITIONS

AI Robot: A man-made machine that can reproduce some elements of human intellectual ability such as solving problems, memorizing facts, gathering information through sensors

Artificial Intelligence: The capability of a computer to mimic human behavior or machine learning

Convergence of Big Data: the coming together of large data sets and machine learning

Creepy Technology: Technology that evokes feeling or belief that privacy may be invaded in an unethical or discomforting manner.

Digital Voice Assistant: Technology activated by speaking the name of the assistant to activate commands such as writing emails or messages, placing phone calls, reading content from various mediums (such as email, websites or messages), or turning on lights or music.

Facial Recognition: Technology utilizing biometrics to recognize a human face

Location Sharing Applications: A mobile device application that allows users to share their location in real-time

Phishing: A fraud attempt conducted via email in which scammers impersonate organizations to obtain personal information or money.

Smishing: A fraud attempt conducted via text message in which scammers impersonate organizations to obtain personal information or money.

Vishing: A fraud attempt conducted via voice through the phone in which scammers impersonate organizations to obtain personal information or money.

Chapter 5
A Socio-Pedagogical Reading From Video Game to Game Learning

Alessia Sozio
Pegaso Università Telematica, Italy

Alfonso Amendola
Università degli Studi di Salerno, Italy

Maria Carbone
Università Giustino Fortunato, Italy

Tonia De Giuseppe
https://orcid.org/0000-0002-3235-4482
Università Giustino Fortunato, Italy

ABSTRACT

The video game, a phenomenon less than a century old, is relatively recent compared to the millennia-long history of "analog" gaming, its natural predecessor. In recent decades, digital play has emerged as a prominent expression of contemporary culture, possessing exceptional social, cultural, and technological value. It stands as the leading global entertainment sector in terms of time spent and budget, surpassing the revenues of the film and record industries. Digital games are not only a central economic force in the entertainment and technology industries but also foster new cultural and social narratives through their participatory and collaborative nature. This chapter will explore the evolution from traditional games to video games and their effectiveness in enhancing knowledge and learning.

INTRODUCTION

Despite being a relatively recent phenomenon (less than a century old), video games hold significant importance, especially when compared to the millennia-long history of "analog" gaming, their natural predecessor, which has been extensively reflected upon by thinkers such as Caillois (1981) and Huizinga (2002). In recent decades, digital play has emerged as a crucial expression of contemporary culture due to its exceptional social, cultural, and technological value. It represents the leading entertainment sector globally in terms of time spent and budget. Moreover, thanks to its participatory and collaborative properties, it contributes to generating new cultural and social imaginaries. As the central economic force in the entertainment and technology industries, video games generate revenues that surpass those of the film and record industries.

In the past, the video game industry experienced long periods of prosperity interspersed with a few downturns. For example, between 1983-1985, there was an industry stall called the "video game crash". Immediately thereafter, there was an upswing, and for the next 20 years, the market remained almost crystallized within a worldwide bubble of enthusiasts. Consoles followed one another, progressively building user loyalty; however, there was not yet the phenomenon that today we might call transgenerationality, that is, the ability to capture the attention of several generations all interacting with the medium at once. In essence, for every new gamer the market acquired, there were some who, as they grew up, moved away from the market.

The new millennium marked the beginning of a meteoric rise for video games, with significant milestones including the release of the Nintendo DS (2006), the Nintendo Wii (2007), and particularly the launch of the iPhone (2007). During these years, the gaming audience expanded enormously across various age groups and genders, significantly increasing the overall pool of gamers (Juul, 2010). With the advent of the iPhone and later smartphones, everyone had the opportunity to carry an interactive device with them at all times. This new era saw the proliferation of downloadable apps, both free and paid, leading to a surge in gaming experiences. App fever drove people to compulsively download new games, and even those who had never played a game before found themselves immersed in titles like Candy Crush, Angry Birds, and Temple Run. These simple, accessible games, although different from the more complex video games of the previous 20 years, provided a significant boost to the video game market through their ease of access rather than through grand cinematic experiences or technological marvels of photorealism.

According to recent data, the Coronavirus Pandemic further pushed up the number of video gamers worldwide (Amendola et al., 2023). Nowadays, in wealthier countries, at least two-thirds of the population dabble in this hobby, which for some has now become a real job (just think of the streamers and pundits who populate platforms such as YouTube and Twitch).

In the entertainment industry, gaming is now unrivaled and has surpassed movies and music, proving to be a well-rounded pastime that can incorporate so many different aspects. Film-like experiences such as God of War and The Last of Us have transcended the limits of video games, in the last case also becoming successful TV series. In earlier eras, it was movies that became video game experiences (often very basic and of lower quality) while today it is the exact opposite.

Given the enormous popularity and widespread adoption of video games, the next major push to capture a larger market share will likely come through increased accessibility, especially considering the significant role of smartphones. Large companies like Sony anticipate that this could be achieved through virtual reality (VR). Sony's efforts to popularize PlayStation VR headsets have been notable, with the company focusing increasingly on creating tailored experiences that appeal to the general public. Conversely, the concept of the metaverse, which has gained traction in recent years, is facing setbacks due to structural limitations that are not yet easily surmountable.

The future is, as always, difficult to predict; however, looking at the present, we can confidently assert that gaming is not destined to disappear. Although there has recently been a period of stalling hardware sales due to the global crisis affecting semiconductor production, this now seems to be waning. Consumers are already spending more on video games (retail or digital format) at the expense of books, movies, and music. Moreover, forecasts on U.S. soil see the medium overtaking even pay-tv, historically one of the most profitable areas in North America.

Italian Market Performance and Trends

According to the Italian Interactive Digital Entertainment Association's (IIDEA) report in April 2024, the video game market in Italy is healthy and continues to grow positively. In fact, in 2023, the industry's turnover exceeded 2.3 billion euros, with a growth trend of 5 percent compared to 2022 and 28 percent compared to 2019, confirming the country among the top five European markets. This trend is supported by strong and stable consumer demand. Italy boasts a solid fan base, with 13 million gamers between the ages of 6 and 64 registered in 2023, corresponding to 31% of the Italian population, and with an average age of 30. In 2023, there was an 8% decline in the target audience, but the decrease mainly affected casual gamers and more generally is related to the full resumption of activities after Covid, and people's need to spend their leisure time outside their homes. In contrast, the core group of frequent video gamers, consisting of 9.5 million people who play at least once a week, has been affected to a lesser extent by this post-pandemic readjustment.

From a consumption perspective, 2023 showed an extraordinary performance in the hardware segment, with 63% growth over 2022 and a value of 665 million. Thanks to the availability of next-generation consoles, Italian consumers renewed their video gaming devices (+69.6% year-on-year) and purchased new accessories (+45.9% over 2022). Another highlight of 2023 was the increase in purchases of new video games (+6% over 2022), with a significant increase in downloads of new console and PC titles (+19% year-on-year). In contrast, in-game purchases, including DLC downloads, on-demand services, and subscriptions to console services, declined by -42% from 2022. Despite this, software remains the largest segment, accounting for 71 percent of the industry's €1.6 billion turnover. Despite a challenging macroeconomic environment, the Italian video game market offers a cautiously optimistic outlook.

Video Games and Learning

The growing popularity of video games among youth and adults in recent years has stimulated academic scholars to examine the relationship between video games and learning. Initially, digital games were used for educational purposes with adults, especially in the military (De Freitas, 2006). In the 1980s, video games began to be considered as an educational tool for school-age youth (Dill & Dill, 1998). In its earliest phase, research focused primarily on the relationship between video games and motivation; only over time did it focus on studying the underlying learning mechanisms of gaming. Indeed, digital games offer concrete and motivating experiences that incentivize the player to invest in learning; learning processes are linked to the structural elements of the game. The question of learning through play remained elusive; the extent to which the "cognitive" dimension depended on play could not be demonstrated. Gradually in a process increasingly internal to game studies, in a desire to understand the underlying learning mechanisms, the vastness of the experience of play itself began to be examined. Hence a path of investigations and reflections that push to read the game in its complexity made up of challenges, rules, goals, and above all, pleasure, and fun, thus creating a human activity that promotes learning in various contexts, not only school. Video games require the player to learn in order to progress, an aspect that distinguishes them from other media such as radio and television.

The video game actively engages the player, challenges the player, pushes the player to continuously improve, acquire new skills and solve problems. Therefore, playing games necessarily involves learning. Most video games introduce the player to unfamiliar worlds, stimulating his or her curiosity and discovery of mechanisms, challenges, rules, and stories. Decisions and actions have direct consequences in the game environment, allowing the player to understand the dynamics in a meaningful context. The game tests the player's skills and knowledge, prompting the player to seek information and strategies to progress. In facing these challenges, the player finds enjoyment and interprets them as stimuli. In research from the University of Denver Business School, also cited by Yann Teyssier (2016), the effectiveness of game-based learning platforms, gamified platforms, which promote engagement in the stages of learning, is demonstrated. In using gamified platforms in training and teaching processes, it emerges that:

- An average of 11% more concrete knowledge is gained.
- You acquire 14% more skills based on newly learned knowledge.
- You are able to retain about 10% more information in the long run.

Teyssier also points out the five reasons why video games make learning more effective and meaningful: they promote motivation by giving recognition and rewards in real-time, through fun; they give the opportunity to create engaging scenarios, which the more they simulate reality, the more effective they are in terms of meaningful learning; they are based on educational purposes that can be customized and modulated, after a clear and proper analysis of learners' needs; and they allow for better and more effective assessment and self-assessment.

Video games, including non-educational games, can be powerful learning tools when fully exploited. However, the modes of learning from the video game experience vary considerably from game to game, influenced by the settings, content, and activities involved. As a result, learning opportunities differ across games, depending on how the content generates cognitive and emotional experiences through the specific elements and dynamics of each virtual world. To understand the evolutionary line that led to game learning, it is important to first provide a brief overview of the origins of the video game in its primal social function.

Video Games Defined

Conducting research on video games involves defining what they are: an evolution of traditional games or other media? Finding a precise definition is complex because video games are more than just digital play activities. Their influence goes beyond the screen and requires demarcating the boundaries with rigor and breadth. Video games seem to be the result of influences from two different worlds. On the one hand, they can be seen as an evolution of traditional games found in various ancient, modern, and contemporary cultures. On the other hand, they can be seen as derivatives of other media such as TV, radio, and film. Both of these aspects have contributed to the development of video games.

However, similar to the human life cycle, the video game has acquired unique characteristics that complement and redefine some elements of its predecessors. According to Newman (2004), the analysis of video games as an object of study in the field of media and culture, along with their similarity to other media such as television and film, has led to video games being viewed as an informational medium, closely related to the context in which they are developed, thus placing less emphasis on their ludic aspect. However, as pointed out by some scholars (Frasca, 1999; Juul, 2005), an approach that includes analysis of the internal structures and dynamics of games enriches the understanding of the video game as a whole.

In 1999, Frasca introduced the term "ludology" to promote the study of games in general and video games in particular, focusing on the rules of behavior that characterize them, referring to the classical theories of traditional games by Johan Huizinga and Roger Caillois. But video games, according to Fabricatore (2000), have two distinguishing characteristics from traditional games: the presence of an opposition that motivates the player and the challenge in achieving game goals. In this sense, digital games move away from conceptions of play as a paideia-type activity, centered in pleasure and without a defined goal, to move closer to the concept of ludus proposed by Caillois, as an activity organized according to rules and objectives.

Moreover, video games always take place in a virtual and interactive game environment, capable of responding to the player's actions and choices, which radically changes the way the game is enjoyed; these distinctive features of digital games are a key element in learning processes. Juul's (2005) classic game theory, which synthesizes the main theorizing on gaming developed so far, provides a useful starting point for understanding the video game as a game. The need for a rule system that organizes the game elements is probably the most relevant feature in defining the video game. Since computational systems need technical specifications to represent and manipulate data numerically, rules are an indispensable element of all digital games. In fact, a video game without rules is an impossible game for the sole reason that, unlike non-digital games where the rules are managed by the players, in video games it is the software that governs the rules. This gives greater flexibility since the computer can handle more rules and of greater complexity, and players can be involved in games of which they do not know the rules beforehand. This last feature is, according to Johnson (2005), one of the main differences with traditional games. In digital games, rules are seldom made explicit at the beginning of the game, which only becomes apparent during video play. Variable and quantifiable outcomes are not always present in video games. In some online video games, the player never reaches the end of the game, and only the logout action defines a temporal end of the game. Simulations that have open-ended endings challenge the valorization of the outcome as an essential feature of games since, in these types of games, there is no outcome that is better or worse than another.

Player effort is a common element of both games and video games. However, the digital medium allows for the displacement of types of effort to other player abilities. A soccer video game, for example, shifts effort from the physical plane to a more strategic one. While traditional games are usually limited by space and time, there are many types of video games that mix real and virtual aspects as an essential part of the game (Juul, 2005). Juul (2005) argued that probably the aspect that defines a clear difference between games and video games is the latter's ability to design fictions. Fiction, the imaginary, non-real aspect in a video game, can be designed in a multiplicity of ways (graphics, sound, text), but always depend on rules, the real aspect with which players interact. The author used the term Half-real to refer to the particular characteristic of video games of being situated in the undefined space between the real and the virtual, the abstract and the concrete, the definite and the ambiguous.

Furthermore, the applicability of the four game categories proposed by Caillois appears as another demonstration of the game nature of video games. Those who step in front of a computer to embark on their adventure in the world of gaming usually encounter an immersive environment capable of creating a state of exhilaration and intoxication (ilinx) due to the fluidity that characterizes these environments. In the current lexicon used by researchers in the field of video games, *ilinx* refers to the sensation of vertigo or disorientation in play (Caillois, 1981), while the concept of *flow* (Csikszentmihalyi, 1990) describes the feeling of complete and energetic immersion in an activity, characterized by high enjoyment and self-efficacy.

Defining Video Games in Modern Context

Giving a single definition of what a video game is today is quite complex since its very nature is multifaceted and depends on the point of view from which it is observed: as a technological device, a form of entertainment, an artistic creation, or a commercial product. Accordi Rickards (2020) suggested that video games are interactive multimedia works, functioning as authorial cultural products that express themselves through various media (text, sound effects, music, speech, static images, video, etc.). Interaction with video games requires immersion in a simulated world governed by technical laws (game design), where the actions of the active user are teleologically oriented. Adding to this perspective, Giovanni Boccia Artieri (2008) conceptualizes video games as video worlds, serving as places of observation for society, changing social relations, and transforming communication. Video games are thus primarily works resulting from technical craftsmanship and creative ideation by one or more individuals. They are cultural products that, implicitly, also function as commercial entities, providing possible sources of income. Moreover, video games are unique media through which it is possible to communicate and express oneself.

The video game can be conceived as an environment in which different media interact and merge to create a new entity with distinct characteristics and languages. In a video game, it is possible to amalgamate the languages of other media, such as literature and film, thus generating a new language and, consequently, a new way of expression. The play component undoubtedly represents the distinctive element of the video game, as it incorporates the concept of play, which Marshall McLuhan (1964) already considered a medium in its own right, arguing that:

> Games [...] are contrived and controlled situations, extensions of collective consciousness, that allow a respite from the usual patterns. They are a way through which the whole society speaks to itself [...] Games are situations contrived to permit the simultaneous participation of many people in some signifying scheme of their collective lives (p. 235).

The Video Aspect of Video Games

Examining video games from a media perspective involves analyzing not only the content, but also the impact they have on perception and worldview. According to McLuhan (1964), each era is characterized by a different medium. This medium, after a period of resistance and sometimes rejection, is finally accepted and integrated into the culture in which it develops. Technology plays a crucial role in the way people read and interpret reality, becoming extensions that amplify and mediate their relationship with the world. Indeed, as pointed out in the title of one of his most significant works, McLuhan sees media as extensions of the human being. He stated that "(...) media, by modifying the environment, evoke in us unique relations of sensory perception. The extension of some sense changes the way we act and think, the way we perceive the world. When these relationships change, humans change" (McLuhan & Fiore, 1968, p. 41). In addition to content, attention is paid to the physical, psychological, and social effects inherent in the way they extend human beings: at the bodily level, through the extension of our senses and movements; at the psychological level, by organizing thought forms; and at the level of interpersonal relationships, by determining ways of communicating and structuring the social world. Each medium, depending on the specific characteristics that define it, accomplishes a particular extension. Photography extends the eye, clothing the skin, printing the memory. In this sense, the media are not neutral. As McLuhan's famous phrase, "The medium is the message" (p. 23), indicates, media not only convey content but are the message itself, carrying with them a vision and a way of organizing knowledge and society. Before video games became popular, McLuhan considered gaming as an information medium and a way to extend the collective awareness of human relations as highlighted in the following:

> Any game, like any information medium, is an extension of the individual or group. Its effects on the group or individual consist in giving a new configuration to those parts of the group or individual that have not been extended. A work of art has no existence or function except in its effects on the men who contemplate it. And art, like popular games or arts, and like communication media, has the power to impose its own assumptions by establishing new relationships and new positions in the human community. (...) If finally, we were to ask, 'Are games mass media?' the answer would have to be affirmative. Games are situations contrived to permit the simultaneous participation of many people in some signifying pattern of their collective lives." (McLuhan, 1966/1997, p. 258-260).

We can consider games as a "trans-media" product, extending across different technologies and media. Video games, like media, create an environment. McLuhan (1964/2003) said that an environment is a process, an action that transforms our nervous system and perceptual habits. It is in the digital format that the game becomes a carrier of a culture different from traditional games, creating a new way of thinking about the world. In this case, the specificity of the video game as a medium becomes of central importance in the deep conditioning that, by virtue of its technological characteristics, operates on our ways of perceiving and thinking about the world.

The video game must be analyzed according to its structural criteria, which govern communication. It is precisely the peculiar communicative structure of this medium that makes it non-neutral, since it affects the behavior and mental models of user-spectators, contributing to the formation of a specific mentality. In order to revolutionize the perception and representation of knowledge, new technologies such as video games must integrate into everyday life, influencing social and individual practices. Digital technologies are increasingly present in everyday life, used for activities such as getting information online, reading news, playing games, and maintaining social relationships. This pervasiveness of them, however, should not lead one to believe that other media, the so-called old media, such as print, television, radio, and film, have been abandoned. On the contrary, it has provided for their modification and restructuring. The emergence of video games was no exception to this trend, integrating into itself a vast wealth of media. Text, audio, and images, still and moving, converge in digital games to create not only an entirely original multimedia communication but, as Maragliano (1996) argued, to create a point of interweaving the cultural resources available to the individual. In this logic, video games follow what Bolter and Grusin (1998) referred to this process as remediation, or the tendency of new media to "re-mediate" existing media:

New media are doing exactly what their predecessors have done: presenting themselves as refashioned and improved versions of other media, digital visual media can best be understood through the ways in which they honor, rival, and revise linear-perspective painting, photography, film, television, and print… What is new about new media comes from the particular ways in which they refashion older media and the ways in which older media refashion themselves to answer the challenges of new media" (p. 14-15).

Each new media absorbs into itself the other media that anticipated it, arriving at the definition of a medium as "that which remediates" (Bolter & Grusin, 1998, p. 94). At the same time, old media, in order to meet the challenges of new forms in emergence, are forced to continually reshape themselves, putting into operation a two-way movement. The representation of one medium within another medium is, according to Bolter and Grusin, the engine of development of the entire media system, a dynamic that has been established from the Renaissance to the present day. There is a wide range of video games, so different video games remediate different media. Video games have become more complex by approaching literary fiction and film. Many games adopt a narrative plot that contributes to the unfolding of the game, incorporating elements such as characters, sequenced actions, and setting similar to traditional fiction. Some scholars analyze video games using narrative categories to structure the gaming experience. As Janet Murray (2004) stated:

Games and stories have in common two important structures [contest and puzzle], and so resemble one another whenever they emphasize these structures… Which comes first, the story or the game? For me, it is always the story that comes first, because storytelling is a core human activity (p. 2).

A video game combines variable action rules and outcomes, challenging storytelling. The relationship between the video game and cinema is another arena in which the debate on remediation has taken on particularly impetuous characteristics. There are an increasing number of encroachments between video games and cinema, from aesthetics to narrative, from the representation of space to the use of cut-scenes in video games. Not surprisingly, film theory has become among the most widely used ways to study video games (King & Krzywinska, 2002). In 1997, Wolf stated that,

At present, film and television theory are best equipped for dealing with the medium of video games, which clearly overlaps them in places and extends many of their ideas, such as the active spectator, suture, first person narrative, and spatial orientation (p. 11).

From Code to Interactivity

Thanks to the flexibility offered by computational language, with its characteristics of modularity, variability, automation and transcoding, video games can offer the player free exploration experiences and the creation of different hypermedia paths, supported by a network of virtual information that gives rise to previously nonexistent logical paths (Tagliagambe, 2006). The video game presents itself as an inherently reconfigurable object (Raessens, 2005), at a time when "(…) a player in this process of exploration is invited to give form to these worlds in an active way by selecting one of the many preprogrammed possibilities in a computer game" (p. 380).

Interactivity in Digital Games

Interactivity is a fundamental concept often used to describe digital games, but it is also an ambiguous term that deserves special attention. Interactivity can mean different things depending on the context. For some, it represents the possibility of choice and intervention, allowing the user to take a more active role. For others, it refers to the medium's ability to create or modify itself in real time in response to the user's actions. To clarify these differences, we can look at the definitions of closed and open interactivity described by Manovich (2001).

- **Closed Interactivity**: This type involves selection within a set of predetermined choices. It is a feature found in both old and new media, such as selecting an option from a menu on a webpage, changing TV channels, or adjusting the volume on a radio.
- **Open Interactivity**: This refers to a more complex form of interaction, characteristic of new media. In open interactivity, both the elements and the structure of an object are partially defined initially and are further created or changed in response to specific user choices. The resulting experience is one among many possible outcomes, shaped by the user's actions.

Open interactivity is particularly relevant to video games, as it offers players a flexible experience where they can make creative, free, and personalized choices. This concept aligns closely with the idea of empowerment (De Giuseppe, 2016), positioning the video game as a "cold medium" in McLuhan's terms. In this context, the active participation of the player is not just necessary but essential for shaping the gaming experience.

Video games present themselves to players as a set of possibilities, providing a context for hypermedia experimentation and choices. Players assume the dual roles of spectators and creators, navigating the game without being confined to predetermined routes. This level of interactivity enhances the sense of immersion, which is crucial for a fulfilling gaming experience. While the degree of interactivity depends mainly on game design, the freedom to move and make impactful choices helps players engage deeply with the game, entering the "magic circle" space where the gameplay experience becomes all-encompassing.

From CBT (Computer-Based Training) to Educational Video Games

The significance of video games in education has evolved over time, becoming increasingly integrated into pedagogical processes. Since the inception of the first computer-based training (CBT) systems in the 1960s, which peaked in the 1980s, computer technologies have advanced significantly alongside learning theories. This evolution has profoundly impacted teaching practices, especially through educational games that incorporate mechanisms to foster engaging and motivating learning environments.

Modern popular games often promote constructivist approaches, supporting creativity and encouraging students to explore and derive meaning from their educational experiences. For instance, Massively Multiplayer Online Role-Playing Games (MMORPGs) offer collaborative educational activities in visually rewarding environments, facilitating the formation of virtual communities where participants communicate and collaborate. Some MMORPGs leverage these features to enhance language learning and 21st-century skills, as collaboration and communication are essential for in-game progress.

Early CBT systems were limited by predefined questions and answers, restricting user interaction. Later systems introduced more flexibility, including tutoring capabilities and the ability to monitor student progress while dynamically adapting pedagogical strategies. Although effective, the development costs of these systems were often high, particularly due to the use of advanced AI. Simulators have evolved to allow students to learn through experimentation and mistakes, following a constructivist approach that promotes active learning. VR-based learning environments further enhance collaboration, enabling participants to learn from their own and others' experiences. Games like MMORPGs or virtual communities such as Second Life and Fortnite naturally support these aspects, making them suitable for innovative teaching methodologies.

Video Games and the Cognitive Process

Educational theories and instructional design can help ensure that students achieve learning goals. Such theories have been used to design school curricula and learning programs. Different approaches, drawn from existing educational theories, can be used to achieve successful learning outcomes. Most educational theories fall into the following categories: cognitivist, behaviorist, and constructivist.

In cognitivist theories, subjects possess an internal map (e.g., knowledge), which external events require them to update. In these approaches, emphasis is placed on the underlying cognitive process. In behaviorist approaches, subjects are not directly responsible for their learning activities, but are conditioned to react to a stimulus. Finally, in constructivist theories, subjects learn to interact with their environment and peers. This involves a process of experimentation that requires students to reflect on their past and present experiences to enrich their knowledge. Because they were originally designed for playful purposes, not all video games are based on the theories of instructional design. Nevertheless, some of them incorporate well-known pedagogical concepts. For example, well-designed games often feature many interactions, defined goals, constant challenges, and meaningful engagement. All of these concepts have been associated with successful learning environments. To some extent, all digital games reflect behavioral, cognitive, and constructivist approaches. In the past, early educational software focused primarily on the first two theories, while newer, more complex digital games of varying lengths encourage a constructivist educational approach. In digital games, players can develop new theories, test them, and improve their skills. Video games that feature 3D environments, advanced AI and realistic physics engines offer responsive and highly realistic simulations.

Cognitive Processes and Learning

In the contexts of learning and cognitive processes, video games can be examined through well-known models such as Carroll's minimalist theory, Vygotsky's Zone of Proximal Development (ZSP), and Kolb's Learning Model. For example, Kolb's model illustrates the developmental process in which students adapt their knowledge based on information and responses obtained from previous actions. Through stages of active experimentation, concrete experience, reflective observation, and abstract conceptualization, they finally return to active experimentation. Applying Kolb's educational cycle theory to the educational experience in video games, we can say that players face situations of failure that prompt them to reflect and identify causes, formulating hypotheses and planning actions to solve the problem. According to Vygotsky's Zone of Proximal Development (ZSP), students should receive gradual support to become increasingly autonomous, improving their metacognitive abilities as they gain confidence and skills. This concept is also evident in games that have a gradual learning curve and are forgiving in the early levels, allowing players to acclimate to the game mechanics and gradually improve their skills. Players must acquire new skills to succeed and take responsibility for learning. The ability of video games to engage and motivate players to learn and collaborate to achieve results is one of the most attractive features that educators can exploit to make learning engaging and challenging.

Video games and Motivation

One of the main qualities of video games is their ability to motivate and engage players in an immersive experience. With a rich variety of auditory, tactile, visual, and intellectual stimuli, video games become enjoyable and, in some cases, even addictive. Although engagement can manifest itself in behavioral, emotional, and cognitive "responses," it usually stems from motivation. In other words, if students are motivated to use video games as a tool, the process of learning through video games requires engaging students both cognitively and emotionally so that they take responsibility for their own learning and decisions (Pesare et al., 2016). One characteristic of video games is their ability to motivate and engage players, making them immersive. Through a wide range of auditory, tactile, visual, and intellectual stimuli, video games become appreciative and, in some cases, even engaging. Students may be motivated to use games as a resource, but learning through video games generally requires involvement on a cognitive and emotional level, along with responsibility for learning and personal choices. In this context, both motivation and involvement should be encouraged. It is believed that video games can achieve this goal because they can motivate and engage students, helping them to develop interest in learning, change behaviors and influence educational outcomes. During the game, players are in a state of "flow," in which they can focus solely on the objective without external distractions. Players' motivation can be influenced by several factors such as gameplay, graphics, interface, and game genre. Players' personalities, aspirations, and cultural backgrounds can influence their behavior in video games. However, it is essential to customize the game experience to fit the player's needs and background, effectively addressing the specific challenges to focus on. The key element is to keep the player focused and motivated while playing the game.

Successful Applications of Video Games

Video games are used for training, educational or therapeutic purposes. Some serious games can be used to train firefighters (https://www.xvrsim.com/en/), medical personnel (https://seriousgaming.nl/portfolio/game-projects/clinical-reasoning/), or to recruit and train soldiers (http://www.americasarmy.com). Some also find wide application in fitness and mental health. The highly advanced technology has made it possible to create extremely realistic environments and simulations. This remarkable level of detail has also been used to treat post-traumatic stress or phobias (Rizzo & Shilling, 2017). For example, commercial games have been used to prevent and treat depression through Wii Fit console exergames, or by using mini-games and puzzles with narrative aspects. Some of these games are based on Cognitive Behavioral Therapy (CBT) approaches (Fleming et al., 2017).

Video games can also be used to evolve learners by proposing that they create their own digital game using a programming language or game engine (e.g., Scratch, Unity, Godot, or Game Maker Studio). By designing and creating their own game, students become designers and creators; players make the game they would like to play and, in doing so, gain important skills (e.g., communication, planning, programming, or multimedia production) and a good understanding of game themes (e.g., pollution, waste recycling, biology, physics, etc.). This approach in particular may be relevant for teachers interested in co-designed teaching and motivating their students in collaborative game development. (see http://www.gamesforchange.org/game/myobeatz/, https://www.mukutu.com.br/)

Using augmented reality (AR), relevant information related to the surrounding environment can be obtained through the use of a digital device (e.g., a mobile device or a visor). Due to their popularity, mobile devices are widely used for those games that support health education (Zhu et al., 2014). Many of these games help players understand a specific disease or improve their health. One example is MojoBeatz, a rhythm-game for mobile devices released in 2018 to train neuromuscular prostheses. Alpha Beta Cancer includes several mini games that help address the topic of cancer in younger patients. Some games can stimulate an emotional dimension to learning, raising awareness of taboo topics or controversial issues such as pollution, environmental threats, sexual health, and bullying. For example, in the digital game Global Conflicts: Latin America, the player impersonates a journalist who investigates to uncover the causes and consequences of industrial pollution in South America.

There are also many games created to promote Internet safety, to help children understand the potential risks of using the Internet and to teach them simple but effective moves with which to make sure their surfing is safe. One example is Hinterland, a game developed by Google, which teaches players how important it is to be careful about the information you share online. Some video games are used to support the teaching of school subjects such as languages, math, geography, history, or science. This list includes both games with inherent educational content but intended for entertainment, and games designed from the beginning with educational goals in mind.

Several games have been developed and used to promote language skills such as listening, reading, spoken or written language in order to acquire skills on both the first and second language. Research has shown that commercial video games, such as World of Warcraft, when used for long periods of time, can have a positive impact on second language development, especially when played outside of the school environment or when the game is combined with in-depth sessions (Reinders, 2017). Online and multi-player games, when used for language learning, provide many opportunities to interact, communicate, and collaborate using the player's second language. This is in contrast to the many games created with a specific training goal, which focus only on the language to be learned, rather than the social context in which learning occurs more spontaneously. Some of the commercial games that can be used to learn a language and whose positive result has been scientifically proven are Tibia, Ragnarok, The Sims, and Club Penguin. The conclusions drawn from the evaluation on the ability of these games in teaching a language and their educational value (e.g., Savonitti & Mattar, 2018), show how many of them support engagement and provide a safe environment to experiment and learn. Moreover, not only do they motivate learners to explore the subject further, but they also help create communities where players are enticed to belong to groups and thus improve their language skills through communication.

Video games are being used to teach mathematics, either in the form of stand-alone applications or as part of a classroom program, where teachers can monitor students' progress and motivate them to compete against each other. For example, with Manga High, an online platform stocked with games for learning math, teachers can track each student's progress, make use of analytical tools, identify areas where students need more support, or promote competition among pupils through the use of leaderboards. A number of studies have shown that using video games can be an effective way to teach mathematics (Tokac et al., 2019), although it is generally agreed that many of the studies done on the impact of games on mathematical skills need to be supplemented with additional information on several factors, including: teacher training, alignment with the curriculum, frequency of use, and the type of skills promoted in the game.

Games such as Dimension M (Bai et al., 2012), Brain Age (Gelman, 2010), MySims (Hawkins, 2008), Vmath Live (King, 2011), Sims 2 - Open for Business (Panoutsopoulos & Sampson, 2012), or Lure of the Labyrinth (Starkey, 2013), have been used and evaluated positively for their educational benefits. Many of these games have proven effective in improving the acquisition of mathematical skills and keeping learning motivation high, as well as developing a more positive attitude toward their teachers. The same goes for those games tailored to support mathematics teaching (Masek et al., 2017).

Other video games are used in primary and secondary schools to support the teaching (and reinforce interest in) science, history, and geography. For example, the game Civilization has been used to teach history and allows players to explore concepts related to strategic planning, agriculture, and engineering, as well as the relationships between these subject areas.

Finally, in recent years, many schools have begun to use video game development to introduce coding among students and promote new skills. Video games are effective in motivating students to learn new skills, such as programming, through creativity. Creating games encourages the development of a wide range of skills, involving different stages of understanding and collaboration. Tools such as Scratch, Game Maker Studio and Minecraft are used to teach coding through game creation, offering accessible and engaging resources for students of all ages. Minecraft is considered suitable for ages 7 or 12+, depending on the version used (https://education.minecraft.net/.) Godot on the other hand (http://www.godotengine.org) is a lightweight, open-source game engine that allows users to create both 2D and 3D games.

In this diverse universe we also define a game jam, which is a competition in which teams or individuals create games based on a specific theme in a few days, lasting between 27 and 72 hours. Participants can work together or remotely. Game jams are popular among educators, students, and developers to bring together players with different skills to create interactive games. Studies on game jams highlight the potential to create complicity among participants, promote technical skills, and encourage confidence by helping to assess one's skills.

Toward Game-Based Learning Education

Game-based learning has gained significant attention as an innovative approach to education. It involves the integration of game elements into the learning process to enhance student engagement and motivation (Untari, 2022). The use of game-based learning has been found to lead to differentiated gains in learning outcomes and perceived flow experience, particularly when implemented in competitive and non-competitive game formats (Chan et al., 2021). Additionally, game-based learning has been identified as a strategy that triggers learners' motivation, rather than simply instructing courses, thereby making the learning process more enjoyable and effective (Lai et al., 2014). Furthermore, the application of game-based learning has been shown to improve student learning outcomes and creativity, making it a valuable tool, especially during challenging circumstances such as the Covid-19 pandemic (Wati & Yuniawatika, 2020). Moreover, game-based learning has been recognized as a means to achieve learning goals and adapt to students' needs in study, thereby providing a more attractive environment for teaching and learning (Bigdeli et al., 2023). It has also been associated with the gamification of education, which involves the use of game design techniques to create a more effective and attractive learning environment (Bigdeli et al., 2023).

The influence of gamification technologies on cognition and learning processes has been supported by neurobiological research, demonstrating its potential to enhance learning experiences (Biryukov et al., 2021). Additionally, the use of game-based learning has been extended to various fields, including mathematics education, language learning, and entrepreneurship education, highlighting its versatility and applicability across different domains (Ryu, 2013; Fox et al., 2018). Furthermore, game-based learning has been linked to the concept of play-based learning, particularly in early childhood education, where it has been associated with higher learning gains and improved learning outcomes (Yee et al., 2022; Vogt et al., 2020).

The method of learning through play has been recognized as an effective approach to facilitate the activeness of kindergarten students, aligning with their natural inclination toward play as a mode of learning (Wardhani & Nduru, 2023). Overall, the literature supports the effectiveness of game-based learning as a pedagogical approach that not only enhances learning outcomes but also fosters student engagement and motivation across various educational contexts.

CONCLUSION

Today, emerging technologies like AR, VR, cloud gaming, AI, and machine learning are converging within the gaming industry. Developers are investing in complex narratives, multifaceted characters, and player choices that deeply influence the gaming experience. The primary goal in game-based learning remains to create immersive experiences that leave a lasting impact on players. The discourse on the potential of video games is ongoing, hinting at a future filled with opportunities, particularly in "inclusive didactics" and addressing "special educational needs" (Aiello & Sibilio, 2015; Aiello, 2018; Di Giuseppe, 2016).

As technologies like VR evolve and cloud gaming grows, gamers can expect increasingly immersive and accessible experiences. The industry is also addressing environmental sustainability and exploring new storytelling methods to connect players in shared virtual worlds. These advancements are becoming integral to contemporary educational and training processes.

Our socio-pedagogical focus is on analyzing gaming trends and their development. One certainty is that the world of video games is continually evolving, and the educational apparatus cannot remain static. AI plays a central role in this evolution, representing a tool with unprecedented potential. The thinking is shifting toward video games having a greater social impact rather than merely commercial. The gaming world must represent a plurality beyond economic-cultural hegemony, necessitating the design of accessible, inclusive games that reflect collective choralities. While this path is challenging, linking AI with educational and training dimensions can expand game-based learning's theoretical and operational design. Enhancing educational and training services isn't limited to video games but extends to all multimedia communication processes related to gaming. This convergence and remediation allow video games to adapt and integrate various media, making them a unique cultural and commercial product.

Game-based learning design is becoming more concrete within educational processes due to the video game's adaptive nature. Since their inception, video games have entailed a convergence of separate languages into one medium: text, images, video, and sound. This adaptability has enabled video games to absorb influences from other media while influencing media and society in turn. A critical and analytical perspective is necessary to understand video games' positive and negative impacts. This balanced view helps illuminate their complexities and better comprehend their nature. Educating Generation Z and Generation Alpha about video gaming, particularly in the context of AI development, will enhance their awareness and understanding of their contemporary world.

REFERENCES

Adams, E. (2014). *Fundamentals of game design*. New Riders.

Aiello, P., Corona, F., & Sibilio, M. (2014). Ipotesi di evoluzione funzionale dell'insegnante di sostegno in Italia. *Italian Journal of Special Education for Inclusion*, 2(2), 21–34.

Aiello, P., Di Tore, S., Di Tore, P. A., & Sibilio, M. (2013). Didactics and simplexity: Umwelt as a perceptive interface. *Education Sciences & Society*, 1, 27–35.

Aiello, P., & Sharma, U. (2018). Improving intentions to teach in inclusive classrooms: The impact of teacher education courses on future learning support teachers. *Form@ re-Open Journal per la Formazione in Rete, 18*(1), 207-219.

Amendola, A. (2023). Il METAVERSO TRA CINEMA E GAME. *Journal of Inclusive Methodology and Technology in Learning and Teaching*, 3(2).

Amendola, A., Guerra, A., & Masullo, M. (2022). La Generazione Z e la (nuova) costruzione dell'identità in epoca pandemica e post pandemica. *La Generazione Z e la (nuova) Costruzione dell'Identità in Epoca Pandemica e Post Pandemica*, 141-167.

Anderson, L. W., & Krathwohl, D. R. (2001). *A taxonomy for learning, teaching, and assessing: A revision of Bloom's taxonomy of educational objectives: Complete edition*. Addison Wesley Longman, Inc.

Antinucci, F. (2007). *Musei virtuali: come non fare innovazione tecnologica*. Musei virtuali.

Bandura, A., & Walters, R. H. (1977). *Social learning theory* (Vol. 1). Prentice Hall.

Baoill, A. Ó. (2008). Jenkins, H.(2006). Convergence Culture: Where Old and New Media Collide. New York: New York University Press. *Social Science Computer Review*, 26(2), 252–254. 10.1177/0894439307306088

Baricco, A. (2010). *I barbari*. Feltrinelli Editore.

Baricco, A. (2019). *The game*. Bezige Bij bv, Uitgeverij De.

Bateson, G. (2000). *Steps to an ecology of mind: Collected essays in anthropology, psychiatry, evolution, and epistemology*. University of Chicago Press. 10.7208/chicago/9780226924601.001.0001

Bertalanffy, L. V. (1968). *General system theory: Foundations, development, applications*. G. Braziller.

Biryukov, A. P., Brikoshina, I. S., Mikhalevich, N. V., Sycheva, S. M., & Khalimon, E. A. (2021). Gamification in education: Threats or new opportunities. *SHS Web of Conferences, 103*, 02001. https://doi.org/10.1051/shsconf/202110302001

Bittanti, M. (Ed.). (2008). *Schermi interattivi: il cinema nei videogiochi* (Vol. 73). Meltemi Editore Srl.

Bolter, J. D. (2007). Remediation and the language of new media. *Northern Lights: Film & Media Studies Yearbook*, 5(1), 25–37. 10.1386/nl.5.1.25_1

Bregni, S. (2018). Assassin's Creed taught me Italian: Video games and the quest for lifelong, ubiquitous learning. *Profession*.

Caillois, R., Dossena, G., & Guarino, L. (1981). *I giochi e gli uomini: la maschera e la vertigine*. Bompiani.

Crawford, C. (1984). *The art of computer game design*. Osborne/McGraw-Hill.

Csikszentmihalyi, M., & Csikzentmihaly, M. (1990). *Flow: The psychology of optimal experience* (Vol. 1990). Harper & Row.

De Freitas, S. (2006). Learning in immersive worlds: A review of game-based learning. *JISC report no. 8*. http://www.jisc.ac.uk/media/documents/programmes/elearninginnovation/gamingreport_v3.pdf

De Giuseppe, T. (2016). *Bisogni educativi speciali: Empowerment e didattiche divergenti per decostruirne la complessità*. Avellino: Il Papavero Editions.

Dewey, J. (1986, September). Experience and education. [). Taylor & Francis Group.]. *The Educational Forum*, 50(3), 241–252. 10.1080/00131728609335764

Di Filippo, L. (2014). Contestualizzare le teorie dei giochi di Johan Huizinga e Roger Caillois. *Problemi di Comunicazione*, 25, 281–308.

Di Tore, P. A. (2014). Perception of space, empathy, and cognitive processes: Design of a video game for the measurement of perspective-taking skills. *International Journal of Emerging Technologies in Learning, 9 Form@re - Open Journal for Networked Training, 14*(3), 43-61. https://doi.org/10.13128/formare-15272

Dill, K. E., & Dill, J. C. (1998). Video game violence: A review of the empirical literature. *Aggression and Violent Behavior*, 3(4), 407–428. 10.1016/S1359-1789(97)00001-3

Dondi, C., & Moretti, M. (2007). A methodological proposal for learning games selection and quality assessment. *British Journal of Educational Technology*, 38(3), 502–512. 10.1111/j.1467-8535.2007.00713.x

Fabricatore, C. (2009). *Media, play and videogaming: On the inner nature and the seldom exploited potential of digital entertainment*. Presentation at the *Fielding University graduate meeting*, New York.

Fiore, Q., & McLuhan, M. (1967). *The medium is the massage* (Vol. 10). Random House.

Fowler, A., Khosmood, F., Arya, A., & Lai, G. (2013). The Global Game Jam for Teaching and Learning. *Proceedings of the 4th Annual Conference of Computing and Information Technology Research and Education, Citrenz2013*.

Fox, J., Pittaway, L., & Uzuegbunam, I. (2018). Simulations in entrepreneurship education: Serious games and learning through play. *Entrepreneurship Education and Pedagogy*, 1(1), 61–89. 10.1177/2515127417737285

Frasca, G. (2013). Simulation versus narrative: Introduction to ludology. In *The Video Game Theory Reader* (pp. 221–235). Routledge.

Gagné, R. M. (1990). *Le condizioni dell'apprendimento* (Vol. 11). Armando Editore.

Gardner, H. (2005). *Educazione e sviluppo della mente. Intelligenze multiple e apprendimento*. Edizioni Erickson.

Garris, R., Ahlers, R., & Driskell, J. E. (2002). Games, motivation, and learning: A research and practice model. *Simulation & Gaming*, 33(4), 441–467. 10.1177/1046878102238607

Gee, J. P. (2003). What video games have to teach us about learning and literacy. [CIE]. *Computers in Entertainment*, 1(1), 20–20. 10.1145/950566.950595

Gelman, A. (2010). *Mario math with millennials: The impact of playing the Nintendo DS on student achievement*. University of Denver.

Green, C. S., & Bavelier, D. (2006). The cognitive neuroscience of video games. *Digital Media: Transformations in Human Communication*, 1(1), 211–223.

Hernández-Jiménez, C., Sarabia, R., Paz-Zulueta, M., Paras-Bravo, P., Pellico, A., Ruiz Azcona, L., Blanco, C., Madrazo, M., Agudo, M. J., Sarabia, C., & Santibáñez, M. (2019). Impact of active video games on body mass index in children and adolescents: Systematic review and meta-analysis evaluating the quality of primary studies. *International Journal of Environmental Research and Public Health*, 16(13), 2424. 10.3390/ijerph1613242431288460

Huizinga, J. (2014). *Homo ludens ils 86*. Routledge. 10.4324/9781315824161

IIdea. (2024). *Video games in Italy in 2023. An analysis of the market and video gamers in Italy in 2023*. IIdea. https://iideassociation.com

Infante, C. (2000). *Learning through play. Interactivity between theater and hypermedia*. Bollati Boringhieri.

Ivory, J. D. (2015). A brief history of video games. In *The Video Game Debate* (pp. 1–21). Routledge. 10.4324/9781315736495-1

Jarvis, P. (1995). *Adult and continuing education: Theory and practice*. Psychology Press.

Jenkins, H. (2004). *Game design as narrative architecture. Computer, 44(3), 118-130*. MIT Press., http://web.mit.edu/cms/People/henry3/games&narrative.html

Jenkins, H. (2006). *Fans, bloggers, and gamers: Exploring participatory culture*. NYU Press.

Juul, J. (2010). *A casual revolution: Reinventing video games and their players*. MIT Press.

Kim, Y. J., & Pavlov, O. (2019). Game-based structural debriefing: How can teachers design game-based curricula for systems thinking? *Information and Learning Science*, 120(9/10), 567–588. 10.1108/ILS-05-2019-0039

King, G., & Krzywinska, T. (Eds.). (2002). *Screenplay: Cinema/videogames/interfaces*. Wallflower Press.

Lecce, A., & Tore, D. (2020). Videogames, Serious game, Exergames come strumenti utili alla didattica. *Nuova Secondaria*.

Malliet, S., & De Meyer, G. (2005). *The history of the video game. Handbook of Computer Game Studies*. The MIT Press.

Malone, T. W., & Lepper, M. R. (2021). Making learning fun: A taxonomy of intrinsic motivations for learning. In *Aptitude, Learning, and Instruction* (pp. 223-254). Routledge.

Maragliano, R. (2005). Technology and knowledge. *Italian Journal of Educational Technology*, 13(1), 21–21. https://www.itd.cnr.it/tdmagazine/PDF34/maragliano.pdf

McLuhan, M., & Capriolo, E. (1986). *Gli strumenti del comunicare*. Garzanti.

Morrison, I., & Ziemke, T. (2005). *Empathy with computer game characters: A cognitive neuroscience perspective*. In Proceedings of the Joint Symposium on Virtual Social Agents, Hatfield, UK. http://www.cet.sunderland.ac.uk/~cs0lha/Empathic_Interaction/Morrison.Ziemke.pdf

Murray, J. (2004). From game-story to cyberdrama. *First Person: New Media as Story, Performance, and Game*, 1, 2–11.

Newman, J. (2012). *Videogames*. Routledge. 10.4324/9780203143421

Pallavicini, F., Ferrari, A., & Mantovani, F. (2018). Video games for well-being: A systematic review on the application of computer games for cognitive and emotional training in the adult population. *Frontiers in Psychology*, 9, 407892. 10.3389/fpsyg.2018.0212730464753

Papert, S. (1993). *The children's machine: Rethinking school in the age of the computer*. New York.

Piaget, J. (1967). *Lo sviluppo mentale del bambino*. Einaudi.

Pintrich, P. R. (2003). *Motivation and classroom learning* (Vol. 103). Handbook of Psychology.

Prensky, M. (2003). Digital game-based learning. [CIE]. *Computers in Entertainment*, 1(1), 21–21. 10.1145/950566.950596

Reynolds, W. M., & Miller, G. E. (2003). Handbook of Psychology: Vol. 1-20. *Current perspectives in educational psychology*.

Savonitti, G., & Mattar, J. (2018). Entertainment games for teaching English as a second language: Characteristics and potential. *International Journal for Innovation Education and Research*, 6(2), 188–207. 10.31686/ijier.vol6.iss2.970

Schreiber, I. (2009). *Game design concepts*. Game Design Concepts. https://gamedesignconcepts.wordpress.com/

Schrier, K. (2019). *Learning, education & games, Volume 3: 100 games to use in the classroom & beyond*. Lulu. com.

Simone, R. (2000). *The third phase. Forms of knowledge we are losing*. Laterza.

Squire, K. (2003). *Replaying history: Learning world history through playing Civilization III*. [Unpublished PhD dissertation].

Starkey, P. L. (2013). *The effects of digital games on middle school students' mathematical achievement*. [PhD Dissertation, Lehigh University].

Steinkuehler, C. A. (2008a). Cognition and literacy in massively multiplayer online games. In Coiro, J., Knobel, M., Lankshear, C., & Leu, D. (Eds.), *Handbook of Research on New Literacies* (pp. 611–634). Erlbaum.

Steinkuehler, C. A., & Duncan, S. (2008b). Scientific habits of mind in virtual worlds. *Journal of Science Education & Technology*. https://website.education.wisc.edu/steinkuehler/papers/SteinkuehlerDuncan2008.pdf

Suits, B. (1978). *The grasshopper: Games, life and utopia*. University of Toronto Press. 10.3138/9781487574338

Tyng, C. M., Amin, H. U., Saad, M. N., & Malik, A. S. (2017). The influences of emotion on learning and memory. *Frontiers in Psychology*, 8, 235933. 10.3389/fpsyg.2017.0145428883804

Untari, A. D. (2022). Game-based learning: Alternative 21st century innovative learning models in improving student learning activeness. *Edueksos Jurnal Pendidikan Sosial & Ekonomi*, 11(2). 10.24235/edueksos.v11i2.11919

Van Eck, R. (2007). Building artificially intelligent learning games. In *Games and Simulations in Online Learning: Research and Development Frameworks* (pp. 271-307). IGI Global. 10.4018/978-1-59904-304-3.ch014

Viola, F., & Cassone, V. I. (2017). *L'arte del coinvolgimento: emozioni e stimoli per cambiare il mondo*. Hoepli Editore.

Vogt, F., Hauser, B., Stebler, R., Rechsteiner, K., & Urech, C. (2020). Learning through play–pedagogy and learning outcomes in early childhood mathematics. In *Innovative Approaches in Early Childhood Mathematics* (pp. 127–141). Routledge., 10.4324/9780429331244-10

Vygotsky, L. S. (2016). Play and its role in the mental development of the child. *International Research in Early Childhood Education*, 7(2), 3–25.

Wati, I. F. (2020, December). *Digital game-based learning as a solution to fun learning challenges during the Covid-19 pandemic*. In *1st International Conference on Information Technology and Education (ICITE 2020)* (pp. 202-210). Atlantis Press. https://doi.org/10.2991/assehr.k.201214.237

Webb, E. (2013). *Learning (Together) with Games-Civilization and Empire*. Transformations.

Wittgenstein, L. (2019). *Philosophical investigations*. Wiley-Blackwell.

Chapter 6
Educational Paradigm Shifts in the Era of Rapid Technological Advancement

Sajid Khan
https://orcid.org/0000-0001-5397-9185
Ghulam Ishaq Khan Institute of Engineering Sciences and Technology, Pakistan

Majid Kahn
https://orcid.org/0000-0002-4576-8174
Massey University, New Zealand

Phil Ramsey
https://orcid.org/0000-0003-3609-6254
Massey University, New Zealand

ABSTRACT

In a rapidly evolving world, students are becoming increasingly techno-social, mirroring the changing demands of firms. Educational systems must adapt correspondingly, necessitating innovation in teaching practices which constitute the educational process. As Savian highlights robust theoretical underpinnings lead to more effective practical activities. However, while learning theories evolve, teaching practices lag behind. Amidst disagreements, it's acknowledged that learning is complex and diverse. The solution lies in transitioning from traditional pedagogy to contextualized, personalized, collaborative, and technology-mediated learning. Successful educational innovations are essential to meet stakeholders' heightened demands.

INTRODUCTION

Change has always pervaded human civilization as a constant phenomenon. The current times are distinctive in the sense that change is happening on a vast scale and at a swift pace. The main reason behind this unprecedented rate of change is the rapid advancement in science and technology (Howard

DOI: 10.4018/979-8-3693-3003-6.ch006

Copyright ©2024, IGI Global. Copying or distributing in print or electronic forms without written permission of IGI Global is prohibited.

et al., 2020). Technological innovations contribute to changes in almost all aspects of life, including the individual, social, and economic (Toronto, 2009).

Those born near the turn of the century and onwards have not known life without modern digital and network technologies. They are always connected to the internet, often engaging in multiple activities simultaneously, and have a relentless need for instant gratification and reliance on technology (Turner, 2015). Compared to previous generations, they may have strong visual-spatial skills and information scanning abilities but weaker memory, attention, critical thinking, imagination, and reflection skills (Carr, 2020; Shanmugasundaram & Tamilarasu, 2023).

Digital and network technologies provide users with virtual spaces to create communities where people with similar interests, values, and beliefs can engage in meaningful long-distance relationships (Turner, 2015). Research reveals that these virtual spaces are used for numerous social practices, such as keeping in touch with old friends, making new friends, playing interactive games, sharing information and photos, initiating and/or terminating romantic relationships (Pennington, 2020), entertainment (Bohnert et al., 2013), and social and political activism (Mansour, 2012).

Rapid technological advancement is also contributing to the transformation of the century-old industrial information economy into a networked information economy (Bankler, 2008). The former economic model relies on economies of scale, tight control structures, obedient workers, and passive consumers, whereas the latter requires economies of networks, flexible control structures, active consumers, and knowledge workers—self-driven individuals whose work requires a higher level of expertise and involves complex, problem-solving tasks (Muzam, 2023).

In the face of rapid growing complexity and dynamism of the world, educational institutions are expected to provide students with an educational experience that is appropriate and relevant to the changing world (Kalimullina et al., 2021). Graduates should be able to obtain work in areas of their interest, thereby contributing not only to their own goals but also to their organizational and community goals and objectives (Perez-Encinas & Berbegal-Mirabent, 2023). Achieving this, however, requires educational institutions to replace traditional pedagogy or lecture-and-test form of instruction with an approach that is more responsive to learners' needs (Raelin, 2007; Scott, 2015).

The traditional pedagogy views teachers as the source of knowledge and learners as "empty vessels" (Freire, 2017). The teacher's task is to "fill" the learners' "emptiness", while learners are expected to consume knowledge through rote memorization and drill (Raelin, 2007). This approach does not encourage thinking, generating knowledge, or questioning assumptions (Raelin, 2007). Learners' contexts, values, emotions, and preferences are ignored, and instructional content is detached from relevant contexts (Freire, 2017). Although efficient for transmitting large amounts of information (Howard, 1998), it primarily promotes surface learning (Jess et al., 2011).

At their best the traditional methods can only produce noncritical, conformist, and organized individuals with basic knowledge in science, numeracy, language, and technical skills (McDermott, 2005). Such individuals were suited to the industrial economy, which valued punctuality, obedience, hierarchical control, and basic literacy (Miller, 2011). However, they do not meet the needs of today's knowledge-based economy, which relies on intellectual assets and cognitive skills (Muzam, 2022; Wagner & Compton, 2012). Based on their extensive literature review, Van Laar et al. (2017) identified seven core skills: technical know-how, information management, creativity and innovation, communication, collaboration, critical thinking, and problem-solving, which are in demand in modern organizations.

The field of education has historically undergone significant paradigm shifts, evolving through various theoretical frameworks to address the changing needs of society. According to Kuhn (1962), a paradigm shift occurs when a new paradigm develops and becomes more unified. Education has transitioned through three major paradigms: Behaviorism, Cognitivism, and Constructivism. However, since the early 2000s, there has been a call for a new paradigm to better address the complexities of modern learning environments (Dziubaniuk et al., 2023).

Recent theorists have introduced theories, such as Complexity Theory, Connectivism, and Quantum Learning Theory. Should teachers adhere to learning theories, blend them, or rely on their own reflections and observations? There are no definitive answers to these questions. None of these theories provide a complete explanation of the learning process or account for individual differences in learning (Christensen, Horn & Johnson, 2008).

Each learning theory offers valuable insights (Ertmer & Newby, 2013; Janzen et al. 2011; Belbase, 2014), yet none can claim absolute truth beyond the premises they are based on. The effective use of any theory—whether personal or formal—depends on its ability to help educators understand their unique instructional contexts and create meaningful learning experiences (Brieger et al., 2020; Anderson, 2008). Teachers must strive for genuine, novel, and valuable instructional practices (Robinson, 2017). These practices can be based on formal learning theories, personal insights, or a combination of both. Notably, constructivist and post-constructivist theories are non-prescriptive and do not dictate specific structures or teaching techniques (Applefield et al., 2000).

The next section discusses the concept of paradigms and paradigm shifts and explores these in the light of events and ideas that have influenced and shaped instructional practices to enable pedagogy to respond to the contemporary needs and requirements. Moreover, an important question - why and what assumptions modern learning theories contain and how do these influence the design of instruction and the role of a learner and a teacher? - is also answered. Finally, a conclusion is drawn on the basis of the literature that is reviewed in this chapter.

What is Paradigm and Paradigm Shift?

A paradigm refers to a shared belief system or set of principles about a particular domain (Cohen et al., 2013). It encompasses beliefs, theories, rules, generalizations, and actions (Kuhn, 1962), and is viewed as the broadest unit of consensus within any discipline, shaping individuals' thoughts and behaviors (Capra, 1996; Robinson, 2017). In other words, the worldview promoted by an established paradigm enters people's consciousness as taken-for-granted ideas about the world. These ideas serve as a foundation for shaping new ideas and practices within any discipline. As such, the worldview plays a major role in shaping practices (Goldberg, 2009).

During its evolution, every paradigm encounters certain problems that require consideration of elements beyond its current scope. The accumulation of such problems within a paradigm eventually pushes it into a state of crisis. This crisis creates an opportunity for a new paradigm to emerge (Kuhn, 1962), initiating a process where the old paradigm is replaced by the new one. The process is completed when the change agents of the new paradigm successfully transform the existing ways of thinking across the discipline (Robinson, 2017)

It is important to understand that a paradigm shift does not entail the complete abrogation of all assumptions of the old paradigm. Instead, only those assumptions that have been proven invalid are discarded, while valid principles may be retained in the new paradigm (Applefield et al., 2000). Moreover, in the social sciences, it is unusual for a dominant paradigm to entirely replace a recessive one; rather, paradigms often coexist within a discipline (Reihlen & Schoeneborn, 2022).

Paradigm Shifts in Education

The history of education systems dates to ancient civilizations (Fernandez et al., 2022). However, there was no consensus among people regarding particular assumptions pertaining to instruction and learning until the 1900s. The time prior to 1900 could be termed as pre-paradigm period for instruction. During the twentieth century the field of instruction experienced various paradigm shifts. The Scientific Management Theory along with three distinct schools of thought of psychology - Behaviourism, Cognitivism and Constructivism - that emerged one after the other, played a major role in causing these paradigm shifts (Applefield et al., 2000). The comprehension of those factors paving the way for these paradigm shifts along with the most important presumptions of the three learning perspectives led to an improved understanding of the impact of these perspectives on design and delivery practices. This understanding is essential for change in instructional methods.

Scientific Management and Behaviorism

In the early 1900s, factors like technological development, high demand for industrial goods and market expansion caused a huge increase in demand for trained workers (Zuboff, 1988). Due to time intensive nature the extant methods such as apprenticeship and on-the-job-learning, could not meet skill and knowledge demands of the industry. During the same period the Scientific Management Theory was conceived. Not only did this theory provide a theoretical basis for a rigid managerial hierarchy, specialised division of labour and standardised jobs but also promoted task analysis as an effective tool for analysing jobs (O'Neill, 2017). The task analysis also enabled management experts to figure out one best way of performing tasks that could be efficiently transferred to employees through classroom and off-the-job training. Though the Scientific Management Theory greatly helped the industry to meet its demands pertaining trained staff, it also shrunk the focus of instruction programs to only a certain specific type of knowledge.

Knowledge based on its nature can broadly be divided into two main types – explicit and tacit. Explicit knowledge represents the objective and rational dimension of knowledge (Nonaka & Takeuchi, 2007). It includes documents, procedures, theoretical approaches, and manuals. Explicit knowledge due to its objective nature can be articulated, codified and stored in media. Tacit knowledge refers to a subjective understanding that is deeply rooted in an individual's actions, experiences, values, ideals and emotions (Nonaka & Takeuchi, 2007). Though the acquisition of tacit knowledge is a slow and complex process it can be effectively learned through apprenticeship and on-the-job learning (Ribeiro, 2013).

The Scientific Management Theory basically attempted to capture knowledge, and translate it into rules, principles, and formulae. It remained successful for explicit knowledge because that can be articulated in formal language. However, it failed for tacit knowledge because experience, judgement, ideals, values, and emotions are very difficult to explain in verbal or written form (Nonaka & Takeuchi, 2007). Consequently, only that knowledge was useful which could be formally codified. In 1913, Watson wrote *The Behavioural Learning Theory* which also promoted the same understanding that only explicit knowledge counts as knowledge (Overskeid, 2008). Behaviourism later became the first formal paradigm for designing training and educational systems.

Behaviourism is grounded in objectivism and monism (Schuh & Barab, 2007). Objectivism as an epistemology and ontology renders reality as an objective which is independent of the observer's consciousness whereas monism is a conceptual approach that rejects the mind-body distinction and views man as an absolute basic unit. It is, however, important to note that due to objectivist nature of Behaviourism when it comes to the knower and the world, it views them as separate entities (Harasim, 2023). Some of the major assumptions of Behaviourism are given in Table 1.

Table 1. Relevant assumptions of behaviorism

	Knowledge	**Knowledge is a "repertoire of behaviors" (Wray, 2014, p. 71). All behaviors of organisms are responses to environmental inputs (stimuli) (Clark, 2018).**
	Learning	Learning modifies the form or frequency of learners' overt behaviors (Mechlova & Malcik, 2012).
	Memory	Memory is formed when the brain is "hardwired" by repeated experiences (Janzen et al., 2012, p. 712). Practice and review are essential for maintaining and retaining learned knowledge and skills (Stewart, 2021).
	Influencing factor	Positive (reward) and negative (punishment) reinforcements greatly assist in eliciting desired behaviors (Wray, 2014).
	Objectives of instruction	The objectives of instruction are accomplished when learners demonstrate desired behaviors by adequately responding to environmental stimuli (Weegar & Pacis, 2012).

The instructional design based on the assumptions of Behaviourism contain its fundamental common features pertaining learning material, sequencing and structuring of activities and learner control (Brau et al., 2020). The learning material is divided into small distinct lessons or modules and presented to the learner as rules, principles, formulae, or definitions along with various relevant examples. The structure of the activities and the pace with which they are delivered to learners are decided by the teacher. However, the activities are sequenced in a manner that they progress toward complexity. The skills or operations for which the instruction is undertaken are demonstrated in the form of small parts to make it easy for the learner to assimilate the desired behaviour. Learners are made to frequently review and practice newly learned knowledge and skills respectively so that they become proficient in applying these in that situation where and when they are applicable. Positive and negative reinforcements are used to maintain learners' motivation. Learners are assessed as per performance standards that are explicitly communicated before or during an instructional program.

The job of the teacher in the Behaviorist instructional program is limited to three roles. The first and foremost job of the teacher is to demonstrate associations between targeted stimuli and their responses, by effectively identifying those stimuli that can produce the desired response (Ertmer & Newby, 2013). The second job is to provide a practice environment to the learner where responses are paired with targeted cues. The third and final job is to arrange the environmental settings in such a way that the learners give correct responses by the application of targeted stimuli and receive reinforcement for those responses (Brau et al., 2020).

Behaviorism remained a dominant ideology in the field of instruction from the 1920s through until the early 1970s (Braat et al., 2020). One of the important reasons of this dominance was the adherence of industry to the principles of the Scientific Management Theory. According to Littler (1978), the Scientific Management Theory suggests that workers should be given simple tasks because they are inherently stupid and incapable of doing those jobs that involve high level thinking and decision taking. As a result, many industrial jobs were designed to be comprised of simple tasks. For such tasks, the Behaviourism strategy of 'learning by doing' was quite effective. However, rapid technological advancement in the 1950s and 1960s significantly transformed the nature of the industrial jobs. These new jobs required highly sophisticated skills for which Behaviourism had no adequate response (Berryman, 1993). Moreover, research conducted in the late 1960s and early 1970s also highlighted the importance of attention, motivation, memory, and perception for learning (Braat et al., 2020). The accumulation of failures created a crisis that demanded a new set of assumptions (Yilmaz, 2011).

Second instructional paradigm - Cognitivism

Cognitivism emerged as a dominant epistemology to resolve those issues which Behaviourism failed to address. With having roots in objectivism and rationalism, Cognitivism considers mind and body as two separate and distinct but interactive items. Nonetheless, from the perspective of Cognitivism, the world is real and external (Schuh & Barab, 2007). Some of the relevant assumptions of this perspective are given in Table 2.

Table 2. Relevant assumptions of cognitivism

Knowledge	Knowledge is an entity that exists outside of the learner (Ertmer & Newby, 2013).
Learning	Learning is a mental activity where cognitive structures known as schema reorganize themselves by combining, extending, or altering to process and store new information (Ertmer & Newby, 2013).
Memory	Memory serves three main functions: encoding, storage, and retrieval (Ertmer & Newby, 2013). When a learner is presented with new information, it initially enters their sensory register, then moves to short-term memory, and finally is stored in long-term memory (Mergel, 1998). Factors such as missing or inadequate cues, memory loss, and incorrect inferences can cause learners to forget what they have learned.
Influencing factor	During the learning process, factors like prior schema (Yilmaz, 2011), the meaningfulness and relevance of instruction components to understanding and context (Mergel, 1998), environmental cues, as well as learners' thoughts, beliefs, attitudes, and values play crucial roles (Ertmer & Newby, 2013).
Objectives of instruction	The goal of instruction is to help learners organize and retrieve the information that has been delivered to them through instruction (Ertmer & Newby, 2013).

The instructional program, based on the assumptions of Cognitivism, views learners as intelligent problem solvers and information seekers (Atkin, 1993). sHierarchical task analysis procedures are employed to identify the cognitive requirements of the learners (Ertmer & Newby, 2013). The instruction is designed with a primary emphasis on keeping the learners engaged throughout the learning process (Ertmer & Newby, 2013). Instructional activities are organized and structured according to the learners' learning styles and prior knowledge, allowing and encouraging learners to make associations with previously learned material. Furthermore, learners are given control of goal setting, resource identification, and evaluation of relevance, motivating them to develop appropriate understanding by extracting relevant information personally from provided sources (Atkins, 1993). Additionally, instructional goals are aligned with the learners' personal goals and communicated to them, making lessons seem worthwhile and intrinsically motivating learners to maximize their learning. The tutoring style is also kept flexible, adapting to the situational demands.

The teacher's role in the Cognitivist instructional program is to assess the learner's background in terms of knowledge and skills to organize and structure instruction so that the learner can connect new information with existing knowledge for maximum learning (Ertmer & Newby, 2013). Moreover, the teacher must choose an appropriate teaching approach from cognitive apprenticeship, reciprocal teaching, anchored instruction, inquiry learning, discovery learning, and problem-based learning (Yilmaz,

2011). Frequent use of feedback is necessary to establish, guide, and support proper mental connections (Thompson et al., 1996).

Cognitivism was a dominant ideology in the field of instruction from the early 1970s until the early 1990s (Chyung, 2008), and many of its views are still considered valid. However, some of its assumptions have been found to be incorrect. For example, Cognitivism views knowledge as an objective reality that can be transferred from the instructor to the learners (Zarei, 2011), ignoring the role of context and limiting individual meanings. Cognitivism also posits that reality is represented in symbols, restricting cognition to symbol manipulation, and failing to explain non-symbolic, non-reflective, and first-person psychological activity (Zarei, 2011). While Cognitivism uses the computer as a metaphor for the human mind, mental functions in biological beings are more complex than information processing models can fully represent. Additionally, Cognitivism suggests that the real world can be modeled (Jonassen, 1992), but the real world is too complex and dynamic to be accurately modeled.

The accumulation of these erroneous assumptions created reasons for the emergence of Constructivism.

Third Instructional Paradigm: Constructivism

Constructivism, in terms of epistemology and ontology, is based on objectivistic rationalism, empiricism, realism, and relativism. Objectivistic rationalism suggests that the reality experienced by an individual exists. However, realism suggests that this reality is more complex than it appears and is experienced (Reihlen, 2022). Relativism proposes that knowledge is an interpretation based on the observer's knowledge and experiences (Schuh & Barab, 2007). From the constructivist perspective, there is no single objective reality, but rather an individually constructed reality that depends on the perceptions of the observer (Newby et al., 2000). Some of the major assumptions of Constructivism are given in Table 3.

Table 3. Relevant assumptions of constructivism

Knowledge	**Knowledge is subjective and individualistic, arising from a complex interaction of cognitive, affective, psychomotor, mental, and metacognitive states within the mind and nervous system (Ertmer & Newby, 2013). This mental framework is not fixed but can be enhanced over time (Fearon et al., 2021).**
Learning	Learning is a personal process of creating meaning (Gerpott et al., 2019), not just the repetition of information stored in memory. The learners' actively construct their meaning and knowledge from their experience.
Memory	Memory is not a passive repository of distinct, isolated fragments of information which enable a learner to repeat what he has learned. It plays an active role in helping learners connect prior knowledge to new contexts and understand reality (Davis et al., 2008), continually evolving through interactions (Ertmer & Newby, 2013).
Influencing factor	Various factors like challenge, interest, choice, desire, and social recognition motivate learners to build or enhance their knowledge (Pintrich & Schunk, 002).
Objectives of instruction	The goal of instruction is to support learners in actively constructing knowledge (Herr, 2014).

The Constructivist instructional design values include active engagement, autonomy, generativity, reflectivity, collaboration, personal relevance, and pluralism (Lebow, 1993). The main emphases of Constructivism are identifying the context in which skills are to be learned and applied and giving the learner control and the ability to manipulate information (Ertmer & Newby, 2013). Examples of context-based learning include learning through group reading, participation in conversations, and listening to stories, movies, and media (Alzahrani & Alhomyani, 2023).

Constructivist instructional design involves presenting a problem, project, or case, and providing learners with tools to enhance their understanding and solve the problem (Motallebinejad et al., 2019). These tools include information sources, cognitive aids, collaboration tools, and social resources to help learners construct knowledge (Brooks & Brooks, 1999). A collaborative and pluralistic learning environment is fostered through strategies such as situated learning, multiple perspectives, and flexible learning (Tam, 2000). Learners appreciate diverse viewpoints on a single issue, developing a comprehensive understanding. Formative evaluation is used to assess the transfer of knowledge and skills. Overall, constructivist instruction helps learners develop problem-solving skills, enabling them to apply existing knowledge to create new knowledge (Ertmer & Newby, 2013).

From the constructivist viewpoint, teachers need to consider learners' prior knowledge and develop learner-driven content that gradually advances from basic facts to higher levels of knowledge creation (Kumar, 2011). The curriculum remains flexible to foster a conducive learning environment. Teachers engage learners using strategies such as open-ended questions and exposing them to complex problems (Kumar, 2011). Learners are encouraged to engage in dialogue with both the instructor and peers (Stewart, 2021), fostering a democratic environment where all viewpoints are considered (Kumar, 2011). Lastly, teachers provide learners with ample time to create metaphors and establish relationships (Kumar, 2011).

While Constructivism is widely espoused for designing instructional practices (Motallebinejad et al., 2019), objectivistic theories of behaviorism and cognitivism are predominantly followed in practice (Päuler-Kuppinger & Jucks, 2017; Altbach et al., 2010; Osberg et al., 2008; Saykili, 2018).

Constructivism has theoretically dominated instructional design for nearly three decades. However, with the rapid advancement of technology in recent years, new cognitive, social, and economic needs have emerged (Brown, 2005). Issues such as learning in a non-linear manner, technology performing cognitive operations, and situations requiring performance without complete understanding need to be addressed by learning theory, despite being non-standard or rare occurrences.

Logically, the question of whether there is a need for a new learning perspective clearly poses itself. Constructivism alone, as a guiding theory, does not seem adequate for underpinning contemporary instructional policies, models, and practices. The question that arises is: 'Do we really need a new learning theory or perspective?' The literature does not provide a categorical answer to this question; rather, it presents a variety of opinions. Some scholars argue that rapid technological development has reduced the relevance of learning theories (Ally, 2004; Brieger et al., 2000). They, however, maintain that there is no need for a new learning theory but a model that integrates different learning theories. Others advocate for 'openness-based flexibility,' suggesting that addressing the complexities of the modern world requires drawing from multiple perspectives and methodologies in creative ways that incorporate various elements such as prevailing technologies, learner needs and stakeholder demands (Spiro et al., 2008, p. 18). Additionally, some suggest adopting broader cultural values such as contextualization, personalization, and collaboration (Collins & Halverson, 2010; Ertmer & Newby, 2013; Khan et al., 2024). Several new learning theories have also emerged to fill the gap. Here, three of these theories are briefly explained.

Connectivism

Connectivism, which has its origins in distributed learning, was proposed by two theorists, George Siemens, and Stephen Downes. In his article "Connectivism: Learning as a Network Creation," Siemens explained that Constructivism, along with Behaviourism and Cognitivism, cannot meet the demands of the existing world because they do not take emerging learning issues into consideration. Consequently, he proposed a new theory called Connectivism, which is based on Chaos theory, Network theory, System theory, and Complexity theory (Siemens, 2004). The following year, Downes further elaborated on the theory in his article "An Introduction to Connective Knowledge" (Downes, 2005). Some of the major assumptions of Connectivism are given in Table 4.

Table 4. Relevant assumptions of constructivism

Knowledge	Knowledge is not a stable output; it is a process that continually changes and grows (Siemens, 2005). For an individual, it comprises an information network that feeds into organizations, which in turn feed back into the network, continuing the process. Knowledge and learning reside in both human and non-human entities, such as databases or other information sources (Siemens, 2005).
Learning	Learning is a process undertaken primarily to acquire new, accurate, and up-to-date knowledge by connecting specialized nodes within a complex environment where elements constantly interact and change (Davis et al., 2008). A node can be anything, such as a person, a group of people, a computer, information, thoughts, feelings, images, etc., which can connect to other nodes (Herlo, 2017). To facilitate continual learning, it is essential to maintain and improve connections between nodes (Downes, 2012).
Memory	Memories consist of adaptive patterns of connectivity and await transfer to new learning contexts (Downes, 2006; Davis et al., 2008).
Influencing factor	The learning process enables learners to know more than their existing state of knowledge, provided they have core abilities to seek out new information, filter secondary and extraneous information, and see connections among fields, ideas, and concepts (Davis et al., 2008).
Objectives of instruction	To assist learners in identifying and maintaining connections between different information sources for support continual learning (Duke et al., 2013).

The Connectivism learning environment is based on five values - dialogue, collaboration and cooperation, group work, interaction with online resources and knowledge production. It uses blogs, wikis, and other open, collaborative platforms to facilitate learning (Seimen, 2009). These platforms use two-way processes which allow learners to easily connect with persons and ideas. Learners are also provided with rich information sources and tools to create their own networks. The capacity to learners to learn is improved so that they can navigate the information (Seimen, 2009). Like constructivism, connectivism also uses formative evaluation such as self-assessment, peer-assessment and negotiated assessment, to measure the performance of learners.

According to Downes (2010) the teacher plays a decisive role in the success of any personal learning initiative. In PLE, a teacher is not a "sage on the stage" but a "guide on the side" to facilitate learners in developing adequate understanding with regards to values, beliefs, mannerism, and ways of observations that are associated with the subject. Downes (2010) identifies 23 different broad roles for a teacher in a PLE. These roles include lecturer, mentor, evaluator, coach, facilitator, demonstrator, coordinator, moderator, theoriser, critic, convener, designer, tech support, programmer, connector, learner, collector, curator, sharer, agitator, alchemist, salesperson and bureaucrat. What these different roles indicate is that in PLE the role of teacher is not fixed but changes according to the requirements of a particular situation. Presumably the list has been created to emphasize the need for flexibility, and a readiness to become whatever is needed.

Some scholars view 'Connectivism' as a new form of 'Constructivism', one which tends to philosophically respond to the increasing role technology in our lives (Hendricks, 2019; Matter, 2010). However, it is important to note that Connectivism has thus far failed to achieve wide acceptance among intellectual circles (Ker, 2007; Verhagen 2006). Bell (2010) and Duke et al., (2013) hold that although Connectivism remained unsuccessful in establishing itself as a distinct learning theory, its epistemological stances can significantly contribute to new learning paradigms.

Quantum learning (QL)

The QL is based on David Bhom's Exchange theory and was proposed by Katherine Janzen, Beth Perry, and Margaret Edwards in the year 2011. This theory suggests 'quantum holism' to understand the world. Quantum holism views the interconnectedness of the entire universe as a fundamental reality and the apparent relatively independent parts as mere contingent forms within this whole. In other words, the 'interconnectedness of things extends infinitely in all things, in all places, and always (Janzen et al. 2011, p.471). The main assumptions of the QL are given in Table 5.

Table 5. Main assumptions of the QL

Knowledge	Knowledge refers to meaningless facts.
Learning	Learning is a multi-dimensional process (Janzen et al., 2012). These dimensions can be cognitive, behavioral, social, cultural, and technological. Furthermore, learning is holistic in nature and is patterned within holographic realities (Janzen et al., 2012). The holographic view suggests that individuals, groups, and systems can connect to form an integral whole, thereby creating and translating knowledge. Learning environments are living systems that continuously learn, adapt, and grow.
Memory	Memory, whether conscious or unconscious, is formed through decoding and encoding within a continuous cycle of inputs and outputs.
Influencing factor	Numerous dimensions influence learning, including technology, culture, social interactions, cognition, spirituality, corporeality, and the intersecting perspectives of both teacher and learner (Janzen et al., 2011).
Objectives of instruction	Learners are holistic beings; learning must engage their multiple dimensions.

In the Quantum Learning (QL) environment, the role of the teacher is to provide opportunities for students to learn in their preferred ways. This requires teachers to engage in innovative and creative teaching and learning strategies. According to Janzen et al. (2011), such strategies can be created or adopted from literature that deals with both traditional and online teaching. Some effective strategies for QL include creative learning, Emotional Intelligence, science-based learning, and arts-based learning.

The QL environment is based on nine values: participation, conceptualization, contextualization, systemization, validation, legitimization, transformation, interpretation, and materialization (Janzen et al., 2011). It aims to construct a multidimensional online environment to create a holistic approach that reaches the students' multiple dimensions. Learners are provided with minimal prescription in terms of "assigned" readings. Instead, they are generally given topics and themes and encouraged to seek out information sources and resources to inform themselves.

It is important to note that instructional models based on Constructivism, Connectivism, and Quantum Learning (QL) differ significantly from objectivist theories, which advocate teacher-centred transmission models. Instead, they promote learner-centred learning. In these models, the individual learner, rather than the teacher, has control over the content they study and the ways in which they study it—when, where, how, and at what pace they learn. Thus, these theories promote "flexibility" in learning.

Flexibility in the instructional context is a dynamic concept that has various dimensions (Li & Wong, 2018). Consequently, it is applied to almost any aspect of the instructional initiative (Celaro et al., 2003), to improve the functionality of that aspect and enable it to contribute positively towards the achievement of anticipated goals and objectives of the instruction (Joan, 2013). As different studies have been conducted from different dimensions there is no unanimous agreement among scholars on the definition of flexibility (Tucker & Morris, 2011). Literature reveals its various interpretations from different angles with one central underlying theme: that flexibility is about facilitating learning processes by giving various types of choice to learners.

The term "flexibility" refers to the ability of a phenomenon to change and adapt to different circumstances. In the context of instruction, there is no unanimous agreement among scholars on the definition of the term (Joan, 2013; Tucker & Morris, 2011). The literature reveals various interpretations from different angles with one central underlying theme: flexibility is about facilitating learning processes by providing various types of choices to learners. According to Dermetriadis and Pombortsis (2007), flexibility involves giving learners greater choice and control over their learning to improve the functionality of that aspect and enable it to contribute positively towards achieving the anticipated goals and objectives of the instruction (Celaro et al., 2003; Joan, 2013).

The choices can involve different aspects of the instruction, such as time, content, entry requirements, delivery mechanisms, instructional approaches, assessments, resources and support, and the goals of the course (Smith & Smith, 2004; Li & Wong, 2018). Numerous studies discuss various dimensions of flexibility (Austerschmidt & Bebermeier, 2019; Bergamin et al., 2010; Collis & Moonen, 2001; Li & Wong, 2018; Smith & Smith, 2004; Soffer et al., 2019). An overview of categories and dimensions of flexibility is given in Table 6.

Table 6. Dimensions of flexibility

Type of Flexibility	Dimensions
Time	Greater choices to learners in terms of: • when they want to learn • pace of learning • duration of learning • choosing the assessment timing • timing for study within the course
Instructional content	Greater choices to learners in terms of: • what they want to learn • sequencing the activities • size and scope of the course • level—basic, intermediate, advanced—of the course • assessment standards • study material • learning styles - wholistic, analytical, and wholist-analytical • presentation of information - verbal only, images only, verbal and images
Instructional approach	Greater choices to learners in terms of: • modes of learning (how and where) • language to be used • social organisation of learning • pedagogy of the course (Instructor as teacher or facilitator)
Instructional location	Greater choices to learners in terms of: • location / place for learning (workplace, home or learning centre) • location for the assessment of learning
Entry and exit	Greater choices to learners in terms of: • entry requirements • exiting the training through multiple start and end points
Delivery and logistics	Greater choices to learners in terms of: • methods of obtaining support such as face to face, telephone and email. • delivery channels such as face to face session, video lecture link, broadcast posts etc.

continued on following page

Table 6. Continued

Type of Flexibility	Dimensions
Learning resources	• Greater choices to learners in terms of learning resources such as paper format, multimedia, educational s/w, PowerPoint presentations, demonstration files etc.
Interaction	• Greater choices to learners in terms of interactions with teacher and among learners through face to face interaction, teleconferencing, e-announcements, emailing, forum and chat etc.
Technology	• Greater choices to learners in terms of choosing and using technology

Complexity Perspective of Learning

Complexity theory, developed mainly in mainstream sciences to deal with complex systems, uses various theoretical and conceptual tools (Hansen, 2017). These tools include Catastrophe theory, Chaos theory, and System theory (Mason, 2008). According to Hansen (2017), Complexity theory seeks to understand the behavior of complex systems to identify patterns that can help better appreciate the workings of these systems. Primarily, this theory is used for identifying complex systems, understanding the issues within them, and developing solutions to these problems (Hansen, 2017).

The complexity of a system or environment indicates the presence of various non-linearly interacting elements or components (Sim, 2007). These elements can include ants, human agents, or organizations, forming complex systems like ant colonies, corporations, or economic systems. Geyer (2003) identified six principles of Complexity theory. A phenomenon can sometimes be simplified while the system remains holistic, predictability is uncertain, and outcomes can only be roughly determined by identifying boundaries. Additionally, new behaviors emerge when a system becomes sufficiently complex, and these behaviors cannot be predicted from the initial conditions since they do not exist in the basic elements. Geyer's final principle states that agents within a complex system may be aware of themselves, the system, and their history, and they may strive to interpret and direct themselves and the system.

The intricacy of a complex system is further elucidated by its three main properties identified by Senge (2010): delays between causal relationships, multiple feedback loops, and several stocks. Firstly, time gaps exist between decisions and their impact on the system, which reduces the accumulation of experience and learning and causes instability. Secondly, any intervention in a system creates multiple feedback loops, potentially causing both desired and undesired reactions. Thirdly, a system contains several stocks, which are accumulations with many inflows and outflows.

According to Mason (2024), from a complex perspective, the phenomenon one wants to change should be seen as a dynamic system within its broader context. Applying this perspective to instructional spaces, they consist of numerous elements that interact within and among themselves and with the larger external environment. This larger environment may include rapidly changing technologies, dynamic industry goals and requirements, evolving socio-political and cultural environments, unstable economic situations, and the developing instructional field. The elements of the external environment interact in a non-linear fashion, making the instructional space excessively complex and highly ambiguous. These external elements influence the internal elements and their complex web of connections.

The instructional space itself also accommodates a myriad of different elements and their connections, such as learners, instructional content, media, instructors, peers, and time (Davis & Sumara, 2008). These elements are complex entities within themselves. Dealing with the complexity of instructional spaces through a linear approach is not viable. A broad approach is needed, as achieving instructional objectives depends on the emergence of certain desired behaviors in the system. According to Complexity theory, sustainable behavior within any system requires the accumulation of sufficient complexity (Mason, 2024). Creating sufficient complexity within an instructional space involves influencing its constituent elements in the required direction from all possible levels and angles through deliberate interventions. These demands identifying the maximum number of available factors and their potential influences on the instructional space and carefully designing interventions. Sustained interventions at all levels will create a new, more complex web of interactions among the elements, leading to the desired behavior.

It is worth noting that the Complexity perspective is a descriptive but not predictive approach (Mason, 2008; Morrison, 2008). Therefore, it cannot predict from the initial state of the elements the quantity and direction of interventions needed to cause the required behavior within a system. According to Mason (2008), existing research literature on education can help identify a direction to design interventions. For example, learners with a wholist cognitive style learn better when ideas are presented as a whole, while learners with an analytic cognitive style learn more effectively when a phenomenon is presented as discrete parts. Thus, the inability of Complexity theory to guide specific intervention designs does not undermine its utility as a directed approach for instructional space.

Geyer et al., (2005) suggest that the complexity of a system requires considering all available epistemological stances and methodological approaches, using a broad and open-minded approach when choosing solutions. Spiro, Collins, and Ramchandran (2008) called this 'openness-based' flexibility and deemed it essential for achieving learning objectives. This means that educational initiatives must broaden their focus to include various phenomena, such as prevailing technologies, diverse learning needs, knowledge and skill levels of learners, and the demands of stakeholders. Creative solutions can then be generated using appropriate technology and relevant methodologies. Instruction designers must adopt multiple perspectives to address emerging issues due to complexity effectively (Spector, 2001).

SUMMARY

The chapter provides a brief overview of the journey of education from the Behaviorist paradigm to the Constructivist paradigm and beyond. It is important to note that Constructivism, the dominant paradigm in education today, emerged in the nineties when technology was relatively in its infancy. Over the last three decades, technology has evolved drastically, creating new needs that Constructivism is incapable of meeting. Janzen et al., (2011, p. 57) highlight the need for a new paradigm with the following words:

If it is accepted that there are multiple ways of knowing, then it follows that there are multiple ways of learning. If there are multiple ways of learning, then multiple ways of explaining how individuals learn must be requisite. Considering how consilience has integrated knowledge across disciplines, it is posited that the creation of a learning theory or perspective that has the potential to integrate theories of learning is long overdue. Further, this integration would bridge theory and practice.

To fill this gap, many new learning theories such as Connectivism, Quantum Learning (QL), and Complexity perspectives have emerged, though none have yet established themselves as a new paradigm for education. These theories all assume that people learn differently from one another, and there cannot be one best way to teach everyone. They are non-prescriptive in nature and emphasize the need for contextualization, collaboration, personalization, flexibility, openness, and an understanding of the broader context in which education occurs. In other words, these theories promote educational innovation by suggesting that teachers need to develop teaching methods and activities that align with the diverse learning needs of their students. Thus, this chapter establishes why innovation is crucial for education. It goes beyond the need for fresh ideas in educational institutions; innovation will be central to whatever new paradigm ultimately shapes education.

REFERENCES

Altbach, P. G., Reisberg, L., & Rumbley, L. E. (2010). Introduction: Twenty-first-century global directions. *Trends in Global Higher Education*, 1-21.

Alzahrani, S., & Alhomyani, M. (2023). The Effectiveness of Explicit Vocabulary Instruction on Productive Vocabulary Learning in Writing Among Intermediate School Learners in Saudi Arabia. *Sino-US English Teaching*, 20(8), 289–310. 10.17265/1539-8072/2023.08.001

Anderson, T. (2008). *The theory and practice of online learning*. AU Press. 10.15215/aupress/9781897425084.01

Applefield, J. M., Huber, R., & Moallem, M. (2000). Constructivism in theory and practice: Toward a better understanding. *High School Journal*, 84(2), 35–53.

Atkins, M. J. (1993). Theories of learning and multimedia applications: An overview. *Research Papers in Education*, 8(2), 251–271. 10.1080/0267152930080207

Austerschmidt, K. L., & Bebermeier, S. (2019). Implementation and effects of flexible support services on student achievements in statistics. *Zeitschrift für Hochschulentwicklung*, 14(3), 137–155. 10.3217/zfhe-14-03/09

Bateson, G. (2000). *Steps to an ecology of mind: Collected essays in anthropology, psychiatry, evolution, and epistemology*. University of Chicago Press. 10.7208/chicago/9780226924601.001.0001

Belbase, S. (2014). Radical versus social constructivism: An epistemological pedagogical dilemma. *International Journal of Contemporary Educational Research*, 1(2), 98–112.

Bell, F. (2010). Connectivism: Its place in theory-informed research and innovation in technology-enabled learning. *International Review of Research in Open and Distance Learning*, 12(3), 98–118. 10.19173/irrodl.v12i3.902

Benkler, Y. (2008). *The wealth of networks: How social production transforms markets and freedom*. Yale University Press.

Bergamin, P., Ziska, S., & Groner, R. (2010). Structural equation modeling of factors affecting success in student's performance in ODL-programs: Extending quality management concepts. *Open Praxis*, 4(1), 18–25.

Berryman, S. E. (1993). Learning for the workplace. In Darling-Hammond, L. (Ed.), *Review of research in education* (pp. 343–401). American Educational Research Association.

Bohnert, A. E., Hughes, J. L., & Pulice-Farrow, L. (2013). Motives that predict liking and the usage of Facebook. *Undergraduate Research Journal for the Human Sciences, 12*(1).

Braat, M., Engelen, J., van Gemert, T., & Verhaegh, S. (2020). The rise and fall of behaviorism: The narrative and the numbers. *History of Psychology*, 23(3), 252–280. 10.1037/hop000014632191061

Brau, B., Fox, N., & Robinson, E. (2020). Behaviorism. In R. Kimmons & S. Caskurlu (Eds.), *The students' guide to learning design and research*. EdTech Books. https://edtechbooks.org/studentguide/behaviorism

Brieger, E., Arghode, V., & McLean, G. (2020). Connecting theory and practice: Reviewing six learning theories to inform online instruction. *European Journal of Training and Development*, 44(4/5), 321–329. 10.1108/EJTD-07-2019-0116

Brooks, J. G., & Brooks, M. (1999). *In search of understanding: The case for constructivist classrooms*. ASCD.

Brown, T. (2005). Beyond constructivism: Exploring future learning paradigms. *education today*, 2(2), 1–11.

Capra, F. (1996). *The web of life: A new scientific understanding of living systems*. Anchor Books.

Carr, N. (2020). *The shallows: What the Internet is doing to our brains*. W.W. Norton & Company.

Celaro, M., Paladini, E. P., Rodrigues, R., & Assumpcao, S. (2003). Quality and flexibility in higher education. In *Proceedings of European Distance Education Network Annual Conference (EDEN)* (pp. 35–41). Hungary: Eden Press.

Christensen, C., Johnson, J., & Horn, M. (2008). *Disrupting class: How disruptive innovation will change the way the world learns*. McGraw-Hill.

Chung, S. Y. (2008). *Foundations of instructional and performance technology*. HRD Press.

Clark, K. R. (2018). Learning theories: Behaviorism. *Radiologic Technology*, 90(2), 172–175. 30420574

Cohen, L., Manion, L., & Morrison, K. (2013). *Research methods in education* (7th ed.). Routledge. 10.4324/9780203720967

Collis, B., & Moonen, J. (2001). *Flexible learning in a digital world: Experiences and expectations*. Kogan Page Limited.

Davis, C., Edmunds, E., & Kelly-Bateman, V. (2008). Connectivism – emerging perspectives on learning, teaching, and technology. University of Georgia. Retrieved from http://epltt.coe.uga.edu/index.php?title=Connectivism

Demetriadis, S., & Pombortsis, A. (2007). E-lectures for flexible learning: A study on their learning efficiency. *Journal of Educational Technology & Society*, 10, 147–157.

Downes, S. (2005). The Living Arts: The Future of Learning Online. Moncton: Stephen Downes. Retrieved from http://www.downes.ca/files/guelph.ppt

Downes, S. (2006). Learning networks and connective knowledge. *Collective intelligence and Elearning*, 20(1), 1–26.

Downes, S. (2012). *Connectivism and connective knowledge: Essays on meaning and learning networks*. http://www.downes.ca/files/books/Connective_Knowledge-19May2012.pdf

Duke, B., Harper, G., & Johnston, M. (2013). Connectivism as a digital age learning theory. *The International HETL Review*, 2013(Special Issue), 4–13.

Dziubaniuk, O., Ivanova-Gongne, M., & Nyholm, M. (2023). Learning and teaching sustainable business in the digital era: A connectivism theory approach. *International Journal of Educational Technology in Higher Education*, 20(1), 20. 10.1186/s41239-023-00390-w 37096023

Ertmer, P. A., & Newby, T. J. (2013). Behaviorism, cognitivism, constructivism: Comparing critical features from an instructional design perspective. *Performance Improvement Quarterly*, 26(2), 43–71. 10.1002/piq.21143

Fearon, D., Hughes, S., & Brearley, S. G. (2021). Constructivist Stakian multicase study: Methodological issues encountered in cross-cultural palliative care research. *International Journal of Qualitative Methods*, 20, 1–10. 10.1177/16094069211015075

Fernandez, C. J., Ramesh, R., & Manivannan, A. S. R. (2022). Synchronous learning and asynchronous learning during COVID-19 pandemic: A case study in India. *Asian Association of Open Universities Journal*, 17(1), 1–14. 10.1108/AAOUJ-02-2021-0027

Freire, P. (2017). *Pedagogy of the oppressed*. Penguin Classics.

Gerpott, F. H., Lehmann-Willenbrock, N., Wenzel, R., & Voelpel, S. C. (2019). Age diversity and learning outcomes in organizational training groups: The role of knowledge sharing and psychological safety. *International Journal of Human Resource Management*, 32(18), 3777–3804. 10.1080/09585192.2019.1640763

Geyer, R. (2003). European integration, the problem of complexity and the revision of theory. *Journal of Common Market Studies*, 41(1), 15–35. 10.1111/1468-5965.t01-1-00409

Geyer, R., Mackintosh, A., & Lehmann, K. (2005). *Integrating UK and European social policy: the complexity of Europeanisation*. Radcliffe Publishing.

Goldberg, R. (2009). How Our Worldviews Shape Our Practices. *Conflict Resolution Quarterly*, 26(4), 405–431. 10.1002/crq.241

Hansen, C. (2017). *Shakespeare and complexity theory*. Routledge. 10.4324/9781351967433

Harasim, L. (2023). Learning theories: The role of epistemology, science, and technology. In *Learning, design, and technology: An international compendium of theory, research, practice, and policy* (pp. 75–113). Springer International Publishing. 10.1007/978-3-319-17461-7_48

Hendricks, G. P. (2019). Connectivism as a learning theory and its relation to open distance education. *Progressio*, 41(1), 1–13. 10.25159/2663-5895/4773

Herlo, D. (2017). Connectivism, a new learning theory? In Soare, E., & Langa, C. (Eds.), *Education facing contemporary world issues. European proceedings of social and behavioural sciences* (pp. 330–337). Future Academy.

Herr, C. M. (2014). Radical constructivist structural design education for large cohorts of Chinese learners. *Constructivist Foundations*, 9(3), 393–402.

Howard, P., Corbett, M., Burke-Saulnier, A., & Young, D. (2020). Education futures: Conservation and change. *Paper commissioned for the UNESCO Futures of Education report*. UNESCO.

Janzen, K., Perry, B., & Edwards, M. (2011). Becoming real: Using the artistic pedagogical technology of photo voice as a medium to becoming real to one another in the online educative environment. *International Journal of Nursing Education Scholarship*, 8(1), 32–43. 10.2202/1548-923X.2168

Janzen, K., Perry, B., & Edwards, M. (2012). The entangled web: Quantum learning, quantum learning environments and Web technology. Ubiquitous Learning. *International Journal (Toronto, Ont.)*, 4(2), 1–16. 10.18848/1835-9795/CGP/v04i02/40328

Jess, M., Atencio, M., & Thorburn, M. (2011). Complexity theory: Supporting curriculum and pedagogy developments in Scottish physical education. *Sport Education and Society*, 16(2), 179–201. 10.1080/13573322.2011.540424

Joan, D. R. (2013). Flexible learning as new learning design in classroom process to promote quality education. *Journal of Science Education and Technology*, 9(1), 37–42.

Jonassen, D. H. (1992). Objectivism versus constructivism: Do we need a new philosophical paradigm? *Educational Technology Research and Development*, 39(3), 5–14. 10.1007/BF02296434

Kalimullina, O., Tarman, B., & Stepanova, I. (2021). Education in the context of digitalization and culture. *Journal of Ethnic and Cultural Studies*, 8(1), 226–238. 10.29333/ejecs/629

Khan, S., Ramsey, P., & Khan, M. (2023). Embracing educational transformation: Exploring personalized, collaborative and contextualized education through dilemma theory. *Innovations in Education and Teaching International*, •••, 1–14. 10.1080/14703297.2023.2283614

Kuhn, T. (1962). *The structure of scientific revolutions*. University of Chicago.

Kumar, A. (2011). Towards Realist Constructivism: Implications for Teaching & Training. *Indian Journal of Industrial Relations*, 46(3), 523–535.

Li, K. C., & Wong, B. Y. Y. (2018). Revisiting the definitions and implementation of flexible learning. *Innovations in open and flexible education*, 3–13.

Littler, C. R. (1978). Understanding Taylorism. *The British Journal of Sociology*, 19(2), 185–202. 10.2307/589888

Mansour, E. (2012). The role of social networking sites (SNSs) in the January 5th revolution in Egypt. *Library Review*, 61(2), 128–159. 10.1108/00242531211220753

Mason, M. (2008). Complexity theory and the philosophy of education. *Educational Philosophy and Theory*, 40(1), 4–18. 10.1111/j.1469-5812.2007.00412.x

Mason, M. (2024). Complexity theory and the enhancement of learning in higher education: The case of the University of Cape Town. *Educational Philosophy and Theory*, 56(5), 469–478. 10.1080/00131857.2022.2140042

Mattes, J. (2010). *Innovation in multinational companies: organisational, international and regional dilemmas*. Peter Lang.

McDermott, R. (2005). An Emersonian approach to higher education. *Revision*, 28(2), 6–16. 10.3200/REVN.28.2.6-17

Mechlova, E., & Malcik, M. (2012, November). ICT in changes of learning theories. In *2012 IEEE 10th international conference on emerging eLearning technologies and applications (ICETA)* (pp. 253–262). IEEE. 10.1109/ICETA.2012.6418326

Mergel, B. (1998). *Instructional design and learning theory* (Unpublished paper, USAK). https://www.usask.ca/education/coursework/802papers/mergel/brenda.htm

Morrison, K. (2008). Educational philosophy and the challenge of complexity theory. *Educational Philosophy and Theory*, 40(1), 19–34. 10.1111/j.1469-5812.2007.00394.x

Motallebinejad, A., Hatami, J., Fardanesh, H., & Moazami, S. (2020). Toward More Effective Legal Education for Adolescents: Systematic or Constructivist Instructional Design Models? *Journal of Constructivist Psychology*, 33(4), 406–421. 10.1080/10720537.2019.1641773

Muzam, J. (2023). The challenges of modern economy on the competencies of knowledge workers. *Journal of the Knowledge Economy*, 14(2), 1635–1671. 10.1007/s13132-022-00979-y

Newby, T. J., Stepich, D. A., Lehman, J. D., & Russell, J. D. (2000). *Instructional Technology for Teaching and Learning*. Prentice Hall.

Nonaka, I., & Takeuchi, H. (2007). The knowledge-creating company. *Harvard Business Review*, 85(7/8), 162.

O'Neill, C. (2017). Taylorism, the European science of work, and the quantified self at work. *Science, Technology & Human Values*, 42(4), 600–621. 10.1177/0162243916677083

Osberg, D., Biesta, G., & Cilliers, P. (2008). From representation to emergence: Complexity's challenge to the epistemology of schooling. *Educational Philosophy and Theory*, 40(1), 213–227. 10.1111/j.1469-5812.2007.00407.x

Päuler-Kuppinger, L., & Jucks, R. (2017). Perspectives on teaching: Conceptions of teaching and epistemological beliefs of university academics and students in different domains. *Active Learning in Higher Education*, 18(1), 63–76. 10.1177/1469787417693507

Pennington, N. (2020). An examination of relational maintenance and dissolution through social networking sites. *Computers in Human Behavior*, 105, 1–8. 10.1016/j.chb.2019.106196

Perez-Encinas, A., & Berbegal-Mirabent, J. (2023). Who gets a job sooner? Results from a national survey of master's graduates. *Studies in Higher Education*, 48(1), 174–188. 10.1080/03075079.2022.2124242

Pintrich, P. R., & Schunk, D. H. (2002). *Motivation in education: Theory, research, and applications* (2nd ed.). Merrill/Prentice Hall.

Raelin, J. A. (2007). Toward an epistemology of practice. *Academy of Management Learning & Education*, 6(4), 495–519. 10.5465/amle.2007.27694950

Reihlen, M., & Schoeneborn, D. (2022). The epistemology of management: An introduction. In Neesham, C., Reihlen, M., & Schoeneborn, D. (Eds.), *Handbook of Philosophy of Management* (pp. 17–37). Springer. 10.1007/978-3-030-76606-1_66

Ribeiro, R. (2013). Tacit knowledge management. *Phenomenology and the Cognitive Sciences*, 12(2), 337–366. 10.1007/s11097-011-9251-x

Robinson, K. (2017). *Out of our minds: The power of being creative*. John Wiley & Sons.

Sadler-Smith, E., & Smith, J., P. (. (2004). Strategies for accommodating individuals' styles and preferences in flexible learning programmes. *British Journal of Educational Technology*, 35(4), 395–412. 10.1111/j.0007-1013.2004.00399.x

Saviani, D. (2007). Pedagogy: The space for education at the university. *Cadernos de Pesquisas*, 37(130), 99–134. 10.1590/S0100-15742007000100006

Saykili, A. (2018). Distance education: Definitions, generations, key concepts and future directions. *International Journal of Contemporary Educational Research*, 5(1), 2–17.

Scott, C. L. (2015). *The futures of learning 3: What kind of pedagogies for the 21st century?* UNESCO.

Senge, P. (2010). *The fifth discipline: The art & practice of the learning organization.* Doubleday.

Shanmugasundaram, M., & Tamilarasu, A. (2023). The impact of digital technology, smartphones, social media, and artificial intelligence (AI) on cognitive functions: A review. *Frontiers in Cognition*, 2, 1203077. 10.3389/fcogn.2023.1203077

Siemens, G. (2004). Connectivism: A learning theory for the digital age. *International Journal of Instructional Technology and Distance Learning.* http://www.itdl.org/Journal/Jan_05/article01.htm

Siemens, G. (2005). Meaning making, learning, subjectivity. http://connectivism.ca/blog/2005/12/meaning_making_learning_subjec.html

Siemens, G. (2009). Elearnspace. https://www.elearnspace.org/blog/8

Sim, Y. (2007). *International Relations & Complex Systems Theory. Paper presented at the 51st Annual Meeting of the International Society for the Systems Sciences.* Tokyo Institute of Technology., Retrieved from https://journals.isss.org/index.php/proceedings51st/article/view/607/225

Soffer, T., Kahan, T., & Nachmias, R. (2019). Patterns of students' utilisation of flexibility in online academic courses and their relation to course achievement. *The International Review of Research in Open and Distributed Learning.* 10.19173/irrodl.v20i4.3949

Spector, J. M. (2001). A philosophy of instructional design for the 21st century? *Journal of Structural Learning and Intelligent Systems*, 14(4), 307–318.

Spiro, R. J., Collins, B. P., & Ramchandran, A. R. (2008). Modes of openness and flexibility in cognitive flexibility hypertext learning environments. In *Online and distance learning: Concepts, methodologies, tools, and applications* (pp. 1903–1908). IGI Global. 10.4018/978-1-59904-935-9.ch152

Stewart, M. (2021). Understanding learning: Theories and critique. In Hunt, L., & Chalmers, D. (Eds.), *University teaching in focus: A learning-centred approach* (2nd ed.). Routledge. 10.4324/9781003008330-2

Tam, M. (2000). Constructivism, instructional design, and technology: Implications for transforming distance learning. *Journal of Educational Technology & Society*, 3(2), 50–60.

Tennyson, R. D. (2010). Historical reflection on learning theories and instructional design. *Contemporary Educational Technology*, 1(1), 1–16. 10.30935/cedtech/5958

Thompson, A. D., Simonson, M. R., & Hargrave, C. P. (1996). *Educational technology: A review of the research* (2nd ed.). Association for Educational Communications & Technology.

Toronto, E. (2009). Time out of mind: Dissociation in the virtual world. *Psychoanalytic Psychology*, 26(2), 117–133. 10.1037/a0015485

Tucker, R., & Morris, G. (2011). Anytime, anywhere, anyplace: Articulating the meaning of flexible delivery in built environment education. *British Journal of Educational Technology*, 42(6), 904–915. 10.1111/j.1467-8535.2010.01138.x

Turner, A. (2015). Generation Z: Technology and social interest. *Journal of Individual Psychology*, 71(2), 103–113. 10.1353/jip.2015.0021

Van Laar, E., Van Deursen, A. J., Van Dijk, J. A., & De Haan, J. (2020). Determinants of 21st-century skills and 21st-century digital skills for workers: A systematic literature review. *SAGE Open*, 10(1), 2158244019900176. 10.1177/2158244019900176

Wagner, T., & Compton, R. A. (2012). *Creating innovators: The making of young people who will change the world*. Scribner.

Weegar, M. A., & Pacis, D. (2012). A comparison of two theories of learning—Behaviorism and constructivism as applied to face-to-face and online learning. In *Proceedings E-Leader Conference, Manila*. http://www.gcasa.com/conferences/manila/papers/Weegar.pdf

Wray, D. (2014). Looking at learning. In Cremin, T., & Arthur, J. (Eds.), *Learning to teach in the primary school* (3rd ed., pp. 69–83). Routledge.

Yilmaz, K. (2011). The cognitive perspective on learning: Its theoretical underpinnings and implications for classroom practices. *The Clearing House: A Journal of Educational Strategies, Issues and Ideas*, 84(5), 204–212. 10.1080/00098655.2011.568989

Zarei, G. R. (2011). A constructivist model for the technological enhancement of university materials. *Asian Journal of Information Technology*, 10(1), 26–31. 10.3923/ajit.2011.26.31

Zuboff, S. (1988). *In the age of the smart machine: The future of work and power*. Basic Books, Inc.

Chapter 7
The Small and Rural School Italian Network for Digital Technologies Flourishing in "Non Standard" Educational Context:
Before, During, and After the Pandemic Era

Giuseppina Rita Jose Mangione
INDIRE, Italy

ABSTRACT

The topic of small and rural schools offers numerous investigative perspectives within educational research. Digital technologies hold significant potential for "non-standard" educational contexts, driving the need to reconsider the structure of schools based on regional partnerships. After summarizing key international studies that have identified the challenges of using technology in rural educational settings, this paper adopts a phenomenological approach, based on narratives of exemplary cases, to present a diachronic analysis (before, during, and after the pandemic) and exemplify disruptive use of technologies in small schools. The Italian Network of Small Schools promoted by INDIRE has supported numerous transformative scenarios that extend the use of technologies beyond the emergency period and guide small schools into a future where also AI can helps solidify their role as centers of democratic values and quality education.

INTRODUCTION ON SMALL SCHOOLS: REMOTENESS, ISOLATION, AND DIGITAL OPPORTUNITIES

The topic of small and rural schools offers numerous perspectives for investigation within educational research. Among the most relevant study strands are those that focus on the relationship between school and territory (Bartolini et al., 2021; Corbett & White, 2014), studies that rethink the use of technologies and digital materiality to intervene in situations of remoteness (Mangione & Cannella, 2020; Mangione

DOI: 10.4018/979-8-3693-3003-6.ch007

& Calzone, 2020), as well as research that deepens the understanding of the advantages (small class sizes and proximity of the community) (Mangione & Cannella, 2021) and disadvantages (difficulty in incentivizing and retaining highly qualified teachers, multi-grade management, geographical isolation, and difficulty in including children with difficulties) (Azano & Stewart, 2016; Mangione et al., 2017). This attention to situations of greater fragility also follows the pandemic period and the inequity of solutions for distance education for rural learners (EAC, 2020; Mangione et al., 2022).

A complex picture emerges, as small schools are not only found in remote and isolated places but also in inner areas and even, sometimes, in urban centers, perhaps in suburbs with problems of marginality or in historic centers undergoing depopulation (Bartolini et al., 2021). In these educational contexts, the fundamental problem is that of cultural and geographical isolation resulting from territorial positioning and a deficient level of interaction, generated by the minimum number of students and often by the impossibility of connecting classes and complexes, or even classes and the space of the house where children in difficulty are located, due to health problems or the absence of transport and passable roads to get to school (Hyry-Beihammer & Hascher, 2015). Small and rural schools that experience geographical isolation, racial segregation, and limited school and community resources are asked to confront unique challenges (Johnson & Strange, 2007). In these contexts, the idea of educational fragility emerges (Du Plessis & Bailey, 2000; Ryan, 2001) along with a demand from parents for interventions capable of supporting quality educational programs for their children.

Digital technologies can be a key lever for enabling quality distance learning but are limited by rural-urban gaps in information and communication technology (ICT) resources in schools and beyond (Trendov et al., 2019). Non-Standard Teaching Situations (SDiNS) (home schooling, hospital schooling, "disconnected" schooling), or all those school realities that, for their understanding, escape the model of the "normal class," with attention to rural and peripheral contexts, are better suited than others to interpret the role of digital technologies to promote inclusive, collaborative processes and personalized education (Carenzio & Ferrari, 2021).

For over ten years, the National Institute for Documentation, Innovation and Educational Research (INDIRE) has been contributing, through service research, to the enhancement of educational offerings and teaching and learning experiences in small schools characterized by isolation, remoteness, and limited size (Bray, 1992; Heeralal, 2014). The recognition of benefits, such as small class sizes and close community ties (Barley & Brigham, 2008; Monk, 2007), and drawbacks, like challenges in recruiting and retaining highly skilled teachers, managing multi-grade classrooms, and geographical isolation (Azano & Stewart, 2016; Miller, 2012), guides the research towards outlining potential pathways for a national movement and exploring innovative organizational and instructional models, which are the focus of experimental actions, training, and documentation.

These activities stem, on the one hand, from the need to identify issues and common obstacles in teaching in multi-grade classrooms (Cornish, 2006; Ronksley-Pavia et al., 2019), seeking new forms of curricula and group management strategies for highly diverse settings (Mangione & Garzia, 2021). On the other hand, they reflect an awareness of the need to assist schools in addressing specific challenges associated with isolation, limited access to digital resources (Johnson & Strange, 2007), educational fragility (Du Plessis & Bailey, 2000; Ryan, 2001), unconventional teaching contexts (Mangione et al., 2023; Rivoltella, 2015) to be addressed post-coronavirus pandemic, along with the inequity in distance education solutions for rural learners (EU, 2021).

The international literature emphasizes both the benefits that technology can offer to small schools and the significant challenges associated with its use. These schools often face not only geographical but also cultural isolation. Among the benefits of technology for small schools, besides accessing a wide range of online resources, are connecting classrooms with different contexts (Hargreaves, 2009; Laferrière et al., 2011), facilitating the inclusion process in new educational environments for students (Hannum et al., 2009), and expanding the variety of extracurricular activities available to students (Hawkes et al., 2002).

However, despite these advantages, technology was not widely adopted in small schools before the COVID-19 pandemic lockdown, even though its use could have significantly advanced educational practices. Studies conducted from 2014 to early 2020 in Italy showed that even in the most innovative small schools, where technology was regularly used, it was often limited to specific subjects and dependent on the initiative of individual teachers (Pieri & Repetto, 2019). The pandemic forced technology into all schools and homes of school-age children, resulting in highly varied usage across different schools and teachers (Füller & Spiewak, 2020).

Regarding the challenges, there are few studies that specifically address the barriers to technology use in primary and secondary education in small schools (Fargas-Malet & Bagley, 2022; Pieri, 2022). Key issues identified include a lack of hardware and software (Francom, 2016; Kale & Goh, 2014; Rundel & Salemink, 2021), limited bandwidth (Handal et al., 2018; Rundel & Salemink, 2021), and a shortage of staff to maintain technological equipment and resolve technical issues (Wang et al., 2019). Additionally, teachers often lack the necessary skills to effectively use technology for teaching (Azano et al., 2019).

Even with access to adequate technological infrastructure, intangible factors such as teacher training and support are crucial. Teachers need to develop the skills and awareness to integrate technology according to their students' specific pedagogical needs and create educational pathways that connect school and everyday life (Azano et al., 2019). A study by Goodpaster, Adedokun, and Weaver (2012) highlights that innovation in teaching practices, such as technology-supported active methodologies that center the student's learning process, can be more challenging in remote areas due to isolation. This isolation limits opportunities for teachers to collaborate and participate in professional development.

Digital and technological services have moved to the forefront of public discourse during the COVID-19 pandemic. Technology has great potential for small rural schools by requiring systems to rethink the school form for small schools and promote experiences that recall the basic principles of smart schools. The forms of digital technologies can be the catalyst in the process of transforming small rural schools into smart schools (Jen, 2001; Mangione & Cannella, 2020) through new architectures and environments for teaching and learning.

After summarizing some international studies that analyze the critical issues regarding the use of digital technologies in rural schools teaching, this chapter offers an overview of the experience of digital education in small and rural schools in Italy supported by INDIRE through the National Movement of Small and Rural Schools, a network able to define different disruptive scenarios guiding isolated schools located in remote areas of the country to revalue themselves as extended and community schooling (Mangione & Cannella, 2021; Mangione et al., 2023).

Digital Technologies Studies in Small and Rural Schools

It is possible to examine the digital technologies in small and rural schools from several analytical trajectories or approaches, specifically (Mangione & Cannella, 2020): (1) studies on the employment of ICT by educators in small and rural schools, with an emphasis on the prevailing digital divide (Hohlfeld et al., 2008; Wang, 2013) and the requirement for a digitally competent staff (Thomas & Falls, 2019); (2) studies that underscore the necessity to steer teachers in rural areas towards the integration of network technology into their instruction, in order to better amalgamate students' in-class and extracurricular activities (Hawkes et al., 2002; Songer et al., 2002); and (3) studies that concentrate on ministerial initiatives and programs designed to promote the use of technology by teachers in rural areas (Howley et al., 2011; Mangione & Calzone, 2019).

Digital Divide Concerns in Rural Schools

In relation to the current frameworks on the digital divide, the one suggested by Hohlfeld et al. (2008) emphasized the primary objectives of equipping schools with computer hardware and ensuring the availability of technology. This issue is especially acute for rural schools compared to their urban counterparts. Despite the vast number of online resources available for instruction today, peripheral regions continue to grapple with bandwidth constraints (Page & Hill, 2008), which hinders genuine technological integration in the pedagogical decisions of rural schools. This not only restricts the implementation of distance learning methods such as video conferencing or streaming video, but sometimes even basic web applications are limited (Hannum et al., 2009). However, the digital divide doesn't only concern the presence of technologies in the classroom but also the capacity of small schools to effectively manage both the digital equipment and infrastructures, as mentioned by Wang (2013). Even when rural schools are tasked with bridging the digital divide, they often lack the necessary facilities, ICT skills, and knowledge to incorporate technology into classrooms. While urban schools have a dedicated staff to handle maintenance and resolve technical issues, rural small schools often lack a technical support service (Hawkes et al., 2002; Howley & Howley, 2008). The global digital divide among schools became starkly apparent in March 2020 when the pandemic led to widespread school closures. Many countries turned to online schooling, posing a significant risk of exclusion for those lacking internet connectivity or digital devices (Ferraro et al., 2020; Kaden, 2020).

While some schools were already equipped with online platforms and accustomed to using them, others had to resort to emailing materials to students (Füller & Spiewak, 2020). The lockdown underscored the critical need to bridge digital inequalities within and beyond schools. Some small schools resist adopting technology in educational activities, while others embrace and promote it (Howley et al., 2011; Kormos, 2018). These observations are also backed by several disciplinary studies. For instance, the research presented by Thomas and Falls (2019) underlines that rural schools encounter unique contextual challenges in relation to STEM teaching and technology integration (Mangione, 2023). Unlike urban districts, rural schools rarely employ instructional coaches, professional development coordinators, or other administrators to assist teachers with STEM content (Mangione, 2023; Seltzer & Himley, 1995).

Bottom-Up Initiatives for the Integration of Digital Technology in Education

While access to a suitable and well-maintained technological infrastructure is a factor that can potentially influence teaching innovation in rural schools, other less tangible factors also play a significant role. Examples of this include the opportunity to guide teachers towards developing awareness and the ability to adapt technology to meet specific pedagogical needs and create educational pathways that connect school and everyday life (Songer et al., 2002; Wang, 2013). Regarding digital knowledge and skills, several studies have noted that students often perceive their teachers as "out of touch," thus observing a disconnect between school and out-of-school environments. "If the teacher is not comfortable using it [technology], then the kids won't use it either" (Cullen et al., 2004, p. 139).

Some studies highlighted that one of the main issues is the working time required to plan the integration of technology into educational activities (Francom, 2016). To foster more positive attitudes and beliefs about technology integration (Howley et al., 2011), some authors advocate for the presence of tutors to oversee activities, the creation of sharing environments such as professional learning communities (Kormos, 2018), and situated professional development and mentoring (Kopcha, 2012; Rossi et al., 2023; Wright & Wilson, 2011) for digital innovation.

Top-Down Measures for the Integration of Digital Technology in Education

Not all rural settings are resistant to the incorporation of technology in educational activities. At times, school communities are open to or even promote the use of digital methodologies (Howley et al., 2011; Kormos, 2018). In such instances, efforts to enhance the integration of technology into teachers' educational practice necessitate leveraging ministerial programs. Generally, ministerial programs aim to either acquire technology or utilize it (Howley et al., 2011). In the U.S., federal and state technology grants are provided to rural schools to enhance technology access. Park et al. (2007) noted that government initiatives provide some advantages to rural schools but necessitate them to independently handle hardware and software procurement and teacher training. There are numerous networks of schools, often supported by the Ministries of Education or Education Research Centres, which at an international level support processes of professional growth and improvement of the training offer. In Europe, it is possible to identify networks of schools established to overcome problems of remoteness and isolation (e.g., the e-Island system in Croatia), (mono) thematic networks such as those present in Hungary (Eco school, Talent Point), or even generalist networks created to respond to political challenges related to improvement and innovation such as the Basic School Network (Oktatási Hivatal Bázisintézménye) in Hungary, or the MakerSpace Network of the Czech Republic (Rossi et al., 2023).

In Italy, the National Network of Small Italian Schools, established in 2017 by INDIRE, serves as a qualified observation point to intercept and select new ideas and proposals for rural schools (Mangione et al., 2017; Mangione & Calzone, 2019). The National Network of Small Italian Schools, the result of a research idea serving educational fragility in real contexts (Jones-Devitt et al., 2017), takes as central the concrete problems of the small school (Cannella & Mangione, 2021; Mangione & Cannella, 2018), creating a partnership based on the exchange of knowledge, resources, and skills, and facilitating the diffusion and appropriation of pedagogical innovations (Mangione, 2024).

The service research guided the drafting of a Manifesto in which the principles, or "innovation trajectories," are indicated for the small schools in which over 500 Comprehensive Institutes, 4,000 small buildings, 38,807 teachers, and 275,687 students look to the Network as the place to recognize themselves and take part in "learning networking" processes and collaborative research (Cannella & Belardinelli, 2020; Mortari, 2010).

If on the one hand the Internet leads us to reflect on the conditions of potential advantage that small schools present in order to be able to transform, also through the pedagogical use of communication and information technologies, educational environments into places of inclusion, collaboration, and educational innovation, on the other hand, it highlights the importance of digital technologies for schools that find themselves in conditions of geographical isolation, allowing the enrichment, opening, and extension of the classroom and the creation of common teaching units through their own organizational forms of shared teaching. By allowing the detection of educational inclusion processes and at the same time creating added value in the context of national and international research dealing with teaching in remote situations, the Italian Network supports digital flourishing in education.

The next sections, through a diachronic reading from pre-pandemic to post-pandemic, present different digital school scenarios supported by the National Network of Small Italian Schools. The need to help schools face the challenges associated with isolation and access to digital resources has allowed the identification of different cases over the years for the enrichment, opening, and extension of the classroom (Mangione & Cannella, 2021), where technology facilitates the possibility of rethinking educational and training experiences by proposing indications for rethinking the organizational management of the widespread and digitally integrated learning environment.

Digital Technologies in Italian Smart Small Schools

The National Network of Small Schools supports school governance in exploring educational models that differ from the dominant paradigm (Maulini & Perrenoud, 2005) and in adopting new tools that promote broader and more participatory educational experiences. It encourages social alliances aimed at involving entire communities in addressing situations of hardship and inequality and advocates for schools as expansive learning systems (De Bartolomeis, 2018), where time, space, and relationships are reimagined.

In this vision of a democratic, community-oriented education system that serves both the territory and its people, digital technology plays a crucial role. Digital platforms can become educational hubs, creating a pervasive presence that can reach those who have greater difficulty accessing educational opportunities. From this perspective, digital ecosystems serve as infrastructure for active citizenship. The need to assist schools in addressing challenges related to isolation and access to digital resources has led to the identification, over the years, of models and practices for enriching, opening up, and extending the classroom (Mangione & Cannella, 2021). Here, technology facilitates the possibility to rethink educational and training experiences, providing insights for rethinking the organizational management of the digitally integrated learning environment. The experiences supported by the Small Schools Network help rethink digital technology as an educational hub for connection—a space of widespread presence capable of reaching those with the most difficulty accessing educational opportunities.

Through service research aimed at addressing educational vulnerabilities in real-world contexts (Jones-Devitt et al., 2017), grounded in a phenomenological approach, it becomes feasible to illustrate, through the analysis of "exemplary" cases, a transformative use of technology that redefines schooling beyond the conventional paradigm.

The case narrative methodology is rooted in a systematic and rigorous approach to documenting, analyzing, and presenting the experiences lived by participants. This methodology is designed to ensure that the cases studied not only tell individual stories but also contribute to the scientific understanding of the phenomenon. Cases were selected based on their representativeness and relevance to the research objectives, employing an intentional sampling process aimed at encompassing a variety of contexts and experiences related to technology integration in small schools. This process ensures that the analyzed cases provide a comprehensive and diversified view of the challenges and opportunities encountered.

Each case is presented in a narrative format that includes context, processes, and outcomes. This structured approach not only captures the nuances of each experience but also facilitates a deeper exploration of how technology is applied, adapted, and perceived within educational settings. By detailing the contextual factors influencing technological integration and highlighting both successful strategies and obstacles, this methodology supports a robust scientific inquiry into the complexities of digital integration in small school environments.

Digital Technologies in Italian Smart Small Schools: Before the Pandemic Era

Before the pandemic era, the Small and Rural School Italian Network intervened to support digital collaboration between schools and territory capable of giving back to the community an idea of a "fair and quality school" that avoids a condition of fragility and the risk of closure (Mangione & Cannella, 2020).

Territorial Alliances for the Continuity of the Small School With Digital: The Case of the Aeolian Islands

The geo-environmental complexity of the School on the Aeolian Islands (6 islands, 14 schools, from childhood to middle school, 4 Municipalities), the fragmentation and dissemination of the school buildings require an organizational effort and an extraordinary commitment in the coordination of the forces in the field.

The educational alliance between the school IC Aeolian Islands and the "AttivaStromboli" Associations guarantees the multimedia educational laboratory through which the school is also able to cope with all the inconveniences caused by adverse weather and sea conditions in the winter months. When the hydrofoils do not travel, it is sufficient for a single teacher to remain on the island and bring the classes to the Laboratory, connecting remotely with all the middle school teachers who teach the lessons from home. For primary school, the weekly presence of teachers is more stable and remote connection is required with teachers who travel (see Figure 1).

Figure 1. Multimedia teaching lab form small schools

The association provided daily support (remotely) to less experienced teachers, pupils, and families, also taking care of the delivery of computers to those who did not have them, coordinating digital work, thus ensuring recovery even in fragile social and economic situations (Mangione & Cannella, 2020).

Territorial Alliances for a School as a Digital Civic Center: The Case of the Bibloh Network

The widespread library is configured as a digital school library which was born precisely from the desire to offer, first to students and then to the inhabitants of the inner area, significant and fundamental training opportunities for the personal and cultural development of each one.

"Bibloh! under the bridge," an initiative of Bobbio small school, is part of the national Bibloh! network, responsible for promoting reading for the entire community, especially in those hamlets scattered across the valley, which do not have adequate infrastructure for cultural development.

The school I.O. of Bobbio, through a digital library, allows students to read books that can be downloaded for free and teachers to use the newsstand part during synchronous lessons, and to take advantage of in-depth texts (see Figure 2). A hybrid space that guarantees continuity of the processes of communication, reflection, comparison, and individual and collaborative production.

Figure 2. Virtual library for small schools

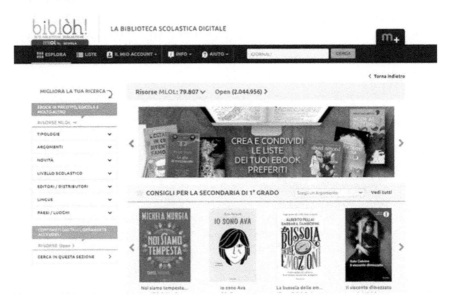

The community actively participates in the maintenance of the library also through crowdfunding actions aimed at increasing the book heritage of the school library. The open library speaks to the territory and will be able to promote cinema, music, and theater, becoming the "cultural center" open to the entire community.

Territorial Alliances for the Valorization of Museum Heritage in the Digital Curriculum

The school-museum relationship and, in our specific research interest, the relationship between small schools and small museums represent a key point in the relaunch of the school which can identify a turning point in the capacity for common work between institutions, overcoming the logic of specialisms, as part of a partnership that makes the museum one of the many learning contexts that can be enjoyed by local schools. Even before the pandemic era, virtuous experiences, a local curriculum that is truly significant, also from the perspective of a traditionally disciplinary curriculum.

The National Network of Small Schools in collaboration with the National Association of Small Museums offers small schools the possibility of building and co-designing, together with small museums located throughout the national territory, educational experiences that meet the rethinking of the curriculum on themes and areas that allow the school to autonomously build the local curriculum, supporting learning about reality that enhances it while respecting territorial vocations (see Figure 3).

Figure 3. Museum environment designed for immersive teaching sessions

The small schools come into contact with a small museum in their region and establish an educational alliance with it to strengthen their training and teaching offer from a planning perspective participated and shared.

Digital Technologies in Italian Smart Small Schools: During the Pandemic Era

Immediately after the closure of schools, the Italian Ministry of Education issued guidelines to regulate distance learning to prevent the isolation of students and to foster a sense of "community," as well as to avoid a long interruption of the learning process (Mangione et al., 2022). INDIRE has made use of the experience of accompanying schools along processes of change and innovation gained over the years and has designed activities and services aimed at teachers, students, and families, focused on the value of the National Network as a system of mentoring different forms of distance education.

Forms of Networking for Teacher Training in Remote Areas

The National Network of Small Schools experiments, adhering to and supporting the Network of Solidarity between Schools ("La scuola per la scuola"), supports, during the pandemic era, a systemic approach to training support and improvement of performance in the use of didactic methodologies and new technologies in distance learning (DAD). The training model experimented recalls the so-called MOOC-Eds (Massive Open Online Course for Educators) (Clark, 2014; Kleiman et al., 2015) widely used in the United States for teacher and educator training. Not simply courses but sharing experiences of professional development that involve participants in implementing new teaching opportunities enabled by technology. The MOOC-Eds experiences have followed one another over time giving rise to numerous initiatives (from "Dove sta di casa la scuola?" to "La scuola allo schermo") including basic resources and supplementary materials on a specific topic, also allowing great customization and flexibility. (see Figure 4).

Figure 4. Resource collection space provided by INDIRE's innovation networks for Italian schools

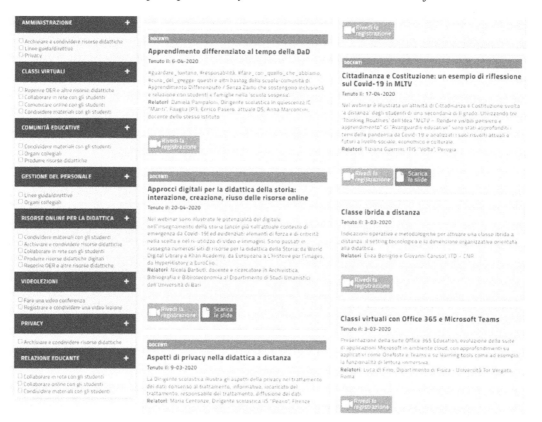

Within the national network, over 20,000 teachers and school principals have been involved in webinars and have experimented with alternative forms of distance education for small schools. Through these initiatives, the National Network of Small Schools aims to empower educators with innovative pedagogical strategies and technological tools, fostering resilience and adaptability in response to the educational challenges posed by the pandemic. By promoting collaborative learning and the exchange of best practices, these programs contribute to a vibrant professional community committed to advancing educational excellence amidst evolving circumstances.

The Home as a Decentralized Classroom for Low Digital Intensity Experiences

During the pandemic era, the Italian Ministry of Education issued guidelines to regulate distance learning to prevent the isolation of students and to foster a sense of "community," as well as to avoid a long interruption of the learning process (Mangione et al., 2022). The first concerns then emerged about whether this model of distance teaching could or could not support the quality of the educational experience, especially in territories where small schools complained about a situation of digital disconnection. The difficulties related to a form of distance schooling that was poorly founded from a methodological point of view and inadequate to meet the needs of all students, together with the obstacles related to the living and housing conditions of their families, risked not guaranteeing a school for all (Nuzzacci et al.,

2020). Access to the digital classroom could become an element of educational inequity. A major concern was the level of autonomy required of students by a model of distance education in emergencies based on technology: for the youngest, access and participation were subject to the presence and digital skills of older caregivers such as parents, siblings, or grandparents. Furthermore, technology and, in general, distance learning could represent a strong limit to the development of the social dimension both on the cognitive and affective levels, to the involvement of different learning styles and, more generally, to any form of experiential and embodied learning (Skulmowski et al., 2018).

The National Network of Small Schools is committed to rethinking the "homes" of children as territories to explore, places rich in "educational facts" capable of crossing sciences, mathematics, Italian, history, art. The home becomes a "low digital intensity" classroom that is more inclusive and democratic where it is possible, in the distance, to recover corporeality, the social dimension of learning, emotional and affective aspects, active teaching methods (laboratory, exploration, and environmental research) (Mangione et al., 2020).

"Where is the school at "home"?" was born, a cycle of webinars dedicated to operational proposals to cross disciplines and major educational themes through phenomena and materials that can be encountered in domestic spaces (see Figure 5). The path of a low digital intensity school at home rests on the concept of transformation. What transformation processes can be observed, can be simulated, can be built at home? Through this theme, various disciplines have been crossed (mathematics, philosophy, music, anthropology, sciences, architecture).

Figure 5. Home instruction modalities in small schools

In online meetings, the identified experts have shed light on numerous activities to be done at home, encouraging greater collaboration of families: activities designed to be carried out in all homes because homes can be very different from each other, to be realized with materials that everyone can have available and with simple and "poor" digital technologies, since many families and many territories struggle to work remotely because they do not have adequate tools and connections. The initiative involved 7,700 participants among teachers, managers, and parents who today continue to animate the dedicated social spaces. The home has thus become for many children and their families a learning environment, an "equipped" place that supports the school by promoting meaningful learning, facilitating operational approaches to knowledge concerning sciences, technology, community languages, music production, theater, pictorial activities, motor skills competences, promoting learning through exploration and discovery.

Devices for Accessing Third Cultural Spaces

The vision of proximity school and the pedagogy of reconciliation supported by the National Network of Small Schools have also given a new boost to heritage pedagogy: cultural spaces, understood as third educational spaces (Mangione et al., 2022; Mangione & De Santis, 2021). In 2021, the National Network of Small Schools proposed a digital proximity school where the audiovisual becomes a transversal language across the various disciplines for active and laboratory-based teaching of atypical sources, films, and documentaries.

The "School on the Screen" project (see Figure 6) presents itself as an inventory made up of over 150 audiovisual materials, divided according to the themes of the 2030 Agenda, audiovisual resources aimed at teachers, school managers, those who study, do research or train in the educational contexts specific to small schools and, more broadly, to anyone in the world of education who wants to delve deeper into social, cultural, and economic issues through audiovisual sources.

Figure 6. Home page di accesso a Piccole scuole - La scuola allo schermo

Films, which are characterized by being one of the most inclusive languages, represent a technology capable of connecting different cultures, to interact with a group of classmates and with the whole class, to discover others and overcome those distances that are not only physical but also cultural ones of the small groups (Mangione & Cannella, 2021). Today, the Network promotes the collection of educational experiences through the resources made available by Scuola alla Screen. The objective of the documentation of the experiences is to share the results of the work carried out with the online inventory but to propose new suggestions for the use of the resources, with the possibility of seeing them published and valorized, becoming an opportunity for comparison and a point of reference for all those who want to be inspired by these activities and propose them in their own teaching practice. The wealth of knowledge made available by the teachers will be a fundamental component of the initiative which thus becomes a window onto a living, collective, constantly updated storytelling thanks to which it will be possible to see, over the years, how the use of cinema as a virtual space capable of strengthening the identity of educational realities in peripheral territories has changed. By distancing itself from an "urban" perspective, digital allows us to reinterpret the most isolated territories and represents an important hub for the school system. In 2022, the initiative, to which a social group participated by around 2000 teachers and school leaders, became part of the European Film Factory network, the European film education platform supported by the MEDIA sub-program of Creative Europe.

Networked Classrooms

"Classi in Rete" (see Figure 7) was born from the study of the École en Réseau model experimented in Québec since 2001 to rethink teaching in small and isolated schools (Mangione, 2022; Pieri, 2022). In the 2020-2021, during and post-pandemic year, INDIRE started the pilot experimentation in small Italian schools to overcome the educational limits that occur in situations of remoteness and to offer an innovative path capable of contrasting the judgment that students and families give to the service "education" as well as on daily pedagogical practices.

Figure 7. "Classi in Rete" experience

The experiences of designing shared teaching practice and working for "delocalized" classes allow to intervene on the definition of new school scenarios, highlighting the changes inherent in the didactic design for "themes" (working in a transdisciplinary and competence-based way), the work for multi-level classes, innovations in the organizational management of the classroom environment and the professional development of teachers in terms of epistemic agency through new technologies (Mangione, 2022).

The classroom context of small schools today presents itself, through forms of online classes and twinning on themes or projects, more inclusive of digital technologies in which the workspace is divided into a continuum that goes from the physical to the virtual (Cannella & Chipa, 2016; Cinnamon, 2017; Mangione, 2023). The Classi in Rete experiences are now offered in different Italian territories where small and isolated schools are located, and the collaboration between the INDIRE and the Québec research group encourages dialogue between the schools of the two networks. The Italia Small and Rural Schools Network supports numerous webinar series to share the model and practices and take part annually in the "Colloque de l'École en réseau," an annual event that represents a very important opportunity to take a look at good practices, project proposals, and international experiences that can enrich the research and training path in small schools.

Digital Technologies in Italian Smart Small Schools: After the Pandemic Era

After the pandemic era, the National Network of Small Schools of INDIRE supports school governance in intercepting alternative school forms to the dominant model (Maulini & Perrenoud, 2005) and consolidates an idea of a widespread proximity school, makes the whole community responsible for the educational project (Cannella & Mangione, 2021). Digital technology, in this vision of a democratic, proximity school at the service of an education to the territory and with the territory, plays a fundamental role.

Forms of Digital Networking for Teacher Training in Remote Areas

Closing ICT skills gaps among teachers in rural areas requires special attention to their professional development. The networking dimension, also analyzed through mentoring practices between rural schools (Chapman & Fullan, 2007; Fazekas & Burns, 2012; Muijs et al., 2010, 2011), can strengthen actions that follow multiple mentoring approaches (top-down, bottom-up, mixed-method) and professional growth (EU, 2021). In 2021, the European School Network (EUN), with the collaboration of numerous education and European ministries (Belgium-Flanders, Croatia, Czech Republic, Hungary, Italy, Portugal) and INDIRE, promoted the creation of a project, "Mentoring for School Improvement (MenSI)," financed by international competitive research funds, in order to experiment with forms of mentoring networking capable of improving the use of ICT in schools. A total of 120 schools, 20 for each country, organized into 4 clusters made up of 1 mentor and 4 mentees (see Figure 8).

Figure 8. The schools involved and the actions supporting the clusters

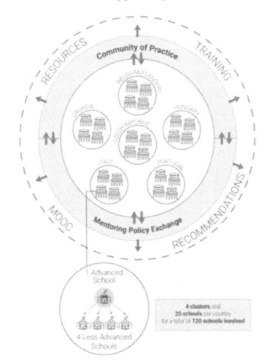

INDIRE took part in the project by involving the schools of the two generalist national networks, creating 4 clusters (2 clusters of Small Schools and 2 clusters of avant-garde education) on specific territories (Emilia-Romagna, Sicily, Campania, and Puglia) and on themes recorded and whose expertise was recognized at the mentor school (Cannella & Laghigna, 2023; Rossi et al., 2023). Each mentor school, in collaboration with the research group, has created its own Continuous Professional Development Toolkit, making resources and skills available in order to offer mentee schools a variety of training opportunities (workshops, pedagogical ateliers, moments of visiting).

During the two years of work, through the involvement of 22 schools, over 150 teachers, and 22 school principals, it was possible to understand the mentoring models implemented by the clusters and to highlight their strengths and weaknesses, and to return in this scientific contribution the enabling factors of the mentoring approach perceived by the clusters of small schools involved. Clusters have adopted the principle of resource exchange. Nothing was "private" or ring-fenced for the benefit of a single school. All participants in the cluster could "take-away" access and use Tookits and ICT solutions made available by the mentor school for their teaching (Mangione et al., 2024). The advantages were obtained in particular for schools located in the most isolated rural locations, even in those territories where the economic slowdown leads to a reduction in funds for the renewal or renewal of ICT (Kurelovic, 2016). By fostering collaborative networks and sharing resources, mentoring within these clusters not only enhanced ICT competencies but also promoted a culture of collective support and innovation among educators in challenging educational environments.

Hybrid Environments for Non-Standard Teaching Situations

Today, a disconnected school, both geographically and in terms of digital connectivity, sees technology as a tool through which to "build or rebuild bonds" (Rivoltella, 2021, p. 61). Non-standard educational situations (SDiNS), such as those found in rural and peripheral contexts, are particularly suited to harnessing the potential of digital technologies to foster inclusive, collaborative, and personalized educational processes. In this context, technology can serve as a tool to build or strengthen connections among members of the educational community (Rivoltella, 2020). The analysis of literature and the national overview of small schools (Mangione et al., 2021) have identified several territorial clusters to which the dBook can be proposed—a tool aimed at overcoming some of the educational challenges related to poor connectivity. These challenges are often raised by teachers and administrators operating in geographically isolated contexts (Garzia & Bassani, 2023).

The little device, developed internally at INDIRE and accepted by an experimental pool of small and peripherally located schools, allows access to a repertoire of tools to be used to build teaching scenarios that respond to an idea of fair and democratic education even in situations of digital divide.

Figure 9. dBook device

In 2022, the dBook was tested in 4 peripheral schools located in the regions of Campania and Tuscany. The teachers included the dBook in the teaching planning of 4 primary school classes for a total of 78 students. The analyzes through multiple case studies allow us to detect an improvement in the educational field, with attention to teaching intentionality and the impact on learning processes (Mangione & Garzia, 2024). The online environment dedicated to experimental schools allows you to upload and download research products and tools as well as encouraging communication between schools that feed a national dBook Community.

Digital for an Educational Milieu Made of Witnesses

Small schools persist in territories at risk of multifactorial early exclusion and educational poverty. It is necessary to start again from what Massa calls the educational milieu, that is, that educational atmosphere characterizing a community that educates (Massa, 2000). If, as well expressed by Rivoltella

(2023), the crisis is of the contexts of experience, and in particular "in the eclipse of the testimony," it is necessary to reevaluate the profile of the witnesses and extend the educational contract to those figures expressing an inclination to reciprocity. Recovering an educational milieu means for small schools today to favor the dialogue between the actors able to guarantee an alliance between school and territory, an educational pluralism, and a targeted coordination (Mangione & Calzone, 2022; Scurati, 2017) of multiple subjects responsible in a social type of educational contract (Cannella & Mangione, 2023). Digital can allow to expand the concept of milieu and to make proximal to the school a network of subjects who commit to intervene in a participatory manner in the educational offer (Bellomi & Mangione, 2023) and to take charge of the "community gifts" by supporting teachers in the recovery of learning and in didactic differentiation. The absence of associations or cultural spaces, as well as a lack of alliance with the local administration, can put a vision characterized by the value of testimony and shared responsibility in crisis. In 2022, the National Network of Small Schools joined the "Volunteers for Education" project and collaborated with Save The Children to support continuity and quality of teaching in small schools, thanks to interprofessionalism (Cannella & Mangione, 2023) that takes root from the collaboration of teachers with university students who decide to accompany the school in recovery actions and strengthening of fragile students through online tutoring, individual and group (see Figure 10).

Figure 10. Home page di accesso a Piccole Scuole - Volontari per l'educazione

University students from all over Italy become part of an important intervention to support situations of fragility and strengthen the bond between school, family, and territory. The support is provided in extra-curricular hours and is not comparable or to be considered an alternative to school obligation but integrative and aimed at supporting moments of differentiation and recovery individually or in small groups. Digital can therefore support and guarantee collaboration between teachers, families, and educators at the base of an open, inclusive and widespread school, capable of feeding on territorial educational alliances, to expand services and the curriculum.

There are many small schools that, through adherence to the "National Movement of Small Schools," access Volunteers for Education, and make extended educational alliances the opportunity to promote a new responsibility of the "witnesses," a form of community engagement to address fragility and social and educational inequalities (Bartolini et al., 2022). In the 2022-2023 school year, the small schools adhering to Volunteers for Education were 48 (belonging to 12 Institutes) and the collaboration led to the support of 80 students. Study aids take place thanks to the help of volunteers, mostly university students, from all over Italy. The small schools, involved in numerous informative and informative webinars, have the opportunity to learn about the project through the voices of peers and to request the activation of support for their students during the school year, in preparation for the middle school exam and during the summer period. During the webinars promoted by the National Network, the "teachers and witnesses" reported their experience by comparing themselves on the key themes of the project: the differences related to the tutoring activated in winter and spring-summer and the different thematic focuses deepened, the involvement of teachers and the relationship with educators and volunteers, the way of managing the platform, the specific situations that involved foreign minors and with disabilities and more generally how, the potential of the project and the digital setting, have been supportive in the school path.

Artificial Intelligence and Future of Italian Smart Small Schools

The recent scientific debate on artificial intelligence (AI) has pushed the INDIRE research group to delve into its main areas of application in the rural educational context, for example, understanding if and how in a non-standard educational context such as that of small schools it is possible to imagine uses of AI aimed at supporting social and cultural inclusion, improving teaching practices, and ensuring educational continuity even in cases of isolation or absence of teachers (Mangione et al., 2023). To investigate the potential application of AI in the context of small and rural schools, a preliminary exploratory study was carried out through a scoping review (Mangione et al., 2024). The main research question addressed was, "What does the international literature reveal about AI and rural education?" with a secondary question focusing on "What are the key areas of AI application in rural educational settings?".

The analysis led to categorization based on common themes of investigation:

- AI to enhance teaching and learning processes and bridge the urban-rural educational gap: This category explores how AI can be leveraged to improve instructional practices, personalize learning experiences, and mitigate disparities between urban and rural schools through innovative technological interventions.
- AI for the professional development of educators: This category focuses on the use of AI to support ongoing professional growth among teachers in rural settings. It includes applications such as AI-powered training modules, personalized learning pathways for educators, and tools for enhancing instructional strategies.
- AI to develop predictive models concerning students' interests and academic achievements: This category examines AI applications that analyze data to predict student preferences, academic performance trends, and potential learning difficulties. It aims to provide early interventions and personalized support strategies to enhance educational outcomes.

- AI for service management and prediction of risks: This category explores how AI technologies can optimize administrative tasks, streamline resource allocation, and predict potential risks or challenges within educational institutions. It encompasses applications like AI-driven management systems, predictive analytics for resource allocation, and risk assessment tools.

These categories provide a structured approach to understanding the diverse applications of AI in rural educational contexts, emphasizing their potential to address specific challenges and enhance educational practices through innovative technological solutions.

This initial scoping review provides a preliminary overview of the literature on AI and "education in rural areas," identifying some predominant themes that can be analyzed across two broad macro-areas where AI can be framed in educational settings: AI as a "content" for teaching and AI as a "tool" to support teaching and learning.

AI as "content" pertains to the necessity of cultivating knowledge and competencies associated with the operation of artificial intelligence to utilize it proficiently and discern potential misuse (OECD, 2018). This entails the need for educational institutions to revamp their curricula to incorporate AI learning. This aspect carries particular significance in rural educational settings to forestall the widening gap with urban counterparts. The importance of implementing standardized curricula integrating AI into compulsory education in both urban and rural contexts becomes apparent in this context. To effectively narrow the rural-urban divide, it is imperative to appropriately tailor AI curricula, encompassing teacher training initiatives and access to suitable technological infrastructure, while acknowledging the influence of geographic context and available resources. The studies reviewed on this subject are geographically situated in China and the USA, where the integration of AI into K12 curricula is already partially developed and implemented (UNESCO, 2022). While their experiences offer valuable insights, it is crucial to consider the specificities of each national context to adeptly and equitably adapt AI integration strategies.

AI as a "tool" represents another significant theme wherein the contributions identified in the review can be categorized. This encompasses AI applications aimed at enriching and refining the teaching-learning process through intelligent tutoring systems (ITS), dialogue-based tutoring systems (DBTS), and exploratory learning environments. These systems can aid in addressing specific challenges prevalent in rural settings, such as assisting educators in crafting educational activities, tailoring student experiences, and refining assessment procedures, often complicated by teacher shortages typical of these environments. Furthermore, AI solutions can assist students in selecting schools based on their aptitudes and needs, supporting families lacking the cultural resources to guide their children. The deployment of online platforms grounded in intelligent systems can also facilitate collaboration among urban and rural educators, bolster school networking, and facilitate teacher training and mentoring.

While the review offers insights into emerging trends and suggests potential avenues for research among scholars and practitioners, particularly within the European context, it is imperative to acknowledge certain limitations. In light of the literature analysis, it was decided to broaden the inquiry in accordance with Arksey and O'Malley's (2005) delineation of the sixth and final optional phase of a scoping review: engaging stakeholders to furnish additional information sources, perspectives, meanings, and applicability (Ghirotto, 2020).

Planned participatory interviews with national and international experts aim to discern opportunities for small schools and elucidate the challenges shaping future educational research endeavors. These experts, selected for their proficiency in small school contexts, will be tasked with addressing key questions emanating from the scoping review. The aim is to identify prospects for small schools and delineate hurdles that could inform forthcoming educational research endeavors. Subsequently, to distill insights gleaned from the research, experts will be engaged in a Delphi study (Green, 2014). This iterative approach aims to establish consensus on focal areas for AI intervention in non-traditional educational settings.

By subsequently aligning key questions with themes identified in the scoping review and challenges highlighted in the Delphi study, it will be possible to design a confirmatory study encompassing a broader participant cohort. A survey questionnaire will be developed and disseminated among all teachers and administrators affiliated with the National Network of Small Schools. The survey seeks to validate key themes and interventions facilitated by AI in small schools, while simultaneously identifying additional areas of interest, capturing preliminary implementation scenarios, or detecting nascent AI-based practices (Miller, 2018).

CONCLUSION

Improving access to digital resources and promoting inclusion and educational equity in small rural schools requires a multifaceted approach. By focusing on teacher training, effective implementation of digital technologies, optimizing existing resources, and advocating for supportive policies, it is possible to create an equitable and inclusive educational environment. These strategies not only enhance the quality of education but also ensure that all students, regardless of their geographic location, have the opportunity to succeed in a digital age.

Today the United Nations Educational, Scientific and Cultural Organization (UNESCO) itself calls for a prudential attitude by underlining that technology can integrate, enrich, and extend school education but not replace it, distancing itself from an absolutist idea of ed-tech capable of drastically improving educational opportunities and results.

The socio-technological approach underpinning the research on a digitally integrated school (Fishman & Dede, 2018) reconsiders the artifact as connected with the educational and social context in which it is embedded (Rossi, 2019). Research conducted over the years by INDIRE (Cannella et al., 2021; Mangione & Cannella, 2020; Mangione et al., 2023) and more recent international analyses (Fargas-Malet & Bagley, 2023) highlight how non-standard educational settings, such as small schools, can particularly benefit from technological solutions.

The Network of Small Schools has launched numerous initiatives, still ongoing, that place digital technology in an idea of militant education (Tomarchi & Ulivieri, 2015) that has not limited its transformative process during times of urgency and emergency such as the pandemic, but still pushes today to question the school as a common good (Locatelli, 2022) and rethinks the role of digital technology in order to guarantee a school of opportunities.

The case narrative methodology employed in this study offers a detailed and contextualized understanding of the dynamics of technological integration in small schools. This approach not only enhances the scientific understanding of the phenomenon but also makes the findings more accessible and relevant to educational professionals. The documented experiences provide valuable insights for developing effective and sustainable support strategies, promoting optimal use of technology to benefit all stakeholders involved. These documented and analyzed experiences provide a wealth of knowledge that can guide the formulation of policies aimed at reducing the digital divide and improving the quality of education in small schools. By capturing nuanced details and practical challenges faced in integrating technology, this methodology supports informed decision-making and fosters a more inclusive educational environment tailored to diverse learning needs and contexts.

Acknowledgments

The author thanks all the schools actively participating in the INDIRE National Network of Small Schools, as well as the entire research team whose efforts over the years have made possible the numerous experiences and case studies narrated in this chapter, fostering innovation and quality in Italian small schools.

REFERENCES

Alpe, Y., & Fauguet, J. L. (2008). Enseigner dans le rural: un «métier» à part?. *Travail et formation en éducation*, 2.

Azano, A. P., Downey, J., & Brenner, D. (2019). Preparing pre-service teachers for rural schools. In *Oxford Research Encyclopedia of Education*. Oxford Press. 10.1093/acrefore/9780190264093.013.274

Azano, A. P., & Stewart, T. T. (2016). Confronting challenges at the intersection of rurality, place, and teacher preparation: Improving efforts in teacher education to staff rural schools. *Global Education Review*, 3(1), 108–128.

Barley, Z. A., & Brigham, N. (2008). Preparing teachers to teach in rural schools. *Issues & Answers Report, REL 2008*. https://ies.ed.gov/ncee/edlabs/regions/central/pdf/REL_2008055_sum.pdf

Bartolini, R., Mangione, G. R. J., De Santis, F., & Tancredi, A. (2021). Piccole scuole e territorio: un'indagine sulla relazione scuola-comune per un progetto formativo allargato. *Scienze del Territorio*, 9, 155-167. https://doi.org/10.13128/sdt-12319

Benigno, V., Fante, C., & Caruso, G. (2021). Approcci, azioni e tecnologie a supporto della classe ibrida inclusiva. *Italian Journal of Educational Technology*, 29(1), 5–25. 10.17471/2499-4324/1182

Bray, M. (1992). Educational planning in small countries. *University of Hong Kong*. https://unesdoc.unesco.org/ark:/48223/pf0000091713

Cannella, G., & Belardinelli, M. (2020). L'importanza delle reti per l'innovazione didattica nelle Piccole Scuole. In Mangione, G. R. J., Cannella, G., Parigi, L., & Bartolini, R. (Eds.), *Comunità di memoria, comunità di futuro. Il valore della piccola scuola* (pp. xx–xx). Carocci.

Cannella, G., & Mangione, G. R. J. (2020). I processi di internazionalizzazione delle piccole scuole come strumenti per l'innovazione didattica e organizzativa. *Formazione & Insegnamento*, 18(1), 128–144. 10.32029/978889002318

Cannella, G., & Mangione, G. R. J. (Eds.). (2021). *A scuola nelle piccole scuole: Storia, metodi, dinamiche*. Morcelliana Scholè.

Cannella, G., & Mangione, G. R. J. (2023). L'interprofessionalità nel contratto educativo sociale. *Essere a Scuola*, 8, 9–14. 10.17471/2499-4324/1322

Carenzio, A., & Ferrari, S. (2021). Situazioni didattiche non standard. In Rivoltella, P. C. (Ed.), *Apprendere a distanza. Teorie e metodi* (pp. xx–xx). Raffaello Cortina Editore.

Chapman, C., & Fullan, M. (2007). Collaboration and partnership for equitable improvement: Towards a networked learning system? *School Leadership & Management*, 27(3), 207–211. 10.1080/13632430701379354

Coppola, A., Del Fabbro, M., Lanzani, A. S., & Pessina, G. (2021). *Ricomporre i divari. Politiche e progetti territoriali contro le disuguaglianze e per la transizione ecologica*. Il Mulino.

Corbett, M., & White, S. (2014). Introduction: Why put the 'rural' in research? In Corbett, M., & White, S. (Eds.), *Doing educational research in rural settings* (pp. 19–22). Routledge. 10.4324/9781315769387

Cornish, L. (2006). Parents' views of composite classes in an Australian primary school. *Australian Educational Researcher*, 33(2), 123–142. 10.1007/BF03216837

Couture, C., Monney, N., Thériault, P., Allaire, S., & Doucet, M. (2013). Enseigner en classe multiâge: Besoins di sviluppo professionale di insegnanti del primario. *Canadian Journal of Education*, 36(3), 108.

Cullen, T., Frey, T., Hinshaw, R., & Warren, S. (2004). Technology grants and rural schools: The power to transform. *Association for Educational Communications and Technology*. https://eric.ed.gov/?id=ED485134

De Bartolomeis, F. (2018). *Fare scuola fuori della scuola*. Aracne Editrice.

Du Plessis, D., & Bailey, J. (2000). Isolated parents' perceptions of the education of their children. *Education in Rural Australia*, 10(2), 1–26. 10.47381/aijre.v10i2.453

Edwards, A. (2009). Relational agency in collaborations for the well-being of children and young people. *Journal of Children's Services*, 4(1), 33–43. 10.1108/17466660200900004

European Commission. Directorate-General for Education, Youth, Sport and Culture, Melstveit Roseme, M., Day, L., & Fellows, T. (2021). *Enhancing learning through digital tools and practices: How digital technology in compulsory education can help promote inclusion: Final report: October 2021*. Publications Office. https://doi.org/doi/10.2766/365846

Fargas Malet, M., & Bagley, C. (2023). Conceptualising small rural school-community relationships within a divided society: People, meanings, practices and spaces. *Oxford Review of Education*, 1–18. 10.1080/03054985.2023.2262383

Fazekas, M., & Burns, T. (2012). *Exploring the complex interaction between governance and knowledge in education*. Paper for the CERI Governing Complex Education Systems Project Launch Meeting, Oslo. 10.1787/19939019

Ferraro, F. V., Ambra, F. I., Aruta, L., & Iavarone, M. L. (2020). Distance learning in the Covid-19 era: Perceptions in Southern Italy. *Education Sciences*, 10(12), 355. 10.3390/educsci10120355

Francom, G. M. (2016). Barriers to technology use in large and small school districts. *Journal of Information Technology Education*, 15(1), 577–591. 10.28945/3596

Giorgi, P., & Zoppi, I. (2021). *La ricerca Indire tra uso didattico del patrimonio storico culturale e promozione delle buone pratiche*.

Giorgi, P., & Zoppi, I. (2021). *Memorie magistrali: memoria, scuola e territorio*. AIPH.

Giroux, H. (2021). *Pandemic pedagogy: Education in time of crisis*. Bloomsbury. 10.5040/9781350184466

Gjelten, T. (1982). *A typology of rural school settings*. Summary of presentation prepared for the Rural Education Seminar, United States Department of Education, Washington, DC.

Gristy, C., Hargreaves, L., & Kučerová, S. R. (Eds.). (2020). *Educational research and schooling in rural Europe: An engagement with changing patterns of education, space, and place*. Information Age Publishing.

Hannum, W. H., Irvin, M. J., Banks, J. B., & Farmer, T. W. (2009). Distance education use in rural schools. *Journal of Research in Rural Education*, 24(3), 1.

Hannum, W. H., Irvin, M. J., Banks, J. B., & Farmer, T. W. (2009). Distance education use in rural schools. *Journal of Research in Rural Education*, 24(3), 1.

Harris, A., & Spillane, J. (2008). Distributed leadership through the looking glass. *Management in Education*, 22(1), 2–6. 10.1177/0892020607085623

Hawkes, M., Halverson, P., & Brockmueller, B. (2002). Technology facilitation in the rural school: An analysis of options. *Journal of Research in Rural Education*, 17(3), 162–170.

Heeralal, P. J. H. (2014). Preparing pre-service teachers to teach in rural schools. *Mediterranean Journal of Social Sciences*, 5(20), 1795–1800. 10.5901/mjss.2014.v5n20p1795

Hohlfeld, T. N., Ritzhaupt, A. D., Barron, A. E., & Kemker, K. (2008, March). *Socio-economic status and technology integration in Florida schools: A longitudinal study*. Paper presented at the annual meeting of the American Educational Research Association, New York.

Howley, A., & Howley, C. (2008). Planning for technology integration: Is the agenda overrated or underappreciated? *Educational Planning*, 17(1), 1–17.

Howley, A., Wood, L., & Hough, B. (2011). Rural elementary school teachers' technology integration. *Journal of Research in Rural Education*, 29(9), 1–18.

Hyry-Beihammer, E. K., & Hascher, T. (2015). Multi-grade teaching practices in Austrian and Finnish primary schools. *International Journal of Educational Research*, 74, 104–113. 10.1016/j.ijer.2015.07.002

INDIRE. (2018). *Manifesto delle Piccole Scuole (Manifesto for Small Schools)*. INDIRE. https://piccolescuole.indire.it/en/the-movement-what-it-is/the-manifesto/

Isidori, M. V., & Vaccarelli, A. (2013). *Pedagogia dell'emergenza/didattica nell'emergenza*. Franco Angeli.

Johnson, J., & Strange, M. (2007). *Why rural matters 2007: The realities of rural education growth*. Rural School and Community Trust. https://files.eric.ed.gov/fulltext/ED498859.pdf

Jones-Devitt, S., Austen, L., & Parkin, H. (2017). Integrative reviewing for exploring complex phenomena. *Social Research Update*, 66.

Kale, U., & Goh, D. (2014). Teaching style, ICT experience and teachers' attitudes toward teaching with web 2.0. *Education and Information Technologies*, 19(1), 41–60. 10.1007/s10639-012-9210-3

Kormos, E. M. (2018). The unseen digital divide: Urban, suburban, and rural teacher use and perceptions of web-based classroom technologies. *Computers in the Schools*, 35(1), 19–31. 10.1080/07380569.2018.1429168

Kurelovic, E. (2016). Advantages and limitations of usage of open educational resources in small countries. *International Journal of Research in Education and Science*, 2(1), 136–142. 10.21890/ijres.92299

Laferrière, T., Hamel, C., Allaire, S., Turcotte, S., Breuleux, A., Beaudoin, J., & Gaudreault Perron, J. (2011). *L'école éloignée en réseau, un modèle. Rapport-synthèse*. CEFRIO. 10.1111/j.1756-8765.2011.01109.x

Locatelli, R. (2019). *Reframing education as a public and common good: Enhancing democratic governance*. Palgrave Macmillan. 10.1007/978-3-030-24801-7

Locatelli, R. (2022). La prospettiva dell'educazione come bene comune quale quadro di riferimento per i Patti educativi di comunità. *Civitas educationis. Education. Política y Cultura*, 10(2). Advance online publication. 10.30444/CE.XX.2022

Mangione, G. R., Fante, C., Dalla Mutta, E., & Benigno, V. (2023). Exploring educational practices for non-standard didactic situations in small schools. In Mangione, P. (Ed.), *Handbook of research on establishing digital competencies in the pursuit of online learning* (pp. 50–72). IGI Global. 10.4018/978-1-6684-7010-7.ch004

Mangione, G. R., Garzia, M., & Pettenati, M. C. (2016). Neoassunti nelle piccole scuole. Sviluppo di competenza e professionalità didattica. *Formazione & Insegnamento*, 14(3), 287–306. 10.32029/11218.14.03.20

Mangione, G. R. J. (2023). STEM in small schools. Organizational and teaching practices. *Journal of Education Technologies and Social Studies*, 15(3). Advance online publication. 10.17471/xxxx-xxxx

Mangione, G. R. J. (2024). Una rete per le piccole scuole. Tra cultura dell'educazione e service research. In Pastori, G., Zecca, L., & Zuccoli, F. (Eds.), *Cantieri aperti e scuola in costruzione. Alla ricerca di nuovi modelli e pratiche di scuola democratica* (pp. xx–xx). FrancoAngeli. 10.17471/xxxx-xxxx

Mangione, G. R. J., & Calzone, S. (2020). Materialities in innovative education: Focus on small Italian schools. In X. X. X (Ed.), *Epistemological approaches to digital learning in educational contexts* (pp. 102-126). Routledge. https://doi.org/10.17471/xxxx-xxxx

Mangione, G. R. J., & Cannella, G. (2020). Small school, smart schools: Distance education in remoteness conditions. *Technology. Knowledge and Learning*, 26(4), 845–865. 10.1007/s10758-020-09480-4

Mangione, G. R. J., & Cannella, G. (2021). La scuola di prossimità. Alleanze territoriali per la realizzazione di nuove forme educative nella piccola scuola. *Archivio di Studi Urbani e Regionali*, 132(Suppl.), 86–109. 10.3280/ASUR2021-SU132006

Mangione, G. R. J., Cannella, G., & De Santis, F. (2021). Piccole scuole, scuole di prossimità. Dimensioni, strumenti e percorsi emergenti. *I Quaderni della Ricerca*, 59. https://doi.org/10.17471/xxxx-xxxx

Mangione, G. R. J., Cannella, G., Parigi, L., & Bartolini, R. (Eds.). (2020). *Comunità di memoria, comunità di futuro. Il valore della piccola scuola*. Carocci.

Mangione, G. R. J., Chipa, S., & Cannella, G. (2022). Il ruolo dei terzi spazi culturali nei patti educativi territoriali. In X. X. X (Ed.), *Il post digitale. Società, culture, didattica* (pp. 171-205). Franco Angeli. https://doi.org/10.17471/xxxx-xxxx

Mangione, G. R. J., & De Santis, F. (2021). La pedagoia del patrimonio per ripensare il curricolo della piccola scuola. Il museo come terzo spazio educativo. *Culture Digitali*, 0, 1–xx. 10.17471/xxxx-xxxx

Mangione, G. R. J., De Santis, F., & Garzia, M. (2023). Le tecnologie per una scuola di comunità aperta e inclusiva. *I Quaderni della Ricerca di Loescher*, 72. https://doi.org/10.17471/xxxx-xxxx

Mangione, G. R. J., & Garzia, M. (2021). Educational measures in multi-grade classroom. Curricular forms and didactic strategies in small Italian schools. *TIMES Journal of Education Technology and Social Studies*, 3. 10.17471/xxxx-xxxx

Mangione, G. R. J., Mughini, E., Sagri, M. T., Rosetti, L., & Zuccaro, A. (2020). La rete come strategia di sistema nel supporto alla scuola italiana in epoca di pandemia: La buona pratica coordinata da INDIRE. *Lifelong Lifewide Learning*, 16(36), 58–75. 10.17471/xxxx-xxxx

Mangione, G. R. J., Parigi, L., & Tonucci, F. (2022). Dove sta di casa la scuola? *Research on Education and Media*, 14(1), 9–24. 10.2478/rem-2022-0003

Mangione, G. R. J., Pieri, M., & De Santis, F. (2023). Intelligenza artificiale ed educazione nei contesti rurali: una scoping review per orientare la ricerca. In *New literacies. Nuovi linguaggi, nuove competenze. Convegno Sirem 2023 Book of Abstracts*. Editrice Morcelliana. https://doi.org/10.17471/xxxx-xxxx

Mangione, G. R. J., Pieri, M., & De Santis, F. (2024). (in press). Revitalizing education in rural and small schools: The role of AI in teachers' professional development. *Italian Journal of Educational Technology*, 31(3).

Maulini, O., & Perrenoud, P. (2005). *La forme scolaire de l'éducation de base: tensions internes et évolutions*. De Boeck., 10.17471/xxxx-xxxx

Melstveit, R., Fellows, S., Staring, F., & Vicentini, L. (2020). *Digital tools and practices: How digital technology in compulsory education can help promote inclusion*. Report EAC Directorate-General for Education, Youth, Sport and Culture.

Miller, L. C. (2012). Situating the rural teacher labor market in the broader context: A descriptive analysis of the market dynamics in New York State. *Journal of Research in Rural Education*, 27, 1.

Monk, D. H. (2007). Recruiting and retaining high-quality teachers in rural areas. *The Future of Children*, 17(1), 155–174. 10.1353/foc.2007.000917407927

Mortari, L. (2010). Cercare il rigore metodologico per una ricerca pedagogica scientificamente fondata. *Education Sciences & Society*, 1(1). 10.17471/xxxx-xxxx

Muijs, D. (2011). Leadership and organisational performance: From research to prescription? *International Journal of Educational Management*, 25(1), 45–60. 10.1108/09513541111100116

Muijs, D., West, M., & Ainscow, M. (2010). Why network? Theoretical perspectives on networking. *School Effectiveness and School Improvement*, 21(1), 5–26. 10.1080/09243450903569692

Nuzzaci, A., Minello, R., Di Genova, N., & Madia, S. (2020). Povertà educativa in contesto italiano tra istruzione e disuguaglianze. Quali gli effetti della pandemia? *Lifelong Lifewide Learning*, 16(36), 76–92. 10.17471/xxxx-xxxx

OECD. (2018). *PISA 2018 database*. Programme for International Student Assessment, OECD. https://www.oecd.org/pisa/data/2018database/

OECD. (2023). *Equity and inclusion in education: Finding strength through diversity*. OECD Publishing. 10.1787/3667c8b0-

Page, G. A., & Hill, M. (2008). Information, communication, and educational technologies in rural Alaska. *New Directions for Adult and Continuing Education*, 117(117), 59–70. 10.1002/ace.286

Rivoltella, P. C. (2015). *Smart future. Didattica, media digitali e inclusione: Didattica, media digitali e inclusione*. FrancoAngeli.

Rivoltella, P. C. (2016). Editoriale. Insegnanti totalmente autonomi. *Scuola Italiana Moderna*, 2(10), 1–2.

Ronksley-Pavia, M., Barton, G., & Pendergast, D. (2019). Multiage education: An exploration of advantages and disadvantages through a systematic review of the literature. *The Australian Journal of Teacher Education*, 44(5), 24–41. 10.14221/ajte.2018v44n5.2

Rossi, F., Storai, F., & Mangione, G. R. J. (2022 in press). Il mentoring basato sul networking per lo sviluppo professionale dei docenti. Analisi delle esperienze del progetto MenSi. In *Apprendere con le tecnologie tra presenza e distanza*. Scholé-Morcelliana., 10.17471/xxxx-xxxx

Ryan, P. (2001). The school-to-work transition: A cross-national perspective. *Journal of Economic Literature*, 39(1), 34–92. 10.1257/jel.39.1.34

Showalter, D., Klein, R., Johnson, J., & Hartman, S. (2017). Why rural matters 2015-2016: Understanding the changing landscape. *Rural School and Community Trust*. https://www.ruraledu.org/user_uploads/file/WRM-2015-16.pdf

Songer, N. B., Lee, H. S., & Kam, R. (2002). Technology-rich inquiry science in urban classrooms: What are the barriers to inquiry pedagogy? *Journal of Research in Science Teaching*, 39(2), 128–150. 10.1002/tea.10013

Steward, S. (2011). Conducting research in educational contexts. *International Journal of Lifelong Education*, 30(4), 565–567. 10.1080/02601370.2011.588469

Sze, S. (2004). Get ahead, get technology: A new idea for rural school success. *Proceedings of the American Council on Rural Special Education*, 24, 118–121.

Thomas, A., & Falls, Z. (2019, March). Rural elementary teachers' access to and use of technology resources in STEM classrooms. In *Society for Information Technology & Teacher Education International Conference* (pp. 2549–2553). Association for the Advancement of Computing in Education (AACE). 10.1007/978-3-030-29736-7_23

Tomarchio, M., & Ulivieri, S. (2015). *Pedagogia militante: Diritti, culture, territori*. ETS.

Trendov, N., Varas, S., & Zeng, M. (2019). *Digital technologies in agriculture and rural areas - Status report*. Food and Agriculture Organization of the United Nations. https://www.fao.org/3/ca4985en/ca4985en.pdf

Tynan, B., & O'Neill, M. (2007). Individual perseverance: A theory of home tutors' management of schooling in isolated settings. *Distance Education*, 28(1), 95–110. 10.1080/01587910701305335

UNESCO. (2023). *Re-immaginare i nostri futuri insieme*. Brescia: La Scuola sei.

UNESCO. (2023). *An ed-tech tragedy? Educational technologies and school closures in the time of COVID-19*. UNESCO., 10.1787/6c2b2b2a-

Wang, P. Y. (2013). Examining the digital divide between rural and urban schools: Technology availability, teachers' integration level and students' perception. *Journal of Curriculum and Teaching*, 2(2), 127–139. 10.5430/jct.v2n2p127

Wright, V. H., & Wilson, E. K. (2011). Teachers' use of technology: Lessons learned from the teacher education program to the classroom. *Journal of Educational Technology Systems*, 40(1), 65–78. 10.2190/ET.40.1.f

Section 2
Disruptive Technologies in Healthcare and Workforce Development

Chapter 8
The Impact of Aligning Artificial Intelligence Large Language Models With Bloom's Taxonomy in Healthcare Education

Matthew Pears
University of Nottingham, UK

Stathis Th Konstantinidis
https://orcid.org/0000-0002-3680-4559
University of Nottingham, UK

ABSTRACT

The innovation of large language models (LLMs) has widened possibilities for renovating healthcare education through AI-powered learning resources, such as chatbots. This chapter explores the assimilation of LLMs with Bloom's taxonomy, demonstrating how this foundational framework for designing and assessing learning outcomes can support the development of critical thinking, problem-solving, and decision-making skills in healthcare learners. Through case examples and research presentations, this chapter illustrates how LLM chatbots provide interactive, scaffolding, and contextually relevant learning experiences. However, it also highlights the importance of designing these tools with key principles in mind, including learner-centeredness, co-creation with domain experts, and principled responsibility. By embracing a collaborative, interdisciplinary, and future-oriented approach to chatbot design and development, the power of LLMs can be harnessed to revolutionize healthcare education and ultimately improve patient care.

METAMORPHOSIS OF EDUCATION AND ARTIFICIAL INTELLIGENCE WITH BLOOM'S TAXONOMY

The advent of breakthroughs in Artificial Intelligence (AI), epitomized by the recent evolution of Large Language Models (LLMs), has precipitated a re-examination of the current approaches in teaching and learning practices. LLMs have demonstrated remarkable capabilities in understanding and generating human-like text. They enable the creation of more sophisticated, powerful learning resources. This chapter conceptualizes and pragmatically highlights that AI is a tool for information delivery and a catalyst for enhancing pedagogical strategies, frameworks, and theories. The methodology draws on author's knowledge and informal narrative review and synthesis of recent literature, drawing on a diverse range of sources including academic articles, case studies, and real-world applications of LLMs in healthcare education. By integrating insights from both theoretical frameworks and practical implementations, we aim to provide a comprehensive understanding of how AI and Bloom's Taxonomy interact in educational settings. The analysis is structured to reflect on different levels of Bloom's Taxonomy, evaluating the integration of LLMs at each stage to address specific pedagogical needs. It first examines the foundations and growth of LLMs in healthcare education, and briefly investigates the technological progression and pedagogical impact. Examples of best practices from research in various healthcare disciplines, such as medicine, nursing, and allied health are presented. The chapter deliberates on the potential impact of AI learning resources, considering the metamorphosis of pedagogical approaches; assessment methods; and the development of key competencies across the cognitive, affective, and psychomotor domains.

A variety of stakeholders in all workforces can find benefits of AI to some extent when approached correctly. In healthcare education, the stakes are particularly high. Integration into healthcare education has begun to address unique challenges faced by learners, such as the need for continuous learning in the face of rapidly evolving medical knowledge (Chan & Zary, 2019). One strength of LLM AI in education is found in their depth of knowledge and flexibility for fostering critical thinking, problem-solving, and decision-making skills, which are essential for professionals navigating an increasingly interprofessional healthcare environment (Flin et al., 2015; Ghorashi, 2008). The demand for precision, contemporaneity, and the ability to apply knowledge in practical settings necessitates innovative educational approaches. AI chatbots represent a promising avenue to fulfil these requisites, providing users with an interactive learning experience that mirrors the complexities of real-world healthcare scenarios.

We proceed to scrutinize how teaching strategies and design standards for deploying LLM-based learning resources in healthcare education align, stressing the need for joint efforts with medical professionals and teaching staff. Ethical considerations and strategies to ensure long-term applicability are evaluated. We outline insights and explanations concerning the repercussions, practical impediments, and trajectories for establishing AI into healthcare education and augmenting the workforce. In reading this chapter of the transformative potential of LLM chatbots in healthcare education, readers will part with the broader discourse on disruptive technologies in education and workforce development. Our aim is to encourage stakeholders to utilize LLMs for constructing innovative, impactful, and sustainable learning resources.

FOUNDATIONS AND EVOLUTION OF LARGE LANGUAGE MODELS

The Emergence of LLMs in Healthcare Education

Large language models are advanced algorithms designed to comprehend, decipher, and produce text, reflecting the expressions of human communication. These models link texts within vast databases to form knowledge, learning patterns, and subtleties to generate responses. Their outputs can vary in responding to queries to producing ideas, marking a substantial advancement in natural language processing technology (Naveed et al., 2023). The prologue of LLMs branched from the broader context of

AI-assisted learning and the development of intelligent tutoring systems (ITS) (Alshaikh & Hewahi, 2021). Traditional AI chatbots have been used in healthcare education for several decades. They are approximately defined as being built on rule-based systems and inherently limited natural language processing capabilities (Sharma et al., 2022). However, these early chatbots often lacked the ability to engage in context-aware conversations, limiting their effectiveness and the acceptability by learners.

The incorporation of LLMs in healthcare education has been driven by several key factors. Increasing complexity of medical knowledge, and the demand for learning resources that are globally scalable yet cost efficient and effective, are just two factors from many (Karabacak et al., 2023). LLM-powered learning resources have the potential to address these challenges by providing learners with on-demand access to up-to-date, evidence-based information, adapting to individual learning needs, and facilitating the development of critical thinking and problem-solving skills through interactive, scenario-based learning (Henderson et al., 2022; Safranek et al., 2023).

The progression of LLMs accelerated from significant innovations in natural language processing, deep learning, and transformer architectures. Language models such as word2vec (Mikolov et al., 2013) concentrated on learning word embeddings. These embeddings captured semantic and syntactic relationships between words and improved the ways machine learning models processed natural language. The introduction of transformer architectures modernized the field of natural language processing, see (Zhou et al, 2023) for an overview. These architectures leveraged the power of self-attention mechanisms and more effectively allow language models to capture long-range dependencies and contextual information. The development of Open AI's GPT (Radford & Narasimhan, 2018) and its subsequent versions up to GPT-4 (OpenAI, 2023) further pushed the boundaries of language modelling.

The application of LLMs for healthcare education has been facilitated by the increasing availability of large-scale medical text datasets, such as PubMed and MIMIC-III (Johnson et al., 2016). These datasets enable fine-tuning of pre-trained LLMs on domain-specific medical knowledge, allowing AI to better understand and generate medically relevant content. The amalgamation of LLMs with other AI techniques, such as vision and reasoning systems, has further enhanced the capabilities of AI chatbots enabling them to provide more accurate, context-aware responses, such as explaining patients' X-ray scans (Lee et al., 2023). As of publication date, the authors label Claude Opus (Anthropic, 2024.) as the strongest model for language and reasoning related use, and GPT-4 features such as add-ins for research use.

Educational Change and Impact of LLMs

At the individual level, AI can engage learners in interactive, dialogue-based learning experiences that adjust to their individual needs, preferences, and prior knowledge (Arif et al., 2023). When prompted to do so, LLMs can support self-regulated learning skills such as goal setting and reflection, by providing learners with immediate feedback and guidance (Sedaghat, 2023). Moreover, it has flexibility in practical application. For example, to facilitate the creation of immersive, scenario-based learning experiences that simulate real-world clinical situations. These interactive learning experiences converge theoretical knowledge and practical application, preparing learners for the challenges of real-world healthcare practice. The implications of continuously monitoring learners' progress and providing real-time feedback means that LLM chatbots can inform the design of learning pathways and facilitate formative assessment strategies (Sharma et al., 2022). In healthcare education's broader ecosystem, encompassing curriculum development and evaluation plus interdisciplinary learning, the significance of instructional impact is magnified within the context of departmental and institutional objectives. By integrating individuals from various healthcare fields into engaging policy and application focussed conversations, the various roles and responsibilities within the healthcare framework are highlighted. Thereby enhancing the educational quality and patient interaction at an institutional level (Stathakarou et al., 2020).

AI is addressing several unique challenges faced by healthcare education. One of the primary challenges is the need to keep pace with the rapidly expanding body of medical knowledge. LLM chatbots can help learners navigate the globally available information by providing them with up-to-date, evidence-based content specific to what they required (Zagabathuni, 2022). Another challenge is the need to develop practical, hands-on skills in addition to theoretical knowledge (Banerjee et al., 2021). Growing evidence shows LLM-based resources boost skill acquisition with their use in interactive, simulation-based learning. Such preparation is essential before engaging with real patients, ensuring they possess both the knowledge and confidence required for delivering optimal care (Larsen et al., 2022). Furthermore, AI driven feedback mechanisms, and even skills prediction forecasting, can help pinpoint areas needing further refinement before learners enter the high-stakes healthcare environment where patient safety is paramount.

With appropriate ethical consideration, this technology can contribute to addressing the challenges of accessibility and equity in healthcare education. By providing learners with on-demand support, regardless of their location or socioeconomic background, LLM chatbots can help democratize access to high-quality educational resources (Tahri Sqalli et al., 2023). This becomes especially pertinent within global health education, where gaps in access to training and resources may impede the cultivation of a proficient healthcare workforce.

Integration of AI with Bloom's Taxonomy in Healthcare Education

Overview of Bloom's Taxonomy

Bloom's Taxonomy is a hierarchical framework for categorising educational objectives into six levels of cognitive complexity: knowledge, comprehension, application, analysis, synthesis, and evaluation (Bloom et al., 1956). The terms within Bloom's Taxonomy underwent revision in 2001, a modification spearheaded by Anderson & Krathwohl, (2001) and Krathwohl, (2010). These revisions aimed to reflect a more dynamic conception of educational processes. The update included changing the nouns to verbs to emphasize the active, process-oriented nature of learning and cognition. The levels developed to become labels of remembering, understanding, applying, analysing, evaluating, and creating. This taxonomy has been broadly adopted in various educational contexts as a tool for designing learning objectives, instructional strategies, and assessment methods. In healthcare education, Bloom's Taxonomy has provided a structured approach to developing and assessing the learning outcomes across the skills continuum. The lower levels of the taxonomy (knowledge and comprehension) focus on the acquisition and transformation of data received by the learner in any format. While the higher levels (application, analysis, synthesis, and evaluation) emphasize the development of critical thinking, problem-solving, and decision-making skills- to name a few.

The success of Bloom's Taxonomy in education relies on how well it is modified to suit the intended project and goals. It supports the design of learning experiences that promote lasting proficiencies (Hidayat & Qamariah, 2023). This has been achieved for those who successfully map and coordinate their learning objectives, instructional strategies, and assessment methods with the appropriate levels of the taxonomy. Educators can produce coherent and effective learning resources that support the progressive skills development. Furthermore, the updated 2001 Taxonomy version provides educators with a unified frame and language for defining learning expectations and assessing student progress. By setting learning objectives at every level of taxonomy, teachers can map out a guide for learners. Helping them to understand what they need to know and be actionable at different points in their learning path, is the key to acceptance and engagement.

In the subsequent section, the integration of LLMs across the taxonomy's levels within healthcare education is discussed. This section is intended to serve as a guide for educators and developers, highlighting the strengths and opportunities. Equally, the unique challenges and threats posed by LLMs at key stages of learning are described.

ALIGNING AI WITH EACH LEVEL OF BLOOM'S TAXONOMY IN HEALTHCARE EDUCATION

Remembering- Level 1

The basal stage of Bloom's Taxonomy, 'Remembering', is necessary for storing the recall of facts, concepts, and answers, which lays the groundwork for higher-order cognitive functions. The ability to effectively encode, store, and retrieve information is essential (Tuma & Nassar, 2021). Surgeons, for example, must accurately recall patient related anatomical details and procedures, which depend on the neural processes involving regions like the prefrontal cortex and hippocampus (Levy, 2024). These brain regions are needed for short-to-long term memory formations, constructing the basis for more complex cognitive tasks (Yan, 2023).

Stathakarou et al., (2020) explored how chatbots could support healthcare education, specifically in aiding the 'Remembering' level of Bloom's Taxonomy. They highlighted chatbots' abilities to quiz students on existing knowledge, thus enhancing the recall of facts and concepts critical in medical and healthcare training. This approach aligns with the foundational need for learners to accurately remember and retrieve essential information, demonstrating the potential of chatbots to reinforce memory retention in healthcare education. However, they suggested that for students and teachers to accept and utilize such solutions, it is the trust towards the performance of a chatbot that is critical.

Evidence at this level is plenty- for example, through the development and implementation of non-LLM chatbots tailored for healthcare curricula, (CEPEH Analysis, 2023) investigated the use of custom chatbots in healthcare education across European institutions. Participants reported improved confidence and knowledge retention of facts and concepts after engaging with the chatbots, indicating their effectiveness in supporting the foundational level of learning. The chatbots were designed to quiz students on existing knowledge, thereby reinforcing memory retention, and aiding in the foundational 'Remembering' stage of Bloom's Taxonomy.

LLM-powered learning resources can further support learning at the 'Remembering' level by engaging learners in interactive question-and-answer sessions that reinforce their understanding and retention of key concepts. Practical uses in medical education are by using an AI model with image recognition capabilities, such as GPT-4 (OpenAI, 2023) or Claude Opus (Anthropic, 2024). They have been shown to query and direct learners to identify specific equipment or describe the features of various organ systems. Such learning resources provide factual, digestible information optimized for storage. With high impact, Ghorashi et al., 2023 demonstrated the value of AI chatbots in simplifying complex medical terminology and procedures, leading to improved student recall, and understanding. These case studies demonstrate AI directly assisting learners to remember targeted information.

However, a threat may form if learners choose to outsource this knowledge base when information is required. This may lead to a 'just-in-time' information retrieval model (Kumaran et al., 2009). This shift could potentially reduce the cognitive load placed on internal memory systems for basic recall, as LLMs provide external cognitive support (Sparrow et al., 2011). Since 'Remembering' forms the foundation of higher order thinking in Bloom's Taxonomy, changes at this level could have subsequent effects on later stages. This is not a new topic in cognition research and application, however as the evolving relationship between human memory and technology arguably accelerates, this warrants investigation on how LLMs impact learning and retention.

Understanding- Level 2

In Bloom's Taxonomy of educational objectives, the 'Understanding' level signifies the ability to create conceptual maps relating to meanings and interpretations of information and recognize the connections between ideas (Anderson et al., 2001). In healthcare education, this level advances the learning journey from rote memorization to the practical application of medical knowledge and adds context for how information is transferred to the learners' environment. The cognitive foundations of understanding have been demonstrated to involve the temporal lobes, particularly Wernicke's area (Astutik et al., 2023). LLM-powered learning resources can personalize explanations and adjust the complexity to match the learner's current knowledge level- ensuring they fully grasp new terminology and concepts. And like any other resource, AI can aid in building and strengthening semantic memory networks through targeted knowledge retrieval practice and presenting information in diverse contexts.

There is a large portion of publications demonstrating efficacy in this level, relative to evidence in subsequent taxonomy levels. Holderried et al (2024) demonstrated that LLMs adapted explanations to the learner's knowledge level, effectively supporting their understanding of medical vocabulary and models. Schubert et al (2023) asserted that LLMs excel in neurology board-style exams, mainly in questions involving 'Understanding'. This indicates that AI-powered simulations engage a learner's working memory as discussed. Sallam (2023) concurred that, particularly in the early stages of training, ChatGPT supports this level of understanding with similar techniques. As a practical example, a chatbot can assume the role of a patient with a specific medical condition and challenge learners to explain the diagnosis, treatment options, and potential risks and benefits in clear, non-technical language.

The apparent success in use cases was investigated by Herrmann-Werner et al., (2024), who better operationalized ChatGPT's proficiency. In psychosomatic medicine examinations, ChatGPT achieved success rates surpassing 90% for various question types particularly in 'remembering' and 'understanding', the findings affirmed ChatGPT's adeptness in these cognitive domains within psychosomatic medicine, indicating its effective application of knowledge. Specifically, it was able to exhibit logical reasoning and the correct use of facts. This was achieved by showcasing its understanding of the relationships of underlying concepts and ability to recognize patterns and different pieces of information from the patient history and the International Classification of Diseases.

These studies highlight the promise of AI in facilitating pedagogy at the second level of the Taxonomy. To optimize the use of AI, specifically Large Language Models (LLMs), for reinforcing the 'Understanding' level within the educational workforce at an institutional or departmental level, consider the following additional recommendations:

- Establish protocols for the regular updating and verification of data used to train/prompt AI models, ensuring the information provided by LLMs is current, accurate, and reflective of the latest medical research and practices, through collaborations between medical professionals, educators, and AI developers.
- Ensure AI technologies, especially LLMs, are designed with advanced customization and adaptability features to cater to diverse learner needs, including accommodations for individuals with disabilities and neurodivergence, by adjusting the presentation of information and the complexity of explanations based on the learner's profile.
- Foster a coherent learning environment with little to no contradictory information produced by educators and AI. This is achieved by aligning AI-generated content with the curriculum, standardizing terminologies, teaching methodologies, and key concepts across courses and AI platforms, and providing regular training sessions for educators on the capabilities and limitations of AI tools.

Applying- Level 3

Bloom's Taxonomy identifies the 'Applying' level as a 3rd stage. At this level, learners develop memorization and actively utilize acquired knowledge and skills in real-world situations they may be experiencing for the first time. This consideration on practical application means that learners must comprehend, demonstrate, and iteratively make use of knowledge in real world contexts. In this section, we present case examples and best practice recommendations to address the challenges learners face at the applying level. This level is arguably considered the most difficult to achieve success in educational settings, due to the significant leap required from theoretical understanding to practical real-world scenarios.

To bridge the gap between theoretical knowledge and its practical application, especially at the 'applying' level of Bloom's Taxonomy, we outline several best practices that foster a deeper engagement with real-world scenarios.

- Foster AI-Supported Collaboration: Launch initiatives that use AI to encourage collaborative problem-solving among learners across different healthcare disciplines. Provide resources for teamwork and recognize achievements in innovative solutions and improvements- Digital escape rooms are one such solution.
- Introduce AI-driven adaptive learning pathways that tailor learning complexity and pace to each learner's progress, enhancing personalized education and knowledge application in real scenarios. Utilize LLMs to create customized learning experiences, improving outcomes and retention.
- Integrate AI-Powered Learning: Deploy AI-driven platforms for scenario-based learning in healthcare that align with curricula, offering realistic simulations for practical knowledge application. These platforms should be continuously updated and include feedback mechanisms to monitor learner progress.

The following case studies exemplify the effective application of these strategies. They offer compelling evidence of how leveraging LLMs within the 'Applying' level can adjust the way learners assimilate knowledge and skills within their workforce role.

At an organizational scale, Rao et al (2023) provided an exciting exploration of ChatGPT's potential in the clinical domain. By assessing its performance across 36 clinical vignettes from the Merck, Sharpe & Dohme (MSD) Clinical Manual, the researchers were the first to comment on the model's capabilities throughout the clinical workflow. This encompasses diagnosis, management, and clinical decision support. An overall accuracy of 71.7% for ChatGPT, which is similar or better in parts than human accuracy, suggests the model's accuracy improves significantly when provided with more clinical context. The implications of this study are far-reaching towards the potential of LLMs to emulate expert-like mental models work in parallel, in various workflow tasks. This capability can be leveraged to support learners in applying their knowledge to real-world scenarios, serving as a valuable supplement to traditional learning methods.

Yuan et al (2023) reviewed applications of LLMs in healthcare, focusing on their potential in knowledge retrieval, clinical workflow automation, and diagnostic assistance. The review is one of the best demonstrations of the application of LLMs in simulating complex healthcare scenarios at the applying level of Bloom's taxonomy. Although illustrating how these models can support medical training and decision-making by offering dynamic, interactive learning experiences, the continuous optimization, and ethical oversight when applying LLMs into clinical practice, should be taken. Challenges were raised related to data limitations, reasoning gaps, and ensuring transparency and fairness. To further ensure transparency, it is essential to implement clear documentation of AI decision processes and criteria used in developing these models. Additionally, fostering fairness requires regular assessment of AI outcomes to identify and correct any biases, thereby safeguarding against discriminatory practices in healthcare delivery.

Analysing- Level 4

At the 4th level of Bloom's Taxonomy, learners are expected to break down complex information into constituent parts, examine their relationships, and identify underlying principles or structures (Anderson et al., 2001). Learners must demonstrate their ability to critically appraise information such as medical research, assess the quality of evidence, and apply the findings to inform their higher-level decision-making.

One study highlighting implemented use of AI is from Pears et al (2024). They performed a double-blinded study in non-technical skills with urology experts and an AI urology feedback provider. Highlighting the capacity of LLMs to replicate the cognitive frameworks of experts and deliver engaging, responsive educational encounters, the aim was to assess LLMs role in augmenting conventional training regimes. The AI was given information about a scenario and learned about key image timepoints from a video. Findings indicate that a custom AI resource using GPT4 can present structured, context-aware training feedback that is analytical in how the trainee understood the scenario events- it likely will be a supplement to human trainers for a more immersive and technology-rich learning milieu.

Such AI-powered case-based learning platforms can present learners with realistic, data-rich patient scenarios, challenging them to analyse the available information. Models are 'cognizant' enough to be able to identify key factors and develop evidence-based recommendations for care if they can search health related databases. Indeed, there is an uptick in the practical capacities of which LLMs can be utilized when they have the capacity to analyse information after digesting, processing, and responding to the learner's queries (Iftimia et al., 2023). For instance, Dolianiti et al (2020) introduced a Conversational Virtual Patient that employed Natural Language Processing techniques to train decision-making skills in medical students regarding thromboembolism. Unlike typical virtual patients, this AI allowed students to formulate their own utterances and interact with analytical intent. From strengthening analytical skills, healthcare professionals can then develop decision-making capacities to adapt to the challenges of modern care delivery. The authors of this chapter perceive AI-powered research assistants to be the most impactful when this uptick develops to mass implementation.

One effect on Bloom's Taxonomy of this capacity is the deviation of progression through different taxonomy levels. Students, staff, academics, and other stakeholders can better shift from this analysis level into the subsequent higher-order tasks of evaluation and creation. At the primary level of assistance, by assigning AI to handle repetitive analytical tasks, such as data processing and literature searches, healthcare professionals can focus on higher-order analytical tasks. Common tasks such as interpreting findings and developing evidence-based recommendations for care, are evaluative tasks which can be attained at a faster rate allowing dedicated time in these cognitive processes. This shift can lead to more innovative solutions and strategies.

The subject areas, data types, stakeholder interactions, and scope of implementation make it difficult to briefly summarize the effect of LLM and other AI types in education and workforce. Yet, consistent behaviour is found in all areas within this level- which is decision-making. Decision-making capabilities, only found after the 'Analysing' level, marks a shift in the potential impact of LLMs on learners, teams, and systems. As LLMs become more adept at processing and analysing a plethora of factors, humans can synthesis to form decisions- they will also provide data-driven insights and recommendations that may improve and directly inform real-world processes (Ninaus & Sailer, 2022).

This means that LLMs can support learners in making evidence-based decisions about patient care, treatment options, and resource allocation. By providing learners with intelligent assistance in analysing data, research findings, or clinical guidelines, LLMs can greatly accelerate the analysis process. This, in turn, allows for more evaluative time, helping learners develop the critical thinking skills essential for making informed decisions in real-world healthcare settings.

To enhance the analysing level of Bloom's Taxonomy in healthcare through LLMs, institutions may consider to:

- Deploy AI-enhanced decision support systems linked with EHRs, offering real-time patient data insights and up-to-date medical research. These systems could be local, but should support not replace human judgment, aiding healthcare professionals in making better-informed decisions.
- Create AI-based knowledge management platforms to aggregate and simplify access to recent medical studies and guidelines, integrating into existing workflows for easier application of this knowledge in daily practices.
- Develop AI-driven training and simulation tools to engage healthcare workers in analysing complex cases and scenarios, fostering critical thinking and evidence-based practices for superior healthcare.

Evaluating – Level 5

The integration of AI and its branch of LLMs in educational settings has shown pragmatic real-world applications that support learners at the evaluation level of Bloom's taxonomy. These novel learning resources can enhance students' ability to critically evaluate information, methodologies, and solutions through innovative learning activities, peer-to-peer interactions, and continuous guidelines and workflow reviews, e.g. see (Sajja et al., 2023). AI-generated content can encourage learners to explore multiple perspectives, consider alternative approaches, and make well-informed decisions.

Researchers have explored LLMs applications to help institutions to evaluate and update clinical guidelines and healthcare workflows. The ability of AI systems to analyse research findings, patient outcomes, and practice efficiencies is growing. The are advancing in providing evidence-based recommendations for guideline updates and workflow optimization. To ensure their assistance does not become problematic or have negative consequence, Mehandru et al. (2023) proposed evaluating LLM agents for their performance on real-world clinical tasks, introducing evaluation frameworks termed "Artificial-intelligence Structured Clinical Examinations" (AI-SCI) for deploying LLM agents into healthcare. In concurrence, we also accentuate the need for additional frameworks, policy analysis, and guidelines to measure the changes in capacities of teams to evaluate information. Basic metrics such as value, effects over time, and accuracy are a starting point of interest. In the context of evaluation of data visualization, Joshi et al. (2024) compared the recommendations of ChatGPT and Google Bard in supporting learners to evaluate hard to interpret graphs named Parallel Coordinate Plots (PCPs). The expert reviewers found that ChatGPT's recommendations were not only appropriate for PCP literacy, but also well-aligned with Bloom's taxonomy in helping learners evaluate these complex images.

As LLMs continue to advance, institutions will need to develop specialized frameworks that guide the ethical and effective use of these technologies. After the analysis phase of Bloom's Taxonomy, these tools can assist learners in contextualizing resultant information, enabling them to explore the breadth and depth of meanings, interpretations, and pathways, thus enhancing their decision-making process in alignment with their goals.

Creating- Level 6

Creating is situated at the highest level of Bloom's Taxonomy. It encompasses the generation, planning, and production of original ideas, products, or perspectives. It necessitates learners to innovatively combine knowledge elements, drawing upon previous processes such as analysis, evaluation, and synthesis (Anderson & Krathwohl, 2001). The main initial component of the creative process in learners at this level is ideation. This involves the generation and manipulation of concepts within the learner's understanding, to form unconventional and innovative outputs. The mental process revolves around the deconstruction and reconstruction of many concepts simultaneously which allow learners to explore new combinations and syntheses, leading to the development of original solutions and perspectives. Ideation in the educational framework can significantly enhance the learning experience and promote higher order thinking skills. To support it, diverse and high-quality educational materials, such as interactive diagrams, simulations, and videos, are typically used. These resources equip learners with the tools and stimuli necessary to engage in creative problem-solving and independently explore new concepts (Halupa, 2020).

In relation to student performance based on this Taxonomy level Prasad & Professor (2021) suggested that many assessments focus on lower cognitive levels, highlighting the need for greater emphasis on higher levels like ideation to foster deeper learning and critical thinking. Educators can address this issue by adopting a methodical approach to evaluating whether educational materials and assessments encompass the full spectrum of cognitive levels, including ideation, ensuring a well-rounded development of cognitive skills among learners (Lourdusamy et al., 2022).

Of course, this is where AI and its branch of LLM usage can alleviate this issue. Most LLMs have an adjustable feature called a 'Temperature' which can support the creativity of learners. Temperature refers to the degree of variability in generated text or visual media, with high temperatures indicating maximal variation and more conducive to creativity, diverging from typical conceptual understanding. Another approach to enhance creativity is through nuclear sampling, which allows for the generation of more diverse and unexpected outputs by sampling from the tail end of the probability distribution. Through such 'outside of the box' suggestions, analogies, metaphors, or images, LLMs enable learners to forge connections between seemingly unrelated ideas, creating novel associations.

Zhao et al (2024) presented a methodical approach to evaluating LLM creativity. By adapting seven tasks from the Torrance Tests of Creative Thinking and introducing an LLM-based evaluation protocol, they constructed a comprehensive analysis framework. This framework measures creativity across fluency, flexibility, originality, and elaboration dimensions. Their dataset, comprising 700 questions, allowed for a detailed examination of divergent thinking capabilities in LLMs. The study indicates that an LLM's architecture, prompt type, and system prompts significantly influence its creative outputs. Moreover, the research unveiled a relationship between the LLMs' creativity levels and their attributed personality traits, observing heightened creativity in various tasks. Enhancements in creativity were also noted with the use of instructive language and Chain-of-Thought prompts. The discoveries from the study should also inform readers that collaboration both with and among different LLMs can amplify creativity, even though this is a new way that everybody has yet to learn the best methods to interface with such tools.

Conversely, lower temperature and more stable/standard settings result in more predictable and coherent outputs, which might be useful for more structured learning tasks but less so for creative ideation. Creativity from a learner could be from a research output in that new findings are obtained through research and large language models conversely need to have no deviation from the data to allow the learner to accurately disseminate the novel knowledge and information they have obtained. Davis et al (2024) investigated ChatGPT's temperature setting and stated that a lower temperature yields consistent outputs, essential for accurately reporting research findings without data distortion. Conversely, a higher temperature encourages creative responses, useful for simplifying complex findings for wider audiences. This dual functionality demonstrates the feature's value in both precise scientific reporting and engaging public dissemination.

Lastly, Large Language Models (LLMs) can serve as powerful tools for generating media based on users' prompts and instructions, enabling learners to express their ideas more effectively. By leveraging the generative capabilities of LLMs, learners can create custom educational content, such as images, videos, or audio, that represents their thoughts and concepts. This AI-generated media can be used to communicate ideas (e.g. see Figure 1), stimulate discussion, and seek feedback from peers and educators. Such tools as Stable Diffusion, Midjourney, and Sora, for image/video generation, Lucid AI for diagramming, and various consumer LLMs (Lucid, 2024; Stable Diffusion, 2024; Midjourney, 2024; OpenAI, 2024) allow learners to quickly and easily produce visual or auditory representations of their ideas empowers learners to engage more deeply with the creative process and iterate on their concepts based on the feedback received. The use and effects of AI on the 6 levels of Bloom's taxonomy are summarized in Table 1. Ultimately, this application of LLMs in healthcare education supports learners in developing and refining their ideas, which may lead to more effective learning outcomes and encourage a more collaborative educational environment.

Figure 1. AI generated image (Dall-E 3) created by the authors, as demonstration for the creative elements of LLMs- prompt: 'Depict an AI-based robot guiding learners through the correct steps to climb Bloom's taxonomies levels, in a paper quilling style'

Table 1. The use and effects of ai on the six levels of Bloom's Taxonomy

Bloom's Taxonomy Level	Verbs & Keywords	Learner's AI Usage	AI Impact	Effect on Taxonomy Progression
Remembering	Define, Recall, Recognize, List, Name, Identify	Quickly access and retrieve information	Accelerates information recall, reducing time spent on memorization	Speeds up progression to understanding level, but may hinder long-term retention if overreliance on AI occurs
Understanding	Explain, Describe, Interpret, Summarize, Classify, Discuss	Employ AI to clarify concepts, generate summaries, and provide context	Enhances comprehension of complex topics, facilitating faster understanding	Accelerates progression to application level, but short-term understanding may occur if learners do not internalize the information
Applying	Apply, Demonstrate, Solve, Use, Illustrate, Implement	Assist in problem-solving, generate examples, and provide guidance	Supports practical application of knowledge, offering insights and solutions	Speeds up progression to analysing level, but may limit development of independent problem-solving skills
Analysing	Analyse, Compare, Contrast, Differentiate, Examine, Investigate	Break down large data, plan analysis strategy, ultimately improve insight and dissemination / presentation	Provides in-depth and efficient analysis, saving time and effort	Overuse may reduce learners' hands-on analysis experience. However, consequences, of lack of, will differ for each system.

continued on following page

Table 1. Continued

Bloom's Taxonomy Level	Verbs & Keywords	Learner's AI Usage	AI Impact	Effect on Taxonomy Progression
Evaluating	Evaluate, Assess, Critique, Judge, Justify, Defend	Use AI-generated analyses and insights to support evaluation and decision-making	Offers diverse perspectives and data-driven insights for more informed evaluations	This level has the largest potential for negative consequences in terms of decision making when included in-patient care or other such high-risk systems.
Creating	Create, Design, Develop, Construct, Produce, Invent	A collaborative tool to generate ideas, iterate on designs, and tool for tasks such as writing code etc	Accelerates the creative process, providing inspiration and novel approaches	Facilitates faster progression through the creating level, but may influence the originality and authenticity of the final product if AI is heavily relied upon

PEDAGOGICAL ALIGNMENT AND DESIGN PRINCIPLES FOR HEALTHCARE EDUCATION

Designing AI resources such as chatbots for healthcare education requires adherence to guiding principles that ensure pedagogical soundness, technological robustness, and ethical responsibility. These principles are important for developing learning resources that effectively support learning outcomes, engage users, and maintain high standards of quality and accuracy.

One key principle is user-centred design, which involves actively engaging stakeholders throughout the development process. Henderson et al (2022) developed an online chatbot development tool allowing learners to create their own chatbots. Focussed on promoting students to identify what topics and content they need additional help within, this tool demonstrates the improvements in the design flows and importance of involving various stakeholders for validating data, development process, and the final product, ensuring the needs and expectations of its users are met.

Another fundamental principle is interactivity, which emphasises designing resources that engage learners in active learning (Dolianiti et al., 2020). This principle involves exploiting the flexibility of LLM features and APIs to create custom learning resources that are multi-modal. The aim is to facilitate dynamic, interactive dialogues that encourage learners to ask questions, explore alternative perspectives, and construct their own understanding (Pears et al., 2021).

Further principles vary based on the project and its needs. However, when identifying the most influential principles for success, the following factors should be considered:

- Established Frameworks for Development and Evaluation: Utilizing proven design and evaluation frameworks, such as ASPIRE (see 4.2) or a similar instructional design model, which aligns AI tool development with the objectives of Bloom's taxonomy- allowing stakeholders to better operationalize how AI inclusion would modify each level of the taxonomy.
- Training Incorporating Ethical and Technical Aspects: Developing comprehensive training programs that address both ethical considerations and technical skills is essential for building confidence and supporting growth in the use of new AI-powered resources.

- Institutional Support for AI Integration: Adequate infrastructure, policies, and support for innovation are necessary for educators to effectively use AI tools to foster learning at each stage of Bloom's taxonomy.
- Commitment to Accessibility and Equity: Designing AI educational tools with a focus on accessibility and equity is crucial for ensuring that all learners can benefit from these technologies and progress through the levels of Bloom's taxonomy without hindrance.

These principles are decisive for supporting learners at all levels of Bloom's taxonomy.

The Importance of Co-Creation With Healthcare Professionals and Educators

Co-creation, co-production, co-design, or participatory design in digital education resources has been a prominent approach in education for many years. These terms, though distinct, can be broadly defined as the collaborative generation of ideas and knowledge by a group of stakeholders (students, academics, content experts, online pedagogists, etc.) towards the development of a digital education resource. Following a participatory approach in the design and development of digital resources is widely accepted to lead to high-quality resources and is considered beneficial for the stakeholders involved (Antoniou., et al, 2021; Pears et al., 2022). Outputs from a plethora of studies in various topics demonstrate that participatory design can be applied for anything- such as re-designing physical and virtual environments, designing learning practices and curricula, empowering professional and local communities through outcomes, and co-designing technologies for learning and teaching (Tuhkala, 2021). Additionally, it can be used for electives provision, crowdsourcing, student-university identification, experience sharing/interaction through university website and online platforms and others (Zarandi et al., 2022).

A literature review of 52 studies by Hamzah & Wahid (2016) identified a set of participatory design principles to guide healthcare system designers when conducting participatory design. These principles provide a framework for effectively engaging stakeholders and ensuring that the resulting systems meet the needs of their intended users. In addition, guidelines for adopting co-creation in open educational practices and resources have been proposed (Antoniou et al., 2021; Atenas et al., 2020), emphasizing the importance of collaborative approaches in the development of educational materials.

Chen (2011) identified over 100 educational design methods or co-design approaches, ranging from linear to iterative (Boyle, 2002; Boyle et al.; Costa, 2013; Dolianiti et al., 2020; Dollinger, Lodge, and Coates., 2018). Most of these methods are based on the ADDIE model (Chen, 2011) and share three common stages: Analysis, Production, and Evaluation (Brown & Green, 2020). The abundance of participatory design principles and co-design approaches in the literature demonstrates the growing recognition of the value of collaboration in the development of healthcare systems and educational resources.

An Effective Co-Creation Framework- ASPIRE

In healthcare education, the ASPIRE framework (Aims, Storyboarding, Population, Implementation, Release, and Evaluation) provides a structured approach for involving stakeholders throughout the development of digital resources (Wharrad, 2021; Ho et al., 2021). This framework has been adapted for chatbot development processes (Dolianiti, 2020; Pears, 2021; Henderson 2022). Grounded in Wenger's community of practice theory, this co-creation approach empowers healthcare professionals and educators to contribute their expertise, leading to more effective and relevant learning outcomes. Such co-creation approaches ensure that the chatbot's content, interactions, and features align with the needs of its users, guaranteeing high quality.

The effectiveness of co-creation is evident in various studies. A meta-analysis associating effectiveness of serious digital games for healthy lifestyle promotion with participatory design revealed that co-design was related to higher effectiveness when used to create the game challenge but to lower game effectiveness when it was applied to game aesthetics (DeSmet et al., 2016). Halvorsrud et al. (2021) conducted a meta-analysis of reviews in healthcare, identifying that co-creation of research may improve several health-related outcomes and public health more broadly, although they noted that reviews rarely tested effectiveness against intended outcomes. In education, single studies found that co-creation assignments had a statistically significant impact on academic performance (Doyle et al., 2021), while student generated content enhance deep learning and engagement leading to conceptual understanding (Doyle et al., 2019; Draper, 2009; Hardy et al., 2014).

A systematic review (Zarandi et al., 2022) on benefits and barriers of student co-creation in higher education identified that co-creation improves student persistence, achievement, and retention (Bond, 2020), and it influences reinforcement and shared emotional connection (Crough & Love, 2019). According to Zarandi et al. (2022), co-creation in higher education improves learning skills, positively contributing to student self-regulated learning, ownership, enjoyment, confidence, deeper understanding of the subject, self-awareness, and self-efficiency. Engaging in co-creation activities also enhances essential soft skills, such as critical thinking, creativity, presentation skills, problem-solving abilities, decision-making capabilities, negotiation techniques, interpersonal communication, and teamwork. These skills are crucial for academic success and highly valuable in students' future professional lives.

However, these frameworks, much like Bloom's Taxonomy, need to consider how LLMs can benefit stakeholders at each step. Pears et al. (2022) suggest developing evidence-based tools grounded in authentic scenarios, such as patient cases and healthcare systems, to support the higher levels of Bloom's taxonomy. When applied in conjunction with the technological advancements of LLMs, these principles have the potential to revolutionize the delivery and experience of healthcare education.

IMPLICATIONS, PRACTICAL CHALLENGES, AND FUTURE DIRECTION IN HEALTHCARE EDUCATION AND WORKFORCE

Ethical and Societal Implications of LLM-Powered AI Chatbots

As healthcare entities and educational institutions increasingly integrate LLMs and AI into their operations, the importance of adopting a flexible, modular, and responsive approach is of utmost important. The Swiss Cheese Model (Reason et al., 2006), an analogy illustrating the multilayered nature of system safeguards against failures, underscores the necessity of regularly updating and enhancing these safeguards in response to emerging challenges and dangers. Although they may be or the specialised tools and models this is a universally applicable and flexible approach towards the evolving functionalities of AI, that present new opportunities and potential vulnerabilities. By employing the Swiss Cheese Model, organizations can gain insights into the impacts of LLMs and AI on healthcare education and workforce dynamics, enabling them to anticipate and navigate the changes brought about by these technologies effectively.

This proactive and adaptive methodology empowers healthcare systems and educational bodies to leverage the capabilities of LLMs and AI not only to bolster existing safeguards but also to improve workflow efficiency and outcomes in patient care and education (Yu et al., 2023). The integration of these technologies reshapes workflow and procedural landscapes, reinforcing specific defensive layers within the healthcare sector through evidence-based recommendations and the reduction of errors associated with human oversight. For example, AI-driven clinical decision support systems analyse extensive patient data to provide medical professionals with informed guidance, with LLMs able to be an interface for patients and other stakeholders- adding a crucial layer of protection against suboptimal treatment decisions.

Moreover, the Swiss Cheese Model emphasizes the critical need to identify and address system vulnerabilities, such as the potential for overreliance on technological solutions or the risk of biased decision-making. Strengthened barriers can weaken other elements within a system. Continuous monitoring and evaluation of LLMs and AI help healthcare organizations address these issues, maintaining the integrity of the system's defences. While AI has already enhanced outputs in healthcare to an extent, the rapid advancements in large language models and other AI technologies necessitate comprehensive assessments to fully understand the implications of these changes. We could only find several evaluations that could be modified to align with LLMs (e.g. (Cummings & Cummings, 2023), however extending other current evaluative techniques such as human factors engineering, failure mode and effects analysis (FMEA), and task analysis before introducing LLM-based resources, organizations can proactively identify and mitigate potential vulnerabilities, ensuring that the adoption of AI aligns with the principles of both the Swiss Cheese Model and Bloom's Taxonomy.

Addressing Cognitive, Affective, and Psychomotor Changes and Maintaining Critical Skills

In the revised version of Blooms taxonomy which introduced the Cognitive, Affective, and Psychomotor domains of learners. To capitalize on AI chatbot benefits while mitigating risks for these 3 domains, a judicious approach is imperative. Individuals, departments, organizations ought to adopt nuanced techniques balancing innovation with core competency preservation. Implementing methods that uphold essential skills while harnessing AI's potential becomes paramount for sustainable progress.

Cognitive Domain

Within the Cognitive domain, LLMs offer assistance for knowledge acquisition, retrieval, and cultivating higher-order cognitive abilities (Kononowicz et al., 2019). However, excessive reliance could lead to cognitive offloading, where learners become overly dependent on the technology for information recall and problem-solving. This is not a new phenomenon as similar evidence for social media in attention span, would be synonymous with the effect of technology. To mitigate this risk, educators should design learning experiences that prioritise active, self-directed learning and metacognitive development. New strategies may be needed specifically for AI, but typically involve prompting learners to generate their own questions, explanations, and predictions, while providing opportunities for reflection and self-assessment (Tsai, 2021).

Affective Domain

Within the Affective domain, LLM chatbots can help cultivate empathy, active listening, and emotional intelligence through simulated patient encounters. We understand more positive impact on learners than negative however this is a very under researched area. However, there is a risk that learners may have less access and practice to real human actors, patients, and other stakeholders. There is a plethora of communication styles and cues and skills needed which is very difficult to facilitate with technology. To mitigate this, educators should create opportunities for real-world, face-to-face interactions with patients and peers, and incorporate debriefing sessions that encourage learners to reflect on their own emotional responses and interpersonal dynamics (Rao, 2023).

Psychomotor Domain

In the Psychomotor domain, LLM chatbots can provide guidance and support for developing skills and competence. However, it is important to recognize the limitations of AI-generated pedagogical outputs in addressing the granular aspects of psychomotor skill acquisition. While AI tools may offer general directions, the development of tactile acuity, muscle memory, and the ability to adapt to unique clinical situations heavily relies on hands-on experience and expert feedback. For instance, when a student is performing a surgical procedure, such as cutting through the Maxilla, the angle of the saw must be determined by the student based on their understanding of the specific case, regardless of any AI-generated suggestions. As AI technologies advance, it is conceivable that future tools incorporating real-time computer vision with LLM voice assistance, or exo-skeletal guidance, to assist in providing more granular direction for psychomotor tasks, akin to a surgical tutor. However, the effectiveness and safety of such tools would depend on rigorous development and assessment processes. There are areas which it may find strength for example in CPR; would care and dressing; medication administration; and scrubbing and gowning, with more standardized techniques and strategies.

To mitigate the risks associated with AI-assisted learning in the Psychomotor Domain, educators should prioritize hands-on, experiential learning opportunities that allow learners to practice and refine their skills in real-world settings, with expert supervision and feedback. AI should not be used as a standalone tool for teaching students; instead, it should be integrated as a parallel resource alongside expert guidance. This approach allows consultants and teachers to leverage the benefits of AI while still providing the necessary human expertise and adaptability. It is crucial to carefully assess its impact on surgical student capabilities and strike a balance between leveraging the benefits of AI-assisted learning and ensuring the development of autonomous, adaptable, and critically thinking healthcare professionals.

Challenges and Future Developments

The integration of AI and LLM chatbots in healthcare education holds immense potential for personalized learning experiences. However, to fully realize this potential, several challenges and limitations must be addressed (Leech et al., 2024). Personalized and adaptive learning is at the forefront of AI and LLM chatbot considerations, yet there is still a lack of resources that effectively enhance these approaches (Chiu et al., 2023). Educators are reported to have lack of digital skills and knowledge to implement AI in educational practice effectively, but frameworks and models to enhance digital competencies have been already proposed (Lameras et al., 2022; Ng et al., 2023).

Since educators are not expected to be technical experts, they choose off-the-shelf AI informed technologies to implement in their educational practice. This result in resources likely not tailored to students' needs, restricted, and are packaged to have dependency. Furthermore, these AI-informed resources are often poorly designed and developed, highlighting the limited input from both educators and students regarding the resource's design, learning objectives, and integration into teaching and learning practices. Pears et al., (2021) proposed an innovative short training the trainers' curriculum on co-creation of chatbots for medical and healthcare education and training which build around the Kolb's learning cycle and targeted not only academics, medical doctors, and researchers, but also IT specialist and learning technologist. Thus, equipping champion teams with the necessary competencies to develop in-house, high quality educational resources.

Need for Interdisciplinarity and Clear Policies

Recent literature (Chiu et al., 2023) concurs that there is a greater need for interdisciplinarity while researching AI in education. Although artificial intelligence is not a new research field, the recent explosion of interest following the release of LLMs has led many researchers, primarily from computer science or engineering backgrounds, to implement such models within educational environments. Thus, there is an evident need for researchers from different disciplines (e.g. Online pedagogist, content experts, learning technologist, AI engineers) to come together to explore the exact needs in the new landscape in education and develop appropriate resources.

Before November 2022, most Higher Education Institutions (HEI) considered AI in education under their Digital Education policies and guidelines. However, the release of ChatGPT and other AI generative applications prompted the creation of urgent policies, often prohibiting the use of AI tools and technologies by students and educators. This resulted in an ambiguous state of what is allowed (Neumann et al., 2023) regarding the use of AI, what is ethical to use in educational practice and what is not. Thus, generic policies and clear guidance are needed in a top-down approach to regulate the use of AI in education in the most effective way for students learning journey.

Theoretical Challenges and Learner Effects

Wu (2023) identified additional challenges based on theoretical roots for education, focusing on the practical application of chatbots in educational practice. As discussed, the use of LLM chatbots can easily lead to a loss of information processing and critical thinking skills. However, designing appropriate chatbots that address specific learning objectives within the Bloom's taxonomy framework can also utilize LLM chatbots to enhance these competencies. Wu's second challenge revolves around "cognitive overload caused by an increase in knowledge availability." This overload can occur when learners are exposed to an overwhelming amount of information through AI-powered resources, leading to difficulty in processing and retaining the knowledge effectively. To mitigate cognitive overload and facilitate effective learning, it is crucial to design AI-powered learning resources that present information in a structured and digestible manner, aligning with learners' cognitive capacities and prior knowledge. Incorporating scaffolding techniques and providing learners with tools to manage and organize the information can further prevent cognitive overload.

As mentioned, the application level of Bloom's taxonomy is arguably the most challenging to achieve in educational settings, as it requires a delicate balance between technology and social elements. Striking this balance is crucial to ensure that learners can benefit from both aspects when applying LLMs in learning situations. For instance, digital escape rooms are primarily socially oriented, allowing learners to collaborate and interact with their peers, thus fostering social learning. However, by incorporating LLMs as facilitators within these digital escape rooms (Fotaris, et al. 2023), educators can leverage the benefits of AI-powered learning while maintaining the social aspects of the experience. This balanced approach enables learners to engage in immersive, collaborative problem-solving activities while receiving personalized support and guidance from the LLMs.

Take Away Insights and Strategies for Integrating AI in Healthcare Education

The rapid advancements in AI particularly Large Language Models (LLMs), are converting the way learners progress through the levels of Bloom's Taxonomy in healthcare education. The integration of LLM chatbots is accelerating the acquisition of knowledge and skills at the lower levels of the taxonomy, such as remembering and understanding. Simultaneously, these AI tools are enhancing learners' abilities to engage in higher order thinking skills, such as applying, analysing, evaluating, and creating. However, as the impact of LLMs on each level of the taxonomy becomes more pronounced, it is crucial for educators and institutions to take actionable steps to maximize the benefits and minimize the risks associated with these changes.

To effectively leverage the transformative potential of AI in healthcare education, educators must design AI resources that support specific learning objectives at each taxonomy level, fostering a more personalized and adaptive learning experience. Collaboration between healthcare professionals and educators in the development process is essential to ensure the creation of authentic, immersive learning experiences that mirror real-world healthcare scenarios. Additionally, implementing comprehensive ethical frameworks and continuous evaluation and improvement processes is crucial to ensure the responsible integration of AI in healthcare education.

In proactively addressing the challenges and opportunities presented by the evolving landscape of AI in education, educators and institutions can cultivate a stronger healthcare workforce. They can be equipped with the critical thinking, problem-solving, and decision-making skills necessary to navigate the complexities of an increasingly AI-driven healthcare environment. Table 2 highlights some key considerations for integrating AI in healthcare education. Ultimately, the strategic integration of AI in healthcare education has the potential to significantly improve patient care and outcomes by empowering learners to apply their knowledge and skills in meaningful, innovative ways.

Table 2. Key considerations for integrating AI chatbots in healthcare education

Area of Focus	Actionable Points for Bloom's Taxonomy Integration	Benefits for Learners
Pedagogical Alignment	Develop a matrix aligning AI chatbot features with specific learning objectives and assessment strategies at each level of Bloom's Taxonomy.	Learners receive targeted support and guidance tailored to their current level of understanding, promoting effective progression through the taxonomy.
Co-Creation and Stakeholder Involvement	Organize workshops and focus groups to gather input from diverse stakeholders, ensuring AI chatbots address the unique needs of each healthcare discipline.	Learners benefit from AI chatbots that incorporate insights from subject matter experts, leading to more relevant and engaging learning experiences.
Personalization and Adaptivity	Implement AI that dynamically adjust the complexity and pace of learning content based on individual learner performance and engagement metrics.	Learners experience a customized learning journey that adapts to their strengths and weaknesses, optimizing their progress through the taxonomy levels.
Authentic and Immersive Learning	Develop AI-powered simulations that present learners with increasingly complex (and purposefully incorrect) scenarios as they progress through the taxonomy.	Learners develop critical thinking and decision-making skills in a safe, controlled environment that closely mimics real-world healthcare settings.
Ethical Considerations	Establish an AI ethics committee to review and approve all AI chatbot content and interactions, ensuring alignment with professional and institutional values.	Learners can trust that the information and guidance provided by AI chatbots adhere to the highest ethical standards, promoting responsible learning and decision-making.
Continuous Evaluation and Improvement	Implement a data-driven feedback loop that collects learner performance data, stakeholder feedback, and AI chatbot usage metrics to inform iterative improvements.	Learners benefit from AI chatbots that continuously evolve and improve based on real-world performance data, ensuring a consistently high-quality learning experience.

CONCLUSION

In this chapter, we have examined how the integration of Artificial Intelligence (AI), specifically Large Language Models (LLMs), into healthcare education can be beneficial. Aligning AI chatbots with Bloom's Taxonomy enables the creation of effective learning tools. These tools enhance skills such as critical thinking, problem solving, and decision making. Through case studies and recommended practices, we've seen how LLM chatbots can offer interactive, layered, and relevant learning experiences in various healthcare fields. Addressing challenges like aligning teaching methods, involving stakeholders in co-creation, understanding ethical concerns, and focusing on continual assessment and refinement is vital for maximizing the advantages of AI in this sector. Looking ahead, adopting a cooperative, cross-disciplinary, and student-focused strategy in designing and applying AI chatbots is desired for leveraging their potential to innovate healthcare education. Thoughtful application of LLMs and AI chatbots can enable learners to master healthcare practice's challenges, leading to enhanced patient care and results. This chapter encourages educators, scholars, and healthcare practitioners to engage in creating and applying AI-driven educational tools, using the insights and practices shared as a foundation for a responsive, individualized, and effective healthcare education future, rooted in Bloom's Taxonomy's core principles.

REFERENCES

Anderson, L. W., & Krathwohl, D. R. (2001). *A taxonomy for learning, teaching, and assessing: A revision of Bloom's taxonomy of educational objectives: Complete edition.* Addison Wesley Longman, Inc. https://fintechsociety.comp.nus.edu/lyfh30syqkpx/20-prof-aaron-hoppe-2/a-9780801319037-a-taxonomy-for-learning-teaching-and-assessing-a.pdf

Anderson, L. W., & Krathwohl, D. R. (2021). *A taxonomy for learning, teaching, and assessing: A revision of Bloom's taxonomy of educational objectives.* Longman. http://dspace.vnbrims.org:13000/xmlui/handle/123456789/4570

Anthropic. (2024). *Introducing Claude 3.* Anthropic. https://www.anthropic.com/news/claude-3-family

Antoniou, P. E., Konstantinidis, S. Th., & Bamidis, P. D. (2021). Panel Session-Co-creative Virtual Reality Content Development in Healthcare: Tackling the content availability problem. *2021 7th International Conference on Immersive Learning Research Network (iLRN)*, (pp. 1–3). IEEE. 10.23919/iLRN52045.2021.9459401

Arif, T. B., Munaf, U., & Ul-Haque, I. (2023). The future of medical education and research: Is ChatGPT a blessing or blight in disguise? *Medical Education Online*, 28(1), 1052. 10.1080/10872981.2023.218105236809073

Astutik, I., Jonathans, P. M., Ratri, D. P., & Devanti, Y. M. (2023). Understanding neuroscience, how the brain works, and the implication on grammar teaching and learning. *ELLITE: Journal of English Language, Literature, and Teaching*, 8(1), 61–73.

Atenas, J., Havemann, L., Neumann, J., & Stefanelli, C. (2020). *Open education policies: Guidelines for co-creation.*

Banerjee, M., Chiew, D., Patel, K. T., Johns, I., Chappell, D., Linton, N., Cole, G. D., Francis, D. P., Szram, J., Ross, J., & Zaman, S. (2021). The impact of artificial intelligence on clinical education: Perceptions of postgraduate trainee doctors in London (UK) and recommendations for trainers. *BMC Medical Education*, 21(1), 1–10. 10.1186/s12909-021-02870-x34391424

Bloom, B. S. (Ed.). (1956). *Taxonomy of educational objectives: The classification of educational goals. Handbook I: Cognitive domain.* David McKay Company.

Bond, M. (2020). Facilitating student engagement through the flipped learning approach in K-12: A systematic review. *Computers & Education*, 151, 103819. 10.1016/j.compedu.2020.103819

Boyle, T. (2002). Towards a theoretical base for educational multimedia design. *Journal of Interactive Media in Education*, 2002(3). 10.5334/2002-2

Boyle, T., Cook, J., Windle, R., Wharrad, H., Leeder, D., & Alton, R. (2007). *Agile methods for developing learning objects.*

Brown, A. H., & Green, T. D. (2019). *The essentials of instructional design: Connecting fundamental principles with process and practice.* Routledge. 10.4324/9780429439698

Chan, K. S., & Zary, N. (2019). Applications and challenges of implementing artificial intelligence in medical education: Integrative review. *JMIR Medical Education*, 5(1), e13930. 10.2196/1393031199295

Chen, I. (2011). Instructional design methodologies. In *Instructional Design: Concepts, Methodologies, Tools and Applications* (pp. 80-94). IGI Global. 10.4018/978-1-60960-503-2.ch108

Chiu, T. K. F., Xia, Q., Zhou, X., Chai, C. S., & Cheng, M. (2023). Systematic literature review on opportunities, challenges, and future research recommendations of artificial intelligence in education. *Computers and Education: Artificial Intelligence*, 4, 100118. 10.1016/j.caeai.2022.100118

Costa, F. A. (2013). Designing educational multimedia resources. In Moreira, A., Benavides, O., & Mendes, A. J. (Eds.), *Media in Education: Results from the 2011 ICEM and SIIE joint Conference* (pp. 29–40). Springer New York., 10.1007/978-1-4614-3175-6_3

Crough, J., & Love, C. A. (2019). Improving student engagement and self-regulated learning through technology-enhanced student partnerships. *International Conference on Information Communication Technologies in Education*, Crete, Greece.

Cummings, M., & Cummings, M. L. (2023). *Identifying AI hazards and responsibility gaps*. Research Gate. https://www.researchgate.net/publication/372051108

Davis, J., Van Bulck, L., Durieux, B. N., & Lindvall, C. (2024). The temperature feature of ChatGPT: Modifying creativity for clinical research. *JMIR Human Factors*, 11(1), e53559. 10.2196/5355938457221

DeSmet, A., Thompson, D., Baranowski, T., Palmeira, A., Verloigne, M., & De Bourdeaudhuij, I. (2016). Is participatory design associated with the effectiveness of serious digital games for healthy lifestyle promotion? A meta-analysis. *Journal of Medical Internet Research*, 18(4), e94. 10.2196/jmir.444427129447

Dolianiti, F., Tsoupouroglou, I., Antoniou, P., Konstantinidis, S., Anastasiades, S., & Bamidis, P. (2020). Chatbots in healthcare curricula: The case of a conversational virtual patient. *Lecture Notes in Computer Science (including Subseries Lecture Notes in Artificial Intelligence and Lecture Notes in Bioinformatics)*, 12462 LNAI, 137–147. 10.1007/978-3-030-60735-7_15

Dollinger, M., Lodge, J., & Coates, H. (2018). Co-creation in higher education: Towards a conceptual model. *Journal of Marketing for Higher Education*, 28(2), 210–231. 10.1080/08841241.2018.1466756

Doyle, E., Buckley, P., & McCarthy, B. (2021). The impact of content co-creation on academic achievement. *Assessment & Evaluation in Higher Education*, 46(3), 494–507. 10.1080/02602938.2020.1782832

Doyle, E., Buckley, P., & Whelan, J. (2019). Assessment co-creation: An exploratory analysis of opportunities and challenges based on student and instructor perspectives. *Teaching in Higher Education*, 24(6), 739–754. 10.1080/13562517.2018.1498077

Draper, S. W. (2009). Catalytic assessment: Understanding how MCQs and EVS can foster deep learning. *British Journal of Educational Technology*, 40(2), 285–293. 10.1111/j.1467-8535.2008.00920.x

Flin, R., Youngson, G. G., & Yule, S. (Eds.). (2015). *Enhancing surgical performance: A primer in non-technical skills*. CRC Press. 10.1201/b18702

Fotaris, P., Mastoras, T., & Lameras, P. (2023, September). Designing educational escape rooms with generative AI: A framework and ChatGPT prompt engineering guide. In *Proceedings of the 17th European Conference on Game-Based Learning: ECGBL 2023*. Academic Conferences and Publishing Limited. 10.34190/ecgbl.17.1.1870

Ghorashi, N., Ismail, A., Ghosh, P., Sidawy, A., Javan, R., & Ghorashi, N. S. (2023). AI-powered chatbots in medical education: Potential applications and implications. *Cureus*, 15(8). 10.7759/cureus.4327137692629

Halupa, C. (2020). Reaching "creating" in Bloom's taxonomy: The merging of heutagogy and technology in online learning. In *Research Anthology on Developing Critical Thinking Skills in Students* (pp. 15–35). IGI Global. 10.4018/978-1-7998-3022-1.ch002

Halvorsrud, K., Kucharska, J., Adlington, K., Rüdell, K., Brown Hajdukova, E., Nazroo, J., Haarmans, M., Rhodes, J., & Bhui, K. (2021). Identifying evidence of effectiveness in the co-creation of research: A systematic review and meta-analysis of the international healthcare literature. *Journal of Public Health (Oxford, England)*, 43(1), 197–208. 10.1093/pubmed/fdz12631608396

Hamzah, A., Almed, & Wahid, F. (2016, November). Participatory design in the development of healthcare systems: A literature review. In *Proceedings of the 2nd International Conference on Communication and Information Processing* (pp. 60-64). ACM. 10.1145/3018009.3018010

Hardy, J., Bates, S. P., Casey, M. M., Galloway, K. W., Galloway, R. K., Kay, A. E., Kirsop, P., & McQueen, H. A. (2014, September 2). Student-generated content: Enhancing learning through sharing multiple-choice questions. *International Journal of Science Education*, 36(13), 2180–2194. 10.1080/09500693.2014.916831

Henderson, J., Pears, M., Bamidis, P. D., Tsoupouroglou, I., Schiza, E., Pattichis, C. S., Stathakarou, N., Karlgren, K., & Konstantinidis, S. T. (2022). Development of a bespoke chatbot design tool to facilitate a crowd-based co-creation process. *2022 International Conference on Interactive Media, Smart Systems and Emerging Technologies, IMET 2022 - Proceedings*. IEEE. 10.1109/IMET54801.2022.9929752

Henderson, J., Pears, M., & Konstantinidis, S. (2022, September). *Done in 60 minutes! Best practices, crowdsourcing, co-creation, and design principals of educational chatbots*. Presented at ALT Annual Conference 2022, Manchester, UK. https://nottingham-repository.worktribe.com/index.php/output/13179986/done-in-60-minutes-best-practices-crowdsourcing-co-creation-and-design-principals-of-educational-chatbots

Herrmann-Werner, A., Festl-Wietek, T., Holderried, F., Herschbach, L., Griewatz, J., Masters, K., Zipfel, S., & Mahling, M. (2024). Assessing ChatGPT's mastery of Bloom's taxonomy using psychosomatic medicine exam questions: Mixed-methods study. *Journal of Medical Internet Research*, 26(1), e52113. 10.2196/5211338261378

Hidayat, S., & Qamariah, Z. (2023). The role of Bloom's taxonomy in curriculum approach. [JIMNU]. *Jurnal Ilmiah Multidisiplin Nusantara*, 1(3), 162–167. 10.59435/jimnu.v1i3.183

Ho, M., Taylor, M., McSharry, E., Bergmann-Tyacke, I., Santos, M. R., Dhaeze, M., Brown, M., Hall, C., & Konstantinidis, S. T. (2021). The role of stakeholders' evaluation on the quality of reusable learning objects following the aspire participatory framework. In *INTED2021 Proceedings* (pp. 7950-7960). IATED.

Holderried, F., Stegemann-Philipps, C., Herschbach, L., Moldt, J.-A., Nevins, A., Griewatz, J., Holderried, M., Herrmann-Werner, A., Festl-Wietek, T., & Mahling, M. (2024). A generative pretrained transformer (GPT)-powered chatbot as a simulated patient to practice history taking: Prospective, mixed methods study. *JMIR Medical Education*, 10(1), e53961. 10.2196/5396138227363

Iftimia, N., Pandya, R., & Mahoney, F. (2023). New advances in artificial intelligence for biomedical research and clinical decision-making. *Preprints,* 2023060243. https://doi.org/10.20944/preprints202306.0243.v1

Johnson, A. E. W., Pollard, T. J., Shen, L., Lehman, L. W. H., Feng, M., Ghassemi, M., Moody, B., Szolovits, P., Celi, L. A., & Mark, R. G. (2016). MIMIC-III, a freely accessible critical care database. *Scientific Data*, 3(1), 1–9. 10.1038/sdata.2016.3527219127

Joshi, A., Srinivas, C., Firat, E. E., & Laramee, R. S. (2024). *Evaluating the recommendations of LLMs to teach a visualization technique using Bloom's taxonomy.* USFCA. https://www.cs.usfca.edu/~apjoshi/papers/2024_VDA_LLM_Evaluation_PCP.pdf

Karabacak, M., & Margetis, K. (2023). Embracing large language models for medical applications: Opportunities and challenges. *Cureus*, 15(5). 10.7759/cureus.3930537378099

Klein, G. (2008). Naturalistic decision making. *Human Factors*, 50(3), 456–460. 10.1518/001872008X28838518689053

Kononowicz, A. A., Woodham, L. A., Edelbring, S., Stathakarou, N., Davies, D., Saxena, N., Tudor Car, L., Carlstedt-Duke, J., Car, J., & Zary, N. (2019). Virtual patient simulations in health professions education: Systematic review and meta-analysis by the digital health education collaboration. *Journal of Medical Internet Research*, 21(7), e14676. 10.2196/1467631267981

Krathwohl, D. R. (2002). A revision of Bloom's taxonomy: An overview. *Theory into Practice*, 41(4), 212–218. 10.1207/s15430421tip4104_2

Kumaran, D., Summerfield, J. J., Hassabis, D., & Maguire, E. A. (2009). Tracking the emergence of conceptual knowledge during human decision making. *Neuron*, 63(6), 889–901. 10.1016/j.neuron.2009.07.03019778516

Lameras, P., Paraskakis, I., & Konstantinidis, S. (2022). A rudimentary progression model for artificial intelligence in education competencies and skills. *Lecture Notes in Networks and Systems, 411 LNNS*, 927–936. 10.1007/978-3-030-96296-8_84

Larsen, T. M., Endo, B. H., Yee, A. T., Do, T., & Lo, S. M. (2022). Probing internal assumptions of the revised Bloom's taxonomy. *CBE Life Sciences Education*, 21(4), ar66. 10.1187/cbe.20-08-017036112622

Lee, S., Youn, J., Kim, H., Kim, M., & Yoon, S. H. (2023). CXR-LLAVA: A multimodal large language model for interpreting chest X-ray images. https://arxiv.org/abs/2310.18341v3

Leech, G., Garfinkel, S., Yagudin, M., Briand, A., Zhuravlev, A., & Research, A. (2024). Ten hard problems in artificial intelligence we must get right. https://arxiv.org/abs/2402.04464v1

Levy, R. (2024). The prefrontal cortex: From monkey to man. *Brain*, 147(3), 794–815. 10.1093/brain/awad38937972282

Lourdusamy, R., Magendiran, P., & Fonceca, C. M. (2022). Analysis of cognitive levels of questions with Bloom's taxonomy: A case study. *International Journal of Software Innovation*, 10(1), 1–22. 10.4018/IJSI.297922

Mehandru, N., Miao, B. Y., Almaraz, E. R., Sushil, M., Butte, A. J., & Alaa, A. (2023). Large language models as agents in the clinic. *arXiv preprint arXiv:2309.10895*. https://doi.org//arXiv.2309.1089510.48550

Midjourney. (2023). *Home*. Midjourney. https://www.midjourney.com/home

Mikolov, T., Chen, K., Corrado, G., & Dean, J. (2013). Efficient estimation of word representations in vector space. *1st International Conference on Learning Representations, ICLR 2013 - Workshop Track Proceedings*. https://arxiv.org/abs/1301.3781v3

Naveed, H., Khan, A. U., Qiu, S., Saqib, M., Anwar, S., Usman, M., Barnes, N., & Mian, A. (2023). A comprehensive overview of large language models. *arXiv preprint arXiv:2307.06435*.

Neumann, O., Guirguis, K., & Steiner, R. (2023). Exploring artificial intelligence adoption in public organizations: A comparative case study. *Public Management Review*, 1–28.

Ng, D. T. K., Leung, J. K. L., Su, J., Ng, R. C. W., & Chu, S. K. W. (2023). Teachers' AI digital competencies and twenty-first century skills in the post-pandemic world. *Educational Technology Research and Development*, 71(1), 137–161. 10.1007/s11423-023-10203-636844361

Ninaus, M., & Sailer, M. (2022). Closing the loop–The human role in artificial intelligence for education. *Frontiers in Psychology*, 13, 956798. 10.3389/fpsyg.2022.95679836092115

Open A. I. (2023). *GPT-4*. OpenAI. https://openai.com/research/gpt-4

Open A. I. (2024). *Sora*. OpenAI. https://openai.com/sora

Pears, M., Henderson, J., & Konstantinidis, S. T. (2021, May 27). Repurposing case-based learning to a conversational agent for healthcare cybersecurity. *Studies in Health Technology and Informatics*, 281, 1066–1070. 10.3233/SHTI21034834042842

Pears, M., Henderson, J., Wharrad, H., & Konstantinidis, S. (2022, September). *The journey from co-creation to impact for digital resources in healthcare*. Presented at ALT Annual Conference 2022, Manchester, UK. https://nottingham-repository.worktribe.com/index.php/output/13179801/the-journey-from-co-creation-to-impact-for-digital-resources-in-healthcare

Pears, M., Wadhwa, K., Hanchanale, V., Jain, S., Elmamoun, M. H., Payne, S. R., Konstantinidis, S., Rochester, M., Doherty, R., & Biyani, C. S. (2024). *Surgical consultants and ChatGPT characteristics in training: A repeated-measures double-blinded study in non-technical skills for urology trainees*. Manuscript submitted for publication.

Prasad, G. N. R., & Professor, S. A. (2021). Evaluating student performance based on Bloom's taxonomy levels. *Journal of Physics: Conference Series*, 1797(1), 12063. 10.1088/1742-6596/1797/1/012063

Radford, A., & Narasimhan, K. (2018). *Improving language understanding by generative pre-training*. Semantic Scholar. https://semanticscholar.org/paper/49313245

Rao, A., Pang, M., Kim, J., Kamineni, M., Lie, W., Prasad, A. K., Landman, A., Dreyer, K. J., Succi, M. D., & Hospital, M. G. (2023). Assessing the utility of ChatGPT throughout the entire clinical workflow. *MedRxiv*. 10.1101/2023.02.21.23285886

Reason, J., Hollnagel, E., & Paries, J. (2006). Revisiting the Swiss cheese model of accidents. *Journal of Clinical Engineering*, 27(4), 110–115.

Safranek, C. W., Sidamon-Eristoff, A. E., Gilson, A., & Chartash, D. (2023). The role of large language models in medical education: Applications and implications. *JMIR Medical Education*, 9(1), e50945. 10.2196/5094537578830

Sajja, R., Sermet, Y., Cikmaz, M., Cwiertny, D., & Demir, I. (2023). Artificial intelligence-enabled intelligent assistant for personalized and adaptive learning in higher education. *arXiv preprint arXiv:2309.10892*. https://doi.org//arxiv.2309.1089210.48550

Sallam, M. (2023). ChatGPT utility in healthcare education, research, and practice: Systematic review on the promising perspectives and valid concerns. *Healthcare (Basel)*, 11(6), 887. 10.3390/healthcare1106088736981544

Schubert, M. C., Wick, W., & Venkataramani, V. (2023). Performance of large language models on a neurology board-style examination. *JAMA Network Open*, 6(12), e2346721. 10.1001/jamanetworkopen.2023.4672138060223

Sedaghat, S. (2023). Early applications of ChatGPT in medical practice, education, and research. *Clinical Medicine (London, England)*, 23(3), 278–279. 10.7861/clinmed.2023-007837085182

Sharma, D., Kaushal, S., Kumar, H., & Gainder, S. (2022). Chatbots in healthcare: Challenges, technologies and applications. In *AIST 2022 - 4th International Conference on Artificial Intelligence and Speech Technology*. IEEE. 10.1109/AIST55798.2022.10065328

Sparrow, B., Liu, J., & Wegner, D. M. (2011). Google effects on memory: Cognitive consequences of having information at our fingertips. *Science*, 333(6043), 776–778. 10.1126/science.120774521764755

Stathakarou, N., Nifakos, S., Karlgren, K., Konstantinidis, S. T., Bamidis, P. D., Pattichis, C. S., & Davoody, N. (2020). Students' perceptions on chatbots' potential and design characteristics in healthcare education. *Studies in Health Technology and Informatics*, 272, 209–212. 10.3233/SHTI20053132604638

Tahri Sqalli, M., Aslonov, B., Gafurov, M., & Nurmatov, S. (2023). Humanizing AI in medical training: Ethical framework for responsible design. *Frontiers in Artificial Intelligence*, 6, 1189914. 10.3389/frai.2023.118991437261331

Tsai, D. C. L., Huang, A. Y. Q., Lu, O. H. T., & Yang, S. J. H. (2021). Automatic question generation for repeated testing to improve student learning outcome. In *Proceedings - IEEE 21st International Conference on Advanced Learning Technologies, ICALT 2021* (pp. 339–341). IEEE. 10.1109/ICALT52272.2021.00108

Tuhkala, A. (2021). A systematic literature review of participatory design studies involving teachers. *European Journal of Education*, 56(4), 641–659. 10.1111/ejed.12471

Tuma, F., & Nassar, A. K. (2021). Applying Bloom's taxonomy in clinical surgery: Practical examples. *Annals of Medicine and Surgery (London)*, 69, 102656. 10.1016/j.amsu.2021.10265634429945

Wharrad, H., Windle, R., & Taylor, M. (2021). Designing digital education and training for health. In Konstantinidis, S. T., Bamidis, P. D., & Zary, N. (Eds.), *Digital Innovations in Healthcare Education and Training* (pp. 31–45). Academic Press. 10.1016/B978-0-12-813144-2.00003-9

Wu, Y. (2023). Integrating generative AI in education: How ChatGPT brings challenges for future learning and teaching. *Journal of Advanced Research in Education*. 10.56397/JARE.2023.07.02

Yan, Z. (2023). Research on the role of hippocampus in memory consolidation. *Theoretical and Natural Science*, 6(1), 108–113. 10.54254/2753-8818/6/20230191

Yu, P., Xu, H., Hu, X., & Deng, C. (2023). Leveraging generative AI and large language models: A comprehensive roadmap for healthcare integration. *Health Care*, 11(20), 2776. 10.3390/healthcare1120277637893850

Yuan, M., Bao, P., Yuan, J., Shen, Y., Chen, Z., Xie, Y., Zhao, J., Chen, Y., Zhang, L., Shen, L., & Dong, B. (2023). Large language models illuminate a progressive pathway to artificial healthcare assistant: A review. *arXiv*. https://doi.org//arXiv.2311.0191810.48550

Zagabathuni, Y. (2022). Applications, scope, and challenges for AI in healthcare. *International Journal of Emerging Trends in Engineering Research*. The World Academy of Research in Science and Engineering. https://www.academia.edu/76121649/Applications_Scope_and_Challenges_for_AI_in_healthcare

Zarandi, N., Soares, A., & Alves, H. (2022). Strategies, benefits, and barriers–a systematic literature review of student co-creation in higher education. *Journal of Marketing for Higher Education*, 1–25. 10.1080/08841241.2022.2134956

Zhao, Y., Zhang, R., Li, W., Huang, D., Guo, J., Peng, S., & Chen, Y. (2024). Assessing and understanding creativity in large language models. *arXiv preprint arXiv:2401.12491*. https://doi.org//arXiv.2401.1249110.48550

Zhou, C., Li, Q., Li, C., Yu, J., Liu, Y., Wang, G., Zhang, K., Ji, C., Yan, Q., He, L., Peng, H., Li, J., Wu, J., Liu, Z., Xie, P., Xiong, C., Pei, J., Yu, P. S., & Sun, L. (2023). A comprehensive survey on pretrained foundation models: A history from BERT to ChatGPT. https://arxiv.org/abs/2302.09419v3

Chapter 9
Transformative Waves:
Exploring Disruptive Technologies in Education and Workforce Development

Nitish Kumar Minz
https://orcid.org/0009-0000-4770-0336
K.R. Mangalam University, India

ABSTRACT

This research explores the transformative impact of disruptive technologies in education and workforce development. Focused on key themes, it investigates how technologies like AI, AR, and VR reshape learning experiences, catalyzing a paradigm shift in education. Examining workforce development, the review highlights initiatives for upskilling and reskilling in the digital age. Balancing opportunities and challenges, the narrative unfolds changes in teaching models towards adaptive, learner-centric approaches. Navigating the evolving digital landscape, stakeholders must embrace innovation while addressing issues of access and equity. Understanding and adapting to these transformative waves are essential for fostering a future-ready education and resilient workforce.

INTRODUCTION

The integration of disruptive technologies into education and workforce development has emerged as a defining phenomenon in contemporary times, reshaping the foundations of how knowledge is acquired, disseminated, and applied. This literature review endeavors to navigate the multifaceted landscape of disruptive technologies, exploring their profound impact on educational paradigms and professional trajectories. As we stand at the precipice of a digital revolution, it becomes imperative to scrutinize the transformative waves generated by technologies such as artificial intelligence (AI), digitization, and innovative learning approaches.

The background of this study is rooted in the dynamic evolution of technology and its pivotal role in restructuring traditional modes of education and professional development. The emergence of disruptive technologies has not only revolutionized pedagogical practices within educational institutions but has also redefined the skill sets essential for success in an increasingly digitized workforce. This transformation is characterized by a departure from conventional teaching methods, marking a shift towards personalized, adaptive, and technology-driven learning experiences.

DOI: 10.4018/979-8-3693-3003-6.ch009

A comprehensive understanding of the disruptive technology landscape requires an exploration of various scholarly perspectives. Agrawal (2021) underscores the ubiquity of technology in educational settings, setting the stage for an in-depth exploration of its role in transforming the learning landscape. In tandem, Amos (2019) delves into the digitization of the global education industry, signaling the intricate interplay between disruptive technologies and the broader educational ecosystem.

Within specific educational niches, Avni (2017) examines the impact of disruptive technologies on Jewish education, providing a nuanced lens into the intersection of technology and cultural learning practices. Flavin's research (2016, 2017) extends the discourse to higher education, unraveling the social and pedagogical implications of disruptive technologies. Harris and Short (2014) shift the focus to the workforce, emphasizing the transformative potential of aligning professional development with technological advancements.

This review encapsulates a diverse array of scholarly contributions, each offering a unique perspective on the intricate relationship between disruptive technologies, education, and workforce development. Through an in-depth analysis of these works, this exploration aims to unveil the transformative potential and challenges posed by disruptive technologies, laying the groundwork for a nuanced understanding of their implications on the educational and professional landscapes.

LITERATURE REVIEW

The integration of disruptive technologies into the realms of education and workforce development marks a pivotal juncture in the evolution of traditional practices. The advent of transformative waves, propelled by these technological interventions, has heralded a paradigm shift in how individuals acquire knowledge, skills, and navigate their professional trajectories. This comprehensive literature review delves into the multifaceted impact of disruptive technologies on education and workforce development, examining key themes across a spectrum of scholarly works.

In recent years, technological advancements have permeated every facet of contemporary society, and the domains of education and workforce development are no exceptions. The amalgamation of digital innovations, AI, and other disruptive technologies has not only altered the landscape of traditional educational practices but has also redefined the dynamics of the modern workforce. As we stand at the intersection of the digital age and the pursuit of knowledge and skills, understanding the profound implications of these transformative waves becomes imperative.

A vital aspect of this examination lies in recognizing the transformative potential embedded within disruptive technologies. Agrawal's (2021) exploration of the role of technology in education provides insights into the transformative potential that technology carries. The study elucidates the multifaceted ways in which technology has the capacity to reshape educational landscapes, influencing pedagogical approaches, and altering the dynamics of student engagement. Such transformations extend beyond the classroom, resonating deeply in the corridors of workforce development.

The global landscape of education has witnessed a profound restructuring, with digitization and disruptive innovation acting as catalysts for change. Amos (2019) contemplates the digitization phenomenon, specifically its transformative power in the global education industry. The research accentuates the intricate relationship between digitization, disruption, and the emergence of a "Society of Singularities." Within this context, the very fabric of education undergoes a metamorphosis, intertwining with disruptive forces to create a tapestry of new possibilities and challenges.

Consideration of disruptive and transformative forces extends into diverse educational settings. Avni's (2017) investigation into Jewish education reflects on the impact of disruptive elements in shaping learning experiences. The study provides a nuanced understanding of how educational paradigms, when subjected to disruptive influences, can lead to transformative outcomes. It sheds light on the intricate dance between tradition and innovation, highlighting the potential of disruptive technologies to redefine the cultural and social dimensions of education.

Moving beyond the confines of traditional education, the influence of disruptive technologies permeates higher education institutions, sparking a discourse on conduct and relations within these spaces. Flavin's work (2016) examines the impact of disruptive technologies on social relations in higher education. The study underscores the need to grapple with the societal shifts induced by disruptive forces, emphasizing the complex interplay between technological advancements and social dynamics within educational institutions.

In the pursuit of knowledge, Flavin (2017) extends the discourse to explore the implications of disruptive innovation. The question of "Why Can't I Just Google It?" becomes emblematic of a broader conversation about the evolving nature of higher education in the face of disruptive forces. This inquiry transcends the realm of mere information retrieval, delving into the deeper transformations that disruptive technologies introduce into the very fabric of educational methodologies.

As the discussion unfolds, considerations extend to the intersection of disruptive technologies and workforce development. Harris and Short (2014) navigate the notion of workforce development within the context of disruptive technologies. Their exploration intricately weaves the threads of workforce dynamics and the transformative potential inherent in disruptions, providing a holistic view of the evolving nature of contemporary workplaces.

The impact of disruptive technologies also extends into the future of education, as envisioned by Her anu (2020). The study peers into the horizon of education, where disruptive technologies cast their shadows, offering a glimpse of the evolving educational landscape. It contemplates the fusion of disruptive elements and future educational developments, opening avenues for anticipatory reflections on the transformative trajectories that education may traverse.

In the exploration of American education, Horn and Mackey (2011) contribute to the narrative by scrutinizing the transformative potential of disruptive technologies. The transformation they envision transcends the immediate confines of classrooms, reaching into the core of the American educational system. Their work underscores the interconnectedness of disruptive technologies and the overarching goal of transforming education at a national level.

In tandem, Horn and Carl (2015) widen the scope to encompass the transformative aspirations embedded within U.S. workforce development policies. Their exploration traverses the policy landscape, contemplating the ways in which disruptive technologies can be harnessed to shape the future trajectory of workforce development. This perspective aligns with broader societal aspirations, where the integration of disruptive technologies becomes instrumental in sculpting a workforce that aligns with the demands of the 21st century.

The disruptive waves of technological innovation are not confined to national boundaries; they permeate global educational ecosystems. Horvath's (2016) examination of disruptive technologies in higher education captures the global dimensions of this transformative phenomenon. The study sheds light on the diverse manifestations of disruptive technologies, emphasizing the need for a nuanced understanding that transcends geographical constraints.

From the vantage point of industry, Jordan (2017) explores the digital workforce and the transformative potential of disruptive technologies within professional domains. The digital workforce, as envisaged by Jordan, becomes a manifestation of the changing nature of work itself. This exploration extends beyond the traditional realms of education, illustrating the symbiotic relationship between education and the workforce, both subject to the transformative forces of disruptive technologies.

The transformative power of disruptive technologies unfolds within the pages of Kirkwood's work (2011), which examines the myths and realities associated with the adoption of transformative technologies. The study unravels the complexities surrounding the integration of technology into collaborative learning environments, challenging preconceived notions and offering a nuanced understanding of the transformative journey.

As the design of education's workforce takes center stage, Lee et al.'s (2020) research navigates the intricate terrain of designing the education workforce. This exploration is rooted in the acknowledgment that the workforce responsible for imparting knowledge plays a pivotal role in shaping the transformative potential of education. The study offers a glimpse into the strategic considerations and design principles that underscore the evolution of the education workforce in the era of disruptive technologies.

Liu and Chen's (2018) investigation brought attention to the enhanced learning experiences facilitated by disruptive technologies. Their study delved into the transformative potential of digital technologies, emphasizing the need for a nuanced understanding of their role in reshaping educational landscapes. The juxtaposition of use and misuse within the context of higher education reflects the delicate balance that educators must navigate to harness the transformative power of disruptive technologies effectively.

In the realm of classroom technologies, Magana's (2019) exploration of disruptive elements lays the groundwork for innovation in education. The framework presented in the study becomes a compass for educators seeking to navigate the transformative potential of disruptive classroom technologies. It underscores the dynamic interplay between disruption and innovation, fostering an environment where educational practices evolve in tandem with technological advancements.

Within engineering education, Putra and Tan's (2012) work introduced an alternative perspective that draws parallels to disruptive technology. This exploration extends beyond the conventional boundaries of educational discourse, highlighting the disruptive potential inherent in design-based education. The study becomes a testament to the transformative waves that can emanate from alternative pedagogical approaches within specialized educational domains.

The contemporary state of research in engineering education further unfolds in Siddhpura et al.'s (2020) examination. The study paints a vivid picture of the current landscape, emphasizing the application of disruptive technologies in engineering education. It becomes a reflection of the dynamic interplay between educational practices and technological disruptions, setting the stage for further exploration into the transformative potential of disruptive forces.

As the landscape of education transforms, Wilson's (2019) exploration delves into the broader cultural revolution propelled by the amalgamation of the Internet of Things (IoT), blockchain, and AI. The study contemplates the disruptive potential of these technologies, transcending individual domains to reshape the overarching culture of learning. The narrative extends beyond the immediate confines of educational institutions, echoing the transformative ripples that extend into the broader societal and cultural fabric.

The effects of disruptive technologies on higher education become a focal point in Wongleedee's (2019) research. The study unfolds the nuanced ways in which disruptive technology shapes the higher education landscape. It becomes a canvas on which the transformative impacts are painted, illustrating the intricate dance between technology and higher education, where the disruptive waves redefine traditional boundaries and challenge established norms.

Furthermore, Yeung's (2023) investigation into transformative learning adds a nuanced layer to the discourse. The study explores the integration of sustainable development goals and innovations into integrated projects, offering a lens through which the transformative potential of disruptive technologies in education becomes tangible. The research becomes a testament to the multifaceted dimensions of transformative learning, illustrating how disruptive technologies can serve as catalysts for holistic and sustainable educational transformations.

This literature review embarks on a comprehensive journey, unraveling the diverse dimensions of disruptive technologies in education and workforce development. As we navigate the transformative waves emanating from technological disruptions, the intricate interplay between innovation, education, and workforce dynamics becomes a focal point for exploration. The subsequent sections of this review will delve deeper into specific themes and findings, shedding light on the nuanced ways in which disruptive technologies reshape the educational and professional landscapes.

DISRUPTIVE TECHNOLOGIES IN EDUCATION

The landscape of education has witnessed a profound transformation with the integration of disruptive technologies, fundamentally altering traditional paradigms and ushering in a new era of interactive and personalized learning experiences. This exploration focuses on key disruptive technologies, including AI, augmented reality (AR), and virtual reality (VR), and their impact on educational methodologies.

Artificial Intelligence (AI)

AI has emerged as a cornerstone in educational innovation, offering intelligent tools that adapt to individual learning needs. Agrawal (2021) underscores the pervasive influence of AI in transforming education. AI algorithms can analyze student performance data, identify learning patterns, and customize content delivery, thereby creating adaptive learning environments. This adaptability caters to diverse learning styles, fostering a more inclusive and effective educational experience (Agrawal, 2021).

Furthermore, AI facilitates the automation of administrative tasks, enabling educators to allocate more time to personalized interactions with students. The integration of AI-driven chatbots and virtual assistants streamlines administrative processes, providing timely and personalized support to learners (Agrawal, 2021).

Augmented Reality (AR) and Virtual Reality (VR)

Augmented reality (AR) and virtual reality (VR) technologies introduce immersive learning experiences that transcend the limitations of traditional classrooms. Lee et al., (2020) emphasized the transformative potential of these technologies in designing the education workforce. AR overlays digital information onto the physical world, enhancing real-time learning experiences. VR, on the other hand, creates simulated environments, enabling learners to engage with content in three-dimensional spaces.

The application of AR and VR in education goes beyond theoretical concepts. For instance, these technologies are employed in medical education to simulate surgeries and provide hands-on training in a risk-free environment (Lee et al., 2020). Such applications demonstrate how disruptive technologies bridge the gap between theoretical knowledge and practical skills.

Interactive and Personalized Learning

The interactive nature of disruptive technologies fosters engagement and active participation. Avni's exploration (2017) of disruptive technologies in Jewish education illustrates the effectiveness of interactive learning tools. These technologies enable educators to design dynamic lessons, incorporating multimedia elements and interactive simulations. Students are no longer passive recipients but active participants in their learning journey.

Additionally, disruptive technologies contribute to the rise of personalized learning pathways. Adaptive learning platforms powered by AI analyze individual progress and tailor content to address specific learning needs (Agrawal, 2021). This personalization enhances the efficiency of education delivery, ensuring that each learner receives a customized educational experience.

Breaking Geographical Barriers

Disruptive technologies eliminate geographical constraints, opening up opportunities for global collaboration and knowledge exchange. Online platforms and virtual classrooms powered by AI, AR, and VR enable students to connect with peers and educators from around the world (Agrawal, 2021). This not only diversifies learning perspectives but also prepares students for a globalized workforce.

Disruptive technologies in education, encompassing AI, AR, and VR, redefine the educational landscape by offering interactive, personalized, and globally connected learning experiences. The integration of these technologies heralds a paradigm shift, emphasizing adaptability, engagement, and inclusivity in education.

WORKFORCE DEVELOPMENT IN THE DIGITAL AGE

The contemporary workforce landscape is undergoing a profound metamorphosis propelled by the integration of disruptive technologies. This review critically examines how these technologies have become integral to workforce development strategies, responding to the escalating demand for a digitally adept and agile workforce.

Upskilling and Reskilling Imperatives

In the digital age, the nature of work is evolving rapidly, driven by technological advancements. To meet the demands of this dynamic landscape, organizations are compelled to adopt workforce development strategies that prioritize upskilling and reskilling. Flavin's research (2017) emphasizes the imperative of disruptive innovation in the context of higher education, stating that a workforce equipped with contemporary skills is pivotal for sustained innovation and competitiveness.

Disruptive technologies act as catalysts for this upskilling and reskilling paradigm. The traditional model of static skill sets is rendered obsolete by the rapid evolution of technologies such as AI and automation. As Jordan (2017) notes, the digital workforce is experiencing a transformative shift, demanding competencies aligned with the demands of disruptive technologies.

E-Learning Platforms and Adaptive Learning

The emergence of e-learning platforms represents a pivotal advancement in workforce development. These platforms, often powered by AI and machine learning algorithms, play a central role in facilitating targeted skill development. Lee et al.'s (2020) exploration of designing the education workforce acknowledges the transformative role of e-learning in the broader context of workforce development. These platforms provide adaptive learning experiences, tailoring content delivery based on individual learner profiles.

Adaptive learning, a product of disruptive technologies, addresses the diverse skill levels and learning paces within the workforce. By leveraging AI, these platforms assess individual competencies, identify skill gaps, and deliver personalized learning pathways (Lee et al., 2020). This not only optimizes the learning experience but also ensures that workforce development initiatives are precisely aligned with the evolving needs of industries.

Aligning Skills With Job Market Dynamics

One of the key objectives of workforce development is aligning individual skills with the dynamic needs of the job market. Her anu's (2020) exploration of future education within disruptive technologies developments emphasizes the need for a synchronized approach between education and industry requirements. Disruptive technologies play a pivotal role in achieving this synchronization by providing real-time insights into emerging skills demanded by industries.

Machine learning algorithms analyze market trends, job postings, and industry reports to identify the most sought-after skills. This data-driven approach allows workforce development initiatives to focus on cultivating skills that are not only relevant today but also anticipated to be in high demand in the future (Her anu, 2020).

Agility and Flexibility in Learning

Disruptive technologies introduce agility and flexibility into traditional learning models. Traditional methods often struggle to keep pace with the rapid changes in the digital landscape. Magana's exploration (2019) of disruptive classroom technologies highlights the role of agility in adapting to new educational paradigms. E-learning platforms, coupled with AI, enable on-the-go learning, breaking away from rigid schedules and physical constraints.

Moreover, disruptive technologies facilitate just-in-time learning, allowing individuals to acquire skills precisely when they are needed (Magana, 2019). This aligns with the principles of agile workforce development, ensuring that individuals remain adaptable to evolving job roles and industry dynamics.

Disruptive technologies are redefining workforce development strategies by promoting upskilling, leveraging e-learning platforms, aligning skills with job market demands, and introducing agility and flexibility into learning models. The integration of these technologies is essential for cultivating a workforce equipped to navigate the complexities of the digital age and contribute meaningfully to the evolving landscape of work.

CHALLENGES AND OPPORTUNITIES

The integration of disruptive technologies into education and workforce development brings forth a nuanced landscape characterized by a duality of challenges and opportunities. This section critically explores the existing literature to illuminate the multifaceted nature of this dual narrative.

Opportunities Unleashed

Disruptive technologies, encompassing AI, VR, and AR, have ushered in a wave of transformative opportunities. The potential for interactive and personalized learning experiences is a central theme in the literature. Yeung's study (2023) on transformative learning through integrated projects underscores how disruptive technologies can revolutionize education by offering engaging and sustainable learning experiences. These technologies enable adaptive learning paths, catering to individual learning styles and preferences.

Moreover, the opportunities extend to the democratization of education. Avni's exploration (2017) into disruptive and transformative Jewish education highlights how digital platforms break down geographical barriers, providing access to education irrespective of physical location. This globalization of education aligns with the broader goals of inclusivity and accessibility.

Equity and Access Challenges

However, alongside these opportunities, challenges related to equity and access emerge prominently. The digital divide, often accentuated by economic disparities, creates a scenario where certain demographics may not have equal access to disruptive technologies. Flavin's research (2016) on the impact of disruptive technologies on social relations in higher education points out that the benefits of these technologies are not uniformly distributed. Students from economically disadvantaged backgrounds may face barriers to accessing the necessary devices and high-speed internet required for effective engagement with digital learning tools.

The literature underscores the importance of considering diverse learning needs. Jordan's examination (2017) of the digital workforce emphasizes that not all individuals adapt to digital learning environments at the same pace. Learners with varying degrees of digital literacy may struggle to navigate complex technological interfaces, potentially exacerbating existing educational inequalities.

Digital Literacy Imperatives

Digital literacy emerges as a critical factor in navigating the opportunities and challenges presented by disruptive technologies. Liu and Chen's study (2018) on disruptive technology-enhanced learning underscores the need for individuals to be adept in utilizing digital tools effectively. The literature suggests that the absence of digital literacy can hinder the realization of the potential benefits of disruptive technologies.

Educational institutions and policymakers are challenged to integrate digital literacy education into curricula to ensure that learners are not only proficient in subject matter but also equipped with the skills to navigate the digital landscape. This aligns with the broader discussions on the evolving nature of literacy in the 21st century.

Balancing Innovation and Drawbacks

In navigating the landscape of disruptive technologies, finding a delicate balance between innovation, and addressing potential drawbacks becomes paramount. Harris and Short's exploration (2014) of the notion of workforce development emphasizes the importance of a holistic approach that considers both the positive and negative aspects of disruptive innovations.

Policymakers and educators must be vigilant in mitigating the challenges posed by disruptive technologies, ensuring that initiatives aimed at reaping the benefits are not inadvertently exacerbating existing educational inequalities. Addressing issues related to access, equity, and digital literacy requires collaborative efforts, involving educators, policymakers, and industry leaders.

IMPACT ON TEACHING AND LEARNING MODELS

The integration of disruptive technologies into education has instigated profound transformations in teaching and learning models. This section delves into the literature to unravel the multifaceted impact on educational approaches, from traditional classrooms to evolving blended and online learning environments.

Shift From Rote Memorization to Critical Thinking

One significant impact of disruptive technologies is the paradigm shift from traditional rote memorization to fostering critical thinking and problem-solving skills. Flavin's exploration (2016) of the impact of disruptive technologies on social relations in higher education underscores this shift. The dynamic nature of digital learning tools allows educators to move beyond traditional pedagogical methods, encouraging students to engage with the learning material critically. The emphasis on critical thinking aligns with the broader goals of preparing learners for a rapidly evolving, knowledge-driven landscape.

Transformation of Classroom Dynamics

The traditional classroom setup is undergoing a metamorphosis, propelled by the integration of disruptive technologies. Lee et al.'s study (2020) on designing the education workforce highlights the move toward learner-centric approaches facilitated by adaptive learning platforms. These platforms utilize AI algorithms to tailor educational content to individual learning styles, preferences, and pace. The literature suggests that this personalization of learning experiences enhances student engagement and comprehension.c

Moreover, the advent of VR and AR technologies contributes to immersive learning experiences. Yeung's research (2023) on transformative learning via integrated projects exemplifies how VR and AR applications transcend traditional boundaries, providing students with hands-on experiences and practical insights into complex concepts. This transformative potential of immersive technologies aligns with the evolving expectations of a digitally literate workforce.

Blended and Online Learning Environments

Disruptive technologies have paved the way for the evolution of learning environments, with a notable shift towards blended and online models. Horn and Mackey's exploration (2011) of transforming American education emphasizes the increasing prevalence of digital platforms in educational settings. The flexibility offered by online learning environments accommodates diverse learning needs, allowing individuals to engage with educational content at their convenience. Furthermore, Siddhpura et al.'s study (2020) on the application of disruptive technologies in engineering education accentuates the role of e-learning platforms powered by AI and machine learning algorithms. These platforms enable targeted skill development, aligning individuals with the dynamic requirements of the job market. The literature suggests that the integration of disruptive technologies in online learning environments not only expands access to education but also provides avenues for upskilling and reskilling initiatives.

Challenges and Considerations

While the impact on teaching and learning models is profound, challenges and considerations must be acknowledged. Harris and Short's examination (2014) of the notion of workforce development emphasizes the importance of addressing potential drawbacks. The digital divide, varying degrees of digital literacy, and the need for educators to adapt to new pedagogical approaches pose challenges that need thoughtful consideration.

The impact of disruptive technologies on teaching and learning models is multifaceted, influencing a shift towards learner-centric approaches, personalized learning, and the evolution of online environments. As educators navigate this transformative landscape, it becomes imperative to address challenges and strike a balance that maximizes the benefits of disruptive technologies in fostering an innovative and effective educational experience.

CONCLUSION

In summary, the integration of disruptive technologies in education and workforce development marks a paradigm shift, bringing forth transformative waves in traditional approaches. The influential role of technologies like AI, AR, and VR goes beyond being mere tools; they act as catalysts for educational and professional metamorphosis, offering adaptive learning paths and breaking geographical barriers (Flavin, 2017; Yeung, 2023). This shift extends to the workforce, where disruptive technologies are integral to strategies for upskilling and reskilling. The demand for a digitally adept workforce has led to the rise of e-learning platforms, powered by AI and machine learning, facilitating targeted skill development in alignment with dynamic job market needs (Horn & Carl, 2015; Siddhpura et al., 2020).

Examining the literature also uncovers a dual narrative of challenges and opportunities. While disruptive technologies present unprecedented opportunities, they also pose challenges related to access, equity, and digital literacy. Striking a balance between innovation and addressing potential drawbacks becomes crucial for educators, policymakers, and industry leaders (Avni, 2017; Flavin, 2016). Furthermore, changes in teaching and learning models are evident, with traditional classrooms evolving into blended and online learning environments. The emphasis is shifting from rote memorization to critical thinking and problem-solving skills, leveraging adaptive learning platforms that foster a learner-centric approach (Harris & Short, 2014; Siddhpura et al., 2020).

The synthesis of literature indicates that disruptive technologies hold the key to a future-ready educational and professional landscape. By embracing innovation while proactively addressing challenges, stakeholders can collectively shape an environment that prepares individuals to thrive in the digital age. This narrative serves as a compass, guiding stakeholders toward a nuanced and adaptive approach to harnessing the transformative power of disruptive technologies.

REFERENCES

Agrawal, S. (2021). A short survey on the role of technology in transforming education. *International Journal of Educational Technology in Higher Education*, 18(1), 3. 10.1186/S41239-020-00242-0

Amos, S. K. (2019). Digitization, disruption, and the "society of singularities": The transformative power of the global education industry. *Digital Transformation and Innovation in Chinese Education*, 87(1), 198–210. 10.1007/978-3-030-04236-3_11

Avni, S. (2017). Considering disruptive and transformative Jewish education. *Journal of Jewish Education*, 83(4), 342–357. 10.1080/15244113.2017.1346949

Flavin, M. (2016). Disruptive conduct: The impact of disruptive technologies on social relations in higher education. *Innovations in Education and Teaching International*, 53(5), 485–495. 10.1080/14703297.2013.866330

Flavin, M. (2017). Why can't I just Google it? What disruptive innovation means for higher education. In *Handbook of Research on Cross-Cultural Business Education*, 1(1), 46-64. 10.1057/978-1-137-57284-4_3

Harris, R., & Short, T. (2014). Exploring the notion of workforce development. In *Handbook of Research on Workforce Diversity in a Global Society*, 1(1), 1-21. 10.1007/978-981-4560-58-0_1

Her anu, C.-L. (2020). Future education within disruptive technologies developments. *Knowledge-Based Organizations*, 26(1), 117–124. 10.2478/kbo-2020-0092

Horn, M. B., & Mackey, K. (2011). Transforming American education. *E-Learning and Digital Media*, 8(2), 133–140. 10.2304/elea.2011.8.2.133

Horn, V., & Carl, E. (2015). Transforming US workforce development policies for the 21st century. *New Directions for Adult and Continuing Education*, 148(1), 9–17.

Horvath, I. (2016). Disruptive technologies in higher education. *IEEE INFOCOM 2016 - The 35th Annual IEEE International Conference on Computer Communications*. IEEE. 10.1109/CogInfoCom.2016.7804574

Jordan, C. (2017). The digital workforce – disruptive technologies changing the way work gets done. *APPEA Journal*, 57(1), 443–449. 10.1071/AJ16150

Kirkwood, A. (2011). Transformational technologies: Exploring myths and realities. *International Journal of Computer-Supported Collaborative Learning*, 6(3), 329–347.

Lee, J.-H., Steer, L., Jimenez, E., King, E. M., & Erikson, E. (2020). Designing the education workforce. *Social Science Research Network*. https://doi.org/10.2139/SSRN.3588221

Liu, X., & Chen, X. (2018). Disruptive technology enhanced learning: The use and misuse of digital technologies in higher education. *Innovations in Education and Teaching International*, 55(6), 605–613. 10.1080/14703297.2018.1405550

Magana, A. J. S. (2019). Disruptive classroom technologies. In *The SAGE Encyclopedia of Educational Technology*, 2(1), 391-395. 10.1093/acrefore/9780190264093.013.423

Putra, A. S., & Tan, K. K. (2012). An alternative perspective in engineering education: A parallel to disruptive technology. *International Journal of Engineering Education*, 28(3), 726–732.

Siddhpura, A., Siddhpura, I., & Siddhpura, M. (2020). Current state of research in the application of disruptive technologies in engineering education. *Procedia Computer Science*, 168(1), 177–184. 10.1016/j.procs.2020.05.163

Wilson, J. H. (2019). Andragogy and the learning-tech culture revolution: The Internet of Things (IoT), blockchain, AI, and the disruption of learning. In *Handbook of Research on Cross-Cultural Business Education,* 1(1), 31-50. 10.4018/978-1-5225-3474-7.ch015

Wongleedee, K. (2019). The effects of disruptive technology on higher education. *Journal of Learning and Teaching in Digital Age*, 4(2), 47–62.

Yeung, S. M. (2023). Transformative learning via integrated projects with sustainable development goals and innovations. *Corporate Governance and Sustainability Review*, 7(2), 3. 10.22495/cgsrv7i2p3

Chapter 10
A Service-Based Measurement Model for Determining Disruptive Workforce Training Technology Value:
Return on Investment Calculations and Example

Scott Joseph Warren
https://orcid.org/0000-0003-4920-3960
University of North Texas, USA

Christina Churchill
Southern Methodist University, USA

Aleshia Hayes
University of North Texas, USA

ABSTRACT

Are the training outcomes of innovative technologies worth their investment cost? How can managers determine a company's valuable profits resulting from employing virtual, mixed, and augmented reality tools? This chapter presents metrics for evaluating information technologies' operations and business value relative to their service contributions in support of worker task efficacy and efficiency, reduced operations downtime due to training, and other benefits. The authors provide sample calculations that can help managers and researchers better explain the service-dominant logic-defined affordances of these innovative tools and their expected benefits in supporting corporate strategy, organizational performance measures, and operational performance in manufacturing knowledge production. Finally, the authors provide extended reality-supported worker training examples to model these calculations to determine the value of innovative technology assets for training and workplace performance improvements.

DOI: 10.4018/979-8-3693-3003-6.ch010

Copyright ©2024, IGI Global. Copying or distributing in print or electronic forms without written permission of IGI Global is prohibited.

INTRODUCTION

Business firms invest significant funds in information technology assets to support yearly operational objectives and provide on-the-job tools for daily work or training. Training and education spending was $6 trillion in 2018 and is estimated to rise to $8 trillion by 2025 (HolonIQ, 2019). Business leaders make technology investments with tools like business analytics systems with an expectation of financial or other employee performance returns to the organization, such as training efficiency (Sharma et al., 2014); that is, a return on investment that financially benefits the company (Shin, 2006). Positive outcomes from information technology in academic research and real-world corporate settings are measured using observable learning or training performance improvements (Means et al., 2009). These improvements should then transfer from the employee to desired firm outcomes such as profit, efficiency gains, or another measurable advantage (Crossan & Apaydin, 2010; Park et al., 2018). Through this lens, workers acquire knowledge, skills, or other intelligence that are absorbed by and benefit the firm (Cohen & Levinthal, 1990; West & Bogers, 2014; Volberda et al., 2010). The evaluation of innovations should focus on the services technology provides rather than assuming tangible goods carry innate value (Vargo & Lusch, 2004; Vargo et al., 2008). Instead, the technology's consumer determines the service value a tool provides. That value results from a user's perception of the benefit they receive from technology-supported experiences. In addition, these services are delivered through digital devices (i.e., information technologies), providing an information-centric outcome (Glazer, 1991) that may be difficult to transfer to performance improvement. Technology-based experiences are often high in informational content, sometimes resulting in a high cognitive load that harms user performance.

The costs and potential training or work performance benefits from using information technology tools vary, as well as the expectations of a return on the investment in these assets. Return on investment (ROI) results from calculating profit after taxes divided by total assets (Oscan, 2017). Since training is commonly prepared for groups of workers by experts who define applied behavioral objectives, it is logical to determine earnings from investment in innovative training technology in terms of *training return on assets* (T-ROA). The traditional ROA calculation is *net income divided by average total assets* (Chopra & Meindl, 2014). Adapting this concept in innovative technology-based training contexts, we can calculate the T-ROA by *net income* (i.e., total measured training improvement or "profit") *divided by the average total cost of assets*.

Innovative technology implementations are commonly instantiated as a diverse, aggregate set of uses that employs a non-standardized mix of information technology tools. With exploratory uses of VR, for example, organizations may employ *Hololens, Oculus,* and one or more other technologies or variations of offerings from the same company. This way, companies can test the best fit for their needs and users. Different extended reality tools from vendors commonly serve the same training or use purposes but at different price points and levels of effectiveness in a particular setting. Therefore, it is important to calculate the average cost of all employed assets to determine whether one XR tool performs better than others so investment decisions can be made with a consistent technological selection that best supports worker training. The results of companies implementing various extended reality tools from vendors serving the same purpose but at different price points led to a lack of standardization and increased costs. However, these tools often significantly vary in usability and service affordances (i.e., digital benefits from use). This situation arises because newer, untested technologies are frequently purchased over time as financial resources are available for testing to determine if they meet the company's needs. Organizations then examine the different options to decide which tool provides the most substantial service benefit to their employees and the firm (Elbanna & Child, 2007). However, this leads to a mismatched portfolio of technologies with different benefits, software and hardware requirements, and applications. Therefore, purchasing decision criteria should include whether the tool's affordances align with supporting the firm's competitive strategy, organizational structure, budget, operations, and desired outcomes (Yoo & Kim, 2018).

From the perspective of human performance improvement, there needs to be more literature regarding how firms measure a return on investments in extended reality technology assets (e.g., virtual, augmented, mixed reality). Therefore, it is crucial to determine which qualitative or quantitative data is best to evaluate the degree to which desired work performance returns are produced by employees when using a particular training information technology. The academic literature includes limited quantitative metrics for measuring the benefits of employing a specific information technology for training. Because these performance support tools include hardware in the form of personal computers, digital displays, and software such as simulation and game products, each information technology has different expected workplace benefits or training affordances (Robertson, 2011; Greeno, 1994).

BACKGROUND

Training costs with technology innovations can be high because, beyond the hardware, which tends to have an average three-to-five-year life cycle, vendors are increasingly charging more for different components of software solutions once bundled into packages that now have annual subscription costs [e.g., Adobe Creative Cloud] (Costello, 2019). In addition, many companies today seek training improvements that positively impact their financial returns that result from employing technologies such as learning management systems, computer-based instruction (Knowlton & Simms, 2010; Steinberg, 2003; Kulik & Kulik, 1991), serious training games (Connolly et al., 2012), and augmented, mixed, and virtual reality tools (Fourtane, 2019; Akçayır, M., & Akçayır, G., 2016; Merchant et al., 2014). Each new technology is a means to transform the training experience. However, there are conflicting views among business leaders, researchers, and academics regarding the value and financial viability of technology-supported training, ranging from highly positive to extremely harmful (Jenkins, 2019; Herold & Molnar, 2018).

Defining the Profits of Technology Use for Organizational Operations

Information technology is vital for economic development delivered through social media, streaming, and other intangible services when viewed from a service-dominant logic perspective (Lusch & Nambisan, 2015). Technology investment and use value outcomes focus on whether a physical product or service provides measurable improvements relative to a firm's objectives, including behavioral, training, or other quantifiable performance improvements. Positive outcomes from service or technological innovation include desirable corporate aims such as greater profitability, business-level outcomes such as reduced employee turnover, or system operations efficiencies such as reduced task error rates (Barney & Hesterly, 2012). Regarding operational and strategic benefits, managers should develop calculations that define straightforward, valuable returns from stakeholders' technology-focused value co-creation activities during processes in which they develop tangible and operant firm resources. Extended reality tools deliver immersive experiences and tend to focus on the user experience (Prahalad & Ramaswamy, 2004), which makes measuring their benefits more challenging than other physical training tools since each user often defines their value. The service-dominant logic (S-D logic) worldview is one in which the end-user (i.e., service recipient) defines and co-creates value when using innovative information technologies (Vargo et al., 2008). Measuring a technology's value stems from whether it effectively supports employee outcomes (e.g., reduced task error rates) or applies resulting firm capabilities to achieve desired outcomes (e.g., greater profits linked to fewer product returns).

Measurable Training Outcomes Instead of Profits

Training and learning technologies commonly derive their perceived service value from whether the user finds that the educational practice activities in digital environments transfer to real-world workplaces (Crichton-Sumners et al., 2013). As such, valuable outcomes are constrained by how well they provide functional training benefits to each employee without expecting them to impact all employees positively. This lens contrasts with the absorptive capacity view of the firm and training benefits expected in many businesses that assume and measure the technology's use value in aggregate by determining whether the tool positively impacts individual employees and, therefore, transfers to the whole company (Cohen & Levinthal, 1990). The field of learning sciences has sought to identify the valuable outcomes of learning activities from a cognitive science perspective since at least the late 1990s (National Research Council, 1999). However, that field's approach is framed primarily through behavioral, cognitive, and psychological terminology (Sawyer, 2006). The calculation of financial or human resources investment cost is not a component of the field's view of learning "profits," which would require determining the cost to benefit in terms of the unit of learning received compared to an existing, lower-cost approach

EXTENDED REALITY TECHNOLOGIES

Analog stereoscopic experiences date to the 1830s, when Wheatstone's images gave viewers depth and immersion in still images. In comparison, the View-Master was a children's toy used in the 1970s and 1980s. Hellig's (1958) *Sensorama* device used film to immerse users in experiences ranging from riding a motorcycle to flying in a helicopter (Merchant et al., 2014). However, virtual reality (VR) experiences using computer-based digital media emerged in the late 1960s with Ivan Sutherland and Bob Sproull's *Sword of Damocles. This head-mounted, computer-based display* influenced today's systems (Virtual Reality Society UK, 2020). Over the last 60 years, VR simulations have expanded from simple wireframe 2.5-dimensional (2.5D) screen renderings used for *subLOGIC's* Microsoft flight simulators in the late 1970s and early 1980s (Al-Riyami, 2014). Today's immersive tools commonly include 3-D headsets and haptic-sensor-fueled Oculus *Rift* and *Go,* which are used increasingly for personal entertainment or as simulators of real-world training experiences. In immersive training, the field passed through at least three phases starting in the 1990s. The first phase included simple tools like the Active Worlds visual browser to present trainees with 2.5D multi-user environment (MUVE) experiences (Dede et al., 2006; Barab et al., 2005). From 2002-2008, trainers and educators experimented with visually robust immersive environments such as *Second Life, Blue Mars*, and others that provided higher resolution, readily programmable virtual world-building technologies to the masses (Warren & Lin, 2012).

Current Phase of XR Technology

The most recent phase of XR, with the onset of advanced tools such as *Playstation VR* Meta *Quest and HTV Vive*, again shows promise to provide learners with high fidelity, immersive training experiences that mimic real-world settings and simulate work settings to provide low-threat, repeatable skills practice. However, the costs remain potentially prohibitively high for many smaller companies who seek to use the new wave of extended reality hardware, software, and development that emerged around 2015 (Nagel, 2019), with the new Apple Vision Pro headset priced around $ 3,500 per unit (Leswing, 2023). Over the last ten years, commercial traditional hardware manufacturers like Samsung and Sony and other entrants like Meta have introduced various VR tool offerings at different price points.

Measurement Challenge With XR Training Tools as a Potentially Beneficial Disruption

A central challenge to determining a technology's return on investment is that academic research historically focuses on whether an approach achieved statistically significant outcomes regarding learning improvement. However, due to the logistical difficulty of locating and testing hypotheses with technology users, academic research often takes place with small user samples, limiting the findings' generalizability. The previous wave of virtual reality releases (i.e., 2.5D) was from 1995 to 2009. It included products such as Linden Labs' *Second Life* (Warren & Wakefield, 2011) and *ActiveWorlds* (Warren et al., 2009). Then, vendors promised that those 2.5D VR tools would transform training and education experiences (Wecker, 2014). However, a meta-analysis of their impact and value indicated little statistical significance regarding learning and training improvement (Mikropoulos & Natsis, 2011; Salmon, 2009). This finding begs the question: Does the investment in today's goggle-based, often expensive information technologies for training result in satisfactory positive outcomes that justify their cost?

Measuring Training Benefits From Extended Reality Information Technologies

Determining whether information technology improves performance and training outcomes is challenging for companies (Damodaran, 2009). For example, translating training improvements from information technologies into quantitative measures of business returns to determine innovative technologies' strategic or operational value is limited due to the ability to contextualize the calculations for actual use (Tabas & Beranová, 2014). Therefore, this article offers suggested metrics for measuring valuable employee training performance outcomes that may result from extended reality (e.g., augmented reality) information technology tools applied in real-world contexts. Using these metrics, we model the calculation of return on investment (ROI) for the demonstrated extended reality asset to produce calculations that allow for the determination of cost-to-benefit from a class of technology assets (i.e., return on assets or ROA) that is traditionally scarce and often expensive to acquire. The metrics created are developed from supply chain and operations management (Chopra & Meindl, 2014). Each measurement calculation is concerned with how efficiently or effectively technologies produce performance results (Warren, 2018), the cycle time of total use of a learning product based on throughput (i.e., number of distinct uses), and with flow defined as time-in-use (i.e., minutes) to produce a desired training outcome.

Determining Performance Data for Evaluating Training Returns

Performance data resulting from training includes outcomes such as a technology asset's in-use time recorded by users tracked within the software whenever employed for training activities to determine their training time-on-task. Data collection may be automated by tracking discrete digital asset uses, as expected with analytics in today's learning management systems. This data and analysis allow the measurement of VR asset use efficiency per training course to identify which version of an XR tool is best for a situation. For virtual reality asset returns (ROA), we provide a mathematical calculation for determining the cost-to-benefit outcomes employed with many different VR types (e.g., Vive, Oculus). This calculation allows for a determination of the asset per-unit-of-learning outcome change from the original non-XR version to the new course relative to the price of the outcome. This performance result relates to the detected variance in trainee performance within the same course. In the following metric, the between-groups comparison equation expands to account for training returns relative to the total cost of XR assets used in all or a training segment during the period of interest. A cycle is a defined period of training use (e.g., one hour or two weeks). Suppose the VR assets fail to show statistically significant returns on the technology investment. In that case, confounding factors may limit improvement from the training model developed for a study. The outcome defined as in-use time reporting determines the cost-to-use efficiency values for 1.) each XR asset, 2.) each asset class, and 3.) all assets used in conjunction with an XR training experience (e.g., laptop, mobile phone, headset, software). This approach supports determining return on assets (ROA) and overall return on investment (ROI) for advanced information technologies used for training by determining their operational value to support desired behavioral outcomes.

Innovative Technology Asset Cost Estimates

The financial outlays for innovative information technology assets aggregate across spending on hardware, software, training, and related expenses. Whether the cost of information technology equipment used for workplace training benefits (e.g., viewing augmented reality product schematics) or training (e.g., virtual simulation practice) is sufficient compared with performance improvement can be examined in different ways such as by using measuring active time-in-use, training gains per minute, or other defined benefit of interest to the organization. Such metrics allow calculations of stakeholder demand for technologies in the extended reality (XR) family, including virtual reality (VR) (Baker et al., 2016), mixed reality (MR) (Serino et al., 2017), and augmented reality (AR) (Wang et al., 2013; Squire, 2010). For this paper, VR, MR, and AR all employ reality virtualization or simulation, collectively called extended reality (XR) technologies (Kaplan et al., 2021; Steel et al., 2020).

Cost-to-Benefit from Technology Investment

To determine the cost-to-benefit from an investment, we must evaluate the financial cost compared with defined gains when accounting for financial outlays for equipment and training experience development. Quantifying the cost-to-learning-benefit from employing VR assets provides decision-makers with empirical support regarding whether the learning outcomes are sufficient to justify the recurring costs. Doing so should allow researchers and instructional units to justify future, continued investment by their institutions in new learning technologies and software, especially when marketers fail to produce research to back up the claims of learning efficacy regarding the tools they sell to businesses of all types. Using such metrics can help reduce the cost of learning technologies for higher education institutions by investing in the right tools to support learners, not just those appearing in the latest industry journals.

METRICS DEVELOPMENT METHODOLOGY

Organizations employ business metrics to gather and analyze data to determine whether to invest in recurring capital expenditures or associated human resources to support them, especially with information technology innovations (Zhu et al., 2006). Therefore, it is appropriate to employ standard metrics from the area of operations and supply chain management analytics as a method of measurement to establish whether there are adequate learning or instructional support returns from investing in XR devices and associated support technologies or software such as high-performance laptops, games, or simulations. Managers can employ the organizational and operations profit metrics developed in this paper to determine the value of learning technologies by facing questions about which innovative technologies provide valuable service returns in support of training and operational performance measures. These metrics are derived or synthesized from both Chopra and Meindl's (2014) operations and supply chain text and Damodaran's (2009) handbook of business valuation measures. The authors developed measures rooted in learning and media affordances of XR technologies for calculating individual and aggregate expected returns on assets. The goal was to help readers better determine the return on investment in extended reality tools for training.

Defining the Measurable Benefits of XR Technologies

Commercial vendors and educational technology companies offer extended reality tools with the potential to impact learning and training. Such prospective improvements are due to extended reality technology's perceived positive *learning affordances* (Greeno, 1994) that assist users with learning tasks through planned, coordinated media and cognitive interface aspects. These learning affordances are benefits that include immersive, auditory, and interactive simulated experiences where students may repeatedly practice complex skills in a low-threat environment (Martín-Gutiérrez et al., 2017). It is also an innovation that received significant investment in its different forms over the last 30 years (Kaplan et al., 2021), so it may act as a model for other future innovative technologies adopted in educational organizations. However, like challenges of achieving measurable outcomes from other complex learning technologies that resulted from open innovation (West & Bogers, 2014), virtual reality experiences that leverage headsets and high-resolution graphics also offer a mix of potentially confounding cognitive, pedagogical, affective, and psychomotor factors that make measuring a training technologies' value challenging, but not impossible (Makransky & Lilleholt, 2018; Martín-Gutiérrez et al., 2018; Reale, 2014). Figure 1 presents examples of potential digital affordances of XR tools.

Figure 1. Potential technology affordances associated with VR tools and organizational performance gains

Psychomotor/ Behavioral	Psychomotor example	Cognitive	Cognitive example	Affective	Affective example
Reflexive movement training	Practice correctly hooking up components of dangerous equipment	Memorize step-based process knowledge	Learn new safety checks before starting the forklift	Stress due to complex workplace	Provide coping strategies for dealing with complexity
Provide repeated physical skills practice	Improve hand, arm, and leg muscle memory with common driving skills	Simulate new environments	Practice driving in the simulated, reconfigured warehouse with robots	Stress due to learning new procedures	Teach through a low-stress learning process
Motor skills development	New forklift operator fine motor skills control development	Improve worker communication	Reinforce rules/ norms of warehouse safety communication	Interpersonal dynamics stressors	Provide models of supportive peer-to-peer workplace communication
Support visual-Physical ability development	Improve linkages between visual/spatial skills and physical labor	Increase awareness of peer behaviors	Teach peer drivers the driving actions concerning own	Stress due to the introduction of innovative technologies	Provide operational models with the addition of robotics / augmented reality

While these benefit/affordance definitions are broad and can be difficult to conceptualize in financially measurable terms, they can translate into behavioral and operational outcomes. For example, those behaviors and operations improvements (e.g., gained efficiencies) are measurable firm worker performance outcomes resulting from positive worker training after using the information technology or system.

Learning Outcomes in Place of Profits With XR

These outcomes are associated with assumptions from past studies on teaching and learning in educational research. In addition, the following assumptions derive from psychological theory and research related to XR use in training and education settings:

- Assumption 1: Learning results from focused time-on-task engagement with educational activities (Kaplan et al., 2021; Warren et al., 2008).
- Assumption 2: Learning improves from timely, specific feedback on student performance (Gan & Hattie, 2014; Kluger & DiNisi, 1996).
- Assumption 3: Predicted learning improvements result from tool use by students, trainers, or instructional faculty and associated training (Chittaro & Sioni, 2015; Dell'Acqua et al., 2023; Grundmeyer & Peters, 2016).

- Assumption 4: Learning improvements cannot be assumed to occur because of educational tool use automatically; however, we can infer that no learning improvements will occur if there is no tool use (Small et al., 2020; Van Bruggen, 2005).
- Assumption 5: Therefore, decision-makers should first determine if the tools are being used in a setting before a researcher studies performance improvement impacts; without evidence of use, there is no need to proceed to the second step (Angst et al., 2010; Bose & Luo, 2011; Zhu et al., 2006).

Our assumptions are linked to performance outcome expectations defined by different authors working in augmented and virtual reality or advanced simulation game training technologies (i.e., extended reality or XR). Following the initial assumptions, metrics derived from the concept of learning or media affordance were developed (Gibson, 1977; Kozma, 1991; Shin, 2017). Learning affordances are acquired benefits from tool use (Greeno, 1994; Wells, 2002) and are linked to likely profitable workplace training outcomes from an XR technology, and examples are included in Figure 2.

Figure 2. Sample return on investment profits from workplace training with XR technologies

Identifier	Activity/Use	Learning affordance	Measurable Outcome	Calculation
Profit A	High fidelity of experience within simulated driver training experience	Attention increased from auditory and visual media cues	Increase in learner time-on-task (minutes) resulting from VR learning technology use vs non-VR experience	$\sum = Minutes\ of\ attention$
Profit B	Comparison of pre-test knowledge vs. post-test knowledge to determine whether a statistically significant gain occurred because of tech use	Results from processes of text or visual materials (documents and images) in support of memory	Increase in total information acquired from use ranged Time A (pre-) to Time B (post-use) for individual learner or an aggregate (unit/course section/class)	$\sum = Posttest\ score - Pretest\ score$
Profit C	Comparison of total pre-test knowledge vs. post-test knowledge at different lengths of time to determine whether a statistically significant gain was retained period	Long-term memory support resulting from media exposure	Increase in total information retained after use from ranged Time B (immediate) to Time C (close), D (near), E (proximal), F (distal), G (Remote)	$\sum = Information\ Retained\ Time\ C - Information\ Retained\ Time\ A$
Profit D	Comparison of total information acquired by students at fixed periods (e.g., 1 hour, 3 hours, 9 hours, 3 days) with VR vs. non-XR	Reduced time to acquire information from exposure to organized media	Increase in information acquisition speed from ranged Time A (pre-) to Time B (post-use)	$\sum = Time\ to\ retention\ (Group\ B) - Time\ to\ retention\ (Group\ A)$
Profit E	Comparison of total number of learners served in one section vs. another section restricted by physical size limits	More learners served at same learning outcomes at comparable cost	Increased access by a larger number of learners with approximately the same learning acquisition outcomes	$\sum = Total\ n\ Group\ B - Total\ n\ Group\ A$
Profit F	Align simulated VR/MR/AR tasks to real world work and reduce support scaffold over time	Due to higher VR/MR/AR engagement with simulated activities and practice time, workers make fewer task errors in transfer setting	Decrease in applied transfer task error rates	$\sum = Total\ task\ errors\ (Group\ B) - Total\ task\ errors$

While not exhaustive, these profits are example calculations linked to potential learning outcomes grounded in assessable cognitive and behavioral science constructs. Each can serve in place of traditional financial gains and offers a measurable benefit when contextualized as a productive profit for the firm. Each measure is next discussed in further detail using the lens of performance improvements, defined either through productivity gains or decreased losses of efficiency or effectiveness on the part of systems or employees. Each metric is framed through an illuminative example with a fictional trucking company to show how they apply in a concrete use case.

ILLUMINATIVE EXAMPLE METRICS APPLICATION: XR DRIVER TRAINING

To illustrate the use applications of the model investment returns calculations, we provide a practical model application. To do so, we employ an imagined national commercial vehicle manufacturer called *Halcyon Heavy Duty Trucks*. This scenario was created by reviewing descriptions of companies in business publications where training and research were conducted with XR (Chowdhury et al., Kaplan et al., 2021; Shafiqul Islam et al., 2023; Yuen et al., 2010).

Worker Return on Investment Profits With Disruptive Training Technologies

In the example, company leaders seek to use one or more XR tools to train different types of drivers, including long-haul commercial, forklift, and last-mile drivers. In this case, management seeks to determine whether investing in one or more extended reality tools yields training benefits for truck drivers facing ever more complex environments, increasing cognitive loads in their everyday work (Lee et al., 2007). Commercial and industrial drivers today perform tasks in increasingly complex warehouse and outdoor settings alongside robots and other forms of autonomous technology (Moniz & Krings, 2016). This situation creates significant dangers for driver safety as workers cope with industrial automation, increasingly hazardous road conditions, and more complex technologies integrated into their vehicles. For forklift and last-mile drivers, damaging pallets of merchandise can cost companies thousands to millions of dollars (Shafiqul Islam et al., 2023), especially when transporting medical supplies and costly electronics. In this simulated case, Halcyon's management is considering a.) simulation games, b.) virtual reality simulation, c.) and augmented reality because they are most appropriate to their performance improvement goals linked to four desired profits: time-on-task, total information retained, length of information retention, and task error reduction.

Increased Productive Time-on-Task

Time-on-task increases student learning (Martin et al., 2007). Measuring productive attention to training activities or materials stems from collecting data regarding minutes on task or *minutes of attention* to training. The more of a desired task the learner does and for a more extended period, the more likely a measured performance improvement resulted from a practice task (Warren et al., 2008). As such, if using a particular XR training technology is correlated with increased time on task, this is evidence that the technology provided the organization with valuable returns on the technology investment.

For example, Halcyon, the total rounded minutes of active time-on-task safety training, not counting setup and non-productive wait time, was higher for the simulation game (n=8,300) than for the AR (n = 2,600) or VR technologies (n=5,000). Part of the reason for this outcome is the extensive training time required to familiarize workers with the AR and VR tools. At the same time, fewer units could be employed concurrently because of the financial cost of the computers needed to run those AR and VR simulations. By comparison, each employee could play the simulation game on separate, low-powered computers in a browser when they had time and improve their performance through low-risk feedback. Further, employees in this model needed help with understanding the AR and VR tool setup, or they had to be set up by trainers, leading to significantly more wait time and requiring more personnel for less time on task than with the simulation game. As such, the simulation game delivered more training, which was the most efficient of the options.

Increased Total Information Acquired

Because many training tasks today are information acquisition-focused, activities aim to increase the employee's total amount of information at the end of a learning period (Schmidt, 2023). This outcome is often related to the total information trainees acquire as measured on a standardized performance test. A desired outcome for firms is that workers receive information more efficiently or effectively, and employees can then apply this information or new technologies to improve the company's productive outcomes (Shin, 2006). For the trucking company, determining whether an XR safety training resulted in more safety information acquired per employee than existing web-based training provides evidence that the technology is effective at supporting learning and may profit the firm. In this model case, augmented reality provided the most total information to employees as measured on a post-use test (87%). This result may have been because the trainer had more guidance and fewer users. The tool provided videos as overlays, which employees reported could replay. With the virtual reality tool, the score was 82% on the post-test, likely because the VR system allowed for notetaking in the space in addition to repeated practice. The simulation game required repeated practice, so while driving performance improved, the lack of time to review information-based materials for the assessment may have resulted in a post-score of only 72%.

Increased Information Retention

Another goal with information technologies in organizations is that the information acquired is not only retained in the short term but for a more extended period (i.e., long-term memory) that allows employees to apply what they learned to daily tasks using what they can access through working memory (Johnson & Dickinson, 2012; Ross et al., 2014). With extended reality technologies, the contextual elements of the digital learning space may foster improved information acquisition and retention in a manner that improves the transfer efficiency from the training to actual application.

For the Halcyon company trainees, safety information retention scores on the same post-training test after three months were 67% for the AR group, 62% for the VR group, and 38% for the simulation game group. However, this outcome should be compared with skill-based performance because safety knowledge may be less valuable to the company than safe driving skills resulting from repeat practice. In an information acquisition-focused job like that in the legal department, information retention may be more critical than for forklift drivers who may need lower task failure rates on skills, so managers must determine which profit is most important for each group of employees.

Reduced Task Error Rate

Since employee task errors in warehouses often reduce firm profits due to spoiled or damaged products, a benefit to the simulated tasks in extended reality training should be lowered task error rates in real-world workspaces (Ron-Angevin & Diaz-Estrella, 2009). Like benefits found when using traditional simulations (Levant et al., 2016; Ross et al., 2014), the lowered cognitive distance between training tasks performed in the virtual space and those they will complete in the real world, task error should decrease when employees transition from training to engaged work practice in the target transfer setting (Cook et al., 2013). For example, by lowering distractions in the virtual space to increase trainee focus with a virtual forklift, simulated practice can increase worker task automaticity and spatial awareness by increasing attention to specific learner objectives (Shafiqul Islam et al., 2023). Training managers then add simulated distractions meant to improve the fidelity of the simulated space until it matches natural world proportions to ensure employees are likely to transfer the training experience to the actual workspace. Once workers achieve a certain level of competence in the extended reality practice space, they are more likely to transfer the skills learned in the virtual space to the real world. Therefore, task error rates in the real-world setting should similarly decrease once employees meet the desired threshold for task error rates in the extended reality setting.

For Halcyon, the simulation game reduced error rates by about one-third (93) compared with the current training (286), with VR around the same results (89) and augmented reality performing best with only 74 errors. However, with all three tools providing similar training gains, deciding on a product based on this metric is not helpful. Instead, managers should determine the best value from different XR options by calculating beneficial returns from those they believe are most desirable to achieve company performance improvements that result in profits.

Determining Training-Focused Information Technology Asset Returns

While the learning profits (i.e., benefits) of a disruptive training technology are an essential marker of their quality and should drive part of the decision-making around information technology adoption, it remains necessary to determine whether these benefits offset the sometimes-high cost of the tools. Therefore, it is necessary to determine if the learning returns are cost-effective. If a manager or trainer sought to define measurable learning benefit returns from the disruptive technology investment, analysts could start with a single cycle of use: a day, a week, or longer. However, there is an assumption that a technology's active training indicates user time on task. In that case, it is necessary to consider a.) tool use frequency and b.) tool in-use time if we are to correlate that use with learning outcomes relative to the asset's value. For example, the cycle time is calculated for total VR learning product use as follows:

D is throughput (i.e., number of distinct uses), and flow is defined as *time-in-use* (i.e., minutes) completing course tasks, which is included as **T**. For each course, data captured for analysis may consist of an asset's in-use time on a tracking sheet or automatically tracked within the software each time it is employed for course activities or automated tracking by the digital asset, as is common in today's learning management systems. This equation allows any potentially disruptive asset (e.g., XR) to create a use efficiency measurement per course or training set.

Return on Assets Calculation from a Disruptive Training Technology

Reality asset returns (ROA) for single information technology are an aggregate measure of returns on a subset of, in our case, all tools included in a comprehensive strategic technology investment in extended reality technologies for an organization. ROA for an XR-enhanced training course is calculated as follows:

A cycle is defined as an in-use period for training in a calendar year. This calculation allows for a cost determination of the asset per-unit-of-learning or performance demonstration outcome change from the original training design to the new, technology-enhanced experience. This result is relative to the detected variance in student performance within the same course.

Value of ROA Measures to Inform Technology Replacement or Discontinuation

In the following metric, the between-groups comparison equation accounts for learning returns relative to the total cost of technology assets used in an organization's courses during the period of interest, allowing comparisons between this set of training resources and other types, such as augmented reality with similar affordances but lower costs.

Suppose all XR asset types failed to show statistically significant returns on the investment for training the drivers as evaluated. In that case, we must understand potential confounding factors that may enable improvement to the curricular model developed for a study. The outcomes of in-use time reporting will be used to calculate b cost-to-use efficiency values for 1.) each XR asset, 2.) each asset class, and 3.) all assets used in conjunction for an XR learning experience (e.g., laptop, headset) if there is a need for equipment beyond what is available in the training space.

ROI Evaluation Results and Decision-Making

This approach to measurement allows an instructor or manager to explain the return on assets (ROA) and overall return on investment (ROI) for groups of equipment. Further, as justification for the replacement of equipment, this approach allows a precise definition of the operational value of a tool (e.g., XR equipment) to support learning and teaching in a manner that is easy to report and explain to managers with less knowledge of educational outcomes. Using this process, an analyst can determine the total financial cost associated with learning gains based on total costs associated with equipment and curricular development needed for the tool to function since few instructional technologies function alone and rely on connections to electricity, other hardware, cloud-based software, or other resources during use. Determining whether to replace XR training tools as they reach the end of their useful life depends on the value of the benefits provided to the company and whether the data shows that their return on investment has met expectations.

Three real-world products were used to illustrate the application of these metrics. The first is a widely used simulation game for forklift driver safety training, compatible with low-cost Chromebooks. The second is virtual reality training software, which requires physical hardware with monitors, pedals, and controls. The third involves a custom augmented reality technology, with cost estimates obtained by examining the projected development expenses from various vendors' websites. Given the need for tailored simulation development, standard pricing data from pre-made solutions was unavailable. Additionally, augmented reality requires a forklift, necessitating a vehicle for each training deployment.

Decision-Making Using Training Profits From a Disruptive Technology

After reviewing the training profits and costs for each, the model Halcyon Trucking company determined the following based on all outcomes they collected. However, they were mainly focused on profits A-C and J, as included in Figure 3, and additional potential metrics the company examined as secondary affordances of the different XR tool options.

Figure 3. Halcyon heavy duty's training results per training profit

Learning Benefit	Metric	2.5D Simulation Game	Augmented Reality	Immersive Virtual Reality	Current Training
Profit A: Time-on-Task	Minutes / Throughput	**n=8,300**	n = 2,600	n=5,000	n=1250
Profit B: Total Information Acquired	Memory-based Test score	72%	87%	**82%**	70%
Profit C: Information Retention (3 months later)	Memory-based Test score	38%	**67%**	62%	22%
Profit D: Information Acquisition Speed	Time to train (hours)	11	9	12	16
Profit E: Increased Access for More Trainees	# trained / Throughput	**45**	14	32	22
Profit F: Greater Training Access Distance	# at a Distance Trained / month	**500**	30	240	4
Profit G: Increased Learner Independence	Reduced trainers	**4 fewer trainers**	1 less trainer	2 fewer trainers	N/A
Profit H: Lower Frustration with Training Assignments	Number of complaints regarding training	94	**31**	72	390
Profit I: Lower Frustration with Technology	Number of complaints regarding tech	57	**22**	61	221
Profit J: Lower Task Error Rate	Task errors	104	**74**	89	286

For Halcyon's training outcomes, augmented reality had the most distinct profits (6) across all collected data. The most significant improvements were a.) lowered task rates and decreased frustration with b.) technology or c.) training, d.) improved information acquisition speed, e.) better information acquisition, and f.) retention. By comparison, the VR group only had one, and the game tool showed four improvements.

Cost Consideration to Inform Future Investment in Disruptive Training Technologies

However, augmented reality may still not be the best service value to the company. Instead, the decision should be determined using cost-to-benefit analysis, which requires acquiring information regarding the costs for each asset and how many the company can implement considering affordability and facilities availability. These costs were derived from real-world vendors of XR technologies for forklift driver training, with prices captured in February 2024, as noted in Figure 4.

Figure 4. Asset costs per XR training technology

XR Tool	Simulation Game	Augmented Reality	Immersive Virtual Reality	Current Training
Title	Apex Safety & Compliance Forklift Safety Game	CG Markerless AR Training (Custom est.)	Vista Forklift Simulator V2	NSC Lift Truck Operator
Number of units or licenses	n=50	n=2	n=4	n=300
Cost per unit (software)	$148	$200,000	Included	$531 for 10 licenses ($53 / license)
Cost per unit (hardware)	$350 (Chromebook)	iPad $1,100 Forklift (2) $35,000	$11,000 (est.)	$350 (Chromebook)
Total cost/user	$498	$36,100	$11,000	$881
Total aggregate cost	$24,900	$272,000	$44,000	$264,300

Applying the metrics of Halcyon's experiment with XR training products, the simulation game had the highest use at the lowest cost per user and, in the aggregate, concurrently served 50 users. In contrast, augmented and virtual reality options served only two and four users concurrently at much higher price points. Further, these costs are cyclical, so licenses must be renewed, and hardware replaced periodically.

Further, the simulation game costs almost $400 per user, less than the current training and significantly less than the custom augmented reality and off-the-shelf virtual reality training. While there are more desired benefits from the augmented reality tool, the requirement of customization and actual world equipment makes it 72 times more expensive than the simulation game for only two users. In contrast, VR, which also requires equipment and software, is around six times more costly for four users. Both require fixed locations to implement the equipment and can serve far fewer users. The VR and AR options are too costly compared to Halcyon's current training. By comparison, the simulation game has benefits similar to those of the other XR tools but at a much lower cost. No tool will improve every profitable training outcome when returns are measured compared to investments, but some will perform better than others at a desired price point.

DISCUSSION AND IMPLICATIONS

Extended reality tools are innovations that can increase valuable business outcomes or improve operational effectiveness or efficiencies. However, as with any learning tool, managers must define the intended benefits or expected performance outcomes they expected before purchase and implementation (Bell, 1999; Saad et al., 2013). This approach allows performance-based data gathering throughout the product's life cycle to ensure value from expenditures on training tools. As noted with the profit calculations, defining an information technology's valuable returns before purchasing for a business provides several potential benefits to the company. These benefits should be aligned with strategic operations objectives so that tool efficacy and return-on-investment measures are logically linked to the described learning affordances or other technology advantages (Webster & Gardner, 2019).

Balancing Positive and Negative Aspects of a Disruptive Technology

For example, a possible benefit to acquiring or developing a technology innovation such as extended reality simulations is that, if designed well, such a tool may decrease negative aspects of training, such as worker frustration with training technologies (Holm & Dahl, 2011) or lack of available training units due to poor IT governance (Huang et al., 2010). On the other hand, such challenges can harm the rate of worker preparation to work with and the adoption of new processes (e.g., safety measures) or more effective workplace tools (MacVaugh & Schiavone, 2010). In this case, managers analyze their available training technology options and decide to improve their operating efficiency by choosing and allocating better-aligned XR information technology training resources or return to analog options. The effectiveness and efficiency of an XR training instance are compared with static web-based or face-to-face training to determine returns based on historical use data, which helps managers decide whether to make future investments in the technology.

Limitations

Adopted extended reality tools should be standardized in training portfolios to ensure they are effectively used and financially efficient. Having various options may be psychologically positive regarding user choice. However, it can complicate training and purchasing cycles because of the diverse tools available that may only sometimes be valuable to support desired training outcomes. Therefore, a significant limitation of this ROI measurement model is the many potential implementation modes that a company may use to achieve different desired training outcomes. As such, applying the fictional model to illustrate how to evaluate the ROI for one training XR implementation will likely not be generalized to other company uses for different training purposes. In addition, training technology efficacy declines due to misuse, especially when practice is unaligned with an XR tool's affordances or benefits.

Further, failure to train users properly or choosing an incorrect metric may mean evaluators draw incorrect conclusions about an XR tool's effectiveness. Further, the training experience's design may need improvement; the chosen tool had an inadequate level of immersion, a poor level of experiential training fidelity (De Giovanni et al., 2009; Lohmann et al., 2019), or an overly complex level of user interactivity, resulting in an excessive cognitive load that harmed performance. Such confounding factors should be considered as possible reasons for an implementation failure.

Hardware, Software, or Training Failures: Which Limited the Tool's Value?

When measuring training during an active XR experience, it is vital to discriminate between failures attributed to the software-based training experience (e.g., simulated forklift driving) and those resulting from hardware engineering failures (e.g., motion sickness from the XR simulation) (Chang et al., 2020; Kaplan et al., 2021). While XR training systems may be highly effective with modification, they may need improved usability, error prevention, or training (Kaplan et al., 2021; Stamm et al., 2022). This is the case with many training technologies that are not fully ready when provided directly by vendors, but only after a training unit determines how it best fits for adoption in their situation and intended implementation (Webster & Gardner, 2019) and whether employees are ready for the disruption (Ahmed et al., 2019). When applying this model of return on investment for XR in education and training, it is necessary to be mindful that no single implementation should determine the efficacy of an information technology enactment. Instead, any information technology is part of the whole training experience. According to service-dominant logic, whether the tool is valuable should be determined by the end-user as they review available performance data and consider whether the use of a new technology-supported transfer of training to their real-world work is worthwhile (Lin et al., 2015).

Future Research

With information technology innovation research historically focusing on efficiency or effectiveness outcomes, there remain few cases of business metrics applied to using information technology for education and training innovations to determine their organizational value in terms of readiness, life-cycle costs, or benefits to companies (Kauffman et al., 2018; Schwabe et al., 2015). To holistically capture employees' experiences using these tools, it will be necessary to expand beyond the behavioral measures presented in this piece by adding survey, interview, and artifact analysis from the qualitative research traditions to provide depth of understanding regarding why one disruptive tool is effective in a context, and another is not. In addition, significant research remains to understand how companies successfully use disruptive technologies to drive employee performance and provide adequate investment returns that justify continued financial outlays for hardware and software. Other studies should examine limitations due to accessibility challenges, digital system integration, and training human resources to properly leverage disruptive technology innovations such as XR, simulation games, generative artificial intelligence (Sahoo et al., 2024), and future disruptive training tools. Improper integration and accessibility could reduce profitable returns on any technology, so understanding these limitations through formal research can help adopters better understand whether and how to implement these tools. Within the immersive innovation training space, there is a need to study the use of different disruptive technologies in the XR class to provide immersive simulation experiences to improve users' operational performance after engaging in these digital training tasks in areas such as accounting (Carenys et al., 2017; Levant et al., 2016), marketing (Beuk, 2016; Buil et al., 2018; Vos, 2015), management (Lohmann et al., 2019;), operations management (Riley et al., 2017), and other business disciplines where training takes place to improve company and worker performance outcomes tied to learning and knowledge dissemination for competitive advantage (Warren et al., 2021; Warren & Churchill, 2024).

CONCLUSION

Determining the cost-to-learning-benefit from employing disruptive training technology assets provides decision-makers with empirical support regarding whether the learning outcomes are sufficient to justify the recurring costs. This approach should allow data-supported arguments for continued organizational investment in new learning technologies and software. The collection of such information is needed, especially when marketers fail to provide research to support claims of a tool's training efficacy. Using such metrics can help organizations reduce the cost of information technologies by allowing them to invest scarce resources in tools to support training, not just those in the latest industry journals. Important takeaways from this chapter are:

1.) Managers must define what outcomes they desire from technology assets before purchase
2.) Managers must define what level of performance is desired for each beneficial outcome
3.) A technology may offer the greatest number of training benefits but not be the best value
4.) Training technology costs are cyclical, not fixed
5.) Knowing the total cost of a workplace training tool, individually and in aggregate, is needed to make sound investment decisions
6.) Some technologies will serve a larger number of users at a lower cost
7.) Balancing costs with beneficial returns on technology investment is central to making sound management decisions

Collecting the correct data to calculate the valuable returns from investing in information technology can help managers decide which innovative resources to acquire, where, when, and why best to apply them for strategic competitive advantage in training and everyday work tasks.

REFERENCES

Ahmed, F., Qin, Y. J., & Martínez, L. (2019). Sustainable change management through employee readiness: Decision support system adoption in technology-intensive British e-businesses. *Sustainability (Basel)*, 11(11), 2998. 10.3390/su11112998

Akçayır, M., & Akçayır, G. (2016). Advantages and challenges associated with augmented reality for education: A systematic review of the literature. *Educational Research Review*, 20, 1–11. 10.1016/j.edurev.2016.11.002

Al-Riyami, F. (2014). *A history of the Microsoft Flight Simulator franchise: the origins, the end, and a new beginning*. ONMSFT. https://www.onmsft.com/news/history-microsoft-flight-simulator-franchise-origins-end-and-new-beginning

Aleven, V., Stahl, E., Schworm, S., Fischer, F., & Wallace, R. (2003). Help Seeking and Help Design in Interactive Learning Environments. *Review of Educational Research*, 73(3), 277–320. 10.3102/00346543073003277

Angst, C. M., Agarwal, R., Sambamurthy, V., & Kelley, K. (2010). Social Contagion and Information Technology Diffusion: The Adoption of Electronic Medical Records in US Hospitals. *Management Science*, 56(8), 1219–1241. 10.1287/mnsc.1100.1183

Baker, R. S., Clarke-Midura, J., & Ocumpaugh, J. (2016). Towards general models of effective science inquiry in virtual performance assessments. *Journal of Computer Assisted Learning*, 32(3), 267–280. 10.1111/jcal.12128

Barab, S., Thomas, M., Dodge, T., Carteaux, R., & Tuzun, H. (2005). Making learning fun: Quest Atlantis, a game without guns. *Educational Technology Research and Development*, 53(1), 86–107. 10.1007/BF02504859

Barney, J., & Hesterly, W. (2012). *Strategic management and competitive advantage: Concepts and Cases* (4th ed.). Pearson.

Bell, S. (1999). Finding out rapidly: A soft systems approach to training needs analysis in Thailand. *Development in Practice*, 9(1–2), 18–32. 10.1080/09614529953188

Beuk, F. (2016). Sales Simulation Games: Student and Instructor Perceptions. *Journal of Marketing Education*, 38(3), 170–182. 10.1177/0273475315604686

Bose, R., & Luo, X. (2011). Integrative framework for assessing firms' potential to undertake Green IT initiatives via virtualization - A theoretical perspective. *The Journal of Strategic Information Systems*, 20(1), 38–54. 10.1016/j.jsis.2011.01.003

Buil, I., Catalán, S., & Martínez, E. (2018). Exploring students' flow experiences in business simulation games. *Journal of Computer Assisted Learning*, 34(2), 183–192. Advance online publication. 10.1111/jcal.12237

Carenys, J., Moya, S., & Perramon, J. (2017). Is it worth it to consider video games in accounting education? A comparison of a simulation and a videogame in attributes, motivation, and learning outcomes. *Revista de Contabilidad*, 20(2), 118–130. 10.1016/j.rcsar.2016.07.003

Chang, E., Kim, H. T., & Yoo, B. (2020). Virtual Reality Sickness: A Review of Causes and Measurements. *International Journal of Human-Computer Interaction*, 36(17), 1658–1682. 10.1080/10447318.2020.1778351

Chittaro, L., & Sioni, R. (2015). Serious games for emergency preparedness: Evaluation of an interactive vs. a non-interactive simulation of a terror attack. *Computers in Human Behavior*, 50, 508–519. 10.1016/j.chb.2015.03.074

Chopra, S., & Meindl, P. (2014). Supply Chain Management: Strategy, Planning, and Operations. In *Pearson Education*. Pearson Education.

Chowdhury, S., Mubarrat, S. T., & Fernandes, A. (2023). A Physics-based Virtual Reality System Design and Evaluation by Simulating Human-Robot Collaboration. *Tech Rchiv*. https://doi.org/10.36227/techrxiv.18972773.v1

Cohen, W. M., & Levinthal, D. A. (1990). Absorptive Capacity: A New Perspective on Learning and Innovation. *Administrative Science Quarterly*, 35(1), 128–152. 10.2307/2393553

Connolly, T. M., Boyle, E. A., MacArthur, E., Hainey, T., & Boyle, J. M. (2012). A systematic literature review of empirical evidence on computer games and serious games. *Computers & Education*, 59(2), 661–686. 10.1016/j.compedu.2012.03.004

Cook, D. A., Hamstra, S. J., Brydges, R., Zendejas, B., Szostek, J. H., Wang, A. T., Erwin, P. J., & Hatala, R. (2013). Comparative effectiveness of instructional design features in simulation-based education: Systematic review and meta-analysis. In *Medical Teacher, 35*(1). https://doi.org/10.3109/0142159X.2012.714886

Costello, K. (2019). *Gartner Forecasts Worldwide Public Cloud Revenue to Grow 17.5 Percent in 2019*. Stamford, CT. https://www.gartner.com/en/newsroom/press-releases/2019-04-02-gartner-forecasts-worldwide-public-cloud-revenue-to-g

Crichton-Sumners, C., Mansouri, M., & Sauser, B. (2013). Systems Thinking for Knowledge Transfer in Organic and Mechanistic Organizations. *Transportation Research Record: Journal of the Transportation Research Board*, 2399(1), 112–120. 10.3141/2399-12

Crossan, M. M., & Apaydin, M. (2010). A multi-dimensional framework of organizational innovation: A systematic review of the literature. *Journal of Management Studies*, 47(6), 1154–1191. 10.1111/j.1467-6486.2009.00880.x

Damodaran, A. (2009). *The Dark Side of Valuation: Valuing Young, Distressed, and Complex Businesses* (2nd ed.). Pearson FT Press.

De Giovanni, D., Roberts, T., & Norman, G. (2009). Relative effectiveness of high- versus low-fidelity simulation in learning heart sounds. *Medical Education*, 43(7), 661–668. 10.1111/j.1365-2923.2009.03398.x19573189

Dede, C., Ketelhut, D., & Ruess, K. (2006). *Designing for motivation and usability in a museum-based multi-user virtual environment* (Vol. 2006, Issue 3/11/2006). Harvard University. https://www.gse.harvard.edu/~dedech/muvees/documents/AELppr.pdf

Dell'Acqua, F., McFowland, E., Mollick, E. R., Lifshitz-Assaf, H., Kellogg, K., Rajendran, S., Krayer, L., Candelon, F., & Lakhani, K. R. (2023). Navigating the Jagged Technological Frontier: Field Experimental Evidence of the Effects of AI on Knowledge Worker Productivity and Quality. SSRN *Electronic Journal*. 10.2139/ssrn.4573321

Elbanna, S., & Child, J. (2007). Influences on Strategic Decision Effectiveness: Development and Test of an Integrative Model. *Strategic Management Journal*, 28(4), 431–453. 10.1002/smj.597

Fourtane, S. (2019, April 22). Augmented Reality: The Future of Education. *Interesting Engineering*.

Gan, M. J. S., & Hattie, J. (2014). Prompting secondary students' use of criteria, feedback specificity, and feedback levels during an investigative task. *Instructional Science*, 42(6), 861–878. 10.1007/s11251-014-9319-4

Gibson, J. J. (1977). The theory of affordances. In Shaw, R., & Bransford, J. (Eds.), *Perceiving, acting, and knowing: Toward on ecological psychology* (pp. 67–82). Erlbaum and Associates.

Glazer, R. (1991). Marketing in an Information Intensive Environment: Strategic Implications of Knowledge as an Asset. *Journal of Marketing*, 55(4), 1–19. 10.1177/002224299105500401

Greeno, J. G. (1994). Gibson's affordances. *Psychological Review*, 101(2), 336–342. 10.1037/0033-295X.101.2.3368022965

Grundmeyer, T., & Peters, R. (2016). Learning from the Learners: Preparing Future Teachers to Leverage the Benefits of Laptop Computers. *Computers in the Schools*, 33(4), 253–273. 10.1080/07380569.2017.1249757

Herold, B., & Molnar, M. (2018, February 8). Virtual Reality for Learning Raises High Hopes and Serious Concerns. *Education Week*.

Holm, L. B., & Dahl, F. A. (2011). Using soft systems methodology as a precursor for an emergency department simulation model. *OR Insight*, 24(3), 168–189. 10.1057/ori.2011.8

Holon, I. Q. (2019). *10 charts that explain the global education technology market*. San Francisco, CA. https://www.holoniq.com/edtech/10-charts-that-explain-the-global-education-technology-market/

Huang, R., Zmud, R. W., & Price, R. L. (2010). Influencing the effectiveness of IT governance practices through steering committees and communication policies. *European Journal of Information Systems*, 19(3), 288–302. 10.1057/ejis.2010.16

Jenkins, A. (2019, June 20). The Fall and Rise of VR: The Struggle to Make Virtual Reality Get Real. *Fortune*. https://fortune.com/longform/virtual-reality-struggle-hope-vr/

Johnson, D. A., & Dickinson, A. M. (2012). Using Postfeedback Delays to Improve Retention of Computer-based Instruction. *The Psychological Record*, pp. 62, 485–496. http://alycedickinson.com/publications/Johnson2012.pdf

Kaplan, A. D., Cruit, J., Endsley, M., Beers, S. M., Sawyer, B. D., & Hancock, P. A. (2021). The Effects of Virtual Reality, Augmented Reality, and Mixed Reality as Training Enhancement Methods: A Meta-Analysis. *Human Factors*, 63(4), 706–726. 10.1177/001872082090422932091937

Kauffman, R. J., Ma, D., & Yu, M. (2018). A metrics suite of cloud computing adoption readiness. *Electronic Markets*, 28(1), 11–37. 10.1007/s12525-015-0213-y

Kirschner, P. A., Sweller, J., Kirschner, F., & Zambrano, J. R. (2018). From Cognitive Load Theory to Collaborative Cognitive Load Theory. *International Journal of Computer-Supported Collaborative Learning*, 13(2), 213–233. 10.1007/s11412-018-9277-y30996713

Kluger, A. N., & DeNisi, A. (1996). The effects of feedback interventions on performance: A historical review, a meta-analysis, and a preliminary feedback intervention theory. *Psychological Bulletin*, 119(2), 254–284. 10.1037/0033-2909.119.2.254

Knowlton, D. S., & Simms, J. (2010). Computer-based instruction and generative strategies: Conceptual framework & illustrative example. *Computers in Human Behavior*, 26(5), 996–1003. 10.1016/j.chb.2010.02.013

Kozma, R. (1991). Learning with media. *Review of Educational Research*, 61(2), 179–211. 10.3102/00346543061002179

Kulik, C., & Kulik, J. (1991). Effectiveness of Computer-based instruction: An updated analysis. *Computers in Human Behavior*, 7(1-2), 75–94. 10.1016/0747-5632(91)90030-5

Lee, Y. C., Lee, J. D., & Boyle, L. N. (2007). Visual attention in driving: The effects of cognitive load and visual disruption. *Human Factors*, 49(4), 721–733. 10.1518/001872007X215791117702223

Leswing, K. (2023, June 9). *Apple Vision Pro: Impressive specs, new way of interacting could help it break the VR curse*. CNBC.

Levant, Y., Coulmont, M., & Sandu, R. (2016). Business simulation as an active learning activity for developing soft skills. *Accounting Education*, 25(4), 368–395. Advance online publication. 10.1080/09639284.2016.1191272

Lin, Y., Pekkarinen, S., & Ma, S. (2015). Service-dominant logic for managing the interface: A case study. *International Journal of Logistics Management*, 26(1), 195–214. 10.1108/IJLM-08-2013-0095

Lohmann, G., Pratt, M. A., Benckendorff, P., Strickland, P., Reynolds, P., & Whitelaw, P. A. (2019). Online business simulations: Authentic teamwork, learning outcomes, and satisfaction. *Higher Education*, 77(3), 455–472. 10.1007/s10734-018-0282-x

Lusch, R. F., & Nambisan, S. (2015). Service Innovation: A service-dominant logic perspective. *Management Information Systems Quarterly*, 39(1), 155–175. 10.25300/MISQ/2015/39.1.07

MacVaugh, J., & Schiavone, F. (2010). Limits to the diffusion of innovation: A literature review and integrative model. *European Journal of Innovation Management*, 13(2), 197–221. 10.1108/14601061011040258

Makransky, G., & Lilleholt, L. (2018). A structural equation modeling investigation of the emotional value of immersive virtual reality in education. *Educational Technology Research and Development*, 66(5), 1141–1164. 10.1007/s11423-018-9581-2

Martin, F., Klein, J. D., & Sullivan, H. (2007). The impact of instructional elements in computer-based instruction. *British Journal of Educational Technology*, 38(4), 623–636. 10.1111/j.1467-8535.2006.00670.x

Martín-Gutiérrez, J., Mora, C. E., Añorbe-Díaz, B., & González-Marrero, A. (2017). Virtual technologies trends in education. *Eurasia Journal of Mathematics, Science and Technology Education*, 13(2), 469–486. 10.12973/eurasia.2017.00626a

Means, B., Toyama, Y., Murphy, R., Bakia, M., & Jones, K. (2009). Evaluation of Evidence-Based Practices in Online Learning. *Structure (London, England)*, 15(20), 94. http://newrepo.alt.ac.uk/629/

Merchant, Z., Goetz, E. T., Cifuentes, L., Keeney-Kennicutt, W., & Davis, T. J. (2014). Effectiveness of virtual reality-based instruction on students' learning outcomes in K-12 and higher education: A meta-analysis. *Computers & Education*, 70, 29–40. 10.1016/j.compedu.2013.07.033

Mikropoulos, T. A., & Natsis, A. (2011). Educational virtual environments: A ten-year review of empirical research (1999-2009). *Computers & Education*, 56(3), 769–780. 10.1016/j.compedu.2010.10.020

Moniz, A. B., & Krings, B. J. (2016). Robots working with humans or humans working with robots? Searching for social dimensions in new human-robot interaction in industry. *Societies (Basel, Switzerland)*, 6(3), 23. 10.3390/soc6030023

Nagel, D. (2019). Funding Is Top Roadblock to AR & VR in Schools. *T.H.E. Journal*.

National Research Council. (1999). *How people learn: Bridging research and practice* (Donovan, M. S., Bransford, J. D., & Pellegrino, J. W., Eds.). National Academy Press.

Oscan, Y. (2017). *Analytics and decision support in health care operations management: History, Diagnosis, and Empirical Foundations* (3rd ed.). Jossey-Bass.

Park, S., Jeong, S., & Ju, B. (2018). Employee learning and development in virtual HRD: Focusing on MOOCs in the workplace. *Industrial and Commercial Training*, 50(5), 261–271. 10.1108/ICT-03-2018-0030

Ramadhani, W. A., Wooldridge, A. R., Roychowdhury, J., Mitchell, A., Hanson, K., Vazquez-Melendez, E., Kendhari, H., Shaikh, N., Riech, T., Mischler, M., Krzyzaniak, S., Barton, G., Formella, K. T., Abbott, Z. R., Farmer, J. N., Ebert-Allen, R., & Croland, T. (2020). Negotiating Time and Space: Investigating the Pediatric Code Cart Augmented Reality Application. *Proceedings of the Human Factors and Ergonomics Society Annual Meeting*, 64(1), 1365–1366. 10.1177/1071181320641326

Reale, E. (2014). Challenges in higher education research: The use of quantitative tools in comparative analyses. *Higher Education*, 67(4), 409–422. 10.1007/s10734-013-9680-2

Riley, J. M., Ellegood, W. A., Solomon, S., & Baker, J. (2017). How mode of delivery affects comprehension of an operations management simulation Online vs face-To-face classrooms. *Journal of International Education in Business*, 10(2), 183–200. 10.1108/JIEB-09-2016-0025

Robertson, J. (2011). The educational affordances of blogs for self-directed learning. *Computers & Education*, 57(2), 1628–1644. 10.1016/j.compedu.2011.03.003

Ron-Angevin, R., & Díaz-Estrella, A. (2009). Brain-computer interface: Changes in performance using virtual reality techniques. *Neuroscience Letters*, 449(2), 123–127. 10.1016/j.neulet.2008.10.09919000739

Ross, V., Jongen, E. M. M., Wang, W., Brijs, T., Brijs, K., Ruiter, R. A. C., & Wets, G. (2014). Investigating the influence of working memory capacity when driving behavior is combined with cognitive load: An LCT study of young novice drivers. *Accident; Analysis and Prevention*, 62, 377–387. 10.1016/j.aap.2013.06.03223915472

Sahoo, S., Kumar, S., Donthu, N., & Singh, A. K. (2024). Artificial intelligence capabilities, open innovation, and business performance – Empirical insights from multinational B2B companies. *Industrial Marketing Management, 117*(May 2023), 28–41. 10.1016/j.indmarman.2023.12.008

Salmon, G. (2009). The future for (second) life and learning. *British Journal of Educational Technology*, 40(3), 526–538. 10.1111/j.1467-8535.2009.00967.x

Sawyer, R. K. (2006). *The Cambridge Handbook of the Learning Sciences* (3rd, 2009th ed., p. 627). Cambridge University Press.

Schmidt, V., Konig, S., Dilawar, R., Sanchez Pacheco, T., & Konig, P. (2023). Improved Spatial Knowledge Acquisition through Sensory Augmentation. *Brain Sciences*, 13(720), 1–29. 10.3390/brainsci1305072037239192

Schwabe, O., Shehab, E., & Erkoyuncu, J. (2015). Uncertainty quantification metrics for whole product life cycle cost estimates in aerospace innovation. *Progress in Aerospace Sciences*, 77, 1–24. 10.1016/j.paerosci.2015.06.002

Serino, A., Noel, J. P., Mange, R., Canzoneri, E., Pellencin, E., Ruiz, J. B., Bernasconi, F., Blanke, O., & Herbelin, B. (2017). Peripersonal space: An index of multisensory body-environment interactions in real, virtual, and mixed realities. *Frontiers in ICT (Lausanne, Switzerland)*, 4(JAN), 1–12. 10.3389/fict.2017.00031

Shafiquil Islam, M. D., Jamshid Nezhad Zahabi, S., Kim, S., Lau, N., Nussbaum, M. A., & Lim, S. (2023). Forklift Driving Performance of Novices with Repeated VR-based Training. *Proceedings of the Human Factors and Ergonomics Society Annual Meeting*, 67(1), 1480–1481. 10.1177/21695067231193664

Sharma, R., Mithas, S., & Kankanhalli, A. (2014). Transforming decision-making processes: A research agenda for understanding the impact of business analytics on organisations. *European Journal of Information Systems*, 23(4), 433–441. 10.1057/ejis.2014.17

Shin, D. H. (2017). The role of affordance in the experience of virtual reality learning: Technological and affective affordances in virtual reality. *Telematics and Informatics*, 34(8), 1826–1836. 10.1016/j.tele.2017.05.013

Shin, N. (2006). The impact of information technology on the financial performance of diversified firms. *Decision Support Systems*, 41(4), 698–707. 10.1016/j.dss.2004.10.003

Small, G. W., Lee, J., Kaufman, A., Jalil, J., Siddarth, P., Gaddipati, H., Moody, T. D., & Bookheimer, S. Y. (2020). Brain health consequences of digital technology use. *Dialogues in Clinical Neuroscience*, 22(2), 179–187. 10.31887/DCNS.2020.22.2/gsmall32699518

Squire, K. D. (2010). From Information to Experience: Place-Based Augmented Reality Games as a Model for Learning in a Globally Networked Society. *Teachers College Record*, 112(10), 2565–2602. https://website.education.wisc.edu/kdsquire/tenure-files/01-TCR-squire-edits.pdf. 10.1177/016146811011201001

Stamm, O., Vorwerg, S., Haink, M., Hildebrand, K., & Buchem, I. (2022). Usability and Acceptance of Exergames Using Different Types of Training among Older Hypertensive Patients in a Simulated Mixed Reality. *Applied Sciences (Basel, Switzerland)*, 12(22), 11424. 10.3390/app122211424

Steinberg, R. (2003). Effects of Computer-based Laboratory Instruction on Future Teachers' Understanding of the Nature of Science City College of New York. *Science*, 22, 185–205.

Tabas, J., & Beranová, M. (2014). Innovations Effect on the Company's Value. *Procedia Economics and Finance*, 12(March), 695–701. 10.1016/S2212-5671(14)00395-5

Tully, M. (2015). Investigating the role of innovation attributes in the adoption, rejection, and discontinued use of open-source software for development. *Information Technologies and International Development*, 11(3), 55–69.

Van Bruggen, J. (2005). Theory and practice of online learning. In T. Anderson & F. Elloumi (Eds.), *British Journal of Educational Technology, 36*(1). Athabasca University. 10.1111/j.1467-8535.2005.00445_1.x

Vargo, S. L., & Lusch, R. F. (2004). Evolving to a New Dominant Logic for Marketing. *Journal of Marketing*, 68(1), 1–17. 10.1509/jmkg.68.1.1.24036

Vargo, S. L., Maglio, P. P., & Archpru, M. (2008). *On value and value co-creation: A service systems and service logic perspective*. 145–152. https://doi.org/10.1016/j.emj.2008.04.003

Virtual Reality Society UK. (2020). *History Of Virtual Reality*. Virtual Reality Society Web Page. https://www.vrs.org.uk/virtual-reality/history.html

Volberda, H. W., Foss, N. J., & Lyles, M. A. (2010). PERSPECTIVE—Absorbing the Concept of Absorptive Capacity: How to Realize Its Potential in the Organization Field. *Organization Science*, 21(4), 931–951. 10.1287/orsc.1090.0503

Vos, L. (2015). Simulation games in business and marketing education: How educators assess student learning from simulations. *International Journal of Management Education*, 13(1), 57–74. 10.1016/j.ijme.2015.01.001

Wang, Y., Vincenti, G., Braman, J., & Dudley, A. (2013). The ARICE Framework: Augmented Reality in Computing Education. *International Journal of Emerging Technologies in Learning*, 8(6), 27–34. 10.3991/ijet.v8i6.2809

Warren, S. J. (2018). *Measuring the Effects of VR/AR/MR*. IMLS Lib3D/VR Forum B.

Warren, S. J., & Churchill, C. (2024). A Model for Applying Cognitive Theory to Firm to Improve Organizational Learning for Sustained Knowledge Production and Competitive Advantage. *Performance Improvement Journal*. https://doi.org/https://doi.org/10.56811/PFI-21-0036

Warren, S. J., Dondlinger, M. J., & Barab, S. A. (2008). A MUVE Towards PBL Writing: Effects of a Digital Learning Environment Designed To Improve Elementary Student Writing. *Journal of Research on Technology in Education*, 41(1), 113–140. 10.1080/15391523.2008.10782525

Warren, S. J., & Lin, L. (2012). Ethical considerations for learning game, simulation, and virtual world design and development. In S. C. Yang, H. H., & Yuen (Ed.), *Practices and Outcomes in Virtual Worlds and Environments* (pp. 1–18). IGI Global. 10.4018/978-1-60960-762-3.ch001

Warren, S. J., Roy, M., & Robinson, H. (2021). Business simulation games: Three cases from supply chain management, marketing, and business strategy. In Ifenthaler, D. (Ed.), *Game-based learning across the disciplines*. Springer. 10.1007/978-3-030-75142-5_5

Warren, S. J., Stein, R. A., Dondlinger, M. J., & Barab, S. A. (2009). A Look Inside a MUVE Design Process: Blending Instructional Design and Game Principles To Target Writing Skills. *Journal of Educational Computing Research*, 40(3), 295–321. 10.2190/EC.40.3.c

Warren, S. J., & Wakefield, J. S. (2011). Instructional design frameworks for Second Life virtual learning. In Hinrichs, R., & Wankel, C. (Eds.), *Transforming Virtual World Learning: Cutting-edge Technologies in Higher Education* (pp. 115–163). Emerald Group Publisher. 10.1108/S2044-9968(2011)0000004010

Webster, A., & Gardner, J. (2019). Aligning technology and institutional readiness: The adoption of innovation. *Technology Analysis and Strategic Management*, 31(10), 1229–1241. 10.1080/09537325.2019.1601694

Wecker, M. (2014, April 22). Whatever happened to Second Life? *ChronicleVitae*. https://chroniclevitae.com/news/456-what-ever-happened-to-second-life

Wells, A. J. (2002). Gibson's affordances and Turing's theory of computation. *Ecological Psychology*, 14(3), 141–180. 10.1207/S15326969ECO1403_3

West, J., & Bogers, M. (2014). Leveraging external sources of innovation: A review of research on open innovation. *Journal of Product Innovation Management*, 31(4), 814–831. 10.1111/jpim.12125

Yoo, S. K., & Kim, B. Y. (2018). A decision-making model for adopting a cloud computing system. *Sustainability (Basel)*, 10(8), 2952. 10.3390/su10082952

Yuen, K. K., Choi, S. H., & Yang, X. B. (2010). A full-immersive CAVE-based VR simulation system of forklift truck operations for safety training. *Computer-Aided Design and Applications*, 7(2), 235–245. 10.3722/cadaps.2010.235-245

Zhu, K., Kraemer, K. L., & Xu, S. (2006). The process of innovation assimilation by firms in different countries: A technology diffusion perspective on e-business. *Management Science*, 52(10), 1557–1576. 10.1287/mnsc.1050.0487

Chapter 11
Technological Disruptions in the Service Sector

Archana Parashar
Indian Institute of Management, Raipur, India

Shivangi Dhiman
University of Delhi, India

ABSTRACT

Technological advancement has greatly shaped the service sector, with the most disruptive technologies in their infancy. The broad arena of the service industry includes several sections, each of which has been disrupted by technological advancements, resulting in transformed process mechanisms and market paradigms. The present chapter included a comprehensive narrative review of literature aimed at broadly analysing the status of technological disruption in the service sector with the help of relevant research studies and real-world applications. Four service sectors, namely financial services, tourism and hospitality, legal services, and the health industry, were investigated to highlight the advent of disruptive technologies across the service industry. Further, consumer and employee behaviour changes concerning technological disruption were highlighted. The prevalent trend of technological disruption has immense practical and academic implications, encouraging experts to provide future directions in the area.

INTRODUCTION

The present chapter aims to provide a comprehensive understanding of technological disruptions in the service sector, examining the diverse disruptive technologies. A comprehensive narrative review was conducted to analyse the status of technological disruption by focusing on major service sectors, namely, financial services, tourism and hospitality, legal services, and the health industry. The phenomenon has been examined using empirical research studies and real-world instances to highlight the changes these disruptive technologies have brought about in the processing of the service industry. Special emphasis was placed on the impact of technological disruptions on consumer and employee behaviour and the consequent changes in human resource practice in sync with disruptive trends. Considering the above objectives, future directions highlighting the practical implications and research opportunities in the field of technological disruption have been discussed.

DOI: 10.4018/979-8-3693-3003-6.ch011

Copyright ©2024, IGI Global. Copying or distributing in print or electronic forms without written permission of IGI Global is prohibited.

DISRUPTIVE TECHNOLOGY

Technological innovation has been associated with productive growth and sustainable development (Jones et al., 2018). In 1995, Christensen and Bower formally introduced the disruptive-innovation model in their article 'Disruptive Technologies: Catching the Wave', and since then, the model has been extended to business proposals and technological advancements. Disruptive technologies include extensive changes resulting from specific automation and robotics technologies (Hynes & Elwell, 2016). They create novel market and technological trends (Abernathy & Utterback, 1978). These technologies are usually inferior to existing ones, but specific improvements make them highly appealing to customers, resulting in disrupted markets. These disruptive technologies interact with each other and with diverse demographic and social factors, amplifying each other's impact on market paradigms (Jones et al., 2018).

Technological disruption has three characteristics: generating new values and challenging the existing status quo, displaying innovative traits that produce radical transformations and having relative effects. Scholars debate whether disruptive technologies result in new opportunities or job losses and unemployment (Jones et al., 2018). It largely impacts employment status such that Manyika et al. (2013) predicted that by 2025, around 140 million workers may experience high job insecurity because of growing artificial intelligence technologies. Further, the impact of disruptive technologies is felt unequally across the workforce (Bennett et al., 2004). Over time, the concept of disruptive technology has widened to include disruptive services and business innovation (Jones et al., 2018).

Focusing on the Service Sector

While pondering the theory of evolutionary science, over fifty profound scholars belonging to the service sectors of marketing, management, tourism and hospitality reached the consensus that in this technologically-driven world, the most responsive has the best chances of survival (Aksoy et al., 2019). The consensus summed up the essence of disruptive technology well. Technological advancement has greatly shaped the service sector such that the global economy's computerisation and digitalisation have major consequences (Klausner & Antia, 2021). Particularly in the service sector, disruptive innovations are the intentional application of technology to benefit producers and consumers (Khan & Khan, 2009). They significantly determine behavioural actions and customer experiences (Su, 2011). Disruptive technologies like cloud computing, machine learning, big data analytics and artificial intelligence have transformed the service industry (Klausner & Antia, 2021).

Service management was greatly impacted by technological advancements and smartness such that the resultant shared economy built a highly interconnected network of customers and service providers, as evidenced in the case of Deliversoo or Uber Eats that were developed to fulfil service requirements (Buhalis et al., 2019). Four key factors drive technological disruption in the service industry (Klausner & Antia, 2021). Primarily disruptive technologies are still evolving, with many in their infancy stage. Further, various associated legal and regulatory challenges need attention, for instance, personal data privacy risks in applying big data analytics. Strong regulatory supervision results in "tech inertia", as experienced in financial and healthcare services. The ongoing patterns of structural dependency limit technological disruption since replacing the global networks of infrastructure, transportation and logistics is difficult.

Buhalis et al. (2019) proposed that virtual and/or augmented reality, autonomous devices and location-based services carry the potential to disrupt the service industry. The authors provide a comprehensive system review of technological disruption in the tourism and hospitality industry in specific research development areas of extra-sensory experience, hyper-personalised experiences and beyond-automated experiences, emphasising customer value-creation. They have further emphasised seven technological advancements, namely, fifth-generation mobile network, artificial intelligence, radio frequency identification, mobile devices, smartphones and wearables, applications or apps, cryptocurrency and blockchain that carry the potential to disrupt the service marketing and management processes technologically.

The next sections examine the status of technological disruption in four service areas: financial services, hospitality and tourism industry, legal services and health industry, to understand the concept through empirical evidence and real-world instances.

Disruptive Financial Services

Disruptive technologies can potentially affect the dynamics among customers, markets and businesses such that market trends and customer behaviour transform. Service sectors such as finance, marketing and human resource management have rapidly integrated many disruptive technologies such as artificial intelligence, chatbots, cloud computation and robotics process automation to produce cost-effective and highly functional business climates in the service industry (Mookerjee & Rao, 2021).

Technological dependence on daily functions requires banking services to transform to keep up with the digital era. Financial technology companies (Fintech) proved to be a disruptive technology, giving birth to innovations such as crowdfunding, peer-to-peer lending, payment getaways and the like (Sila & Martini, 2020). Fintech technologies have displaced conventional processes in the financial sector, such as efficient online loan services, blockchain-influenced payment services (e.g. Paytm and Google Pay), global money transfers, and disruptive trends of personal finance, equity financing (e.g. virtual fundraising), new products (e.g. cryptocurrencies) and consumer banking. Their implementation results in decreased operational costs and credit risks, enhanced productivity and better customer interactions (Kabra & Jadhav, 2023).

Insurance services have also been disrupted by applying artificial intelligence and big data analytics to cost-effectively transform underwriting and claims management. Automated insurance providers, such as Root, use mobile telematics applications to monitor driving habits and offer discounts and suitable claims accordingly. Life insurance companies use artificial intelligence-powered algorithms for underwriting and pricing mechanisms, which are then used by big data analytics to come up with periodic evaluation systems. Constant data supply from wearables such as Apple Watches allows efficient risk evaluation such that customers exhibiting consistent healthy behaviour can be rewarded. In the case of claims management, Lemonade uses digital images to settle claims in a time-efficient manner. The combination of "high tech and high touch" will cause extensive technological disruption in the insurance industry (Klausner & Antia, 2021).

Branchless banking services carry disruptive potential, allowing customers to innovatively go about banking transactions and create new markets (Sila & Martini, 2020). Digitalisation has majorly impacted the banking industry, resulting in enhanced customer services. Digitalisation successfully increases the customer base by providing convenient, largely error-free, cost-effective banking services (Bhosle et al., 2020). Neobanks have gained popularity because they are digitally driven and partner with online platforms to create need-based financial services (Klausner & Antia, 2021). Online payment systems such as Google Pay, Paytm and PhonePe have disrupted banking services, facilitating international trade transactions and simplifying security and intelligence systems (Bhosale et al., 2020). Indian consumers highly prefer the Google Pay payment platform because it includes a conveniently efficient method to conduct business through easy monitoring of inventories, sales and payments (Kabra & Jadhav, 2023).

Hospitality and Tourism Industry

Hospitality services are unique since they require analysis of simultaneous production and service that must be considered to produce efficient service systems (Su, 2011). Technological disruptions have revolutionised the tourism industry by determining marketing strategies and setting competitive advantages (Buhalis, 2020). Poon (1993) predicted the all-encompassing impact of these technologies on the tourism industry. The introduction of computerised information and distribution systems, such as travel agencies, permitted productive and efficient operations whilst providing personalised services. The era of eTourism was based on internet networking and opened diverse service avenues in the form of online travel systems and review websites, influencing tourism organisations' business performance concerning their reputation and brand establishment (Buhalis, 2020).

The introduction of information and communication technologies allows co-creation of value, resulting in increased destination familiarity, mitigated travelling risks and reduced hostility perceptions. Virtual reality facilitates pre-examining destination accessibility by individuals with disabilities from their homes. It also allows individuals with autism spectrum disorders to familiarise themselves with the destination and establish a routine, leading to better customer experiences (Weissenberg, 2017). Apple app store includes over 450 travel and tourism-related applications, helping customers better plan their trips (Xia et al., 2018).

Smart tourism, facilitated by big data analytics and software agents, utilised global interconnectivity platforms to create innovative tourism services such that these services were accessible to diverse population segments irrespective of physical barriers (Buhalis et al., 2019). Additionally, service gamification increases customer engagement and satisfaction. For instance, Starbucks includes a gamified reward system to build customer loyalty (Xu et al., 2017). Several disruptive technologies, such as the Internet of Things, fifth-generation mobile networks, mobile services, artificial intelligence, machine learning and the like, combine to form ambient intelligence tourism (Buhalis et al., 2019). Here, the tourism ecosystem promotes personalised services through automated services of robots, drones and augmented and virtual realities. Hence, smart tourism environments have the disruptive potential for service transformation by targeting strategic, management and marketing operations (Buhalis, 2020). Singapore Tourism Board has successfully built a tourism analytics network (STAN) to personalise tourist offers concerning time, price and location by examining tourist data from phones and transportation systems (GovInsider, 2018).

The Case of Airbnb

In 2008, San Francisco witnessed the launch of Airbnb, following which digital platforms encouraging short-term letting gained global fame for building a network of hosts and guests worldwide (Crommelin et al., 2018). Airbnb greatly impacts the traditional tourism industry. It is an online platform allowing ordinary individuals to rent their spaces as tourist accommodations. Its innovative transformation of tourism accommodation made it a disruptive innovation (Guttentag, 2015).

Airbnb shook the traditional tourism industry by creating an online market, following the trend of peer-to-peer accommodation based on a shared economy wherein access to underused assets is provided on rentals. It includes a technological framework that effectively connects hosts with willing guests and simultaneously eliminates the bigger marking challenge of attracting customers. Airbnb's public review feature establishes trust between the customers and the hosts (Guttentag, 2015). Such a reputation mechanism allows thorough examination on the customers' end, creating incentives to behave appropriately (Jøsang et al., 2007). Further, technological features of direct communication between hosts and customers via messages and user authenticity verification through online profiles, which include photographs, personal information and links on other social media accounts, establish trust between the involved parties. Additionally, Airbnb attracts guests because they are cost-effective and include additional benefits of staying in local accommodations, enhancing the tourist experience (Guttentag, 2015).

Airbnb has disrupted the accommodation market catering to short-term visitors, such as the hotel industry. The disruptive power of Airbnb includes using technology to economically facilitate millions of individuals to indulge in hospitality entrepreneurship by allowing them to use long-term housing accommodations innovatively. It has, most importantly, sparked intense competition in the housing markets, especially in tourist-friendly sites and raised valid concerns for housing affordability (Crommelin et al., 2018).

Disruptive Restaurant Services

Disruptive innovation in restaurant services is driven by online platforms that must be appealing and include timely orders and error-free transactions to increase customer satisfaction. Technological disruption has created new restaurant terminologies such as cloud, virtual, and dark kitchens. For instance, ghost DoorDash Kitchen provides rental spaces to restaurant brands to expand their off-restaurant sales (Khan, 2020). Creating competitive advantages, robots have invaded restaurant positions such that they can cook hamburgers, as done by Caliburger (Graham, 2018). Creator involves a robotic service delivery system such that robots perform diverse cooking operations and filter the kitchen smoke, reducing labour costs (Peters, 2018). Lee and Lee (2019) highlight the advent of digitalised delivery services called "untact technology" because they do not include direct communication with restaurants. These have disrupted restaurant services by creating quick, convenient and customised value while maintaining customer privacy (Kim et al., 2019).

Khan (2020) introduced six types of disruptive technologies in restaurant services. At the foremost stage, restaurants include limited technology use service types, including fast-casual dining, fine dining and fast foods, eliciting different customer experiences. This is followed by technology-facilitated services, which include mobile applications or internal machines for ordering restaurant food. Pick-up services are categorised under technology-mediated services, whereas using third-party (e.g. Zomato and Swiggy) or restaurant delivery services are categorised under technology-generated services. These were followed by technology-enable services in the form of freestanding delivery services and highly technology-dependent delivery services such as drone delivery services.

The National Restaurant Association (2019) has predicted the integration of technology and data in restaurant services such that smooth digital customer services will be provided on a customisation basis. The association proposes the increased popularity of restaurant services in the coming decades for socialisation purposes due to the expected decline of shopping malls. Virtualisation, autonomous vehicles, provision of food services by non-food companies and automated food preparation will disrupt restaurant services majorly. By 2030, technology will be effectively used to enhance management productivity and monitor costs, making takeout and delivery services highly sophisticated and digitalised.

Glancing Into the Future: Robotics and Artificial Intelligence

Bowen and Morosan (2018) predicted that by 2030, the hospitality industry would encompass a 25 percent robotic workforce, resulting in a disruptive trend that will tackle the challenges of labour shortage, management of huge consumer data and handling international travellers. Japan's Henn-na hotel was the first to introduce a front desk managed by robots, which resulted in their CEO predicting that over half of the hospitality jobs will be taken over by machines soon (Semuels, 2018). The robotic systems will disrupt the traditional service systems since humans will be replaced by machines such that lobby robots will perform front desk functions of payment, security checking and guest authentication. With advancements in voice-recognition algorithms, robotic systems can create personalised, customer-friendly experiences (Bowen & Morosan, 2018).

The future disruptive robotic and artificial intelligence technologies will address critical hospitality service tasks. These include "front-of-the-house robots" that are well-versed in diverse languages and perform behaviours that enhance customer experience. These technologies also facilitate workers' productivity by recognising the most efficient periods for individual employees, sending them heuristically automated tasks and tasks requiring maximum attention accordingly. While the millennials and generations following them will readily accept this disruptive trend, boomers will require human assistance. Additionally, value-conscious customers will be provided with inexpensive quality services because robotic technology will reduce costs in the hospitality industry. In this robotic future, luxury services will be defined by hospitality services provided by an all-human staff (Bowen & Morosan, 2018).

Legal Services

The last three decades have evidenced the impact of disruptive technologies on legal services, transforming the legal profession (Susskind & Susskind, 2015; Webley et al., 2019; Webb, 2020). In the digital age, law firms are rapidly integrating information management technologies and social media to enhance decision-making processes concerning scoping, cost-effective pricing, impeccable customer service and competitive advantages. The legal industry has reported increased implementation of intrants, virtual court and content management systems and knowledge management technologies, allowing effective information discovery, management and retrieval across internal and external fields (Evans et al., 2018).

Technological disruption became possible in the legal industry because many legal tasks were broken down into smaller segments automated using technology. The disruptive technologies range from artificial intelligence, social networking, cloud computing, robotics and the like (Evans et al., 2018). Some legal sectors are much more prone to technological disruption than others, namely, reviewing legal documents (discover), precisely searching for legal cases and examining them for persuasiveness (legal search), automated document generation to produce tailored legal arguments, using predictive analytics to predict case outcomes and generating brief, precise memos (McGinnis & Pearce, 2019). Further, technological disruption may be driven by external advancements such that law firms respond by being adaptive (Evans et al., 2018).

Technological disruption targets the culture of the legal industry such that it continuously becomes sustainable, serving its clients effectively (Evans et al., 2018). It has made the industry increasingly hybrid and complex, specifically targeting legal information management, automated legal support and legal infrastructure (Webb, 2020).

Major Disruptive Technologies

Webb (2020) highlights how technological disruption has created a decentralised, flexible law industry. Technological disruption impacts the legal sector at micro levels by transforming the professional work processes and at macro levels by examining how these processes impact the whole profession and its governance. Specialist legal technology or law tech has emerged, intending to automate the legal process through disruptive technologies to effectively provide legal decision support and directly advise clients (Webb, 2020).

Data, information and knowledge form the core of the legal industry (Evans & Price, 2017) and the primary objective of disruptive technologies is to provide accurate data to the right population segments at the right time (Evans et al., 2018). The top management, consisting of chief executives, needs to perceive technological advancement with an open mind such that its implementation benefits them and results in many creative opportunities (Nirell, 2014; Evans et al., 2018). Additionally, technological disruption has transformed the legal structure through paralegals, remote functioning and the incoming trend of client-centred financial reporting (White & Grueger, 2017). It has transformed the billing systems and enhanced the client experiences through customisation (Evans et al., 2018).

The legal industry has been flooded with diverse software for various purposes, such as billing (e.g. Freshbooks), document management (e.g. Clio), analysis (e.g. Relativity) and the like. Lawyers use blockchain technology to track transactions, maintain process transparency, and create smart contracts. Big data applications facilitate the maintenance of billions of client data whilst maintaining confidentiality. Based on artificial intelligence, software bots and machine-drive legal services facilitate the smooth information structuring, prediction of case outcomes and production of algorithmically perfect case presentations. Client communication has become simple through cloud computing, allowing efficient data management (Evans et al., 2018). Virtual and augmented reality allows the delivery of online legal services through Virtual Law Firms, whereas Virtual Courtrooms help simulate proceedings beyond geographical constraints (Press, 2017). Further, online dispute resolution systems have reduced the number of trials (Carneiro et al., 2014).

Specifically, blockchain technology, artificial intelligence, cloud computing, and digitalised court processes have increased start-up activity. For instance, the Australian law tech market doubled between 2015-2018, and Brazil reported 150 law tech start-ups. The growth has been attributed to the beneficial impact of disruptive technologies that permit flexible functioning (Webb, 2020).

Pertinent Challenges and Resulting Implications

An Australian law practitioner emphasises that the legal industry is immensely risk averse because the disbalance between the firms' needs and disruptive technology's impact may result in lost work and a diminishing client base. He emphasises how employees responsible for technology report to senior executives who impulsively shut down technological proposals due to low awareness and knowledge, resulting in restrictive and unhealthy dynamics (Evans et al., 2018). Such a trait results in lawyers being resistant to change in the name of maintaining the history and legacy of law firms (Croft, 2017; Evans et al., 2018).

Further, law employees performing tasks that may be easily automated, such as formulating routine wills or standard contracts, face job insecurity, reinforcing employee resistance to change (Evans et al., 2018). The latest Deloitte data proposed that artificial intelligence will make over a lakh legal jobs redundant in the next twenty years (White & Grueger, 2017). Medium-sized law firms, as opposed to large and small-sized ones, face a higher risk of failure if they fail to incorporate disruptive technologies into daily functioning (Evans et al., 2018).

Governance and regulation of technological disruption of legal services is a major concern such that legal jurisdictions indirectly shape technological advancement by restricting non-lawyer people from providing legal advice, basing external investment on firm size and prohibiting market practices such as advertising or referral fees based on cultural norms. Further, regulatory provisions are not up-to-date with technological advancement to produce legal and ethical occupational competence and may result in jurisdictional restrictions for local regulators (Webb, 2020).

The most efficient way to survive technological disruption is to accept change to their advantage and innovatively create quality services by meeting client demands and considering employee wellness. It would be beneficial to measure the readiness of law firms to deal openly with digital disruption and drive innovation internally. Further, disruptive technologies will allow customers to identify exceptional lawyers and produce cost-effective services through machine intelligence. It is imperative to understand that only a combination of human and machine intelligence will allow effective problem-solving and accommodation of diverse clients (Evans et al., 2018).

Healthcare Industry

The disruptive technology of telehealth has threatened traditional healthcare delivery by integrating electronic services to provide cost-effective and equitable care. Most telehealth innovations, such as virtual healthcare visits, aim to make healthcare safer and more convenient, while others generate novel healthcare delivery methods, such as remote patient monitoring (Schwamm, 2014). Telecommunication has connected clients and health providers globally, improving healthcare and reducing costs. Most importantly, telecommunication empowers individuals in underdeveloped regions, making healthcare systems efficient and accountable in response to knowledgeable clients. The concept of "connected health", encompassing telemedicine, mHeath and telehealth, has gained much popularity (Iglehart, 2014).

Technological disruptive programs like Veterans Health Administration and Partners Healthcare that introduce home telemonitoring have produced successful results concerning client satisfaction and health outcomes (Iglehart, 2014). TeleStroke, an affordable telehealth application by Mayo Clinic (2006), uses interactive videoconferencing and digital images to bridge the access gap between urban health centres and rural hospitals wherein acute stroke patients may require advanced interventions. Since TeleStroke uniquely established a hospital-to-hospital relationship, it created a financially efficient method of healthcare delivery (Schwamm, 2014). Clinical laboratory services such as Prodia also faced technological disruption when online consultation was introduced and resorted to digitalising its services to enhance customer satisfaction through online communication and result delivery, chatbots and mobile applications. Customers perceived these digital services as convenient and time-efficient, wherein further digital advancements such as 24-hour doctor availability virtually or online radiology results were demanded (Narolita & Darma, 2020).

In their systematic analysis, Sounderajah et al. (2021) investigated the healthcare industry for traces of disruptive innovations since its inception till 2019. Technological disruptions such as mobile healthcare applications, telemedicine and health informatics were the most popular innovations. Hence, digital health has immensely disrupted the healthcare industry by introducing digital information and communication technology. Junaid et al. (2022) conducted a comprehensive survey examining the application of smart sensors, the Internet of Things, artificial technology and blockchain technologies in healthcare management. Their implementation has formulated personalised healthcare services, improving overall patient well-being.

Disruptive Medical Delivery Systems

Innovative technological advancements such as advanced air mobility systems have greatly impacted the service of trauma surgery. Medical drones have popularised the "last mile delivery" concept, wherein critical medical supplies such as medications can be delivered within time constraints. These technological disruptions will help overcome urban congestion in densely populated areas and provide access to remote areas by facilitating effective transportation of medical services, especially in emergency cases. The most recent pandemic raised the demand for time-efficient delivery services that include minimum physical contact to lower transmission risks, a criterion fulfilled by medical drones. Implementing medical drones will decrease ambulance response times, allowing medical officers to effectively address emergencies such as cardiac arrest and childbirth (Sigari & Biberthaler, 2019).

Many exemplary advanced air mobility systems have disrupted medical delivery services. For instance, Zipline has largely decentralised patient therapy by delivering chemotherapy medication to patients' homes, reducing hospital visits and increasing medication adherence. Volansi, a drone delivery start-up, primarily delivers cold-chain medicines such as eye drops or vaccines as per on-demand delivery. These start-ups have also successfully set global delivery systems, proving detrimental in worldwide emergencies, as witnessed during the COVID-19 pandemic. Customers respond optimistically to drone delivery and show great possibilities for using these services. Such preferences will majorly disrupt traditional healthcare services (Sigari & Biberthaler, 2019).

Artificial Intelligence in Dentistry

Innovative dental medicine aims to provide patient-driven, personalised healthcare to monitor oral diseases through customised interventions that facilitate early diagnosis and effective treatment. Artificial intelligence systems carry the potential to develop personalised dentistry services by facilitating the systematic generation and management of healthcare data, increasing the accuracy of diagnosis and overall work efficiency. These systems are being rapidly incorporated to improve the quality of services and operational processes. Research in dental and oral healthcare is also driven by machine learning and deep learning advances that help develop image-based intelligent systems that aid diagnosis and treatment. Dentistry has also utilised social media to reach diverse population targets to create dentist-patient networks and spread dental education among students and patients. Social media platforms facilitate research by allowing the expression of opinion, resulting in peer support, information exchange and feedback generation (Joda et al., 2021).

Artificial intelligence algorithms help examine health data to modify policy decisions such as research-based programs. Dental medicine uses prototyping in combination with intraoral optical scanning to produce digital dental data for customised tooth replication or future dental reconstruction. Virtual and augmented reality technologies allow dentists to demystify complex treatment options as they visually demonstrate the impact of several therapeutic alternatives. Further, artificial intelligence has facilitated guided implant surgery and prosthetic-driven implant surgery in dentistry (Joda et al., 2021).

Teledentistry permits patients to perform dental care without physical visits to the dentist (Joda et al., 2021). Smartphone applications have resulted in efficient communication networks between dentists and patients, wherein digital images and videos assist clinical diagnosis, monitoring, and treatment planning (Petruzzi & De Benedittis, 2016). Removing economic and geographic constraints, telecommunication has made dental care greatly accessible (Fricton & Chen, 2009). Hence, teledentistry has immense disruptive potential in providing remote dental care services (Joda et al., 2021).

Disruptive Psychiatry

Innovative, disruptive thinking is required to produce effective psychiatric treatment plans to address the ongoing mental health pandemic and the dearth of effective pharmacological options (Sarris, 2022). Telepsychiatry has expanded recently, especially during the COVID-19 pandemic (Ee et al., 2020). Technological disruption will enable effective mental healthcare delivery across diagnosis, therapy and follow-up care phases. Most importantly, it will help bridge the gap between biological data and psychosocial symptoms by using machine learning, artificial intelligence and quantum computing. For instance, healthcare data collection using blockchain technology can help integrate clinical and biomarker indicators to produce effective client care (Sarris, 2022).

Technology is essential in producing microbiome-altering and digital therapies, improved drug delivery systems or nanotechnology and advanced brain-stimulation technology. In the case of therapies, digital technologies, especially smartphones, facilitate digital phenotyping, allowing the development of customised, remote and cost-effective interventions delivered through applications (Sarris, 2022). An effective combination of artificial intelligence and digital data tracking may produce interactive psychological chatbots that reinforce the importance of a healthy lifestyle (Sarris et al., 2020; Firth et al., 2020). In their comprehensive study, Bourla et al. (2018) reported moderate acceptability of disruptive technologies, namely machine learning, ecological momentary assessment and computerised adaptive testing, and digital phenotype among psychiatrists. Their apprehension of disruptive technologies is driven by a lack of knowledge and the associated medical and ethical risks concerning data security and storage, client-therapist relationships and confidentiality concerns.

Impact On Employees and Consumers

The fourth wave of the Industrial Revolution has transformed business models in the service industry, impacting employee functioning and consumer behaviour (Kavia-oja et al., 2020). Extensive globalisation and standardisation severely impact technical development, which influences daily functioning. Digitalisation and platform economy have transformed the lives of employees and consumers because many daily operations have become automated (Jakosuo, 2019). Platform economy means utilising operational platforms for novel value creation, such as relaying rentals, as done by Uber, or relaying the supply of private services, as done by Upwork (Farrell & Greig, 2016).

Schmidthuber et al. (2018) applied the technology acceptance model to the disruptive technology of mobile payment to investigate the factors influencing consumer intention to use a disruptive technology. The results indicated that the intention to use a disruptive technology is positively driven by the technology's perceived usefulness and perceived compatibility. Individuals who perceive themselves as innovative and think using these technologies will enhance their social status have a higher intention to use disruptive technologies. However, the impact of these variables is countered by the influence of perceived risks, which may reduce consumer willingness to use disruptive technology.

Jakosuo (2019) conducted a qualitative analysis to understand the impact of technological disruption, mainly digitalisation and platform economy, on employee and consumer behaviour. For instance, the application of Honda's humanoid robot will result in automated work, increased occupational safety and decreased social interaction on the employee forefront, whereas it will provide easy and detailed information access to customers. On the customers' end, digitalisation has removed geographical limitations and has provided convenient access to information at low costs. Online consumer communities allow opinion expression and price comparisons, empowering customers. Customers may also personalise and customise the available services per their needs and expectations through direct communication with the producers.

Increased work automation may decrease work satisfaction, resulting in uncertainty among employees. Digitalisation demands technological expertise from employees, who may have created polarised groups with highly skilled jobs on one end and low-skilled occupations on the other. While the platform economy increases work flexibility, it is connected with low wages and job security, negatively impacting employee well-being (Valenduc & Vendramin, 2016). Digitalisation and platform economy prove fruitful in developing countries (Yordanova, 2015). Such consequences have immense implications for human resource practices. HR practices have also been hit by technological disruption, as discussed below.

Human Resource (HR) Technological Disruptions

HR technologies, namely, Human Resource Information Systems (HRIS) and People Analytics, help manage workforce data to provide effective solutions. They result in disruptive innovations because they facilitate actionable analytics (Tursunbayeva, 2019). HRIS is an essential disruptive technology because it produces actionable insights concerning employee management, from recruitment and selection to career and retirement planning (McLaren, 2018). The HR industry has shifted its focus from automation to increasing employee productivity, resulting in technology-driven working models called smart-/tele-/remote-/agile-working (Tursunbayev, 2019). The adoption of these models by May Clinic and Texas Health enhanced employee satisfaction, increased employee retention and expanded popularity among prospective employees (It's tough to…, 2023). Additionally, social media tools such as Workplace by Facebook allow simplification of daily tasks, as reported by Tan Tock Seng Hospital (Tursunbayev, 2019).

HRIS has facilitated performance management processes, reducing manual errors, total costs and chances of data misplacement by managers. The disruptive potential of technological HR practices is further influenced by employee feedback mechanisms such as Qualtrics by SAP. Disruptive HR proposals such as "TV/Netflix-alike" training modules, microlearning and virtual and/or augmented reality technology-based educational practices have produced customised and personalised services. These technologies improve HR practices by reinforcing strategic workforce planning, addressing employee well-being, and including standardised procedures (Tursunbayev, 2019).

Ethical Considerations and Future Directions

The current chapter provides a comprehensive overview of the status of technological disruption in the service industry. The overwhelming adoption of artificial intelligence in the service sector, such as financial services, involves ethical and societal implications such as data privacy, biased decision-making and potential for risky outcomes, making ethical oversight and regulation of disruption of disruptive technology all the more necessary. Hopster (2021) outlined four descriptive levels of disruptive technology–technology, artefact, application and society–emphasising the corresponding ethical dilemmas that must be considered precisely. The most general technology level involves disruptive material techniques which may include side-effects, raising ethical worries and can be effectively tackled using an ethical foresight approach. Next, the artefact level deals with ethical issues surrounding disruptive products that may be nullified using ethical designs. Thirdly, the application level includes ethical challenges surrounding the purposeful use of disruptive procedures and products that require an ethical mediation approach, focusing on mindful implementation. Lastly, at the societal level, societal experimentation approaches readily regulate the impact of disruptive technology on society (Hopster, 2021). The developers of disruptive technology must not overall these ethical challenges and efficiently incorporate the suitable ethical approaches to produce a technologically social atmosphere wherein societal benefit and technological advancement move hand in hand.

Introducing disruptive technologies has several theoretical and practical implications, opening many research opportunities. For instance, virtual assistants, location-based services, and virtual and augmented reality technologies have immense implications in the tourism and hospitality industry. Virtual and augmented reality will assist in bridging the bridge gap between physical and virtual tourism and help simulate experiences such that presence in virtual settings can help determine tourists' perceptions towards destinations and satisfaction levels. Location-based services will enhance tourist experiences by providing real-time information about current trends. Virtual assistants may be developed to examine tourist tolerance levels regarding presented prices (Buhalis et al., 2019).

Ghawe and Chan (2022) thoroughly examined the implementation of disruptive technology frameworks and came up with several theoretical and practical implications. They identified the implementation process as an organisational phenomenon such that several internal and external barriers drove it. Further, it was emphasised that technical and human aspects of disruptive technologies combine to determine the outcome of framework implementation. Hence, organisations prioritising technology-framework fitness will successfully identify and eliminate challenges. Digital disruptive technologies were identified as adaptive technologies that readily responded to dynamic environmental demands whose successful implementation required paying considerable attention to structural and strategic challenges. Digital technologies will disrupt knowledge management systems by producing pragmatic applications and novel social and technical challenges (Kaivo-oja et al., 2020).

In their analysis of digital evolution in the service sector, Chin et al., (2023) recommends longitudinal examinations of innovative technologies' journeys to identify key contributors. Future studies may also expand the scope of research such that the concept of digital technologies is not limited to service sector-wise division. Further, it would benefit to highlight the customers' motivation behind their use of disruptive technologies. A proposed research programme focuses on the decision-making considerations required to select the most appropriate disruptive technology in organisations. It would help examine the rationale behind leaders' emphasis on benefits gained from disruptive technology implementation rather than the associated challenges and develop tools to mitigate the implementation risks before project initiation. Future research may be focused on customised implementation of disruptive technologies by holistically considering the interactions among social and technical challenges (Ghawe & Chan, 2022).

Various investment implications of technological disruption result in critical issues for executive members that require effective, actionable recommendations. Business leaders worldwide must enhance their knowledge of the concept by involving senior members in developing next-generation technologies. The impact of technology risks and opportunities across security processes and asset selection must be analysed to identify the prominent incumbents leading technological disruption. Investment leaders worldwide need to be connected via a virtual or physical link to carry intellectual discussions on the investment implications of technological disruptions based on the insights from forward-thinking business players such as start-ups and venture capitalists. Since regulatory uncertainty is often associated with new technologies, it would be beneficial to prepare for the regulatory backlash (Klausner & Antia, 2021).

CONCLUSION

In this chapter, the process of technological disruption has been highlighted concerning the service industry. Many sections of the service sector have utilised the disruptive power of technological advancements to automate routine tasks and increase customer satisfaction. Financial services stand disrupted with the advent of technological evolution such that including disruptive technologies has resulted in enhanced productivity and satisfactory customer interactions. The tourism and hospitality industry includes several instances of technological disruption, including Airbnb, disrupted restaurant delivery services and future possibilities of robotic hosts. The legal services have incorporated disruptive technologies to produce effective billing, document management and client communication processes. Similarly, the healthcare industry has widely accepted technological disruption, as evidenced in density and psychiatry subdivisions. Introducing disruptive technologies largely impacts the operational process, customer behaviour and employee functioning, resulting in immense practical implications. The chapter reiterates the prevalence of technological disruption in the service industry, raising questions about the future outlook of a highly technologically disrupted service sector.

REFERENCES

Abernathy, W. J., & Utterback, J. M. (1978). Patterns of industrial innovation. *Technology Review*, 80(7), 40–47.

Aksoy, L., King, C., & Chun, H. H. (2019). Evolving service thinking: Disruption and opportunity in hospitality and tourism. *Journal of Service Management*, 30(4), 449–451. 10.1108/JOSM-07-2019-413

Bennett, B., Brunker, D., & Hodges, R. (2004). Innovation, economic growth and vocational education and training. Vocational Education and Training. Research Readings, Australian National Training Authority, 68-83.

Bhosale, T., Kadam, V., & Jagtap, S. (2020). A Study on Relevance of Digitalization in the Banking Sector. *Advance and Innovative Research*, 7(1), 192–198.

Bourla, A., Ferreri, F., Ogorzelec, L., Peretti, C. S., Guinchard, C., & Mouchabac, S. (2018). Psychiatrists' attitudes toward disruptive new technologies: Mixed-methods study. *JMIR Mental Health*, 5(4), e10240. 10.2196/1024030552086

Bowen, J., & Morosan, C. (2018). Beware hospitality industry: The robots are coming. *Worldwide Hospitality and Tourism Themes*, 10(6), 726–733. 10.1108/WHATT-07-2018-0045

Bower, J. L., & Christensen, C. M. (1995). Disruptive technologies: Catching the wave. *Harvard Business Review*.

Buhalis, D. (2020). Technology in tourism-from information communication technologies to eTourism and smart tourism towards ambient intelligence tourism: A perspective article. *Tourism Review*, 75(1), 267–272. 10.1108/TR-06-2019-0258

Buhalis, D., Harwood, T., Bogicevic, V., Viglia, G., Beldona, S., & Hofacker, C. (2019). Technological disruptions in services: Lessons from tourism and hospitality. *Journal of Service Management*, 30(4), 484–506. 10.1108/JOSM-12-2018-0398

Carneiro, D., Novais, P., Andrade, F., Zeleznikow, J., & Neves, J. (2014). Online dispute resolution: An artificial intelligence perspective. *Artificial Intelligence Review*, 41(2), 211–240. 10.1007/s10462-011-9305-z

Chin, H., Marasini, D. P., & Lee, D. (2023). Digital transformation trends in service industries. *Service Business*, 17(1), 11–36. 10.1007/s11628-022-00516-6

Croft, J. (2017). Law firms programmed for more technological disruption. *Financial Times, 2*.

Crommelin, L., Troy, L., Martin, C., & Parkinson, S. (2018). *Technological disruption in private housing markets: the case of Airbnb*.

Ee, C., Lake, J., Firth, J., Hargraves, F., De Manincor, M., Meade, T., Marx, W., & Sarris, J. (2020). An integrative collaborative care model for people with mental illness and physical comorbidities. *International Journal of Mental Health Systems*, 14(1), 1–16. 10.1186/s13033-020-00410-633292354

Evans, N., & Price, J. (2017). Managing information in law firms: Changes and challenges. *Information Research*, 22(1).

Evans, N., Price, J., & Pender, D. (2018, October). Digital Disruption and Innovation in the Legal Industry: Management Considerations. In *ECMLG 2018 14th European Conference on Management, Leadership and Governance* (p. 66). Academic Conferences and publishing limited.

Farrell, D., & Greig, F. (2016, January). Paychecks, paydays, and the online platform economy. In *Proceedings. Annual Conference on Taxation and Minutes of the Annual Meeting of the National Tax Association*. National Tax Association.

Firth, J., Solmi, M., Wootton, R. E., Vancampfort, D., Schuch, F. B., Hoare, E., Gilbody, S., Torous, J., Teasdale, S. B., Jackson, S. E., Smith, L., Eaton, M., Jacka, F. N., Veronese, N., Marx, W., Ashdown-Franks, G., Siskind, D., Sarris, J., Rosenbaum, S., & Stubbs, B. (2020). A meta-review of "lifestyle psychiatry": The role of exercise, smoking, diet and sleep in the prevention and treatment of mental disorders. *World Psychiatry; Official Journal of the World Psychiatric Association (WPA)*, 19(3), 360–380. 10.1002/wps.2077332931092

Fricton, J., & Chen, H. (2009). Using teledentistry to improve access to dental care for the underserved. *Dental Clinics of North America*, 53(3), 537–548. 10.1016/j.cden.2009.03.00519482128

Ghawe, A. S., & Chan, Y. (2022). Implementing Disruptive Technologies: What Have We Learned? *Communications of the Association for Information Systems*, 50(1), 36. 10.17705/1CAIS.05030

GovInsider. (2018, October 12). *How the Singapore tourism board uses data to personalise tourism?* Retrieved from https://govinsider.asia/intl-en/article/how-the-singapore-tourism-board-uses-data-to-personalise-tourism

Graham, J. (2018). Hamburger-making robot Flippy is back at Calif. Chain. *USA Today*.

Guttentag, D. (2015). Airbnb: Disruptive innovation and the rise of an informal tourism accommodation sector. *Current Issues in Tourism*, 18(12), 1192–1217. 10.1080/13683500.2013.827159

Hopster, J. (2021, September). The ethics of disruptive technologies: towards a general framework. In *International Conference on Disruptive Technologies, Tech Ethics and Artificial Intelligence* (pp. 133-144). Cham: Springer International Publishing. 10.2139/ssrn.3903839

Hynes, N., & Elwell, A. D. (2016). The role of inter-organizational networks in enabling or delaying disruptive innovation: A case study of mVoIP. *Journal of Business and Industrial Marketing*, 31(6), 722–731. 10.1108/JBIM-10-2012-0168

Iglehart, J. K. (2014). Connected health: Emerging disruptive technologies. *Health Affairs*, 33(2), 190–190. 10.1377/hlthaff.2014.004224493758

It's tough to telecommute in health care. Here's how Mayo Clinic does it. (2023, March, 18). *Advisory Board*.

Jakosuo, K. (2019). Digitalisation And Platform Economy-Disruption In Service Sector. In *Joint Conference Ismc 2018-Icltibm 2018-14th International Strategic Management Conference 8th International Conference On Leadership, Technology, Innovation And Business Management*. Future Academy. 10.15405/epsbs.2019.01.02.7

Joda, T., Yeung, A. W. K., Hung, K., Zitzmann, N. U., & Bornstein, M. M. (2021). Disruptive innovation in dentistry: What it is and what could be next. *Journal of Dental Research*, 100(5), 448–453. 10.1177/00220345209787743332997

Jones, J., Seet, P., Spoehr, J., & Hordacre, A. (2018). The Fourth Industrial Revolution: the implications of technological disruption for Australian VET, NCVER. *Adelaide. Australia. Recuperado em, 25*.

Jøsang, A., Ismail, R., & Boyd, C. (2007). A survey of trust and reputation systems for online service provision. *Decision Support Systems*, 43(2), 618–644. 10.1016/j.dss.2005.05.019

Kabra, A., & Jadhav, B. (2023). FINTECH AND BEYOND. *The Online Journal of Distance Education and e-Learning : TOJDEL*, 11(1).

Kaivo-oja, J., Kuusi, O., Knudsen, M. S., & Lauraéus, I. T. (2020). Digital twin: Current shifts and their future implications in the conditions of technological disruption. *International Journal of Web Engineering and Technology*, 15(2), 170–188. 10.1504/IJWET.2020.109730

Khan, M., & Khan, M. A. (2009). How technological innovations extend services outreach to customers: The changing shape of hospitality services taxonomy. *International Journal of Contemporary Hospitality Management*, 21(5), 509–522. 10.1108/09596110910967773

Khan, M. A. (2020). Technological disruptions in restaurant services: Impact of innovations and delivery services. *Journal of Hospitality & Tourism Research (Washington, D.C.)*, 44(5), 715–732. 10.1177/1096348020908636

Kim, E., Libaque-Saenz, C., & Park, M. (2019). Understanding shopping routes of offline purchasers: Selection of search-channels (online vs. offline) and search-platforms (mobile vs. PC) based on product types. *Service Business*, 13(2), 305–338. 10.1007/s11628-018-0384-7

Klausner, D., & Antia, S. (2021). *Reshaping Services: The Investment Implications of Technological Disruption*. PGIM Megatrends-October.

Lee, S. M., & Lee, D. (2019). "Untact": A new customer service strategy in the digital age. *Service Business*. Advance online publication.

Manyika, J., Chui, M., Bughin, J., Dobbs, R., Bisson, P., & Marrs, A. (2013). *Disruptive technologies: Advances that will transform life, business, and the global economy, 180, 17-21*. McKinsey Global Institute.

McGinnis, J. O., & Pearce, R. G. (2019). The great disruption: How machine intelligence will transform the role of lawyers in the delivery of legal services. *Actual Probs.Econ.*, L, 1230.

McLaren, S. (2018). *How Hilton, Google, and more have dramatically reduced their time to hire*.

Mookerjee, J., & Rao, O. (2021). A review of the impact of disruptive innovations on markets and business performance of players. *International Journal of Grid and Distributed Computing*, 14(1), 605–630.

Narolita, D., & Darma, G. S. (2020). Prodia: disruption in clinical laboratory service system. *International research journal of management, IT and social sciences, 7*(1), 9-18.

National Restaurant Association. (2019, November 14). *Restaurant Industry 2030: Actionable insights for the future*. National Restaurant Association. https://restaurant.org/research/reports/Restaurant-Industry-2030

Nirell, L. (2014). *The mindful marketer: How to stay present and profitable in a data-driven world*. Springer. 10.1057/9781137386311

Peters, A. (2018). *This crazy-looking robot is the chef at a new burger joint*. Fast Company.

Petruzzi, M., & De Benedittis, M. (2016). WhatsApp: A telemedicine platform for facilitating remote oral medicine consultation and improving clinical examinations. *Oral Surgery, Oral Medicine, Oral Pathology and Oral Radiology*, 121(3), 248–254. 10.1016/j.oooo.2015.11.00526868466

Poon, A. (1993). *Tourism, technology and competitive strategies, CAB*. International Oxford. 10.1079/9780851989501.0000

Press, G. (2017). Top technologies for digital disruption. *Forbes*.

Sarris, J. (2022). Disruptive innovation in psychiatry. *Annals of the New York Academy of Sciences*, 1512(1), 5–9. 10.1111/nyas.1476435233789

Sarris, J., Thomson, R., Hargraves, F., Eaton, M., de Manincor, M., Veronese, N., Solmi, M., Stubbs, B., Yung, A. R., & Firth, J. (2020). Multiple lifestyle factors and depressed mood: A cross-sectional and longitudinal analysis of the UK Biobank (N= 84,860). *BMC Medicine*, 18(1), 1–10. 10.1186/s12916-020-01813-533176802

Schmidthuber, L., Maresch, D., & Ginner, M. (2020). Disruptive technologies and abundance in the service sector-toward a refined technology acceptance model. *Technological Forecasting and Social Change*, 155, 119328. 10.1016/j.techfore.2018.06.017

Schwamm, L. H. (2014). Telehealth: Seven strategies to successfully implement disruptive technology and transform health care. *Health Affairs*, 33(2), 200–206. 10.1377/hlthaff.2013.102124493761

Semuels, A. (2018). Robots will transform fast food that might not be a bad thing. *Atlantic (Boston, Mass.)*.

Sigari, C., & Biberthaler, P. (2021). Medical drones: Disruptive technology makes the future happen. *Der Unfallchirurg*, 124(12), 974–976. 10.1007/s00113-021-01095-334714357

Sila, I. K., & Martini, I. A. (2020). Transformation and revitalization of service quality in the digital era of revolutionary disruption 4.0. *JMBI UNSRAT (Jurnal Ilmiah Manajemen Bisnis dan Inovasi Universitas Sam Ratulangi)*., 7(1).

Sounderajah, V., Patel, V., Varatharajan, L., Harling, L., Normahani, P., Symons, J., Barlow, J., Darzi, A., & Ashrafian, H. (2021). Are disruptive innovations recognised in the healthcare literature? A systematic review. *BMJ Innovations*, 7(1), 208–216. 10.1136/bmjinnov-2020-00042433489312

Su, C. S. (2011). The role of service innovation and customer experience in ethnic restaurants. *Service Industries Journal*, 31(3), 425–440. 10.1080/02642060902829302

Susskind, R. E., & Susskind, D. (2015). *The future of the professions: How technology will transform the work of human experts*. Oxford University Press. 10.1093/oso/9780198713395.001.0001

Tursunbayeva, A. (2019). Human resource technology disruptions and their implications for human resources management in healthcare organisations. *BMC Health Services Research*, 19(1), 1–8. 10.1186/s12913-019-4068-330606168

Valenduc, G., & Vendramin, P. (2016). Work in the digital economy: sorting the old from the new. *ETUI Research Paper-Working Paper*.

Webb, J. (2020). Legal Technology: The Great Disruption? *U of Melbourne Legal Studies Research Paper*, (897).

Webley, L., Flood, J., Webb, J., Bartlett, F., Galloway, K., & Tranter, K. (2019). The profession (s)'engagements with lawtech: Narratives and archetypes of future law. *Law. Technology and Humans*, 1(1), 6–26. 10.5204/lthj.v1i0.1314

Weissenberg, A. (2017). Trends defining the global travel industry in 2017. *Global Economic Impact and Issue 2017*.

White, N., & Grueger, D. (2017). *Managing the digital workforce*. Deloitte.

Xia, M., Zhang, Y., & Zhang, C. (2018). A TAM-based approach to explore the effect of online experience on destination image: A smartphone user's perspective. *Journal of Destination Marketing & Management*, 8, 259–270. 10.1016/j.jdmm.2017.05.002

Xu, F., Buhalis, D., & Weber, J. (2017). Serious games and the gamification of tourism. *Tourism Management*, 60, 244–256. 10.1016/j.tourman.2016.11.020

Yordanova, G. (2015). Global Digital Workplace as an Opportunity for Bulgarian Woman to Achieve Work-Family Balance. *The Dynamics of Virtual Work*, 5, 1–12.

Section 3
Inclusive and Sustainable Educational Innovations

Chapter 12
Inclusive E-Tutoring Between Artificial Intelligence, Corporaty, and Emotionality:
Flipped Inclusion and New Research Perspectives

Silvia Tornusciolo
Mercatorum University, Italy

Enzapaola Catalano
Pegaso University, Italy

Tonia De Giuseppe
https://orcid.org/0000-0002-3235-4482
Giustino Fortunato University, Italy

ABSTRACT

The report on the digital decade prompted the European Commission to issue recommendations to Italy aimed at encouraging investment in high quality education that leads to the development of the transversal skills necessary to keep pace with the digital transformation of society. AI is revolutionising the world, and, with it, education. Learning that passes through the corporeity and the senses is therefore destined to disappear and be replaced by the perception of the three-dimensional world? Will it still be necessary to aim towards literacy emotional literacy and inclusion, the result of a skillful application of inclusive teaching methodologies such as flipped inclusion? These are the questions the authors will try to reflect on, analysing in particular flipped inclusion, in order to of exploring, devising, designing and testing inclusive models of ecological development.

DOI: 10.4018/979-8-3693-3003-6.ch012

DIGITAL SKILLS, VIRTUAL LEARNING ENVIRONMENT, AND KNOWLEDGE PRODUCTION: HISTORICAL EVOLUTIONARY FRAMEWORK

On September 27, 2023, the European Commission (EC) published the first *State of the Digital Decade* report. The report assessed the progress of member states, providing specific country recommendations. It highlighted that, under current conditions, only 59% of the population will have basic digital skills by 2030, against a target population of 80%. Furthermore, the number of information and communication technology (ICT) specialists may not exceed 12 million, whereas the target is 20 million. Consequently, the report recommended prioritizing investment in high-quality education and skills, particularly promoting women's participation in science, technology, engineering, and mathematics (STEM) disciplines from an early age (Di Marco, 2023).

Given these findings, renewing the educational system to match the dynamic future society is imperative. This entails implementing new learning and teaching models and optimizing existing ones across various life and knowledge areas (De Benedictis et al., 2019). Such renewal should capitalize on experiential innovations and adopt educational practices that acknowledge the pervasive interconnections in formal, informal, and non-formal learning contexts (De Giuseppe et al., 2023). Thus, new emoeducational perspectives concerning artificial intelligent (AI) systems should transform differences into potentialities through responsible administration of new technologies (Zellini, 2018), amplifying subjective potentialities (Aiello et al., 2017) and moving away from compensatory logic linked to diversity, adaptation, and integration (Sibilio & Aiello, 2016).

Artificial Intelligence (AI) is revolutionizing society and education, necessitating an understanding of how pedagogy can benefit from it. Reflecting on Alan Turing (1950), who is considered the founding father of computer science and AI, it is useful to compare the results of a process rather than defining intelligence. According to the "Imitation Game" method, if a process is considered intelligent when performed by a human, it can be considered intelligent when performed by a machine. Thus, AI can be defined as the science that enables computers to perform tasks requiring human-like intelligence. This technological intervention has redefined learning, knowledge acquisition, and the roles and methodologies of teachers, reshaping learning environments (Petruccelli, 2017). However, there are advantages and risks, including the potential anthropomorphizing of AI (Finocchiaro, 2022), where students might imagine replacing a teacher or tutor with a machine.

The school, traditionally seen as the primary place of learning (Barbi, 2014), must adapt to the new reality of accessible culture anytime, anywhere. This adaptation is in line with the concept of a virtual learning environment (VLE), moving away from exclusive face-to-face classes and the traditional transmission of knowledge. A learning community is seen as a process that unites individual actions of self-education for common goals (Batini & Fontana, 2003). The web is now an environment for mutual interaction and collaborative knowledge production (Calvani & Menichetti, 2013), where learners are no longer passive consumers but active producers of knowledge (Panciroli, 2008).

Corporeity, Emotional Illiteracy, and Educational Challenges Between Digitalization and AI

Understanding that learning involves processing raw sensory data into abstract ideas applicable in new situations is fundamental (Dehaene, 2020). Merleau-Ponty (1945) and Sartre (2003) emphasized the body's role in human experience and self-understanding. According to Butler (1990), cultural and social frameworks influence our perception of our bodies and identities. In contrast, today's youth can often do without physical presence, even in work and relationships, replaced by virtual forms of corporeity (Digennaro, 2023).

The concept of community has evolved. Traditionally characterized by defined territorial boundaries and shared cultures, communities now include virtual ones marked by dynamic, chosen belonging (Tosoni, 2019). However, despatialized simultaneity (Thompson, 1998) has altered perceptions of time, space, and community belonging, necessitating effective relationship-building in this new context. This shift requires learning methodologies that develop social skills for collective well-being and foster cooperative learning where everyone is responsible for each other's knowledge.

Living a "hived-off" existence (Digennaro, 2023), where physical interaction is mediated by digital screens, blurs the lines between real and virtual experiences, leading to the concept of "onlife" (Floridi, 2014). This hybrid existence combines online and offline actions, necessitating organic policies for skill development and collective understanding to shape a sustainable, inclusive future. Technological competence becomes crucial to avoid the risks associated with unchecked innovation.

A strategy for an effective educational system must consider the rapid response of the brain to direct interaction with objects (Rizzolati, 2019). Hands-on learning activates brain areas related to memorization and abstract thought processing (Bramati, 2022). In contrast, flat-screen interactions without tactile correlation hinder sensory learning. The role of the body in learning, emphasized by pedagogists like Cousinet, Freinet, and Montessori, underscores space as an action place intertwined with bodily experience (Merleau-Ponty, 2003).

Machine Learning, Educator Training, and Inclusive E-Tutoring With AI: Theoretical Research Framework

AI aims to understand human intelligence—our ability to reason, plan, solve problems, and learn from experience. In AI learning, machine learning involves statistical techniques that improve through experience. Supervised learning uses pre-labeled data to build decision models, while unsupervised learning detects patterns in unlabeled data to create models.

For example, teaching a computer to recognize a dog in photos requires thousands of labeled images (dog and not dog) to train machine learning algorithms. Unlike humans, who learn through sensory perception and interactive experiences, AI needs extensive data for pattern recognition (Di Tore, 2023). In eLearning, AI personalizes user experiences by learning from user interactions, improving learning and portal experiences tailored to individual needs.

Machine learning educates algorithms to learn from diverse situations, fostering meaningful learning that relates prior knowledge to new information (Ausubel, 2004). However, AI's autonomy and learning abilities pose risks, including cognitive overload and informational bubbles leading to cultural polarization and diminished critical thinking (De Giuseppe & Iannello, 2023).

Ethical considerations in AI involve maintaining control over AI uses and consequences, known as meaningful control (Taddeo, 2016). Ethics-by-design integrates ethical considerations into AI design and development, ensuring new technologies follow societal norms and values (Niglia, 2020). The UN Agenda 2030 emphasizes balancing economic, social, and environmental dimensions for sustainable development, recognizing these factors as indivisible for realizing human rights.

E-Tutors and Inclusive Methodologies

In the networked knowledge approach, emotions play a crucial role in learning (Moors, 2019). Positive emotions enhance motivation, gratification, and self-efficacy, while negative emotions hinder learning, leading to learned helplessness (Seligman, 2017). The e-tutor supports positive emotions and empathy, crucial for well-being in the learning process (Edith, 2014). Empathy, as a virtue of the educator, fosters cognitive development and ethical relationships, essential for emotional connection and avoiding emotional disconnection (Sorce, 2023).

Traditional didactics emphasize competitive performance standards, often leading to labeling and exclusion. Inclusive education values everyone's abilities, strengthened through relationships and targeted teaching methodologies in consonant learning environments. Technologies facilitate flexible, inclusive learning, enhancing skills according to individual needs (Sibilio & Aiello, 2016).

The Flipped Inclusion model explores, ideates, designs, and experiments with inclusive ecological development models, considering the dynamic interaction between individuals and environments (De Giuseppe, 2020). This method, tested at Giustino Fortunato Telematic University, embraces an ecological perspective with concentric structures (microsystem, mesosystem, exosystem, macrosystem) influencing individual development. These interrelationships affect actions, events, and emotions in a multidimensional perspective, applicable in formal, informal, and non-formal learning contexts.

CONCLUSION

In analyzing the role of Artificial Intelligence (AI) in education, it becomes evident that AI cannot fully replace the humanity of teachers who convey learning through sensory experiences, thereby promoting systemic ecological well-being. While AI can serve as a valuable tool or partner in facilitating new forms of distributed knowledge, it also poses risks such as the proliferation of generic information and social isolation.

To mitigate these risks and enhance the benefits of AI, it is essential to pursue systemic ecological well-being through the promotion of pro-social behaviors and the adoption of inclusive design models like Flipped Inclusion. This approach not only leverages the strengths of AI but also ensures that education remains holistic and centered on human values.

Furthermore, the importance of emotional education cannot be overstated. As emphasized by Randazzo (2018), integrating cognitive and emotional skills is crucial for modern education. Collaboration between family, school, and educational organizations is necessary to cultivate emotional intelligence, which is a key determinant of success in both interpersonal and social contexts (Buccolo, 2020). Emotional education enhances motivation, fosters effective learning strategies, and promotes positive mindsets. In this context, the role of the e-tutor becomes pivotal. By guiding emotional exploration, the e-tutor contributes significantly to the balanced development of individuals.

In conclusion, in a world that is constantly changing and enriched by the advancements of AI, emotional education remains an invaluable resource. It enables individuals to address challenges and seize opportunities with greater awareness and balance, ensuring that the integration of AI in education enhances rather than detracts from the human experience.

REFERENCES

Aiello, P. (2017). *Insegnare a leggere la mente: progettazione di un edugame per lo sviluppo di abilità sociali in studenti con Disturbi dello Spettro Autistico. Giornale Italiano della Ricerca Educativa* (Multimedia, P., Ed.).

Alberti, R. E., & Emmons, M. C. (2003). *Essere assertivi. Come imparare a farsi rispettare senza prevaricare gli altri*. Il Sole 24 Ore.

Alexandre, L. (2018). *La guerra delle intelligenze. Intelligenza artificiale contro l'intelligenza umana*. EDT.

Allport, G. W. (1962). *The general and unique in psychological science*. Harvard University.

Amato, M. (2013). *La costruzione del Sé, il luogo educativo tra scuola "in presenza" e "a distanza"*. Lamezia Terme.

American Psychiatric Association. (2000). *Diagnostic and statistical manual of mental disorders* (4th ed.). American Psychiatric Publishing.

American Psychiatric Association. (2013). *Diagnostic and statistical manual of mental disorders* (5th ed.). American Psychiatric Publishing.

Anchisi, R., & Gambotto Dessy, M. (1995). *Non solo comunicare. Teoria e pratica del comportamento assertivo*. Libreria Cortina.

Aragona, M. (2006). *Aspettando la rivoluzione. Oltre il DSM-V: le nuove idee sulla diagnosi tra filosofia della scienza e psicopatologia*. University Press, Editori Riuniti.

Arntz, A. (2005). Pathological dependency: Distinguishing functional from emotional dependency. *Clinical Psychology : a Publication of the Division of Clinical Psychology of the American Psychological Association*, 12(4), 411–416. 10.1093/clipsy.bpi051

Asbury, K., & Plomin, R. (2015). *G come geni. L'impatto della genetica sull'apprendimento*. Raffaello Cortina Editore.

Augusti, F., & Bonavolontà, G. (2021). *Intelligenza Artificiale e Educazione: le percezioni degli studenti del Dipartimento di Scienze dell'Educazione dell'Università Roma Tre sul concetto di Intelligenza Artificiale. QTimes – webmagazine*.

Ausubel, D. P. (2004). *Educazione e processi cognitivi*. Franco Angeli.

Barbi, A. (2014). Ambiente virtuale per un apprendimento reale. *EL.LE*, *3*(1).

Basti, G. (n.d.). La sfida etica dell'intelligenza artificiale e il ruolo della filosofia. In V. C. Müller (Ed.), *Ethics of artificial intelligence and robotics*. In E. N. Zalta (Ed.), *Stanford Encyclopedia of Philosophy*. Stanford Press. https://plato.stanford.edu/archives/sum2021/entries/ethics-ai/

Batini, F., & Fontana, A. (2003). *Comunità di apprendimento. Un nuovo modo di imparare*. Editore Zona.

Bauman, Z. (2014). *La vita tra reale e virtuale. Meet the media guru*. Egea.

Bramati, A. (2022, July 4). *Il ruolo dei sensi nell'apprendimento e nello sviluppo linguistico*. Dire Fare Insegnare. https://www.direfareinsegnare.education/didattica/il-ruolo-dei-sensi-nell-apprendimento-e-nello-sviluppo-linguistico/

Brieger, P., Sommer, S., Bloink, R., & Marneros, A. (2000). The relationship between five-factor personality measurements and ICD-10 personality disorder dimensions: Results from a sample of 229 subjects. *Journal of Personality Disorders*, 14(3), 282–290. 10.1521/pedi.2000.14.3.28211019751

Bronfenbrenner, U. (1979). *The ecology of human development*. Harvard University Press. 10.4159/9780674028845

Bronfenbrenner, U. (1986). Ecology of the family as a context for human development: Research perspectives. *Developmental Psychology*, 22(6), 723–742. 10.1037/0012-1649.22.6.723

Buccolo, M. (2020). L'educatore emozionale e la promozione del benessere nei contesti di cura. *Medical Humanities & Medicina Narrativa*, 99-107.

Buccolo, M. (2020). La gestione delle emozioni nel lavoro educativo con gli adolescenti e le famiglie. *Consultori Familiari Oggi*, 24-33.

Butler, J. (1990). *Gender trouble: Feminism and the subversion of identity*. Routledge.

Caligiuri, M. (2018). *Educazione per popoli superflui? L'avvento dell'intelligenza artificiale e gli studenti plusdotati: per una pedagogia consapevole*. Formazione & Insegnamento.

Calvani, M., & Menichetti, M. (2013). Quali scenari per le pratiche e-learning nell'università? Gli "Open Educational Path." Firenze.

Carr, N. (2011). *Internet ci rende stupidi? Come la Rete sta cambiando il nostro cervello*. Raffaello Cortina.

Corona, F., & De Giuseppe, T. (2017). La Flipped Inclusion, tra impianto teoretico e didattica sperimentale di aula aumentata per una didattica inclusiva. [Trento: Centro Studi Erickson.]. *Pedagogia Più Didattica*, 3, 2–7.

Costamagna, C. (n.d.). *Mappe concettuali e apprendimento significativo*. Verga via grande. https://www.vergaviagrande.edu.it/scuola/per/formazione/ponD1_09/mappe/Mappe_concettuali_e_apprend_significativo.pdf

D'Alessi, C. (2021). Empatia ed intelligenza emotiva per una sostenibilità affettivo-sociale: Dalla teoria alla prassi. *Formazione & Insegnamento*.

De Bartolomeis, F., & Cousinet, R. (1973). *Il metodo di lavoro libero per gruppi*. La Nuova Italia.

De Benedictis, R., et al. (2019). Tecnologie intelligenti per la formazione a supporto dell'invecchiamento attivo. *Forma@re-Open Journal per la formazione in rete*, 19(1), 301-311.

De Giuseppe, T. (2016). *Metodologia Flipped tra sistemica inclusione e prospettive didattico-assertive*. Il Papavero.

De Giuseppe, T. (2023). *Flipped Inclusion e disturbo borderline di personalità: tra Empowerment, Consapevolezza Assertiva e Cura Pedagogica*. Il Papavero.

De Giuseppe, T. (2023). *Educational science tra digital transformation e sfide interdisciplinari per professionalità inclusive.* Il Papavero.

De Giuseppe, T., & Corona, F. (2017). Metodologia Flipped tra sistemica inclusione e prospettive didattico-assertive. [Pensa Multimedia.]. *Formazione e Insegnamento*, 15(2), 409–420.

De Giuseppe, T., & Iannello, A. (2023). *I paradigmi eco-pedagogico-inclusivi tra Accessibility e Design for All: il modello Flipped Inclusion.* Il Papavero.

Deakin, J. F. (1998). Il ruolo della serotonina in casi di panico, ansia e depressione. *Clinical Psychopharmacology*, 13(4), S1–S5.

Dehaene, S. (2020). *How We Learn: Why Brains Learn Better Than Any Machine... for Now.* London.

Dennenburg, V. H. (1981). Lateralità emisferica negli animali e effetti della prima esperienza. *Behavioral and Brain Sciences*, 4, 1–49.

Di Marco, L. (2023, October 3). I risultati dell'Ue per il decennio digitale 2030, Raccomandazioni all'Italia. ASVIS. https://asvis.it/rubrica-europa-e-agenda-2030/1339-17867/i-risultati-dellue-per-il-decennio-digitale-2030-raccomandazioni-allitalia

Di Tore, P. A. (2023). *Intelligenza Artificiale e processi educativi secondo l'Intelligenza Artificiale.* Anicia.

Di Tore, S. (2017). *Utilizzo della tecnologia dei display montati sulla testa per supportare l'insegnamento attraverso ambienti di apprendimento virtuale in contesti non formali. Giornale Italiano della Ricerca Educativa.* Pensa Multimedia.

Digennaro, S. (2018). Corpi emotivi: riflessioni sull'educazione emotiva nella scuola. *Encyclopaideia – Journal of Phenomenology and Education*, 22(52).

Digennaro, S. (2023). *Corpo, vita onlife e dualismo: una nuova sfida per le professioni educative.* Pensa MultiMedia.

Doidge, N. (2008). *The Brain That Changes Itself.* Penguin.

Dollar, J., & Miller, N. E. (1950). *Personality and psychotherapy.* McGraw-Hill.

Ehrensaft, M. K. (2005). Interpersonal relationship and sex differences in the development of conduct problems. *Clinical Child and Family Psychology Review*, 8(1), 39–63. 10.1007/s10567-005-2341-y15898304

Finocchiaro, G. (2022). *La regolazione dell'intelligenza artificial. Riv. Trimest. Dirit. Pubblico.* Digital Media Laws.

Floridi, L. (2014). *The fourth revolution: How the infosphere is reshaping human reality.* Oxford University Press.

Fonagy, P. (2000). Attaccamento, sviluppo del Sé e sua patologia nei disturbi di personalità. Psychomedia. www.psychomedia.it

Fonagy, P., & Target, M. (1996). Playing with reality: 1 Theory of mind and the normal development of psychic reality. *The International Journal of Psycho-Analysis*, 77, 217–233.8771375

Freinet, C. (1978). *La scuola del fare*. Ed. Emme.

Freud, S. (1900). *Die traumdeutung*. Franz Deuticke.

Giacomantonio, M. (2020). Intelligenza artificiale e apprendimento. *Innovatio Educativa*, 51-56.

Grice, H. P. (1993). *Logica e conversazione. Saggi su intenzione, significato e comunicazione*. Il Mulino.

Grinker, R. R., Werble, B., & Dyre, R. C. (1968). *The Borderline Syndrome*. Basic Books.

Gunderson, J. G., & Singer, M. (1975). Defining borderline patients: An overview. *The American Journal of Psychiatry*, 132(1), 1–10. 10.1176/ajp.132.1.1802958

Hay, L. (1994). *Puoi guarire la tua vita*.

Lewandowski, K. E., Barrantes-Vidal, N., Nelson-Gray, R., Clacy, C., Kepley, H. O., & Kwapil, T. R. (2006). Anxiety and depression symptoms in psychometrically identified schizotypy. *Schizophrenia Research*, 8(2-3), 225–235. 10.1016/j.schres.2005.11.02416448805

Lewin, K. (1948). *Resolving social conflicts*. Harper.

Linehan, M. (1993). *Cognitive behavioural therapy for borderline personality disorder*. Guilford Press.

Linehan, M. (2001). *Il trattamento cognitivo-comportamentale del disturbo borderline: il modello dialettico*. Milano: Cortina.

Linehan, M. M., & Dimeff, L. (2001). Terapia dialettica comportamentale in breve. *Lo psicologo californiano*, *34*, 10-13.

Livesley, W. J., Schroeder, M. L., & Jackson, D. N. (1990). Dependent personality disorder and attachment problems. *Journal of Personality Disorders*, 3, 292–306. 10.1521/pedi.1989.3.4.292

Longo, G. O. (2003). *Il Simbionte. Prove di umanità future*. Meltemi.

Lorenz, K. (1967). *L'anello di re Salomone*. Milano: Adelphi.

Lucangeli, D. (2019). *Cinque lezioni leggere sull'emozione di apprendere*. Erickson.

Mahler, M. S., Pine, F., & Bergman, A. (1978). *La nascita del bambino*. Boringhieri.

Martini, E. R., & Sequi, R. (1999). *Il lavoro nella comunità*. Carocci.

Marx, K., & Engels, F. (1970). *Selected Works*. International.

Maslow, A. H. (1955). Deficiency motivation and growth motivation. In Jones, M. R. (Ed.), *Nebraska symposium on motivation* (pp. 1–39). Univ. Nebraska Press.

Masterson, J. F. (1972). *Treatment of the Borderline Adolescent*. Wiley.

Maton, K. I., & Salem, D. (1995). Organizational characteristics of empowerment-community settings: A multiple case study approach. *American Journal of Community Psychology*, 23(5), 631–656. 10.1007/BF025069858851343

Mead, G. H. (1934). *Mind, Self, and Society*. University of Chicago Press.

Megginson, D., & Clutterbuck, D. (1995). *Mentoring in action*. Kogan Page.

Meissner, W. W. (1988). *Treatment of Patients in the Borderline Spectrum*. Aronson.

Merleau-Ponty, M. (2003). *Fenomelogia della percezione*. Bompiani.

Meyer, B., Ajchenbrenner, M., & Bowles, D. P. (2005). Sensory sensitivity, attachment experiences, and rejection responses among adults with borderline and avoidant features. *Journal of Personality Disorders*, 19(6), 641–658. 10.1521/pedi.2005.19.6.64116553560

Montessori, M. (1970). *L'autoeducazione*. Garzanti.

Morey, L. C., Gunderson, J. G., Quigley, B. D., Shea, M. T., Skodol, A. E., McGlashan, T. H., Stout, R. L., & Zanarini, M. C. (2002). The representation of borderline, avoidant, obsessive-compulsive, and schizotypal personality disorders by the five-factor model. *Journal of Personality Disorders*, 16(3), 215–234. 10.1521/pedi.16.3.215.2254112136679

Niglia, F. (2020, November 10). Ethics by Design (EbD), la responsabilità sociale nell'industria 4.0. *Network Digital 360*. https://www.industry4business.it/smart-manufacturing/ethics-by-design-ebd-la-responsabilita-sociale-nellindustria-4-0/

Novak, J. D. (2001). *L'apprendimento significativo*. Erickson.

Nussbaum, M. C. (2006). *Coltivare l'umanità. I classici, il multiculturalismo, l'educazione contemporanea*. Carocci.

OECD. (2010). *The High Cost of Low Educational Performance. The Long-Run Economic Impact of Improving PISA Outcomes*. OECD. https://www.oecd.org/pisa/44417824.pdf

Panciroli, C. (2008). E-learning e learning-e Riflessioni sulla formazione. *Ricerche di Pedagogia e Didattica*, 3. Bologna.

Petruccelli, I. (2017). *Psicologia architettonica e ambientale dei luoghi scolastici*. Il Mulino.

Plutchik, R. (2001). The Nature of Emotions. *American Scientist*, 89(4), 344–350. 10.1511/2001.28.344

Randazzo, M. (2018). Intelligenza emotiva ed empatia: l'ultima frontiera della didattica. *Laboratorio di sociologia del diritto*, Motta, G. (Ed.).

Rapport, J. (1981). In Praise of Paradox. A Social Policy of Empowerment over Prevention. *American Journal of Community Psychology*, 1(1), 1–25. 10.1007/BF008963577223726

Raskin, R. N., & Terry, H. (1998). A principal components analysis of the Narcissistic Personality Inventory and further evidence of its construct validity. *Journal of Personality and Social Psychology*, 54(5), 890–902. 10.1037/0022-3514.54.5.8903379585

Rizzolati, G. (2019). *Specchi nel cervello*. Milano: Cortina.

Rogers, C. R. (1961). *On becoming a person*. Houghton Mifflin.

Rogers, C. R. (1978). *Potere personale. La forza interiore e il suo effetto rivoluzionario*. Astrolabio, Ubaldini.

Sadin, E. (2019). *Critica della ragione artificiale*. Luiss University Press.

Sampson, E. E. (1988). The debate on individualism: Indigenous psychologies of the individual and their role in personal and societal functioning. *The American Psychologist*, 43(1), 15–22. 10.1037/0003-066X.43.1.15

Sibilio, M., & Aiello, P. (Eds.). (2016). *Formazione e ricerca per una didattica inclusiva*. Franco Angeli.

Spitzer, M. (2015). *Solitudine digitale*. Corbaccio.

Stern, A. (1938). Psychoanalytic investigations and therapy in the borderline group of neuroses. *The Psychoanalytic Quarterly*, 7(4), 467–489. 10.1080/21674086.1938.11925367

Stone, M. H. (1987). Treatment of patients in the borderline spectrum. In Tasman, A., Hales, R. E., & Frances, A. J. (Eds.), *American Psychiatric Press review of psychiatry* (Vol. 8, pp. 103–122). Psychiatric Press.

Taddeo, M. (2016). Costruire l'etica dell'intelligenza artificiale. *Università degli studi di Firenze*. Retrieved from https://www.openstarts.units.it/server/api/core/bitstreams/bad34fc9-cd4c-4be2-957a-68d436f6657e/content

Thompson, J. B. (1998). *Mezzi di comunicazione e modernità. Una teoria sociale dei media*.

Weinschenk, S. M. (2010). *Neuro web design. L'inconscio ci guida nel web*. Apogeo.

Zellini, P. (2018). *La dittatura del calcolo*. Milano: Adelphi.

Zimmerman, M. A. (2000). Empowerment Theory: Psychological, Organizational and Community Levels of Analysis. In Rapport, J., & Seidman, E. (Eds.), *Handbook of Community Psychology*. Kluwer Academic/Plenum Publishers. 10.1007/978-1-4615-4193-6_2

Zuckerman, M. (2005). Psychobiology of personality (2nd ed.). New York: Cambridge 10.1017/CBO9780511813733

Chapter 13
Community-Driven Governance:
Between Complex Education and Flipped Inclusion – Research Perspectives for an Eco-Sustainable Economic Pedagogy

Maria Carbone
Pegaso Telematic University, Italy

Alessia Sozio
Pegaso Università Telematica, Italy

Tonia De Giuseppe
https://orcid.org/0000-0002-3235-4482
Giustino Fortunato University, Italy

ABSTRACT

Technological progress and, in particular, the spread of artificial intelligence, constitutes in the context an element of innovation no longer only at the level of production but also at the level of administration and control. This chapter explores the potential and risks that directors are faced with as a result of the entry of artificial intelligence into the boardroom, proposing to investigate whether in the corporate governance of small and medium-sized companies it is possible to act pedagogically to form an organizational culture devoted to inclusion through the application of cooperative learning methodologies that allow, in fact, to achieve greater inclusiveness among the individuals working there. The project proposes to apply the methodology of flipped inclusion, and more specifically Cohen's method of complex instruction because through the creation of heterogeneous teamwork and interdependence of roles, the resources of all group members can be enhanced.

INTRODUCTION

The transformation of economic activities due to artificial intelligence (AI) technologies has been underway for some time but has become particularly pronounced in recent years. This evolution has prompted experts in corporate law and business organizations to globally confront the effects of this

DOI: 10.4018/979-8-3693-3003-6.ch013

Copyright ©2024, IGI Global. Copying or distributing in print or electronic forms without written permission of IGI Global is prohibited.

technological revolution. AI is not only opening up new opportunities but also posing unprecedented interpretative problems and innovative regulatory demands on legislators and supervisory authorities. Many believe AI is central to the "fourth industrial revolution," irrevocably changing daily life.

More interconnected societies will base decision-making processes on big data analysis; firms in competitive markets will access resources at lower costs, and goods and services can be purchased from anywhere through automated services. The organization and management of modern enterprises are undergoing a metamorphosis (Rossi, 2012), leading to a modified genetic code of corporate governance. This is characterized by a renewed balance between inter-organic dynamics and positioning in a globalized, digital market. Accessibility and interoperability among communication platforms support technological democratization, fostering shared value and well-being.

Corporate governance, understood as the institutional framework regulating corporate decision-making, is in flux. Questions abound regarding the impact of new AI technologies on corporate structures, particularly governance itself. AI-driven disruptive innovation benefits corporate governance in various ways (Sickle et al., 2018). Companies utilize new technologies not just for production and distribution but also for management and control, enhancing market performance and decision-making processes internally.

Entrusting "machines" with corporate compliance could refocus administrators on business while mitigating conflicts of interest inherent in human decision-makers. Terms like "roboboard," "corp-tech," and "self-driving corporations" indicate an impending dehumanization of the corporate legal person (Abriani, 2020). The risk is that corporations dominating markets through digital interaction, enabled by big data analytics, may prevail (Mancuso Hobey, 2020).

This debate is ongoing, influenced by regulatory developments and behavioral changes among governance actors, aimed at sustainable value creation. Major market players, aware of the importance of innovation and change, are reviewing business models and internal organization, redefining strategic goals, strengthening culture and engagement, and balancing recruitment with retraining. A shift from platform governance to community-driven governance is evident. The largest economic players use AI technologies not only to facilitate economic exchanges but also to enable stakeholder participation in corporate assets. This practice, implemented through feedback (Scarchillo, 2019), involves a process where system action results impact the system itself, influencing future behavior.

The perspectives of "algo-governance"

Top management's needs and available tools to respond to strategic challenges are changing, along with internal organizational relationships, customer responses, and stakeholder engagement. The ongoing technological transformation creates a new balance of values. Debates on business purpose and social responsibility must consider the genetic mutation of the corporate organism and the ethical limits of AI use.

While humans may experience illness, cognitive and behavioral limitations, bias, and emotions, AI is resilient to such variables, especially in scenarios of systemic shocks. Currently, AI primarily supports directors, auditors, and investors in analyzing and controlling financial information (Montagnani & Passador, 2021). However, AI's contribution includes:

- Integration of investigative activities for more informed decisions
- Automated prediction supporting strategic direction and management choices
- Corporate reporting enhancement through efficient data analysis and report generation
- Compliance monitoring with real-time legislative updates

- Management of internal information flows, including data protection
- Board self-assessment
- Identification of the best candidates for co-option or nomination
- Management of shareholder dialogue and participation

AI applications in corporate governance are numerous, aiding but not replacing governing bodies, subject to human oversight. To continue "algo-governance" while respecting the human-centric vision, investment in AI culture, trust-building, accountability, and verifiability is essential. Automating company administration allows for managing complex situations and making optimal decisions for a variety of shareholders, protecting, and pursuing social interests.

Legally, recognizing AI in director roles relates to broader debates on granting legal subjectivity to AI tools. While direct appointment of AI to boards is challenging, indirect appointment through specialized companies is plausible. Legal entities can hold directorial positions, operating through natural representatives with AI expertise. Corporate governance rules on conflict of interest, related party transactions, and majority abuse may need adaptation to prevent distortions from algorithmic administration. Conversely, rules on corporate social responsibility and crisis prevention could be strengthened by appropriately structured algorithms.

Thus, the impact of new algorithmic technologies on corporate governance is multifaceted, requiring an assessment of which rules may be compromised and which may be enhanced by AI. Effective incorporation into technological frameworks is hindered by the often-vague content of regulatory criteria, challenging their translation into computer codes. Pursuing normative objectives via AI remains an open question, raising further issues such as the liability of AI administrators and the corporate structures using them.

Roles of Artificial Intelligence and Corporate Compliance

The COVID-19 pandemic has accelerated business digitization, with AI increasingly entering daily life. Since early 2023, we've seen an explosion of AI-based services, such as ChatGPT, Midjourney, Stable Diffusion, and DALL-E, prompting regulatory attention. AI technologies significantly change how enterprises approach information analytics and compliance. In the short term, AI systems assist in corporate monitoring, aiding administrative bodies in compliance and accountability processes by processing large amounts of data (Hilb, 2020).

AI technologies play a growing role in companies and boards of directors, influencing decision-making processes and outcomes. This is especially true for companies relying on platforms like Amazon, Google, Uber, YouTube, Netflix, and Facebook. AI helps achieve streamlined strategic decisions aligned with corporate goals and social responsibility. AI's role in corporate governance requires reinterpretation to become a concrete resource for directors in administration and control functions, considering AI's potential and risks.

AI can structure organizational, administrative, and accounting arrangements, constituting essential components within companies. In the medium to long term, with proper regulations (Mosco, 2019), we can envision "roboboards" entirely composed of AI entities. Advanced companies should consider enhancing IT and digital expertise in-house, potentially through specialized corp-tech committees. These committees would develop and monitor AI systems, protecting the governing body from potential liability when using AI tools in business.

A balanced approach to AI in corporate governance views it as a support for human directors, fostering interaction between intelligent machines and people. AI research distinguishes between Assisted, Augmented, and Autonomous AI based on their roles in decision-making:

- **Assisted AI** automates specific tasks, identifying patterns and applying solutions.
- **Augmented AI** supports human decision-making, approximating outcomes.
- **Autonomous AI** processes recommendations and makes decisions independently, acting as operational substitutes for human intelligence (Rao, 2016).

Blockchain, Social Responsibility Processes, and Disintermediation

Recent corporate practices show increasing algorithm use for director selection and decision-making support. Future scenarios may include algorithms as administrative body components, even in fully AI-driven roboboards (Moslein, 2017). Research by the World Economic Forum in 2015 predicted massive robotization of corporate governance by 2025. For example, deep knowledge ventures appointed an AI algorithm, Vital, as a board member to automate due diligence, although Vital remains an observer (Fenwick & Vermeulen, 2018).

Blockchain can facilitate corporate changes, increasing transparency and simplifying monitoring activities. It can streamline bookkeeping and decision-making processes, promoting decentralized governance where employees have a say in company strategy. AI can foster shareholder activism, help directors manage complex organizations, and provide unbiased assessments.

The legitimacy of AI as an administrator relates to recognizing AI tools' legal subjectivity (Teubner, 2019). The shift from traditional corporate governance to platform governance (Fenwick et al., 2018) highlights AI's role in decentralized, community-driven governance models. AI's involvement can improve board efficiency without compromising oversight quality or corporate transparency.

AI must be integrated into board processes, with supervision ensuring effective use. Human factors remain crucial in algorithmic design for administration, and management automation poses risks, particularly in conflict-of-interest situations. Transparency in AI-driven managerial operations is vital.

Pedagogical Research in Companies: Theoretical Frameworks and Inclusive Methodologies

The research project at the Telematic University "Giustino Fortunato" in Benevento applies the Flipped Inclusion model (Corona & De Giuseppe, 2017) combined with Cohen's cooperative method to corporate governance. Flipped Inclusion (De Giuseppe, 2018) follows computational thinking logic to foster systemic inclusiveness in lifelong learning. Computational thinking involves problem decomposition, pattern recognition, abstraction, and algorithmic design, enhancing problem-solving, data analysis, system design, and adaptability to technological challenges.

Promoting knowledge-building communities with technology partners enables authentic social-communicative interactions, fostering prosocial inclusive behaviors. The Flipped Inclusion model supports systemic inclusivity through:

- **Explore:** Identify challenges through inquiry learning (Kuhn et al., 2000).

- **Ideate:** Discover aspects for hypothesis generation (Bruner, 1960).
- **Planning:** Master tools and resources for goal achievement (Bloom, 1994).
- **Experiment:** Collect feedback to implement inclusivity models (Kolb, 2014).

Flipped Inclusion and Cohen's Complex Instruction (Cohen, 1994) aim to create inclusive corporate governance through cooperative learning. AI technologies in corporate governance, supported by these methodologies, foster an inclusive organizational culture.

The research questions include:
1. Can corporate governance foster a participatory environment with AI tools?
2. Can cooperative learning models (Complex Instruction and Flipped Inclusion) develop an inclusive corporate culture?

The hypothesis is that integrating these methods promotes an inclusive organizational climate, forming corporate governance marked by participatory styles and highly inclusive cultures.

CONCLUSIONS: INCLUSIVE EDUCATION IN DEMOCRATIZATION AND MULTI-PERFORMANCE INTEROPERABILITY FOR A WELL-BEING SOCIETY

AI's influence on corporate information and management is increasing, raising questions about information requirements and specific regulations. The digital revolution introduces unexplored content and reflections in corporate structures. The legitimacy of IT tools for administrative purposes must be scrutinized legally and ethically, with potential guidelines like those from the European Commission for the Efficiency of Justice (CEPEJ, 2018).

Computational thinking in education is essential for understanding innovative events, detecting critical elements, and enhancing individual and contextual specialties from a prosocial perspective. Teaching computational thinking fosters personal growth, social participation, and skills to navigate technological challenges. Training activities should integrate emotional-affective-motivational skills for socio-relational management and cognitive-metacognitive reworking of inclusive prosocial skills.

Corporate governance's approach to AI should initially be experimental, benefiting from corporate governance codes' flexibility. This allows progressive adaptation to technological support, fostering structural standardization. Human sensitivity will focus on high corporate strategy, addressing major issues and fundamental aspects of the enterprise. Highlighting interdependencies between digitization and corporate sustainability, digital technologies present risks and opportunities. Proper management and risk mitigation of digital tools are essential for sustainable success. Furthermore, corporate digital responsibility ensures good governance of algorithmic codes, balancing the technological and human dimensions of corporate purposes.

REFERENCES

Abriani, N. (2020). *Corporate governance in the age of the algorithm. Prolegomena to a study on the impact of artificial intelligence on corporate governance.* The New Corporate Law. Giappichelli.

Bloom, B. S. (1994). *Bloom's taxonomy: A forty-year retrospective.*

Bruner, J. (1960). *The process of education.* Harvard University Press. 10.4159/9780674028999

Buemi, M., Conte, M., & Guazzo, G. (2015). *Diversity management for inclusive growth: Strategies and tools.* Franco Angeli.

CEPEJ. (2018). *European ethical charter on the use of artificial intelligence in justice systems and related fields.* European Commission for the Efficiency of Justice.

Cohen, E. (1994). Restructuring the classroom: Conditions for productive small groups. *Review of Educational Research*, 64(1), 1–35. 10.3102/00346543064001001

Corona, F., & De Giuseppe, T. (2017). *Flipped methodology between systemic inclusion and didactic-assertive perspectives.* Pensa Multimedia.

De Giuseppe, T. (2016). *Special educational needs: Empowerment and divergent didactics to deconstruct their complexity.* Avellino: Il Papavero.

De Giuseppe, T. (2016). Well-being between prosocial vicariousness, subjective perceptions and situated values. In F. Corona & T. De Giuseppe (Eds.), *Prosociality, inclusive technologies, and universal design in specific learning disorders* (pp. 108-119). Avellino: Il Papavero.

De Giuseppe, T., & Corona, F. (2017). Flipped teaching for inclusion. In Limone, P., & Parmigiani, D. (Eds.), *Pedagogical models and teaching practices for initial and in-service teacher education* (pp. 409–420). Progedit.

Enriques, L., & Zetzsche, D. (2019). Corporate technologies and the tech nirvana fallacy. *European Corporate Governance Institute, Law Working Paper No. 457/2019.*

Fenwick, M., McCahery, J. A., & Vermeulen, P. M. (2018). The end of corporate governance (Hello "platform governance"). *European Business Organization Law Review*, 19(1), 57–77.

Fenwick, M., & Vermeulen, P. M. (2018). Technology and corporate governance: Blockchain, crypto, and artificial intelligence. *ECGI Law Working Paper*, No. 424/2018.

Hilb, M. (2020). Toward artificial governance? The role of artificial intelligence in shaping the future of corporate governance. *The Journal of Management and Governance*, 24(2), 265–286. 10.1007/s10997-020-09519-9

Kolb, D. A. (2014). *Experiential learning: Experience as the source of learning and development.* FT Press.

Kuhn, D., Cheney, R., & Weinstock, M. (2000). The development of epistemological understanding. *Cognitive Development*, 15(3), 309–328. 10.1016/S0885-2014(00)00030-7

Mancuso Hobey, E. (2020). Interview: Finch Capital Co-Founder/Partner Radboud Vlaar discusses disruptive and enabling financial technology post-COVID-19. *EKMH Innovators Interview Series*. https://ekmhinnovators.com/interview-finch-capital-co-founder-partner-radboud-vlaar-discusses-disruptive-and-enabling-financial-technology-post-covid-19/

Montagnani, M. L. (2020). Artificial intelligence and governance of the 'new' large shareholder firm: Potential and endoconsiliar issues. *Journal of Corporations*, 29(3), 234–251.

Montagnani, M. L., & Passador, M. L. (2021). The board of directors in the age of artificial intelligence: Between corporate reporting, composition, and accountability. *Journal of Corporations*, 30(2), 312–329.

Mosco, G. D. (2019). Roboboard. Artificial intelligence in boards of directors. *Legal Analysis of Economics*, 8(1), 45–67.

Moslein, P. (2017). Robots in the boardroom: Artificial intelligence and corporate law. *Columbia Business Law Review*, 3, 435–474.

Nicotra, M. (2023). *Artificial intelligence: What it is, how it works, and applications in Italy and Europe*. Agenda Digitale. https://www.agendadigitale.eu/sicurezza/privacy/intelligenza-artificiale-la-via-delleuropa-su-regole-e-investimenti/

Nuzzo, A., & Olivieri, G. (2019). Algorithms. If you know them, you regulate them. *Legal Analysis of Economics*, 9(2), 78–91.

Pellegrini, M. (2019). Technological innovation and economic law. *Quarterly Journal of Economic Law*, 31(1), 12–29.

Petrin, M. (2019). Corporate management in the age of AI. *UCL Working Paper Series Corporate Management in the Age of AI*, No. 3/2019.

Rao, A. (2016). *AI everywhere/nowhere*. Insurance Thought Leadership. https://www.insurancethoughtleadership.com/ai-everywherenowhere/

Rossi, G. (2012). The metamorphosis of the corporation. *Journal of Corporations*, 24(4), 67–89.

Sacco Ginevri, A. (2022). Artificial intelligence and corporate governance. *Journal of Business Law*, 33(2), 201–219.

Scarchillo, G. (2019). Corporate governance and artificial intelligence. *The New Annotated Civil Jurisprudence*, 9(3), 289–302.

Schneider, G. (2022). Artificial intelligence, corporate governance, and corporate social responsibility: Risks and opportunities. *The New Annotated Civil Jurisprudence*, 10(1), 112–130.

Solenne, V. (2020, April 28). *The impact of AI on corporate aspects of corporate governance*. PandesLegal. https://www.pandslegal.it/business/intelligenza-artificiale-e-corporate-governance/

Teubner, G. (2019). *Digital legal subjects? On the private status of autonomous software agents*. ESI.

Weill, P., Woerner, T., Stephanie, L., & Banner, J. (2019). Assessing the impact of digital savvy boards on company performance. *MIT Sloan CISR Working Paper, 433*. Cambridge: MIT Sloan.

Zoppini, A. (2021). *The firm as an organization and the system of controls. Metamorphosis of Company Law*. ESI.

Chapter 14
Sustainable Development Between Artificial Intelligence and Education:
The Inclusive Perspective of the Flipped Inclusion Model

Tonia De Giuseppe
https://orcid.org/0000-0002-3235-4482
Giustino Fortunato University, Italy

Silvia Tornusciolo
Università Mercatorum, Italy

Enza paola Catalano
University Pegaso, Italy

ABSTRACT

This chapter, starting from the United Nation's (UN) 2030 agenda, analyzes the current stage of implementing its objectives, focusing on the milestones. The UN Agenda 2030 aims to overcome inequalities, poverty, and disparities. This ambitious goal, especially considering the social transformations caused by the pandemic, requires new models of sustainable development. Sustainability and inclusion are key: how can artificial intelligence (AI) support sustainable development and create an inclusive society? AI's pervasiveness can become a risk without a society democratically oriented toward awareness of its centrality and the common good. The emergence of new inclusion models, such as flipped inclusion, can address this challenge and make the ambitious project of the UN Agenda 2030 a concrete reality.

DOI: 10.4018/979-8-3693-3003-6.ch014

INTRODUCTION: THE CULTURE OF SUSTAINABILITY CONNECTIVENESS FOR INCLUSIVE SOCIETIES

An ideal model of society is one that can adapt to various natural and human crises, face challenges and negative impacts arising from environmental, social, and economic changes, while simultaneously preserving natural resources and ensuring the well-being of people. This enables individuals to live full and creative lives, develop their potential, and organize meaningful lives that honor their equal human dignity (Nussbaum, 2011).

The culture of sustainability represents a form of social capital that indicates the degree of civic cohesion, institutional collaboration, and bonds of solidarity (Malavasi, 2017) within the planetary community. Defining sustainability as a pedagogical paradigm occurs in a historical period characterized by weakened relationships with others and the environment. Sustainability requires profound anthropological and ethical reflection that crosses social and economic sciences, not just a cultural adaptation to climate change data (Alessandrini, 2021). The theme of human development connected to the capabilities approach can be considered a substantive point for rethinking educational practices from a "generative" perspective, emphasizing new educational values centered on inclusivity and fighting inequalities, including gender (Alessandrini, 2021).

The term "new humanism" or "humanism of commitment" is used to describe a new model of development. Sustainable development is an inspiring social doctrine that respects humanity and serves as the roadmap for the future. The goal is to build a generation committed to a vision of knowledge networks towards progress and an inclusive, sustainable, and accessible future. This generation of commitment aligns with the United Nation's (UN) Agenda 2030, realizing a "development model" with 2050 as its horizon, overcoming inequalities, promoting work, green initiatives, digital cities, the knowledge society, the fight against poverty, gender equality, and sustainable prosperity (Malavasi, 2022).

The UN Agenda 2030, often referred to as the World Charter of Progressivism, introduces a new formula of "geo-reformism" that outlines a "New Human Agenda" (Harari, 2017). The concept of "pars pro toto" emphasizes that our connectivity is linked to a whole, reminding us that defending the common home is our collective responsibility. The survival of the human race depends on mutual responsibility towards ecological transition, which develops through continuous interaction between individuals and their environment, value orientations, and responsible actions (Iavarone, et al., 2017).

Transitioning to the role of AI in this context, Artificial Intelligence (AI), particularly generative intelligence, represents a significant cultural shift (Accoto, 2021) as it undertakes activities long considered exclusive to humans, necessitating cultural renewal. The social value of this transition emphasizes the qualitative relationships involved, expanding the concept of collaboration between educational contexts, and fostering positive interactions (Triani, 2018). A sustainable society aims for peace and prosperity for all, ensuring inclusivity that "leaves no one behind," integrating AI's pervasiveness with these principles..

In this context, pedagogical-didactic activity should encompass theoretical research and applied experimentation, focusing on creativity as the foundation of individual connectivity (Bauman, 2003). There is a growing need for an ecological perspective on development to ensure social inclusion, recognizing the uncertainties consumerist society has introduced. The interconnected systems of macro, meso, exo, and micro propaedeutics (Bronfenbrenner, 2002) determine the context's significance. The ability to connect and interact through generative networks, promoting a culture of proximity and encounter, is vital for fostering a humanism of life from an eco-systemic perspective, countering the planetary crisis, and prioritizing the relational dimension.

In relationships, based on care, support, listening, and interrelation (Mariani, 2021), essential networks of reciprocity are created, promoting significant human growth through shared experiences (Dewey, 2014). Pedagogy, the science of education and training, integrates theoretical and practical knowledge, fostering a new anthropological model that emphasizes safeguarding human dignity and caring for creation. This analysis underscores the importance of critical thinking and the need to redefine it: questioning the objective of efficiency and prioritizing human values. The functioning of educational platforms heavily depends on education for democracy, as highlighted by various studies.

The *culture of sustainability* today indicates the degree of civic cohesion, institutional collaboration, and bonds of solidarity within the planetary community (Malavasi, 2017). This effort occurs during a historical period marked by weakened relationships with others and the environment, leading to degraded forms of living, resource overconsumption, environmental degradation, and new forms of poverty. A pedagogical approach to sustainability supports the ability to ally for a just and inclusive environmental, economic, and social transition for future prosperity. The *sustainability paradigm* and the *capability approach* converge on community, especially regarding the meaning of "common" that binds people within specific territorial contexts. Agenda 2030 identifies community cohesion as crucial for enabling environments that realize rights and capabilities.

Exploring community education emphasizes its strong connection with education for democracy: viewing citizenship as belonging and participation highlights the need for democracy to find roots in territorial communities. A more specific analysis of AI and education literature recognizes the need to redefine educational research lines related to AI. Interdisciplinary fields must synchronize and mutually influence each other, finding space for discussion and joint negotiation of models, intentions, actions, practices, and effective and ethical results for participatory and concrete methods.

Pervasiveness of AI and Educational Awareness

The generation of commitment aims to defeat poverty and hunger, ensure healthy lives, promote well-being at all ages, ensure inclusive and equitable education, achieve gender equality, guarantee sustainable water and sanitation management, promote accessible and sustainable energy, inclusive economic growth, full and productive employment, decent work for all, build solid infrastructure, foster inclusive industrialization, reduce inequalities, create sustainable cities, ensure sustainable consumption and production, combat climate change, conserve marine resources, protect terrestrial ecosystems, manage forests sustainably, combat desertification, halt biodiversity loss, and strengthen global partnerships for sustainable development (Derinaldis, 2021).

These topics, long discussed in philosophical circles, have gained new attention due to AI's progress and societal impact. Managing AI platforms without a common good orientation can generate negative consequences (Benanti et al., 2021). Democratic education is crucial for proactive citizenship (Nuzzaci, 2021; Vorhaus, 2005), developing soft skills and self-determination in learning (Wood et al., 2004), and encouraging conscious political participation (Wehmeyer & Schalock, 2001).

The scientific community agrees on AI's pervasiveness and the need to define its reliability boundaries. The European Commission highlights fundamental requirements for reliable AI systems, including human supervision, technical robustness, data confidentiality, transparency, non-discrimination, fairness, social and environmental well-being, and responsibility (OECD, 2019). The Organization for Economic Co-operation and Development (OECD) has identified five principles to protect the interests of those involved:

1. AI should benefit people and the planet, promoting inclusive growth and well-being.
2. AI systems should respect the rule of law, human rights, democratic values, and diversity, with appropriate safeguards for a just society.
3. There should be transparency and responsible disclosure to ensure understanding of AI-based results.
4. AI systems should operate safely throughout their lifecycle, continuously assessing and managing risks.
5. Organizations and individuals developing AI systems should be accountable for their proper functioning.

Education must go beyond critical smartphone use, developing awareness of digital capitalism's influence on thought and behavior. The challenge for Media Education lies in the logic governing content circulation and behavior definition (Rivoltella, 2020). Data's growing importance transforms society, forming a "society of code" (Accoto, 2019). An ethic of care is needed to explore algorithmic decision-making systems in education (Prinsloo, 2017).

New Humanism emphasizes the importance of considering individuals within new technological contexts. The advent of AI necessitates the development of new skills and knowledge, reaffirming the centrality of training. Contemporary challenges require an interdisciplinary or transdisciplinary approach (Colicchi, 2021). Participation in the construction of knowledge entails a responsibility towards the common good, which is crucial for active citizenship and broader democratic involvement. The influence of new technologies on cultural and environmental transformations requires an educational perspective emphasizing connectivity across various contexts (Cerrocchi & Dozza, 2018).

Agenda 2030 Between Machine Learning and Artificial Intelligence

In September 2015, over 150 international leaders met at the UN to contribute to global development, promote human well-being, and protect the environment. The community of states approved the 2030 Agenda for Sustainable Development, encompassing 17 sustainable development goals (SDGs) and 169 sub-goals, aiming to end poverty, fight inequalities, tackle climate change, and build peaceful societies respecting human rights by 2030. The national sustainable development strategy addresses economic, environmental, and social inequalities for balanced and inclusive development. This approach uses fiscal policies and structural reforms, emphasizing the three dimensions of sustainable development: economic, social, and ecological.

The "Benessere Italia" control room coordinates and monitors policies for citizen well-being, promoting fair and sustainable well-being through new approaches and policies. Equitable sustainable regeneration, mobility, territorial cohesion, energy transition, quality of life, and the circular economy are key programmatic areas centered on human development and continuous training. Achieving the SDGs requires overcoming the paradigm of selfish individualism and fostering enabling educational contexts for civic engagement (Nussbaum, 2021). The objectives are clear, but reaching them requires a paradigm shift in economic, cultural, and social levels (Ceruti, 2018).

The concept of intelligent machines dates back to Alan Turing's hypothesis of a stored-program machine capable of improving its program (Turing, 1950). The Turing Test, which assesses machines' ability to simulate human intelligence, raised philosophical and ethical questions about intelligence and consciousness. John McCarthy later coined the term "Artificial Intelligence," marking the beginning of a new research field (McCarthy et al., 1955).

Machine learning (ML), or automatic learning, emerged in the mid-1950s with the idea of replicating biological neurons' behavior using mathematical models. ML allows machines to learn and improve over time, enhancing their capabilities and responses through experience. For machines to be intelligent, they must autonomously extend their knowledge and skills, performing tasks more effectively over time (Simon, 1984). ML reduces the need for human instruction, allowing machines to learn independently.

Artificial Intelligence and Democratic Models of Inclusivity: Big Data and Direct Applications of AI

Inclusion, derived from the Latin term "inclusiono-onis," signifies the act of incorporating an element within a group or set. Socially, it represents a state where all individuals experience fairness and equal opportunities in education, work, and economics, regardless of disadvantages. Inclusion enhances individuals' quality of life, fostering productive coexistence of differences (Gardou, 2012). However, AI's impact on intelligence and consciousness raises ethical and social concerns that need to be addressed.

New learning contexts, characterized by web-database interactions using AI, enable synergistic interactions with the semantic web, advancing from Web 1.0 to Web 4.0. This evolution facilitates collaboration through shared resources and skills, achieving common goals. Semantic intelligence interprets and processes data, enabling automatic reasoning and inferences (DE Giuseppe, 2016).

In the realms of education, corporate, and social sectors, virtual assistants show significant potential. For example, Caterina, the first humanoid virtual assistant in the Italian public administration, demonstrates advanced interaction levels using natural language processing. Similarly, the Decidim platform in Barcelona exemplifies AI's role in promoting transparency and inclusion in the political sphere, facilitating citizen engagement, and integrating community voices into decision-making (Severino, 2022).

Given these advancements, educational contexts must be rethought to address contemporary challenges more effectively and creatively. Concepts of collective intelligence, emphasizing individual knowledge and participation in knowledge construction, contrast with connective intelligence, which fosters relationships between individual intelligences (Cadei, 2021; De Kerckhove, 1998).

Moreover, investigating AI's direct applications for sustainable development reveals data's growing importance, forming a "society of code" (Accoto, 2017). Data actively guide researchers' intentions, emphasizing the need for a data-driven approach to sustainable development models (Accoto, 2019). AI-driven data analytics systems require comprehensive and up-to-date data, enabling predictive and machine learning algorithms. However, data availability alone is insufficient; accurate data are crucial for effective AI systems (Pedró et al., 2019).

Furthermore, household data and data from other ministries can provide insights into exogenous factors affecting learning, underscoring the importance of data integration. Technological advancements in data capture can be costly, particularly for low- and middle-income countries. Therefore, institutional capacity-building is essential for producing consistent, relevant, and timely data (Custer et al., 2018). Investments in institutional processes and capacity-building are crucial for effective data-dependent systems, including AI technology (Pedró et al., 2019).

CONCLUSION: AI AND QUALITY OF LIFE - THE INCLUSIVE MODELS FLIPPED INCLUSION

Sharing knowledge in educational contexts involves cooperative learning to enhance educational and training professions' imaginative and planning capacities. This approach aims to propose transformative experiences in lifelong and life-wide educational terms, highlighting the relationship between critical reflection and individual and social change processes (Striano, 2018).

The digitalized society's transformative processes necessitate integrating quantitative and qualitative educational research models. A new pedagogical paradigm requires intent and action awareness to educate in political and digital eco-sustainability (Benanti, 2021), encouraging lifelong learning models aligned with collective well-being (De Giuseppe, 2018). Empowerment processes, emphasizing proactive participation of context resources, aim to transform socio-educational fabrics into inclusive ones (Dovigo, 2007). Media education models can implement inclusive system learning (Alberici, 2002).

Integrating culture and digital tools can generate pro-social and economic value, breaking down stereotypes and promoting systemic inclusiveness cultures (Calveri & Sacco, 2021; Sibilio, 2023). AI impacts life models, highlighting the need for eco-pedagogical-participatory research to support co-generative digital welfare and quality of life (Fannizza, 2022).

The Flipped Inclusion model, promoting permanent qualitative well-being of life through a holistic approach, emphasizes educational paths for managing postmodern challenges. This model follows the EIPS phases: Explore, Ideate, Design, and Experiment (De Giuseppe, 2020). Flipped Inclusion aligns with sustainable development, following the EIPS macrophases:

1. Explore problems related to achieving Agenda 2030 goals.
2. Ideate solutions to overcome disparities and inequalities.
3. Design proactive citizen participation platforms using AI.
4. Experiment and collect feedback to identify and overcome critical issues.

Furthermore, a monitoring body is crucial for understanding tools' phenomenological impact, documenting problems, and evaluating interventions. The pandemic negatively impacted Agenda 2030 goals, particularly affecting women and youth in service, care, and precarious work sectors. Accelerated actions and policies are needed to achieve economic and social transformation for the SDGs (Alessandrini, 2021). Education for sustainability and democracy consolidation is essential to overcome inequalities. Investment in human and social capital, starting from pre-school, is crucial for understanding immaterial capitalism and Big Data's predictive capabilities (Cunha & Heckman, 2007; Mayer-Schönberger & Cukier, 2013; Putnam, 1993). Addressing functional illiteracy and fostering critical thinking are urgent educational needs (Morin, 2001; OECD, 2016). AI can contribute to sustainable development through responsible elites addressing human capital formation and biosphere preservation. New job creation and meaningful engagement in free time are necessary for sustainable prosperity (Keynes, 2009). The educational system must be reinvented to address anthropological metamorphosis and prevent regression (Caligiuri, 2018). Given AI's significant impact on education and democracy, responsible and ethical practices are essential to building an inclusive and sustainable society (Chomsky, 2005; Dewey, 2018). In this context, the Flipped Inclusion model offers a strategic revolution to manage socio-educational emergencies and promote sustainability values for the future (De Giuseppe, 2020).

REFERENCES

Accoto, C. (2017). *The given world. Five short lessons in digital philosophy.* Egea.

Accoto, C. (2019). *The ex machina world. Five short lessons on the philosophy of automation.* Egea.

Alberici, A. (2002). *Always learning in the knowledge society* (2nd ed.). Bruno Mondadori.

Alessandrini, G. (2021). *Civic and citizenship education in plural contexts Martha Nussbaum.*

Alessandrini, G. (2021). Education for sustainability as "civic engagement": From Agenda 2030 to Martha Nussbaum's lesson. *Pedagogy Today*, 19(2), 13–21.

Aragón, P., Kaltenbrunner, A., Calleja-López, A., Pereira, A., Monterde, A., Barandiaran, X. E., & Gómez, V. (2017). Deliberative platform design: The case study of online discussions in Decidim Barcelona, Social Informatics 9th International Conference, SocInfo, Oxford, UK, September 13-15, Proceedings, Part II. *Cornell University.*

Baker, T., & Smith, L. (2019). *Educ-AI-tion rebooted? Exploring the future of artificial intelligence in schools and colleges.* NESTA. https://www.nesta.org.uk/report/education-rebooted/

Baldacci, M. (2022). *Praxis and concept. The language of pedagogy.* FrancoAngeli.

Bauman, Z. (2003). *Liquid modernity.* Laterza.

Beetham, D., & Boyle, K. (1995). *Introducing democracy: 80 questions and answers.* Polity Press.

Beetham, D., & Boyle, K. (1995). *Introducing democracy: 80 questions and answers.* Politics Press.

Benanti, P., & Maffettone, S. (2021). Sustainability D. The consequences of the digital revolution in our lives. *The Mill.*

Benanti, P., & Maffettone, S. (2021). *Sustainability D. The consequences of the digital revolution in our lives.* The Mill.

Berkeley, G. (1998). *A treatise concerning the principles of human knowledge.* Oxford University Press Academic.

Booth, T., & Ainscow, M. (2008). *The Index for Inclusion.* Trent: Erickson.

Bronfenbrenner, U. (1986). *Ecology of human development.* Bologna: il Mulino. (Original work published 1979).

Bronfenbrenner, U. (2002). *Ecology of human development.* Bologna: il Mulino.

Buckingham, D. (2009). The future of media literacy in the digital age: Some challenges for policy and practice. *Medienimpulse, 47*(2). 10.21243/mi-02-09-13

Calveri, C., & Sacco, P. L. (2021). *The digital transformation of culture. Cultural Geographies.* Bibliographic Publisher.

Cambi, F. (2014). *The pedagogies of the twentieth century.* Edizioni Laterza.

Canevaro, A. (2009). *The long road to integration into society for a new independent life, in Scholastic and social integration.* Trent: Erickson.

Ceruti, M. (2018). *The time of complexity.*

Chinnici, G. (2016). *Turing. The enigma of a genius.* Hoepli.

Chomsky, N. (2005). *Big brother democracy.* Casale Monferrato: Piemme.

Corona, F., & De Giuseppe, T. (2016). Mutism between electivity and selectivity in an etiological process of inclusive recognition. *Italian Journal of Special Education for Inclusion*, 4(1).

Corona, F., & De Giuseppe, T. (2017). *Flipped inclusion, between theoretical framework and experimental augmented classroom teaching for inclusive teaching. Pedagogy More Didactics* (Vol. III). Erickson.

Cunha, F., & Heckman, J. J. (2007). The technology of skill training. *The American Economic Review*, 97(2), 31–47. 10.1257/aer.97.2.31

Custer, S. (2018). *Towards data-driven education systems: Insights into using information to measure results and manage change.* Brookings Center for Universal Education.

Dardot, P., & Laval, C. (2015). *Del comune, o della Rivoluzione nel XXI secolo.* DeriveApprodi.

Davies, L., Harber, C., & Schweisfurth, M. (2002). *Democracy through teacher education.* CIER/CfBT.

De Giuseppe, T. (2016). Selective mutism and flipped inclusion, between ecological-systemic perspectives and modeling inclusive reversals. *Italian Journal of Special Education for Inclusion*, 4(1).

De Giuseppe, T. (2020). *Flipped inclusion: Computational thinking and transformative phenomenologies in the society of knowledge.* Avellino: The Poppy.

De Giuseppe, T., Ciambrone, R., & Corona, F. (2018). The inclusive experimentation of systemic approaches in flipped teaching. *Training and Teaching, 16.*

De Giuseppe, T., & Corona, F. (2020). *Emerging and disruptive technological trends in education and the world of work.* IGI Global.

De Giuseppe, T., Ianniello, R., Podovšovnik, E., & Corona, F. (2020). The educational research flipped inclusion between social metamorphosis and technocratic hybridizations. In Podovšovnik, E. (Ed.), *Examining the roles of teachers and students in mastering new technologies.* IGI Global Publication. 10.4018/978-1-7998-2104-5.ch002

De Toni, A. F., Siagri, R., & Battistella, C. (2015). *Anticipate the future. Corporate foresight.* EGEA.

Del Serto, G. (2024). *Critical analysis of the impact of artificial intelligence on social and gender dynamics: Between inequalities and ethical challenges.*

Delello, J., & McWhorter, R. R. (2020). *Disruptive and emerging technology trends across education and the workplace.*

Derinaldis, A. (2021). *The humanism of commitment for a new development model: Paths of reformism.*

Dewey, J. (2014). *Experience and education.* Raffaello Cortina.

Dewey, J. (2018). *Democracy and education: An introduction to the philosophy of education* (Spadafora, G., Ed.). Anicia.

Di Tore, A. P. (2023). *Metawelt. Bodies, interactions, educations*. Studium. *Culture (Québec)*.

Di Tore, P. A. (2023). *Artificial intelligence and educational processes according to intelligence*.

Di Tore, S. (2017). *Using head-mounted display technology to support teaching through virtual learning environments in non-formal contexts. Giornale Italiano della Ricerca Educativa*. Think Multimedia.

Diamond, L. (1999). *Developing democracy: Toward consolidation*. The Johns Hopkins University Press. 10.56021/9780801860140

Donati, P. (2019). *Scoprire i beni relazionali. Per generare una nuova socialità*. Soveria Mannelli: Rubbettino.

Donati, P., & Socli, R. (2011). *I beni relazionali. Che cosa sono e quali effetti producono*. Bollati Boringhieri.

Dovigo, F. (2007). *Make differences*. Erickson.

Dovigo, F. (2008). *The Index for inclusion: A proposal for the inclusive development of schools*. Erickson.

Educause. (2019). Horizon report: 2019 higher education edition. *EDUCAUSE Horizon Report: 2019 Higher Education Edition*. EduCause. https://library.educause.edu/-/media/files/library/2019/4/2019horizonreport.pdf

Esposito, R. (2002). *Immunitas*. Einaudi.

Fannizza, F. (2022). *Artificial intelligence: Promises, current affairs, controversies*. Franco Angeli.

Feigenbaum, E., & Feldman, J. (1963). *Computers and thought*. McGraw-Hill.

Gardou, C. (2012). *Inclusive society, parlons-*. Érès.

Giovanazzi, T. (2021). *Educate for human development*. Expo Dubai 2020. Lecce: Think MultiMedia.

Giovanazzi, T. (2023). *Educating in connective contexts. Between knowledge sharing and ecological transition of human communities*.

Goffman, E. (2001). *Frame analysis. The organization of the experience*. Armando.

Harari, Y. N. (2017). *Homo Deus: Brief history of the future*. Bompiani. 10.17104/9783406704024

Haugeland, J. (1985). *Artificial intelligence: The very idea*. MIT Press.

Hinojo-Lucena, F. J., Aznar-Díaz, I., Cáceres-Reche, M. P., & Romero-Rodríguez, J. M. (2019). Artificial intelligence in higher education: A bibliometric study on its impact in the scientific literature. *Education Sciences*, 9(1), 51. 10.3390/educsci9010051

Hoskins, B. (2006). Draft framework on indicators for active citizenship. *CRELL*. https://legalinstruments.oecd.org/en/instruments/OECD-LEGAL-0449

Iavarone, M. L., Malavasi, P., Orefice, P., & Pinto Minerva, F. (Eds.). (2017). *Environmental pedagogy 2017: Between human development and social responsibility*. Think MultiMedia.

Johnson-Laird, P. (1988). *The computer and the mind: An introduction to cognitive science*. Harvard University Press.

Kaplan, J. (2016). *People are useless: Work and wealth in the age of artificial intelligence*. Luiss University.

Kennedy, G. E., Judd, T., Churchward, A., & Krause, K. (2008). First-year students' experiences with technology: Are they really digital natives? *Australasian Journal of Educational Technology*, 24(1), 108–122. 10.14742/ajet.1233

Keynes, J. M. (2009). *Financial possibilities for our grandchildren*. Milan: Adelphi.

Kolb, D. A. (2014). *Experiential learning: Experience as the source of learning and development*. FT Press.

Kurzweil, R. (1990). *The age of intelligent machines*. MIT Press.

Luckin, R., Holmes, W., Griffiths, M., & Forcier, L. B. (2016). *Intelligence unleashed: An argument for AI in education*. UCL. https://discovery.ucl.ac.uk/1475756/

Malavasi, P. (2017). Introduzione. In Iavarone, M. L., Malavasi, P., Orefici, P., & Pinto Minerva, F. (Eds.), *Pedagogia dell'ambiente 2017: Tra sviluppo umano e responsabilità sociale* (pp. 9–14). Pensa MultiMedia.

Malavasi, P. (2022). *PNRR and training. The path of ecological transition*. Life and Thought.

Manovich, L. (2001). *T.*

Marchesini, R. (2014). Hybridizations and evolutionary processes. In Barone, P., Ferrante, A., & Sartori, D. (Eds.), *Education and post-humanism: Pedagogical paths in the era of technology* (pp. 69–86). Raffaello Cortina.

Mariani, A. (2021). Introduction. The educational relationship between human sciences and advanced democratic society. In Mariani, A. (Ed.), *The educational relationship: Contemporary perspectives* (pp. 13–26). Carocci.

Maritain, J. (1963). *The person and the common good*. Morcelliana.

Mayer-Schönberger, V., & Cukier, K. N. (2013). *Big data: A revolution that will transform how we live, work, and think*. Garzanti.

McKeachie, W. J. (2002). *Teaching tips: Strategies, research, and theory for college and university teachers* (9th ed.). D.C. Heath and Co.

Morin, E. (2001). *I sette saperi necessari all'educazione del futuro*. Raffaello Cortina.

Morin, E. (2015). *Insegnare a vivere: Manifesto per cambiare l'educazione*. Raffaello Cortina.

Mounier, E. (1999). *Il personalismo*. AVE.

Mura, A. (2020). *Inclusione e collaborazione a scuola: un'occasione per insegnanti e famiglia*. Pensa MultiMedia., 10.7346/sipes-01-2020-19

Nichols, T. (2018). *La conoscenza e i suoi nemici: L'era dell'incompetenza e i rischi per la democrazia.* Luiss University.

Nussbaum, M. C. (2012). *Creare capacità. Liberarsi dalla dittatura del Pil.* Bologna: il Mulino.

Nuzzaci, A. (Ed.). (2011). *Patrimoni culturali, educazioni, territori: verso un'idea di multiliteracy.* Pensa MultiMedia Editore s.r.l.

Nuzzaci, A. (2021). *Educazione democratica.*

OECD. (2016). *Skills matter: Further results from the survey of adult skills.* OECD. https://www.oecd-ilibrary.org/education/skills-matter_9789264258051-en

OECD. (2019). *Recommendation of the Council on OECD Legal Instruments Artificial Intelligence.* OECD/LEGAL/0449. https://legalinstruments.oecd.org/en/instruments/OECD-LEGAL-0449

Orr, K. (1998). Data quality and systems. *Communications of the ACM*, 41(2), 66–71. 10.1145/269012.269023

Panciroli, C. (2018). *Educare nella città.* FrancoAngeli.

Panciroli, C., et al. (2020). Intelligenza artificiale e educazione: nuove prospettive di ricerca. *Form@re - Open Journal per la formazione in rete,* 20(3), 1-12.

Pedró, F., Subosa, M., Rivas, A., & Valverde, P. (2019). *Artificial intelligence in education: Challenges and opportunities for sustainable development.* Unesco.

Prinsloo, P. (2017). Fleeing from Frankenstein's monster and meeting Kafka on the way: Algorithmic decision-making in higher education. *E-Learning and Digital Media*, 14(3), 138–163. 10.1177/2042753017731355

Putnam, R. D. (1993). *La tradizione civica nelle regioni italiane.* Mondadori.

Rivoltella, P. C. (2020). La didattica al tempo della mediatizzazione: Tra retrotopia e innovazione. 3° Convegno EDUIA, Università Roma Tre, 6 novembre 2020.

Russell, S., & Norvig, P. (1998). *Intelligenza artificiale: un approccio moderno.* UTET.

Searle, J. (1984). Menti, cervelli e programmi. *Behavioral and Brain Sciences.*

Severino, P. (2022). *Artificial intelligence: Politics, economics, law, technology.* Luiss University Press.

Sibilio, M. (2014). *La didattica semplessa.* Liguori.

Sibilio, M. (2023). *La semplessità: Proprietà e principi per agire il cambiamento.* Morcelliana.

Simon, H. (1981). *The science of artificial.* MIT Press.

Tognazzi, B. (2022). *Educazione, ambienti e apprendimento nella cultura della complessità.*

Turing, A. M. (1950). Computing machinery and intelligence. *Mind*, LIX(236), 433–460. 10.1093/mind/LIX.236.433

UNESCO (1978). *Towards a methodology for projecting rates of literacy and educational attainment.* (Current Surveys and Research in Statistics, No. 28). UNESCO.

UNESCO. (1979). *Records of the General Conference Twentieth Session (Vol. 1 - Paris, 24 October to 28 November 1978).* United Nations.

Vischi, A. (2021). Introduzione: Impatto, educazione, ecologia integrale. In Vischi, A. (Ed.), *Impatto sul territorio: Lavoro, giovani, ecologia integrale* (pp. 19–27). Pensa MultiMedia.

Vorhaus, J. (2005). Citizenship, competence and profound disability. *Journal of Philosophy of Education*, 39(3), 461–475. 10.1111/j.1467-9752.2005.00448.x

Vygotskij, L. S. (1990). *Storia dello sviluppo delle funzioni psichiche superiori. E altri scritti.* Florence: Giunti-Barbèra. (Original work published 1930-31).

Wehmeyer, M. L., & Schalock, R. (2001). Self-determination and quality of life: Implications for special education services and supports. *Focus on Exceptional Children*, 33(8), 1–16.

Winograd, T., & Flores, F. (1987). *Calcolatori e conoscenza.* Mondadori.

Wood, W. M., Karvonen, M., Test, D. W., Browder, D., & Algozzine, B. (2004). Promoting student self-determination skills in IEP planning. *Teaching Exceptional Children*, 36(3), 8–16. 10.1177/004005990403600301

Zawacki-Richter, O., Marín, V. I., Bond, M., & Gouverneur, F. (2019). Systematic review of research on artificial intelligence applications in higher education – Where are the educators? *International Journal of Educational Technology in Higher Education*, 16(1), 39. 10.1186/s41239-019-0171-0

Compilation of References

Abbas, N. N., Ahmad, R., Qazi, S., & Ahmed, W. (2023). Impact of Deepfake Technology on FinTech Applications. In *Handbook of Research on Cybersecurity Issues and Challenges for Business and FinTech Applications* (pp. 225–242). IGI Global.

Abernathy, W. J., & Utterback, J. M. (1978). Patterns of industrial innovation. *Technology Review*, 80(7), 40–47.

Abriani, N. (2020). *Corporate governance in the age of the algorithm. Prolegomena to a study on the impact of artificial intelligence on corporate governance*. The New Corporate Law. Giappichelli.

Abulibdeh, A., Zaidan, E., & Abulibdeh, R. (2024). Navigating the confluence of artificial intelligence and education for sustainable development in the era of industry 4.0: Challenges, opportunities, and ethical dimensions. *Journal of Cleaner Production*, 437(140527), 1–15. 10.1016/j.jclepro.2023.140527

Accoto, C. (2017). *The given world. Five short lessons in digital philosophy*. Egea.

Accoto, C. (2019). *The ex machina world. Five short lessons on the philosophy of automation*. Egea.

ACLU. (2023, June 7). *The fight to stop face recognition technology*. American Civil Liberties. https://www.aclu.org/news/topic/stopping-face-recognition-surveillance

Adams, D. (2019). *Guida galattica per gli autostoppisti. Il ciclo completo*. Edizioni Mondadori.

Adams, E. (2014). *Fundamentals of game design*. New Riders.

Agrawal, S. (2021). A short survey on the role of technology in transforming education. *International Journal of Educational Technology in Higher Education*, 18(1), 3. 10.1186/S41239-020-00242-0

Ahmed, F., Qin, Y. J., & Martínez, L. (2019). Sustainable change management through employee readiness: Decision support system adoption in technology-intensive British e-businesses. *Sustainability (Basel)*, 11(11), 2998. 10.3390/su11112998

Aiello, P., & Sharma, U. (2018). Improving intentions to teach in inclusive classrooms: The impact of teacher education courses on future learning support teachers. *Form@ re-Open Journal per la Formazione in Rete*, 18(1), 207-219.

Aiello, P. (2017). *Insegnare a leggere la mente: progettazione di un edugame per lo sviluppo di abilità sociali in studenti con Disturbi dello Spettro Autistico*. Giornale Italiano della Ricerca Educativa (Multimedia, P., Ed.).

Aiello, P., Corona, F., & Sibilio, M. (2014). Ipotesi di evoluzione funzionale dell'insegnante di sostegno in Italia. *Italian Journal of Special Education for Inclusion*, 2(2), 21–34.

Aiello, P., Di Tore, S., Di Tore, P. A., & Sibilio, M. (2013). Didactics and simplicity: Umwelt as a perceptive interface. *Education Sciences & Society*, 1, 27–35.

Akçayır, M., & Akçayır, G. (2016). Advantages and challenges associated with augmented reality for education: A systematic review of the literature. *Educational Research Review*, 20, 1–11. 10.1016/j.edurev.2016.11.002

Aksoy, L., King, C., & Chun, H. H. (2019). Evolving service thinking: Disruption and opportunity in hospitality and tourism. *Journal of Service Management*, 30(4), 449–451. 10.1108/JOSM-07-2019-413

Alberici, A. (2002). *Always learning in the knowledge society* (2nd ed.). Bruno Mondadori.

Alberti, R. E., & Emmons, M. C. (2003). *Essere assertivi. Come imparare a farsi rispettare senza prevaricare gli altri*. Il Sole 24 Ore.

Alessandrini, G. (2021). *Civic and citizenship education in plural contexts Martha Nussbaum*.

Alessandrini, G. (2021). Education for sustainability as "civic engagement": From Agenda 2030 to Martha Nussbaum's lesson. *Pedagogy Today*, 19(2), 13–21.

Aleven, V., Stahl, E., Schworm, S., Fischer, F., & Wallace, R. (2003). Help Seeking and Help Design in Interactive Learning Environments. *Review of Educational Research*, 73(3), 277–320. 10.3102/00346543073003277

Alexandre, L. (2018). *La guerra delle intelligenze. Intelligenza artificiale contro l'intelligenza umana*. EDT.

Aljohani, N. F., Daud, A., Abbasi, R. A., Alowibdi, J. S., Basheri, M., & Aslam, M. A. (2019). An integrated framework for course adapted student learning analytics dashboard. *Computers in Human Behavior*, 92, 679–690. 10.1016/j.chb.2018.03.035

Allport, G. W. (1962). *The general and unique in psychological science*. Harvard University.

Alpe, Y., & Fauguet, J. L. (2008). Enseigner dans le rural: un «métier» à part?. *Travail et formation en éducation*, 2.

Al-Riyami, F. (2014). *A history of the Microsoft Flight Simulator franchise: the origins, the end, and a new beginning*. ONMSFT. https://www.onmsft.com/news/history-microsoft-flight-simulator-franchise-origins-end-and-new-beginning

Altbach, P. G., Reisberg, L., & Rumbley, L. E. (2010). Introduction: Twenty-first-century global directions. *Trends in Global Higher Education*, 1-21.

AlZahrani, N. A., Hussain, R. F., & Alabdulkarim, S. (2018). A Blockchain-based Architecture for Securing Student Records and Data Privacy. In *Proceedings of the 2018 International Conference on Computational Science and Computational Intelligence (CSCI 2018)* (pp. 626-631). Reseearch Gate.

Alzahrani, S., & Alhomyani, M. (2023). The Effectiveness of Explicit Vocabulary Instruction on Productive Vocabulary Learning in Writing Among Intermediate School Learners in Saudi Arabia. *Sino-US English Teaching*, 20(8), 289–310. 10.17265/1539-8072/2023.08.001

Amadeo, R. (2024, April 18). *Boston dynamics' new humanoid moves like no robot you've ever seen*. Ars Technica. https://arstechnica.com/gadgets/2024/04/boston-dynamics-debuts-humanoid-robot-destined-for-commercialization/?comments=1

Amato, M. (2013). *La costruzione del Sé, il luogo educativo tra scuola "in presenza" e "a distanza"*. Lamezia Terme.

Amazon Web Services. (2024). *What is facial recognition? - facial recognition technology explained - AWS*. Amazon Web Services Machine Learning and AI. https://aws.amazon.com/what-is/facial-recognition/ \

Amazon. (2023, September 21). *Introducing a new era for the Alexa smart home*. US About Amazon. https://www.aboutamazon.com/news/devices/amazon-smart-home-announcements-2023

Amazon. (n.d.) *What is natural language understanding? - Alexa skills kit official site*. Amazon Alexa. https://developer.amazon.com/en-US/alexa/alexa-skills-kit/nlu

Amendola, A., Guerra, A., & Masullo, M. (2022). La Generazione Z e la (nuova) costruzione dell'identità in epoca pandemica e post pandemica. *La Generazione Z e la (nuova) Costruzione dell'Identità in Epoca Pandemica e Post Pandemica*, 141-167.

Amendola, A. (2023). Il METAVERSO TRA CINEMA E GAME. *Journal of Inclusive Methodology and Technology in Learning and Teaching*, 3(2).

American Psychiatric Association. (2000). *Diagnostic and statistical manual of mental disorders* (4th ed.). American Psychiatric Publishing.

Amos, S. K. (2019). Digitization, disruption, and the "society of singularities": The transformative power of the global education industry. *Digital Transformation and Innovation in Chinese Education*, 87(1), 198–210. 10.1007/978-3-030-04236-3_11

Anchisi, R., & Gambotto Dessy, M. (1995). *Non solo comunicare. Teoria e pratica del comportamento assertivo*. Libreria Cortina.

Anderson, L. W., & Krathwohl, D. R. (2001). *A taxonomy for learning, teaching, and assessing: A revision of Bloom's taxonomy of educational objectives: Complete edition*. Addison Wesley Longman, Inc. https://fintechsociety.comp.nus.edu/lyfh30syqkpx/20-prof-aaron-hoppe-2/a-9780801319037-a-taxonomy-for-learning-teaching-and-assessing-a.pdf

Anderson, L. W., & Krathwohl, D. R. (2021). *A taxonomy for learning, teaching, and assessing: A revision of Bloom's taxonomy of educational objectives*. Longman. http://dspace.vnbrims.org:13000/xmlui/handle/123456789/4570

Anderson, L. W., & Krathwohl, D. R. (2001). *A taxonomy for learning, teaching, and assessing: A revision of Bloom's taxonomy of educational objectives: Complete edition*. Addison Wesley Longman, Inc.

Anderson, T. (2008). *The theory and practice of online learning*. AU Press. 10.15215/aupress/9781897425084.01

Angst, C. M., Agarwal, R., Sambamurthy, V., & Kelley, K. (2010). Social Contagion and Information Technology Diffusion: The Adoption of Electronic Medical Records in US Hospitals. *Management Science*, 56(8), 1219–1241. 10.1287/mnsc.1100.1183

Anthropic. (2024). *Introducing Claude 3*. Anthropic. https://www.anthropic.com/news/claude-3-family

Antinucci, F. (2007). *Musei virtuali: come non fare innovazione tecnologica*. Musei virtuali.

Antoniou, P. E., Konstantinidis, S. Th., & Bamidis, P. D. (2021). Panel Session-Co-creative Virtual Reality Content Development in Healthcare: Tackling the content availability problem. *2021 7th International Conference on Immersive Learning Research Network (iLRN)*, (pp. 1–3). IEEE. 10.23919/iLRN52045.2021.9459401

Applefield, J. M., Huber, R., & Moallem, M. (2000). Constructivism in theory and practice: Toward a better understanding. *High School Journal*, 84(2), 35–53.

Aragón, P., Kaltenbrunner, A., Calleja-López, A., Pereira, A., Monterde, A., Barandiaran, X. E., & Gómez, V. (2017). Deliberative platform design: The case study of online discussions in Decidim Barcelona, Social Informatics 9th International Conference, SocInfo, Oxford, UK, September 13-15, Proceedings, Part II. *Cornell University*.

Aragona, M. (2006). *Aspettando la rivoluzione. Oltre il DSM-V: le nuove idee sulla diagnosi tra filosofia della scienza e psicopatologia*. University Press, Editori Riuniti.

Arghire, I. (2024, March 13). Just a moment... Just a moment... *Security Week*. https://www.securityweek.com/stanford-university-data-breach-impacts-27000-individuals/

Arif, T. B., Munaf, U., & Ul-Haque, I. (2023). The future of medical education and research: Is ChatGPT a blessing or blight in disguise? *Medical Education Online*, 28(1), 1052. 10.1080/10872981.2023.218105236809073

Arntz, A. (2005). Pathological dependency: Distinguishing functional from emotional dependency. *Clinical Psychology : a Publication of the Division of Clinical Psychology of the American Psychological Association, 12*(4), 411–416. 10.1093/clipsy.bpi051

Arsenault, B. (2023, March 1). Your biggest cybersecurity risks could be inside your organization. *Harvard Business Review*. https://hbr.org/2023/03/your-biggest-cybersecurity-risks-could-be-inside-your-organization

Arts Education Data Project. (2022). *Millions of U.S. students denied access to music education, according to first-ever national study conducted by Arts Education Data Project*. Cision PRWeb. https://www.prweb.com/releases/millions-of-u-s-students-denied-access-to-music-education-according-to-first-ever-national-study-conducted-by-arts-education-data-project-876709378.html

Asbury, K., & Plomin, R. (2015). *G come geni. L'impatto della genetica sull'apprendimento*. Raffaello Cortina Editore.

Asimily. (2024, March 1). *4 cyberattacks that shook universities and colleges*. Asimily. https://asimily.com/blog/4-cyberattacks-universities-and-colleges/

Astutik, I., Jonathans, P. M., Ratri, D. P., & Devanti, Y. M. (2023). Understanding neuroscience, how the brain works, and the implication on grammar teaching and learning. *ELLITE: Journal of English Language, Literature, and Teaching, 8*(1), 61–73.

Atenas, J., Havemann, L., Neumann, J., & Stefanelli, C. (2020). *Open education policies: Guidelines for co-creation*.

Atkins, M. J. (1993). Theories of learning and multimedia applications: An overview. *Research Papers in Education, 8*(2), 251–271. 10.1080/0267152930080207

Augusti, F., & Bonavolontà, G. (2021). *Intelligenza Artificiale e Educazione: le percezioni degli studenti del Dipartimento di Scienze dell'Educazione dell'Università Roma Tre sul concetto di Intelligenza Artificiale*. QTimes – webmagazine.

Austerschmidt, K. L., & Bebermeier, S. (2019). Implementation and effects of flexible support services on student achievements in statistics. *Zeitschrift für Hochschulentwicklung, 14*(3), 137–155. 10.3217/zfhe-14-03/09

Ausubel, D. P. (2004). *Educazione e processi cognitivi*. Franco Angeli.

Avni, S. (2017). Considering disruptive and transformative Jewish education. *Journal of Jewish Education, 83*(4), 342–357. 10.1080/15244113.2017.1346949

Azano, A. P., Downey, J., & Brenner, D. (2019). Preparing pre-service teachers for rural schools. In *Oxford Research Encyclopedia of Education*. Oxford Press. 10.1093/acrefore/9780190264093.013.274

Azano, A. P., & Stewart, T. T. (2016). Confronting challenges at the intersection of rurality, place, and teacher preparation: Improving efforts in teacher education to staff rural schools. *Global Education Review, 3*(1), 108–128.

Baker, T., & Smith, L. (2019). *Educ-AI-tion rebooted? Exploring the future of artificial intelligence in schools and colleges*. NESTA. https://www.nesta.org.uk/report/education-rebooted/

Baker, R. S., Clarke-Midura, J., & Ocumpaugh, J. (2016). Towards general models of effective science inquiry in virtual performance assessments. *Journal of Computer Assisted Learning, 32*(3), 267–280. 10.1111/jcal.12128

Baker, R., & Siemens, G. (2014). Educational data mining and learning analytics. In Sawyer, R. K. (Ed.), *The Cambridge handbook of the learning sciences* (2nd ed., pp. 253–272). Cambridge University Press. 10.1017/CBO9781139519526.016

Baldacci, M. (2022). *Praxis and concept. The language of pedagogy*. FrancoAngeli.

Baldwin, R. (2019). *The globotics upheaval: Globalization, robotics, and the future of work*. Oxford University Press.

Banday, M. T., Lone, S. A., Ahmad, A., & Malik, H. (2021). Blockchain in Education: A Review of the State-of-the-Art and Research Challenges. In *Proceedings of the International Conference on Machine Learning, Big Data, Cloud and Parallel Computing (COMITCon)* (pp. 52-61). Research Gate.

Bandura, A., & Walters, R. H. (1977). *Social learning theory* (Vol. 1). Prentice Hall.

Banerjee, M., Chiew, D., Patel, K. T., Johns, I., Chappell, D., Linton, N., Cole, G. D., Francis, D. P., Szram, J., Ross, J., & Zaman, S. (2021). The impact of artificial intelligence on clinical education: Perceptions of postgraduate trainee doctors in London (UK) and recommendations for trainers. *BMC Medical Education*, 21(1), 1–10. 10.1186/s12909-021-02870-x34391424

Baoill, A. Ó. (2008). Jenkins, H.(2006). Convergence Culture: Where Old and New Media Collide. New York: New York University Press. *Social Science Computer Review*, 26(2), 252–254. 10.1177/0894439307306088

Barab, S., Thomas, M., Dodge, T., Carteaux, R., & Tuzun, H. (2005). Making learning fun: Quest Atlantis, a game without guns. *Educational Technology Research and Development*, 53(1), 86–107. 10.1007/BF02504859

Barbi, A. (2014). Ambiente virtuale per un apprendimento reale. *EL.LE*, 3(1).

Barbot, B., & Webster, P. R. (2018). Creative thinking in music. In T. Lubart (Ed.), *The Creative Process* (Palgrave Studies in Creativity and Culture). Palgrave Macmillan. 10.1057/978-1-137-50563-7_10

Baricco, A. (2019). *The game*. Bezige Bij bv, Uitgeverij De.

Baricco, A. (2010). *I barbari*. Feltrinelli Editore.

Barley, Z. A., & Brigham, N. (2008). Preparing teachers to teach in rural schools. *Issues & Answers Report, REL 2008*. https://ies.ed.gov/ncee/edlabs/regions/central/pdf/REL_2008055_sum.pdf

Barney, J., & Hesterly, W. (2012). *Strategic management and competitive advantage: Concepts and Cases* (4th ed.). Pearson.

Barocas, S., & Selbst, A. D. (2016). Big data's disparate impact. *California Law Review*, 104(3), 671–732. 10.15779/Z38BG31

Bartolini, R., Mangione, G. R. J., De Santis, F., & Tancredi, A. (2021). Piccole scuole e territorio: un'indagine sulla relazione scuola-comune per un progetto formativo allargato. *Scienze del Territorio*, 9, 155-167. https://doi.org/10.13128/sdt-12319

Basti, G. (n.d.). La sfida etica dell'intelligenza artificiale e il ruolo della filosofia. In V. C. Müller (Ed.), *Ethics of artificial intelligence and robotics*. In E. N. Zalta (Ed.), *Stanford Encyclopedia of Philosophy*. Stanford Press. https://plato.stanford.edu/archives/sum2021/entries/ethics-ai/

Bateson, G. (2000). *Steps to an ecology of mind: Collected essays in anthropology, psychiatry, evolution, and epistemology*. University of Chicago Press. 10.7208/chicago/9780226924601.001.0001

Batini, F., & Fontana, A. (2003). *Comunità di apprendimento. Un nuovo modo di imparare*. Editore Zona.

Bauman, Z. (2003). *Liquid modernity*. Laterza.

Bauman, Z. (2014). *La vita tra reale e virtuale. Meet the media guru*. Egea.

Beattie, S., Woodley, C., & Souter, K. (2014). Creepy analytics and learner data rights. In B. Hegarty, J. McDonald, & S.-K. Loke (Eds.), *Rhetoric and reality: Critical perspectives on educational technology*. Proceedings ascilite Dunedin 2014 (pp. 421-425).

Beetham, D., & Boyle, K. (1995). *Introducing democracy: 80 questions and answers*. Polity Press.

Belbase, S. (2014). Radical versus social constructivism: An epistemological pedagogical dilemma. *International Journal of Contemporary Educational Research*, 1(2), 98–112.

Belda-Medina, J., & Kokošková, V. (2023). Integrating chatbots in education: Insights from the chatbot-human interaction satisfaction model (CHISM). *International Journal of Educational Technology in Higher Education*, 20(1), 62. 10.1186/s41239-023-00432-3

Bell, F. (2010). Connectivism: Its place in theory-informed research and innovation in technology-enabled learning. *International Review of Research in Open and Distance Learning*, 12(3), 98–118. 10.19173/irrodl.v12i3.902

Bell, S. (1999). Finding out rapidly: A soft systems approach to training needs analysis in Thailand. *Development in Practice*, 9(1–2), 18–32. 10.1080/09614529953188

Belpaeme, T., Kennedy, J., Ramachandran, A., Scassellati, B., & Tanaka, F. (2018). Social robots for education: A review. *Science Robotics*, 3(21), 1–9. https://www.science.org/doi/10.1126/scirobotics.aat5954. 10.1126/scirobotics.aat595433141719

Benanti, P., & Maffettone, S. (2021). Sustainability D. The consequences of the digital revolution in our lives. *The Mill*.

Benanti, P., & Maffettone, S. (2021). *Sustainability D. The consequences of the digital revolution in our lives*. The Mill.

Benigno, V., Fante, C., & Caruso, G. (2021). Approcci, azioni e tecnologie a supporto della classe ibrida inclusiva. *Italian Journal of Educational Technology*, 29(1), 5–25. 10.17471/2499-4324/1182

Benjamin, R. (2019). Assessing risk, automating racism. *Science*, 366(6464), 421–422. 10.1126/science.aaz387331649182

Benkler, Y. (2008). *The wealth of networks: How social production transforms markets and freedom*. Yale University Press.

Bennett, B., Brunker, D., & Hodges, R. (2004). Innovation, economic growth and vocational education and training. Vocational Education and Training. Research Readings, Australian National Training Authority, 68-83.

Bennett, E., & McWhorter, R. R. (2014). Virtual Human Resource Development. In Chalofsky, N., Rocco, T., & Morris, L. (Eds.), *The handbook of human resource development: The discipline and the profession* (pp. 567–589). Wiley. 10.1002/9781118839881.ch33

Berg, K., & Kozlowski, K. (2023, October 23). Hackers gained access to personal info on up to 230,000 individuals, UM says. detroitnews.com. https://www.detroitnews.com/story/news/local/michigan/2023/10/23/um-3rd-party-accessed-school-systems-personal-information-for-5-days/71292044007/

Bergamin, P., Ziska, S., & Groner, R. (2010). Structural equation modeling of factors affecting success in student's performance in ODL-programs: Extending quality management concepts. *Open Praxis*, 4(1), 18–25.

Berkeley, G. (1998). *A treatise concerning the principles of human knowledge*. Oxford University Press Academic.

Berryman, S. E. (1993). Learning for the workplace. In Darling-Hammond, L. (Ed.), *Review of research in education* (pp. 343–401). American Educational Research Association.

Bertalanffy, L. V. (1968). *General system theory: Foundations, development, applications*. G. Braziller.

Beuk, F. (2016). Sales Simulation Games: Student and Instructor Perceptions. *Journal of Marketing Education*, 38(3), 170–182. 10.1177/0273475315604686

Bhosale, T., Kadam, V., & Jagtap, S. (2020). A Study on Relevance of Digitalization in the Banking Sector. *Advance and Innovative Research*, 7(1), 192–198.

Bhuiyan, J. (2023). Rite aid facial recognition misidentified Black, Latino and Asian people as 'likely' shoplifters. *The Guardian*. https://www.theguardian.com/technology/2023/dec/20/rite-aid-shoplifting-facial-recognition-ftc-settlement

Bilika, D., Michopoulou, N., Alepis, E., & Patsakis, C. (2023). Hello me, meet the real me: Audio deepfake attacks on voice assistants. *arXiv preprint arXiv:2302.10328*.

Biryukov, A. P., Brikoshina, I. S., Mikhalevich, N. V., Sycheva, S. M., & Khalimon, E. A. (2021). Gamification in education: Threats or new opportunities. *SHS Web of Conferences, 103*, 02001. https://doi.org/10.1051/shsconf/202110302001

Bittanti, M. (Ed.). (2008). *Schermi interattivi: il cinema nei videogiochi* (Vol. 73). Meltemi Editore Srl.

Bitter, A. (2024) Facial recognition tech is widespread now, but still might not recognize you. *Business Insider*. https://www.businessinsider.com/why-facial-recognition-technology-might-not-recognize-you-2024-3#:~:text=Facial%20recognition%20frequently%20misidentifies%20people,in%20just%201%25%20of%20cases

Bloom, B. S. (1994). *Bloom's taxonomy: A forty-year retrospective*.

Bloom, B. S. (Ed.). (1956). *Taxonomy of educational objectives: The classification of educational goals. Handbook I: Cognitive domain*. David McKay Company.

Blose, A. (2023, April 12). *As ChatGPT enters the classroom, teachers weigh pros and cons*. NEA Today. https://www.nea.org/nea-today/all-news-articles/chatgpt-enters-classroom-teachers-weigh-pros-and-cons

Bohnert, A. E., Hughes, J. L., & Pulice-Farrow, L. (2013). Motives that predict liking and the usage of Facebook. *Undergraduate Research Journal for the Human Sciences, 12*(1).

Bolter, J. D. (2007). Remediation and the language of new media. *Northern Lights: Film & Media Studies Yearbook, 5*(1), 25–37. 10.1386/nl.5.1.25_1

Bond, M. (2020). Facilitating student engagement through the flipped learning approach in K-12: A systematic review. *Computers & Education, 151*, 103819. 10.1016/j.compedu.2020.103819

Booth, T., & Ainscow, M. (2008). *The Index for Inclusion*. Trent: Erickson.

Borel, É. (1913). La mécanique statique et l'irréversibilité. *J. Phys. Theor. Appl., 3*(1), 189–196. 10.1051/jphystap:019130030018900

Bornstein, S. (2018). Antidiscriminatory algorithms. *Alabama Law Review, 70*, 519.

Bose, R., & Luo, X. (2011). Integrative framework for assessing firms' potential to undertake Green IT initiatives via virtualization - A theoretical perspective. *The Journal of Strategic Information Systems, 20*(1), 38–54. 10.1016/j.jsis.2011.01.003

Bosker, B. (2013, Jan. 22). SIRI RISING: The inside story of Siri's origins—and why she could overshadow the iPhone. *HUFFPOST*. https://www.huffpost.com/entry/siri-do-engine-apple-iphone_n_2499165

Bourla, A., Ferreri, F., Ogorzelec, L., Peretti, C. S., Guinchard, C., & Mouchabac, S. (2018). Psychiatrists' attitudes toward disruptive new technologies: Mixed-methods study. *JMIR Mental Health, 5*(4), e10240. 10.2196/1024030552086

Bowen, J., & Morosan, C. (2018). Beware hospitality industry: The robots are coming. *Worldwide Hospitality and Tourism Themes, 10*(6), 726–733. 10.1108/WHATT-07-2018-0045

Bower, J. L., & Christensen, C. M. (1995). Disruptive technologies: Catching the wave. *Harvard Business Review*.

Boyle, T. (2002). Towards a theoretical base for educational multimedia design. *Journal of Interactive Media in Education, 2002*(3). 10.5334/2002-2

Boyle, T., Cook, J., Windle, R., Wharrad, H., Leeder, D., & Alton, R. (2007). *Agile methods for developing learning objects.*

Braat, M., Engelen, J., van Gemert, T., & Verhaegh, S. (2020). The rise and fall of behaviorism: The narrative and the numbers. *History of Psychology*, 23(3), 252–280. 10.1037/hop000014632191061

Bramati, A. (2022, July 4). *Il ruolo dei sensi nell'apprendimento e nello sviluppo linguistico.* Dire Fare Insegnare. https://www.direfareinsegnare.education/didattica/il-ruolo-dei-sensi-nell-apprendimento-e-nello-sviluppo-linguistico/

Brau, B., Fox, N., & Robinson, E. (2020). Behaviorism. In R. Kimmons & S. Caskurlu (Eds.), *The students' guide to learning design and research.* EdTech Books. https://edtechbooks.org/studentguide/behaviorism

Bray, M. (1992). Educational planning in small countries. *University of Hong Kong.* https://unesdoc.unesco.org/ark:/48223/pf0000091713

Bregni, S. (2018). Assassin's Creed taught me Italian: Video games and the quest for lifelong, ubiquitous learning. *Profession.*

Bridle, J. (2016). Algorithmic citizenship, digital statelessness. *GeoHumanities*, 2(2), 377–381. 10.1080/2373566X.2016.1237858

Brieger, E., Arghode, V., & McLean, G. (2020). Connecting theory and practice: Reviewing six learning theories to inform online instruction. *European Journal of Training and Development*, 44(4/5), 321–329. 10.1108/EJTD-07-2019-0116

Brieger, P., Sommer, S., Bloink, R., & Marneros, A. (2000). The relationship between five-factor personality measurements and ICD-10 personality disorder dimensions: Results from a sample of 229 subjects. *Journal of Personality Disorders*, 14(3), 282–290. 10.1521/pedi.2000.14.3.28211019751

Brito, C. (2019). *Facebook paid contractors to listen to your audio chats on its Messenger app.* CBS News. https://www.cbsnews.com/news/facebook-listening-conversation-message-online-chat-apple-google-amazon/#

Bronfenbrenner, U. (1986). *Ecology of human development.* Bologna: il Mulino. (Original work published 1979).

Bronfenbrenner, U. (2002). *Ecology of human development.* Bologna: il Mulino.

Bronfenbrenner, U. (1979). *The ecology of human development.* Harvard University Press. 10.4159/9780674028845

Bronfenbrenner, U. (1986). Ecology of the family as a context for human development: Research perspectives. *Developmental Psychology*, 22(6), 723–742. 10.1037/0012-1649.22.6.723

Brooks, J. G., & Brooks, M. (1999). *In search of understanding: The case for constructivist classrooms.* ASCD.

Brooks, R. A. (1991). Intelligence without representation. *Artificial Intelligence*, 47(1-3), 139–159. 10.1016/0004-3702(91)90053-M

Brown, T. (2005). Beyond constructivism: Exploring future learning paradigms. *education today, 2*(2), 1–11.

Brown, A. H., & Green, T. D. (2019). *The essentials of instructional design: Connecting fundamental principles with process and practice.* Routledge. 10.4324/9780429439698

Bruner, J. (1960). *The process of education.* Harvard University Press. 10.4159/9780674028999

Buccolo, M. (2020). L'educatore emozionale e la promozione del benessere nei contesti di cura. *Medical Humanities & Medicina Narrativa*, 99-107.

Buccolo, M. (2020). La gestione delle emozioni nel lavoro educativo con gli adolescenti e le famiglie. *Consultori Familiari Oggi*, 24-33.

Buckingham, D. (2009). The future of media literacy in the digital age: Some challenges for policy and practice. *Medienimpulse, 47*(2). 10.21243/mi-02-09-13

Buemi, M., Conte, M., & Guazzo, G. (2015). *Diversity management for inclusive growth: Strategies and tools*. Franco Angeli.

Buhalis, D. (2020). Technology in tourism-from information communication technologies to eTourism and smart tourism towards ambient intelligence tourism: A perspective article. *Tourism Review, 75*(1), 267–272. 10.1108/TR-06-2019-0258

Buhalis, D., Harwood, T., Bogicevic, V., Viglia, G., Beldona, S., & Hofacker, C. (2019). Technological disruptions in services: Lessons from tourism and hospitality. *Journal of Service Management, 30*(4), 484–506. 10.1108/JOSM-12-2018-0398

Buil, I., Catalán, S., & Martínez, E. (2018). Exploring students' flow experiences in business simulation games. *Journal of Computer Assisted Learning, 34*(2), 183–192. Advance online publication. 10.1111/jcal.12237

Buolamwini, J., & Gebru, T. (2018). Gender shades: Intersectional accuracy disparities in commercial gender classification. In *Proceedings of the Conference on Fairness, Accountability, and Transparency* (pp. 77-91). Research Gate.

Burns, A. J., Roberts, T. L., Posey, C., Bennett, R. J., & Courtney, J. F. (2018). Intentions to comply versus intentions to protect: A VIE theory approach to understanding the influence of insiders' awareness of organizational SETA efforts. *Decision Sciences, 49*(6), 1187–1228. 10.1111/deci.12304

Burroughs, A. (2018). EDUCAUSE 2018: Top IT issues emphasize data and funding challenges. *EdTech Magazine*. https://edtechmagazine.com/higher/article/2018/11/educause-2018-top-10-it-issues-emphasize-data-and-funding-challenges

Butler, J. (1990). *Gender trouble: Feminism and the subversion of identity*. Routledge.

Butler, L., & Starkey, L. (2024). OK Google, help me learn: An exploratory study of voice-activated artificial intelligence in the classroom. *Technology, Pedagogy and Education, 33*(2), 135–148. 10.1080/1475939X.2024.2311779

Caillois, R., Dossena, G., & Guarino, L. (1981). *I giochi e gli uomini: la maschera e la vertigine*. Bompiani.

Caligiuri, M. (2018). *Educazione per popoli superflui? L'avvento dell'intelligenza artificiale e gli studenti plusdotati: per una pedagogia consapevole*. Formazione & Insegnamento.

Caliskan, A., Bryson, J. J., & Narayanan, A. (2017). Semantics derived automatically from language corpora contain human-like biases. *Science, 356*(6334), 183–186. 10.1126/science.aal423028408601

Calvani, M., & Menichetti, M. (2013). Quali scenari per le pratiche e-learning nell'università? Gli "Open Educational Path." Firenze.

Calveri, C., & Sacco, P. L. (2021). *The digital transformation of culture. Cultural Geographies*. Bibliographic Publisher.

Cambi, F. (2014). *The pedagogies of the twentieth century*. Edizioni Laterza.

Campbell, J. P., DeBlois, P. B., & Oblinger, D. G. (2007). Academic analytics: A new tool for a new era. *EDUCAUSE Review, 42*(4), 40–42. https://er.educause.edu/articles/2007/7/academic-analytics-a-new-tool-for-a-new-era

Campell, R. (2023). *Utilizing AI In the classroom: 11 innovative strategies with ChatGPT*. Richard Campbell. https://richardccampbell.com/utilizing-ai-in-the-classroom-11-innovative-strategies-with-chatgpt/

Canevaro, A. (2009). *The long road to integration into society for a new independent life, in Scholastic and social integration*. Trent: Erickson.

Cannella, G., & Belardinelli, M. (2020). L'importanza delle reti per l'innovazione didattica nelle Piccole Scuole. In Mangione, G. R. J., Cannella, G., Parigi, L., & Bartolini, R. (Eds.), *Comunità di memoria, comunità di futuro. Il valore della piccola scuola* (pp. xx–xx). Carocci.

Cannella, G., & Mangione, G. R. J. (2020). I processi di internazionalizzazione delle piccole scuole come strumenti per l'innovazione didattica e organizzativa. *Formazione & Insegnamento*, 18(1), 128–144. 10.32029/978889002318

Cannella, G., & Mangione, G. R. J. (2023). L'interprofessionalità nel contratto educativo sociale. *Essere a Scuola*, 8, 9–14. 10.17471/2499-4324/1322

Cannella, G., & Mangione, G. R. J. (Eds.). (2021). *A scuola nelle piccole scuole: Storia, metodi, dinamiche*. Morcelliana Scholè.

Canva. (2024). *Free online AI image generator*. https://www.canva.com/ai-image-generator/

Capra, F. (1996). *The web of life: A new scientific understanding of living systems*. Anchor Books.

Carenys, J., Moya, S., & Perramon, J. (2017). Is it worth it to consider video games in accounting education? A comparison of a simulation and a videogame in attributes, motivation, and learning outcomes. *Revista de Contabilidad*, 20(2), 118–130. 10.1016/j.rcsar.2016.07.003

Carenzio, A., & Ferrari, S. (2021). Situazioni didattiche non standard. In Rivoltella, P. C. (Ed.), *Apprendere a distanza. Teorie e metodi* (pp. xx–xx). Raffaello Cortina Editore.

Carneiro, D., Novais, P., Andrade, F., Zeleznikow, J., & Neves, J. (2014). Online dispute resolution: An artificial intelligence perspective. *Artificial Intelligence Review*, 41(2), 211–240. 10.1007/s10462-011-9305-z

Carr, N. (2011). *Internet ci rende stupidi? Come la Rete sta cambiando il nostro cervello*. Raffaello Cortina.

Carr, N. (2020). *The shallows: What the Internet is doing to our brains*. W.W. Norton & Company.

Celaro, M., Paladini, E. P., Rodrigues, R., & Assumpcao, S. (2003). Quality and flexibility in higher education. In *Proceedings of European Distance Education Network Annual Conference (EDEN)* (pp. 35–41). Hungary: Eden Press.

CEPEJ. (2018). *European ethical charter on the use of artificial intelligence in justice systems and related fields*. European Commission for the Efficiency of Justice.

Ceruti, M. (2018). *The time of complexity*.

Chang, T. S., Li, Y., Huang, H. W., & Whitfield, B. (2021, March). Exploring EFL students' writing performance and their acceptance of AI-based automated writing feedback. In *2021 2nd International Conference on Education Development and Studies* (pp. 31–35). 10.1145/3459043.3459065

Chang, E., Kim, H. T., & Yoo, B. (2020). Virtual Reality Sickness: A Review of Causes and Measurements. *International Journal of Human-Computer Interaction*, 36(17), 1658–1682. 10.1080/10447318.2020.1778351

Chan, K. S., & Zary, N. (2019). Applications and challenges of implementing artificial intelligence in medical education: Integrative review. *JMIR Medical Education*, 5(1), e13930. 10.2196/1393031199295

Chapman, C., & Fullan, M. (2007). Collaboration and partnership for equitable improvement: Towards a networked learning system? *School Leadership & Management*, 27(3), 207–211. 10.1080/13632430701379354

Chen, I. (2011). Instructional design methodologies. In *Instructional Design: Concepts, Methodologies, Tools and Applications* (pp. 80-94). IGI Global. 10.4018/978-1-60960-503-2.ch108

Cheney-Lippold, J. (2011). A new algorithmic identity: Soft biopolitics and the modulation of control. *Theory, Culture & Society*, 28(6), 164–181. 10.1177/0263276411424420

Chen, L., Geng, X., Lu, M., Shimada, A., & Yamada, M. (2023). How students use learning analytics dashboards in higher education: A learning performance perspective. *SAGE Open*, 13(3), 21582440231192151. 10.1177/21582440231192151

Chilton, J., Dey, A., & Ho, D. (2018). Blockchain-based system for educational records management. *IEEE Transactions on Learning Technologies*, 11(2), 197–206.

China, C. (2023). *Leveraging user-generated social media content with text-mining examples*. IBM. https://www.ibm.com/blog/text-mining-examples/

Chin, H., Marasini, D. P., & Lee, D. (2023). Digital transformation trends in service industries. *Service Business*, 17(1), 11–36. 10.1007/s11628-022-00516-6

Chinnici, G. (2016). *Turing. The enigma of a genius*. Hoepli.

Chittaro, L., & Sioni, R. (2015). Serious games for emergency preparedness: Evaluation of an interactive vs. a non-interactive simulation of a terror attack. *Computers in Human Behavior*, 50, 508–519. 10.1016/j.chb.2015.03.074

Chiu, T. K. F. (2023). The impact of Generative AI (GenAI) on practices, policies, and research direction in education: A case of ChatGPT and Midjourney. *Interactive Learning Environments*, 1–17. 10.1080/10494820.2023.2253861

Chiu, T. K. F., Xia, Q., Zhou, X., Chai, C. S., & Cheng, M. (2023). Systematic literature review on opportunities, challenges, and future research recommendations of artificial intelligence in education. *Computers and Education: Artificial Intelligence*, 4, 100118. 10.1016/j.caeai.2022.100118

Choi, S. P. M., Lam, S. S., Li, K. C., & Wong, B. T. M. (2018). Learning analytics at low cost: At-risk student prediction with clicker data and systematic proactive interventions. *Journal of Educational Technology & Society*, 21(2), 273–290. https://www.jstor.org/stable/26388407

Choi, W. J., Jerath, K., & Sarvary, M. (2023). Consumer privacy choices and (un) targeted advertising along the purchase journey. *JMR, Journal of Marketing Research*, 60(5), 889–907. 10.1177/00222437221140052

Chomsky, N. (2005). *Big brother democracy*. Casale Monferrato: Piemme.

Chomsky, N., Roberts, I., & Watumull, J. (2023, March 8). Noam Chomsky: The false promise of ChatGPT. *The New York Times*. https://www.nytimes.com/2023/03/08/opinion/noam-chomsky-chatgpt.html

Chopra, S., & Meindl, P. (2014). Supply Chain Management: Strategy, Planning, and Operations. In *Pearson Education*. Pearson Education.

Chouldechova, A. (2017). Fair prediction with disparate impact: A study of bias in recidivism prediction instruments. *Big Data*, 5(2), 153–163. 10.1089/big.2016.004728632438

Chowdhury, S., Mubarrat, S. T., & Fernandes, A. (2023). A Physics-based Virtual Reality System Design and Evaluation by Simulating Human-Robot Collaboration. *Tech Rchiv*. https://doi.org/10.36227/techrxiv.18972773.v1

Christensen, C., Johnson, J., & Horn, M. (2008). *Disrupting class: How disruptive innovation will change the way the world learns*. McGraw-Hill.

Chung, S. Y. (2008). *Foundations of instructional and performance technology*. HRD Press.

CISA. (2023, May 11). *CISA and FBI release joint advisory in response to active exploitation of PaperCut vulnerability | CISA*. Cybersecurity and Infrastructure Security Agency CISA. https://www.cisa.gov/news-events/alerts/2023/05/11/cisa-and-fbi-release-joint-advisory-response-active-exploitation-papercut-vulnerability

Clark, K. R. (2018). Learning theories: Behaviorism. *Radiologic Technology*, 90(2), 172–175.30420574

Coeckelbergh, M. (2021). Time machines: Artificial intelligence, process, and narrative. *Philosophy & Technology*, 34(4), 1623–1638. 10.1007/s13347-021-00479-y

Cohen, E. (1994). Restructuring the classroom: Conditions for productive small groups. *Review of Educational Research*, 64(1), 1–35. 10.3102/00346543064001001

Cohen, L., Manion, L., & Morrison, K. (2013). *Research methods in education* (7th ed.). Routledge. 10.4324/9780203720967

Cohen, W. M., & Levinthal, D. A. (1990). Absorptive Capacity: A New Perspective on Learning and Innovation. *Administrative Science Quarterly*, 35(1), 128–152. 10.2307/2393553

Collis, B., & Moonen, J. (2001). *Flexible learning in a digital world: Experiences and expectations*. Kogan Page Limited.

Connolly, T. M., Boyle, E. A., MacArthur, E., Hainey, T., & Boyle, J. M. (2012). A systematic literature review of empirical evidence on computer games and serious games. *Computers & Education*, 59(2), 661–686. 10.1016/j.compedu.2012.03.004

Cook, D. A., Hamstra, S. J., Brydges, R., Zendejas, B., Szostek, J. H., Wang, A. T., Erwin, P. J., & Hatala, R. (2013). Comparative effectiveness of instructional design features in simulation-based education: Systematic review and meta-analysis. In *Medical Teacher, 35*(1). https://doi.org/10.3109/0142159X.2012.714886

Coppola, A., Del Fabbro, M., Lanzani, A. S., & Pessina, G. (2021). *Ricomporre i divari. Politiche e progetti territoriali contro le disuguaglianze e per la transizione ecologica*. Il Mulino.

Corbett, M., & White, S. (2014). Introduction: Why put the 'rural' in research? In Corbett, M., & White, S. (Eds.), *Doing educational research in rural settings* (pp. 19–22). Routledge. 10.4324/9781315769387

Cornish, L. (2006). Parents' views of composite classes in an Australian primary school. *Australian Educational Researcher*, 33(2), 123–142. 10.1007/BF03216837

Corona, F., & De Giuseppe, T. (2016). Mutism between electivity and selectivity in an etiological process of inclusive recognition. *Italian Journal of Special Education for Inclusion*, 4(1).

Corona, F., & De Giuseppe, T. (2017). *Flipped inclusion, between theoretical framework and experimental augmented classroom teaching for inclusive teaching. Pedagogy More Didactics* (Vol. III). Erickson.

Corona, F., & De Giuseppe, T. (2017). *Flipped methodology between systemic inclusion and didactic-assertive perspectives*. Pensa Multimedia.

Corona, F., & De Giuseppe, T. (2017). La Flipped Inclusion, tra impianto teoretico e didattica sperimentale di aula aumentata per una didattica inclusiva. [Trento: Centro Studi Erickson.]. *Pedagogia Più Didattica*, 3, 2–7.

Costa, F. A. (2013). Designing educational multimedia resources. In Moreira, A., Benavides, O., & Mendes, A. J. (Eds.), *Media in Education: Results from the 2011 ICEM and SIIE joint Conference* (pp. 29–40). Springer New York., 10.1007/978-1-4614-3175-6_3

Costamagna, C. (n.d.). *Mappe concettuali e apprendimento significativo*. Verga via grande. https://www.vergaviagrande.edu.it/scuola/per/formazione/ponD1_09/mappe/Mappe_concettuali_e_apprend_significativo.pdf

Costello, K. (2019). *Gartner Forecasts Worldwide Public Cloud Revenue to Grow 17.5 Percent in 2019*. Stamford, CT. https://www.gartner.com/en/newsroom/press-releases/2019-04-02-gartner-forecasts-worldwide-public-cloud-revenue-to-g

Couture, C., Monney, N., Thériault, P., Allaire, S., & Doucet, M. (2013). Enseigner en classe multiâge: Besoins di sviluppo professionale di insegnanti del primario. *Canadian Journal of Education*, 36(3), 108.

Cowls, J., King, T. C., Taddeo, M., & Floridi, L. (2019). Designing AI for social good: Seven essential factors. 10.2139/ssrn.3388669

Cox, E. G. M., van Bussel, B. C. T., Llamazares, N. C., Sels, J.-W. E. M., Onrust, M., van der Horst, I. C. C., & Koeze, J.SICS Study Group. (2024). Facial appearance associates with longitudinal multi-organ failure: An ICU cohort study. *Critical Care*, 28(1), 106. 10.1186/s13054-024-04891-638566179

Crawford, C. (1984). *The art of computer game design*. Osborne/McGraw-Hill.

Crawford, K., & Calo, R. (2016). There is a blind spot in AI research. *Nature*, 538(7625), 311–313. 10.1038/538311a27762391

Creaser, A. V., Frazer, M. T., Costa, S., Bingham, D. D., & Clemes, S. A. (2023). The use of wearable activity trackers in schools to promote child and adolescent physical activity: A descriptive content analysis of school staff's perspectives. *International Journal of Environmental Research and Public Health*, 19(21), 14067. 10.3390/ijerph192114067363609444

Crichton-Sumners, C., Mansouri, M., & Sauser, B. (2013). Systems Thinking for Knowledge Transfer in Organic and Mechanistic Organizations. *Transportation Research Record: Journal of the Transportation Research Board*, 2399(1), 112–120. 10.3141/2399-12

Croft, J. (2017). Law firms programmed for more technological disruption. *Financial Times*, 2.

Crommelin, L., Troy, L., Martin, C., & Parkinson, S. (2018). *Technological disruption in private housing markets: the case of Airbnb*.

Crossan, M. M., & Apaydin, M. (2010). A multi-dimensional framework of organizational innovation: A systematic review of the literature. *Journal of Management Studies*, 47(6), 1154–1191. 10.1111/j.1467-6486.2009.00880.x

Crough, J., & Love, C. A. (2019). Improving student engagement and self-regulated learning through technology-enhanced student partnerships. *International Conference on Information Communication Technologies in Education*, Crete, Greece.

Csikszentmihalyi, M., & Csikzentmihaly, M. (1990). *Flow: The psychology of optimal experience* (Vol. 1990). Harper & Row.

Cuador, C. (2017). From street photography to face recognition: Distinguishing between the right to be seen and the right to be recognized. *Nova Law Review*, 41(2), 237–264.

Cullen, T., Frey, T., Hinshaw, R., & Warren, S. (2004). Technology grants and rural schools: The power to transform. *Association for Educational Communications and Technology*. https://eric.ed.gov/?id=ED485134

Cummings, M., & Cummings, M. L. (2023). *Identifying AI hazards and responsibility gaps*. Research Gate. https://www.researchgate.net/publication/372051108

Cunha, F., & Heckman, J. J. (2007). The technology of skill training. *The American Economic Review*, 97(2), 31–47. 10.1257/aer.97.2.31

Custer, S. (2018). *Towards data-driven education systems: Insights into using information to measure results and manage change*. Brookings Center for Universal Education.

da Silva, F. S. C., & Coelho, I. M. (2020). Blockchain and Smart Contracts for the Education Sector. *InProceedings of the 2020 3rd International Conference on Education and E-Learning (ICEEL 2020)* (pp. 67-72). Research Gate.

D'Alessi, C. (2021). Empatia ed intelligenza emotiva per una sostenibilità affettivo-sociale: Dalla teoria alla prassi. *Formazione & Insegnamento*.

Damodaran, A. (2009). *The Dark Side of Valuation: Valuing Young, Distressed, and Complex Businesses* (2nd ed.). Pearson FT Press.

Dang, S. S. (2019). Artificial intelligence in humanoid robots. *Forbes*. https://www.forbes.com/sites/cognitiveworld/2019/02/25/artificial-intelligence-in-humanoid-robots/#6a7cd2b724c7

Dardot, P., & Laval, C. (2015). *Del comune, o della Rivoluzione nel XXI secolo*. DeriveApprodi.

Darvishi, A., Khosravi, H., Sadiq, S., & Gašević, D. (2022). Incorporating AI and learning analytics to build trustworthy peer assessment systems. *British Journal of Educational Technology*, 53(4), 844–875. 10.1111/bjet.13233

Davies, L., Harber, C., & Schweisfurth, M. (2002). *Democracy through teacher education*. CIER/CfBT.

Davis, C., Edmunds, E., & Kelly-Bateman, V. (2008). Connectivism – emerging perspectives on learning, teaching, and technology. University of Georgia. Retrieved from http://epltt.coe.uga.edu/index.php?title=Connectivism

Davis, J., Van Bulck, L., Durieux, B. N., & Lindvall, C. (2024). The temperature feature of ChatGPT: Modifying creativity for clinical research. *JMIR Human Factors*, 11(1), e53559. 10.2196/5355938457221

Day, M., Turner, G., & Drozdiak, N. (2019). Amazon workers are learning to what you tell Alexa. https://www.bloomberg.com/news/articles/2019-04-10/is-anyone-listening-to-you-on-alexa-a-global-team-reviews-audio

De Bartolomeis, F. (2018). *Fare scuola fuori della scuola*. Aracne Editrice.

De Bartolomeis, F., & Cousinet, R. (1973). *Il metodo di lavoro libero per gruppi*. La Nuova Italia.

De Benedictis, R., et al. (2019). Tecnologie intelligenti per la formazione a supporto dell'invecchiamento attivo. *Forma@re-Open Journal per la formazione in rete*, 19(1), 301-311.

De Freitas, S. (2006). Learning in immersive worlds: A review of game-based learning. *JISC report no. 8*. http://www.jisc.ac.uk/media/documents/programmes/elearninginnovation/gamingreport_v3.pdf

De Giovanni, D., Roberts, T., & Norman, G. (2009). Relative effectiveness of high- versus low-fidelity simulation in learning heart sounds. *Medical Education*, 43(7), 661–668. 10.1111/j.1365-2923.2009.03398.x19573189

De Giuseppe, T. (2016). *Bisogni educativi speciali: Empowerment e didattiche divergenti per decostruirne la complessità*. Avellino: Il Papavero Editions.

De Giuseppe, T. (2016). *Special educational needs: Empowerment and divergent didactics to deconstruct their complexity*. Avellino: Il Papavero.

De Giuseppe, T. (2016). Well-being between prosocial vicariousness, subjective perceptions and situated values. In F. Corona & T. De Giuseppe (Eds.), *Prosociality, inclusive technologies, and universal design in specific learning disorders* (pp. 108-119). Avellino: Il Papavero.

De Giuseppe, T. (2020). *Flipped inclusion: Computational thinking and transformative phenomenologies in the society of knowledge*. Avellino: The Poppy.

De Giuseppe, T., Ciambrone, R., & Corona, F. (2018). The inclusive experimentation of systemic approaches in flipped teaching. *Training and Teaching, 16*.

De Giuseppe, T. (2016). *Metodologia Flipped tra sistemica inclusione e prospettive didattico-assertive*. Il Papavero.

De Giuseppe, T. (2016). Selective mutism and flipped inclusion, between ecological-systemic perspectives and modeling inclusive reversals. *Italian Journal of Special Education for Inclusion*, 4(1).

De Giuseppe, T. (2023). *Educational science tra digital transformation e sfide interdisciplinari per professionalità inclusive*. Il Papavero.

De Giuseppe, T. (2023). *Flipped Inclusion e disturbo borderline di personalità: tra Empowerment, Consapevolezza Assertiva e Cura Pedagogica*. Il Papavero.

De Giuseppe, T., & Corona, F. (2017). Flipped teaching for inclusion. In Limone, P., & Parmigiani, D. (Eds.), *Pedagogical models and teaching practices for initial and in-service teacher education* (pp. 409–420). Progedit.

De Giuseppe, T., & Corona, F. (2017). Metodologia Flipped tra sistemica inclusione e prospettive didattico-assertive. [Pensa Multimedia.]. *Formazione e Insegnamento*, 15(2), 409–420.

De Giuseppe, T., & Corona, F. (2020). *Emerging and disruptive technological trends in education and the world of work*. IGI Global.

De Giuseppe, T., & Iannello, A. (2023). *I paradigmi eco-pedagogico-inclusivi tra Accessibility e Design for All: il modello Flipped Inclusion*. Il Papavero.

De Giuseppe, T., Ianniello, R., Podovšovnik, E., & Corona, F. (2020). The educational research flipped inclusion between social metamorphosis and technocratic hybridizations. In Podovšovnik, E. (Ed.), *Examining the roles of teachers and students in mastering new technologies*. IGI Global Publication. 10.4018/978-1-7998-2104-5.ch002

De Toni, A. F., Siagri, R., & Battistella, C. (2015). *Anticipate the future. Corporate foresight*. EGEA.

Deakin, J. F. (1998). Il ruolo della serotonina in casi di panico, ansia e depressione. *Clinical Psychopharmacology*, 13(4), S1–S5.

Dede, C., Ketelhut, D., & Ruess, K. (2006). *Designing for motivation and usability in a museum-based multi-user virtual environment* (Vol. 2006, Issue 3/11/2006). Harvard University. https://www.gse.harvard.edu/~dedech/muvees/documents/AELppr.pdf

Dehaene, S. (2020). *How We Learn: Why Brains Learn Better Than Any Machine... for Now*. London.

Del Serto, G. (2024). *Critical analysis of the impact of artificial intelligence on social and gender dynamics: Between inequalities and ethical challenges*.

Delello, J., & McWhorter, R. R. (2020). *Disruptive and emerging technology trends across education and the workplace*.

Delello, J. A., Sung, W., Mokhtari, K., & De Giuseppe, T. (2023). Exploring college students' awareness of AI and ChatGPT: Unveiling perceived benefits and risks. *Journal of Inclusive Methodology and Technology in Learning and Teaching*, 3(4), 1–25. https://www.inclusiveteaching.it/index.php/inclusiveteaching/article/view/132

Delello, J. A., Sung, W., Mokhtari, K., & De Giuseppe, T. (2024). Are K-16 educators prepared to address the educational and ethical ramifications of artificial intelligence software? *Advances in Information and Communication*, 921, 1–27. 10.1007/978-3-031-54053-0_28

Dell'Acqua, F., McFowland, E., Mollick, E. R., Lifshitz-Assaf, H., Kellogg, K., Rajendran, S., Krayer, L., Candelon, F., & Lakhani, K. R. (2023). Navigating the Jagged Technological Frontier: Field Experimental Evidence of the Effects of AI on Knowledge Worker Productivity and Quality. SSRN *Electronic Journal*. 10.2139/ssrn.4573321

Demetriadis, S., & Pombortsis, A. (2007). E-lectures for flexible learning: A study on their learning efficiency. *Journal of Educational Technology & Society*, 10, 147–157.

Dennenburg, V. H. (1981). Lateralità emisferica negli animali e effetti della prima esperienza. *Behavioral and Brain Sciences*, 4, 1–49.

Derinaldis, A. (2021). *The humanism of commitment for a new development model: Paths of reformism*.

DeSmet, A., Thompson, D., Baranowski, T., Palmeira, A., Verloigne, M., & De Bourdeaudhuij, I. (2016). Is participatory design associated with the effectiveness of serious digital games for healthy lifestyle promotion? A meta-analysis. *Journal of Medical Internet Research*, 18(4), e94. 10.2196/jmir.444427129447

Dewey, J. (1986, September). Experience and education. []. Taylor & Francis Group.]. *The Educational Forum*, 50(3), 241–252. 10.1080/00131728609335764

Dewey, J. (2014). *Experience and education*. Raffaello Cortina.

Dewey, J. (2018). *Democracy and education: An introduction to the philosophy of education* (Spadafora, G., Ed.). Anicia.

Di Filippo, L. (2014). Contestualizzare le teorie dei giochi di Johan Huizinga e Roger Caillois. *Problemi di Comunicazione*, 25, 281–308.

Di Marco, L. (2023, October 3). I risultati dell'Ue per il decennio digitale 2030, Raccomandazioni all'Italia. ASVIS. https://asvis.it/rubrica-europa-e-agenda-2030/1339-17867/i-risultati-dellue-per-il-decennio-digitale-2030-raccomandazioni-allitalia

Di Tore, P. A. (2023). *Artificial intelligence and educational processes according to intelligence*.

Di Tore, A. P. (2023). *Metawelt. Bodies, interactions, educations*. Studium. *Culture (Québec)*.

Di Tore, P. A. (2014). Perception of space, empathy, and cognitive processes: Design of a video game for the measurement of perspective-taking skills. *International Journal of Emerging Technologies in Learning, 9 Form@re - Open Journal for Networked Training, 14*(3), 43-61. https://doi.org/10.13128/formare-15272

Di Tore, P. A. (2023). *Intelligenza Artificiale e processi educativi secondo l'Intelligenza Artificiale*. Anicia.

Di Tore, S. (2017). *Using head-mounted display technology to support teaching through virtual learning environments in non-formal contexts. Giornale Italiano della Ricerca Educativa*. Think Multimedia.

Di Tore, S. (2017). *Utilizzo della tecnologia dei display montati sulla testa per supportare l'insegnamento attraverso ambienti di apprendimento virtuale in contesti non formali. Giornale Italiano della Ricerca Educativa*. Pensa Multimedia.

Di Tore, S., Aiello, P., Sibilio, M., & Berthoz, A. (2020). Simplex didactics: Promoting transversal learning through the training of perspective taking. *Journal of e-Learning and Knowledge Society, 16*(3), 34-49. https://doi.org/10.20368/1971-8829/1135221

Diakopoulos, N. (2016). Accountability in algorithmic decision making. *Communications of the ACM*, 59(2), 56–62. 10.1145/2844110

Diamond, L. (1999). *Developing democracy: Toward consolidation*. The Johns Hopkins University Press. 10.56021/9780801860140

Digennaro, S. (2018). Corpi emotivi: riflessioni sull'educazione emotiva nella scuola. *Encyclopaideia – Journal of Phenomenology and Education*, 22(52).

Digennaro, S. (2023). *Corpo, vita onlife e dualismo: una nuova sfida per le professioni educative*. Pensa MultiMedia.

Dill, K. E., & Dill, J. C. (1998). Video game violence: A review of the empirical literature. *Aggression and Violent Behavior*, 3(4), 407–428. 10.1016/S1359-1789(97)00001-3

Dix, A., & Hainey, T. (2020). Blockchain in Education: A Critical Review of the Literature. *InProceedings of the 2020 IEEE Global Engineering Education Conference (EDUCON)* (pp. 1116-1122). IEEE.

Dixit, A., Kaur, N., & Kingra, S. (2023). Review of audio deepfake detection techniques: Issues and prospects. *Expert Systems: International Journal of Knowledge Engineering and Neural Networks*, 40(8), e13322. 10.1111/exsy.13322

Dizon, G. (2017). Using intelligent personal assistants for second language learning: A case study of Alexa. *TESOL Journal*, 8(4), 811–830. 10.1002/tesj.353

Dizon, G., & Gayed, J. M. (2021). Examining the impact of Grammarly on the quality of mobile L2 writing. *The JALT CALL Journal*, 17(2), 74–92. 10.29140/jaltcall.v17n2.336

Doidge, N. (2008). *The Brain That Changes Itself*. Penguin.

Dolianiti, F., Tsoupouroglou, I., Antoniou, P., Konstantinidis, S., Anastasiades, S., & Bamidis, P. (2020). Chatbots in healthcare curricula: The case of a conversational virtual patient. *Lecture Notes in Computer Science (including Subseries Lecture Notes in Artificial Intelligence and Lecture Notes in Bioinformatics)*, 12462 LNAI, 137–147. 10.1007/978-3-030-60735-7_15

Dollar, J., & Miller, N. E. (1950). *Personality and psychotherapy*. McGraw-Hill.

Dollinger, M., Lodge, J., & Coates, H. (2018). Co-creation in higher education: Towards a conceptual model. *Journal of Marketing for Higher Education*, 28(2), 210–231. 10.1080/08841241.2018.1466756

Donati, P. (2019). *Scoprire i beni relazionali. Per generare una nuova socialità*. Soveria Mannelli: Rubbettino.

Donati, P., & Socli, R. (2011). *I beni relazionali. Che cosa sono e quali effetti producono*. Bollati Boringhieri.

Dondi, C., & Moretti, M. (2007). A methodological proposal for learning games selection and quality assessment. *British Journal of Educational Technology*, 38(3), 502–512. 10.1111/j.1467-8535.2007.00713.x

Dousay, T. A., & Hall, C. (2018). Alexa, tell me about using a virtual assistant in the classroom. In *EdMedia + Innovate Learning* (pp. 1413–1419). Amsterdam, Netherlands.

Dovigo, F. (2007). *Make differences*. Erickson.

Dovigo, F. (2008). *The Index for inclusion: A proposal for the inclusive development of schools*. Erickson.

Downes, S. (2005). The Living Arts: The Future of Learning Online. Moncton: Stephen Downes. Retrieved from http://www.downes.ca/files/guelph.ppt

Downes, S. (2006). Learning networks and connective knowledge. *Collective intelligence and Elearning*, 20(1), 1–26.

Downes, S. (2012). *Connectivism and connective knowledge: Essays on meaning and learning networks*. http://www.downes.ca/files/books/Connective_Knowledge-19May2012.pdf

Doyle, E., Buckley, P., & McCarthy, B. (2021). The impact of content co-creation on academic achievement. *Assessment & Evaluation in Higher Education*, 46(3), 494–507. 10.1080/02602938.2020.1782832

Doyle, E., Buckley, P., & Whelan, J. (2019). Assessment co-creation: An exploratory analysis of opportunities and challenges based on student and instructor perspectives. *Teaching in Higher Education*, 24(6), 739–754. 10.1080/13562517.2018.1498077

Draper, S. W. (2009). Catalytic assessment: Understanding how MCQs and EVS can foster deep learning. *British Journal of Educational Technology*, 40(2), 285–293. 10.1111/j.1467-8535.2008.00920.x

Du Plessis, D., & Bailey, J. (2000). Isolated parents' perceptions of the education of their children. *Education in Rural Australia*, 10(2), 1–26. 10.47381/aijre.v10i2.453

Duke, B., Harper, G., & Johnston, M. (2013). Connectivism as a digital age learning theory. *The International HETL Review*, 2013(Special Issue), 4–13.

Duolingo Team. (2023). *Introducing Duolingo Max, a learning experience powered by GPT-4*. Duolingo Team. https://blog.duolingo.com/duolingo-max/

Dwork, C., & Ilvento, C. (2018). Fairness under composition. *arXiv preprint arXiv:1806.06122*. https://arxiv.org/abs/1806.06122

Dziubaniuk, O., Ivanova-Gongne, M., & Nyholm, M. (2023). Learning and teaching sustainable business in the digital era: A connectivism theory approach. *International Journal of Educational Technology in Higher Education*, 20(1), 20. 10.1186/s41239-023-00390-w37096023

Educause. (2019). Horizon report: 2019 higher education edition. *EDUCAUSE Horizon Report: 2019 Higher Education Edition.* EduCause. https://library.educause.edu/-/media/files/library/2019/4/2019horizonreport.pdf

Edwards, A. (2009). Relational agency in collaborations for the well-being of children and young people. *Journal of Children's Services*, 4(1), 33–43. 10.1108/17466660200900004

Ee, C., Lake, J., Firth, J., Hargraves, F., De Manincor, M., Meade, T., Marx, W., & Sarris, J. (2020). An integrative collaborative care model for people with mental illness and physical comorbidities. *International Journal of Mental Health Systems*, 14(1), 1–16. 10.1186/s13033-020-00410-633292354

Ehrensaft, M. K. (2005). Interpersonal relationship and sex differences in the development of conduct problems. *Clinical Child and Family Psychology Review*, 8(1), 39–63. 10.1007/s10567-005-2341-y15898304

Elbanna, S., & Child, J. (2007). Influences on Strategic Decision Effectiveness: Development and Test of an Integrative Model. *Strategic Management Journal*, 28(4), 431–453. 10.1002/smj.597

Enriques, L., & Zetzsche, D. (2019). Corporate technologies and the tech nirvana fallacy. *European Corporate Governance Institute, Law Working Paper No. 457/2019.*

Ertmer, P. A., & Newby, T. J. (2013). Behaviorism, cognitivism, constructivism: Comparing critical features from an instructional design perspective. *Performance Improvement Quarterly*, 26(2), 43–71. 10.1002/piq.21143

Esposito, R. (2002). *Immunitas*. Einaudi.

European Commission. Directorate-General for Education, Youth, Sport and Culture, Melstveit Roseme, M., Day, L., & Fellows, T. (2021). *Enhancing learning through digital tools and practices: How digital technology in compulsory education can help promote inclusion: Final report: October 2021*. Publications Office. https://doi.org/doi/10.2766/365846

Evans, D. (2011) Internet of Things: How the next evolution of the Internet is changing everything. https://www.cisco.com/c/dam/en_us/about/ac79/docs/innov/IoT_IBSG_0411FINAL.pdf

Evans, N., Price, J., & Pender, D. (2018, October). Digital Disruption and Innovation in the Legal Industry: Management Considerations. In *ECMLG 2018 14th European Conference on Management, Leadership and Governance* (p. 66). Academic Conferences and publishing limited.

Evans, N., & Price, J. (2017). Managing information in law firms: Changes and challenges. *Information Research*, 22(1).

Fabricatore, C. (2009). *Media, play and videogaming: On the inner nature and the seldom exploited potential of digital entertainment*. Presentation at the *Fielding University graduate meeting*, New York.

Fagan, N. (2019). Privacy emerges as a top concern for higher education IT. *EdTech Magazine.* https://edtechmagazine.com/higher/article/2019/01/privacy-emerges-top-concern-higher-education-it

Fannizza, F. (2022). *Artificial intelligence: Promises, current affairs, controversies*. Franco Angeli.

Fargas Malet, M., & Bagley, C. (2023). Conceptualising small rural school-community relationships within a divided society: People, meanings, practices and spaces. *Oxford Review of Education*, 1–18. 10.1080/03054985.2023.2262383

Farrell, D., & Greig, F. (2016, January). Paychecks, paydays, and the online platform economy. In *Proceedings. Annual Conference on Taxation and Minutes of the Annual Meeting of the National Tax Association*. National Tax Association.

Fazekas, M., & Burns, T. (2012). *Exploring the complex interaction between governance and knowledge in education.* Paper for the CERI Governing Complex Education Systems Project Launch Meeting, Oslo. 10.1787/19939019

Fearon, D., Hughes, S., & Brearley, S. G. (2021). Constructivist Stakian multicase study: Methodological issues encountered in cross-cultural palliative care research. *International Journal of Qualitative Methods*, 20, 1–10. 10.1177/16094069211015075

Feigenbaum, E., & Feldman, J. (1963). *Computers and thought*. McGraw-Hill.

Fenwick, M., & Vermeulen, P. M. (2018). Technology and corporate governance: Blockchain, crypto, and artificial intelligence. *ECGI Law Working Paper*, No. 424/2018.

Fenwick, M., McCahery, J. A., & Vermeulen, P. M. (2018). The end of corporate governance (Hello "platform governance"). *European Business Organization Law Review*, 19(1), 57–77.

Fernandez, C. J., Ramesh, R., & Manivannan, A. S. R. (2022). Synchronous learning and asynchronous learning during COVID-19 pandemic: A case study in India. *Asian Association of Open Universities Journal*, 17(1), 1–14. 10.1108/AAOUJ-02-2021-0027

Ferraro, F. V., Ambra, F. I., Aruta, L., & Iavarone, M. L. (2020). Distance learning in the Covid-19 era: Perceptions in Southern Italy. *Education Sciences*, 10(12), 355. 10.3390/educsci10120355

Finocchiaro, G. (2022). *La regolazione dell'intelligenza artificial. Riv. Trimest. Dirit. Pubblico*. Digital Media Laws.

Fiore, Q., & McLuhan, M. (1967). *The medium is the massage* (Vol. 10). Random House.

Firth, J., Solmi, M., Wootton, R. E., Vancampfort, D., Schuch, F. B., Hoare, E., Gilbody, S., Torous, J., Teasdale, S. B., Jackson, S. E., Smith, L., Eaton, M., Jacka, F. N., Veronese, N., Marx, W., Ashdown-Franks, G., Siskind, D., Sarris, J., Rosenbaum, S., & Stubbs, B. (2020). A meta-review of "lifestyle psychiatry": The role of exercise, smoking, diet and sleep in the prevention and treatment of mental disorders. *World Psychiatry; Official Journal of the World Psychiatric Association (WPA)*, 19(3), 360–380. 10.1002/wps.2077332931092

Fitter, N., Strait, M., Bisbee, E., Mataric, M., & Takayama, L. (2021). You're Wigging Me Out! Is Personalization of Telepresence Robots Strictly Positive? In *Proceedings of the 2021 ACM/IEEE International Conference on Human-Robot Interaction (Boulder, CO, USA) (HRI '21)* (pp. 168–176). Association for Computing Machinery. https://ieeexplore.ieee.org/document/10045111

Flavin, M. (2017). Why can't I just Google it? What disruptive innovation means for higher education. In *Handbook of Research on Cross-Cultural Business Education*, 1(1), 46-64. 10.1057/978-1-137-57284-4_3

Flavin, M. (2016). Disruptive conduct: The impact of disruptive technologies on social relations in higher education. *Innovations in Education and Teaching International*, 53(5), 485–495. 10.1080/14703297.2013.866330

Flin, R., Youngson, G. G., & Yule, S. (Eds.). (2015). *Enhancing surgical performance: A primer in non-technical skills*. CRC Press. 10.1201/b18702

Floridi, L. (2008). The method of levels of abstraction. *Minds and Machines*, 18(3), 303–329. 10.1007/s11023-008-9113-7

Floridi, L. (2014). *The fourth revolution: How the infosphere is reshaping human reality*. Oxford University Press.

Floridi, L. (2015). *The onlife manifesto: Being human in a hyperconnected era*. Springer Nature. 10.1007/978-3-319-04093-6

Floridi, L. (2022). *Etica dell'intelligenza artificiale: Sviluppi, opportunità, sfide*. Raffaello Cortina Editore.

Fonagy, P. (2000). Attaccamento, sviluppo del Sé e sua patologia nei disturbi di personalità. Psychomedia. www.psychomedia.it

Fonagy, P., & Target, M. (1996). Playing with reality: 1 Theory of mind and the normal development of psychic reality. *The International Journal of Psycho-Analysis*, 77, 217–233.8771375

Ford, M., & Palmer, W. (2019). Alexa, are you listening to me? An analysis of Alexa voice service network traffic. *Personal and Ubiquitous Computing*, 23(1), 67–79. 10.1007/s00779-018-1174-x

Fotaris, P., Mastoras, T., & Lameras, P. (2023, September). Designing educational escape rooms with generative AI: A framework and ChatGPT prompt engineering guide. In *Proceedings of the 17th European Conference on Game-Based Learning: ECGBL 2023*. Academic Conferences and Publishing Limited. 10.34190/ecgbl.17.1.1870

Fourtane, S. (2019, April 22). Augmented Reality: The Future of Education. *Interesting Engineering*.

Fowler, A., Khosmood, F., Arya, A., & Lai, G. (2013). The Global Game Jam for Teaching and Learning. *Proceedings of the 4th Annual Conference of Computing and Information Technology Research and Education, Citrenz2013*.

Fox, J., Pittaway, L., & Uzuegbunam, I. (2018). Simulations in entrepreneurship education: Serious games and learning through play. *Entrepreneurship Education and Pedagogy*, 1(1), 61–89. 10.1177/2515127417737285

Francom, G. M. (2016). Barriers to technology use in large and small school districts. *Journal of Information Technology Education*, 15(1), 577–591. 10.28945/3596

Frasca, G. (2013). Simulation versus narrative: Introduction to ludology. In *The Video Game Theory Reader* (pp. 221–235). Routledge.

Freinet, C. (1978). *La scuola del fare*. Ed. Emme.

Freire, P. (2017). *Pedagogy of the oppressed*. Penguin Classics.

Freud, S. (1900). *Die traumdeutung*. Franz Deuticke.

Fricton, J., & Chen, H. (2009). Using teledentistry to improve access to dental care for the underserved. *Dental Clinics of North America*, 53(3), 537–548. 10.1016/j.cden.2009.03.00519482128

Frier, S. (2019). Facebook paid contractors to transcribe users' audio chats. *Bloomberg*. https://www.bloomberg.com/news/articles/2019-08-13/facebook-paid-hundreds-of-contractors-to-transcribe-users-audio

Gagné, R. M. (1990). *Le condizioni dell'apprendimento* (Vol. 11). Armando Editore.

Gan, M. J. S., & Hattie, J. (2014). Prompting secondary students' use of criteria, feedback specificity, and feedback levels during an investigative task. *Instructional Science*, 42(6), 861–878. 10.1007/s11251-014-9319-4

Gardner, H. (2005). *Educazione e sviluppo della mente. Intelligenze multiple e apprendimento*. Edizioni Erickson.

Gardou, C. (2012). *Inclusive society, parlons-*. Érès.

Garris, R., Ahlers, R., & Driskell, J. E. (2002). Games, motivation, and learning: A research and practice model. *Simulation & Gaming*, 33(4), 441–467. 10.1177/1046878102238607

Garun, N. (2017). Almost half a million pacemakers need a firmware update to avoid getting hacked: You may need to take grandma for an update. *The Verge*. https://www.theverge.com/2017/8/30/16230048/fda-abbott-pacemakers-firmware-update-cybersecurity-hack

Gee, J. P. (2003). What video games have to teach us about learning and literacy. [CIE]. *Computers in Entertainment*, 1(1), 20–20. 10.1145/950566.950595

Gelman, A. (2010). *Mario math with millennials: The impact of playing the Nintendo DS on student achievement*. University of Denver.

Gerpott, F. H., Lehmann-Willenbrock, N., Wenzel, R., & Voelpel, S. C. (2019). Age diversity and learning outcomes in organizational training groups: The role of knowledge sharing and psychological safety. *International Journal of Human Resource Management*, 32(18), 3777–3804. 10.1080/09585192.2019.1640763

Geyer, R. (2003). European integration, the problem of complexity and the revision of theory. *Journal of Common Market Studies*, 41(1), 15–35. 10.1111/1468-5965.t01-1-00409

Geyer, R., Mackintosh, A., & Lehmann, K. (2005). *Integrating UK and European social policy: the complexity of Europeanisation*. Radcliffe Publishing.

Ghawe, A. S., & Chan, Y. (2022). Implementing Disruptive Technologies: What Have We Learned? *Communications of the Association for Information Systems*, 50(1), 36. 10.17705/1CAIS.05030

Ghorashi, N., Ismail, A., Ghosh, P., Sidawy, A., Javan, R., & Ghorashi, N. S. (2023). AI-powered chatbots in medical education: Potential applications and implications. *Cureus*, 15(8). 10.7759/cureus.4327137692629

Giacomantonio, M. (2020). Intelligenza artificiale e apprendimento. *Innovatio Educativa*, 51-56.

Gibson, J. J. (1977). The theory of affordances. In Shaw, R., & Bransford, J. (Eds.), *Perceiving, acting, and knowing: Toward on ecological psychology* (pp. 67–82). Erlbaum and Associates.

Gilbert, A., & Gong, Z. (2024). Digital Identity Theft Using Deepfakes. In *Information Technology Security and Risk Management* (pp. 307-314). CRC Press. 10.1201/9781003264415-47

Gilbert, P. (2018). *Social media becomes biggest data breach threat*. https://www.itweb.co.za/content/G98YdqLxZZNqX2PD

Giorgi, P., & Zoppi, I. (2021). *La ricerca Indire tra uso didattico del patrimonio storico culturale e promozione delle buone pratiche*.

Giorgi, P., & Zoppi, I. (2021). *Memorie magistrali: memoria, scuola e territorio*. AIPH.

Giovanazzi, T. (2021). *Educate for human development*. Expo Dubai 2020. Lecce: Think MultiMedia.

Giovanazzi, T. (2023). *Educating in connective contexts. Between knowledge sharing and ecological transition of human communities*.

Gira, M., Zhang, R., & Lee, K. (2022). Debiasing pre-trained language models via efficient fine-tuning. In *Proceedings of the Second Workshop on Language Technology for Equality, Diversity, and Inclusion* (pp. 85-95). Research Gate. 10.18653/v1/2022.ltedi-1.8

Giroux, H. (2021). *Pandemic pedagogy: Education in time of crisis*. Bloomsbury. 10.5040/9781350184466

Gittlen, S. (2011). Schools use biometrics to enhance student services. *EdTech Magazine*. https://edtechmagazine.com/k12/article/2011/07/schools-use-biometrics-enhance-student-services

Gjelten, T. (1982). *A typology of rural school settings*. Summary of presentation prepared for the Rural Education Seminar, United States Department of Education, Washington, DC.

Glazer, R. (1991). Marketing in an Information Intensive Environment: Strategic Implications of Knowledge as an Asset. *Journal of Marketing*, 55(4), 1–19. 10.1177/002224299105500401

Goertzel, Mossbridge, Monroe, Hanson & Yu, (2017). *Loving AI: Humanoid robots as agents of human consciousness expansion.* https://arxiv.org/pdf/1709.07791.pdf

Goffman, E. (2001). *Frame analysis. The organization of the experience.* Armando.

Goldberg, R. (2009). How Our Worldviews Shape Our Practices. *Conflict Resolution Quarterly, 26*(4), 405–431. 10.1002/crq.241

Goodfellow, I., Pouget-Abadie, J., Mirza, M., Xu, B., Warde-Farley, D., Ozair, S., Courville, A., & Bengio, Y. (2014). Generative adversarial nets. In Vol. 27, pp. 2672–2680). Advances in Neural Information Processing Systems. Neural Information Processing Systems Foundation.

GovInsider. (2018, October 12). *How the Singapore tourism board uses data to personalise tourism?* Retrieved from https://govinsider.asia/intl-en/article/how -the-singapore -tourism-board-uses-data-to-personalise-tourism

Graham, J. (2018). Hamburger-making robot Flippy is back at Calif. Chain. *USA Today.*

Grech, A., & Xu, D. (2019). Blockchain for Education: Lifelong Learning Passport. *Proceedings of the 2019 International Conference on Blockchain Technology and Applications (ICBTA 2019)* (pp. 71-76).

Green, C. S., & Bavelier, D. (2006). The cognitive neuroscience of video games. *Digital Media: Transformations in Human Communication, 1*(1), 211–223.

Greeno, J. G. (1994). Gibson's affordances. *Psychological Review, 101*(2), 336–342. 10.1037/0033-295X.101.2.3368022965

Grice, H. P. (1993). *Logica e conversazione. Saggi su intenzione, significato e comunicazione.* Il Mulino.

Grinker, R. R., Werble, B., & Dyre, R. C. (1968). *The Borderline Syndrome.* Basic Books.

Gristy, C., Hargreaves, L., & Kučerová, S. R. (Eds.). (2020). *Educational research and schooling in rural Europe: An engagement with changing patterns of education, space, and place.* Information Age Publishing.

Grundmeyer, T., & Peters, R. (2016). Learning from the Learners: Preparing Future Teachers to Leverage the Benefits of Laptop Computers. *Computers in the Schools, 33*(4), 253–273. 10.1080/07380569.2017.1249757

Gunderson, J. G., & Singer, M. (1975). Defining borderline patients: An overview. *The American Journal of Psychiatry, 132*(1), 1–10. 10.1176/ajp.132.1.1802958

Gupta, A., Saini, V., Kumar, R., & Kumar, V. (2019). Blockchain-based decentralized education system. *International Journal of Computer Applications, 182*(4), 14–18. 10.5120/1833-2457

Guttentag, D. (2015). Airbnb: Disruptive innovation and the rise of an informal tourism accommodation sector. *Current Issues in Tourism, 18*(12), 1192–1217. 10.1080/13683500.2013.827159

Halupa, C. (2020). Reaching "creating" in Bloom's taxonomy: The merging of heutagogy and technology in online learning. In *Research Anthology on Developing Critical Thinking Skills in Students* (pp. 15–35). IGI Global. 10.4018/978-1-7998-3022-1.ch002

Halvorsrud, K., Kucharska, J., Adlington, K., Rüdell, K., Brown Hajdukova, E., Nazroo, J., Haarmans, M., Rhodes, J., & Bhui, K. (2021). Identifying evidence of effectiveness in the co-creation of research: A systematic review and meta-analysis of the international healthcare literature. *Journal of Public Health (Oxford, England), 43*(1), 197–208. 10.1093/pubmed/fdz12631608396

Hamzah, A., Almed, & Wahid, F. (2016, November). Participatory design in the development of healthcare systems: A literature review. In *Proceedings of the 2nd International Conference on Communication and Information Processing* (pp. 60-64). ACM. 10.1145/3018009.3018010

Hannum, W. H., Irvin, M. J., Banks, J. B., & Farmer, T. W. (2009). Distance education use in rural schools. *Journal of Research in Rural Education*, 24(3), 1.

Hansen, C. (2017). *Shakespeare and complexity theory*. Routledge. 10.4324/9781351967433

Harari, Y. N. (2017). *Homo Deus: Brief history of the future*. Bompiani. 10.17104/9783406704024

Harasim, L. (2023). Learning theories: The role of epistemology, science, and technology. In *Learning, design, and technology: An international compendium of theory, research, practice, and policy* (pp. 75–113). Springer International Publishing. 10.1007/978-3-319-17461-7_48

Hardy, J., Bates, S. P., Casey, M. M., Galloway, K. W., Galloway, R. K., Kay, A. E., Kirsop, P., & McQueen, H. A. (2014, September 2). Student-generated content: Enhancing learning through sharing multiple-choice questions. *International Journal of Science Education*, 36(13), 2180–2194. 10.1080/09500693.2014.916831

Harris, R., & Short, T. (2014). Exploring the notion of workforce development. In *Handbook of Research on Workforce Diversity in a Global Society, 1*(1), 1-21. 10.1007/978-981-4560-58-0_1

Harris, A., & Spillane, J. (2008). Distributed leadership through the looking glass. *Management in Education*, 22(1), 2–6. 10.1177/0892020607085623

Harris, J. (2005). Our agenda for technology integration: It's time to choose. *Contemporary Issues in Technology & Teacher Education*, 5(2), 116–122. https://scholarworks.wm.edu/cgi/viewcontent.cgi?article=1092&context=educationpubs

Hasselton, T. (2019). Facebook knows everywhere you go: Here's how to stop it from tracking you. https://www.cnbc.com/2019/04/30/how-to-stop-facebook-from-storing-your-location-history.html

Haugeland, J. (1985). *Artificial intelligence: The very idea*. MIT Press.

Hawkes, M., Halverson, P., & Brockmueller, B. (2002). Technology facilitation in the rural school: An analysis of options. *Journal of Research in Rural Education*, 17(3), 162–170.

Hay, L. (1994). *Puoi guarire la tua vita*.

Heeralal, P. J. H. (2014). Preparing pre-service teachers to teach in rural schools. *Mediterranean Journal of Social Sciences*, 5(20), 1795–1800. 10.5901/mjss.2014.v5n20p1795

Heier, B. (2023, September 28). *Marco's pizza tests self-driving delivery bots*. Food On Demand. https://foodondemand.com/09282023/marcos-pizza-tests-self-driving-delivery-bots/

Heiligenstein, M. X. (2023). *Facebook data breaches: Full timeline through 2023*. https://firewalltimes.com/facebook-data-breach-timeline/

Henderson, J., Pears, M., & Konstantinidis, S. (2022, September). *Done in 60 minutes! Best practices, crowdsourcing, co-creation, and design principals of educational chatbots*. Presented at ALT Annual Conference 2022, Manchester, UK. https://nottingham-repository.worktribe.com/index.php/output/13179986/done-in-60-minutes-best-practices-crowdsourcing-co-creation-and-design-principals-of-educational-chatbots

Henderson, J., Pears, M., Bamidis, P. D., Tsoupouroglou, I., Schiza, E., Pattichis, C. S., Stathakarou, N., Karlgren, K., & Konstantinidis, S. T. (2022). Development of a bespoke chatbot design tool to facilitate a crowd-based co-creation process. *2022 International Conference on Interactive Media, Smart Systems and Emerging Technologies, IMET 2022 - Proceedings*. IEEE. 10.1109/IMET54801.2022.9929752

Hendricks, G. P. (2019). Connectivism as a learning theory and its relation to open distance education. *Progressio*, 41(1), 1–13. 10.25159/2663-5895/4773

Herlo, D. (2017). Connectivism, a new learning theory? In Soare, E., & Langa, C. (Eds.), *Education facing contemporary world issues. European proceedings of social and behavioural sciences* (pp. 330–337). Future Academy.

Hernandez-de-Menendez, M., Morales-Menendez, R., Escobar, C. A., & Arinez, J. (2021). Biometric applications in education. [IJIDeM]. *International Journal on Interactive Design and Manufacturing*, 15(2-3), 365–380. 10.1007/s12008-021-00760-6

Hernández-Jiménez, C., Sarabia, R., Paz-Zulueta, M., Paras-Bravo, P., Pellico, A., Ruiz Azcona, L., Blanco, C., Madrazo, M., Agudo, M. J., Sarabia, C., & Santibáñez, M. (2019). Impact of active video games on body mass index in children and adolescents: Systematic review and meta-analysis evaluating the quality of primary studies. *International Journal of Environmental Research and Public Health*, 16(13), 2424. 10.3390/ijerph1613242431288460

Herodotou, C., Hlosta, M., Boroowa, A., Rienties, B., Zdrahal, Z., & Mangafa, C. (2019). Empowering online teachers through predictive learning analytics. *British Journal of Educational Technology*, 50(6), 3064–3079. 10.1111/bjet.12853

Herold, B., & Molnar, M. (2018, February 8). Virtual Reality for Learning Raises High Hopes and Serious Concerns. *Education Week*.

Herr, C. M. (2014). Radical constructivist structural design education for large cohorts of Chinese learners. *Constructivist Foundations*, 9(3), 393–402.

Herrmann-Werner, A., Festl-Wietek, T., Holderried, F., Herschbach, L., Griewatz, J., Masters, K., Zipfel, S., & Mahling, M. (2024). Assessing ChatGPT's mastery of Bloom's taxonomy using psychosomatic medicine exam questions: Mixed-methods study. *Journal of Medical Internet Research*, 26(1), e52113. 10.2196/5211338261378

Her anu, C.-L. (2020). Future education within disruptive technologies developments. *Knowledge-Based Organizations*, 26(1), 117–124. 10.2478/kbo-2020-0092

Heylighen, F. (2016). Stigmergy as a universal coordination mechanism I: Definition and components. *Cognitive Systems Research*, 38, 4–13. 10.1016/j.cogsys.2015.12.002

Hidayat, S., & Qamariah, Z. (2023). The role of Bloom's taxonomy in curriculum approach. [JIMNU]. *Jurnal Ilmiah Multidisiplin Nusantara*, 1(3), 162–167. 10.59435/jimnu.v1i3.183

Hilb, M. (2020). Toward artificial governance? The role of artificial intelligence in shaping the future of corporate governance. *The Journal of Management and Governance*, 24(2), 265–286. 10.1007/s10997-020-09519-9

Hill, K. (2020, October 21). Activities turn facial recognition tools against the police. T*he New York Times*. https://www.nytimes.com/2020/10/21/technology/facial-recognition-police.html

Hinojo-Lucena, F. J., Aznar-Díaz, I., Cáceres-Reche, M. P., & Romero-Rodríguez, J. M. (2019). Artificial intelligence in higher education: A bibliometric study on its impact in the scientific literature. *Education Sciences*, 9(1), 51. 10.3390/educsci9010051

Ho, J., Chan, W., Saharia, C., Whang, J., Gao, R., Gritsenko, A., Kingma, D. P., Poole, B., Norouzi, M., Fleet, D. J., & Salimans, T. (2022). *Imagen Video: High definition video generation with diffusion models.* https://imagen.research.google/video/paper.pdf

Ho, M., Taylor, M., McSharry, E., Bergmann-Tyacke, I., Santos, M. R., Dhaeze, M., Brown, M., Hall, C., & Konstantinidis, S. T. (2021). The role of stakeholders' evaluation on the quality of reusable learning objects following the aspire participatory framework. In *INTED2021 Proceedings* (pp. 7950-7960). IATED.

Hockenbary, L. (2024, February 21). *2024: The year of generative AI.* eSchool News. https://www.eschoolnews.com/digital-learning/2024/02/21/2024-the-year-of-gen-ai/

Hohlfeld, T. N., Ritzhaupt, A. D., Barron, A. E., & Kemker, K. (2008, March). *Socio-economic status and technology integration in Florida schools: A longitudinal study.* Paper presented at the annual meeting of the American Educational Research Association, New York.

Holderried, F., Stegemann-Philipps, C., Herschbach, L., Moldt, J.-A., Nevins, A., Griewatz, J., Holderried, M., Herrmann-Werner, A., Festl-Wietek, T., & Mahling, M. (2024). A generative pretrained transformer (GPT)-powered chatbot as a simulated patient to practice history taking: Prospective, mixed methods study. *JMIR Medical Education*, 10(1), e53961. 10.2196/5396138227363

Holloway, K. (2020). Big Data and learning analytics in higher education: Legal and ethical considerations. *Journal of Electronic Resources Librarianship*, 32(4), 276–285. 10.1080/1941126X.2020.1821992

Holm, L. B., & Dahl, F. A. (2011). Using soft systems methodology as a precursor for an emergency department simulation model. *OR Insight*, 24(3), 168–189. 10.1057/ori.2011.8

Holon, I. Q. (2019). *10 charts that explain the global education technology market.* San Francisco, CA. https://www.holoniq.com/edtech/10-charts-that-explain-the-global-education-technology-market/

Hopster, J. (2021, September). The ethics of disruptive technologies: towards a general framework. In *International Conference on Disruptive Technologies, Tech Ethics and Artificial Intelligence* (pp. 133-144). Cham: Springer International Publishing. 10.2139/ssrn.3903839

Horn, M. B., & Mackey, K. (2011). Transforming American education. *E-Learning and Digital Media*, 8(2), 133–140. 10.2304/elea.2011.8.2.133

Horn, V., & Carl, E. (2015). Transforming US workforce development policies for the 21st century. *New Directions for Adult and Continuing Education*, 148(1), 9–17.

Horvath, I. (2016). Disruptive technologies in higher education. *IEEE INFOCOM 2016 - The 35th Annual IEEE International Conference on Computer Communications*. IEEE. 10.1109/CogInfoCom.2016.7804574

Hoskins, B. (2006). Draft framework on indicators for active citizenship. *CRELL*. https://legalinstruments.oecd.org/en/instruments/OECD-LEGAL-0449

Hou, B. C., & Houstman, N. E. (2018). A Distributed Learning Record Store using Blockchain Technology. *InProceedings of the 2018 IEEE Frontiers in Education Conference (FIE)* (pp. 1-4). IEEE.

Howard, P., Corbett, M., Burke-Saulnier, A., & Young, D. (2020). Education futures: Conservation and change. *Paper commissioned for the UNESCO Futures of Education report.* UNESCO.

Howley, A., & Howley, C. (2008). Planning for technology integration: Is the agenda overrated or underappreciated? *Educational Planning*, 17(1), 1–17.

Howley, A., Wood, L., & Hough, B. (2011). Rural elementary school teachers' technology integration. *Journal of Research in Rural Education*, 29(9), 1–18.

Huang, R., Zmud, R. W., & Price, R. L. (2010). Influencing the effectiveness of IT governance practices through steering committees and communication policies. *European Journal of Information Systems*, 19(3), 288–302. 10.1057/ejis.2010.16

Huizinga, J. (2014). *Homo ludens ils 86*. Routledge. 10.4324/9781315824161

Hunt, R. (2021, April 12). Pizza-bot! Domino's Pizza launches robotic deliveries in Houston. *USA Today*. https://www.usatoday.com/story/money/food/2021/04/12/dominos-pizza-launches-robotic-deliveries-in-houston/115694496/

Hynes, N., & Elwell, A. D. (2016). The role of inter-organizational networks in enabling or delaying disruptive innovation: A case study of mVoIP. *Journal of Business and Industrial Marketing*, 31(6), 722–731. 10.1108/JBIM-10-2012-0168

Hyry-Beihammer, E. K., & Hascher, T. (2015). Multi-grade teaching practices in Austrian and Finnish primary schools. *International Journal of Educational Research*, 74, 104–113. 10.1016/j.ijer.2015.07.002

Iavarone, M. L., Malavasi, P., Orefice, P., & Pinto Minerva, F. (Eds.). (2017). *Environmental pedagogy 2017: Between human development and social responsibility*. Think MultiMedia.

IBM. (2023). *Cost of a data breach report 2023*. IBM. https://www.ibm.com/reports/data-breach

Ifenthaler, D., Gibson, D., Prasse, D., Shimada, A., & Yamada, M. (2021). Putting learning back into learning analytics: Actions for policy makers, researchers, and practitioners. *Educational Technology Research and Development*, 69(4), 2131–2150. 10.1007/s11423-020-09909-8

Iftimia, N., Pandya, R., & Mahoney, F. (2023). New advances in artificial intelligence for biomedical research and clinical decision-making. *Preprints*, 2023060243. https://doi.org/10.20944/preprints202306.0243.v1

Iglehart, J. K. (2014). Connected health: Emerging disruptive technologies. *Health Affairs*, 33(2), 190–190. 10.1377/hlthaff.2014.004224493758

IIdea. (2024). *Video games in Italy in 2023. An analysis of the market and video gamers in Italy in 2023*. IIdea. https://iideassociation.com

Ikromovich, H. O., & Mamatkulovich, B. B. (2023). Facial recognition using transfer learning in the deep CNN. *Web of Scientist: International Scientific Research Journal*, 4(3), 502-507. https://wos.academiascience.org/index.php/wos/article/view/3483

Impact Research. (2023, March 1). *Teachers and students embrace ChatGPT for education*. Walton Family Foundation. https://www.waltonfamilyfoundation.org/learning/teachers-and-students-embrace-chatgpt-for-education

INDIRE. (2018). *Manifesto delle Piccole Scuole (Manifesto for Small Schools)*. INDIRE. https://piccolescuole.indire.it/en/the-movement-what-it-is/the-manifesto/

Infante, C. (2000). *Learning through play. Interactivity between theater and hypermedia*. Bollati Boringhieri.

Insights, C. B. (2019). Like it or not facial recognition is already here. These are the industries it will transform first. https://www.cbinsights.com/research/facial-recognition-disrupting-industries/

Instructure (2023). *Accelerating the learning process with AI tools for teachers*. Instructure. https://www.instructure.com/resources/blog/accelerating-learning-process-ai-tools-teachers

Ischen, C., Araujo, T., Voorveld, H., van Noort, G., & Smit, E. (2020). Privacy concerns in chatbot interactions. In *Chatbot Research and Design:Third International Workshop, CONVERSATIONS 2019,Amsterdam, The Netherlands*, (pp. 34-48). Springer International Publishing.

Isidori, M. V., & Vaccarelli, A. (2013). *Pedagogia dell'emergenza/didattica nell'emergenza*. Franco Angeli.

Islam, S. M. R., Hasan, M. R., Amin, M. B., & Alam, M. A. (2019). Blockchain-based Education Certificate Verification System. *InProceedings of the 2019 International Conference on Innovations in Science, Engineering and Technology (ICISET 2019)* (pp. 1-6). IEEE.

It's tough to telecommute in health care. Here's how Mayo Clinic does it. (2023, March, 18). *Advisory Board*.

Ivory, J. D. (2015). A brief history of video games. In *The Video Game Debate* (pp. 1–21). Routledge. 10.4324/9781315736495-1

Jain, A. K., Ross, A., & Prabhakar, S. (2004). An introduction to biometric recognition. *IEEE Transactions on Circuits and Systems for Video Technology*, 14(1), 4–20. 10.1109/TCSVT.2003.818349

Jakosuo, K. (2019). Digitalisation And Platform Economy-Disruption In Service Sector. In *Joint Conference Ismc 2018-Icltibm 2018-14th International Strategic Management Conference 8th International Conference On Leadership, Technology, Innovation And Business Management*. Future Academy. 10.15405/epsbs.2019.01.02.7

Janzen, K., Perry, B., & Edwards, M. (2011). Becoming real: Using the artistic pedagogical technology of photo voice as a medium to becoming real to one another in the online educative environment. *International Journal of Nursing Education Scholarship*, 8(1), 32–43. 10.2202/1548-923X.2168

Janzen, K., Perry, B., & Edwards, M. (2012). The entangled web: Quantum learning, quantum learning environments and Web technology. Ubiquitous Learning. *International Journal (Toronto, Ont.)*, 4(2), 1–16. 10.18848/1835-9795/CGP/v04i02/40328

Jarvis, P. (1995). *Adult and continuing education: Theory and practice*. Psychology Press.

Javaid, M., Haleem, A., Singh, R. P., Khan, S., & Khan, I. H. (2023). Unlocking the opportunities through ChatGPT tool towards ameliorating the education system. *BenchCouncil Transactions on Benchmarks. Standards and Evaluations*, 3(2), 100115. 10.1016/j.tbench.2023.100115

Jenkins, A. (2019, June 20). The Fall and Rise of VR: The Struggle to Make Virtual Reality Get Real. *Fortune*. https://fortune.com/longform/virtual-reality-struggle-hope-vr/

Jenkins, H. (2004). Game design as narrative architecture. *Computer, 44(3), 118-130*. MIT Press., http://web.mit.edu/cms/People/henry3/games&narrative.html

Jenkins, H. (2006). *Fans, bloggers, and gamers: Exploring participatory culture*. NYU Press.

Jess, M., Atencio, M., & Thorburn, M. (2011). Complexity theory: Supporting curriculum and pedagogy developments in Scottish physical education. *Sport Education and Society*, 16(2), 179–201. 10.1080/13573322.2011.540424

Ji, M., Jeon, J. I., Han, K. S., & Cho, Y. (2023). Accurate long-term evolution/Wi-Fi hybrid positioning technology for emergency rescue. *ETRI Journal*, 45(6), 939–951. https://onlinelibrary.wiley.com/doi/10.4218/etrij.2022-0234. 10.4218/etrij.2022-0234

Joan, D. R. (2013). Flexible learning as new learning design in classroom process to promote quality education. *Journal of Science Education and Technology*, 9(1), 37–42.

Joda, T., Yeung, A. W. K., Hung, K., Zitzmann, N. U., & Bornstein, M. M. (2021). Disruptive innovation in dentistry: What it is and what could be next. *Journal of Dental Research*, 100(5), 448–453. 10.1177/00220345209787743332997

Johnson, D. A., & Dickinson, A. M. (2012). Using Postfeedback Delays to Improve Retention of Computer-based Instruction. *The Psychological Record*, pp. 62, 485–496. http://alycedickinson.com/publications/Johnson2012.pdf

Johnson, J., & Strange, M. (2007). *Why rural matters 2007: The realities of rural education growth*. Rural School and Community Trust. https://files.eric.ed.gov/fulltext/ED498859.pdf

Johnson, T., & Johnson, N. (2023, May 18). Police facial recognition technology can't tell Black people apart. *Scientific American*. https://www.scientificamerican.com/article/police-facial-recognition-technology-cant-tell-black-people-apart/

Johnson, A. E. W., Pollard, T. J., Shen, L., Lehman, L. W. H., Feng, M., Ghassemi, M., Moody, B., Szolovits, P., Celi, L. A., & Mark, R. G. (2016). MIMIC-III, a freely accessible critical care database. *Scientific Data*, 3(1), 1–9. 10.1038/sdata.2016.3527219127

Johnson-Laird, P. (1988). *The computer and the mind: An introduction to cognitive science*. Harvard University Press.

Jonassen, D. H. (1992). Objectivism versus constructivism: Do we need a new philosophical paradigm? *Educational Technology Research and Development*, 39(3), 5–14. 10.1007/BF02296434

Jones, J., Seet, P., Spoehr, J., & Hordacre, A. (2018). The Fourth Industrial Revolution: the implications of technological disruption for Australian VET, NCVER. *Adelaide. Australia. Recuperado em*, 25.

Jones-Devitt, S., Austen, L., & Parkin, H. (2017). Integrative reviewing for exploring complex phenomena. *Social Research Update*, 66.

Jones, K. M., & Salo, D. (2018). Learning analytics and the academic library: Professional ethics commitments at a crossroads. *College & Research Libraries*, 79(3), 304–323. 10.5860/crl.79.3.304

Jordan, C. (2017). The digital workforce – disruptive technologies changing the way work gets done. *APPEA Journal*, 57(1), 443–449. 10.1071/AJ16150

Jøsang, A., Ismail, R., & Boyd, C. (2007). A survey of trust and reputation systems for online service provision. *Decision Support Systems*, 43(2), 618–644. 10.1016/j.dss.2005.05.019

Joshi, A., Srinivas, C., Firat, E. E., & Laramee, R. S. (2024). *Evaluating the recommendations of LLMs to teach a visualization technique using Bloom's taxonomy*. USFCA. https://www.cs.usfca.edu/~apjoshi/papers/2024_VDA_LLM_Evaluation_PCP.pdf

Juul, J. (2010). *A casual revolution: Reinventing video games and their players*. MIT Press.

Kabra, A., & Jadhav, B. (2023). FINTECH AND BEYOND. *The Online Journal of Distance Education and e-Learning : TOJDEL*, 11(1).

Kabudi, T., Pappas, I., & Olsen, D. H. (2021). AI-enabled adaptive learning systems: A systematic mapping of the literature. *Computers and Education: Artificial Intelligence*, 2, 100017. 10.1016/j.caeai.2021.100017

Kaivo-oja, J., Kuusi, O., Knudsen, M. S., & Lauraéus, I. T. (2020). Digital twin: Current shifts and their future implications in the conditions of technological disruption. *International Journal of Web Engineering and Technology*, 15(2), 170–188. 10.1504/IJWET.2020.109730

Kale, U., & Goh, D. (2014). Teaching style, ICT experience and teachers' attitudes toward teaching with web 2.0. *Education and Information Technologies*, 19(1), 41–60. 10.1007/s10639-012-9210-3

Kalimullina, O., Tarman, B., & Stepanova, I. (2021). Education in the context of digitalization and culture. *Journal of Ethnic and Cultural Studies*, 8(1), 226–238. 10.29333/ejecs/629

Kamiran, F., & Calders, T. (2012). Data preprocessing techniques for classification without discrimination. *Knowledge and Information Systems*, 33(1), 1–33. 10.1007/s10115-011-0463-8

Kan, M. (2023). *ChatGPT may be the fastest growing app of all time, beating TikTok*. PCMagazine. https://www.pcmag.com/news/chatgpt-may-be-the-fastest-growing-app-of-all-time-beating-tiktok

Kaplan, A. D., Cruit, J., Endsley, M., Beers, S. M., Sawyer, B. D., & Hancock, P. A. (2021). The Effects of Virtual Reality, Augmented Reality, and Mixed Reality as Training Enhancement Methods: A Meta-Analysis. *Human Factors*, 63(4), 706–726. 10.1177/0018720820904229320919 37

Kaplan, J. (2016). *Artificial intelligence: What everyone needs to know*. Oxford University Press. 10.1093/wentk/9780190602383.001.0001

Kaplan, J. (2016). *People are useless: Work and wealth in the age of artificial intelligence*. Luiss University.

Karabacak, M., & Margetis, K. (2023). Embracing large language models for medical applications: Opportunities and challenges. *Cureus*, 15(5). 10.7759/cureus.3930537378099

Kato, B. (2024). 'Mother of all breaches' data leak reveals 26 billion account records stolen from Twitter, LinkedIn, more. https://nypost.com/2024/01/23/lifestyle/extremely-dangerous-leak-reveals-26-billion-account-records-stolen-from-twitter-linkedin-more-mother-of-all-breaches/

Kauffman, R. J., Ma, D., & Yu, M. (2018). A metrics suite of cloud computing adoption readiness. *Electronic Markets*, 28(1), 11–37. 10.1007/s12525-015-0213-y

Kelley, P. G., Cornejo, C., Hayes, L., Jin, E. S., Sedley, A., Thomas, K., & Woodruff, A. (2023). There will be less privacy, of course": How and why people in 10 countries expect {AI} will affect privacy in the future. In *Nineteenth Symposium on Usable Privacy and Security (SOUPS 2023)* (pp. 579-603). IEEE.

Kennedy, G. E., Judd, T., Churchward, A., & Krause, K. (2008). First-year students' experiences with technology: Are they really digital natives? *Australasian Journal of Educational Technology*, 24(1), 108–122. 10.14742/ajet.1233

Keynes, J. M. (2009). *Financial possibilities for our grandchildren*. Milan: Adelphi.

Khalifa, N. E. M., & Salem, A. B. M. (2021). Blockchain Technology in Education: A Systematic Review. *IEEE Access : Practical Innovations, Open Solutions*, 9, 19134–19145.

Khan, M. A. (2020). Technological disruptions in restaurant services: Impact of innovations and delivery services. *Journal of Hospitality & Tourism Research (Washington, D.C.)*, 44(5), 715–732. 10.1177/1096348020908636

Khan, M. A., & Mehmood, R. (2021). Blockchain for education: Current status, challenges, and future directions. *IEEE Access : Practical Innovations, Open Solutions*, 9, 5586–5605.

Khan, M., & Khan, M. A. (2009). How technological innovations extend services outreach to customers: The changing shape of hospitality services taxonomy. *International Journal of Contemporary Hospitality Management*, 21(5), 509–522. 10.1108/09596110910967773

Khan, S., Ramsey, P., & Khan, M. (2023). Embracing educational transformation: Exploring personalized, collaborative and contextualized education through dilemma theory. *Innovations in Education and Teaching International*, •••, 1–14. 10.1080/14703297.2023.2283614

Kim, E., Libaque-Saenz, C., & Park, M. (2019). Understanding shopping routes of offline purchasers: Selection of search-channels (online vs. offline) and search-platforms (mobile vs. PC) based on product types. *Service Business*, 13(2), 305–338. 10.1007/s11628-018-0384-7

Kim, J., Shin, S., Bae, K., Oh, S., Park, E., & del Pobil, A. P. (2020). Can AI be a content generator? Effects of content generators and information delivery methods on the psychology of content consumers. *Telematics and Informatics*, 55, 101452. 10.1016/j.tele.2020.101452

Kim, Y. J., & Pavlov, O. (2019). Game-based structural debriefing: How can teachers design game-based curricula for systems thinking? *Information and Learning Science*, 120(9/10), 567–588. 10.1108/ILS-05-2019-0039

King, G., & Krzywinska, T. (Eds.). (2002). *Screenplay: Cinema/videogames/interfaces*. Wallflower Press.

King, N. J., & Forder, J. (2016). Data analytics and consumer profiling: Finding appropriate privacy principles for discovered data. *Computer Law & Security Report*, 32(5), 696–714. 10.1016/j.clsr.2016.05.002

Kiran, N. R., Sharma, S., & Chandra, P. (2020). Blockchain in Education: Use Cases, Implications, and Challenges. In*Proceedings of the 2020 International Conference on Emerging Trends in Information Technology and Engineering (ICETITE 2020)* (pp. 27-32). IEEE.

Kirkwood, A. (2011). Transformational technologies: Exploring myths and realities. *International Journal of Computer-Supported Collaborative Learning*, 6(3), 329–347.

Kirschner, P. A., Sweller, J., Kirschner, F., & Zambrano, J. R. (2018). From Cognitive Load Theory to Collaborative Cognitive Load Theory. *International Journal of Computer-Supported Collaborative Learning*, 13(2), 213–233. 10.1007/s11412-018-9277-y30996713

Kjeldgaard-Christiansen, J. (2024). What is creepiness, and what makes ChatGPT creepy? *Leviathan: Interdisciplinary Journal in English*, 10(10), 1–15. 10.7146/lev102024144284

Klausner, D., & Antia, S. (2021). *Reshaping Services: The Investment Implications of Technological Disruption*. PGIM Megatrends-October.

Kleinberg, J., Lakkaraju, H., Leskovec, J., Ludwig, J., & Mullainathan, S. (2018). Human decisions and machine predictions. *The Quarterly Journal of Economics*, 133(1), 237–293. 10.1093/qje/qjx03229755141

Klein, G. (2008). Naturalistic decision making. *Human Factors*, 50(3), 456–460. 10.1518/001872008X28838518689053

Kluger, A. N., & DeNisi, A. (1996). The effects of feedback interventions on performance: A historical review, a meta-analysis, and a preliminary feedback intervention theory. *Psychological Bulletin*, 119(2), 254–284. 10.1037/0033-2909.119.2.254

Knowlton, D. S., & Simms, J. (2010). Computer-based instruction and generative strategies: Conceptual framework & illustrative example. *Computers in Human Behavior*, 26(5), 996–1003. 10.1016/j.chb.2010.02.013

Koh, P. W., & Liang, P. (2017). Understanding black-box predictions via influence functions. In *Proceedings of the International Conference on Machine Learning* (pp. 1885-1894).

Kolb, D. A. (2014). *Experiential learning: Experience as the source of learning and development*. FT Press.

Kononowicz, A. A., Woodham, L. A., Edelbring, S., Stathakarou, N., Davies, D., Saxena, N., Tudor Car, L., Carlstedt-Duke, J., Car, J., & Zary, N. (2019). Virtual patient simulations in health professions education: Systematic review and meta-analysis by the digital health education collaboration. *Journal of Medical Internet Research*, 21(7), e14676. 10.2196/1467631267981

Kormos, E. M. (2018). The unseen digital divide: Urban, suburban, and rural teacher use and perceptions of web-based classroom technologies. *Computers in the Schools*, 35(1), 19–31. 10.1080/07380569.2018.1429168

Kostka, G., Steinacker, L., & Meckel, M. (2023). Under big brother's watchful eye: Cross-country attitudes toward facial recognition technology. *Government Information Quarterly*, 40(1), 101761. https://www.sciencedirect.com/science/article/pii/S0740624X22000971. 10.1016/j.giq.2022.101761

Kozma, R. (1991). Learning with media. *Review of Educational Research*, 61(2), 179–211. 10.3102/00346543061002179

Krathwohl, D. R. (2002). A revision of Bloom's taxonomy: An overview. *Theory into Practice*, 41(4), 212–218. 10.1207/s15430421tip4104_2

Kuhn, D., Cheney, R., & Weinstock, M. (2000). The development of epistemological understanding. *Cognitive Development*, 15(3), 309–328. 10.1016/S0885-2014(00)00030-7

Kuhn, T. (1962). *The structure of scientific revolutions*. University of Chicago.

Kulik, C., & Kulik, J. (1991). Effectiveness of Computer-based instruction: An updated analysis. *Computers in Human Behavior*, 7(1-2), 75–94. 10.1016/0747-5632(91)90030-5

Kulik, J. A., & Fletcher, J. D. (2016). Effectiveness of intelligent tutoring systems: A meta-analytic review. *Review of Educational Research*, 86(1), 42–78. https://psycnet.apa.org/doi/10.3102/0034654315581420. 10.3102/0034654315581420

Kumar, A. (2011). Towards Realist Constructivism: Implications for Teaching & Training. *Indian Journal of Industrial Relations*, 46(3), 523–535.

Kumaran, D., Summerfield, J. J., Hassabis, D., & Maguire, E. A. (2009). Tracking the emergence of conceptual knowledge during human decision making. *Neuron*, 63(6), 889–901. 10.1016/j.neuron.2009.07.03019778516

Kurelovic, E. (2016). Advantages and limitations of usage of open educational resources in small countries. *International Journal of Research in Education and Science*, 2(1), 136–142. 10.21890/ijres.92299

Kurni, M., Mohammed, M. S., & Srinivasa, K. G. (2023). AI-assisted remote proctored examinations. In *A Beginner's Guide to Introduce Artificial Intelligence in Teaching and Learning* (pp. 199–211). Springer. 10.1007/978-3-031-32653-0_11

Kurzweil, R. (1990). *The age of intelligent machines*. MIT Press.

Laferrière, T., Hamel, C., Allaire, S., Turcotte, S., Breuleux, A., Beaudoin, J., & Gaudreault Perron, J. (2011). L'école éloignée en réseau, un modèle. Rapport-synthèse. CEFRIO. 10.1111/j.1756-8765.2011.01109.x

Lameras, P., Paraskakis, I., & Konstantinidis, S. (2022). A rudimentary progression model for artificial intelligence in education competencies and skills. *Lecture Notes in Networks and Systems, 411 LNNS*, 927–936. 10.1007/978-3-030-96296-8_84

Langreo, L. (2023, July 28). *What educators think about using AI in schools*. Education Week. https://www.edweek.org/technology/what-educators-think-about-using-ai-in-schools/2023/04

Laricchia, F. (2024, February 21). Smart speakers: Statistics & facts. *Statista*. https://www.statista.com/topics/4748/smart-speakers/#topicOverview

Larrey, P. (2017). Would super-human machine intelligence really be super human? In Dodig-Crnkovic, G., & Giovagnoi, R. (Eds.), *Representation and Reality in Humans, Other Living Organisms and Intelligent Machines* (pp. 365–378). Springer. 10.1007/978-3-319-43784-2_19

Larsen, T. M., Endo, B. H., Yee, A. T., Do, T., & Lo, S. M. (2022). Probing internal assumptions of the revised Bloom's taxonomy. *CBE Life Sciences Education*, 21(4), ar66. 10.1187/cbe.20-08-017036112622

Latour, B. (2007). *Reassembling the social: An introduction to actor-network-theory*. Oup Oxford.

Lecce, A., & Tore, D. (2020). Videogames, Serious game, Exergames come strumenti utili alla didattica. *Nuova Secondaria*.

Leech, G., Garfinkel, S., Yagudin, M., Briand, A., Zhuravlev, A., & Research, A. (2024). Ten hard problems in artificial intelligence we must get right. https://arxiv.org/abs/2402.04464v1

Lee, J.-H., Steer, L., Jimenez, E., King, E. M., & Erikson, E. (2020). Designing the education workforce. *Social Science Research Network*. https://doi.org/10.2139/SSRN.3588221

Lee, S. M., & Lee, D. (2019). "Untact": A new customer service strategy in the digital age. *Service Business*. Advance online publication.

Lee, S., Youn, J., Kim, H., Kim, M., & Yoon, S. H. (2023). CXR-LLAVA: A multimodal large language model for interpreting chest X-ray images. https://arxiv.org/abs/2310.18341v3

Lee, Y. C., Lee, J. D., & Boyle, L. N. (2007). Visual attention in driving: The effects of cognitive load and visual disruption. *Human Factors*, 49(4), 721–733. 10.1518/001872007X215791 17702223

Leswing, K. (2023, June 9). *Apple Vision Pro: Impressive specs, new way of interacting could help it break the VR curse*. CNBC.

Levant, Y., Coulmont, M., & Sandu, R. (2016). Business simulation as an active learning activity for developing soft skills. *Accounting Education*, 25(4), 368–395. Advance online publication. 10.1080/09639284.2016.1191272

Lévi-Strauss, C. (2010). *Lo sguardo da lontano* (Vol. 715). Il Saggiatore.

Levy, R. (2024). The prefrontal cortex: From monkey to man. *Brain*, 147(3), 794–815. 10.1093/brain/awad389 37972282

Lewandowski, K. E., Barrantes-Vidal, N., Nelson-Gray, R., Clacy, C., Kepley, H. O., & Kwapil, T. R. (2006). Anxiety and depression symptoms in psychometrically identified schizotypy. *Schizophrenia Research*, 8(2-3), 225–235. 10.1016/j.schres.2005.11.024 16448805

Lewin, K. (1948). *Resolving social conflicts*. Harper.

Li, K. C., & Wong, B. Y. Y. (2018). Revisiting the definitions and implementation of flexible learning. *Innovations in open and flexible education*, 3–13.

Liao, H., Chen, C., & Sun, X. (2020). Application of blockchain in education: A systematic review. *Sustainability*, 12(11), 4418.

Li, C., & Xing, W. (2021). Natural language generation using deep learning to support MOOC learners. *International Journal of Artificial Intelligence in Education*, 31(2), 186–214. 10.1007/s40593-020-00235-x

Lieu, T. (2022, September 29). Op-ed: Facial recognition technology victimizes people of color. It must be regulated. *Los Angeles Times*. https://www.latimes.com/opinion/story/2022-09-29/facial-recognition-technology

Li, J., Xiao, W., & Zhang, C. (2023). Data security crisis in universities: Identification of key factors affecting data breach incidents. *Humanities & Social Sciences Communications*, 10(1), 1–18. 10.1057/s41599-023-01757-0 37273415

Linehan, M. (2001). *Il trattamento cognitivo-comportamentale del disturbo borderline: il modello dialettico*. Milano: Cortina.

Linehan, M. M., & Dimeff, L. (2001). Terapia dialettica comportamentale in breve. *Lo psicologo californiano*, 34, 10-13.

Linehan, M. (1993). *Cognitive behavioural therapy for borderline personality disorder*. Guilford Press.

LinkedIn. (2023). *What are the emerging trends and opportunities for location intelligence in social media analytics?* https://www.linkedin.com/advice/1/what-emerging-trends-opportunities-location

Lin, Y., Pekkarinen, S., & Ma, S. (2015). Service-dominant logic for managing the interface: A case study. *International Journal of Logistics Management*, 26(1), 195–214. 10.1108/IJLM-08-2013-0095

Li, P., & Wang, B. (2023). Artificial intelligence in music education. *International Journal of Human-Computer Interaction*, 1–10. 10.1080/10447318.2023.2209984

Lipton, Z. C. (2018). The mythos of model interpretability: In machine learning, the concept of interpretability is both important and slippery. *ACM Queue; Tomorrow's Computing Today*, 16(3), 31–57. 10.1145/3236386.3241340

Li, T. W., Hsu, S., Fowler, M., Zhang, Z., Zilles, C., & Karahalios, K. (2023). Am I wrong, or is the autograder wrong? Effects of AI grading mistakes on learning. In *Proceedings of the 2023 ACM Conference on International Computing Education Research* - Volume 1 (pp. 159–176). Association for Computing Machinery. 10.1145/3568813.3600124

Littler, C. R. (1978). Understanding Taylorism. *The British Journal of Sociology*, 19(2), 185–202. 10.2307/589888

Liu, X., & Chen, X. (2018). Disruptive technology enhanced learning: The use and misuse of digital technologies in higher education. *Innovations in Education and Teaching International*, 55(6), 605–613. 10.1080/14703297.2018.1405550

Livesley, W. J., Schroeder, M. L., & Jackson, D. N. (1990). Dependent personality disorder and attachment problems. *Journal of Personality Disorders*, 3, 292–306. 10.1521/pedi.1989.3.4.292

Locatelli, R. (2019). *Reframing education as a public and common good: Enhancing democratic governance*. Palgrave Macmillan. 10.1007/978-3-030-24801-7

Locatelli, R. (2022). La prospettiva dell'educazione come bene comune quale quadro di riferimento per i Patti educativi di comunità. *Civitas educationis. Education. Política y Cultura*, 10(2). Advance online publication. 10.30444/CE.XX.2022

Lohmann, G., Pratt, M. A., Benckendorff, P., Strickland, P., Reynolds, P., & Whitelaw, P. A. (2019). Online business simulations: Authentic teamwork, learning outcomes, and satisfaction. *Higher Education*, 77(3), 455–472. 10.1007/s10734-018-0282-x

Longo, G. O. (2003). *Il Simbionte. Prove di umanità future*. Meltemi.

Long, P., & Siemens, G. (2011). Penetrating the fog: Analytics in learning and education. *EDUCAUSE Review*, 46(5), 31–40.

Lorenz, K. (1967). *L'anello di re Salomone*. Milano: Adelphi.

Lourdusamy, R., Magendiran, P., & Fonceca, C. M. (2022). Analysis of cognitive levels of questions with Bloom's taxonomy: A case study. *International Journal of Software Innovation*, 10(1), 1–22. 10.4018/IJSI.297922

Lucangeli, D. (2019). *Cinque lezioni leggere sull'emozione di apprendere*. Erickson.

Luckin, R., Holmes, W., Griffiths, M., & Forcier, L. B. (2016). *Intelligence unleashed: An argument for AI in education*. UCL. https://discovery.ucl.ac.uk/1475756/

Lungarella, M., Metta, G., Pfeifer, R., & Sandini, G. (2003). Developmental robotics: A survey. *Connection Science*, 15(4), 151–190. 10.1080/09540090310001655110

Lusch, R. F., & Nambisan, S. (2015). Service Innovation: A service-dominant logic perspective. *Management Information Systems Quarterly*, 39(1), 155–175. 10.25300/MISQ/2015/39.1.07

Lyon, D. (2014). Surveillance, Snowden, and Big Data: Capacities, consequences, critique. *Big Data & Society*, 1(2). 10.1177/2053951714541861

MacVaugh, J., & Schiavone, F. (2010). Limits to the diffusion of innovation: A literature review and integrative model. *European Journal of Innovation Management*, 13(2), 197–221. 10.1108/14601061011040258

Magana, A. J. S. (2019). Disruptive classroom technologies. In *The SAGE Encyclopedia of Educational Technology, 2*(1), 391-395. 10.1093/acrefore/9780190264093.013.423

Magid, L. (2018). *The good and bad of location sharing*. Connect Safely. https://www.connectsafely.org/the-good-and-bad-of-location-sharing/

Mahler, M. S., Pine, F., & Bergman, A. (1978). *La nascita del bambino*. Boringhieri.

Makransky, G., & Lilleholt, L. (2018). A structural equation modeling investigation of the emotional value of immersive virtual reality in education. *Educational Technology Research and Development*, 66(5), 1141–1164. 10.1007/s11423-018-9581-2

Malavasi, P. (2017). Introduzione. In Iavarone, M. L., Malavasi, P., Orefici, P., & Pinto Minerva, F. (Eds.), *Pedagogia dell'ambiente 2017: Tra sviluppo umano e responsabilità sociale* (pp. 9–14). Pensa MultiMedia.

Malavasi, P. (2022). *PNRR and training. The path of ecological transition*. Life and Thought.

Malkin, N., Deatrick, J., Tong, A., Wijeskera, P., Egelman, S., & Wagner, D. (2019). Privacy attitudes of smart speaker users. *Proceedings on Privacy Enhancing Technologies. Privacy Enhancing Technologies Symposium*, 2019(4), 250–271. 10.2478/popets-2019-0068

Malliet, S., & De Meyer, G. (2005). *The history of the video game. Handbook of Computer Game Studies*. The MIT Press.

Malone, T. W., & Lepper, M. R. (2021). Making learning fun: A taxonomy of intrinsic motivations for learning. In *Aptitude, Learning, and Instruction* (pp. 223-254). Routledge.

Ma, M., & Xu, Z. (2020). Blockchain in education: A review and a case study. *Journal of Educational Technology Development and Exchange*, 13(2), 1–19.

Mancuso Hobey, E. (2020). Interview: Finch Capital Co-Founder/Partner Radboud Vlaar discusses disruptive and enabling financial technology post-COVID-19. *EKMH Innovators Interview Series*. https://ekmhinnovators.com/interview-finch-capital-co-founder-partner-radboud-vlaar-discusses-disruptive-and-enabling-financial-technology-post-covid-19/

Mangione, G. R. J. (2023). STEM in small schools. Organizational and teaching practices. *Journal of Education Technologies and Social Studies*, 15(3). Advance online publication. 10.17471/xxxx-xxxx

Mangione, G. R. J., & Cannella, G. (2020). Small school, smart schools: Distance education in remoteness conditions. *Technology. Knowledge and Learning*, 26(4), 845–865. 10.1007/s10758-020-09480-4

Mangione, G. R. J., & Cannella, G. (2021). La scuola di prossimità. Alleanze territoriali per la realizzazione di nuove forme educative nella piccola scuola. *Archivio di Studi Urbani e Regionali*, 132(Suppl.), 86–109. 10.3280/ASUR2021-SU132006

Mangione, G. R. J., Parigi, L., & Tonucci, F. (2022). Dove sta di casa la scuola? *Research on Education and Media*, 14(1), 9–24. 10.2478/rem-2022-0003

Mangione, G. R. J., Pieri, M., & De Santis, F. (2024). (in press). Revitalizing education in rural and small schools: The role of AI in teachers' professional development. *Italian Journal of Educational Technology*, 31(3).

Mangione, G. R., Fante, C., Dalla Mutta, E., & Benigno, V. (2023). Exploring educational practices for non-standard didactic situations in small schools. In Mangione, P. (Ed.), *Handbook of research on establishing digital competencies in the pursuit of online learning* (pp. 50–72). IGI Global. 10.4018/978-1-6684-7010-7.ch004

Mangione, G. R., Garzia, M., & Pettenati, M. C. (2016). Neoassunti nelle piccole scuole. Sviluppo di competenza e professionalità didattica. *Formazione & Insegnamento*, 14(3), 287–306. 10.32029/11218.14.03.20

Manovich, L. (2001). *T*.

Mansour, E. (2012). The role of social networking sites (SNSs) in the January 5th revolution in Egypt. *Library Review*, 61(2), 128–159. 10.1108/00242531211220753

Manyika, J., Chui, M., Bughin, J., Dobbs, R., Bisson, P., & Marrs, A. (2013). *Disruptive technologies: Advances that will transform life, business, and the global economy, 180, 17-21*. McKinsey Global Institute.

Maragliano, R. (2005). Technology and knowledge. *Italian Journal of Educational Technology*, 13(1), 21–21. https://www.itd.cnr.it/tdmagazine/PDF34/maragliano.pdf

Marchesini, R. (2014). Hybridizations and evolutionary processes. In Barone, P., Ferrante, A., & Sartori, D. (Eds.), *Education and post-humanism: Pedagogical paths in the era of technology* (pp. 69–86). Raffaello Cortina.

Mariani, A. (2021). Introduction. The educational relationship between human sciences and advanced democratic society. In Mariani, A. (Ed.), *The educational relationship: Contemporary perspectives* (pp. 13–26). Carocci.

Maritain, J. (1963). *The person and the common good*. Morcelliana.

Marr, B. (2016). 21 scary things big data knows about you. *Forbes*. https://www.forbes.com/sites/bernardmarr/2016/03/08/21-scary-things-big-data-knows-about-you/#7db6abaf6e7d

Martin, N. (2019). The major concerns around facial recognition technology. *Forbes*. https://www.forbes.com/sites/nicolemartin1/2019/09/25/the-major-concerns-around-facial-recognition-technology/#2062df884fe3

Martin, F., Klein, J. D., & Sullivan, H. (2007). The impact of instructional elements in computer-based instruction. *British Journal of Educational Technology*, 38(4), 623–636. 10.1111/j.1467-8535.2006.00670.x

Martín-Gutiérrez, J., Mora, C. E., Añorbe-Díaz, B., & González-Marrero, A. (2017). Virtual technologies trends in education. *Eurasia Journal of Mathematics, Science and Technology Education*, 13(2), 469–486. 10.12973/eurasia.2017.00626a

Martini, E. R., & Sequi, R. (1999). *Il lavoro nella comunità*. Carocci.

Marx, K., & Engels, F. (1970). *Selected Works*. International.

Marzuki, W., Widiati, U., Rusdin, D., Darwin, , & Indrawati, I. (2023). The impact of AI writing tools on the content and organization of students' writing: EFL teachers' perspective. *Cogent Education*, 10(2), 2236469. 10.1080/2331186X.2023.2236469

Maslow, A. H. (1955). Deficiency motivation and growth motivation. In Jones, M. R. (Ed.), *Nebraska symposium on motivation* (pp. 1–39). Univ. Nebraska Press.

Mason, M. (2008). Complexity theory and the philosophy of education. *Educational Philosophy and Theory*, 40(1), 4–18. 10.1111/j.1469-5812.2007.00412.x

Mason, M. (2024). Complexity theory and the enhancement of learning in higher education: The case of the University of Cape Town. *Educational Philosophy and Theory*, 56(5), 469–478. 10.1080/00131857.2022.2140042

Masterson, J. F. (1972). *Treatment of the Borderline Adolescent*. Wiley.

Maton, K. I., & Salem, D. (1995). Organizational characteristics of empowerment-community settings: A multiple case study approach. *American Journal of Community Psychology*, 23(5), 631–656. 10.1007/BF025069858851343

Mattes, J. (2010). *Innovation in multinational companies: organisational, international and regional dilemmas*. Peter Lang.

Maturana, H. R., & Varela, F. J. (1980). *Autopoiesis and cognition: The realization of the living.* D. Reidel Publishing Company. (Original work published 1972)

Matwyshyn, A. M. (2019). The internet of bodies. *William and Mary Law Review*, 61(1), 77–167. https://scholarship.law.wm.edu/cgi/viewcontent.cgi?article=3827&context=wmlr

Mayer-Schönberger, V., & Cukier, K. N. (2013). *Big data: A revolution that will transform how we live, work, and think.* Garzanti.

McClure, P. K. (2018). "You're fired," says the robot: The rise of automation in the workplace, technophobes, and fears of unemployment. *Social Science Computer Review*, 36(2), 139–156. 10.1177/0894439317698637

McDermott, R. (2005). An Emersonian approach to higher education. *Revision*, 28(2), 6–16. 10.3200/REVN.28.2.6-17

McGinnis, J. O., & Pearce, R. G. (2019). The great disruption: How machine intelligence will transform the role of lawyers in the delivery of legal services. *Actual Probs.Econ.*, L, 1230.

McKeachie, W. J. (2002). *Teaching tips: Strategies, research, and theory for college and university teachers* (9th ed.). D.C. Heath and Co.

McLaren, S. (2018). *How Hilton, Google, and more have dramatically reduced their time to hire.*

McLaren, T., & Ellis, R. (2020). Blockchain and Education: A Critical Appraisal. *InProceedings of the 2020 10th International Conference on Information and Communication Technology and Accessibility (ICTA 2020)* (pp. 1-8). IEEE.

McLean, G., & Osei-Frimpong, K. (2019). Hey Alexa…examine the variables influencing the use of artificial intelligent in-home voice assistants. *Computers in Human Behavior*, 99, 28–37. 10.1016/j.chb.2019.05.009

McLuhan, M., & Capriolo, E. (1986). *Gli strumenti del comunicare.* Garzanti.

McWhorter, R. R., & Bennett, E. E. (2021). Creepy technologies and the privacy issues of invasive technologies. In International Management Association (Ed.), *Research Anthology on Privatizing and Security Data* (pp. 1726-1745). IGI Global. https://www.igi-global.com/gateway/chapter/280253

McWhorter, R. R. (2023). Virtual human resource development: Definitions, challenges, and opportunities.*Human Resource Development Review*, 22(4), 582–601. 10.1177/15344843231188820

McWhorter, R. R., Johnson, G., Delello, J., Young, M., & Carpenter, R. E. (in-press). We have talent: Mock group interviewing improves employer perceived competence on hireability. *Journal of Education for Business.* 10.1080/08832323.2024.2366782

Mead, G. H. (1934). *Mind, Self, and Society.* University of Chicago Press.

Means, B., Toyama, Y., Murphy, R., Bakia, M., & Jones, K. (2009). Evaluation of Evidence-Based Practices in Online Learning. *Structure (London, England)*, 15(20), 94. http://newrepo.alt.ac.uk/629/

Mechlova, E., & Malcik, M. (2012, November). ICT in changes of learning theories. In *2012 IEEE 10th international conference on emerging eLearning technologies and applications (ICETA)* (pp. 253–262). IEEE. 10.1109/ICETA.2012.6418326

Megahed, F. M., Chen, Y.-J., Ferris, J. A., Knoth, S., & Jones-Farmer, L. A. (2023). How generative AI models such as ChatGPT can be (mis)used in SPC practice, education, and research? An exploratory study. *Quality Engineering*, 36(2), 287–315. 10.1080/08982112.2023.2206479

Megginson, D., & Clutterbuck, D. (1995). *Mentoring in action.* Kogan Page.

Mehrabian, A., & Russell, J. A. (1974). *An approach to environmental psychology.* MIT Press.

Meissner, W. W. (1988). *Treatment of Patients in the Borderline Spectrum*. Aronson.

Melstveit, R., Fellows, S., Staring, F., & Vicentini, L. (2020). *Digital tools and practices: How digital technology in compulsory education can help promote inclusion*. Report EAC Directorate-General for Education, Youth, Sport and Culture.

Menezes, D. (2024, March 3). *Student fights AI cheating allegations for using Grammarly*. NewsNation. https://www.newsnationnow.com/business/tech/ai/student-fights-academic-probation-ai-tool/

Merchant, Z., Goetz, E. T., Cifuentes, L., Keeney-Kennicutt, W., & Davis, T. J. (2014). Effectiveness of virtual reality-based instruction on students' learning outcomes in K-12 and higher education: A meta-analysis. *Computers & Education*, 70, 29–40. 10.1016/j.compedu.2013.07.033

Mergel, B. (1998). *Instructional design and learning theory* (Unpublished paper, USAK). https://www.usask.ca/education/coursework/802papers/mergel/brenda.htm

Merleau-Ponty, M. (2003). *Fenomelogia della percezione*. Bompiani.

Meyer, B., Ajchenbrenner, M., & Bowles, D. P. (2005). Sensory sensitivity, attachment experiences, and rejection responses among adults with borderline and avoidant features. *Journal of Personality Disorders*, 19(6), 641–658. 10.1521/pedi.2005.19.6.64116553560

Midjourney. (2023). *Home*. Midjourney. https://www.midjourney.com/home

Mikhalchuk, O. (2020, January 14). Using AI and biometrics to enhance exam proctoring. *Biometric Update*. https://www.biometricupdate.com/202001/using-ai-and-biometrics-to-enhance-exam-proctoring

Mikolov, T., Chen, K., Corrado, G., & Dean, J. (2013). Efficient estimation of word representations in vector space. *1st International Conference on Learning Representations, ICLR 2013 - Workshop Track Proceedings*. https://arxiv.org/abs/1301.3781v3

Mikropoulos, T. A., & Natsis, A. (2011). Educational virtual environments: A ten-year review of empirical research (1999-2009). *Computers & Education*, 56(3), 769–780. 10.1016/j.compedu.2010.10.020

Miller, L. C. (2012). Situating the rural teacher labor market in the broader context: A descriptive analysis of the market dynamics in New York State. *Journal of Research in Rural Education*, 27, 1.

Mironov, D. (2024). *From Posts to Patterns: Mastering Social Media Data Mining*. https://improvado.io/blog/what-is-social-media-data-mining

Mitchell, M., Wu, S., Zaldivar, A., Barnes, P., Vasserman, L., Hutchinson, B., & Gebru, T. (2019). Model cards for model reporting. In *Proceedings of the Conference on Fairness, Accountability, and Transparency* (pp. 220-229). ACM. 10.1145/3287560.3287596

Mittal, A. (2024, Jan. 9). *The plagiarism problem: How generative AI models reproduce copyrighted content*. Unite.AI.

Moniz, A. B., & Krings, B. J. (2016). Robots working with humans or humans working with robots? Searching for social dimensions in new human-robot interaction in industry. *Societies (Basel, Switzerland)*, 6(3), 23. 10.3390/soc6030023

Monk, D. H. (2007). Recruiting and retaining high-quality teachers in rural areas. *The Future of Children*, 17(1), 155–174. 10.1353/foc.2007.000917407927

Montagnani, M. L. (2020). Artificial intelligence and governance of the 'new' large shareholder firm: Potential and endoconsiliar issues. *Journal of Corporations*, 29(3), 234–251.

Montagnani, M. L., & Passador, M. L. (2021). The board of directors in the age of artificial intelligence: Between corporate reporting, composition, and accountability. *Journal of Corporations*, 30(2), 312–329.

Montessori, M. (1970). *L'autoeducazione*. Garzanti.

Mookerjee, J., & Rao, O. (2021). A review of the impact of disruptive innovations on markets and business performance of players. *International Journal of Grid and Distributed Computing*, 14(1), 605–630.

Moorhouse, B. L., Yeo, M. A., & Wan, Y. (2023). Generative AI tools and assessment: Guidelines of the world's top-ranking universities. *Computers and Education Open*, 5, 100151. 10.1016/j.caeo.2023.100151

Morey, L. C., Gunderson, J. G., Quigley, B. D., Shea, M. T., Skodol, A. E., McGlashan, T. H., Stout, R. L., & Zanarini, M. C. (2002). The representation of borderline, avoidant, obsessive-compulsive, and schizotypal personality disorders by the five-factor model. *Journal of Personality Disorders*, 16(3), 215–234. 10.1521/pedi.16.3.215.2254112136679

Morin, E. (2001). *I sette saperi necessari all'educazione del futuro*. Raffaello Cortina.

Morin, E. (2015). *Insegnare a vivere: Manifesto per cambiare l'educazione*. Raffaello Cortina.

Morrison, I., & Ziemke, T. (2005). *Empathy with computer game characters: A cognitive neuroscience perspective*. In Proceedings of the Joint Symposium on Virtual Social Agents, Hatfield, UK. http://www.cet.sunderland.ac.uk/~cs0lha/Empathic_Interaction/Morrison.Ziemke.pdf

Morrison, K. (2008). Educational philosophy and the challenge of complexity theory. *Educational Philosophy and Theory*, 40(1), 19–34. 10.1111/j.1469-5812.2007.00394.x

Mosco, G. D. (2019). Roboboard. Artificial intelligence in boards of directors. *Legal Analysis of Economics*, 8(1), 45–67.

Moslein, P. (2017). Robots in the boardroom: Artificial intelligence and corporate law. *Columbia Business Law Review*, 3, 435–474.

Mosqueira-Rey, E., Hernández-Pereira, E., Alonso-Ríos, D., Bobes-Bascarán, J., & Fernández-Leal, Á. (2023). Human-in-the-loop machine learning: A state of the art. *Artificial Intelligence Review*, 56(4), 3005–3054. 10.1007/s10462-022-10246-w

Motallebinejad, A., Hatami, J., Fardanesh, H., & Moazami, S. (2020). Toward More Effective Legal Education for Adolescents: Systematic or Constructivist Instructional Design Models? *Journal of Constructivist Psychology*, 33(4), 406–421. 10.1080/10720537.2019.1641773

Mounier, E. (1999). *Il personalismo*. AVE.

Mousavinasab, E., Zarifsanaiey, N., & Niakan, S. R, Kalhori, Rakhshan, M., Keikha, L., & Saeedi, M.G. (2021). Intelligent tutoring systems: A systematic review of characteristics, applications, and evaluation methods. *Interactive Learning Environments*, 29(1), 142–163. 10.1080/10494820.2018.1558257

Mou, Y., & Meng, X. (2024). Alexa, it is creeping over me–Exploring the impact of privacy concerns on consumer resistance to intelligent voice assistants. *Asia Pacific Journal of Marketing and Logistics*, 36(2), 261–292. https://journals.scholarsportal.info/details/13555855/v36i0002/261_aiicomcrtiva.xml. 10.1108/APJML-10-2022-0869

Muijs, D. (2011). Leadership and organisational performance: From research to prescription? *International Journal of Educational Management*, 25(1), 45–60. 10.1108/09513541111100116

Muijs, D., West, M., & Ainscow, M. (2010). Why network? Theoretical perspectives on networking. *School Effectiveness and School Improvement*, 21(1), 5–26. 10.1080/09243450903569692

Mullaney, T. (2024). *Pedagogy and the AI guest speaker or what teachers should know about the Eliza Effect*. Tom Mullaney. https://tommullaney.com/2024/02/20/pedagogy-the-eliza-effect/?fbclid=IwAR0vDdDrcZ7HqaAm2ahf56hsE3To2VjWtLWvYAzt9Z44SGULcEnmqWWXdwY

Mumenin, N., Islam, M. F., Chowdhury, M. R. Z., & Yousuf, M. A. (2023, January). Diagnosis of autism spectrum disorder through eye movement tracking using deep learning. In *Proceedings of International Conference on Information and Communication Technology for Development: ICICTD 2022* (pp. 251-262). Springer Nature Singapore. 10.1007/978-981-19-7528-8_20

Mura, A. (2020). *Inclusione e collaborazione a scuola: un'occasione per insegnanti e famiglia*. Pensa MultiMedia., 10.7346/sipes-01-2020-19

Murray, J. (2004). From game-story to cyberdrama. *First Person: New Media as Story, Performance, and Game*, 1, 2–11.

Muzam, J. (2023). The challenges of modern economy on the competencies of knowledge workers. *Journal of the Knowledge Economy*, 14(2), 1635–1671. 10.1007/s13132-022-00979-y

Nagel, D. (2019). Funding Is Top Roadblock to AR & VR in Schools. *T.H.E. Journal*.

Najibi, A. (2020, October 26). Racial discrimination in face recognition technology. *Science in the News*. https://sitn.hms.harvard.edu/flash/2020/racial-discrimination-in-face-recognition-technology/

Narolita, D., & Darma, G. S. (2020). Prodia: disruption in clinical laboratory service system. *International research journal of management, IT and social sciences, 7*(1), 9-18.

Nash, J. (2024, March 7). AI surveillance in US schools becoming the safe bet. *Biometric Update*. https://www.biometricupdate.com/202403/ai-surveillance-in-us-schools-becoming-the-safe-bet

National Research Council. (1999). *How people learn: Bridging research and practice* (Donovan, M. S., Bransford, J. D., & Pellegrino, J. W., Eds.). National Academy Press.

National Restaurant Association. (2019, November 14). *Restaurant Industry 2030: Actionable insights for the future*. National Restaurant Association. https://restaurant.org/research/reports/Restaurant-Industry-2030

Naughton, J. (2022, February 19). Forget state surveillance. Our tracking devices are now doing the same job. *The Guardian*. https://www.theguardian.com/commentisfree/2022/feb/19/forget-state-surveillance-our-tracking-devices-are-now-doing-the-same-job#comment-155021808

Naveed, H., Khan, A. U., Qiu, S., Saqib, M., Anwar, S., Usman, M., Barnes, N., & Mian, A. (2023). A comprehensive overview of large language models. *arXiv preprint arXiv:2307.06435*.

Neumann, M. M. (2020). Social robots and young children's early language and literacy learning. *Early Childhood Education Journal*, 48(2), 157–170. 10.1007/s10643-019-00997-7

Neumann, O., Guirguis, K., & Steiner, R. (2023). Exploring artificial intelligence adoption in public organizations: A comparative case study. *Public Management Review*, 1–28.

Newby, T. J., Stepich, D. A., Lehman, J. D., & Russell, J. D. (2000). *Instructional Technology for Teaching and Learning*. Prentice Hall.

Newman, J. (2012). *Videogames*. Routledge. 10.4324/9780203143421

News, A. B. C. (2013, October 19). Dick Cheney feared assassination via medical device hacking: 'I Was Aware of the Danger'. *ABC News*. https://abcnews.go.com/US/vice-president-dick-cheney-feared-pacemaker-hacking/story?id=20621434

Ng, D. T. K., Leung, J. K. L., Su, J., Ng, R. C. W., & Chu, S. K. W. (2023). Teachers' AI digital competencies and twenty-first century skills in the post-pandemic world. *Educational Technology Research and Development*, 71(1), 137–161. 10.1007/s11423-023-10203-636844361

Nichols, T. (2018). *La conoscenza e i suoi nemici: L'era dell'incompetenza e i rischi per la democrazia*. Luiss University.

Nicotra, M. (2023). *Artificial intelligence: What it is, how it works, and applications in Italy and Europe*. Agenda Digitale. https://www.agendadigitale.eu/sicurezza/privacy/intelligenza-artificiale-la-via-delleuropa-su-regole-e-investimenti/

Niglia, F. (2020, November 10). Ethics by Design (EbD), la responsabilità sociale nell'industria 4.0. *Network Digital 360*. https://www.industry4business.it/smart-manufacturing/ethics-by-design-ebd-la-responsabilita-sociale-nellindustria-4-0/

Ninaus, M., & Sailer, M. (2022). Closing the loop–The human role in artificial intelligence for education. *Frontiers in Psychology*, 13, 956798. 10.3389/fpsyg.2022.95679836092115

Nirell, L. (2014). *The mindful marketer: How to stay present and profitable in a data-driven world*. Springer. 10.1057/9781137386311

Noble, S. U. (2018). *Algorithms of oppression: How search engines reinforce racism*. New York University Press. 10.18574/nyu/9781479833641.001.0001

Nonaka, I., & Takeuchi, H. (2007). The knowledge-creating company. *Harvard Business Review*, 85(7/8), 162.

Novak, J. D. (2001). *L'apprendimento significativo*. Erickson.

Nussbaum, M. C. (2012). *Creare capacità. Liberarsi dalla dittatura del Pil*. Bologna: il Mulino.

Nussbaum, M. C. (2006). *Coltivare l'umanità. I classici, il multiculturalismo, l'educazione contemporanea*. Carocci.

Nuzzaci, A. (2021). *Educazione democratica*.

Nuzzaci, A. (Ed.). (2011). *Patrimoni culturali, educazioni, territori: verso un'idea di multiliteracy*. Pensa MultiMedia Editore s.r.l.

Nuzzo, A., & Olivieri, G. (2019). Algorithms. If you know them, you regulate them. *Legal Analysis of Economics*, 9(2), 78–91.

Nwana, H. S. (1990). Intelligent tutoring systems: An overview. *Artificial Intelligence Review*, 4(4), 251–277. https://link.springer.com/article/10.1007/BF00168958. 10.1007/BF00168958

Nye, B. D., Graesser, A. C., & Hu, X. (2014). AutoTutor and family: A review of 17 years of natural language tutoring. *International Journal of Artificial Intelligence in Education*, 24(4), 427–469. 10.1007/s40593-014-0029-5

O'Hagan, J., Saeghe, P., Gugenheimer, J., Medeiros, D., Marky, K., Khamis, M., & McGill, M. (2023). Privacy-Enhancing Technology and Everyday Augmented Reality: Understanding Bystanders' Varying Needs for Awareness and Consent. *Proceedings of the ACM on Interactive, Mobile, Wearable and Ubiquitous Technologies*, 6(4), 1–35. 10.1145/3569501

O'Neill, C. (2017). Taylorism, the European science of work, and the quantified self at work. *Science, Technology & Human Values*, 42(4), 600–621. 10.1177/0162243916677083

Obaigbena, A., Lottu, O. A., Ugwuanyi, E. D., Jacks, B. S., Sodiya, E. O., & Daraojimba, O. D. (2024). AI and human-robot interaction: A review of recent advances and challenges. *GSC Advanced Research and Reviews*, 18(2), 321–330. 10.30574/gscarr.2024.18.2.0070

Obermeyer, Z., Powers, B., Vogeli, C., & Mullainathan, S. (2019). Dissecting racial bias in an algorithm used to manage the health of populations. *Science*, 366(6464), 447–453. 10.1126/science.aax234231649194

OECD. (2010). *The High Cost of Low Educational Performance. The Long-Run Economic Impact of Improving PISA Outcomes*. OECD. https://www.oecd.org/pisa/44417824.pdf

OECD. (2016). *Skills matter: Further results from the survey of adult skills*. OECD. https://www.oecd-ilibrary.org/education/skills-matter_9789264258051-en

OECD. (2018). *PISA 2018 database*. Programme for International Student Assessment, OECD. https://www.oecd.org/pisa/data/2018database/

OECD. (2019). *Recommendation of the Council on OECD Legal Instruments Artificial Intelligence*. OECD/LEGAL/0449. https://legalinstruments.oecd.org/en/instruments/OECD-LEGAL-0449

OECD. (2023). *Equity and inclusion in education: Finding strength through diversity*. OECD Publishing. 10.1787/3667c8b0-

Open A. I. (2023). *GPT-4*. OpenAI. https://openai.com/research/gpt-4

Open A. I. (2024). *Sora*. OpenAI. https://openai.com/sora

Open A. I. (2024a). *Introducing ChatGPT*. OpenAI. https://openai.com/blog/chatgpt

Open A. I. (2024b). *Sora*. OpenAI. https://openai.com/sora

Open A. I. (2024c). *ChatGPT*. (March 11 version) [Large language model]. OpenAI. https://chat.openai.com/chat

Oregon Department of Education. (2023). *Generative artificial intelligence (AI) in K-12 classrooms*. Oregon Department of Education. https://www.oregon.gov/ode/educator-resources/teachingcontent/Documents/ODE_Generative_Artificial_Intelligence_%28AI%29_in_K-12_Classrooms_2023.pdf

Orike, S., Bakare, B. I., & Sampson, J. U. (2023). An artificial intelligence-based fingerprint biometric application for students attendance register. *Research and Reviews: Advancement in Robotics*, 6(3), 19–27. 10.5281/zenodo.8317744

Orr, K. (1998). Data quality and systems. *Communications of the ACM*, 41(2), 66–71. 10.1145/269012.269023

Osberg, D., Biesta, G., & Cilliers, P. (2008). From representation to emergence: Complexity's challenge to the epistemology of schooling. *Educational Philosophy and Theory*, 40(1), 213–227. 10.1111/j.1469-5812.2007.00407.x

Oscan, Y. (2017). *Analytics and decision support in health care operations management: History, Diagnosis, and Empirical Foundations* (3rd ed.). Jossey-Bass.

Ouyang, F., Wu, M., Zheng, L., Zhang, L., & Jiao, P. (2023). Integration of artificial intelligence performance prediction and learning analytics to improve student learning in online engineering course. *International Journal of Educational Technology in Higher Education*, 20(4), 4. 10.1186/s41239-022-00372-436683653

Page, G. A., & Hill, M. (2008). Information, communication, and educational technologies in rural Alaska. *New Directions for Adult and Continuing Education*, 117(117), 59–70. 10.1002/ace.286

Pallavicini, F., Ferrari, A., & Mantovani, F. (2018). Video games for well-being: A systematic review on the application of computer games for cognitive and emotional training in the adult population. *Frontiers in Psychology*, 9, 407892. 10.3389/fpsyg.2018.0212730464753

Panciroli, C. (2008). E-learning e learning-e Riflessioni sulla formazione. *Ricerche di Pedagogia e Didattica*, 3. Bologna.

Panciroli, C., et al. (2020). Intelligenza artificiale e educazione: nuove prospettive di ricerca. *Form@re - Open Journal per la formazione in rete, 20*(3), 1-12.

Panciroli, C. (2018). *Educare nella città*. FrancoAngeli.

Panciroli, C., & Rivoltella, P. C. (2023). Can an algorithm be fair? Intercultural biases and critical thinking in generative artificial intelligence social uses. In Pasta, S., & Zoletto, D. (Eds.), *Postdigital Intercultures. Interculture Postdigitali* (pp. 19–46). SCHOLÉ.

Papert, S. (1993). *The children's machine: Rethinking school in the age of the computer*. New York.

Park, S., Jeong, S., & Ju, B. (2018). Employee learning and development in virtual HRD: Focusing on MOOCs in the workplace. *Industrial and Commercial Training*, 50(5), 261–271. 10.1108/ICT-03-2018-0030

Pataranutaporn, P., Danry, V., Leong, J., Punpongsanon, P., Novy, D., Maes, P., & Sra, M. (2021). AI-generated characters for supporting personalized learning and well-being. *Nature Machine Intelligence*, 3(12), 1013–1022. 10.1038/s42256-021-00417-9

Päuler-Kuppinger, L., & Jucks, R. (2017). Perspectives on teaching: Conceptions of teaching and epistemological beliefs of university academics and students in different domains. *Active Learning in Higher Education*, 18(1), 63–76. 10.1177/1469787417693507

Pears, M., Henderson, J., Wharrad, H., & Konstantinidis, S. (2022, September). *The journey from co-creation to impact for digital resources in healthcare*. Presented at ALT Annual Conference 2022, Manchester, UK. https://nottingham-repository.worktribe.com/index.php/output/13179801/the-journey-from-co-creation-to-impact-for-digital-resources-in-healthcare

Pears, M., Wadhwa, K., Hanchanale, V., Jain, S., Elmamoun, M. H., Payne, S. R., Konstantinidis, S., Rochester, M., Doherty, R., & Biyani, C. S. (2024). *Surgical consultants and ChatGPT characteristics in training: A repeated-measures double-blinded study in non-technical skills for urology trainees*. Manuscript submitted for publication.

Pears, M., Henderson, J., & Konstantinidis, S. T. (2021, May 27). Repurposing case-based learning to a conversational agent for healthcare cybersecurity. *Studies in Health Technology and Informatics*, 281, 1066–1070. 10.3233/SHTI21034834042842

Pedró, F., Subosa, M., Rivas, A., & Valverde, P. (2019). *Artificial intelligence in education: Challenges and opportunities for sustainable development*. Unesco.

Pellegrini, M. (2019). Technological innovation and economic law. *Quarterly Journal of Economic Law*, 31(1), 12–29.

Pennington, N. (2020). An examination of relational maintenance and dissolution through social networking sites. *Computers in Human Behavior*, 105, 1–8. 10.1016/j.chb.2019.106196

Pereira, J. (2016). Leveraging chatbots to improve self-guided learning through conversational quizzes. In García-Peñalvo, F. J. (Ed.), *Proceedings of the Fourth International Conference on Technological Ecosystems for Enhancing Multiculturality* (pp. 911–918). Association for Computing Machinery. 10.1145/3012430.3012625

Perez-Encinas, A., & Berbegal-Mirabent, J. (2023). Who gets a job sooner? Results from a national survey of master's graduates. *Studies in Higher Education*, 48(1), 174–188. 10.1080/03075079.2022.2124242

Peters, K. (2024, April 9). Texas will use computers to grade written answers on this year's STAAR tests. *The Texas Tribune*. https://www.texastribune.org/2024/04/09/staar-artificial-intelligence-computer-grading-texas/

Peters, A. (2018). *This crazy-looking robot is the chef at a new burger joint*. Fast Company.

Petrin, M. (2019). Corporate management in the age of AI. *UCL Working Paper Series Corporate Management in the Age of AI*, No. 3/2019.

Petruccelli, I. (2017). *Psicologia architettonica e ambientale dei luoghi scolastici*. Il Mulino.

Petruzzi, M., & De Benedittis, M. (2016). WhatsApp: A telemedicine platform for facilitating remote oral medicine consultation and improving clinical examinations. *Oral Surgery, Oral Medicine, Oral Pathology and Oral Radiology*, 121(3), 248–254. 10.1016/j.oooo.2015.11.00526868466

Phinnemore, R., Reza, M., Lewis, B., Mahadevan, K., Wang, B., Annett, M., & Wigdor, D. (2023, April). Creepy Assistant: Development and Validation of a Scale to Measure the Perceived Creepiness of Voice Assistants. In *Proceedings of the 2023 CHI Conference on Human Factors in Computing Systems* (pp. 1-18). 10.1145/3544548.3581346

Piaget, J. (1967). *Lo sviluppo mentale del bambino*. Einaudi.

Picciano, A. G. (2012). The evolution of big data and learning analytics in American higher education. *Online Learning : the Official Journal of the Online Learning Consortium*, 16(3), 9–20. 10.24059/olj.v16i3.267

Pictory. (2023). *Case study: Teacher enhances student learning and engagement with video*. Pictory. https://pictory.ai/case-studies/pippa-teacher-helps-students

Pintrich, P. R. (2003). *Motivation and classroom learning* (Vol. 103). Handbook of Psychology.

Pintrich, P. R., & Schunk, D. H. (2002). *Motivation in education: Theory, research, and applications* (2nd ed.). Merrill/Prentice Hall.

Platone. (2011). *Fedro* (A. Iezzi, Ed.). REA.

Plutchik, R. (2001). The Nature of Emotions. *American Scientist*, 89(4), 344–350. 10.1511/2001.28.344

Poon, A. (1993). *Tourism, technology and competitive strategies, CAB*. International Oxford. 10.1079/9780851989501.0000

Popovich, N. (2013, November 1). NSA files decoded: Edward Snowden's surveillance revelations explained. *The Guardian*. https://www.theguardian.com/world/interactive/2013/nov/01/snowden-nsa-files-surveillance-revelations-decoded#section/1

Prasad, G. N. R., & Professor, S. A. (2021). Evaluating student performance based on Bloom's taxonomy levels. *Journal of Physics: Conference Series*, 1797(1), 12063. 10.1088/1742-6596/1797/1/012063

Prensky, M. (2003). Digital game-based learning. [CIE]. *Computers in Entertainment*, 1(1), 21–21. 10.1145/950566.950596

Press, G. (2017). Top technologies for digital disruption. *Forbes*.

Prinsloo, P. (2017). Fleeing from Frankenstein's monster and meeting Kafka on the way: Algorithmic decision-making in higher education. *E-Learning and Digital Media*, 14(3), 138–163. 10.1177/2042753017731355

Putnam, R. D. (1993). *La tradizione civica nelle regioni italiane*. Mondadori.

Putra, A. S., & Tan, K. K. (2012). An alternative perspective in engineering education: A parallel to disruptive technology. *International Journal of Engineering Education*, 28(3), 726–732.

Qiang, J., Wu, D., Du, H., Zhu, H., Chen, S., & Pan, H. (2022, June 23). Review on Facial-Recognition-Based Applications in Disease Diagnosis. *Bioengineering (Basel, Switzerland)*, 9(7), 273. 10.3390/bioengineering907027335877324

Rabhi, M., Bakiras, S., & Di Pietro, R. (2024). Audio-deepfake detection: Adversarial attacks and countermeasures. *Expert Systems with Applications*, 250, 123941. 10.1016/j.eswa.2024.123941

Radford, A., & Narasimhan, K. (2018). *Improving language understanding by generative pre-training*. Semantic Scholar. https://semanticscholar.org/paper/49313245

Raelin, J. A. (2007). Toward an epistemology of practice. *Academy of Management Learning & Education*, 6(4), 495–519. 10.5465/amle.2007.27694950

Rainie, L., Funk, C., Anderson, M., & Tyson, A. (2022). *Public more likely to see facial recognition use by police as good, rather than bad for society.* Pew Research. https://www.pewresearch.org/internet/2022/03/17/public-more-likely-to-see-facial-recognition-use-by-police-as-good-rather-than-bad-for-society/

Ramadhani, W. A., Wooldridge, A. R., Roychowdhury, J., Mitchell, A., Hanson, K., Vazquez-Melendez, E., Kendhari, H., Shaikh, N., Riech, T., Mischler, M., Krzyzaniak, S., Barton, G., Formella, K. T., Abbott, Z. R., Farmer, J. N., Ebert-Allen, R., & Croland, T. (2020). Negotiating Time and Space: Investigating the Pediatric Code Cart Augmented Reality Application. *Proceedings of the Human Factors and Ergonomics Society Annual Meeting*, 64(1), 1365–1366. 10.1177/1071181320641326

Randazzo, M. (2018). Intelligenza emotiva ed empatia: l'ultima frontiera della didattica. *Laboratorio di sociologia del diritto*, Motta, G. (Ed.).

Rao, A. (2016). *AI everywhere/nowhere.* Insurance Thought Leadership. https://www.insurancethoughtleadership.com/ai-everywherenowhere/

Rao, A., Pang, M., Kim, J., Kamineni, M., Lie, W., Prasad, A. K., Landman, A., Dreyer, K. J., Succi, M. D., & Hospital, M. G. (2023). Assessing the utility of ChatGPT throughout the entire clinical workflow. *MedRxiv*. 10.1101/2023.02.21.23285886

Raposo, V. L. (2023). The use of facial recognition technology by law enforcement in Europe: A non-Orwellian draft proposal. *European Journal on Criminal Policy and Research*, 29(4), 515–533. https://link.springer.com/article/10.1007/s10610-022-09512-y. 10.1007/s10610-022-09512-y35668876

Rapport, J. (1981). In Praise of Paradox. A Social Policy of Empowerment over Prevention. *American Journal of Community Psychology*, 1(1), 1–25. 10.1007/BF008963577223726

Raskin, R. N., & Terry, H. (1998). A principal components analysis of the Narcissistic Personality Inventory and further evidence of its construct validity. *Journal of Personality and Social Psychology*, 54(5), 890–902. 10.1037/0022-3514.54.5.8903379585

Reale, E. (2014). Challenges in higher education research: The use of quantitative tools in comparative analyses. *Higher Education*, 67(4), 409–422. 10.1007/s10734-013-9680-2

Reason, J., Hollnagel, E., & Paries, J. (2006). Revisiting the Swiss cheese model of accidents. *Journal of Clinical Engineering*, 27(4), 110–115.

Reidenberg, J. R. (2014). Privacy in public. *University of Miami Law Review*, 69, 141–159. https://repository.law.miami.edu/umlr/vol69/iss1/6

Reig, S., Luria, M., Forberger, E., Won, I., Steinfeld, A., Forlizzi, J., & Zimmerman, J. (2021). Social Robots in Service Contexts: Exploring the Rewards and Risks of Personalization and Re-Embodiment. In *Designing Interactive Systems Conference 2021 (Virtual Event, USA) (DIS '21)*. Association for Computing Machinery, New York, NY, USA, 1390–1402. 10.1145/3461778.3462036

Reihlen, M., & Schoeneborn, D. (2022). The epistemology of management: An introduction. In Neesham, C., Reihlen, M., & Schoeneborn, D. (Eds.), *Handbook of Philosophy of Management* (pp. 17–37). Springer. 10.1007/978-3-030-76606-1_66

Reynolds, W. M., & Miller, G. E. (2003). Handbook of Psychology: Vol. 1-20. *Current perspectives in educational psychology*.

Ribeiro, R. (2013). Tacit knowledge management. *Phenomenology and the Cognitive Sciences*, 12(2), 337–366. 10.1007/s11097-011-9251-x

Riley, J. M., Ellegood, W. A., Solomon, S., & Baker, J. (2017). How mode of delivery affects comprehension of an operations management simulation Online vs face-To-face classrooms. *Journal of International Education in Business*, 10(2), 183–200. 10.1108/JIEB-09-2016-0025

Rivoltella, P. C. (2020). La didattica al tempo della mediatizzazione: Tra retrotopia e innovazione. 3° Convegno EDUIA, Università Roma Tre, 6 novembre 2020.

Rivoltella, P. C. (2015). *Smart future. Didattica, media digitali e inclusione: Didattica, media digitali e inclusione*. FrancoAngeli.

Rivoltella, P. C. (2016). Editoriale. Insegnanti totalmente autonomi. *Scuola Italiana Moderna*, 2(10), 1–2.

Rizzolati, G. (2019). *Specchi nel cervello*. Milano: Cortina.

Robertson, J. (2011). The educational affordances of blogs for self-directed learning. *Computers & Education*, 57(2), 1628–1644. 10.1016/j.compedu.2011.03.003

Robinson, K. (2017). *Out of our minds: The power of being creative*. John Wiley & Sons.

Rogers, C. R. (1961). *On becoming a person*. Houghton Mifflin.

Rogers, C. R. (1978). *Potere personale. La forza interiore e il suo effetto rivoluzionario*. Astrolabio, Ubaldini.

Ron-Angevin, R., & Díaz-Estrella, A. (2009). Brain-computer interface: Changes in performance using virtual reality techniques. *Neuroscience Letters*, 449(2), 123–127. 10.1016/j.neulet.2008.10.09919000739

Ronksley-Pavia, M., Barton, G., & Pendergast, D. (2019). Multiage education: An exploration of advantages and disadvantages through a systematic review of the literature. *The Australian Journal of Teacher Education*, 44(5), 24–41. 10.14221/ajte.2018v44n5.2

Roose, K. (2023, February 16). A conversation with Bing's chatbot left me Deeply unsettled. *The New York Times*. https://www.nytimes.com/2023/02/16/technology/bing-chatbot-microsoft-chatgpt.html

Rossi, G. (2012). The metamorphosis of the corporation. *Journal of Corporations*, 24(4), 67–89.

Ross, V., Jongen, E. M. M., Wang, W., Brijs, T., Brijs, K., Ruiter, R. A. C., & Wets, G. (2014). Investigating the influence of working memory capacity when driving behavior is combined with cognitive load: An LCT study of young novice drivers. *Accident; Analysis and Prevention*, 62, 377–387. 10.1016/j.aap.2013.06.03223915472

Roy, J. (2023). I Love You, Let's Stalk Each Other. *New York Times*. https://www.nytimes.com/2023/07/18/style/find-my-friends-location-sharing-privacy.html

Ruiz-Rojas, L. I., Acosta-Vargas, P., De-Moreta-Llovet, J., & Gonzalez-Rodriguez, M. (2023). Empowering education with generative artificial intelligence tools: Approach with an instructional design matrix. *Sustainability (Basel)*, 15(15), 11524. 10.3390/su151511524

Russell, S., & Norvig, P. (1998). *Intelligenza artificiale: un approccio moderno*. UTET.

Ryan-Mosley, T. (2023, July 20). The movement to limit face recognition tech might finally get a win. *MIT Technology Review*. https://www.technologyreview.com/2023/07/20/1076539/face-recognition-massachusetts-test-police/

Ryan, P. (2001). The school-to-work transition: A cross-national perspective. *Journal of Economic Literature*, 39(1), 34–92. 10.1257/jel.39.1.34

Sacco Ginevri, A. (2022). Artificial intelligence and corporate governance. *Journal of Business Law*, 33(2), 201–219.

Sadin, E. (2019). *Critica della ragione artificiale*. Luiss University Press.

Sadler-Smith, E., & Smith, J., P. (. (2004). Strategies for accommodating individuals' styles and preferences in flexible learning programmes. *British Journal of Educational Technology*, 35(4), 395–412. 10.1111/j.0007-1013.2004.00399.x

Safranek, C. W., Sidamon-Eristoff, A. E., Gilson, A., & Chartash, D. (2023). The role of large language models in medical education: Applications and implications. *JMIR Medical Education*, 9(1), e50945. 10.2196/5094537578830

Sahoo, S., Kumar, S., Donthu, N., & Singh, A. K. (2024). Artificial intelligence capabilities, open innovation, and business performance – Empirical insights from multinational B2B companies. *Industrial Marketing Management, 117*(May 2023), 28–41. 10.1016/j.indmarman.2023.12.008

Sáiz-Manzanares, M. C., Marticorena-Sánchez, R., & Ochoa-Orihuel, J. (2020). Effectiveness of using voice assistants in learning: A study at the time of COVID-19. *International Journal of Environmental Research and Public Health*, 17(15), 5618. 10.3390/ijerph1715561832759832

Sallam, M. (2023). ChatGPT utility in healthcare education, research, and practice: Systematic review on the promising perspectives and valid concerns. *Healthcare (Basel)*, 11(6), 887. 10.3390/healthcare1106088736981544

Salmon, G. (2009). The future for (second) life and learning. *British Journal of Educational Technology*, 40(3), 526–538. 10.1111/j.1467-8535.2009.00967.x

Sampson, E. E. (1988). The debate on individualism: Indigenous psychologies of the individual and their role in personal and societal functioning. *The American Psychologist*, 43(1), 15–22. 10.1037/0003-066X.43.1.15

Sandulescu, V., & Caraiani, C. (2019). Blockchain technology in education: Opportunities and challenges. *Sustainability*, 11(3), 679.

Sarris, J. (2022). Disruptive innovation in psychiatry. *Annals of the New York Academy of Sciences*, 1512(1), 5–9. 10.1111/nyas.1476435233789

Sarris, J., Thomson, R., Hargraves, F., Eaton, M., de Manincor, M., Veronese, N., Solmi, M., Stubbs, B., Yung, A. R., & Firth, J. (2020). Multiple lifestyle factors and depressed mood: A cross-sectional and longitudinal analysis of the UK Biobank (N= 84,860). *BMC Medicine*, 18(1), 1–10. 10.1186/s12916-020-01813-533176802

Saviani, D. (2007). Pedagogy: The space for education at the university. *Cadernos de Pesquisas*, 37(130), 99–134. 10.1590/S0100-15742007000100006

Savonitti, G., & Mattar, J. (2018). Entertainment games for teaching English as a second language: Characteristics and potential. *International Journal for Innovation Education and Research*, 6(2), 188–207. 10.31686/ijier.vol6.iss2.970

Sawyer, R. K. (2006). *The Cambridge Handbook of the Learning Sciences* (3rd, 2009th ed., p. 627). Cambridge University Press.

Saykili, A. (2018). Distance education: Definitions, generations, key concepts and future directions. *International Journal of Contemporary Educational Research*, 5(1), 2–17.

Scarchillo, G. (2019). Corporate governance and artificial intelligence. *The New Annotated Civil Jurisprudence*, 9(3), 289–302.

Schein, E. H. (2010). *Organizational cultural and leadership, 4th ed.* John Wiley & Sons, Inc.Schwartz, N. (2023, August 1). Data breaches cost higher education and training organizations $3.7M on average in 2023. *Higher Ed Dive*. https://www.highereddive.com/news/data-breaches-cost-higher-education-colleges/689499 /

Schmidthuber, L., Maresch, D., & Ginner, M. (2020). Disruptive technologies and abundance in the service sector-toward a refined technology acceptance model. *Technological Forecasting and Social Change*, 155, 119328. 10.1016/j.techfore.2018.06.017

Schmidt, V., Konig, S., Dilawar, R., Sanchez Pacheco, T., & Konig, P. (2023). Improved Spatial Knowledge Acquisition through Sensory Augmentation. *Brain Sciences*, 13(720), 1–29. 10.3390/brainsci13050720 37239192

Schneider, G. (2022). Artificial intelligence, corporate governance, and corporate social responsibility: Risks and opportunities. *The New Annotated Civil Jurisprudence*, 10(1), 112–130.

Schreiber, I. (2009). *Game design concepts*. Game Design Concepts. https://gamedesignconcepts.wordpress.com/

Schrier, K. (2019). *Learning, education & games, Volume 3: 100 games to use in the classroom & beyond*. Lulu. com.

Schubert, M. C., Wick, W., & Venkataramani, V. (2023). Performance of large language models on a neurology board-style examination. *JAMA Network Open*, 6(12), e2346721. 10.1001/jamanetworkopen.2023.46721 38060223

Schwabe, O., Shehab, E., & Erkoyuncu, J. (2015). Uncertainty quantification metrics for whole product life cycle cost estimates in aerospace innovation. *Progress in Aerospace Sciences*, 77, 1–24. 10.1016/j.paerosci.2015.06.002

Schwamm, L. H. (2014). Telehealth: Seven strategies to successfully implement disruptive technology and transform health care. *Health Affairs*, 33(2), 200–206. 10.1377/hlthaff.2013.1021 24493761

Scott, C. L. (2015). *The futures of learning 3: What kind of pedagogies for the 21st century?* UNESCO.

Searle, J. (1984). Menti, cervelli e programmi. *Behavioral and Brain Sciences*.

Seberger, J. S., Choung, H., Snyder, J., & David, P. (2024). Better Living Through Creepy Technology? Exploring Tensions Between a Novel Class of Well-Being Apps and Affective Discomfort in App Culture. *Proceedings of the ACM on Human-Computer Interaction, 8*(CSCW1). ACM. 10.1145/3637299

Sedaghat, S. (2023). Early applications of ChatGPT in medical practice, education, and research. *Clinical Medicine (London, England)*, 23(3), 278–279. 10.7861/clinmed.2023-0078 37085182

Semuels, A. (2018). Robots will transform fast food that might not be a bad thing. *Atlantic (Boston, Mass.)*.

Senge, P. (2010). *The fifth discipline: The art & practice of the learning organization*. Doubleday.

Serino, A., Noel, J. P., Mange, R., Canzoneri, E., Pellencin, E., Ruiz, J. B., Bernasconi, F., Blanke, O., & Herbelin, B. (2017). Peripersonal space: An index of multisensory body-environment interactions in real, virtual, and mixed realities. *Frontiers in ICT (Lausanne, Switzerland)*, 4(JAN), 1–12. 10.3389/fict.2017.00031

Serve Robotics. (n.d.). Serve Robotics. https://www.serverobotics.com

Severino, P. (2022). *Artificial intelligence: Politics, economics, law, technology*. Luiss University Press.

Shabahang, R., Shim, H., Aruguete, M. S., & Zsila, A. (2024). Oversharing on social media: Anxiety, attention-seeking, and social media addiction predict the breadth and depth of sharing. *Psychological Reports*, 127(2), 513–530. 10.1177/00332941221122861 35993372

Shafiquil Islam, M. D., Jamshid Nezhad Zahabi, S., Kim, S., Lau, N., Nussbaum, M. A., & Lim, S. (2023). Forklift Driving Performance of Novices with Repeated VR-based Training. *Proceedings of the Human Factors and Ergonomics Society Annual Meeting*, 67(1), 1480–1481. 10.1177/21695067231193664

Shanmugasundaram, M., & Tamilarasu, A. (2023). The impact of digital technology, smartphones, social media, and artificial intelligence (AI) on cognitive functions: A review. *Frontiers in Cognition*, 2, 1203077. 10.3389/fcogn.2023.1203077

Sharma, D., Kaushal, S., Kumar, H., & Gainder, S. (2022). Chatbots in healthcare: Challenges, technologies and applications. In *AIST 2022 - 4th International Conference on Artificial Intelligence and Speech Technology*. IEEE. 10.1109/AIST55798.2022.10065328

Sharma, S. (20236). ChatGPT creates mutating malware that evades detection by EDR. CSO. https://www.csoonline.com/article/575487/chatgpt-creates-mutating-malware-that-evades-detection-by-edr.html

Sharma, R., Mithas, S., & Kankanhalli, A. (2014). Transforming decision-making processes: A research agenda for understanding the impact of business analytics on organisations. *European Journal of Information Systems*, 23(4), 433–441. 10.1057/ejis.2014.17

Sharma, V., Sharma, K. K., Vashishth, T. K., Panwar, R., Kumar, B., & Chaudhary, S. (2023). Brain-Computer Interface: Bridging the Gap Between Human Brain and Computing Systems. *2023 International Conference on Research Methodologies in Knowledge Management, Artificial Intelligence and Telecommunication Engineering (RMKMATE)*, Chennai, India. 10.1109/RMKMATE59243.2023.10369702

Shin, D. H. (2017). The role of affordance in the experience of virtual reality learning: Technological and affective affordances in virtual reality. *Telematics and Informatics*, 34(8), 1826–1836. 10.1016/j.tele.2017.05.013

Shin, N. (2006). The impact of information technology on the financial performance of diversified firms. *Decision Support Systems*, 41(4), 698–707. 10.1016/j.dss.2004.10.003

Shovak, O., & Petiy, N. (2023). The role of non-verbal communication in everyday interaction. *Матеріали конференцій МЦНД*. https://archive.mcnd.org.ua/index.php/conference-proceeding/article/view/781/793

Showalter, D., Klein, R., Johnson, J., & Hartman, S. (2017). Why rural matters 2015-2016: Understanding the changing landscape. *Rural School and Community Trust*. https://www.ruraledu.org/user_uploads/file/WRM-2015-16.pdf

Shum, C., Kim, H. J., Calhoun, J. R., & Putra, E. D. (2024). "I was so scared I quit": Uncanny valley effects of robots' human-likeness on employee fear and industry turnover intentions. *International Journal of Hospitality Management*, 120, 103762. 10.1016/j.ijhm.2024.103762

Sibilio, M. (2014). *La didattica semplessa*. Liguori.

Sibilio, M. (2023). *La semplessità: Proprietà e principi per agire il cambiamento*. Morcelliana.

Sibilio, M., & Aiello, P. (Eds.). (2016). *Formazione e ricerca per una didattica inclusiva*. Franco Angeli.

Siddhpura, A., Siddhpura, I., & Siddhpura, M. (2020). Current state of research in the application of disruptive technologies in engineering education. *Procedia Computer Science*, 168(1), 177–184. 10.1016/j.procs.2020.05.163

Siemens, G. (2004). Connectivism: A learning theory for the digital age. *International Journal of Instructional Technology and Distance Learning*. http://www.itdl.org/Journal/Jan_05/article01.htm

Siemens, G. (2005). Meaning making, learning, subjectivity. http://connectivism.ca/blog/2005/12/meaning_making_learning_subjec.html

Siemens, G. (2009). Elearnspace. https://www.elearnspace.org/blog/8

Siemens, G. (2013). Learning analytics. *The American Behavioral Scientist*, 57(10), 1380–1400. 10.1177/0002764213498851

Sigari, C., & Biberthaler, P. (2021). Medical drones: Disruptive technology makes the future happen. *Der Unfallchirurg*, 124(12), 974–976. 10.1007/s00113-021-01095-334714357

Sila, I. K., & Martini, I. A. (2020). Transformation and revitalization of service quality in the digital era of revolutionary disruption 4.0. *JMBI UNSRAT (Jurnal Ilmiah Manajemen Bisnis dan Inovasi Universitas Sam Ratulangi).*, 7(1).

Simone, R. (2000). *The third phase. Forms of knowledge we are losing.* Laterza.

Simon, H. (1981). *The science of artificial.* MIT Press.

Sim, Y. (2007). *International Relations & Complex Systems Theory. Paper presented at the 51st Annual Meeting of the International Society for the Systems Sciences.* Tokyo Institute of Technology., Retrieved from https://journals.isss.org/index.php/proceedings51st/article/view/607/225

Singer, U., Polyak, A., Hayes, T., Yin, X., An, J., Zhang, S., Hu, Q., Yang, H., Ashual, O., Gafni, O., Parikh, D., Gupta, S., & Taigman, Y. (2022). MAKE-A-VIDEO: Text-to-video generation without text-video data. *arXiv:2209.14792*. https://doi.org//arXiv.2209.1479210.48550

Small, G. W., Lee, J., Kaufman, A., Jalil, J., Siddarth, P., Gaddipati, H., Moody, T. D., & Bookheimer, S. Y. (2020). Brain health consequences of digital technology use. *Dialogues in Clinical Neuroscience*, 22(2), 179–187. 10.31887/DCNS.2020.22.2/gsmall32699518

Soffer, T., Kahan, T., & Nachmias, R. (2019). Patterns of students' utilisation of flexibility in online academic courses and their relation to course achievement. *The International Review of Research in Open and Distributed Learning.* 10.19173/irrodl.v20i4.3949

Solenne, V. (2020, April 28). *The impact of AI on corporate aspects of corporate governance.* PandesLegal. https://www.pandslegal.it/business/intelligenza-artificiale-e-corporate-governance/

Songer, N. B., Lee, H. S., & Kam, R. (2002). Technology-rich inquiry science in urban classrooms: What are the barriers to inquiry pedagogy? *Journal of Research in Science Teaching*, 39(2), 128–150. 10.1002/tea.10013

Sounderajah, V., Patel, V., Varatharajan, L., Harling, L., Normahani, P., Symons, J., Barlow, J., Darzi, A., & Ashrafian, H. (2021). Are disruptive innovations recognised in the healthcare literature? A systematic review. *BMJ Innovations*, 7(1), 208–216. 10.1136/bmjinnov-2020-00042433489312

Sparrow, B., Liu, J., & Wegner, D. M. (2011). Google effects on memory: Cognitive consequences of having information at our fingertips. *Science*, 333(6043), 776–778. 10.1126/science.120774521764755

Spector, J. M. (2001). A philosophy of instructional design for the 21st century? *Journal of Structural Learning and Intelligent Systems*, 14(4), 307–318.

Spiro, R. J., Collins, B. P., & Ramchandran, A. R. (2008). Modes of openness and flexibility in cognitive flexibility hypertext learning environments. In *Online and distance learning: Concepts, methodologies, tools, and applications* (pp. 1903–1908). IGI Global. 10.4018/978-1-59904-935-9.ch152

Spitzer, M. (2015). *Solitudine digitale.* Corbaccio.

Squire, K. (2003). *Replaying history: Learning world history through playing Civilization III.* [Unpublished PhD dissertation].

Squire, K. D. (2010). From Information to Experience: Place-Based Augmented Reality Games as a Model for Learning in a Globally Networked Society. *Teachers College Record*, 112(10), 2565–2602. https://website.education.wisc.edu/kdsquire/tenure-files/01-TCR-squire-edits.pdf. 10.1177/016146811011201001

Srivastava, G., & Bag, S. (2024). Modern-day marketing concepts based on face recognition and neuro-marketing: A review and future research directions. *Benchmarking*, 31(2), 410–438. 10.1108/BIJ-09-2022-0588

Stamm, O., Vorwerg, S., Haink, M., Hildebrand, K., & Buchem, I. (2022). Usability and Acceptance of Exergames Using Different Types of Training among Older Hypertensive Patients in a Simulated Mixed Reality. *Applied Sciences (Basel, Switzerland)*, 12(22), 11424. 10.3390/app122211424

Starkey, P. L. (2013). *The effects of digital games on middle school students' mathematical achievement*. [PhD Dissertation, Lehigh University].

Stathakarou, N., Nifakos, S., Karlgren, K., Konstantinidis, S. T., Bamidis, P. D., Pattichis, C. S., & Davoody, N. (2020). Students' perceptions on chatbots' potential and design characteristics in healthcare education. *Studies in Health Technology and Informatics*, 272, 209–212. 10.3233/SHTI200053132604638

Stauffer, J. (2024, January 26). *Meet 'ChemBot': How to design a personalized GPT tutor*. Edutopia. https://www.edutopia.org/article/designing-gpt-tutor

Steels, L. (1990). Components of expertise. *AI Magazine*, 11(2), 28–49. 10.1609/aimag.v11i2.855

Steinberg, R. (2003). Effects of Computer-based Laboratory Instruction on Future Teachers' Understanding of the Nature of Science City College of New York. *Science*, 22, 185–205.

Steinkuehler, C. A., & Duncan, S. (2008b). Scientific habits of mind in virtual worlds. *Journal of Science Education & Technology*. https://website.education.wisc.edu/steinkuehler/papers/SteinkuehlerDuncan2008.pdf

Steinkuehler, C. A. (2008a). Cognition and literacy in massively multiplayer online games. In Coiro, J., Knobel, M., Lankshear, C., & Leu, D. (Eds.), *Handbook of Research on New Literacies* (pp. 611–634). Erlbaum.

Stern, A. (1938). Psychoanalytic investigations and therapy in the borderline group of neuroses. *The Psychoanalytic Quarterly*, 7(4), 467–489. 10.1080/21674086.1938.11925367

Steward, S. (2011). Conducting research in educational contexts. *International Journal of Lifelong Education*, 30(4), 565–567. 10.1080/02601370.2011.588469

Stewart, M. (2021). Understanding learning: Theories and critique. In Hunt, L., & Chalmers, D. (Eds.), *University teaching in focus: A learning-centred approach* (2nd ed.). Routledge. 10.4324/9781003008330-2

Stokel-Walker, C. (2021, October 8). AI-generated deepfake voices can fool both humans and smart assistants. *New Scientist*. https://www.newscientist.com/article/2293138-ai-generated-deepfake-voices-can-fool-both-humans-and-smart-assistants/

Stone, M. H. (1987). Treatment of patients in the borderline spectrum. In Tasman, A., Hales, R. E., & Frances, A. J. (Eds.), *American Psychiatric Press review of psychiatry* (Vol. 8, pp. 103–122). Psychiatric Press.

Su, C. S. (2011). The role of service innovation and customer experience in ethnic restaurants. *Service Industries Journal*, 31(3), 425–440. 10.1080/02642060902829302

Suits, B. (1978). *The grasshopper: Games, life and utopia*. University of Toronto Press. 10.3138/9781487574338

Sulleyman, A. (2017). Google's AI future: So impressive it's scary. *Independent*. https://www.independent.co.uk/life-style/gadgets-and-tech/features/google-lens-ai-preview-features-so-impressive-its-scary-a7745686.html

Susskind, R. E., & Susskind, D. (2015). *The future of the professions: How technology will transform the work of human experts*. Oxford University Press. 10.1093/oso/9780198713395.001.0001

Symanovich, S. (2018). *How does facial recognition work?* Norton. https://us.norton.com/internetsecurity-iot-how-facial-recognition-software-works.html

Sze, S. (2004). Get ahead, get technology: A new idea for rural school success. *Proceedings of the American Council on Rural Special Education*, 24, 118–121.

Tabas, J., & Beranová, M. (2014). Innovations Effect on the Company's Value. *Procedia Economics and Finance*, 12(March), 695–701. 10.1016/S2212-5671(14)00395-5

Taddeo, M. (2016). Costruire l'etica dell'intelligenza artificiale. *Università degli studi di Firenze*. Retrieved from https://www.openstarts.units.it/server/api/core/bitstreams/bad34fc9-cd4c-4be2-957a-68d436f6657e/content

Tahri Sqalli, M., Aslonov, B., Gafurov, M., & Nurmatov, S. (2023). Humanizing AI in medical training: Ethical framework for responsible design. *Frontiers in Artificial Intelligence*, 6, 1189914. 10.3389/frai.2023.118991437261331

Tam, M. (2000). Constructivism, instructional design, and technology: Implications for transforming distance learning. *Journal of Educational Technology & Society*, 3(2), 50–60.

Teasley, S. D. (2017). Student facing dashboards: One size fits all? *Technology. Knowledge and Learning*, 22(3), 377–384. 10.1007/s10758-017-9314-3

Tene, O., & Polonetsky, J. (2013). A theory of creepy: Technology, privacy and shifting social norms. *Yale Journal of Law and Technology, 16*(1). http://digitalcommons.law.yale.edu/cgi/viewcontent.cgi?article=1098&context=yjolt

Tennyson, R. D. (2010). Historical reflection on learning theories and instructional design. *Contemporary Educational Technology*, 1(1), 1–16. 10.30935/cedtech/5958

Teubner, G. (2019). *Digital legal subjects? On the private status of autonomous software agents*. ESI.

The Open Innovation Team & Department for Education. (2023). *Generative AI in education: Educator and expert views.*https://assets.publishing.service.gov.uk/media/65609be50c7ec8000d95bddd/Generative_AI_call_for_evidence_summary_of_responses.pdf

The Partner Alliance for Safer Schools. (2023). *Safety and security guidelines for K-12 schools* (6th ed.). PASSK12. https://passk12.org/wpcontent/uploads/2023/03/PASS_SAFETY_ AND_SECURITY _GUIDELINES_6th_Ed.pdf

Thomas, A., & Falls, Z. (2019, March). Rural elementary teachers' access to and use of technology resources in STEM classrooms. In *Society for Information Technology & Teacher Education International Conference* (pp. 2549–2553). Association for the Advancement of Computing in Education (AACE). 10.1007/978-3-030-29736-7_23

Thompson, J. B. (1998). *Mezzi di comunicazione e modernità. Una teoria sociale dei media.*

Thompson, K. (2023, June 8). *Robotic servers spotted at Austin chick-fil-A*. KXAN Austin. https://www.kxan.com/news/local/austin/robotic-servers-spotted-at-austin-chick-fil-a/

Thompson, A. D., Simonson, M. R., & Hargrave, C. P. (1996). *Educational technology: A review of the research* (2nd ed.). Association for Educational Communications & Technology.

Thurbon, R. (2024). Elon Musk unveils new footage of Tesla's Optimus robot showing improved mobility and speed. *Techspot.*https://www.techspot.com/news/102044-elon-musk-unveils-new-footage-tesla-optimus-robot.html

Time.com. (2019). Amazon is making it easier to delete your Alexa recordings. *Time*. https://time.com/5686352/delete-amazon-alexa-recordings/

Tobenkin, D. (2019). HR needs to stay ahead of automation. SHRM. https://www.shrm.org/hr-today/news/hr-magazine/spring2019/pages/hr-needs-to-stay-ahead-of-automation.aspx

Tognazzi, B. (2022). *Educazione, ambienti e apprendimento nella cultura della complessità.*

Tomarchio, M., & Ulivieri, S. (2015). *Pedagogia militante: Diritti, culture, territori*. ETS.

Toronto, E. (2009). Time out of mind: Dissociation in the virtual world. *Psychoanalytic Psychology*, 26(2), 117–133. 10.1037/a0015485

Trendov, N., Varas, S., & Zeng, M. (2019). *Digital technologies in agriculture and rural areas - Status report*. Food and Agriculture Organization of the United Nations. https://www.fao.org/3/ca4985en/ca4985en.pdf

Tsai, D. C. L., Huang, A. Y. Q., Lu, O. H. T., & Yang, S. J. H. (2021). Automatic question generation for repeated testing to improve student learning outcome. In *Proceedings - IEEE 21st International Conference on Advanced Learning Technologies, ICALT 2021* (pp. 339–341). IEEE. 10.1109/ICALT52272.2021.00108

Tsai, S. C., Chen, C. H., Shiao, Y. T., Ciou, J. S., & Wu, T. N. (2020). Precision education with statistical learning and deep learning: A case study in Taiwan. *International Journal of Educational Technology in Higher Education*, 17(1), 12. https://sci-hub.se/10.1186/s41239-020-00186-2. 10.1186/s41239-020-00186-2

Tucker, R., & Morris, G. (2011). Anytime, anywhere, anyplace: Articulating the meaning of flexible delivery in built environment education. *British Journal of Educational Technology*, 42(6), 904–915. 10.1111/j.1467-8535.2010.01138.x

Tuhkala, A. (2021). A systematic literature review of participatory design studies involving teachers. *European Journal of Education*, 56(4), 641–659. 10.1111/ejed.12471

Tully, M. (2015). Investigating the role of innovation attributes in the adoption, rejection, and discontinued use of open-source software for development. *Information Technologies and International Development*, 11(3), 55–69.

Tulsiani, R. (2024). The art of ChatGPT-driven gamification. *eLearning Industry*. https://elearningindustry.com/the-art-of-chatgpt-driven-gamification

Tuma, F., & Nassar, A. K. (2021). Applying Bloom's taxonomy in clinical surgery: Practical examples. *Annals of Medicine and Surgery (London)*, 69, 102656. 10.1016/j.amsu.2021.10265634429945

Turing, A. M. (1950). Computing machinery and intelligence. *Mind*, LIX(236), 433–460. 10.1093/mind/LIX.236.433

Turnbull, D., Chugh, R., & Luck, J. (2020). Learning management systems: An overview. In Tatnall, A. (Ed.), *Encyclopedia of Education and Information Technologies* (pp. 1052–1058). Springer. 10.1007/978-3-030-10576-1_248

Turner, A. (2015). Generation Z: Technology and social interest. *Journal of Individual Psychology*, 71(2), 103–113. 10.1353/jip.2015.0021

Tursunbayeva, A. (2019). Human resource technology disruptions and their implications for human resources management in healthcare organisations. *BMC Health Services Research*, 19(1), 1–8. 10.1186/s12913-019-4068-330606168

Tynan, B., & O'Neill, M. (2007). Individual perseverance: A theory of home tutors' management of schooling in isolated settings. *Distance Education*, 28(1), 95–110. 10.1080/01587910701305335

Tyng, C. M., Amin, H. U., Saad, M. N., & Malik, A. S. (2017). The influences of emotion on learning and memory. *Frontiers in Psychology*, 8, 235933. 10.3389/fpsyg.2017.0145428883804

U.S. Department of Education, Institute of Education Sciences, What Works Clearinghouse. (2016, June). *Secondary mathematics intervention report: Cognitive Tutor®*. US DoE. http://whatworks.ed.gov

Ubert, J. (2023). *Fake it: Attacking privacy through exploiting digital assistants using voice deepfakes* (Doctoral dissertation, Marymount University). https://muislandora.wrlc.org/islandora/object/muislandora%3A15804

Underwood, J. (2017). Exploring AI language assistants with primary EFL students. In Borthwick, K., Bradley, L., & Thouësny, S. (Eds.), *CALL in a climate of change: Adapting to turbulent global conditions – Short papers from EUROCALL 2017* (pp. 317–321). IEEE. 10.14705/rpnet.2017.eurocall2017.733

Underwood, J. (2021). Speaking to machines: Motivating speaking through oral interaction with intelligent assistants. In Beaven, T., & Rosell-Aguilar, F. (Eds.), *Innovative language pedagogy report* (pp. 127–132)., 10.14705/rpnet.2021.50.1247

UNESCO (1978). *Towards a methodology for projecting rates of literacy and educational attainment*. (Current Surveys and Research in Statistics, No. 28). UNESCO.

UNESCO. (1979). *Records of the General Conference Twentieth Session (Vol. 1 - Paris, 24 October to 28 November 1978)*. United Nations.

UNESCO. (2023). *An ed-tech tragedy? Educational technologies and school closures in the time of COVID-19*. UNESCO., 10.1787/6c2b2b2a-

UNESCO. (2023). *Re-immaginare i nostri futuri insieme*. Brescia: La Scuola sei.

Untari, A. D. (2022). Game-based learning: Alternative 21st century innovative learning models in improving student learning activeness. *Edueksos Jurnal Pendidikan Sosial & Ekonomi*, 11(2). 10.24235/edueksos.v11i2.11919

Valenduc, G., & Vendramin, P. (2016). Work in the digital economy: sorting the old from the new. *ETUI Research Paper-Working Paper*.

Van Bruggen, J. (2005). Theory and practice of online learning. In T. Anderson & F. Elloumi (Eds.), *British Journal of Educational Technology, 36*(1). Athabasca University. 10.1111/j.1467-8535.2005.00445_1.x

van der Pol, J., Janssen, M., & Dondorp, S. (2020). Blockchain-based Educational Credentials: A Feasibility Study in Dutch Higher Education. In *Proceedings of the 2020 15th International Conference on e-Learning (ICEL 2020)* (pp. 185-192).

Van Eck, R. (2007). Building artificially intelligent learning games. In *Games and Simulations in Online Learning: Research and Development Frameworks* (pp. 271-307). IGI Global. 10.4018/978-1-59904-304-3.ch014

van Huijstee, M. (2024). *Enhancing learning management systems: A novel approach to improve usability through learning analytics* [Bachelor's thesis, University of Twente]. https://essay.utwente.nl/98161/

Van Laar, E., Van Deursen, A. J., Van Dijk, J. A., & De Haan, J. (2020). Determinants of 21st-century skills and 21st-century digital skills for workers: A systematic literature review. *SAGE Open*, 10(1), 2158244019900176. 10.1177/2158244019900176

Vance, A., & Arciniega, J. (2023, Sept.). *FERPA & AI: What is protected?* EdAI HQ. https://ai4ed.substack.com/p/ferpa-and-ai-what-is-protected

VanLehn, K. (2006). The behavior of tutoring systems. *International Journal of Artificial Intelligence in Education*, 16(3), 227–265.

VanLehn, K. (2011). The relative effectiveness of human tutoring, intelligent tutoring systems, and other tutoring systems. *Educational Psychologist*, 46(4), 197–221. 10.1080/00461520.2011.611369

Vanlehn, K., Graesser, A. C., Jackson, G. T., Jordan, P., Olney, A., & Rosé, C. P. (2007). When are tutorial dialogues more effective than reading? *Cognitive Science*, 31(1), 3–62. 10.1080/03640210709336984 21635287

Varela, F. J., Thompson, E. T., & Rosch, E. (1992). *The embodied mind: Cognitive science and human experience*. MIT Press.

Vargo, S. L., Maglio, P. P., & Archpru, M. (2008). *On value and value co-creation: A service systems and service logic perspective*. 145–152. https://doi.org/10.1016/j.emj.2008.04.003

Vargo, S. L., & Lusch, R. F. (2004). Evolving to a New Dominant Logic for Marketing. *Journal of Marketing*, 68(1), 1–17. 10.1509/jmkg.68.1.1.24036

Vashishth, T. K., Sharma, V., Sharma, K. K., & Kumar, B. (2024). Enhancing Literacy Education in Higher Institutions with AI Opportunities and Challenges. *AI-Enhanced Teaching Methods*, 198-215.

Vashishth, T. K., Kumar, B., Panwar, R., Kumar, S., & Chaudhary, S. (2023, August). Exploring the Role of Computer Vision in Human Emotion Recognition: A Systematic Review and Meta-Analysis. *In 2023 Second International Conference on Augmented Intelligence and Sustainable Systems (ICAISS)* (pp. 1071-1077). IEEE. 10.1109/ICAISS58487.2023.10250614

Vashishth, T. K., Sharma, V., Sharma, K. K., Kumar, B., Chaudhary, S., & Panwar, R. (2024). Transforming Classroom Dynamics: The Social Impact of AI in Teaching and Learning. In *AI-Enhanced Teaching Methods* (pp. 322–346). IGI Global. 10.4018/979-8-3693-2728-9.ch015

Vashishth, T. K., Sharma, V., Sharma, K. K., Kumar, B., Panwar, R., & Chaudhary, S. (2024). AI-Driven Learning Analytics for Personalized Feedback and Assessment in Higher Education. In *Using Traditional Design Methods to Enhance AI-Driven Decision Making* (pp. 206–230). IGI Global. 10.4018/979-8-3693-0639-0.ch009

Verizon. (2022). *Data breaches Investigation Report - Data Breaches in Education*. Verizon. https://www.verizon.com/business/resources/reports/dbir/2022/data-breaches-in-education/

Verma, P. K., Sharma, V., Kumar, P., Sharma, S., Chaudhary, S., & Preety, P. (2023). IoT Enabled Real Time Appearance System using AI Camera and Deep Learning for Student Tracking. *International Journal on Recent and Innovation Trends in Computing and Communication*, 11(6s), 249–254. 10.17762/ijritcc.v11i6s.6885

Viola, F., & Cassone, V. I. (2017). *L'arte del coinvolgimento: emozioni e stimoli per cambiare il mondo*. Hoepli Editore.

Virtual Reality Society UK. (2020). *History Of Virtual Reality*. Virtual Reality Society Web Page. https://www.vrs.org.uk/virtual-reality/history.html

Vischi, A. (2021). Introduzione: Impatto, educazione, ecologia integrale. In Vischi, A. (Ed.), *Impatto sul territorio: Lavoro, giovani, ecologia integrale* (pp. 19–27). Pensa MultiMedia.

Vogt, F., Hauser, B., Stebler, R., Rechsteiner, K., & Urech, C. (2020). Learning through play–pedagogy and learning outcomes in early childhood mathematics. In *Innovative Approaches in Early Childhood Mathematics* (pp. 127–141). Routledge., 10.4324/9780429331244-10

Vogt, P., de Haas, M., de Jong, C., Baxter, P., & Krahmer, E. (2017). Child-robot interactions for second language tutoring to preschool children. *Frontiers in Human Neuroscience*, 11, 73. 10.3389/fnhum.2017.0007328303094

Volberda, H. W., Foss, N. J., & Lyles, M. A. (2010). PERSPECTIVE—Absorbing the Concept of Absorptive Capacity: How to Realize Its Potential in the Organization Field. *Organization Science*, 21(4), 931–951. 10.1287/orsc.1090.0503

Vorhaus, J. (2005). Citizenship, competence and profound disability. *Journal of Philosophy of Education*, 39(3), 461–475. 10.1111/j.1467-9752.2005.00448.x

Vos, L. (2015). Simulation games in business and marketing education: How educators assess student learning from simulations. *International Journal of Management Education*, 13(1), 57–74. 10.1016/j.ijme.2015.01.001

Vu, H. Q., Law, R., & Li, G. (2019). Breach of traveller privacy in location-based social media. *Current Issues in Tourism*, 22(15), 1825–1840. 10.1080/13683500.2018.1553151

Vygotskij, L. S. (1990). *Storia dello sviluppo delle funzioni psichiche superiori. E altri scritti*. Florence: Giunti-Barbèra. (Original work published 1930-31).

Vygotsky, L. S. (2016). Play and its role in the mental development of the child. *International Research in Early Childhood Education*, 7(2), 3–25.

Wagner, T., & Compton, R. A. (2012). *Creating innovators: The making of young people who will change the world*. Scribner.

Walton Family Foundation. (2023). *ChatGPT used by teachers more than students, new survey from Walton Family Foundation finds*. Walton Family Foundation. https://www.waltonfamilyfoundation.org/chatgpt-used-by-teachers-more-than-students-new-survey-from-walton-family-foundation-finds

Wang, P. Y. (2013). Examining the digital divide between rural and urban schools: Technology availability, teachers' integration level and students' perception. *Journal of Curriculum and Teaching*, 2(2), 127–139. 10.5430/jct.v2n2p127

Wang, Y., Vincenti, G., Braman, J., & Dudley, A. (2013). The ARICE Framework: Augmented Reality in Computing Education. *International Journal of Emerging Technologies in Learning*, 8(6), 27–34. 10.3991/ijet.v8i6.2809

Warren, S. J. (2018). *Measuring the Effects of VR/AR/MR. IMLS Lib3D/VR Forum B*.

Warren, S. J., & Churchill, C. (2024). A Model for Applying Cognitive Theory to Firm to Improve Organizational Learning for Sustained Knowledge Production and Competitive Advantage. *Performance Improvement Journal*. https://doi.org/https://doi.org/10.56811/PFI-21-0036

Warren, S. J., & Lin, L. (2012). Ethical considerations for learning game, simulation, and virtual world design and development. In S. C. Yang, H. H., & Yuen (Ed.), *Practices and Outcomes in Virtual Worlds and Environments* (pp. 1–18). IGI Global. 10.4018/978-1-60960-762-3.ch001

Warren, S. J., Dondlinger, M. J., & Barab, S. A. (2008). A MUVE Towards PBL Writing: Effects of a Digital Learning Environment Designed To Improve Elementary Student Writing. *Journal of Research on Technology in Education*, 41(1), 113–140. 10.1080/15391523.2008.10782525

Warren, S. J., Roy, M., & Robinson, H. (2021). Business simulation games: Three cases from supply chain management, marketing, and business strategy. In Ifenthaler, D. (Ed.), *Game-based learning across the disciplines*. Springer. 10.1007/978-3-030-75142-5_5

Warren, S. J., Stein, R. A., Dondlinger, M. J., & Barab, S. A. (2009). A Look Inside a MUVE Design Process: Blending Instructional Design and Game Principles To Target Writing Skills. *Journal of Educational Computing Research*, 40(3), 295–321. 10.2190/EC.40.3.c

Warren, S. J., & Wakefield, J. S. (2011). Instructional design frameworks for Second Life virtual learning. In Hinrichs, R., & Wankel, C. (Eds.), *Transforming Virtual World Learning: Cutting-edge Technologies in Higher Education* (pp. 115–163). Emerald Group Publisher. 10.1108/S2044-9968(2011)0000004010

Wati, I. F. (2020, December). *Digital game-based learning as a solution to fun learning challenges during the Covid-19 pandemic*. In *1st International Conference on Information Technology and Education (ICITE 2020)* (pp. 202-210). Atlantis Press. https://doi.org/10.2991/assehr.k.201214.237

Webb, J. (2020). Legal Technology: The Great Disruption? *U of Melbourne Legal Studies Research Paper*, (897).

Webb, E. (2013). *Learning (Together) with Games-Civilization and Empire*. Transformations.

Webley, L., Flood, J., Webb, J., Bartlett, F., Galloway, K., & Tranter, K. (2019). The profession (s)'engagements with lawtech: Narratives and archetypes of future law. *Law. Technology and Humans*, 1(1), 6–26. 10.5204/lthj.v1i0.1314

Webster, A., & Gardner, J. (2019). Aligning technology and institutional readiness: The adoption of innovation. *Technology Analysis and Strategic Management*, 31(10), 1229–1241. 10.1080/09537325.2019.1601694

Wecker, M. (2014, April 22). Whatever happened to Second Life? *ChronicleVitae*. https://chroniclevitae.com/news/456-what-ever-happened-to-second-life

Weegar, M. A., & Pacis, D. (2012). A comparison of two theories of learning—Behaviorism and constructivism as applied to face-to-face and online learning. In *Proceedings E-Leader Conference, Manila*. http://www.gcasa.com/conferences/manila/papers/Weegar.pdf

Wehmeyer, M. L., & Schalock, R. (2001). Self-determination and quality of life: Implications for special education services and supports. *Focus on Exceptional Children*, 33(8), 1–16.

Weill, P., Woerner, T., Stephanie, L., & Banner, J. (2019). Assessing the impact of digital savvy boards on company performance. *MIT Sloan CISR Working Paper, 433*. Cambridge: MIT Sloan.

Weinschenk, S. M. (2010). *Neuro web design. L'inconscio ci guida nel web*. Apogeo.

Weissenberg, A. (2017). Trends defining the global travel industry in 2017. *Global Economic Impact and Issue 2017*.

Weitekamp, D., Harpstead, E., & Koedinger, K. R. (2020). An interaction design for machine teaching to develop AI tutors. In *Proceedings of the 2020 CHI Conference on Human Factors in Computing Systems* (pp. 1–11). Association for Computing Machinery. 10.1145/3313831.3376226

Wells, A. J. (2002). Gibson's affordances and Turing's theory of computation. *Ecological Psychology*, 14(3), 141–180. 10.1207/S15326969ECO1403_3

Westerlund, M., Isabelle, D. A., & Leminen, S. (2021). The acceptance of digital surveillance in an age of big data. *Technology Innovation Management Review*, 11(3), 32–44. https://acris.aalto.fi/ws/portalfiles/portal/62347871/TIMReview_2021_March_3.pdf. 10.22215/timreview/1427

West, J., & Bogers, M. (2014). Leveraging external sources of innovation: A review of research on open innovation. *Journal of Product Innovation Management*, 31(4), 814–831. 10.1111/jpim.12125

Westlund, K., Dickens, J. M. K., Jeong, L., Harris, S., DeSteno, P. L., & Breazeal, C. L. (2017). Children use non-verbal cues to learn new words from robots as well as people. *International Journal of Child-Computer Interaction*, 13, 1–9. 10.1016/j.ijcci.2017.04.001

Wharrad, H., Windle, R., & Taylor, M. (2021). Designing digital education and training for health. In Konstantinidis, S. T., Bamidis, P. D., & Zary, N. (Eds.), *Digital Innovations in Healthcare Education and Training* (pp. 31–45). Academic Press. 10.1016/B978-0-12-813144-2.00003-9

White, N., & Grueger, D. (2017). *Managing the digital workforce*. Deloitte.

Wilson, J. H. (2019). Andragogy and the learning-tech culture revolution: The Internet of Things (IoT), blockchain, AI, and the disruption of learning. In *Handbook of Research on Cross-Cultural Business Education, 1*(1), 31-50. 10.4018/978-1-5225-3474-7.ch015

Winne, P. H. (2021). Open learner models working in symbiosis with self-regulating learners: A research agenda. *International Journal of Artificial Intelligence in Education*, 31(3), 446–459. 10.1007/s40593-020-00212-4

Winograd, T., & Flores, F. (1987). *Calcolatori e conoscenza*. Mondadori.

Wittgenstein, L. (2019). *Philosophical investigations*. Wiley-Blackwell.

Wongleedee, K. (2019). The effects of disruptive technology on higher education. *Journal of Learning and Teaching in Digital Age*, 4(2), 47–62.

Wood, W. M., Karvonen, M., Test, D. W., Browder, D., & Algozzine, B. (2004). Promoting student self-determination skills in IEP planning. *Teaching Exceptional Children*, 36(3), 8–16. 10.1177/004005990403600301

Wray, D. (2014). Looking at learning. In Cremin, T., & Arthur, J. (Eds.), *Learning to teach in the primary school* (3rd ed., pp. 69–83). Routledge.

Wright, V. H., & Wilson, E. K. (2011). Teachers' use of technology: Lessons learned from the teacher education program to the classroom. *Journal of Educational Technology Systems*, 40(1), 65–78. 10.2190/ET.40.1.f

Wu, Y. (2023). Integrating generative AI in education: How ChatGPT brings challenges for future learning and teaching. *Journal of Advanced Research in Education*, 2(4), 6–10. https://www.pioneerpublisher.com/jare/article/view/324. 10.56397/JARE.2023.07.02

Xia, M., Zhang, Y., & Zhang, C. (2018). A TAM-based approach to explore the effect of online experience on destination image: A smartphone user's perspective. *Journal of Destination Marketing & Management*, 8, 259–270. 10.1016/j.jdmm.2017.05.002

Xiong, X., Yang, L., Liu, J., & Hu, B. (2021). Smart contract-based educational certificate management system. *Future Generation Computer Systems*, 117, 521–534.

Xu, F., Buhalis, D., & Weber, J. (2017). Serious games and the gamification of tourism. *Tourism Management*, 60, 244–256. 10.1016/j.tourman.2016.11.020

Xu, L., & Duan, Y. (2020). Blockchain and Education: Opportunities and Challenges. *Journal of Educational Technology Development and Exchange*, 13(1), 1–16.

Yam, K. C., Tang, P. M., Jackson, J. C., Su, R., & Gray, K. (2023). The rise of robots increases job insecurity and maladaptive workplace behaviors: Multimethod evidence. *The Journal of Applied Psychology*, 108(5), 850–870. 10.1037/apl000104536222634

Yang, S. J., Ogata, H., Matsui, T., & Chen, N. S. (2021). Human-centered artificial intelligence in education: Seeing the invisible through the visible. *Computers and Education: Artificial Intelligence*, 2(1), 1–5. 10.1016/j.caeai.2021.100008

Yan, Z. (2023). Research on the role of hippocampus in memory consolidation. *Theoretical and Natural Science*, 6(1), 108–113. 10.54254/2753-8818/6/20230191

Yau, K. W., Chai, C. S., Chiu, T. K., Meng, H., King, I., & Yam, Y. (2023). A phenomenographic approach on teacher conceptions of teaching Artificial Intelligence (AI) in K-12 schools. *Education and Information Technologies*, 28(1), 1041–1064. 10.1007/s10639-022-11161-x

Yeung, S. M. (2023). Transformative learning via integrated projects with sustainable development goals and innovations. *Corporate Governance and Sustainability Review*, 7(2), 3. 10.22495/cgsrv7i2p3

Yilmaz, K. (2011). The cognitive perspective on learning: Its theoretical underpinnings and implications for classroom practices. *The Clearing House: A Journal of Educational Strategies, Issues and Ideas*, 84(5), 204–212. 10.1080/00098655.2011.568989

Yoo, S. K., & Kim, B. Y. (2018). A decision-making model for adopting a cloud computing system. *Sustainability (Basel)*, 10(8), 2952. 10.3390/su10082952

Yordanova, G. (2015). Global Digital Workplace as an Opportunity for Bulgarian Woman to Achieve Work-Family Balance. *The Dynamics of Virtual Work*, 5, 1–12.

Yuen, K. K., Choi, S. H., & Yang, X. B. (2010). A full-immersive CAVE-based VR simulation system of forklift truck operations for safety training. *Computer-Aided Design and Applications*, 7(2), 235–245. 10.3722/cadaps.2010.235-245

Yu, P., Xu, H., Hu, X., & Deng, C. (2023). Leveraging generative AI and large language models: A comprehensive roadmap for healthcare integration. *Health Care*, 11(20), 2776. 10.3390/healthcare1120277637893850

Zagabathuni, Y. (2022). Applications, scope, and challenges for AI in healthcare. *International Journal of Emerging Trends in Engineering Research*. The World Academy of Research in Science and Engineering. https://www.academia.edu/76121649/Applications_Scope_and_Challenges_for_AI_in_healthcare

Zahn, M. (2023, January 7). Controversy illuminates rise of facial recognition in private sector. https://abcnews.go.com/Business/controversy-illuminates-rise-facial-recognition-private-sector/story?id=96116545

Zarandi, N., Soares, A., & Alves, H. (2022). Strategies, benefits, and barriers–a systematic literature review of student co-creation in higher education. *Journal of Marketing for Higher Education*, 1–25. 10.1080/08841241.2022.2134956

Zarei, G. R. (2011). A constructivist model for the technological enhancement of university materials. *Asian Journal of Information Technology*, 10(1), 26–31. 10.3923/ajit.2011.26.31

Zawacki-Richter, O., Marín, V. I., Bond, M., & Gouverneur, F. (2019). Systematic review of research on artificial intelligence applications in higher education – Where are the educators? *International Journal of Educational Technology in Higher Education*, 16(1), 39. 10.1186/s41239-019-0171-0

Zellini, P. (2018). *La dittatura del calcolo*. Milano: Adelphi.

Zewe, A. (2023). Explained: Generative AI. *How do powerful generative AI systems like ChatGPT work, and what makes them different from other types of artificial intelligence?* MIT News. https://news.mit.edu/2023/explained-generative-ai-1109

Zhang, J., & Wan, J. (2019). Advances in social science, education, and humanities research. In *International Conference on Education, Economics, and Information Management (ICEEIM 2019)* (Vol. 428, pp. 42-44). Atlantis Press. https://www.atlantis-press.com/article/125938453.pdf

Zhao, F., Hwang, G. J., & Yin, C. (2021). A result confirmation-based learning behavior analysis framework for exploring the hidden reasons behind patterns and strategies. *Journal of Educational Technology & Society*, 24(1), 138–151. https://www.jstor.org/stable/26977863

Zhao, F., Liu, G. Z., Zhou, J., & Yin, C. (2023). A learning analytics framework based on human-centered artificial intelligence for identifying the optimal learning strategy to intervene learning behavior. *Journal of Educational Technology & Society*, 26(1), 132–146. 10.30191/ETS.202301_26(1).0010

Zhou, V. (2023). *AI is already taking video game illustrators' jobs in China*. Rest of World. https://restofworld.org/2023/ai-image-china-video-game-layoffs/

Zhou, C., Li, Q., Li, C., Yu, J., Liu, Y., Wang, G., Zhang, K., Ji, C., Yan, Q., He, L., Peng, H., Li, J., Wu, J., Liu, Z., Xie, P., Xiong, C., Pei, J., Yu, P. S., & Sun, L. (2023). A comprehensive survey on pretrained foundation models: A history from BERT to ChatGPT. https://arxiv.org/abs/2302.09419v3

Zhu, K., Kraemer, K. L., & Xu, S. (2006). The process of innovation assimilation by firms in different countries: A technology diffusion perspective on e-business. *Management Science*, 52(10), 1557–1576. 10.1287/mnsc.1050.0487

Compilation of References

Zimmerman, M. A. (2000). Empowerment Theory: Psychological, Organizational and Community Levels of Analysis. In Rapport, J., & Seidman, E. (Eds.), *Handbook of Community Psychology*. Kluwer Academic/Plenum Publishers. 10.1007/978-1-4615-4193-6_2

Zoppini, A. (2021). *The firm as an organization and the system of controls. Metamorphosis of Company Law*. ESI.

Zotov, V., & Kramkowski, E. (2023). Moving-target intelligent tutoring system for marksmanship training. *International Journal of Artificial Intelligence in Education*, 33(4), 817–842. 10.1007/s40593-022-00308-z

Zuboff, S. (1988). *In the age of the smart machine: The future of work and power*. Basic Books, Inc.

Zuckerman, M. (2005). Psychobiology of personality (2nd ed.). New York: Cambridge 10.1017/CBO9780511813733

About the Contributors

Julie Delello is a Distinguished Teaching Professor in the College of Education and Psychology at The University of Texas at Tyler. She received her Ph.D. in Curriculum and Instruction with a specialization in Science and Technology from Texas A&M University. She has served in education for over 27 years with extensive experience in K-16 teaching, administration, and leadership. She has authored numerous publications, and her professional interests focus on academic innovations, artificial intelligence, emerging technologies, gerontechnology, and social media platforms for authentic learning.

Rochell McWhorter is an Associate Professor of Human Resource Development (HRD) in the Soules College of Business at The University of Texas at Tyler. Her long-term research agenda includes the study of virtual scenario planning (VSP) as the development of leadership capability and capacity within virtual environments for the purpose of preparing organizations for times of uncertainty. Her passion for emerging technologies includes the study of virtual human resource development (VHRD) to discover its implications for research and practice in the field of HRD. She utilizes various techniques in the classroom such as social media, infographics, digital badges, augmented reality, and artificial intelligence; and, she is a champion of service-learning and researcher of eSports.

***

Alfonso Amendola is a professor of Sociology of cultural processes and Sociology of electronic arts at the University of Salerno. He directs the "Open Class" University meetings. The communication professions" and co-directs the "Sociological Dialogues". He is a professor in the Doctorate College of Politics, Culture, and Development (XL cycle) of the University of Calabria. He deals with visual studies, avant-garde cultures, generational consumption, digital innovation, and literary mediology. He directs the sociology of culture series "La Sensitivity Vitale" for Edizioni Rogas in Rome and co-directs the series "Multidisciplinary Approaches to Discourse and Sociology" for Cambridge Scholars.

Jennifer Bailey Watters, Ed.D. is an assistant professor of practice in the School of Education at the University of Texas at Tyler. Serving as a teacher, principal, and central office administrator before moving into higher education, Dr. Watters now prepares instructional coaches and school leaders through graduate studies. Passionate about advancing instructional leadership pedagogy and scholarship, she is engaged in research mentorship and serves in leadership roles for several scholarly organizations. Dr. Watters' research centers around school leadership learning to improve leadership attrition and advance school improvement outcomes.

Maria Carbone born in San Giuseppe Vesuviano (Naples - Italy) on 14/05/9772. Graduated in Economics from the University of Naples "Federico II", certified public accountant, auditor and financial promoter. She has been collaborating with the Telematic University "Giustino Fortunato" as an e-tutor in Business Economics, Financial Statements and Accounting Principles and Budget Analysis since 2006. PhD for the XXXIX cycle "Equity, diversity and inclusion" at the "Pegaso" Telematic University.

Christina Churchill combines three decades of technology leadership experience and 14 years of teaching and learning expertise. Her diverse technology background encompasses K-12, higher education, and corporate. She has taught graduate-level courses since 2017 in instructional technology. Dr. Churchill has spearheaded the implementation of instructional technology and online programs and trained faculty in innovative teaching methods. She led a technology initiative integrating K12 one-to-one technology in 2011. Recently, she was instrumental in building Smart Classrooms that allow students worldwide to join classes virtually at Southern Methodist University's engineering school. A published researcher, Christina holds a Ph.D. in Learning Technologies from the University of North Texas and an M.S. Ed. in Learning Design and Technology from Purdue University.

Tonia De Giuseppe is an Associate Professor SECTOR 11 D2 - Didactics, special pedagogy and educational research, at the Giustino Fortunato University - PhD in Language Sciences, Society, Politics and Education: Corporeality, Technologies and Inclusion, Director of editorial series. Editorial & Scientific Advisory Board scientific platform. Reviewer International Editorial Board. Since 1990 he has been involved in training processes and studies of strategic educational implementations in complex territorial contexts. In particular, since 1998, he has participated in multidisciplinary studies for the creation of systems of intercultural

About the Contributors

inclusiveness, for which he has received national and international recognition of merit. He has been involved in intercultural and inclusive planning since 1998, for which he has received recognition with national and international merit awards. He has held training, planning and evaluation roles for public bodies, for international, governmental and non-governmental cooperation and development education organizations. She is the author of scientific contributions in magazines, texts, monographs, relating to themes of inclusive educational-design innovation. You have participated in training and research activities in the field of cooperation and peace education, including with non-governmental organisations, addressing issues for which you have also obtained various recognitions, which indicate a continuous and coherent commitment, also with the contents of the disciplinary sector 11 / D2. She is currently engaged in scientific and educational-training activities of a theoretical, empirical and experimental nature regarding teaching, training, special pedagogy, orientation and evaluation in different educational, educational and training contexts. In particular, she focused on research relating to: general teaching (Didactics and special pedagogy); educational planning, training and cooperation methodologies and inclusive organizational management; on media education and e-learning; on product, process and system evaluation; on special education aimed at people with disabilities and problems of social and cultural integration; education in socio-motor activities (experimental pedagogy) with constant attention to the theme of teaching innovation, in particular the flipped classroom methodology and others. In fact, the studies concerning some deficits (selective mutism, attention disorders and hyperactivity, autism spectrum disorders) but above all the research activities carried out since 2014 on the flipped inclusion model and innovative analyzes on E-sports education, relating to implementation of systemic inclusiveness models from the lifelong learning approach in an ecological-inclusive perspective, applied through a cultural approach and a research methodology, which has allowed us to prefigure original future heuristic scenarios such as to arouse interest from the national and international scientific community.

Pio Alfredo Di Tore, PhD in Educational Research Methodology, has a degree in literature, with a thesis on "Semantic technologies and literary texts". For several years he worked as a software designer for "Omslearning.it", a software house specializing in elearning solutions. He is currently associate professor of Didactics and Special Pedagogy at the University of Cassino and Southern Lazio. His research interests are mainly aimed at the relationship between corporeality, technologies and teaching, with particular attention to natural interfaces and simulation environments.

Arlene Garcia-Lopez, EdD has over 14 years of experience in higher education. Her areas of research and professional interest include community college student engagement, retention and completion, early alert interventions, faculty development, organizational theory, and developing technologies in education.

Aleshia Hayes is an Assistant Professor of Learning Technologies and founding Director of the SURGE (Simulation, User Research, Game Experience) XR Lab. In the lab, Dr. Hayes leads the design, development, and testing of serious games and simulations for education, training, and behavior change. Dr. Hayes leverages her research funded by the National Science Foundation, the American Association of University Women, and Oculus/Meta to inform learning technology design and implementation across learners from K12 and university levels to the workforce. Her projects have changed lives, won awards, and garnered media attention. Dr. Aleshia Hayes leads the Researching Immersive Technologies for Teaching and Learning Think Tank and directs the design and production of the Immersive Learning Library experience.

Sajid Khan is working as an Assistant Professor of Entrepreneurship and Innovation at School of Management Sciences, Ghulam Ishaq Khan Institute of Engineering Sciences and Technology, Pakistan. He has earned his PhD in Management from Massey University, New Zealand. Sajid's background is in managing innovation, though his interests have broaden to embrace the field of education and the impact of culture on learning and change. He is particularly interested in pedagogic theory, skill transfer, instruction evaluation and dilemma management.

Stathis Konstantinidis is an Associate Professor in e-Learning and Health informatics and the Deputy Digital Learning Director of the Faculty of Medicine and Health Sciences at the University of Nottingham, UK, and an active member of DICE research group and HELM team, which work spans a number of intertwining themes on Digital Innovations in healthCare and Education. In the past, he was a researcher (2012-2015) for more than two years at the Northern Research Institute (NORUT) based at Tromso, Norway. He was teaching at Technological Educational Institute of West Macedonia, Kozani, Greece (2006-2011) and he was a research associate at the Medical School of the Aristotle University of Thessaloniki for 6 years (2006-2012). He served as a member of the Global Healthcare Workforce Council (2015- 2016) and as OKFN ambassador in Norway (2013-2016), while his teaching experience in higher education and CPD spans across different countries including UK, Greece and Norway, and he served as the director of the MSc course Quality and Patient Safety in the University of Nottingham, UK. He had participated in many EU, interregional and national co-funded projects from different roles with the vast majority around the medical informatics education field. He was the project coordinator for CoViRR, CEPEH and HEALTINT4ALL ERASMUS+ projects, CAMEI (FP7 - CSA) (www.camei-project.eu) and PI for University of Nottingham for TBDTHC, EPoCFiNDS and ReHIn ERASMUS+ project, while serves as Co-I in a range of projects including ACoRD (ERASMUS+), TOTEMM(ERASMUS+), TransCoCon (ERASMUS+), CREATE(COT Royal College of Occupational Therapist), technical coordinator for mEducator(EU eContentPlus) and others. He has a great publication portfolio, while he has served as the co-chair of 4 International Conferences: 2nd, 4th and 5th Interantional Conference on Medical Education Informatics (MEI2015, MEI2021, MEI 2024) and IEEE 30th International Symposium on Computer Based Medical Systems(CBMS2017) and the CAMEI Summer School, among other special sessions organisations in multiple international conferences. He is an Associate editor of Health Informatics Journal. His research includes among other conversational agents, internet of things, virtual reality and artificial intelligence in education, collaborative e-learning, co-creation of OER, social media, content sharing, retrieval and repurposing, educational standards, virtual patients, web of data, semantic web, learning analytics, serious games, gamification and exergames.

Bhupendra Kumar completed his Graduation and Post Graduation from Chaudhary Charan Singh University, Meerut, U.P. and Ph.D. in Computer Science and Engineering from Mewar University, Hapur. Presently, he is working as a Professor in the Department of Computer Science and Applications, IIMT University, Meerut, U.P. He has been a huge teaching experience of 19 years. He is the reviewer member of some reputed journals. He has published several book chapters and research papers of national and international reputed journals.

Mandi M. Laurie holds a Bachelor's degree in Psychology from Texas State University, a Master's degree in Human Resource Development from The University of Texas at Tyler, and is currently a PhD Candidate in Human Resource Development at The University of Texas at Tyler. Affiliated with The University of Texas at Tyler, she brings a wealth of experience from her past work in both the corporate world and as a private consultant. Her research interests lie in the innovative use of experiential learning methods, particularly service-learning, to enhance Human Resource Development practices. Mandi also conducts research in the field of Virtual HRD, exploring its potential applications and impact on Human Resource Development practices.

Nitish Kumar Minz is an exceptional Bachelor of Commerce student specializing in Business Administration and Management at K.R. Mangalam University. With an unwavering commitment to excellence and a remarkable work ethic, Mr. Minz has consistently demonstrated his dedication to academic and professional pursuits. His academic achievements extend beyond the classroom, as he has made significant contributions to several research papers and book chapters that are currently in the final stages of publication. His insightful contributions and research expertise have earned him recognition within his field of study. Nitish Kumar Minz, as the President of the Student Council at K.R. Mangalam University, holds a prestigious position. In this leadership role, he has demonstrated exceptional skills in managing various projects and strategic initiatives. His internship at KEIC (KRMU Entrepreneurship & Incubation Center) has allowed him to further refine his project management and strategic planning abilities, providing valuable hands-on experience in the field. Furthermore, he has been selected as NEP SAARTHI- Student Ambassador for Academic Reforms in Transforming Higher Education at K.R. Mangalam University. This esteemed role demonstrates his passion for educational reforms and his commitment to improving the quality of higher education. As a Student Ambassador, Mr. Minz actively engages with fellow students, faculty, and staff, promoting a culture of academic excellence and facilitating positive changes within the university. Recognizing his outstanding accomplishments and exceptional contributions, he has recently been honored with the prestigious CHANCELLOR'S EXCELLENCE AWARD. This esteemed award serves as a testament to his dedication, hard work, and exemplary performance throughout his academic journey. Mr. Nitish Kumar Minz's academic prowess, research contributions, leadership roles, and recognition through awards highlight his exceptional abilities and potential for future success. He continues to inspire and make a significant impact within the academic community, demonstrating his commitment to excellence in all his endeavors.

Archana Parashar is working as an Associate Professor at IIM Raipur since 2014. She is a gold medalist in M.A (English Literature), M. Phil topper and completed her Ph. D on American fiction. Prior to this she was associated with SGSITS, Indore. She has 14 yrs. experience of teaching & corporate training.

Matthew Pears holds a Bachelor of Science in Psychology and advanced degrees including a Master of Science by Research (MRes) and a PhD in Psychology. His extensive research in healthcare pedagogy, innovative technologies, and applied cognition focuses on enhancing learning and healthcare delivery through Large Language Models, Virtual Reality, and human factors techniques. Currently, Dr. Pears is a member of the Health E-learning and Media (HELM) team at the University of Nottingham, where he researches digital educational tools. His research efforts include developing and implementing cutting-edge educational tools, notably using virtual reality for surgical training, and exploring the use of AI through Large Language Models. Dr. Pears has authored numerous publications in journals such as the Journal of Applied Psychology and the Journal of Surgical Education and has presented at significant conferences. His research often bridges psychology, technology, and healthcare education, demonstrating practical applications of innovative technologies in medical settings. In addition to his academic publications, Dr. Pears has contributed to international projects like ERASMUS+ CoViRR and CEPEH, which focus on VR and AI in healthcare education. These projects aim to improve healthcare pedagogy through policy analysis and best practice guidelines. Dr. Pears's technical skills include developing VR applications, using EEG technology, data analysis and visualization with SPSS, R Studio, and Python, and manages large datasets effectively. His experience extends to developing small-scale web applications and utilizing LLM APIs in educational resources. He has been involved in other funded projects and has been awarded funds including the ESCR Impact Accelerator Fund, Leeds Hospital Charity Fund, and Santander Mobility Fund. Dr. Pears actively contributes to the academic community as a reviewer, conference organizer, and disseminating outputs at events to share his knowledge and uphold research standards.

Phil Ramsey is a Senior Lecturer in Organizational Learning at Massey University in New Zealand. His research has focused on application of organizational learning concepts, particularly in education. He is the author of the Billibonk and Frankl series of books, that teach systems thinking to children.

About the Contributors

Kewal Krishan Sharma is a professor in computer sc. in IIMT University, Meerut, U.P, India. He did his Ph.D. in computer network with this he has MCA, MBA and Law degree also. He did variously certification courses also. He has an overall experience of around 33 year in academic, business and industry. He wrote a number of research papers and books.

Vikas Sharma completed his Graduation and Post Graduation from Chaudhary Charan Singh University, Meerut, U.P. Currently Pursuing his Ph.D. in Computer Science and Engineering from Govt. Recognized University. Presently, he is working as an Assistant Professor in the Department of Computer Science and Applications, IIMT University, Meerut, U.P. He has been awarded as Excellence in teaching award 2019. He is the reviewer member of some reputed journals. He has published several book chapters and research papers of national and international reputed journals.

Alessia Sozio is a PhD student in "Equity, diversity and inclusion" at Pegaso University. She was born in Naples on December 12, 1975. Previously graduated in Communication Sciences, she obtained a second degree in Primary Education Sciences.

Tarun Kumar Vashishth is an active academician and researcher in the field of computer science with 22 years of experience. He earned Ph.D. Mathematics degree specialized in Operations Research; served several academic positions such as HoD, Dy. Director, Academic Coordinator, Member Secretary of Department Research Committee, Assistant Center superintendent and Head Examiner in university examinations. He is involved in academic development and scholarly activities. He is member of International Association of Engineers, The Society of Digital Information and Wireless Communications, Global Professors Welfare Association, International Association of Academic plus Corporate (IAAC), Computer Science Teachers Association and Internet Society. His research interest includes Cloud Computing, Artificial Intelligence, Machine Learning and Operations Research; published more than 25 research articles with 2 books and 15 book chapters in edited books. He is contributing as member of editorial and reviewers boards in conferences and various computer journals published by CRC Press, Taylor and Francis, Springer, IGI global and other universities.

Scott Warren is a Professor of Learning Technologies in the College of Information at the University of North Texas. He has studied the design and ethical use of learning with innovative technologies to support complex education and training contexts for more than 20 years. As part of this work, he co-developed the Ethical Choices with Educational Technology frameworks for use in the evaluation of potential information technology adoption for training, instruction, and learning design. As a researcher in logistics and operations management, his research also includes how stakeholders employ systemic evaluation approaches with business firms as part of improving organizational learning and performance improvement through gains to efficiency and effectiveness with information technology adoption. His recent NSF-grant-funded work examines the use of sensor suites and eye-tracking data to inform how best to engage in cognitive load reduction for workers in complex warehouse environments containing autonomous robots, artificial intelligence tools, and extended reality devices for training and learning.

Index

A

AI 1, 2, 3, 4, 5, 6, 7, 8, 9, 10, 11, 12, 13, 14, 15, 16, 17, 18, 19, 20, 21, 22, 23, 24, 25, 26, 49, 51, 52, 53, 54, 55, 56, 57, 58, 59, 60, 61, 62, 63, 64, 65, 66, 67, 69, 71, 72, 73, 74, 75, 76, 77, 78, 80, 81, 82, 83, 85, 86, 87, 88, 90, 92, 93, 104, 108, 109, 134, 136, 154, 155, 156, 162, 166, 167, 168, 169, 170, 171, 172, 173, 174, 175, 176, 177, 178, 179, 180, 181, 182, 183, 184, 185, 187, 188, 190, 191, 192, 193, 194, 196, 197, 198, 199, 200, 202, 203, 205, 226, 251, 252, 253, 254, 255, 261, 262, 263, 264, 265, 267, 269, 270, 271, 272, 273, 274, 275, 278
algorithms 1, 2, 4, 6, 7, 10, 12, 13, 14, 25, 26, 52, 53, 55, 56, 58, 59, 60, 61, 62, 63, 64, 65, 67, 68, 167, 197, 199, 202, 234, 237, 241, 253, 263, 264, 267, 273
Artificial Intelligence 1, 2, 6, 15, 16, 17, 18, 19, 20, 21, 22, 23, 24, 25, 49, 51, 52, 53, 54, 55, 58, 61, 65, 67, 68, 70, 71, 78, 79, 86, 88, 93, 134, 154, 155, 166, 183, 185, 186, 187, 189, 190, 191, 193, 197, 222, 229, 233, 234, 235, 237, 238, 239, 240, 241, 243, 245, 246, 251, 252, 254, 255, 261, 263, 266, 267, 269, 270, 272, 273, 275, 276, 277, 278, 279, 280
augmented reality 10, 90, 106, 197, 206, 210, 211, 215, 216, 217, 218, 219, 220, 224, 226, 228, 230, 234, 238, 241, 242, 243

B

Big Data 5, 19, 22, 48, 52, 64, 67, 70, 71, 79, 83, 89, 92, 93, 233, 234, 235, 238, 262, 273, 274, 278
Blockchain Technology 27, 28, 29, 30, 31, 32, 33, 35, 36, 37, 38, 39, 40, 41, 42, 43, 44, 45, 46, 47, 48, 49, 50, 238, 241
Bloom's Taxonomy 110, 166, 167, 169, 170, 171, 172, 173, 174, 175, 176, 177, 178, 179, 180, 181, 183, 184, 185, 186, 188, 189, 190, 191, 266

C

citizenship 51, 53, 58, 59, 60, 65, 66, 67, 141, 271, 272, 275, 277, 280
Co-creation 166, 179, 180, 183, 185, 186, 187, 188, 190, 192, 208, 230, 235
Cognition 55, 58, 68, 108, 113, 121, 124, 134, 169, 171
collaborative learning 146, 196, 204, 227
computational thinking 264, 265, 276
content generation 9, 10
cooperative learning 253, 261, 265, 274
corporate 79, 205, 206, 207, 208, 261, 262, 263, 264, 265, 266, 267, 273, 276
corporate governance 205, 261, 262, 263, 264, 265, 266, 267
corporeality 51, 124, 147
Creepy Technologies 70, 71, 83, 84, 89

D

Digital Credentials 41
Disruptive Technologies 83, 167, 193, 194, 195, 196, 197, 198, 199, 200, 201, 202, 203, 204, 205, 222, 232, 233, 234, 235, 236, 237, 238, 239, 241, 242, 243, 244, 245, 246, 247, 248
Distributed Ledger 36, 46

E

Education 1, 2, 3, 5, 6, 7, 8, 9, 12, 13, 14, 15, 16, 17, 18, 19, 20, 21, 22, 23, 24, 25, 27, 28, 29, 30, 31, 32, 33, 34, 35, 36, 37, 38, 39, 40, 41, 42, 43, 45, 46, 47, 48, 49, 52, 53, 58, 64, 65, 73, 79, 83, 87, 89, 91, 92, 103, 106, 107, 108, 110, 111, 112, 113, 114, 117, 118, 119, 127, 128, 129, 130, 131, 132, 133, 134, 135, 136, 137, 138, 139, 140, 141, 145, 146, 147, 148, 149, 150, 151, 152, 153, 154, 155, 156, 158, 159, 160, 161, 162, 163, 164, 166, 167, 168, 169, 170, 171, 172, 174, 176, 178, 179, 180, 181, 182, 183, 184, 185, 186, 187, 188, 189, 190, 191, 192, 193, 194, 195, 196, 197, 198, 199, 200, 201, 202, 204, 205, 207, 210, 212, 213, 222, 224, 225, 226, 227, 228, 230, 231, 240, 245, 247, 251, 252, 254, 256, 257, 261, 265, 266, 269, 271, 272, 273, 274, 275, 276, 277, 278, 279, 280
Educational innovation 127, 140, 197
Education Sector 27, 28, 29, 30, 31, 32, 33, 35, 36, 37, 39, 40, 41, 43, 45, 46, 47, 48, 79
educators 1, 4, 6, 9, 10, 11, 13, 14, 15, 16, 18, 20, 25, 30, 31, 34, 35, 39, 45, 46, 50, 52, 59, 62, 64, 66, 79, 83, 84, 105, 107, 117, 138, 145, 146, 151, 153, 154, 155, 169, 170, 172, 175, 176, 179, 181, 182, 183, 184, 185, 196, 197, 198, 201, 202, 203, 209, 230, 280
emotions 15, 57, 116, 118, 254, 259, 262
ethics 16, 19, 52, 56, 57, 62, 63, 64, 66, 185, 246, 253, 255, 259
European 50, 61, 91, 97, 130, 131, 133, 149, 150, 155,

159, 170, 188, 191, 226, 227, 229, 246, 251, 252, 265, 266, 271

Evaluation 21, 32, 35, 64, 106, 120, 122, 123, 168, 169, 174, 175, 176, 178, 179, 181, 184, 185, 187, 188, 207, 218, 225, 228, 234

extended reality 206, 207, 208, 209, 210, 211, 212, 214, 215, 216, 217, 218, 221

F

Flipped Inclusion 251, 254, 256, 257, 261, 264, 265, 269, 274, 276

H

Healthcare 31, 32, 36, 55, 63, 73, 166, 167, 168, 169, 170, 171, 172, 173, 174, 175, 176, 178, 179, 180, 181, 182, 183, 184, 185, 186, 187, 188, 190, 191, 192, 233, 239, 240, 241, 244, 248, 249

healthcare industry 239, 240, 244

hospitality and tourism industry 234, 235

human resource 76, 77, 85, 89, 131, 232, 234, 242, 249

I

Immutability 43, 50

inclusion 64, 68, 110, 138, 140, 141, 154, 156, 159, 162, 163, 178, 251, 254, 256, 257, 261, 264, 265, 266, 269, 270, 273, 274, 275, 276, 277

Innovation 1, 6, 22, 28, 32, 46, 49, 92, 113, 115, 116, 127, 128, 129, 130, 132, 137, 138, 139, 140, 145, 151, 158, 166, 179, 181, 190, 193, 194, 195, 196, 197, 199, 201, 203, 204, 208, 212, 221, 222, 225, 227, 229, 230, 231, 233, 236, 239, 245, 246, 247, 248, 253, 261, 262, 267

innovative 2, 7, 14, 17, 23, 104, 107, 114, 124, 137, 138, 146, 149, 154, 155, 161, 167, 172, 174, 175, 183, 184, 193, 202, 206, 207, 209, 210, 211, 212, 223, 233, 235, 236, 240, 241, 242, 243, 245, 262, 265

Internet of Bodies 71, 89

Internet of Things 71, 83, 87, 196, 205, 235, 240

L

Large Language Models 51, 52, 81, 166, 167, 171, 176, 181, 184, 185, 189, 190, 191, 192

Learning 1, 2, 3, 4, 5, 6, 7, 8, 9, 10, 12, 13, 14, 15, 16, 17, 18, 19, 20, 21, 22, 23, 24, 25, 26, 27, 30, 31, 32, 33, 34, 35, 37, 39, 41, 42, 43, 44, 45, 48, 49, 50, 52, 53, 54, 55, 56, 62, 63, 67, 68, 69, 79, 85, 86, 88, 90, 93, 95, 97, 98, 99, 103, 104, 105, 106, 107, 108, 110, 111, 112, 113, 114, 115, 116, 117, 118, 119, 120, 121, 122, 123, 124, 125, 126, 127, 128, 129, 130, 131, 132, 133, 134, 135, 137, 138, 139, 140, 141, 144, 145, 146, 147, 148, 152, 153, 154, 155, 157, 159, 161, 162, 163, 166, 167, 168, 169, 170, 171, 172, 173, 174, 175, 176, 178, 179, 180, 181, 182, 183, 184, 185, 186, 187, 188, 190, 191, 192, 193, 194, 195, 196, 197, 198, 199, 200, 201, 202, 203, 204, 205, 207, 208, 209, 210, 211, 212, 213, 214, 215, 216, 217, 218, 221, 223, 224, 225, 226, 227, 228, 229, 230, 231, 233, 235, 240, 241, 247, 251, 252, 253, 254, 256, 259, 261, 264, 265, 266, 271, 272, 273, 274, 275, 277, 278, 279

Location-Sharing Applications 72, 83

M

mixed reality 208, 211, 226, 230

P

Pedagogy 17, 21, 23, 111, 114, 115, 116, 117, 125, 131, 132, 134, 148, 160, 163, 171, 252, 261, 271, 275, 276, 278

personalized learning 1, 3, 4, 14, 22, 26, 154, 182, 197, 198, 199, 200, 202

Privacy Concerns 35, 72, 79, 83, 88, 90

R

return-on-investment 221

roboboard 262, 267

S

service industry 232, 233, 234, 241, 243, 244

small and rural schools 136, 137, 138, 150, 154

Smart Contracts 27, 30, 31, 38, 39, 40, 45, 46, 48, 50, 238

Social Media 58, 71, 72, 73, 74, 79, 80, 86, 87, 89, 91, 92, 134, 181, 208, 236, 237, 240, 242

Social Robots 17, 21, 70, 71, 75, 77, 78, 83, 91

students 1, 2, 3, 4, 5, 6, 7, 8, 9, 10, 12, 13, 14, 15, 16, 17, 18, 19, 20, 21, 22, 23, 29, 30, 31, 34, 35, 39, 44, 45, 46, 47, 52, 53, 54, 80, 82, 83, 103, 104, 105, 106, 107, 108, 113, 115, 116, 124, 128, 129, 133, 134, 137, 138, 139, 140, 143, 145, 146, 147, 149, 152, 153, 154, 155, 156, 164, 170, 174, 178, 179, 180, 182, 183, 188, 191, 197, 198, 200, 201, 202, 212, 213, 224, 226, 228, 240, 252, 276, 278

sustainable development 17, 197, 205, 233, 253, 269,

270, 271, 272, 273, 274, 279

T

technological disruption 232, 233, 234, 236, 237, 238, 239, 241, 242, 243, 244, 245, 247

technological integration 139, 142, 156

technology 1, 2, 3, 5, 7, 8, 9, 10, 12, 13, 14, 15, 16, 17, 18, 19, 20, 21, 22, 23, 24, 25, 27, 28, 29, 30, 31, 32, 33, 35, 36, 37, 38, 39, 40, 41, 42, 43, 44, 45, 46, 47, 48, 49, 50, 52, 57, 59, 61, 62, 66, 67, 68, 70, 71, 73, 74, 78, 80, 81, 82, 83, 84, 85, 86, 87, 88, 89, 90, 91, 92, 93, 95, 96, 100, 105, 110, 111, 113, 114, 115, 116, 122, 123, 124, 126, 127, 129, 130, 131, 132, 133, 134, 135, 136, 137, 138, 139, 140, 141, 145, 147, 148, 150, 152, 156, 158, 159, 160, 161, 162, 163, 164, 167, 169, 171, 173, 181, 182, 184, 187, 188, 190, 191, 193, 194, 196, 197, 201, 204, 205, 206, 207, 208, 209, 210, 211, 212, 213, 214, 215, 216, 217, 218, 219, 221, 222, 223, 224, 226, 227, 228, 229, 230, 231, 233, 234, 236, 237, 238, 239, 240, 241, 242, 243, 244, 245, 246, 247, 248, 249, 252, 264, 266, 267, 273, 276, 277, 278, 279, 280

Technology innovation 92, 221, 222

Textuality 51, 52, 65

training 3, 15, 24, 32, 34, 41, 43, 46, 50, 55, 60, 62, 64, 65, 67, 71, 77, 78, 81, 83, 91, 98, 103, 105, 106, 107, 108, 111, 113, 118, 125, 130, 131, 132, 137, 138, 140, 141, 143, 144, 145, 150, 151, 154, 155, 156, 169, 170, 171, 172, 173, 174, 178, 183, 190, 191, 192, 198, 206, 207, 208, 209, 210, 211, 212, 213, 214, 215, 216, 217, 218, 219, 220, 221, 222, 223, 224, 226, 228, 229, 230, 231, 242, 245, 253, 265, 271, 272, 274, 276, 278

Transparency 1, 16, 30, 31, 32, 39, 40, 41, 42, 43, 46, 63, 64, 65, 67, 68, 173, 238, 264, 271, 272, 273

V

Verification 27, 28, 29, 30, 32, 33, 38, 40, 41, 42, 43, 44, 45, 46, 48, 172, 236

Videogames 112, 113

virtual reality 96, 186, 197, 208, 209, 210, 211, 212, 214, 215, 216, 218, 220, 225, 226, 227, 228, 229, 230, 235

W

Workforce Development 41, 42, 167, 193, 194, 195, 197, 198, 199, 200, 201, 202, 204

Publishing Tomorrow's Research Today

Uncover Current Insights and Future Trends in
Business & Management
with IGI Global's Cutting-Edge Recommended Books

Print Only, E-Book Only, or Print + E-Book.
Order direct through IGI Global's Online Bookstore at **www.igi-global.com** or through your preferred provider.

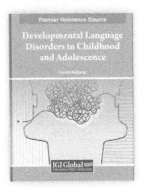

ISBN: 9798369306444
© 2023; 436 pp.
List Price: US$ **230**

ISBN: 9798369300084
© 2023; 358 pp.
List Price: US$ **250**

ISBN: 9781668458594
© 2023; 366 pp.
List Price: US$ **240**

ISBN: 9781668486344
© 2023; 256 pp.
List Price: US$ **280**

ISBN: 9781668493243
© 2024; 318 pp.
List Price: US$ **250**

ISBN: 9798369304181
© 2023; 415 pp.
List Price: US$ **250**

Do you want to stay current on the latest research trends, product announcements, news, and special offers?
Join IGI Global's mailing list to receive customized recommendations, exclusive discounts, and more.
Sign up at: **www.igi-global.com/newsletters**.

Scan the QR Code here to view more related titles in Business & Management.

www.igi-global.com   ✉ Sign up at www.igi-global.com/newsletters   facebook.com/igiglobal   twitter.com/igiglobal   linkedin.com/igiglobal

Ensure Quality Research is Introduced to the Academic Community

Become a Reviewer for IGI Global Authored Book Projects

  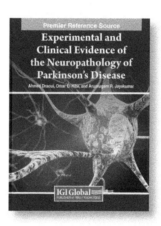 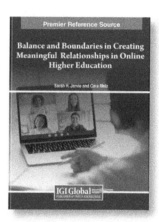

The overall success of an authored book project is dependent on quality and timely manuscript evaluations.

Applications and Inquiries may be sent to:
development@igi-global.com

Applicants must have a doctorate (or equivalent degree) as well as publishing, research, and reviewing experience. Authored Book Evaluators are appointed for one-year terms and are expected to complete at least three evaluations per term. Upon successful completion of this term, evaluators can be considered for an additional term.

If you have a colleague that may be interested in this opportunity, we encourage you to share this information with them.

IGI Global's Open Access Journal Program
Publishing Tomorrow's Research Today

Including Nearly 200 Peer-Reviewed, Gold (Full) Open Access Journals across IGI Global's Three Academic Subject Areas: Business & Management; Scientific, Technical, and Medical (STM); and Education

Consider Submitting Your Manuscript to One of These Nearly 200 Open Access Journals for to Increase Their Discoverability & Citation Impact

Web of Science Impact Factor 6.5	Web of Science Impact Factor 4.7	Web of Science Impact Factor 3.2	Web of Science Impact Factor 2.6
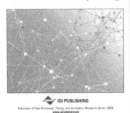 JOURNAL OF Organizational and End User Computing	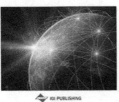 JOURNAL OF Global Information Management	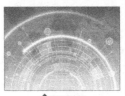 INTERNATIONAL JOURNAL ON Semantic Web and Information Systems	 JOURNAL OF Database Management

Choosing IGI Global's Open Access Journal Program Can Greatly Increase the Reach of Your Research

Higher Usage
Open access papers are 2-3 times more likely to be read than non-open access papers.

Higher Download Rates
Open access papers benefit from 89% higher download rates than non-open access papers.

Higher Citation Rates
Open access papers are 47% more likely to be cited than non-open access papers.

Submitting an article to a journal offers an invaluable opportunity for you to share your work with the broader academic community, fostering knowledge dissemination and constructive feedback.

Submit an Article and Browse the IGI Global Call for Papers Pages

We can work with you to find the journal most well-suited for your next research manuscript.
For open access publishing support, contact: journaleditor@igi-global.com

Are You Ready to Publish Your Research

IGI Global offers book authorship and editorship opportunities across three major subject areas, including Business, STM, and Education.

Benefits of Publishing with IGI Global:

- Free one-on-one editorial and promotional support.
- Expedited publishing timelines that can take your book from start to finish in less than one (1) year.
- Choose from a variety of formats, including Edited and Authored References, Handbooks of Research, Encyclopedias, and Research Insights.
- Utilize IGI Global's eEditorial Discovery® submission system in support of conducting the submission and double-blind peer review process.
- IGI Global maintains a strict adherence to ethical practices due in part to our full membership with the Committee on Publication Ethics (COPE).
- Indexing potential in prestigious indices such as Scopus®, Web of Science™, PsycINFO®, and ERIC – Education Resources Information Center.
- Ability to connect your ORCID iD to your IGI Global publications.
- Earn honorariums and royalties on your full book publications as well as complimentary content and exclusive discounts.

Learn More at: www.igi-global.com/publish
or Contact IGI Global's Aquisitions Team at: acquisition@igi-global.com

Individual Article & Chapter Downloads
US$ 37.50/each

Easily Identify, Acquire, and Utilize Published Peer-Reviewed Findings in Support of Your Current Research

- Browse Over **170,000+ Articles & Chapters**
- **Accurate & Advanced** Search
- Affordably Acquire **International Research**
- **Instantly Access** Your Content
- Benefit from the **InfoSci® Platform Features**

It really provides an excellent entry into the research literature of the field. It presents a manageable number of highly relevant sources on topics of interest to a wide range of researchers. The sources are scholarly, but also accessible to 'practitioners'.

- Ms. Lisa Stimatz, MLS, University of North Carolina at Chapel Hill, USA

Milton Keynes UK
Ingram Content Group UK Ltd.
UKHW010228300724
446304UK00005B/112